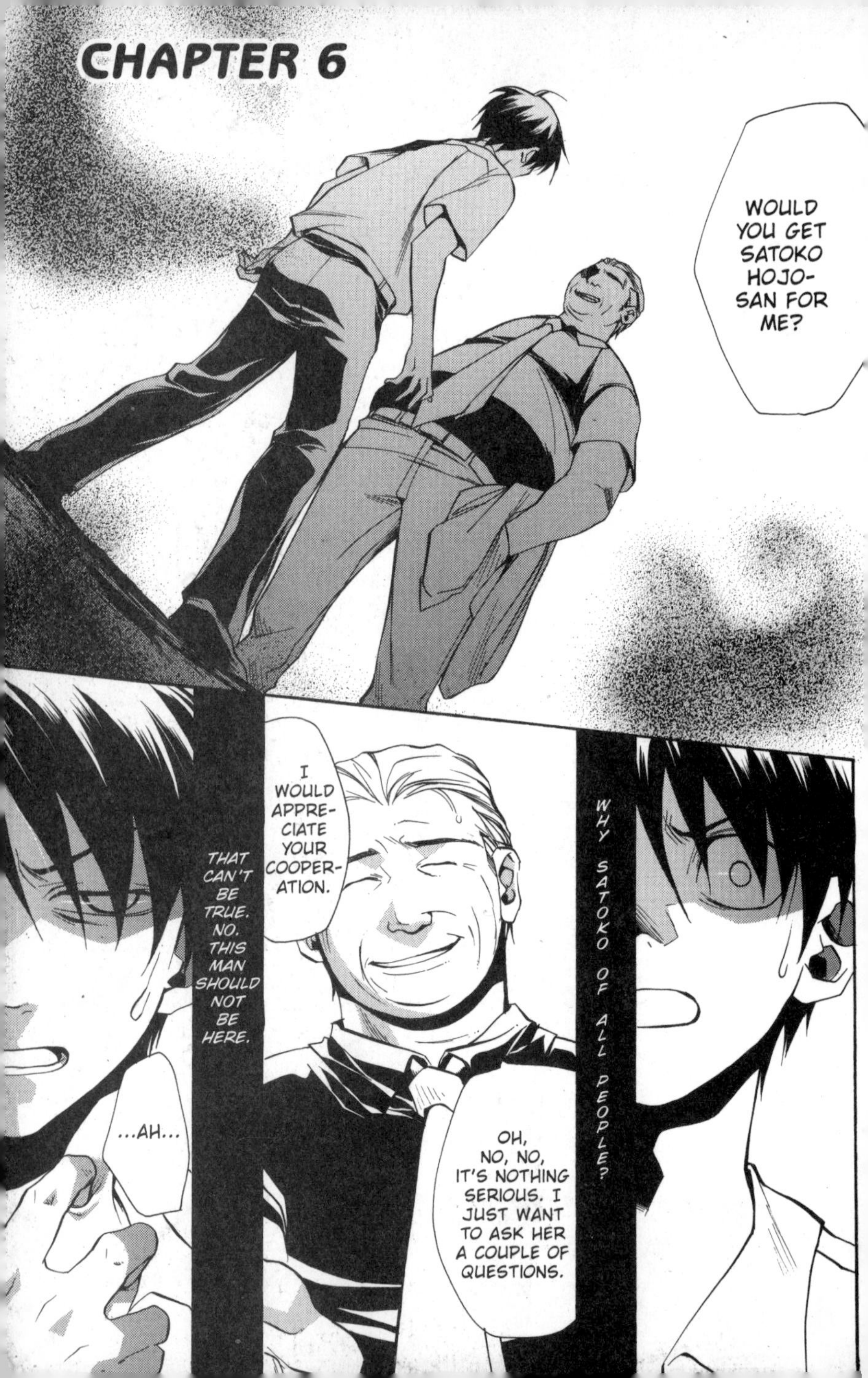
CHAPTER 6
WOULD YOU GET SATOKO HOJO-SAN FOR ME?
WHY SATOKO OF ALL PEOPLE?
OH, NO, NO, IT'S NOTHING SERIOUS. I JUST WANT TO ASK HER A COUPLE OF QUESTIONS.
I WOULD APPRECIATE YOUR COOPERATION.
THAT CAN'T BE TRUE. NO. THIS MAN SHOULD NOT BE HERE.
...AH...

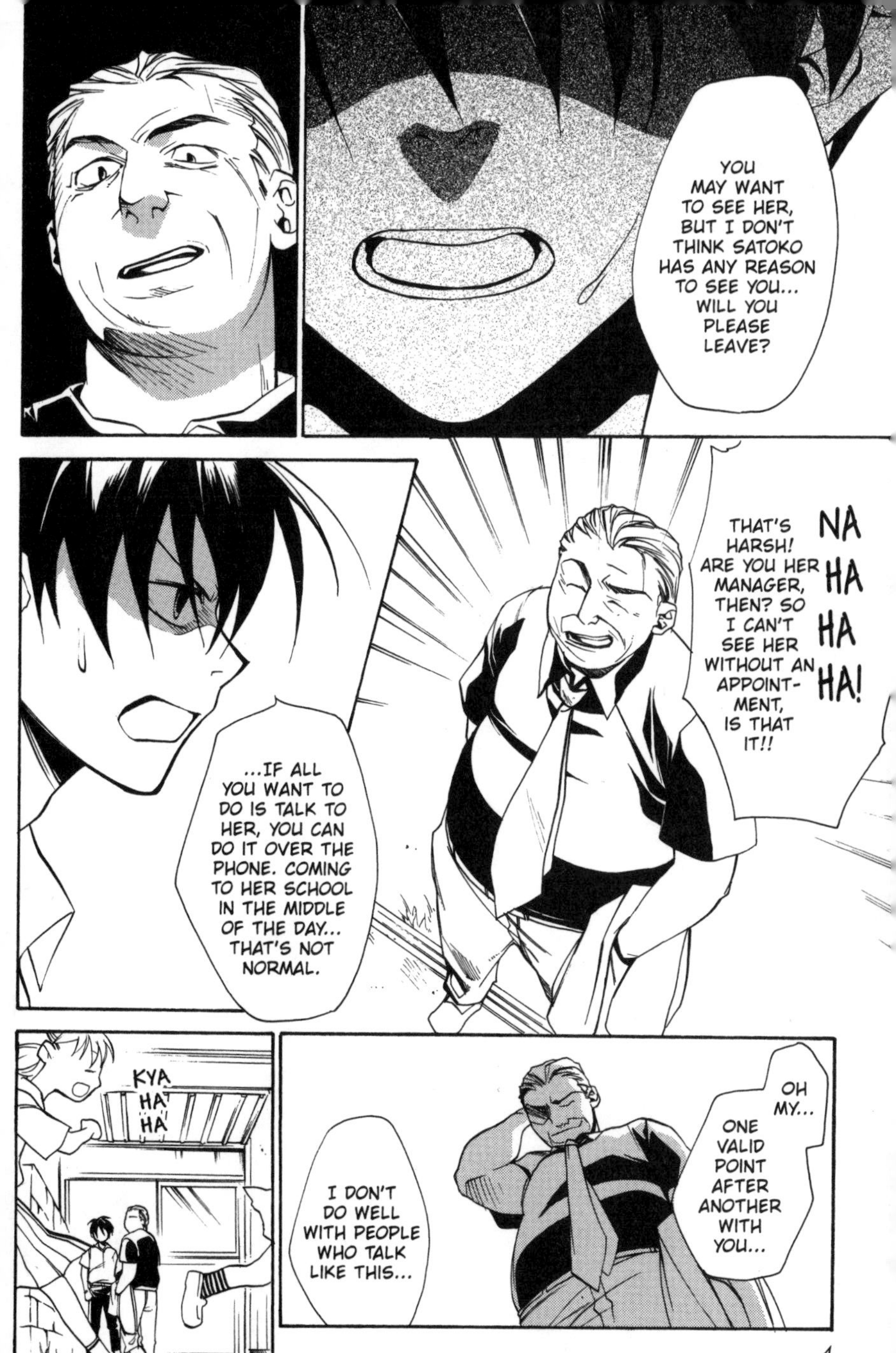
YOU MAY WANT TO SEE HER, BUT I DON'T THINK SATOKO HAS ANY REASON TO SEE YOU... WILL YOU PLEASE LEAVE?
NA HA HA HA!
THAT'S HARSH! ARE YOU HER MANAGER, THEN? SO I CAN'T SEE HER WITHOUT AN APPOINT-MENT, IS THAT IT!!
...IF ALL YOU WANT TO DO IS TALK TO HER, YOU CAN DO IT OVER THE PHONE. COMING TO HER SCHOOL IN THE MIDDLE OF THE DAY... THAT'S NOT NORMAL.
OH MY... ONE VALID POINT AFTER ANOTHER WITH YOU...
I DON'T DO WELL WITH PEOPLE WHO TALK LIKE THIS...
KYA HA HA HA

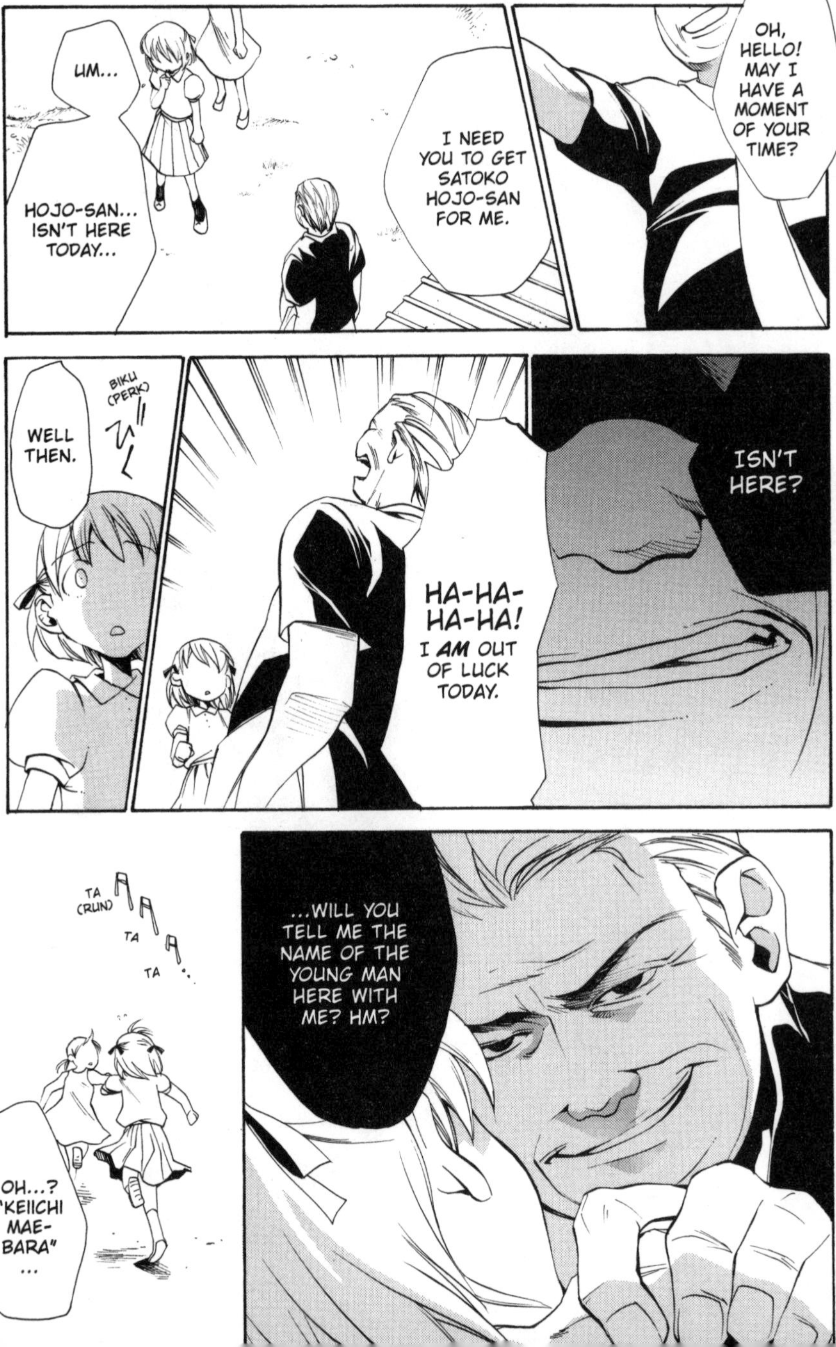
OH, HELLO! MAY I HAVE A MOMENT OF YOUR TIME?
I NEED YOU TO GET SATOKO HOJO-SAN FOR ME.
UM...
HOJO-SAN... ISN'T HERE TODAY...
ISN'T HERE?
HA-HA-HA-HA! I AM OUT OF LUCK TODAY.
BIKU (PERK)
WELL THEN.
...WILL YOU TELL ME THE NAME OF THE YOUNG MAN HERE WITH ME? HM?
TA (RUN)
TA
TA
OH...? "KEIICHI MAE-BARA"...

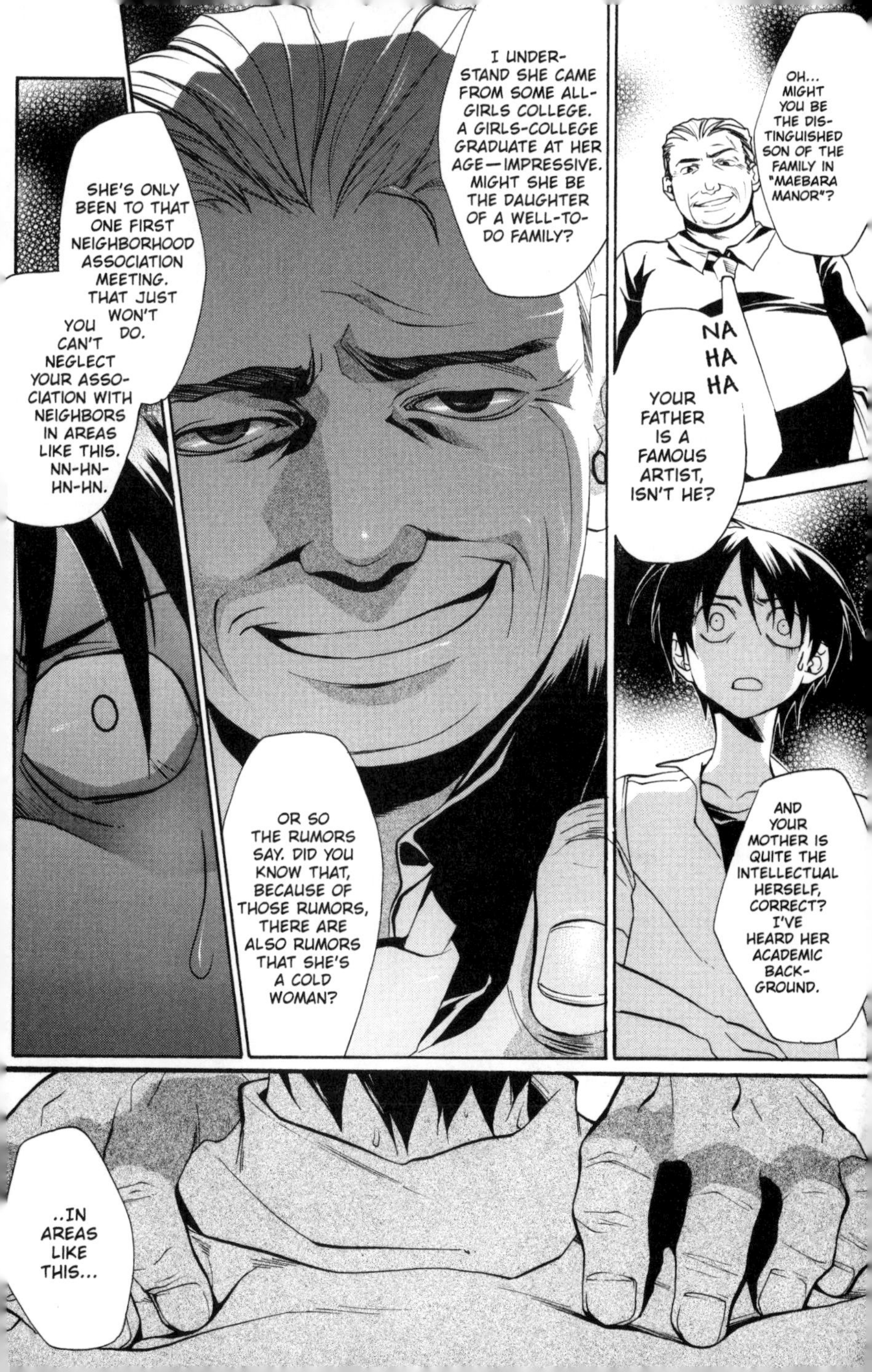
OH... MIGHT YOU BE THE DIS-TINGUISHED SON OF THE FAMILY IN "MAEBARA MANOR"?
NA HA HA
YOUR FATHER IS A FAMOUS ARTIST, ISN'T HE?
AND YOUR MOTHER IS QUITE THE INTELLECTUAL HERSELF, CORRECT? I'VE HEARD HER ACADEMIC BACK-GROUND.
I UNDER-STAND SHE CAME FROM SOME ALL-GIRLS COLLEGE. A GIRLS-COLLEGE GRADUATE AT HER AGE—IMPRESSIVE. MIGHT SHE BE THE DAUGHTER OF A WELL-TO-DO FAMILY?
SHE'S ONLY BEEN TO THAT ONE FIRST NEIGHBORHOOD ASSOCIATION MEETING. THAT JUST WON'T DO.
YOU CAN'T NEGLECT YOUR ASSO-CIATION WITH NEIGHBORS IN AREAS LIKE THIS. NN-HN-HN-HN.
OR SO THE RUMORS SAY. DID YOU KNOW THAT, BECAUSE OF THOSE RUMORS, THERE ARE ALSO RUMORS THAT SHE'S A COLD WOMAN?
..IN AREAS LIKE THIS...

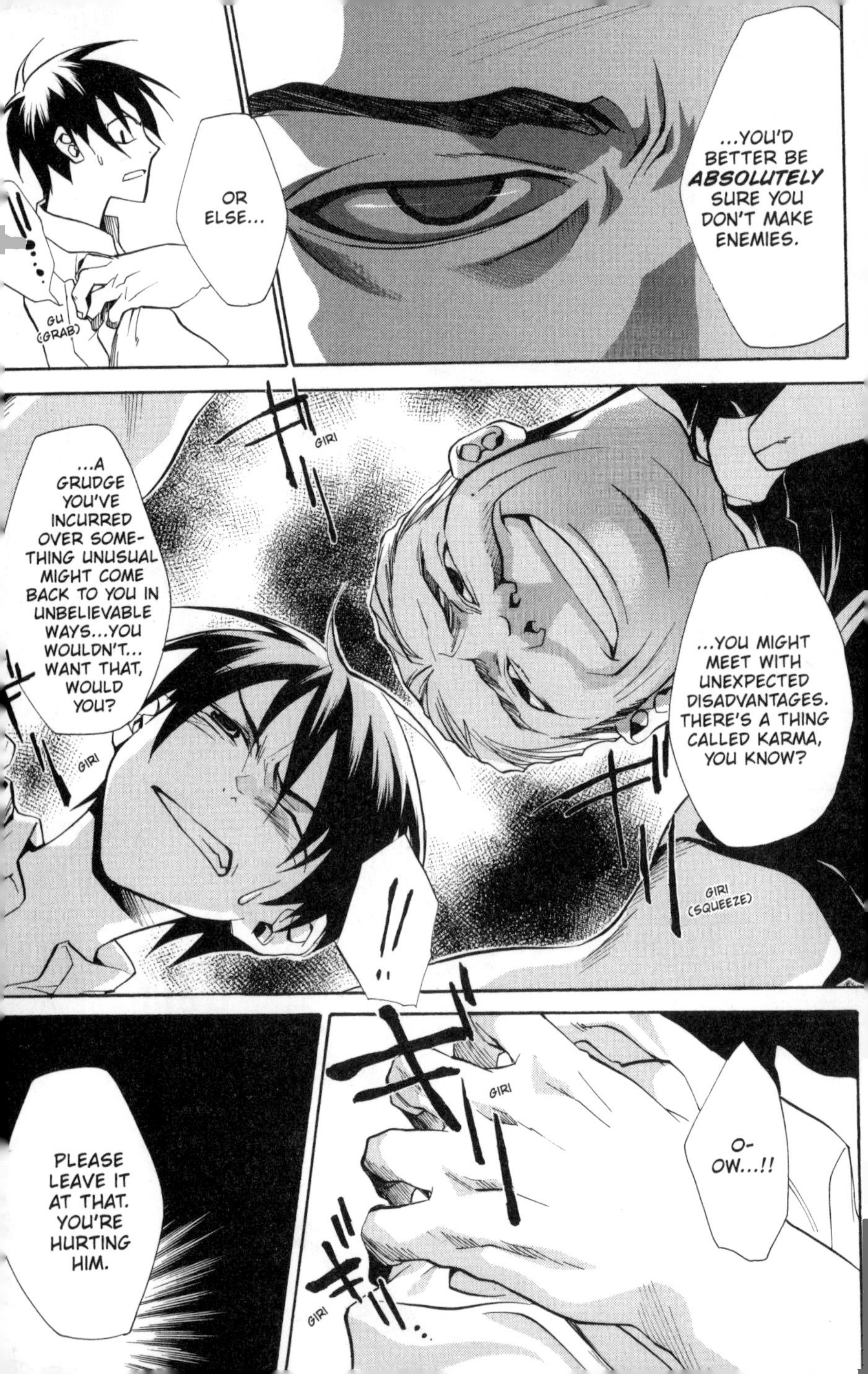
...YOU'D BETTER BE ***ABSOLUTELY*** SURE YOU DON'T MAKE ENEMIES.
OR ELSE...
GU (GRAB)
...YOU MIGHT MEET WITH UNEXPECTED DISADVANTAGES. THERE'S A THING CALLED KARMA, YOU KNOW?
GIRI
...A GRUDGE YOU'VE INCURRED OVER SOME-THING UNUSUAL MIGHT COME BACK TO YOU IN UNBELIEVABLE WAYS...YOU WOULDN'T... WANT THAT, WOULD YOU?
GIRI (SQUEEZE)
GIRI
O-OW...!!
GIRI
GIRI
PLEASE LEAVE IT AT THAT. YOU'RE HURTING HIM.

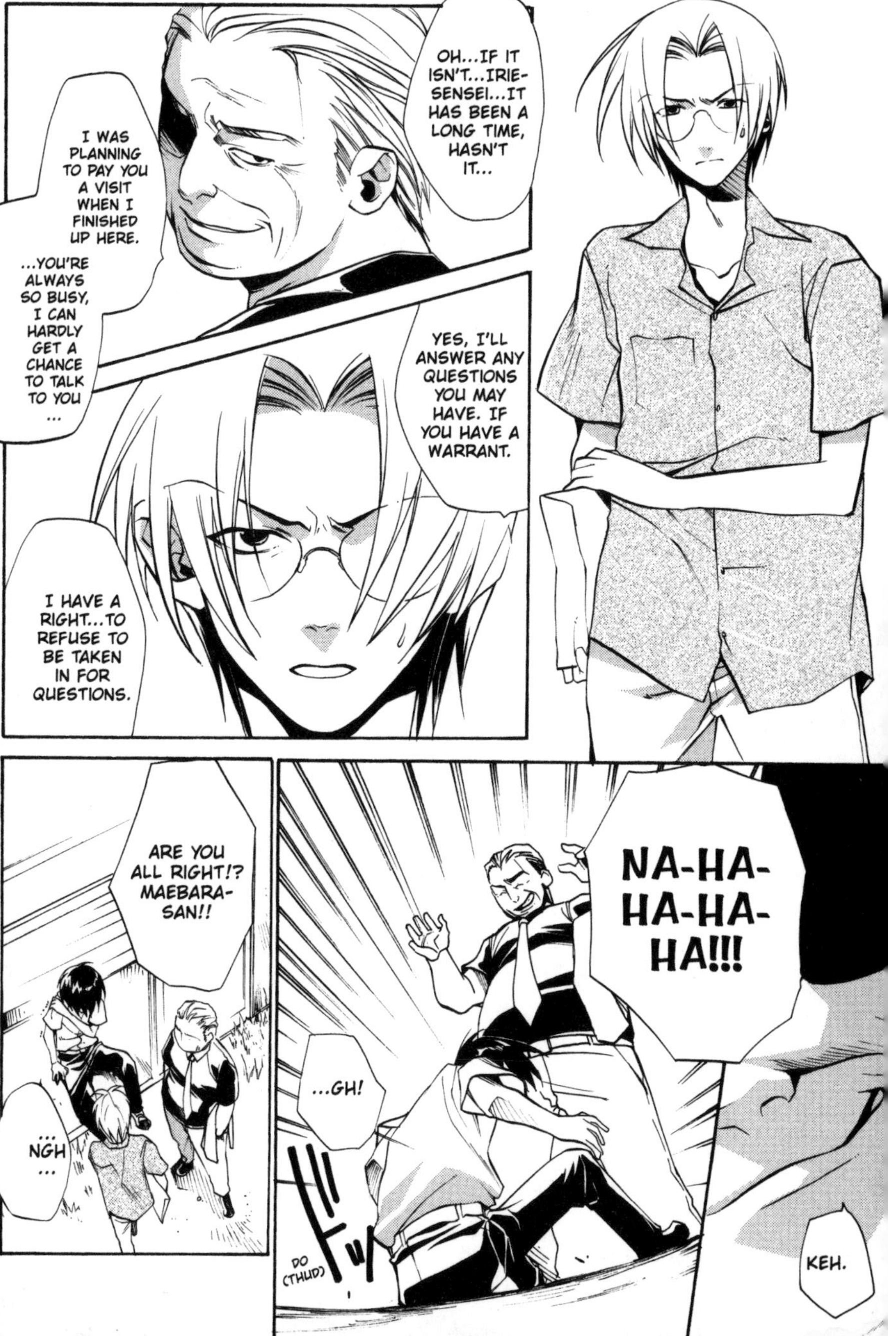
OH...IF IT ISN'T...IRIE-SENSEI...IT HAS BEEN A LONG TIME, HASN'T IT...
I WAS PLANNING TO PAY YOU A VISIT WHEN I FINISHED UP HERE.
...YOU'RE ALWAYS SO BUSY, I CAN HARDLY GET A CHANCE TO TALK TO YOU ...
YES, I'LL ANSWER ANY QUESTIONS YOU MAY HAVE. IF YOU HAVE A WARRANT.
I HAVE A RIGHT...TO REFUSE TO BE TAKEN IN FOR QUESTIONS.
NA-HA-HA-HA-HA-HA!!!
...GH!
KEH.
DO (THUD)
ARE YOU ALL RIGHT!? MAEBARA-SAN!!
...NGH...

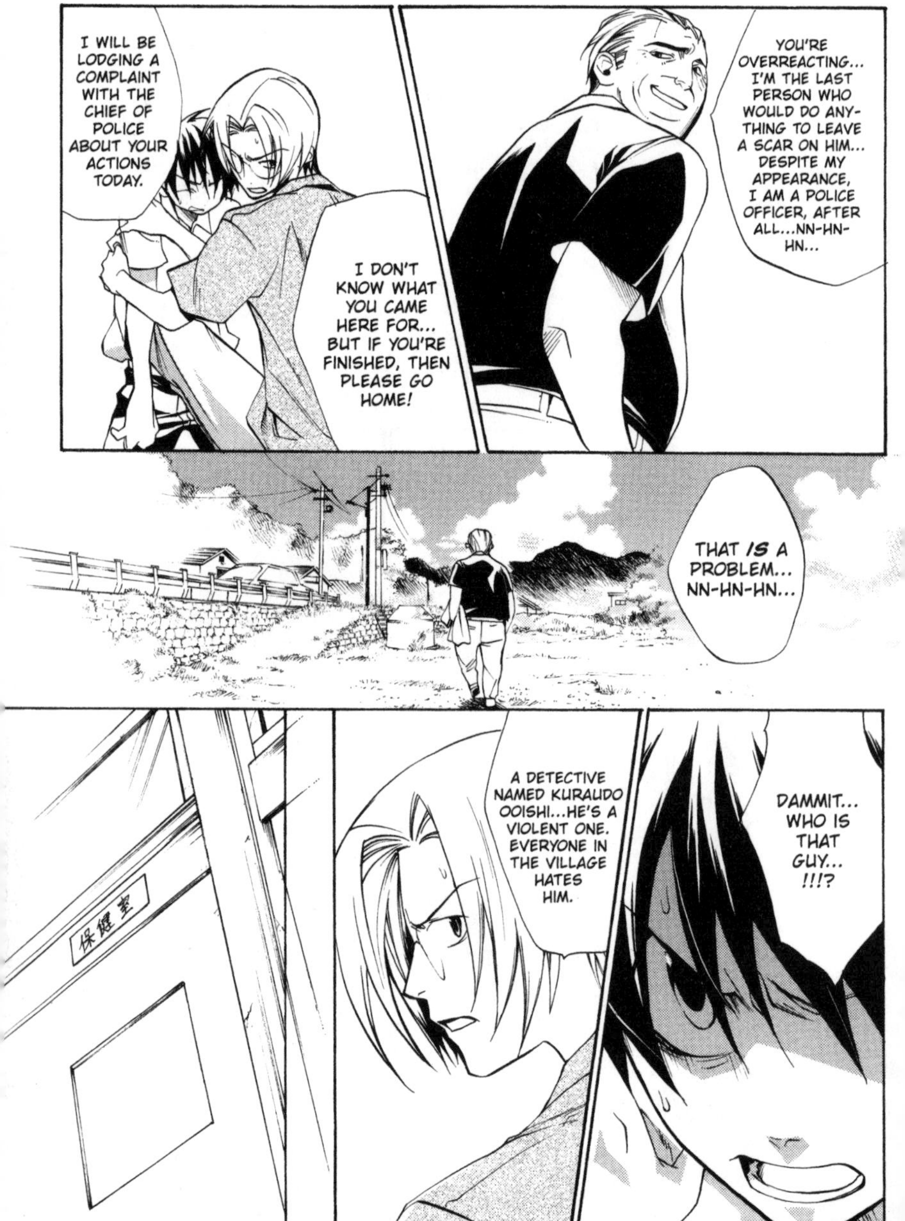
YOU'RE OVERREACTING... I'M THE LAST PERSON WHO WOULD DO ANY-THING TO LEAVE A SCAR ON HIM... DESPITE MY APPEARANCE, I AM A POLICE OFFICER, AFTER ALL...NN-HN-HN...
I WILL BE LODGING A COMPLAINT WITH THE CHIEF OF POLICE ABOUT YOUR ACTIONS TODAY.
I DON'T KNOW WHAT YOU CAME HERE FOR... BUT IF YOU'RE FINISHED, THEN PLEASE GO HOME!
THAT *IS* A PROBLEM... NN-HN-HN...
DAMMIT... WHO IS THAT GUY... !!!?
A DETECTIVE NAMED KURAUDO OOISHI...HE'S A VIOLENT ONE. EVERYONE IN THE VILLAGE HATES HIM.
保健室

SIGN: MEDICAL OFFICE

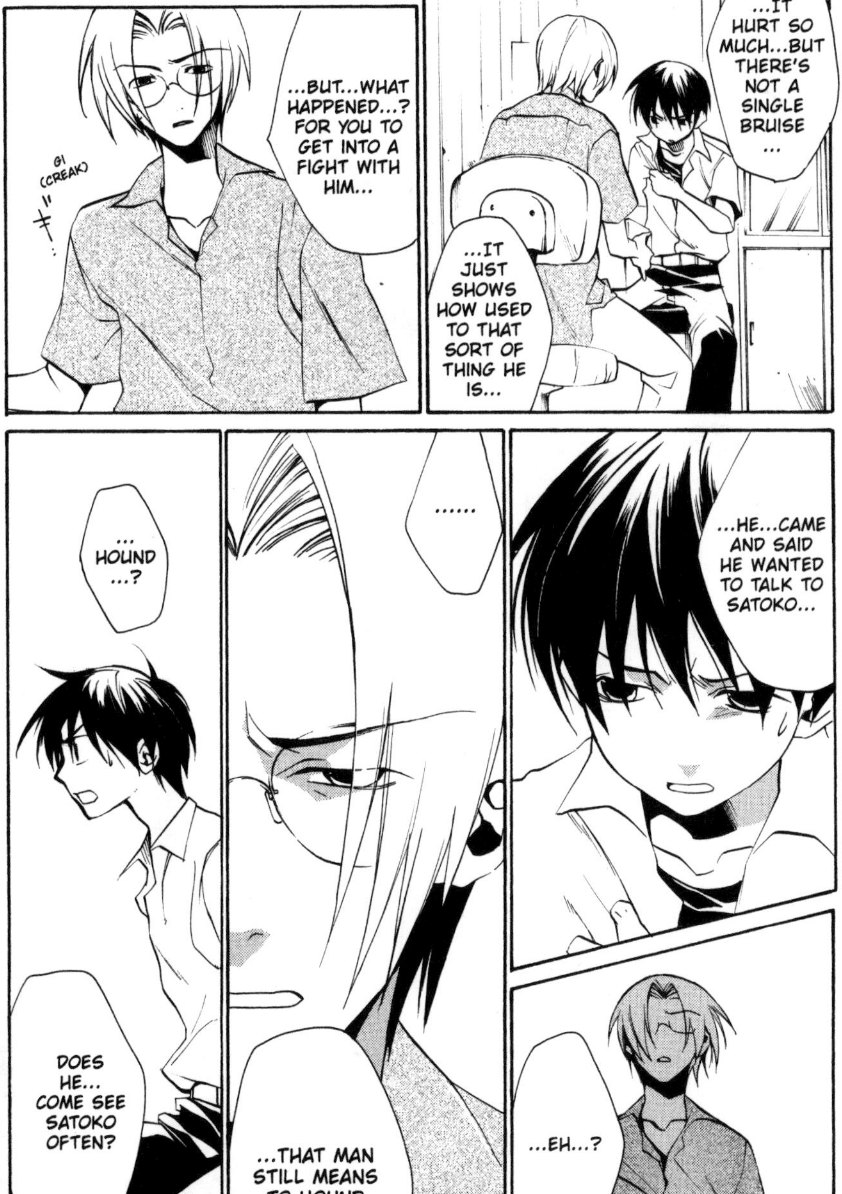
...IT HURT SO MUCH...BUT THERE'S NOT A SINGLE BRUISE ...
...IT JUST SHOWS HOW USED TO THAT SORT OF THING HE IS...
...BUT...WHAT HAPPENED...? FOR YOU TO GET INTO A FIGHT WITH HIM...
GI (CREAK)
ギ
...HE...CAME AND SAID HE WANTED TO TALK TO SATOKO...
...EH...?
......
...THAT MAN STILL MEANS TO HOUND SATOKO-CHAN...?
...HOUND...?
DOES HE... COME SEE SATOKO OFTEN?

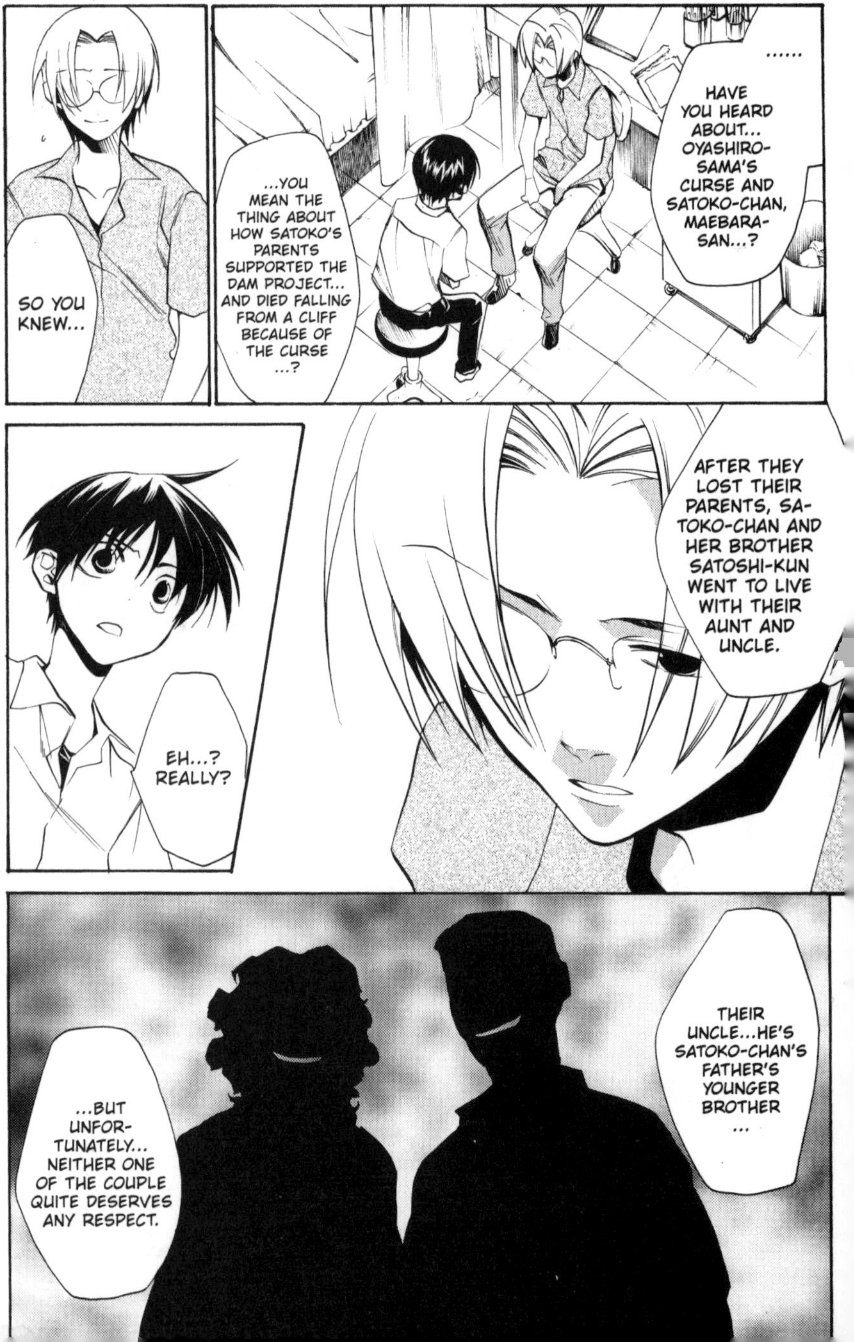
......
HAVE YOU HEARD ABOUT... OYASHIRO-SAMA'S CURSE AND SATOKO-CHAN, MAEBARA-SAN...?
...YOU MEAN THE THING ABOUT HOW SATOKO'S PARENTS SUPPORTED THE DAM PROJECT... AND DIED FALLING FROM A CLIFF BECAUSE OF THE CURSE ...?
SO YOU KNEW...
AFTER THEY LOST THEIR PARENTS, SATOKO-CHAN AND HER BROTHER SATOSHI-KUN WENT TO LIVE WITH THEIR AUNT AND UNCLE.
EH...? REALLY?
THEIR UNCLE...HE'S SATOKO-CHAN'S FATHER'S YOUNGER BROTHER ...
...BUT UNFORTUNATELY... NEITHER ONE OF THE COUPLE QUITE DESERVES ANY RESPECT.

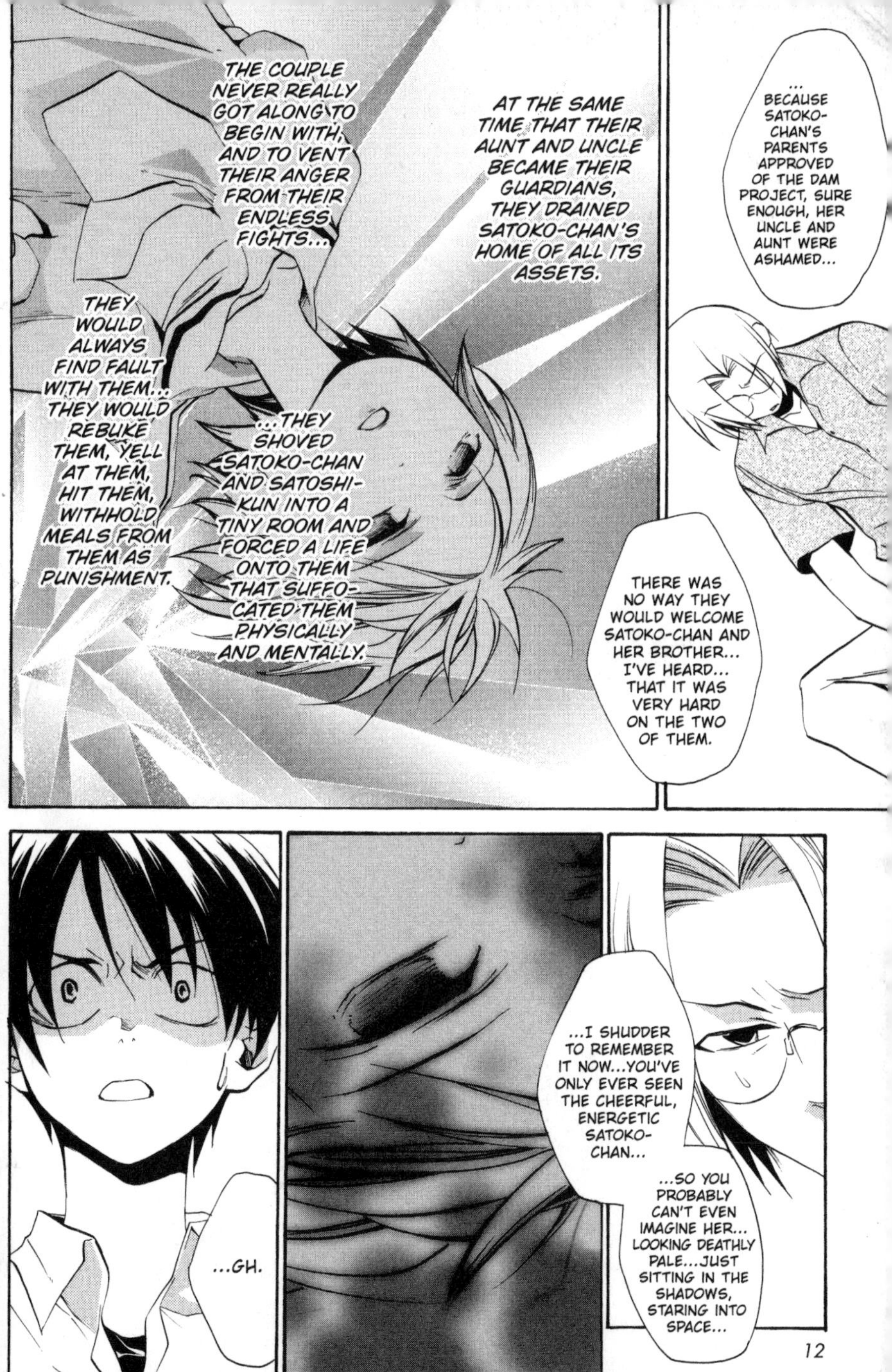
...BECAUSE SATOKO-CHAN'S PARENTS APPROVED OF THE DAM PROJECT, SURE ENOUGH, HER UNCLE AND AUNT WERE ASHAMED...
THERE WAS NO WAY THEY WOULD WELCOME SATOKO-CHAN AND HER BROTHER... I'VE HEARD... THAT IT WAS VERY HARD ON THE TWO OF THEM.
AT THE SAME TIME THAT THEIR AUNT AND UNCLE BECAME THEIR GUARDIANS, THEY DRAINED SATOKO-CHAN'S HOME OF ALL ITS ASSETS.
THE COUPLE NEVER REALLY GOT ALONG TO BEGIN WITH, AND TO VENT THEIR ANGER FROM THEIR ENDLESS FIGHTS...
...THEY SHOVED SATOKO-CHAN AND SATOSHI-KUN INTO A TINY ROOM AND FORCED A LIFE ONTO THEM THAT SUFFO-CATED THEM PHYSICALLY AND MENTALLY.
THEY WOULD ALWAYS FIND FAULT WITH THEM... THEY WOULD REBUKE THEM, YELL AT THEM, HIT THEM, WITHHOLD MEALS FROM THEM AS PUNISHMENT.
...I SHUDDER TO REMEMBER IT NOW...YOU'VE ONLY EVER SEEN THE CHEERFUL, ENERGETIC SATOKO-CHAN...
...SO YOU PROBABLY CAN'T EVEN IMAGINE HER... LOOKING DEATHLY PALE...JUST SITTING IN THE SHADOWS, STARING INTO SPACE...
...GH.

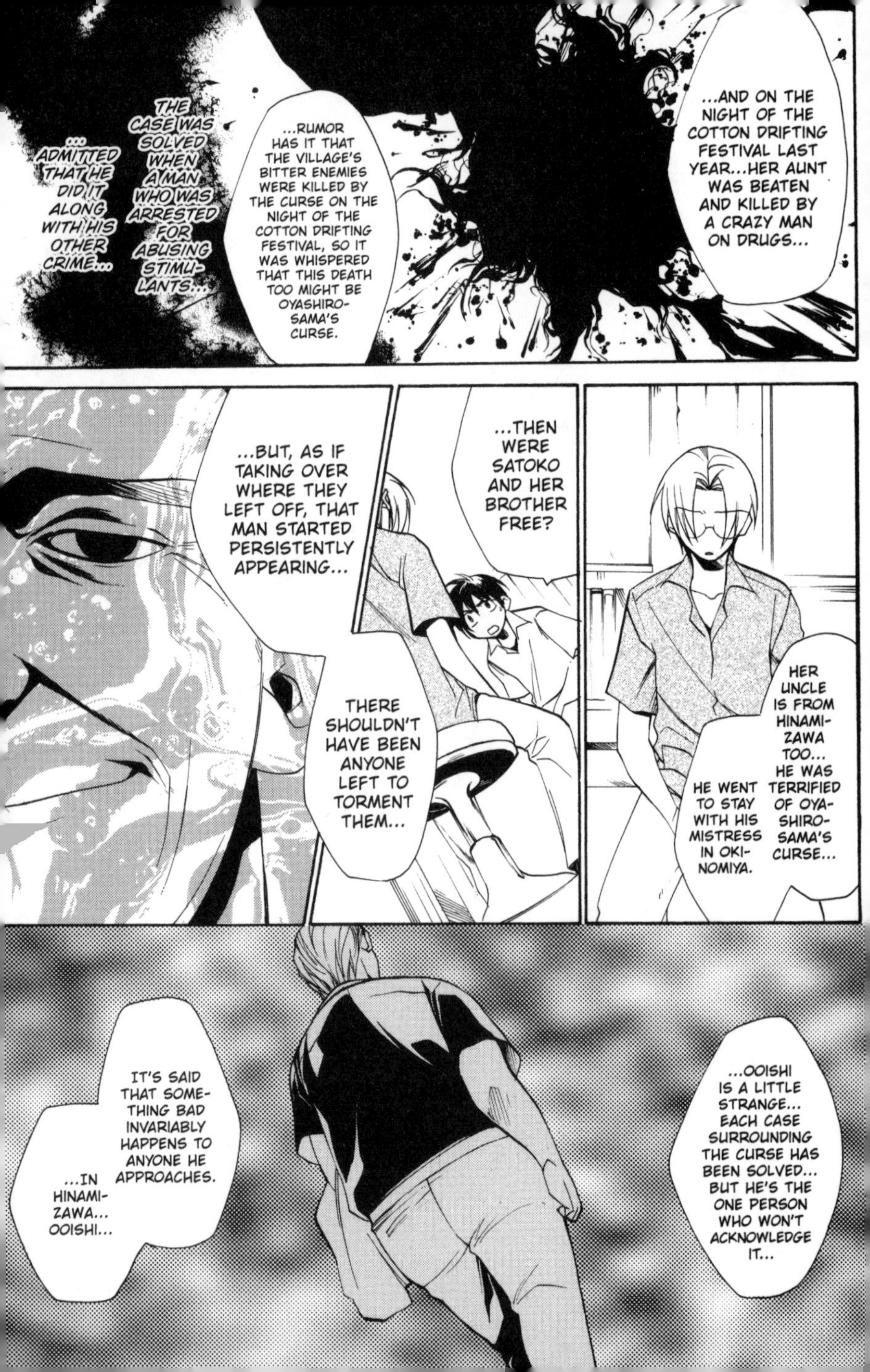
...AND ON THE NIGHT OF THE COTTON DRIFTING FESTIVAL LAST YEAR...HER AUNT WAS BEATEN AND KILLED BY A CRAZY MAN ON DRUGS...
...RUMOR HAS IT THAT THE VILLAGE'S BITTER ENEMIES WERE KILLED BY THE CURSE ON THE NIGHT OF THE COTTON DRIFTING FESTIVAL, SO IT WAS WHISPERED THAT THIS DEATH TOO MIGHT BE OYASHIRO-SAMA'S CURSE.
THE CASE WAS SOLVED WHEN A MAN WHO WAS ARRESTED FOR ABUSING STIMULANTS...
...ADMITTED THAT HE DID IT ALONG WITH HIS OTHER CRIME...
HER UNCLE IS FROM HINAMIZAWA TOO... HE WAS TERRIFIED OF OYASHIRO-SAMA'S CURSE...
HE WENT TO STAY WITH HIS MISTRESS IN OKINOMIYA.
...THEN WERE SATOKO AND HER BROTHER FREE?
THERE SHOULDN'T HAVE BEEN ANYONE LEFT TO TORMENT THEM...
...BUT, AS IF TAKING OVER WHERE THEY LEFT OFF, THAT MAN STARTED PERSISTENTLY APPEARING...
...OOISHI IS A LITTLE STRANGE... EACH CASE SURROUNDING THE CURSE HAS BEEN SOLVED... BUT HE'S THE ONE PERSON WHO WON'T ACKNOWLEDGE IT...
IT'S SAID THAT SOMETHING BAD INVARIABLY HAPPENS TO ANYONE HE APPROACHES.
...IN HINAMIZAWA... OOISHI...

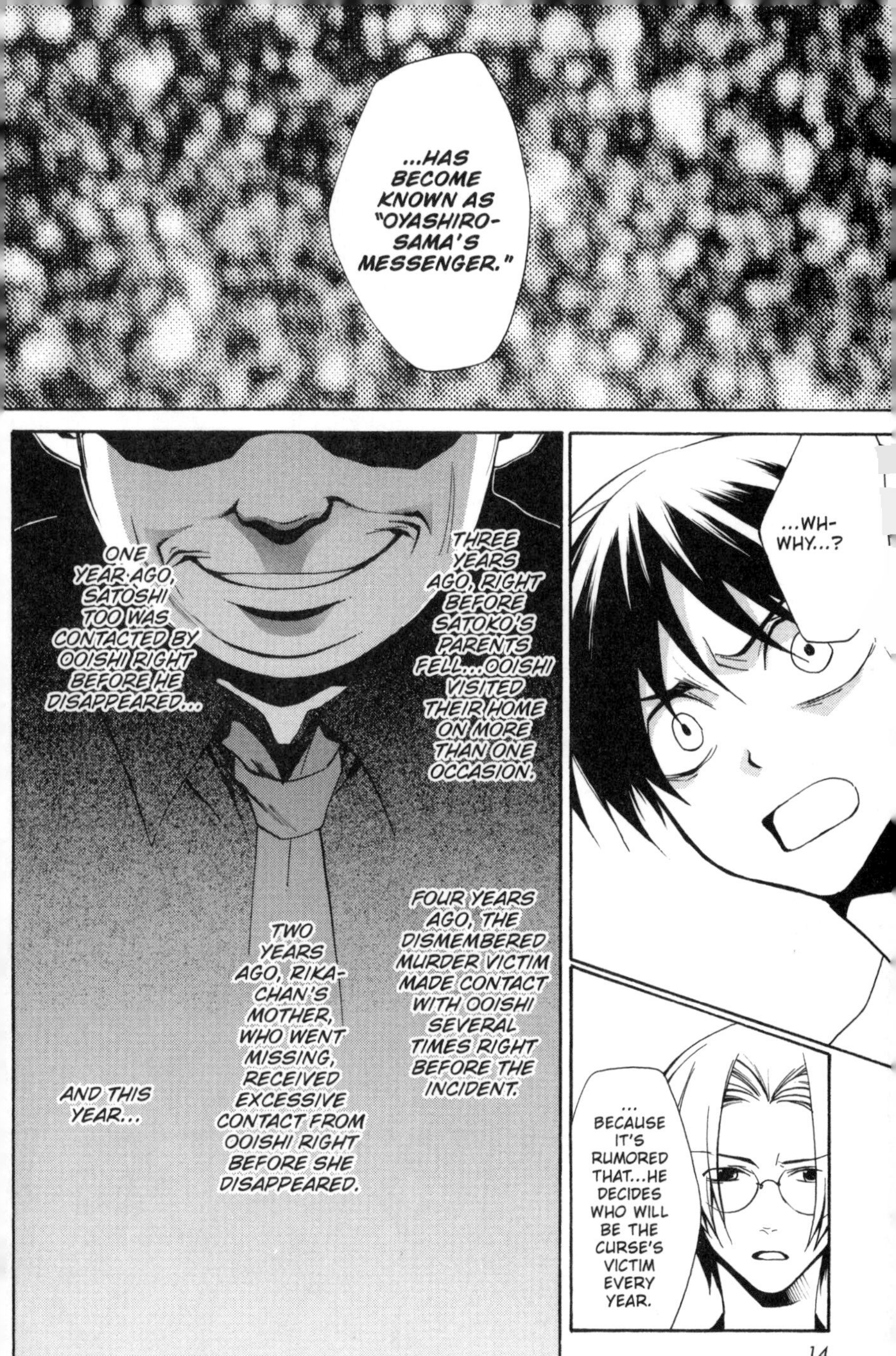
...HAS BECOME KNOWN AS "OYASHIRO-SAMA'S MESSENGER."
...WH- WHY...?
...BECAUSE IT'S RUMORED THAT...HE DECIDES WHO WILL BE THE CURSE'S VICTIM EVERY YEAR.
THREE YEARS AGO, RIGHT BEFORE SATOKO'S PARENTS FELL...OOISHI VISITED THEIR HOME ON MORE THAN ONE OCCASION.
ONE YEAR AGO, SATOSHI TOO WAS CONTACTED BY OOISHI RIGHT BEFORE HE DISAPPEARED...
FOUR YEARS AGO, THE DISMEMBERED MURDER VICTIM MADE CONTACT WITH OOISHI SEVERAL TIMES RIGHT BEFORE THE INCIDENT.
TWO YEARS AGO, RIKA-CHAN'S MOTHER, WHO WENT MISSING, RECEIVED EXCESSIVE CONTACT FROM OOISHI RIGHT BEFORE SHE DISAPPEARED.
AND THIS YEAR...

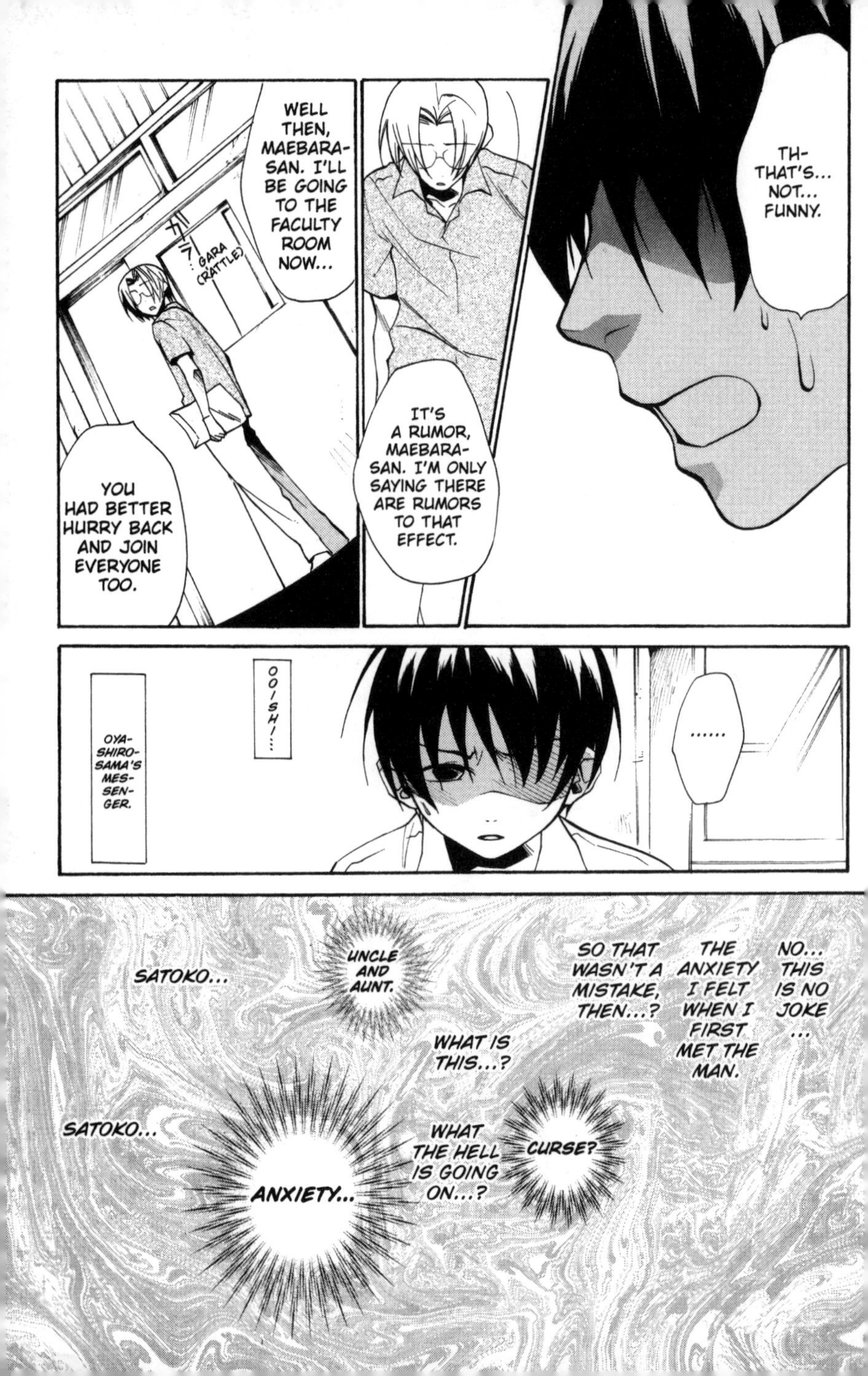
TH- THAT'S... NOT... FUNNY.
IT'S A RUMOR, MAEBARA-SAN. I'M ONLY SAYING THERE ARE RUMORS TO THAT EFFECT.
WELL THEN, MAEBARA-SAN. I'LL BE GOING TO THE FACULTY ROOM NOW...
GARA (RATTLE)
YOU HAD BETTER HURRY BACK AND JOIN EVERYONE TOO.
......
OOISHI...
OYA-SHIRO-SAMA'S MES-SEN-GER.
NO... THIS IS NO JOKE...
THE ANXIETY I FELT WHEN I FIRST MET THE MAN.
SO THAT WASN'T A MISTAKE, THEN...?
UNCLE AND AUNT.
WHAT IS THIS...?
SATOKO...
CURSE?
WHAT THE HELL IS GOING ON...?
ANXIETY...
SATOKO...

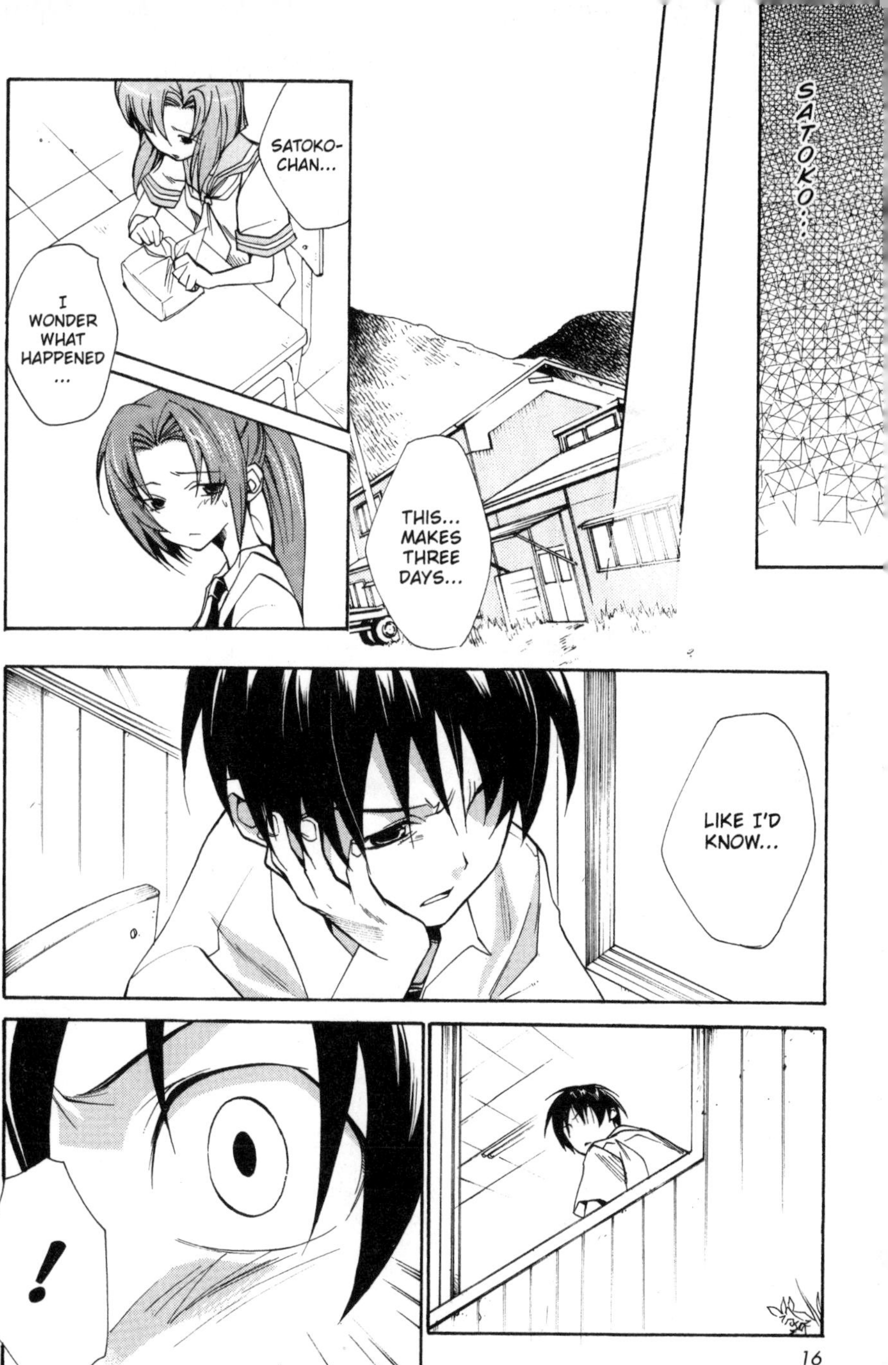
SATOKO...
THIS... MAKES THREE DAYS...
SATOKO-CHAN...
I WONDER WHAT HAPPENED...
LIKE I'D KNOW...
!

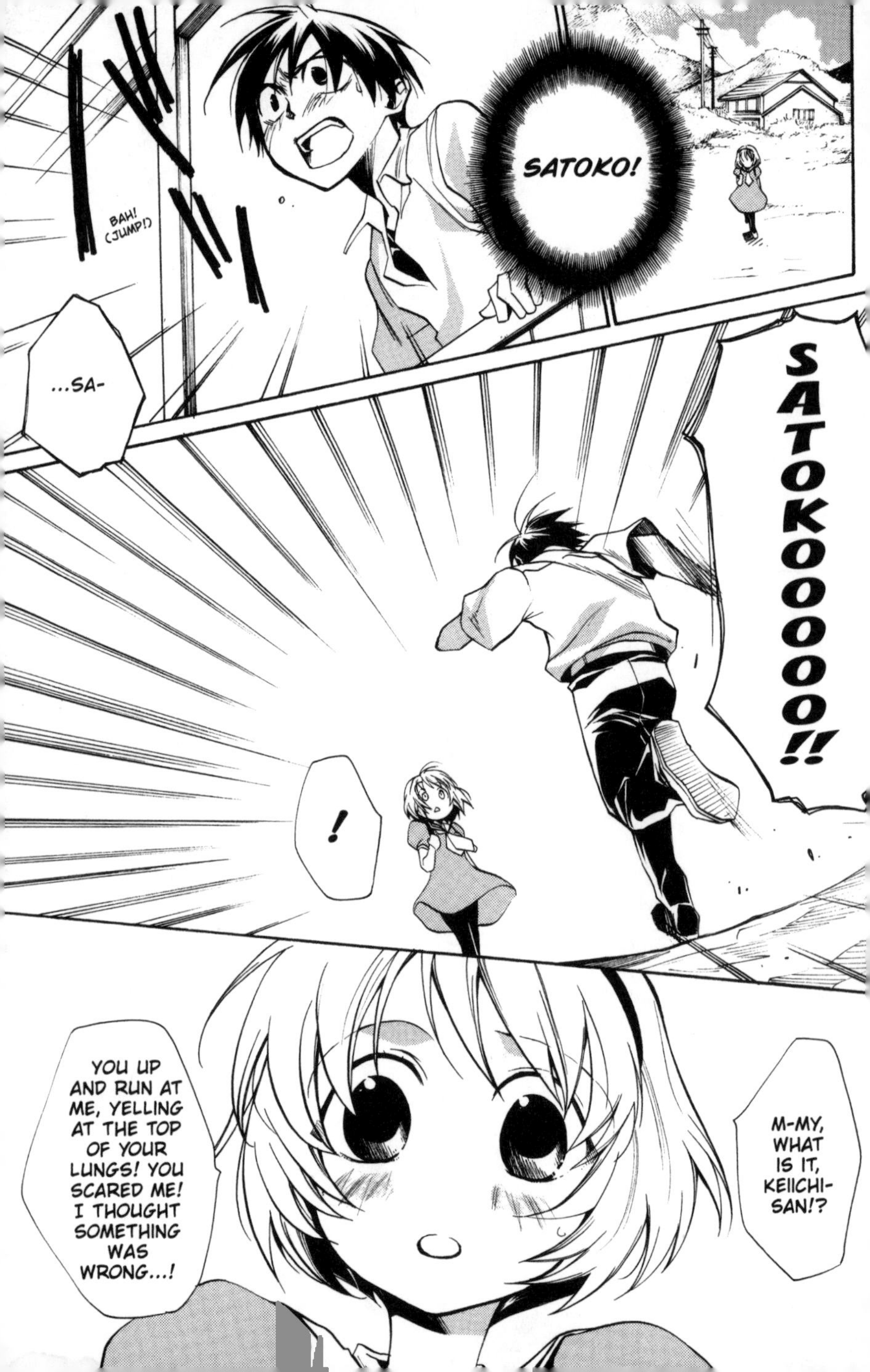
SATOKO!
BAH! (JUMP!)
...SA-
SATOKOOOOOO!!
!
M-MY, WHAT IS IT, KEIICHI-SAN!?
YOU UP AND RUN AT ME, YELLING AT THE TOP OF YOUR LUNGS! YOU SCARED ME! I THOUGHT SOMETHING WAS WRONG...!

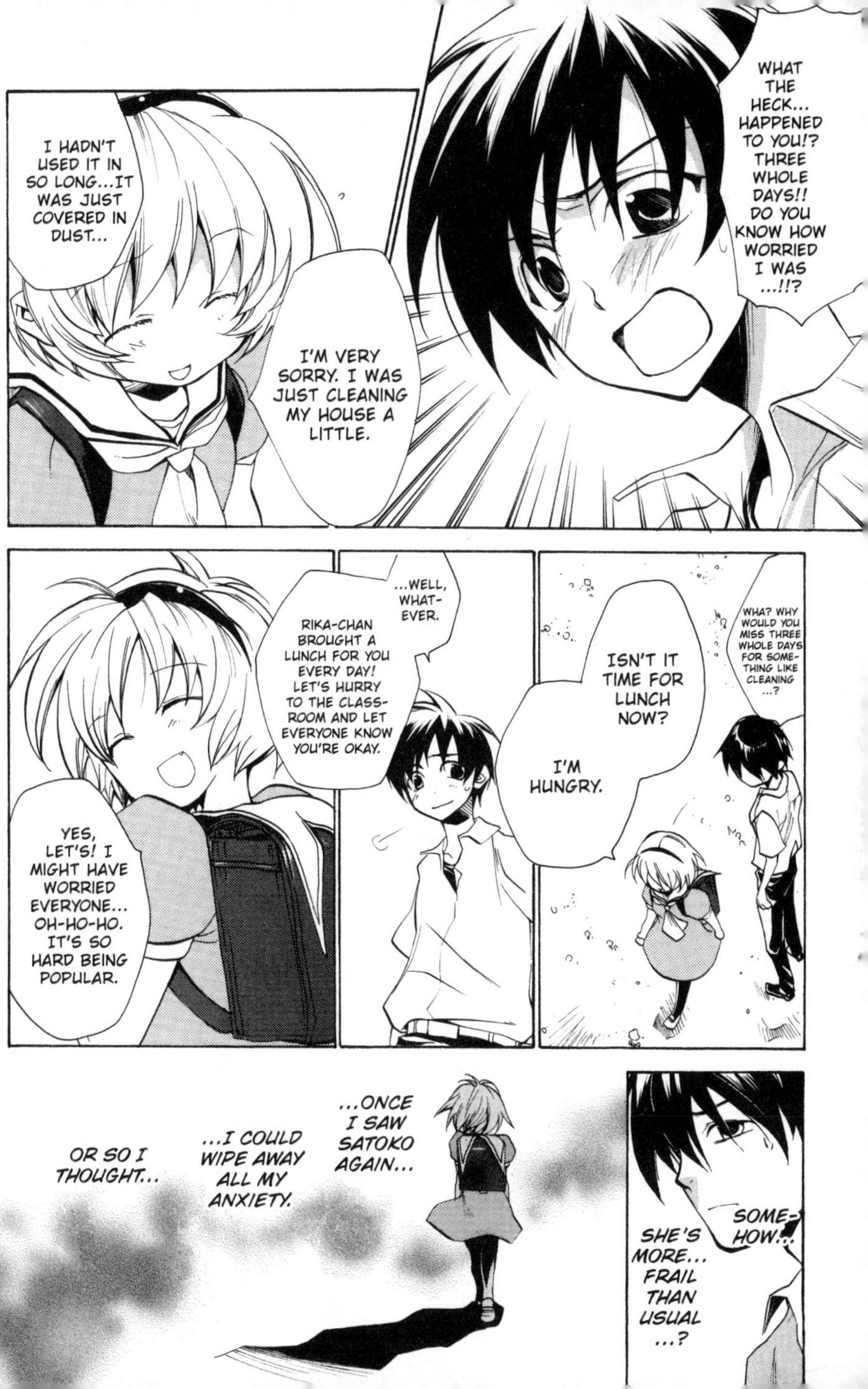
WHAT THE HECK... HAPPENED TO YOU!? THREE WHOLE DAYS!! DO YOU KNOW HOW WORRIED I WAS ...!!?
I'M VERY SORRY. I WAS JUST CLEANING MY HOUSE A LITTLE.
I HADN'T USED IT IN SO LONG...IT WAS JUST COVERED IN DUST...
WHA? WHY WOULD YOU MISS THREE WHOLE DAYS FOR SOMETHING LIKE CLEANING ...?
ISN'T IT TIME FOR LUNCH NOW?
I'M HUNGRY.
...WELL, WHATEVER.
RIKA-CHAN BROUGHT A LUNCH FOR YOU EVERY DAY! LET'S HURRY TO THE CLASSROOM AND LET EVERYONE KNOW YOU'RE OKAY.
YES, LET'S! I MIGHT HAVE WORRIED EVERYONE... OH-HO-HO. IT'S SO HARD BEING POPULAR.
SOMEHOW...
SHE'S MORE... FRAIL THAN USUAL ...?
...ONCE I SAW SATOKO AGAIN...
...I COULD WIPE AWAY ALL MY ANXIETY.
OR SO I THOUGHT...

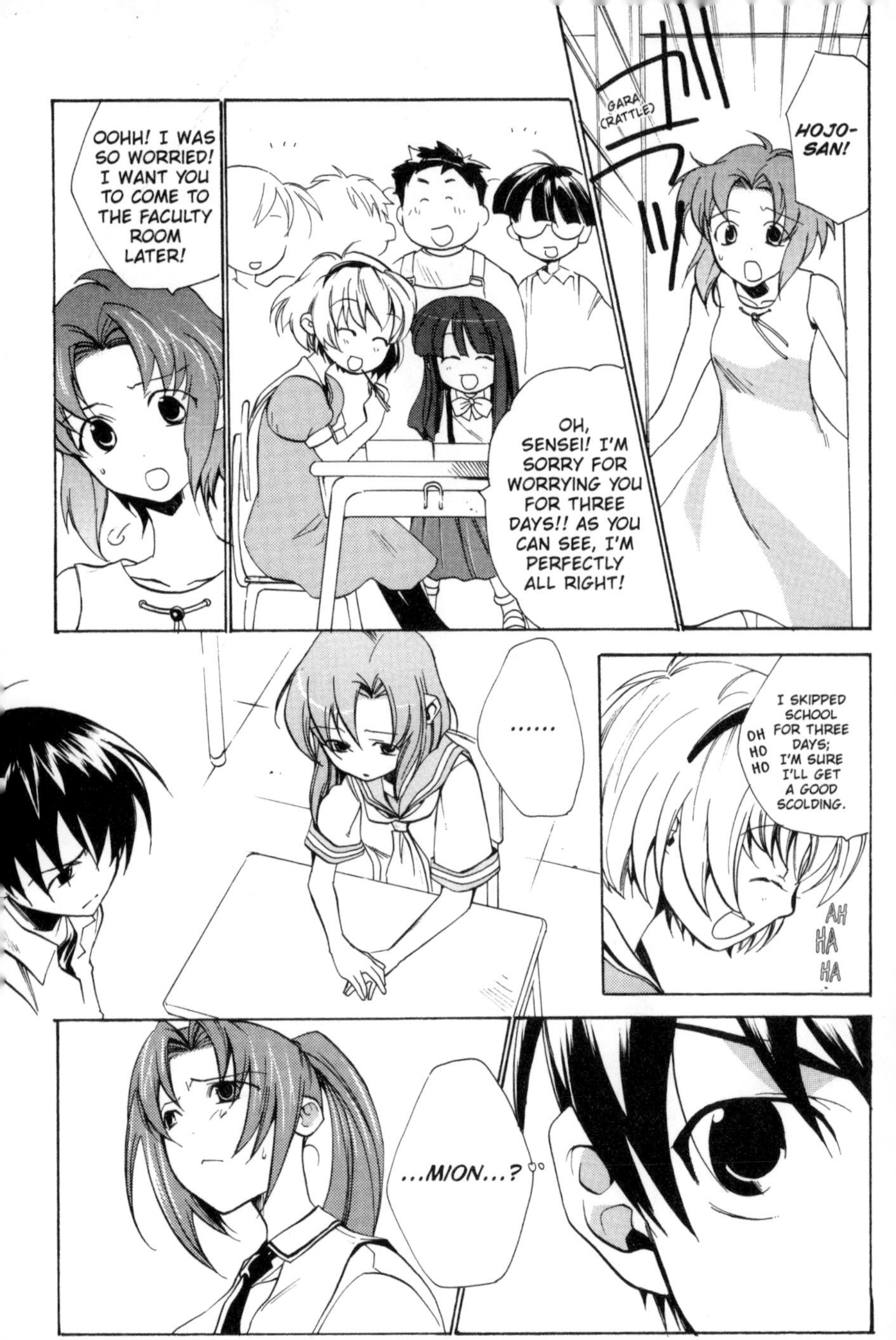
GARA (RATTLE)
HOJO-SAN!
OH, SENSEI! I'M SORRY FOR WORRYING YOU FOR THREE DAYS!! AS YOU CAN SEE, I'M PERFECTLY ALL RIGHT!
OOHH! I WAS SO WORRIED! I WANT YOU TO COME TO THE FACULTY ROOM LATER!
I SKIPPED SCHOOL FOR THREE DAYS; I'M SURE I'LL GET A GOOD SCOLDING.
OH HO HO
AH HA HA
......
...MION...?

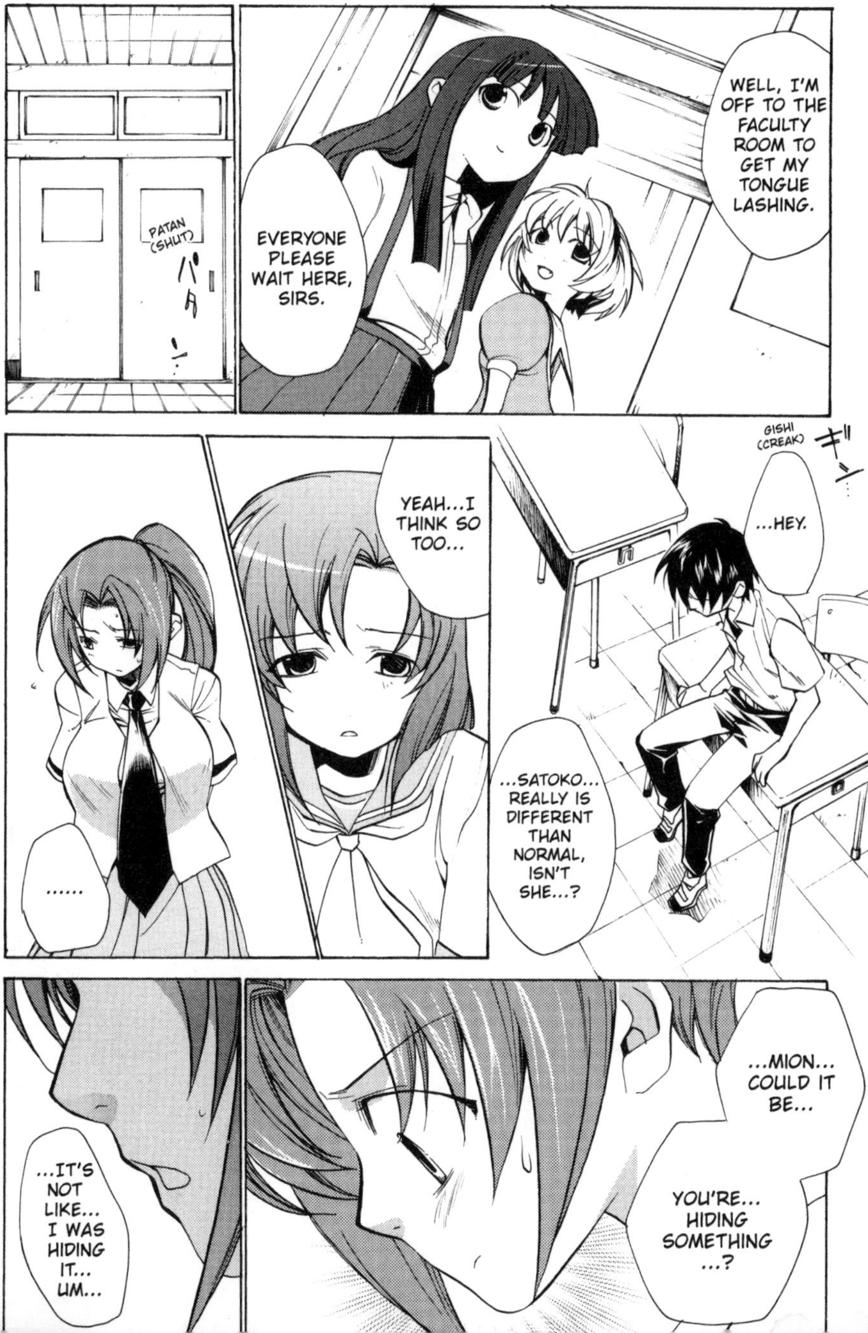
WELL, I'M OFF TO THE FACULTY ROOM TO GET MY TONGUE LASHING.
EVERYONE PLEASE WAIT HERE, SIRS.
PATAN (SHUT)
GISHI (CREAK)
...HEY.
...SATOKO... REALLY IS DIFFERENT THAN NORMAL, ISN'T SHE...?
YEAH...I THINK SO TOO...
......
...MION... COULD IT BE...
YOU'RE... HIDING SOMETHING ...?
...IT'S NOT LIKE... I WAS HIDING IT... UM...

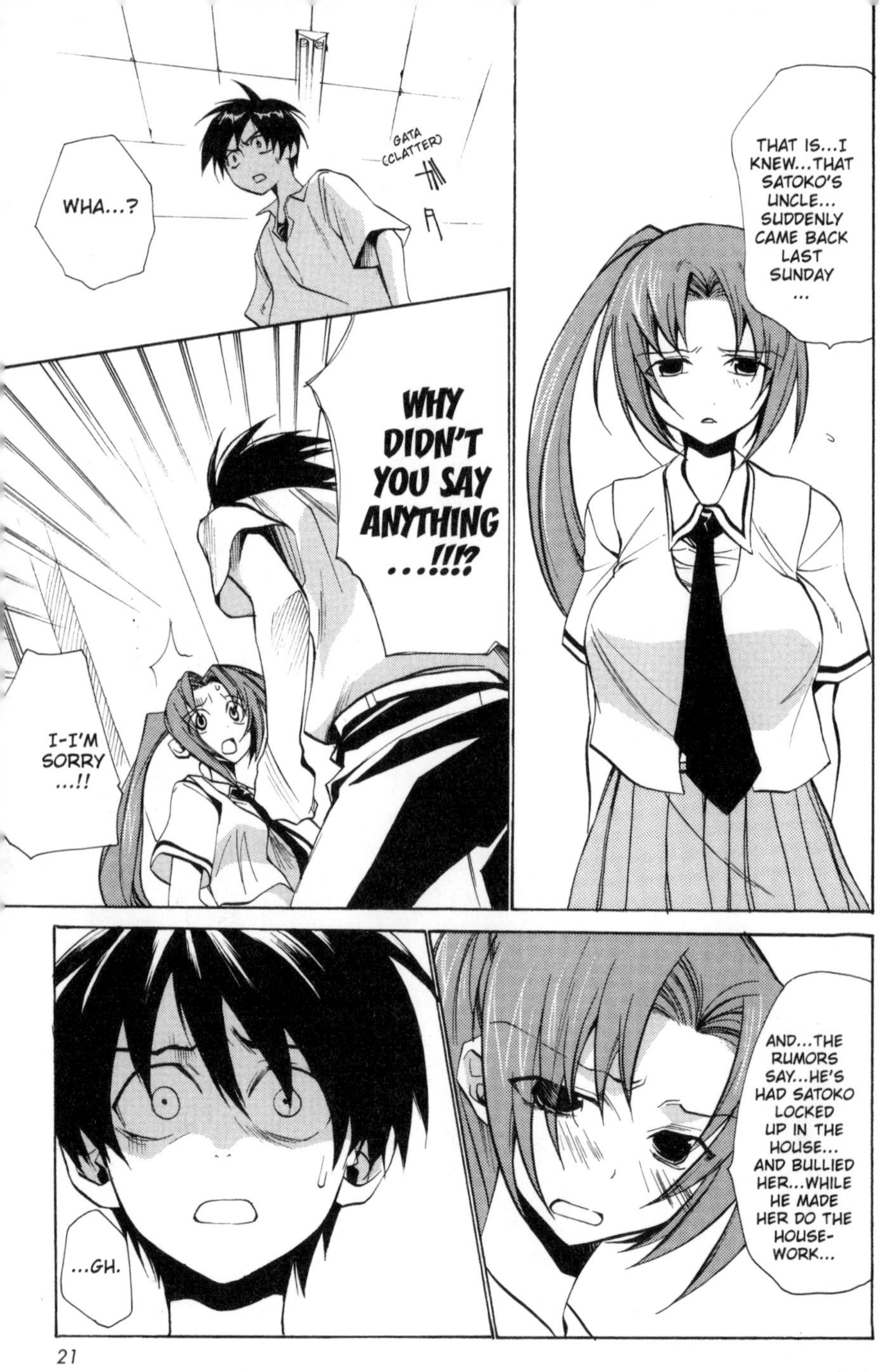
THAT IS...I KNEW...THAT SATOKO'S UNCLE... SUDDENLY CAME BACK LAST SUNDAY ...
GATA (CLATTER)
WHA...?
WHY DIDN'T YOU SAY ANYTHING ...!!!?
I-I'M SORRY ...!!
AND...THE RUMORS SAY...HE'S HAD SATOKO LOCKED UP IN THE HOUSE... AND BULLIED HER...WHILE HE MADE HER DO THE HOUSE-WORK...
...GH.

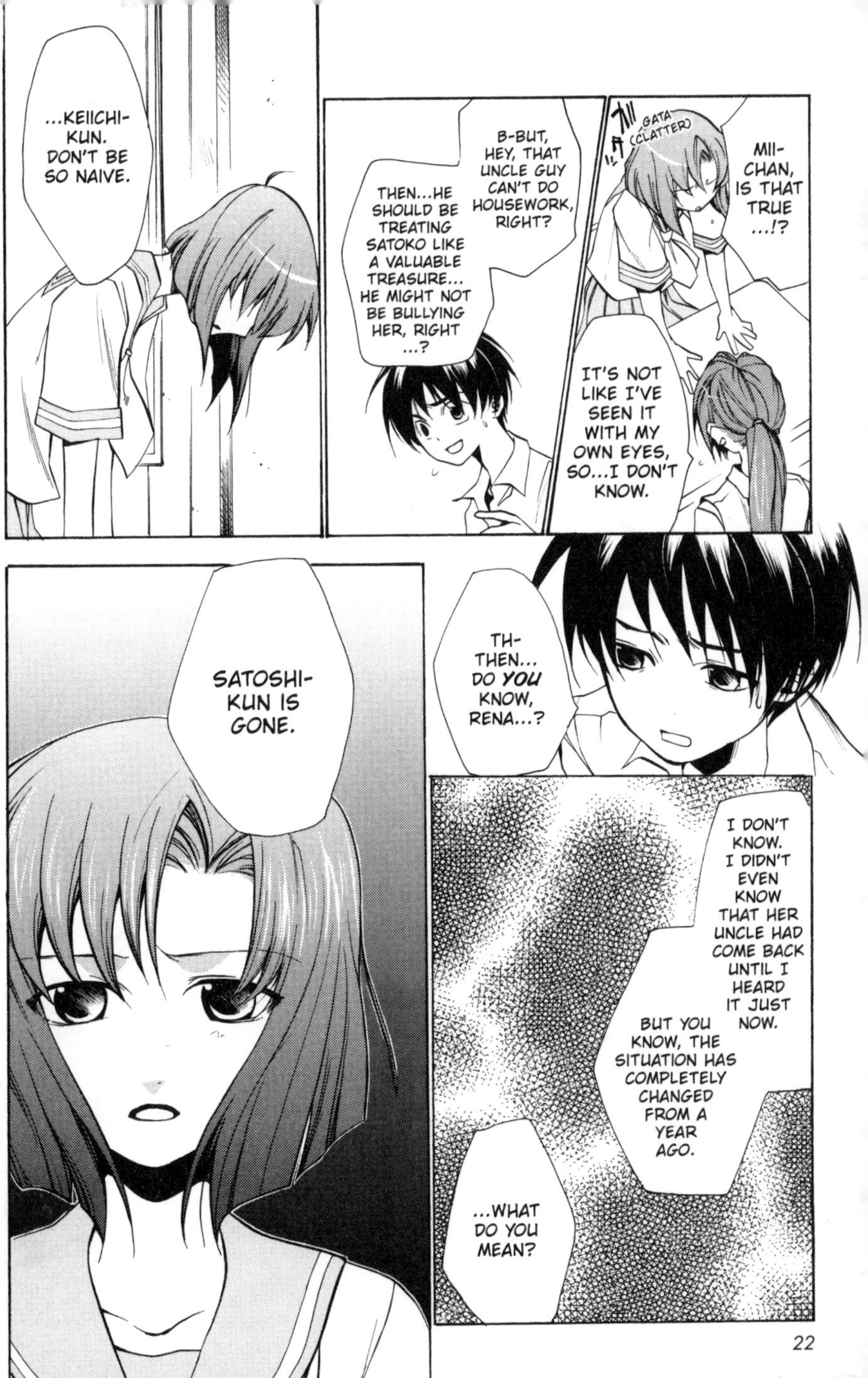
GATA (CLATTER)
MII-CHAN, IS THAT TRUE ...!?
IT'S NOT LIKE I'VE SEEN IT WITH MY OWN EYES, SO...I DON'T KNOW.
B-BUT, HEY, THAT UNCLE GUY CAN'T DO HOUSEWORK, RIGHT?
THEN...HE SHOULD BE TREATING SATOKO LIKE A VALUABLE TREASURE... HE MIGHT NOT BE BULLYING HER, RIGHT ...?
...KEIICHI-KUN. DON'T BE SO NAIVE.
TH-THEN... DO *YOU* KNOW, RENA...?
I DON'T KNOW. I DIDN'T EVEN KNOW THAT HER UNCLE HAD COME BACK UNTIL I HEARD IT JUST NOW.
BUT YOU KNOW, THE SITUATION HAS COMPLETELY CHANGED FROM A YEAR AGO.
...WHAT DO YOU MEAN?
SATOSHI-KUN IS GONE.

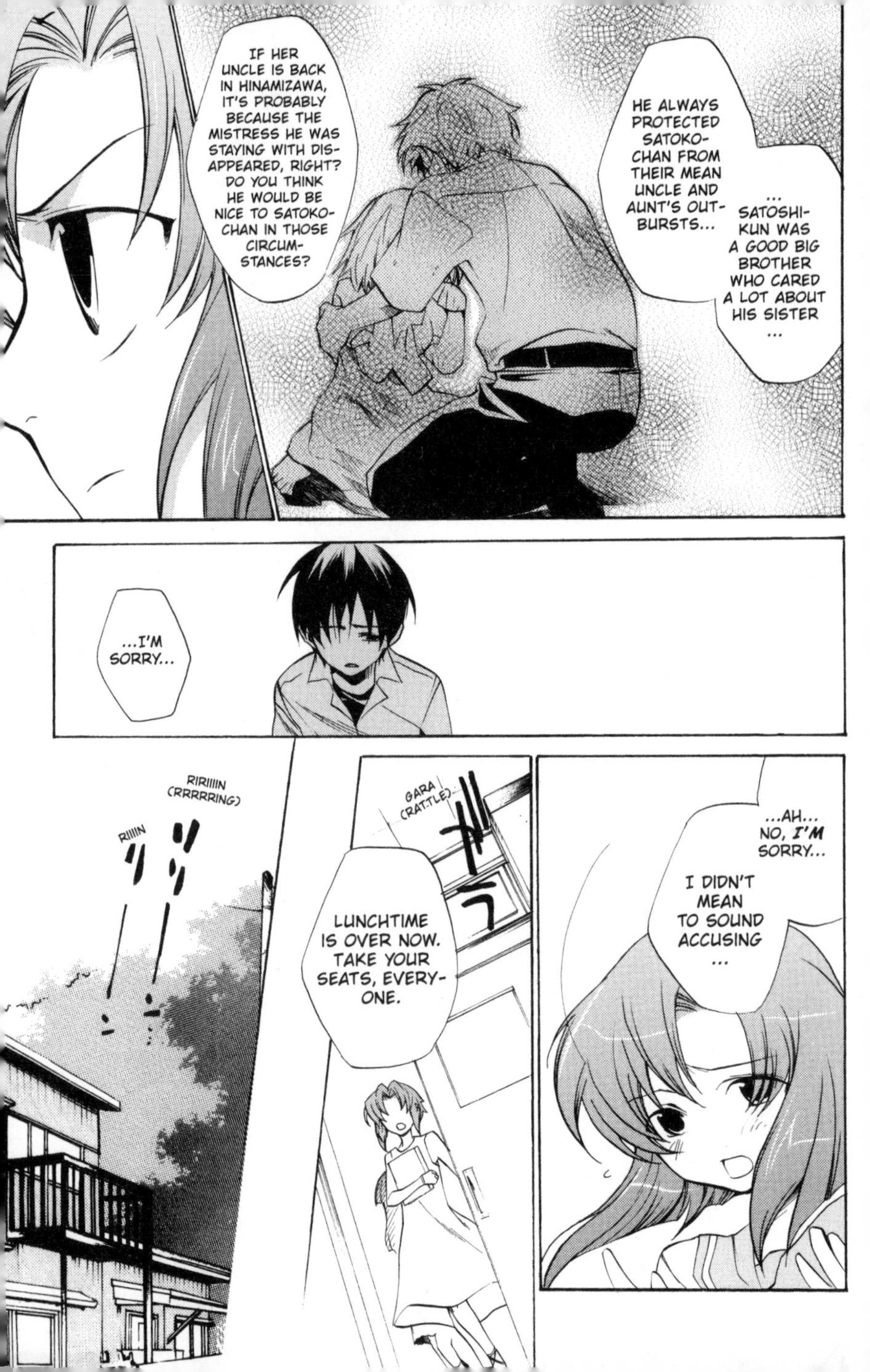
...SATOSHI-KUN WAS A GOOD BIG BROTHER WHO CARED A LOT ABOUT HIS SISTER...
HE ALWAYS PROTECTED SATOKO-CHAN FROM THEIR MEAN UNCLE AND AUNT'S OUTBURSTS...
IF HER UNCLE IS BACK IN HINAMIZAWA, IT'S PROBABLY BECAUSE THE MISTRESS HE WAS STAYING WITH DISAPPEARED, RIGHT? DO YOU THINK HE WOULD BE NICE TO SATOKO-CHAN IN THOSE CIRCUMSTANCES?
...I'M SORRY...
...AH... NO, *I'M* SORRY...
I DIDN'T MEAN TO SOUND ACCUSING...
GARA (RATTLE)
LUNCHTIME IS OVER NOW. TAKE YOUR SEATS, EVERYONE.
RIRIIIN (RRRRRING)
RIIIN

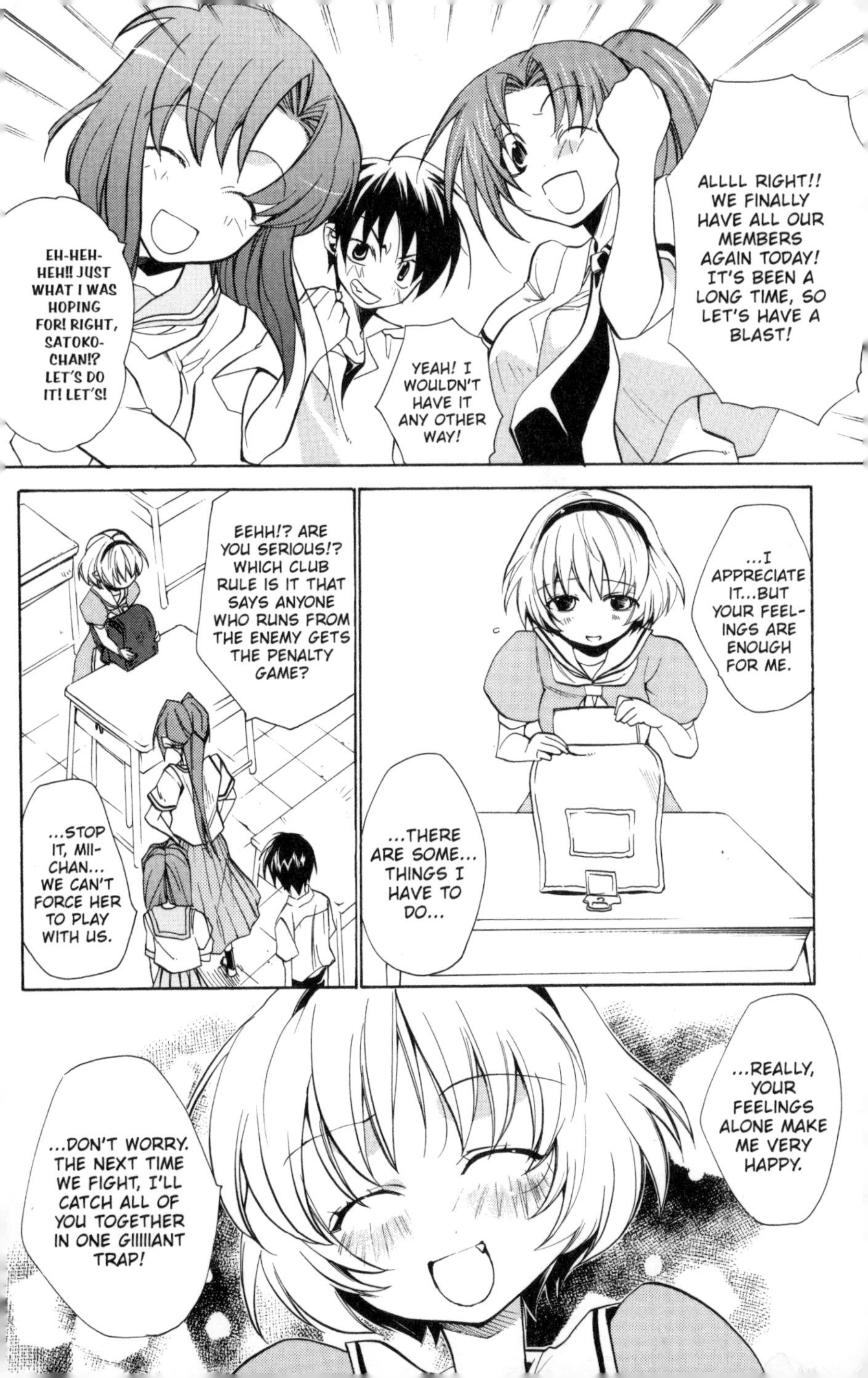
ALLLL RIGHT!! WE FINALLY HAVE ALL OUR MEMBERS AGAIN TODAY! IT'S BEEN A LONG TIME, SO LET'S HAVE A BLAST!
YEAH! I WOULDN'T HAVE IT ANY OTHER WAY!
EH-HEH-HEH!! JUST WHAT I WAS HOPING FOR! RIGHT, SATOKO-CHAN!? LET'S DO IT! LET'S!
...I APPRECIATE IT...BUT YOUR FEEL-INGS ARE ENOUGH FOR ME.
...THERE ARE SOME... THINGS I HAVE TO DO...
EEHH!? ARE YOU SERIOUS!? WHICH CLUB RULE IS IT THAT SAYS ANYONE WHO RUNS FROM THE ENEMY GETS THE PENALTY GAME?
...STOP IT, MII-CHAN... WE CAN'T FORCE HER TO PLAY WITH US.
...REALLY, YOUR FEELINGS ALONE MAKE ME VERY HAPPY.
...DON'T WORRY. THE NEXT TIME WE FIGHT, I'LL CATCH ALL OF YOU TOGETHER IN ONE GIIIIIANT TRAP!

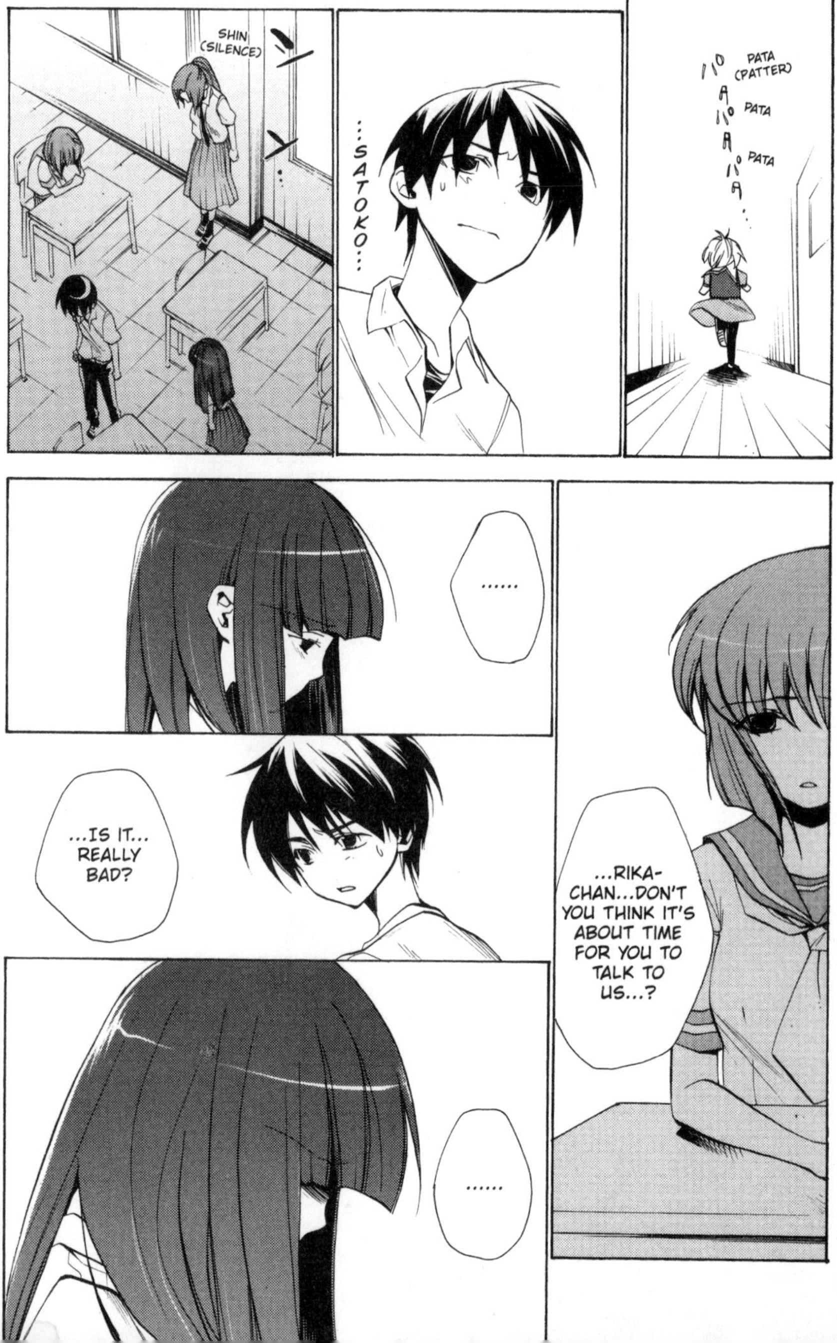
PATA (PATTER)
PATA
PATA
...SATOKO...
SHIN (SILENCE)
...RIKA-CHAN...DON'T YOU THINK IT'S ABOUT TIME FOR YOU TO TALK TO US...?
......
...IS IT... REALLY BAD?
......

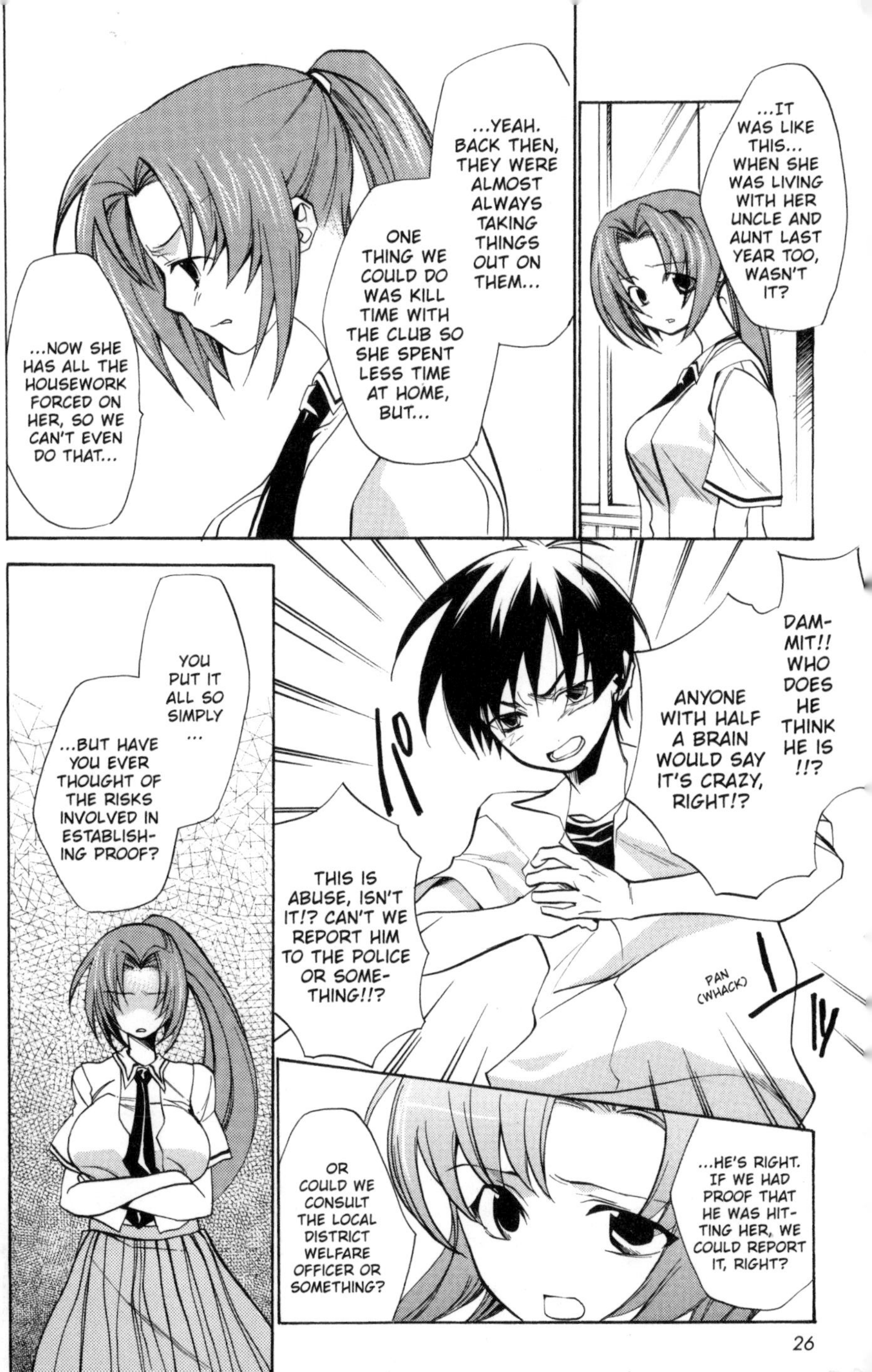
...IT WAS LIKE THIS... WHEN SHE WAS LIVING WITH HER UNCLE AND AUNT LAST YEAR TOO, WASN'T IT?
...YEAH. BACK THEN, THEY WERE ALMOST ALWAYS TAKING THINGS OUT ON THEM...
ONE THING WE COULD DO WAS KILL TIME WITH THE CLUB SO SHE SPENT LESS TIME AT HOME, BUT...
...NOW SHE HAS ALL THE HOUSEWORK FORCED ON HER, SO WE CAN'T EVEN DO THAT...
DAMMIT!! WHO DOES HE THINK HE IS!!?
ANYONE WITH HALF A BRAIN WOULD SAY IT'S CRAZY, RIGHT!?
THIS IS ABUSE, ISN'T IT!? CAN'T WE REPORT HIM TO THE POLICE OR SOMETHING!!?
PAN (WHACK)
...HE'S RIGHT. IF WE HAD PROOF THAT HE WAS HITTING HER, WE COULD REPORT IT, RIGHT?
OR COULD WE CONSULT THE LOCAL DISTRICT WELFARE OFFICER OR SOMETHING?
YOU PUT IT ALL SO SIMPLY ...
...BUT HAVE YOU EVER THOUGHT OF THE RISKS INVOLVED IN ESTABLISHING PROOF?

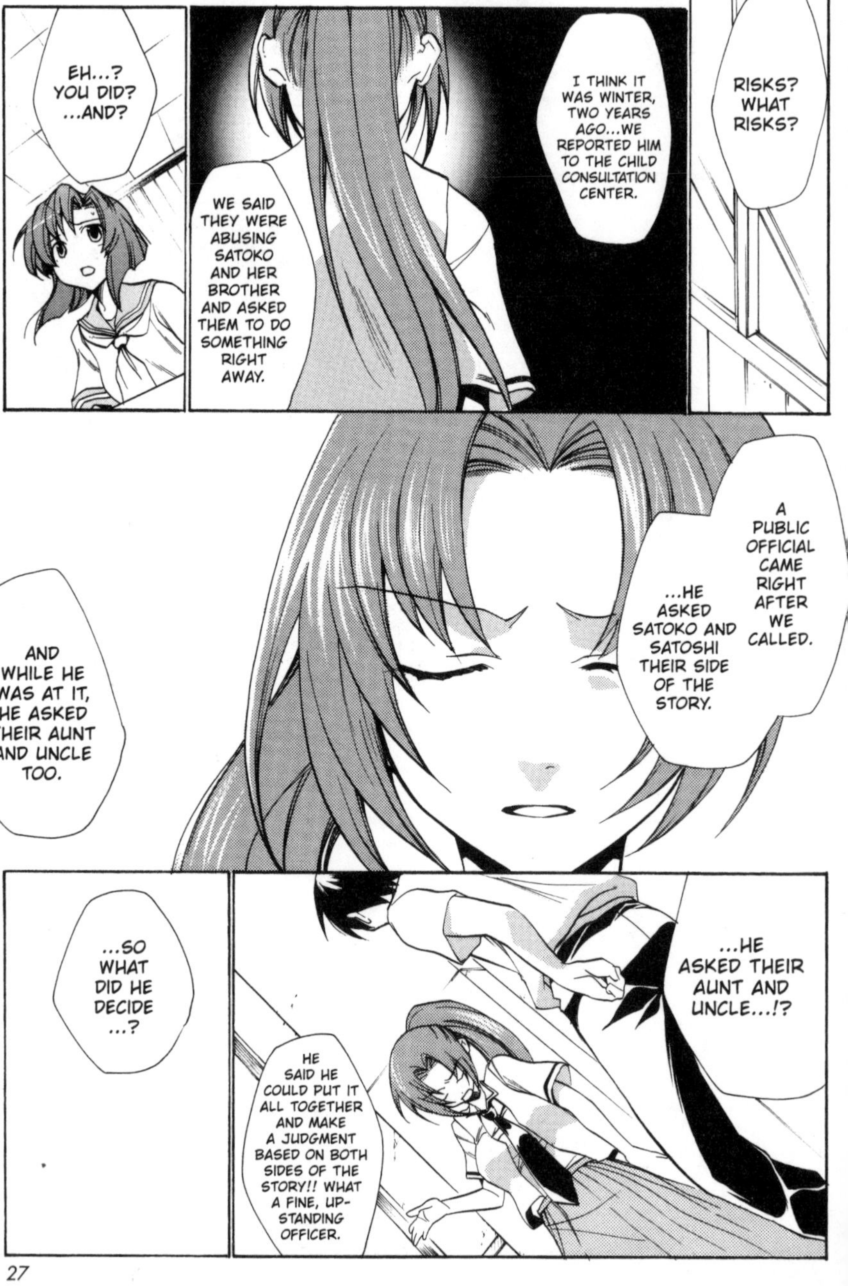
RISKS? WHAT RISKS?
I THINK IT WAS WINTER, TWO YEARS AGO...WE REPORTED HIM TO THE CHILD CONSULTATION CENTER.
WE SAID THEY WERE ABUSING SATOKO AND HER BROTHER AND ASKED THEM TO DO SOMETHING RIGHT AWAY.
EH...? YOU DID? ...AND?
A PUBLIC OFFICIAL CAME RIGHT AFTER WE CALLED.
...HE ASKED SATOKO AND SATOSHI THEIR SIDE OF THE STORY.
AND WHILE HE WAS AT IT, HE ASKED THEIR AUNT AND UNCLE TOO.
...HE ASKED THEIR AUNT AND UNCLE...!?
HE SAID HE COULD PUT IT ALL TOGETHER AND MAKE A JUDGMENT BASED ON BOTH SIDES OF THE STORY!! WHAT A FINE, UP-STANDING OFFICER.
...SO WHAT DID HE DECIDE ...?

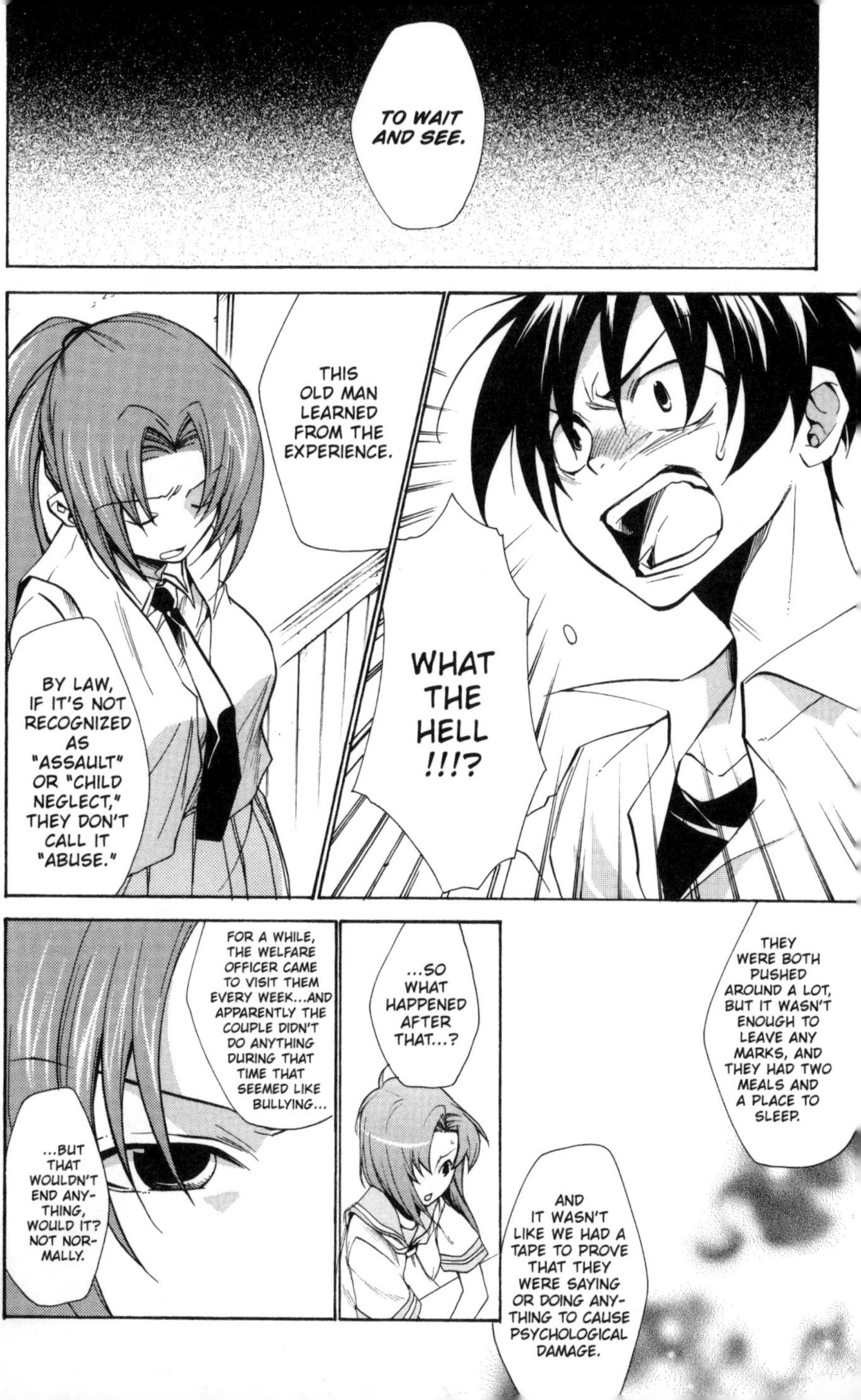
TO WAIT AND SEE.
WHAT THE HELL!!!?
THIS OLD MAN LEARNED FROM THE EXPERIENCE.
BY LAW, IF IT'S NOT RECOGNIZED AS "ASSAULT" OR "CHILD NEGLECT," THEY DON'T CALL IT "ABUSE."
THEY WERE BOTH PUSHED AROUND A LOT, BUT IT WASN'T ENOUGH TO LEAVE ANY MARKS, AND THEY HAD TWO MEALS AND A PLACE TO SLEEP.
AND IT WASN'T LIKE WE HAD A TAPE TO PROVE THAT THEY WERE SAYING OR DOING ANY-THING TO CAUSE PSYCHOLOGICAL DAMAGE.
...SO WHAT HAPPENED AFTER THAT...?
FOR A WHILE, THE WELFARE OFFICER CAME TO VISIT THEM EVERY WEEK...AND APPARENTLY THE COUPLE DIDN'T DO ANYTHING DURING THAT TIME THAT SEEMED LIKE BULLYING...
...BUT THAT WOULDN'T END ANY-THING, WOULD IT? NOT NOR-MALLY.

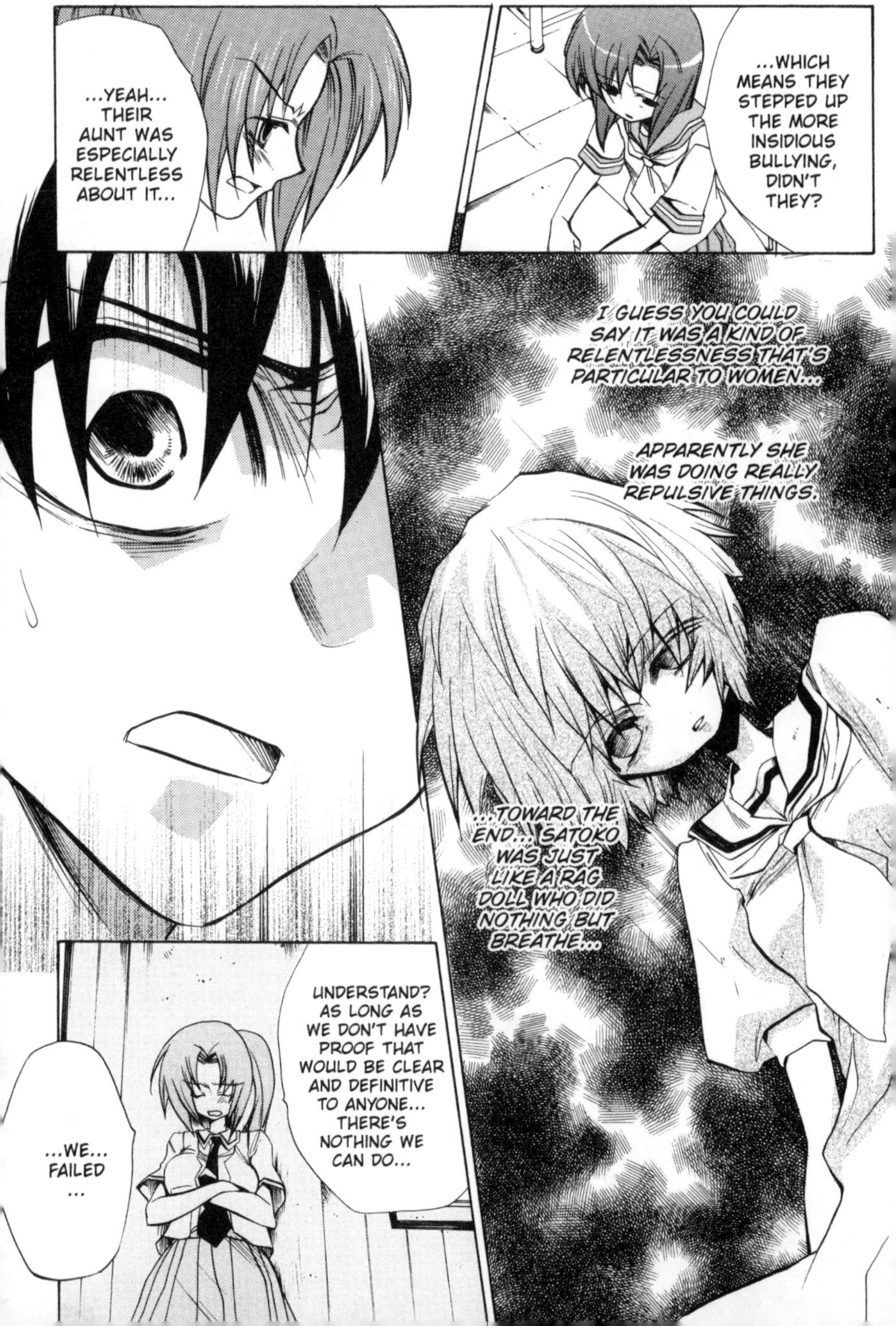
...WHICH MEANS THEY STEPPED UP THE MORE INSIDIOUS BULLYING, DIDN'T THEY?
...YEAH... THEIR AUNT WAS ESPECIALLY RELENTLESS ABOUT IT...
I GUESS YOU COULD SAY IT WAS A KIND OF RELENTLESSNESS THAT'S PARTICULAR TO WOMEN...
APPARENTLY SHE WAS DOING REALLY REPULSIVE THINGS.
...TOWARD THE END... SATOKO WAS JUST LIKE A RAG DOLL WHO DID NOTHING BUT BREATHE...
UNDERSTAND? AS LONG AS WE DON'T HAVE PROOF THAT WOULD BE CLEAR AND DEFINITIVE TO ANYONE... THERE'S NOTHING WE CAN DO...
...WE... FAILED ...

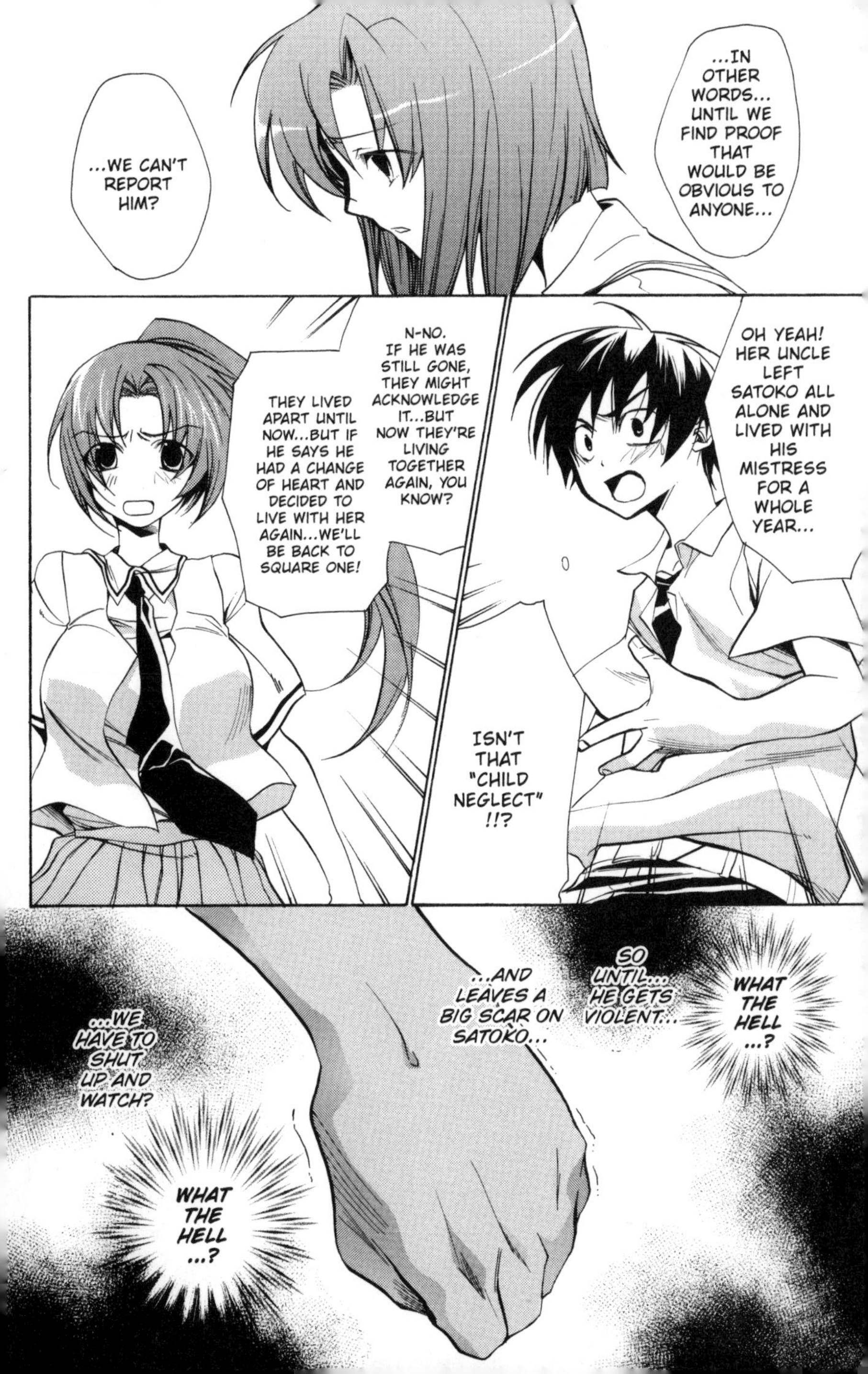
...IN OTHER WORDS... UNTIL WE FIND PROOF THAT WOULD BE OBVIOUS TO ANYONE...
...WE CAN'T REPORT HIM?
OH YEAH! HER UNCLE LEFT SATOKO ALL ALONE AND LIVED WITH HIS MISTRESS FOR A WHOLE YEAR...
ISN'T THAT "CHILD NEGLECT" !!?
N-NO. IF HE WAS STILL GONE, THEY MIGHT ACKNOWLEDGE IT...BUT NOW THEY'RE LIVING TOGETHER AGAIN, YOU KNOW?
THEY LIVED APART UNTIL NOW...BUT IF HE SAYS HE HAD A CHANGE OF HEART AND DECIDED TO LIVE WITH HER AGAIN...WE'LL BE BACK TO SQUARE ONE!
WHAT THE HELL ...?
SO UNTIL... HE GETS VIOLENT...
...AND LEAVES A BIG SCAR ON SATOKO...
...WE HAVE TO SHUT UP AND WATCH?
WHAT THE HELL ...?

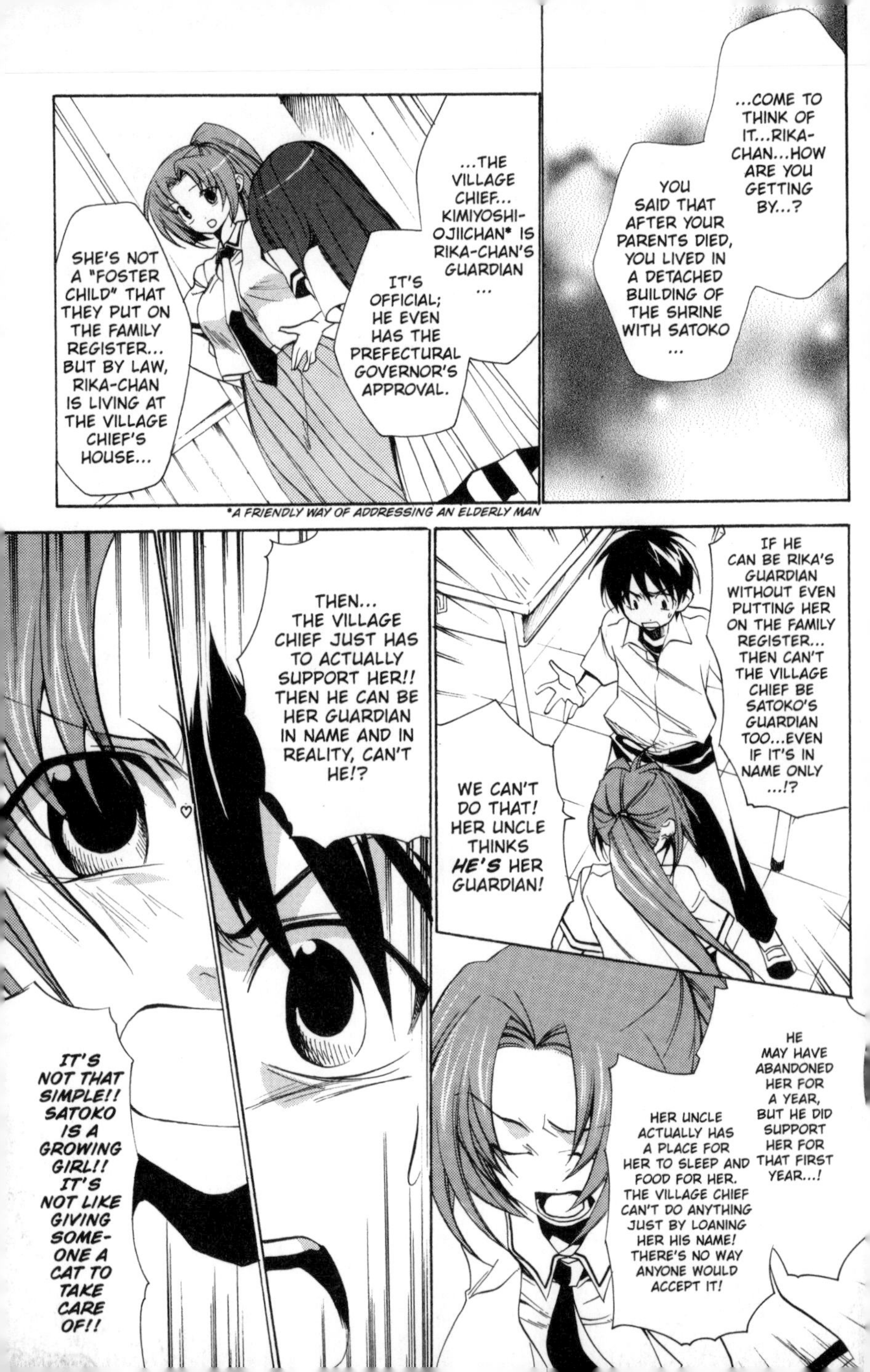
...COME TO THINK OF IT...RIKA-CHAN...HOW ARE YOU GETTING BY...?
YOU SAID THAT AFTER YOUR PARENTS DIED, YOU LIVED IN A DETACHED BUILDING OF THE SHRINE WITH SATOKO...
...THE VILLAGE CHIEF... KIMIYOSHI-OJIICHAN* IS RIKA-CHAN'S GUARDIAN...
IT'S OFFICIAL; HE EVEN HAS THE PREFECTURAL GOVERNOR'S APPROVAL.
SHE'S NOT A "FOSTER CHILD" THAT THEY PUT ON THE FAMILY REGISTER... BUT BY LAW, RIKA-CHAN IS LIVING AT THE VILLAGE CHIEF'S HOUSE...
*A FRIENDLY WAY OF ADDRESSING AN ELDERLY MAN
IF HE CAN BE RIKA'S GUARDIAN WITHOUT EVEN PUTTING HER ON THE FAMILY REGISTER... THEN CAN'T THE VILLAGE CHIEF BE SATOKO'S GUARDIAN TOO...EVEN IF IT'S IN NAME ONLY ...!?
WE CAN'T DO THAT! HER UNCLE THINKS *HE'S* HER GUARDIAN!
HE MAY HAVE ABANDONED HER FOR A YEAR, BUT HE DID SUPPORT HER FOR THAT FIRST YEAR...!
HER UNCLE ACTUALLY HAS A PLACE FOR HER TO SLEEP AND FOOD FOR HER. THE VILLAGE CHIEF CAN'T DO ANYTHING JUST BY LOANING HER HIS NAME! THERE'S NO WAY ANYONE WOULD ACCEPT IT!
THEN... THE VILLAGE CHIEF JUST HAS TO ACTUALLY SUPPORT HER!! THEN HE CAN BE HER GUARDIAN IN NAME AND IN REALITY, CAN'T HE!?
IT'S NOT THAT SIMPLE!! SATOKO IS A GROWING GIRL!! IT'S NOT LIKE GIVING SOME-ONE A CAT TO TAKE CARE OF!!

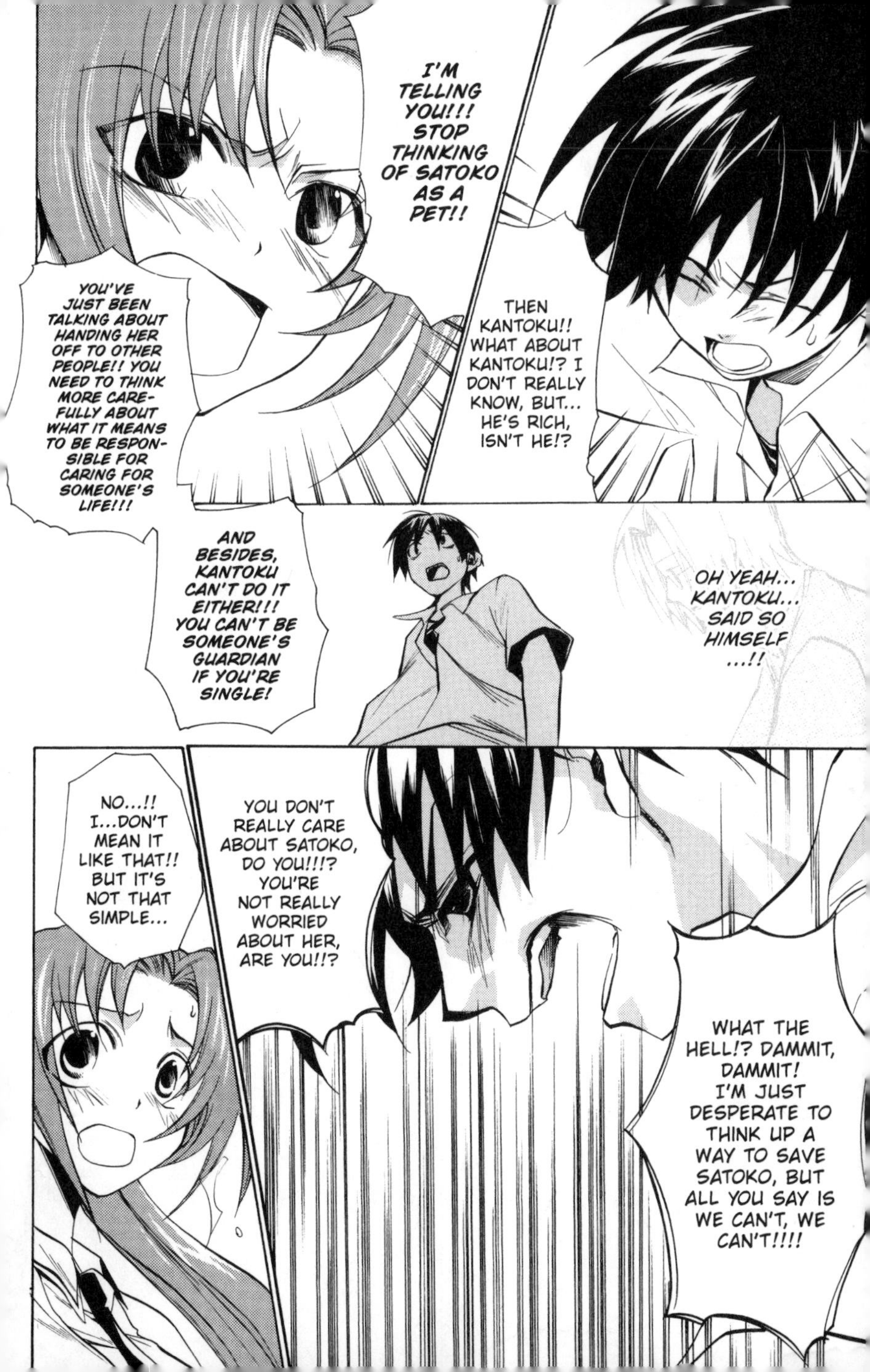
I'M TELLING YOU!!! STOP THINKING OF SATOKO AS A PET!!
THEN KANTOKU!! WHAT ABOUT KANTOKU!? I DON'T REALLY KNOW, BUT... HE'S RICH, ISN'T HE!?
YOU'VE JUST BEEN TALKING ABOUT HANDING HER OFF TO OTHER PEOPLE!! YOU NEED TO THINK MORE CARE-FULLY ABOUT WHAT IT MEANS TO BE RESPON-SIBLE FOR CARING FOR SOMEONE'S LIFE!!!
AND BESIDES, KANTOKU CAN'T DO IT EITHER!!! YOU CAN'T BE SOMEONE'S GUARDIAN IF YOU'RE SINGLE!
OH YEAH... KANTOKU... SAID SO HIMSELF ...!!
WHAT THE HELL!? DAMMIT, DAMMIT! I'M JUST DESPERATE TO THINK UP A WAY TO SAVE SATOKO, BUT ALL YOU SAY IS WE CAN'T, WE CAN'T!!!!
YOU DON'T REALLY CARE ABOUT SATOKO, DO YOU!!!? YOU'RE NOT REALLY WORRIED ABOUT HER, ARE YOU!!?
NO...!! I...DON'T MEAN IT LIKE THAT!! BUT IT'S NOT THAT SIMPLE...

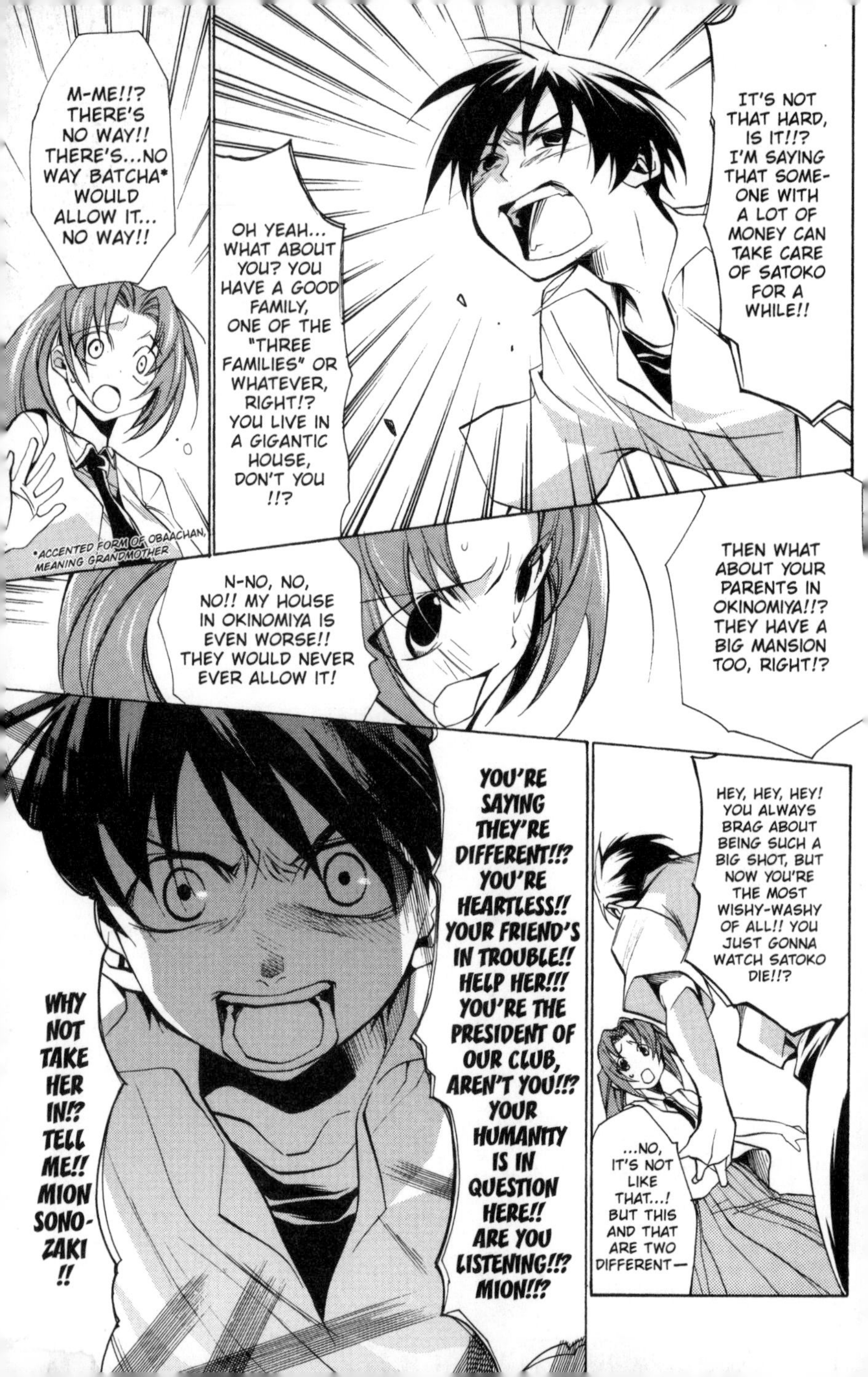
IT'S NOT THAT HARD, IS IT!!? I'M SAYING THAT SOMEONE WITH A LOT OF MONEY CAN TAKE CARE OF SATOKO FOR A WHILE!!
OH YEAH... WHAT ABOUT YOU? YOU HAVE A GOOD FAMILY, ONE OF THE "THREE FAMILIES" OR WHATEVER, RIGHT!? YOU LIVE IN A GIGANTIC HOUSE, DON'T YOU!!?
M-ME!!? THERE'S NO WAY!! THERE'S...NO WAY BATCHA* WOULD ALLOW IT... NO WAY!!
*ACCENTED FORM OF OBAACHAN, MEANING GRANDMOTHER
THEN WHAT ABOUT YOUR PARENTS IN OKINOMIYA!!? THEY HAVE A BIG MANSION TOO, RIGHT!?
N-NO, NO, NO!! MY HOUSE IN OKINOMIYA IS EVEN WORSE!! THEY WOULD NEVER EVER ALLOW IT!
HEY, HEY, HEY! YOU ALWAYS BRAG ABOUT BEING SUCH A BIG SHOT, BUT NOW YOU'RE THE MOST WISHY-WASHY OF ALL!! YOU JUST GONNA WATCH SATOKO DIE!!?
...NO, IT'S NOT LIKE THAT...! BUT THIS AND THAT ARE TWO DIFFERENT—
YOU'RE SAYING THEY'RE DIFFERENT!!? YOU'RE HEARTLESS!! YOUR FRIEND'S IN TROUBLE!! HELP HER!!! YOU'RE THE PRESIDENT OF OUR CLUB, AREN'T YOU!!? YOUR HUMANITY IS IN QUESTION HERE!! ARE YOU LISTENING!!? MION!!?
WHY NOT TAKE HER IN!? TELL ME!! MION SONOZAKI!!

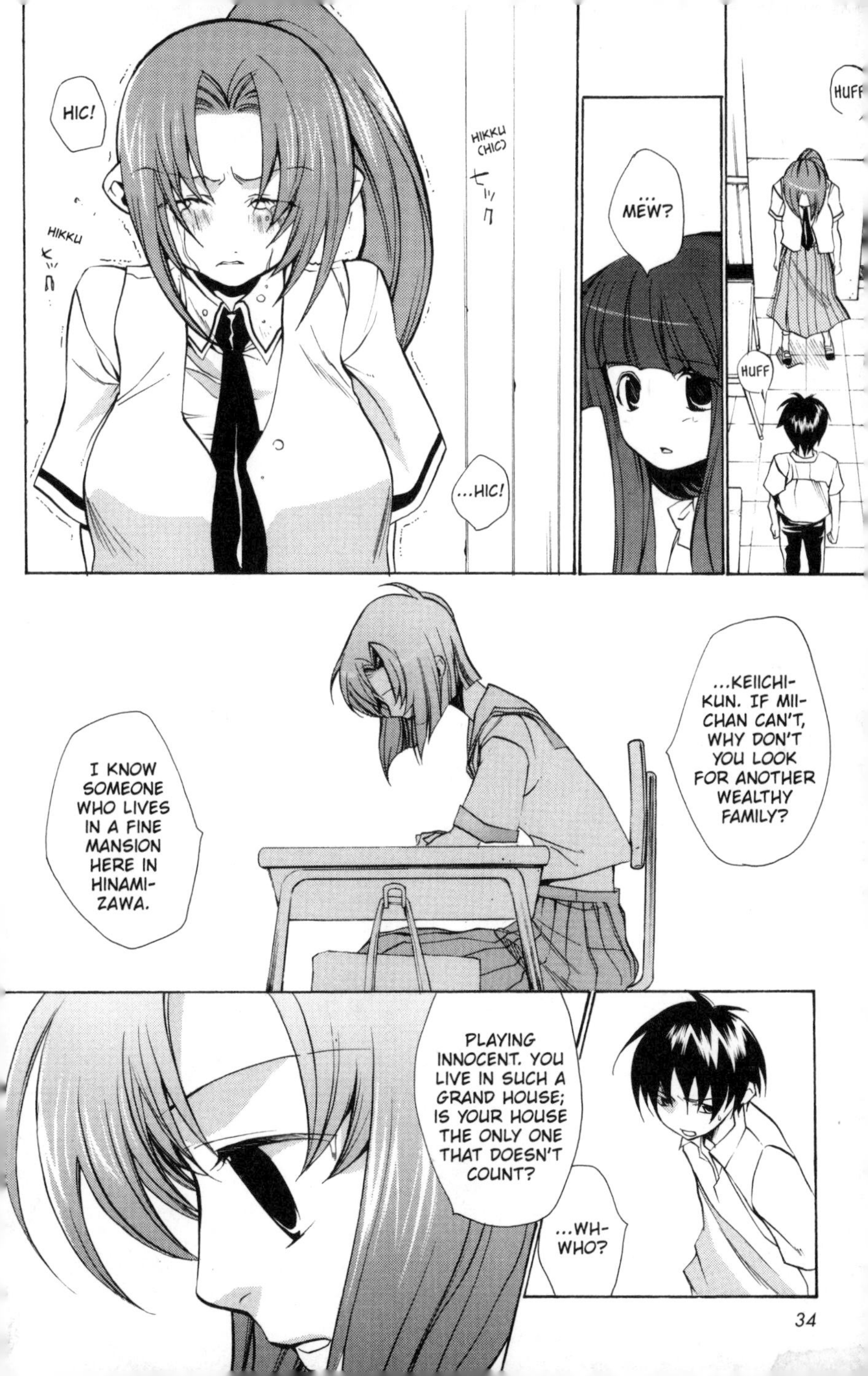
HUFF
HUFF
...MEW?
HIC!
HIKKU (HIC)
HIKKU
...HIC!
...KEIICHI-KUN. IF MII-CHAN CAN'T, WHY DON'T YOU LOOK FOR ANOTHER WEALTHY FAMILY?
I KNOW SOMEONE WHO LIVES IN A FINE MANSION HERE IN HINAMI-ZAWA.
...WH-WHO?
PLAYING INNOCENT. YOU LIVE IN SUCH A GRAND HOUSE; IS YOUR HOUSE THE ONLY ONE THAT DOESN'T COUNT?

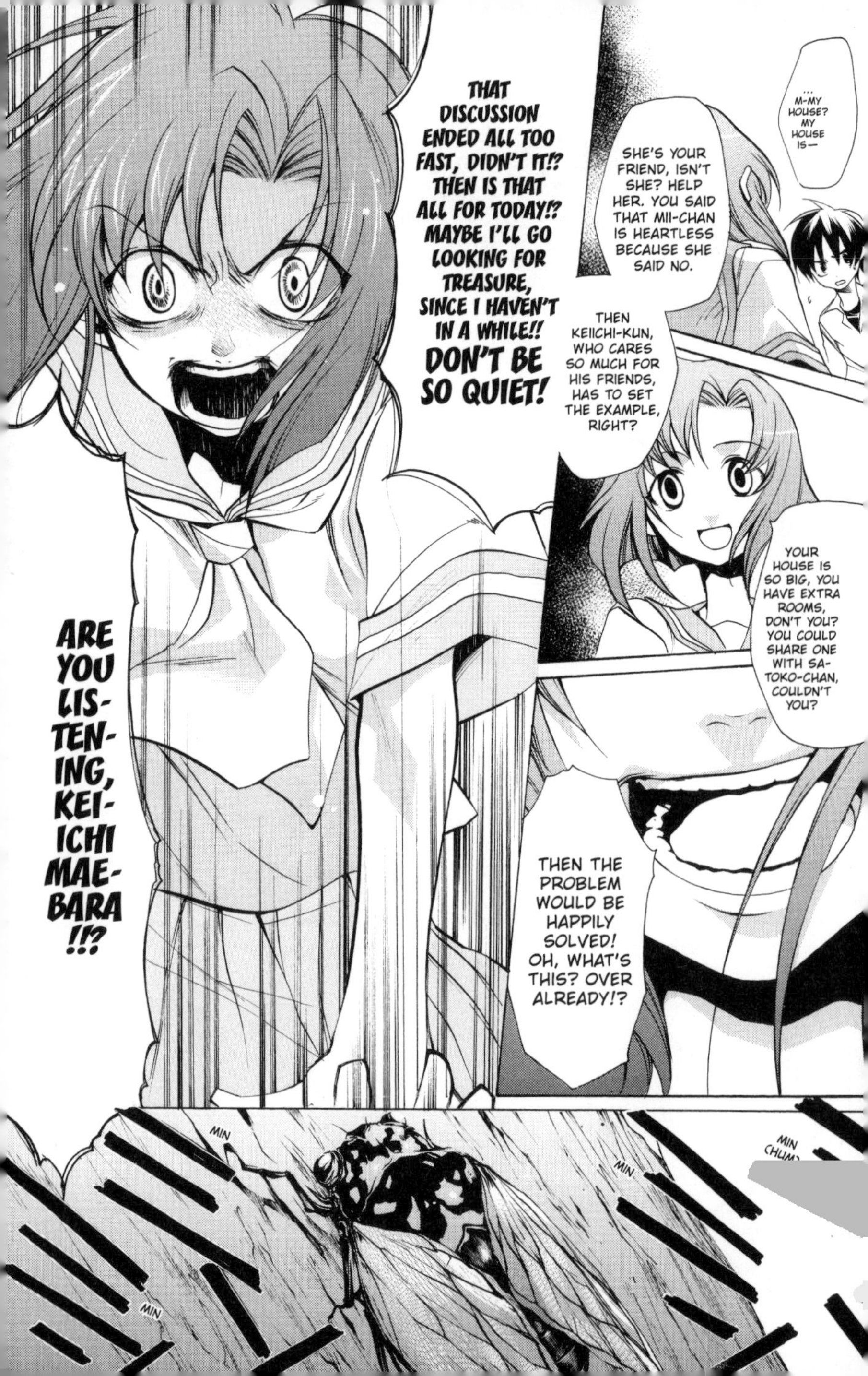
...M-MY HOUSE? MY HOUSE IS—
SHE'S YOUR FRIEND, ISN'T SHE? HELP HER. YOU SAID THAT MII-CHAN IS HEARTLESS BECAUSE SHE SAID NO.
THEN KEIICHI-KUN, WHO CARES SO MUCH FOR HIS FRIENDS, HAS TO SET THE EXAMPLE, RIGHT?
YOUR HOUSE IS SO BIG, YOU HAVE EXTRA ROOMS, DON'T YOU? YOU COULD SHARE ONE WITH SA-TOKO-CHAN, COULDN'T YOU?
THEN THE PROBLEM WOULD BE HAPPILY SOLVED! OH, WHAT'S THIS? OVER ALREADY!?
THAT DISCUSSION ENDED ALL TOO FAST, DIDN'T IT!? THEN IS THAT ALL FOR TODAY!? MAYBE I'LL GO LOOKING FOR TREASURE, SINCE I HAVEN'T IN A WHILE!! DON'T BE SO QUIET!
ARE YOU LIS-TEN-ING, KEI-ICHI MAE-BARA!!?
MIN (CHUM)
MIN
MIN
MIN

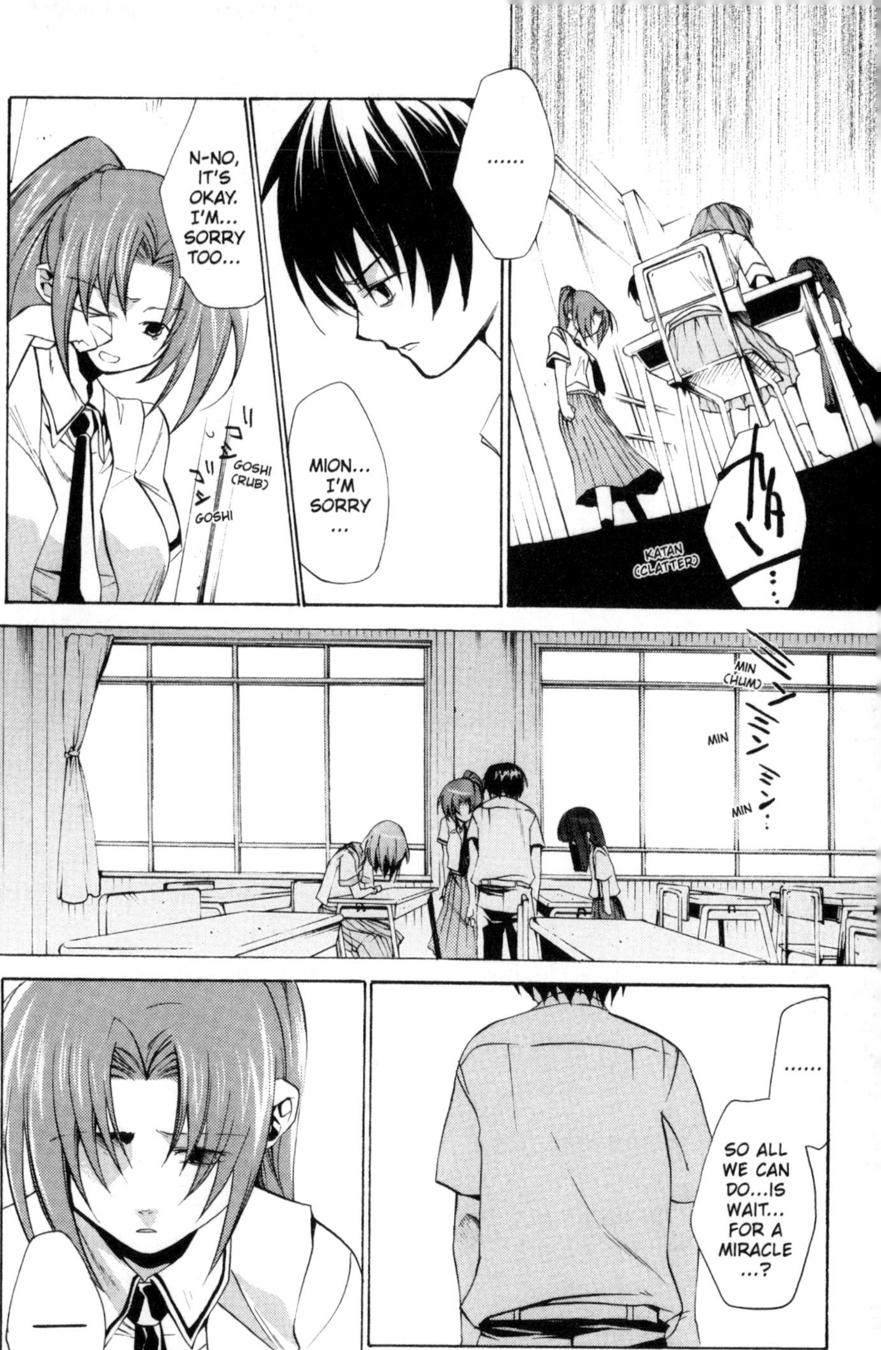

KATAN (CLATTER)
......
MION... I'M SORRY ...
N-NO, IT'S OKAY. I'M... SORRY TOO...
GOSHI (RUB)
GOSHI
MIN (HUM)
MIN
MIN
......
SO ALL WE CAN DO...IS WAIT... FOR A MIRACLE ...?
——

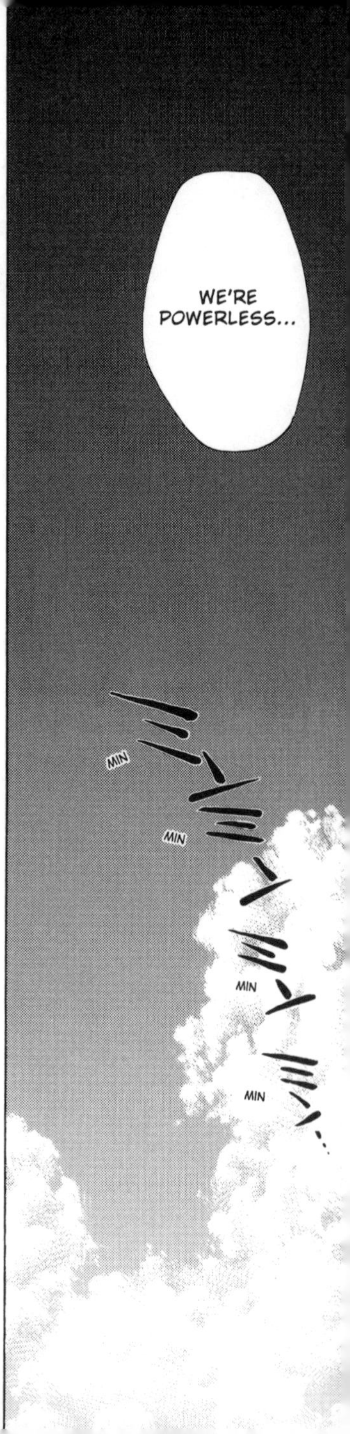
WE'RE POWERLESS...
MIN
MIN
MIN
MIN

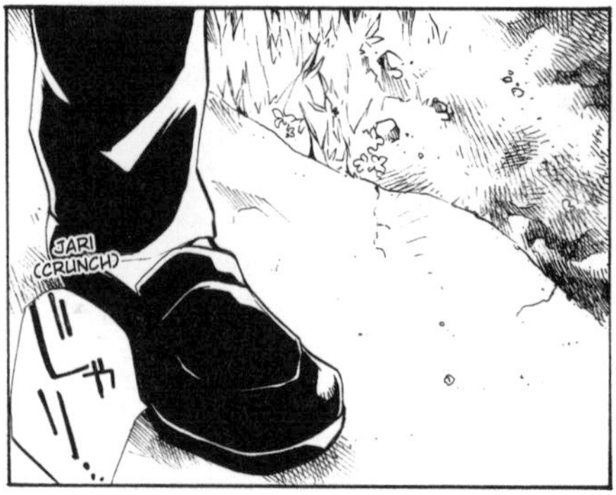
JARI (CRUNCH)

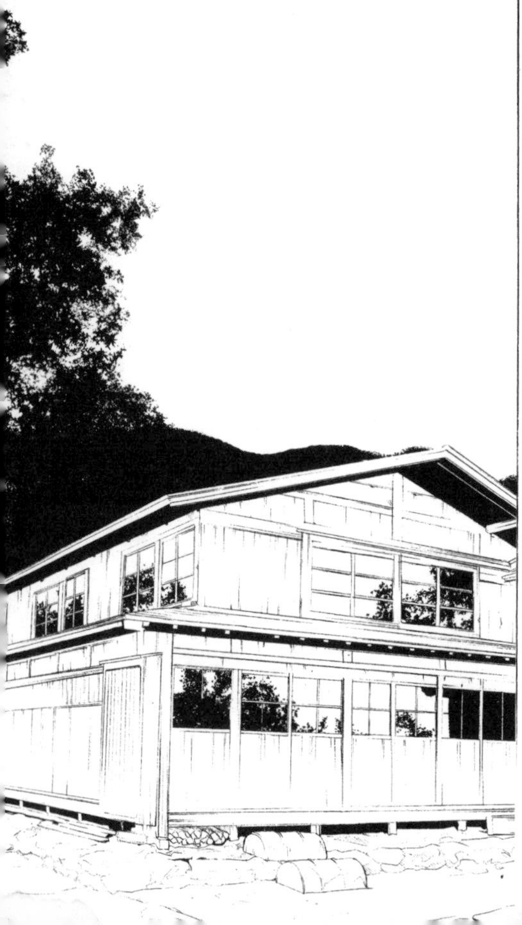

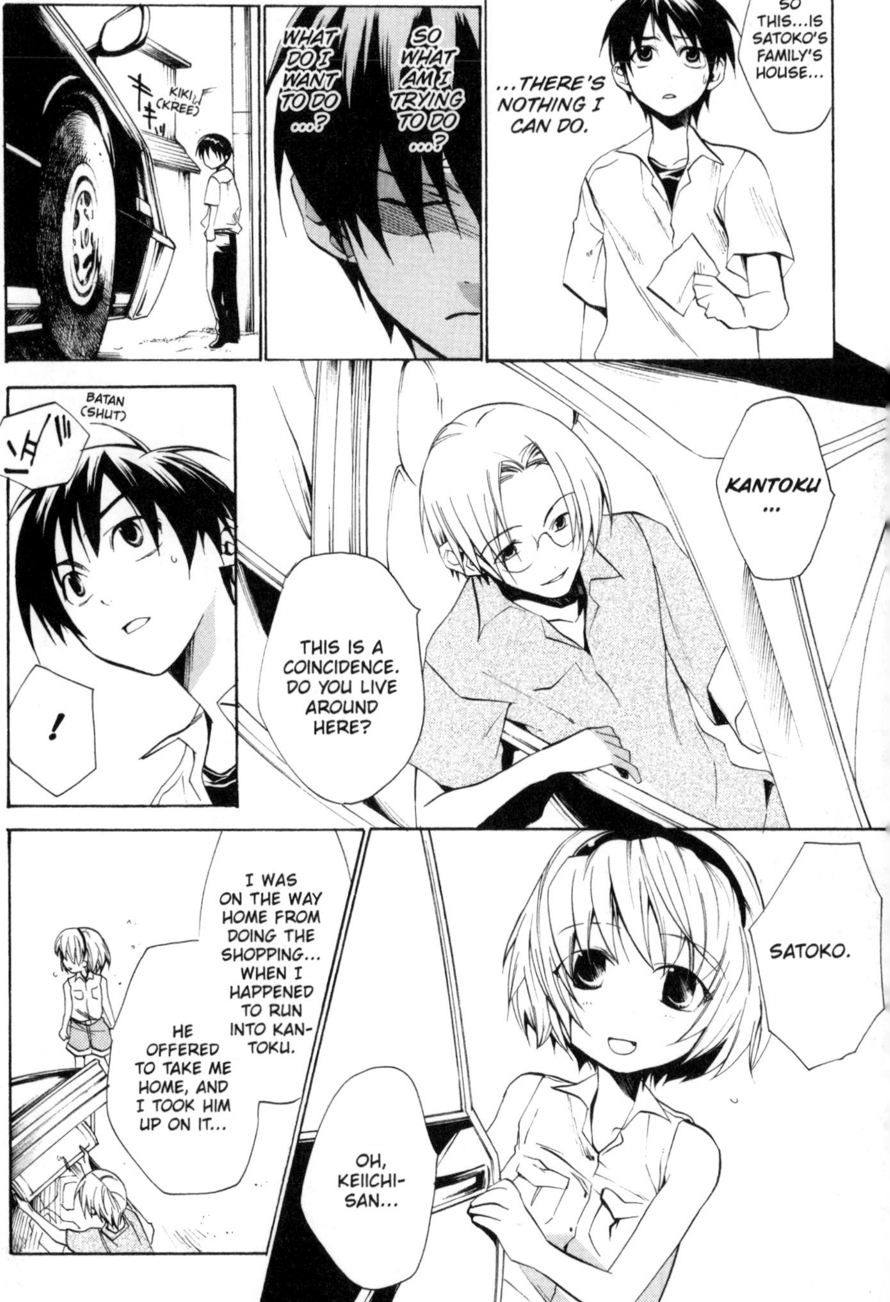
SO THIS...IS SATOKO'S FAMILY'S HOUSE...
...THERE'S NOTHING I CAN DO.
SO WHAT AM I TRYING TO DO ...?
WHAT DO I WANT TO DO ...?
KIKI (KREE)
KANTOKU ...
THIS IS A COINCIDENCE. DO YOU LIVE AROUND HERE?
BATAN (SHUT)
!
SATOKO.
OH, KEIICHI-SAN...
I WAS ON THE WAY HOME FROM DOING THE SHOPPING... WHEN I HAPPENED TO RUN INTO KAN-TOKU.
HE OFFERED TO TAKE ME HOME, AND I TOOK HIM UP ON IT...

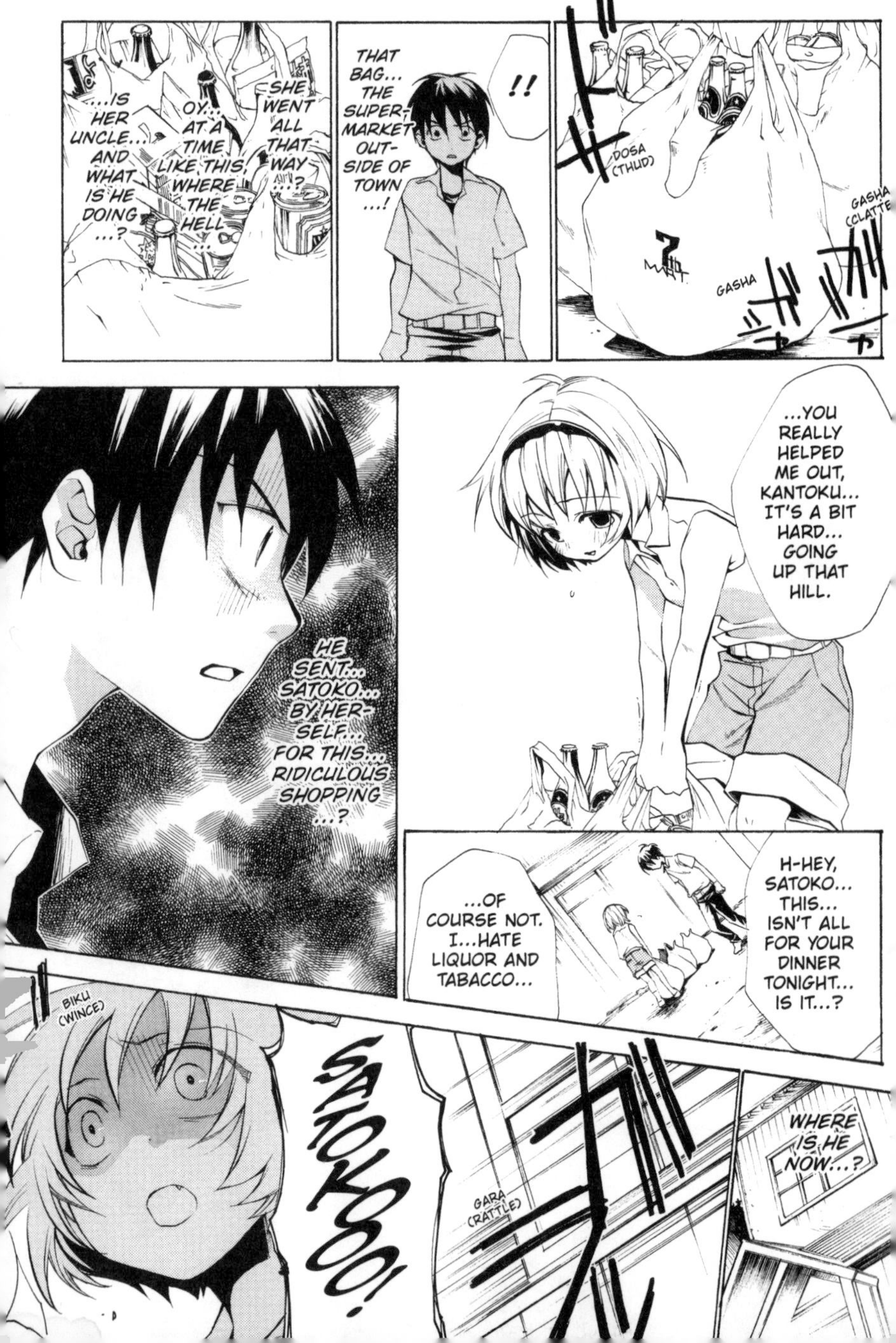
DOSA (THUD)
GASHA (CLATTE
GASHA
!!
THAT BAG... THE SUPER-MARKET OUT-SIDE OF TOWN...!
SHE WENT ALL THAT WAY...?
OY... AT A TIME LIKE THIS, WHERE THE HELL
...IS HER UNCLE... AND WHAT IS HE DOING...?
...YOU REALLY HELPED ME OUT, KANTOKU... IT'S A BIT HARD... GOING UP THAT HILL.
H-HEY, SATOKO... THIS... ISN'T ALL FOR YOUR DINNER TONIGHT... IS IT...?
...OF COURSE NOT. I...HATE LIQUOR AND TABACCO...
HE SENT... SATOKO... BY HER-SELF... FOR THIS... RIDICULOUS SHOPPING ...?
WHERE IS HE NOW...?
GARA (RATTLE)
SATOKOOO!
BIKU (WINCE)

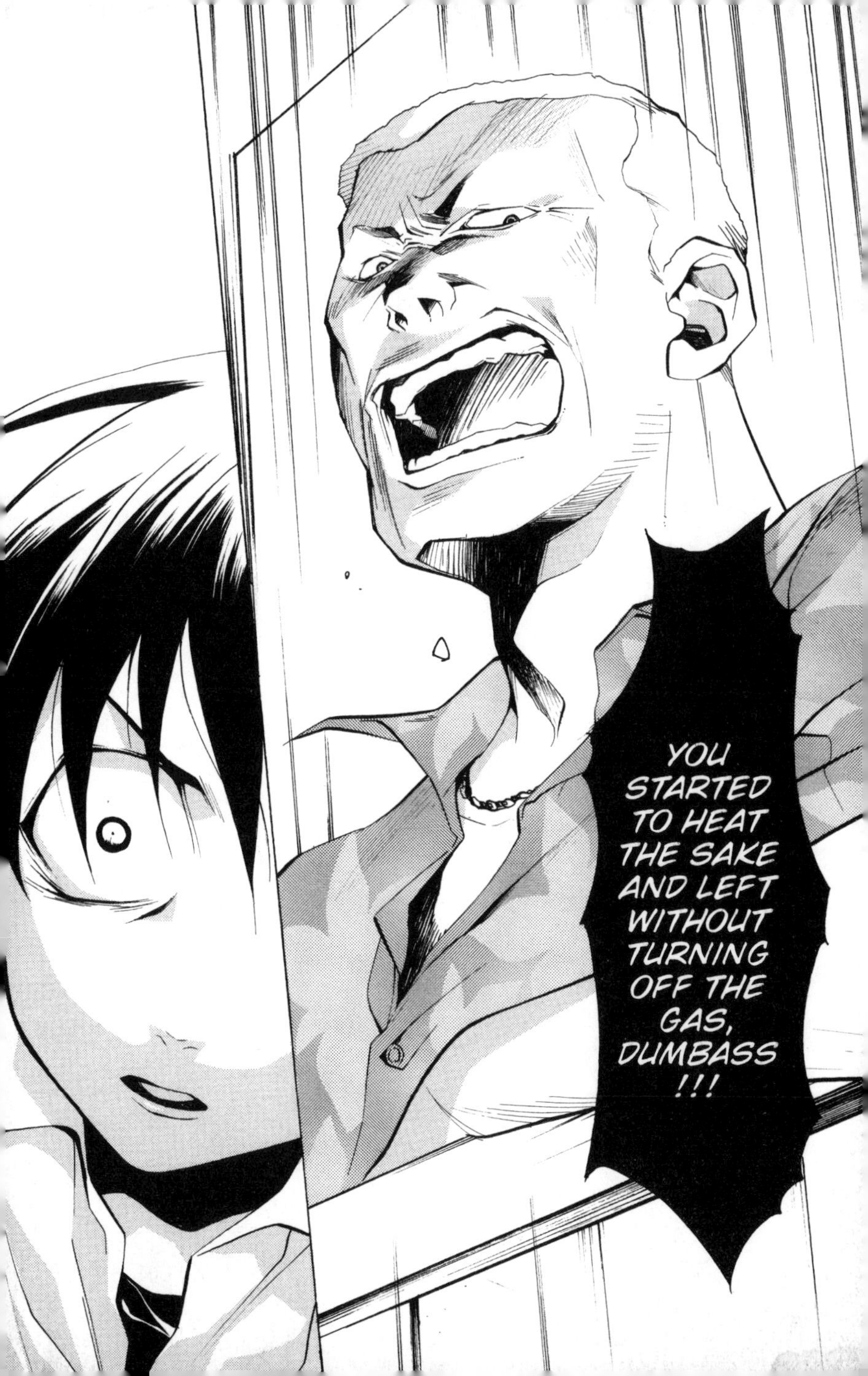
YOU STARTED TO HEAT THE SAKE AND LEFT WITHOUT TURNING OFF THE GAS, DUMBASS!!!

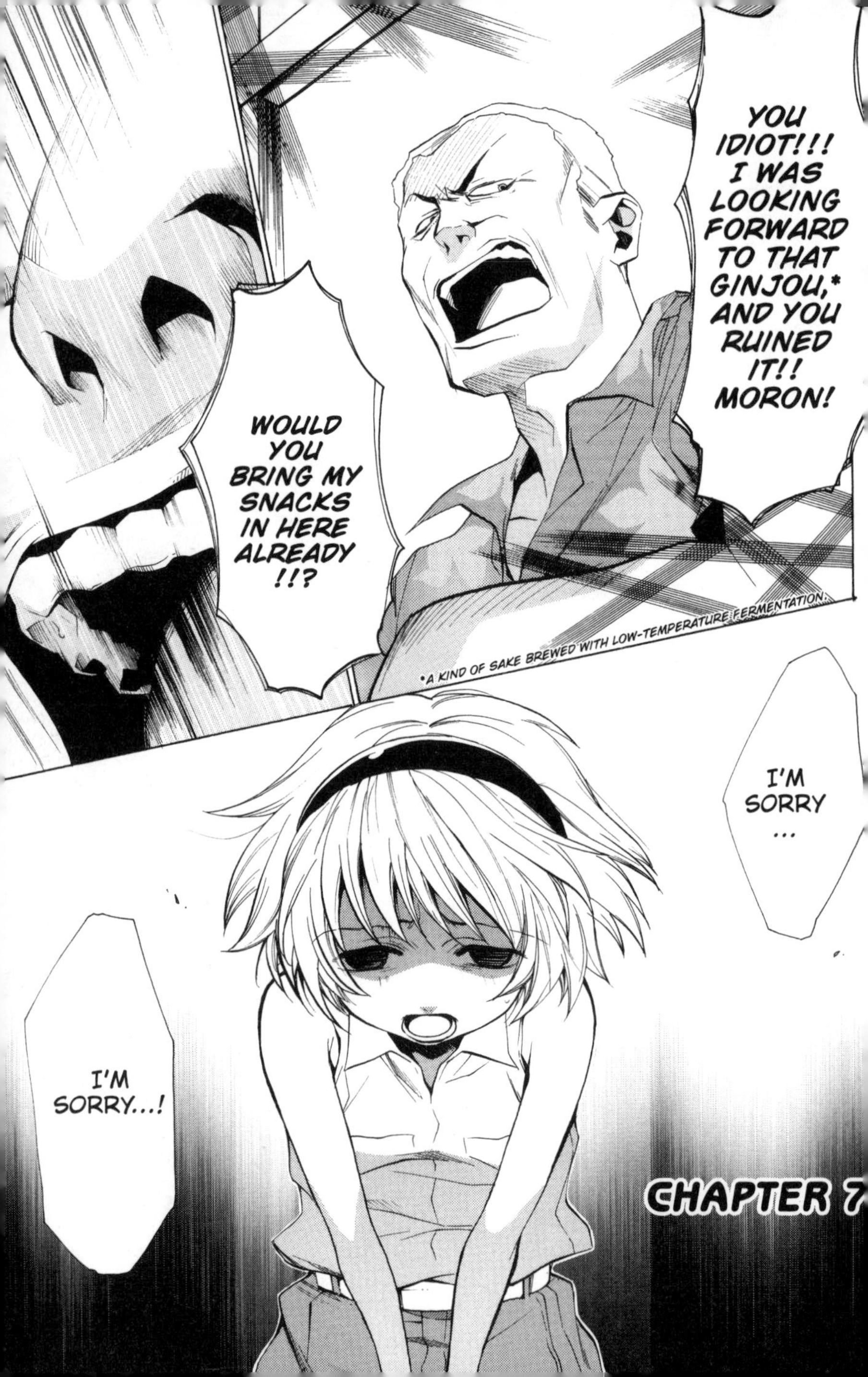
YOU IDIOT!!! I WAS LOOKING FORWARD TO THAT GINJOU,* AND YOU RUINED IT!! MORON!
WOULD YOU BRING MY SNACKS IN HERE ALREADY!!?
*A KIND OF SAKE BREWED WITH LOW-TEMPERATURE FERMENTATION.
I'M SORRY...
I'M SORRY...!
CHAPTER 7

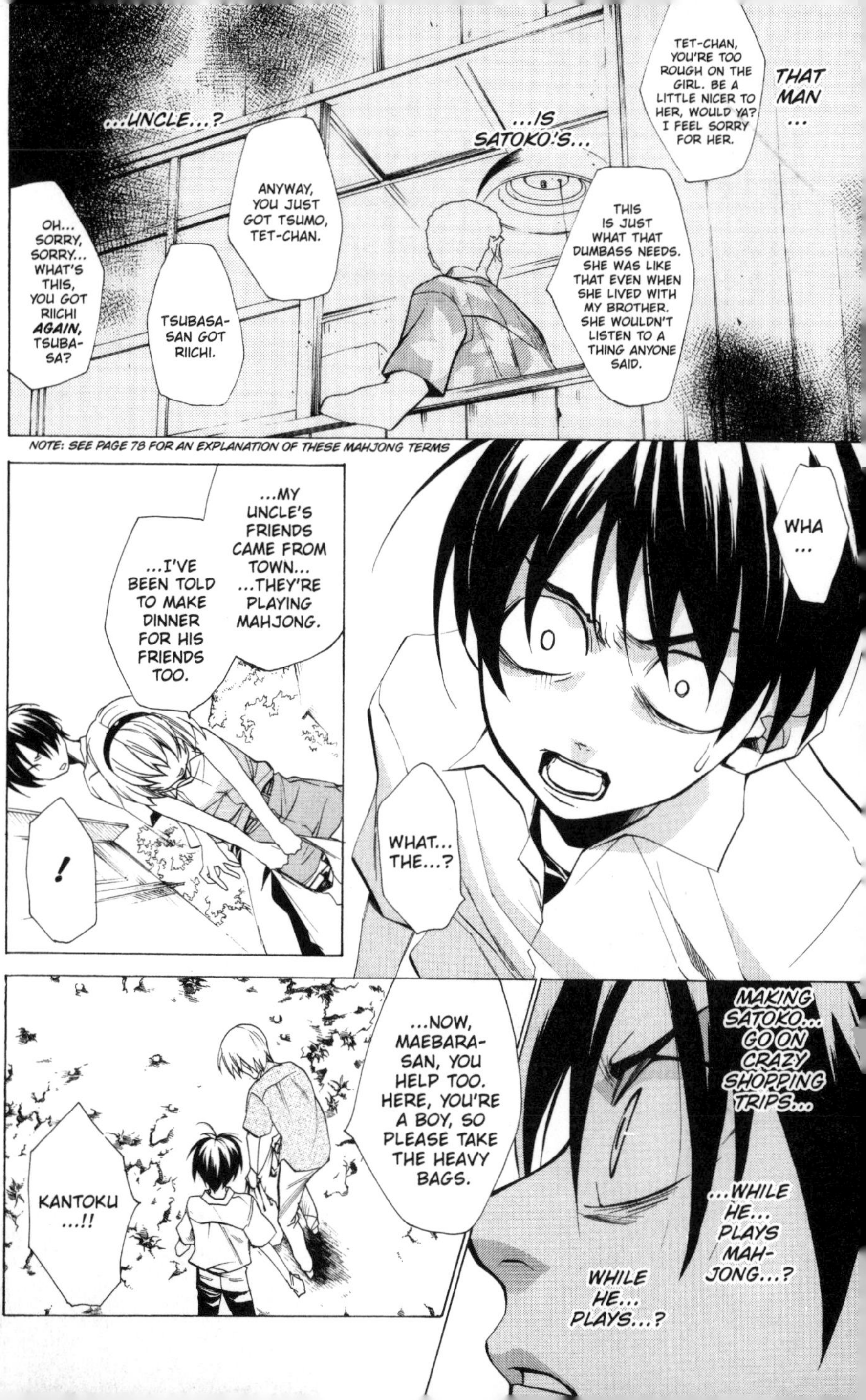
THAT MAN ...
TET-CHAN, YOU'RE TOO ROUGH ON THE GIRL. BE A LITTLE NICER TO HER, WOULD YA? I FEEL SORRY FOR HER.
...IS SATOKO'S...
...UNCLE...?
THIS IS JUST WHAT THAT DUMBASS NEEDS. SHE WAS LIKE THAT EVEN WHEN SHE LIVED WITH MY BROTHER. SHE WOULDN'T LISTEN TO A THING ANYONE SAID.
ANYWAY, YOU JUST GOT TSUMO, TET-CHAN.
TSUBASA-SAN GOT RIICHI.
OH... SORRY, SORRY... WHAT'S THIS, YOU GOT RIICHI AGAIN, TSUBASA-SA?
NOTE: SEE PAGE 78 FOR AN EXPLANATION OF THESE MAHJONG TERMS
WHA ...
WHAT... THE...?
...MY UNCLE'S FRIENDS CAME FROM TOWN... ...THEY'RE PLAYING MAHJONG.
...I'VE BEEN TOLD TO MAKE DINNER FOR HIS FRIENDS TOO.
!
MAKING SATOKO... GO ON CRAZY SHOPPING TRIPS...
...WHILE HE... PLAYS MAH-JONG...?
WHILE HE... PLAYS...?
...NOW, MAEBARA-SAN, YOU HELP TOO. HERE, YOU'RE A BOY, SO PLEASE TAKE THE HEAVY BAGS.
KANTOKU ...!!

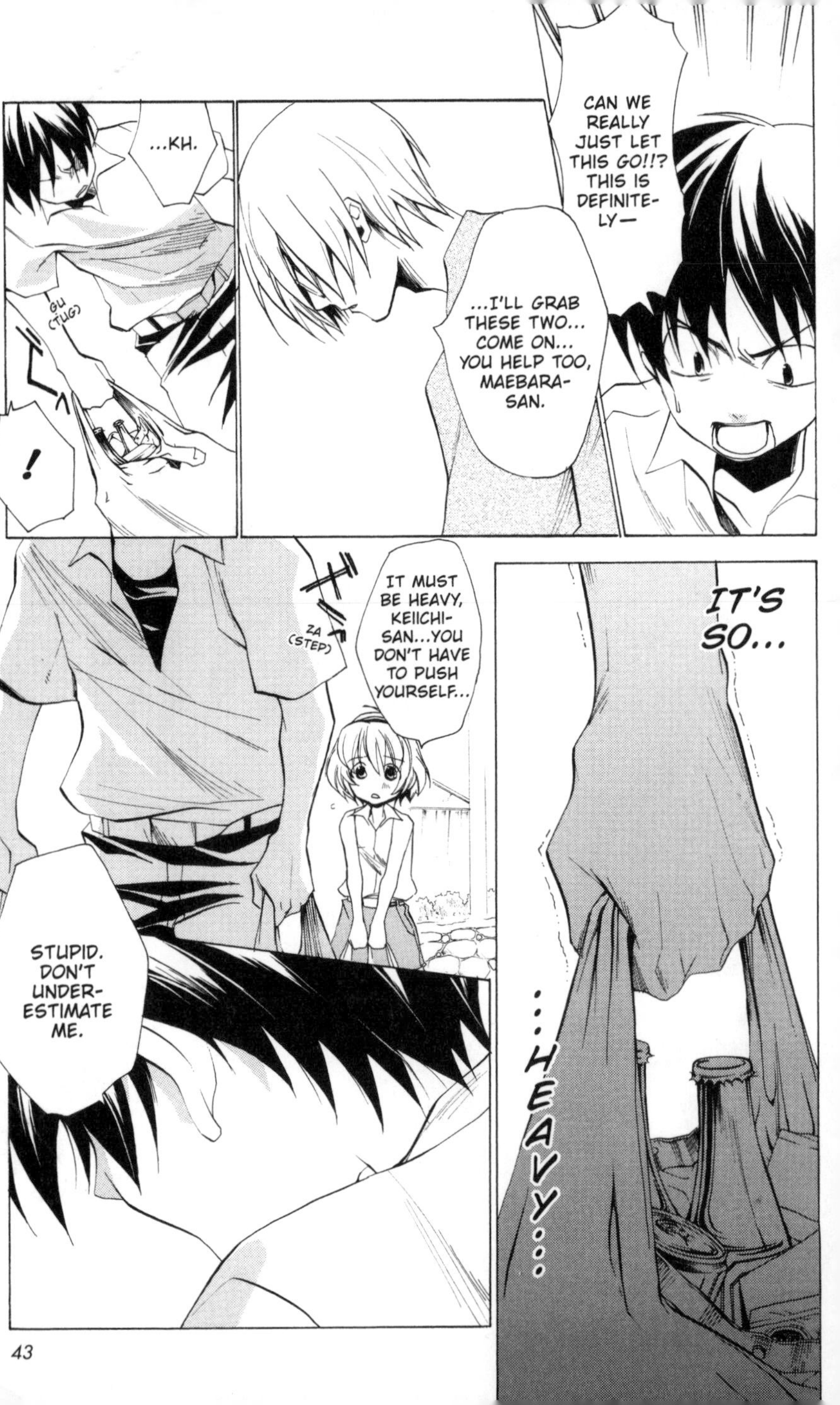
CAN WE REALLY JUST LET THIS GO!!? THIS IS DEFINITELY—
...I'LL GRAB THESE TWO... COME ON... YOU HELP TOO, MAEBARA-SAN.
...KH.
GU (TUG)
!
IT'S SO...
...HEAVY...
ZA (STEP)
IT MUST BE HEAVY, KEIICHI-SAN...YOU DON'T HAVE TO PUSH YOURSELF...
STUPID. DON'T UNDERESTIMATE ME.

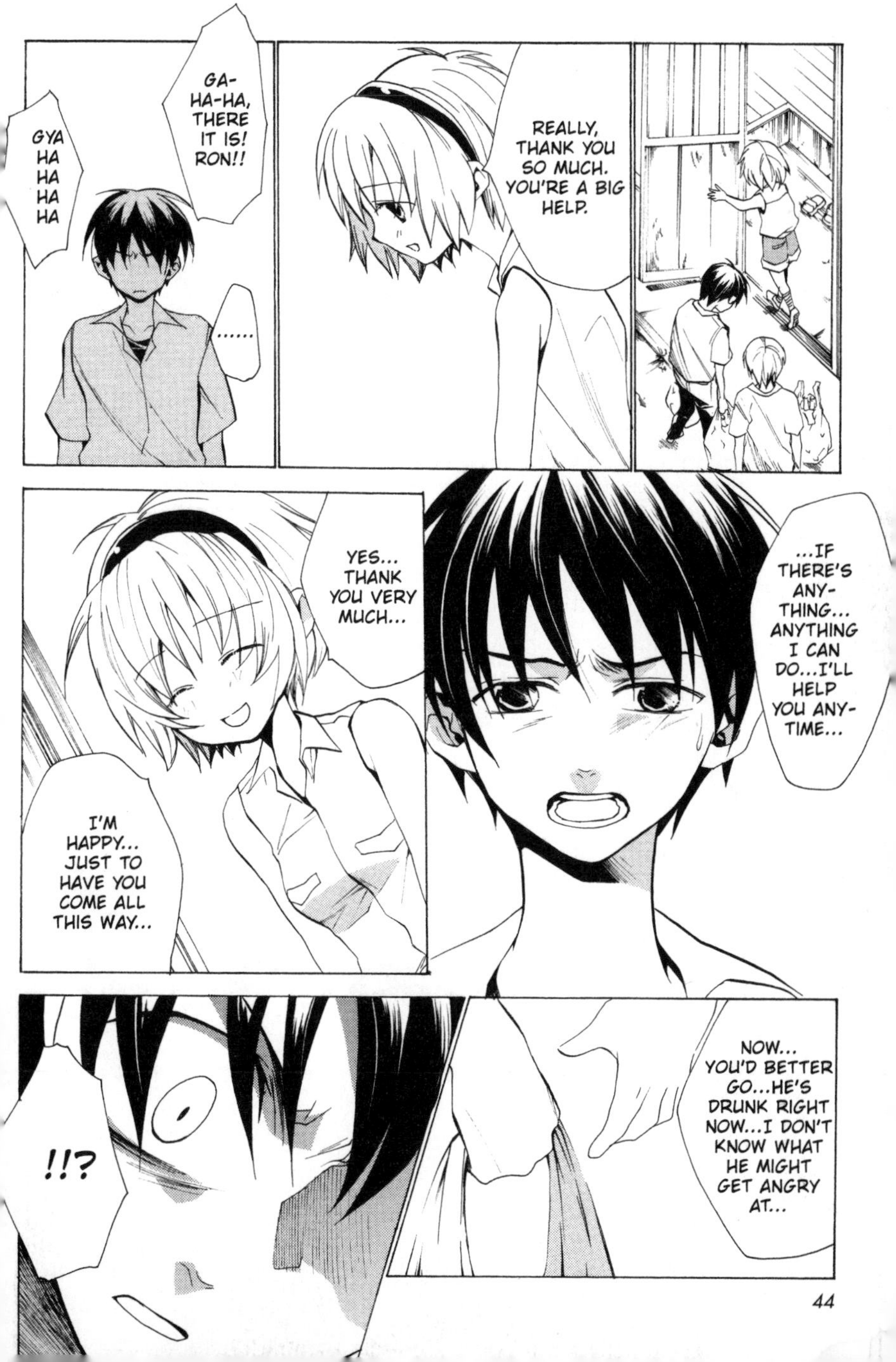
REALLY, THANK YOU SO MUCH. YOU'RE A BIG HELP.
GA-HA-HA, THERE IT IS! RON!!
GYA HA HA HA HA
......
...IF THERE'S ANY-THING... ANYTHING I CAN DO...I'LL HELP YOU ANY-TIME...
YES... THANK YOU VERY MUCH...
I'M HAPPY... JUST TO HAVE YOU COME ALL THIS WAY...
NOW... YOU'D BETTER GO...HE'S DRUNK RIGHT NOW...I DON'T KNOW WHAT HE MIGHT GET ANGRY AT...
!!?

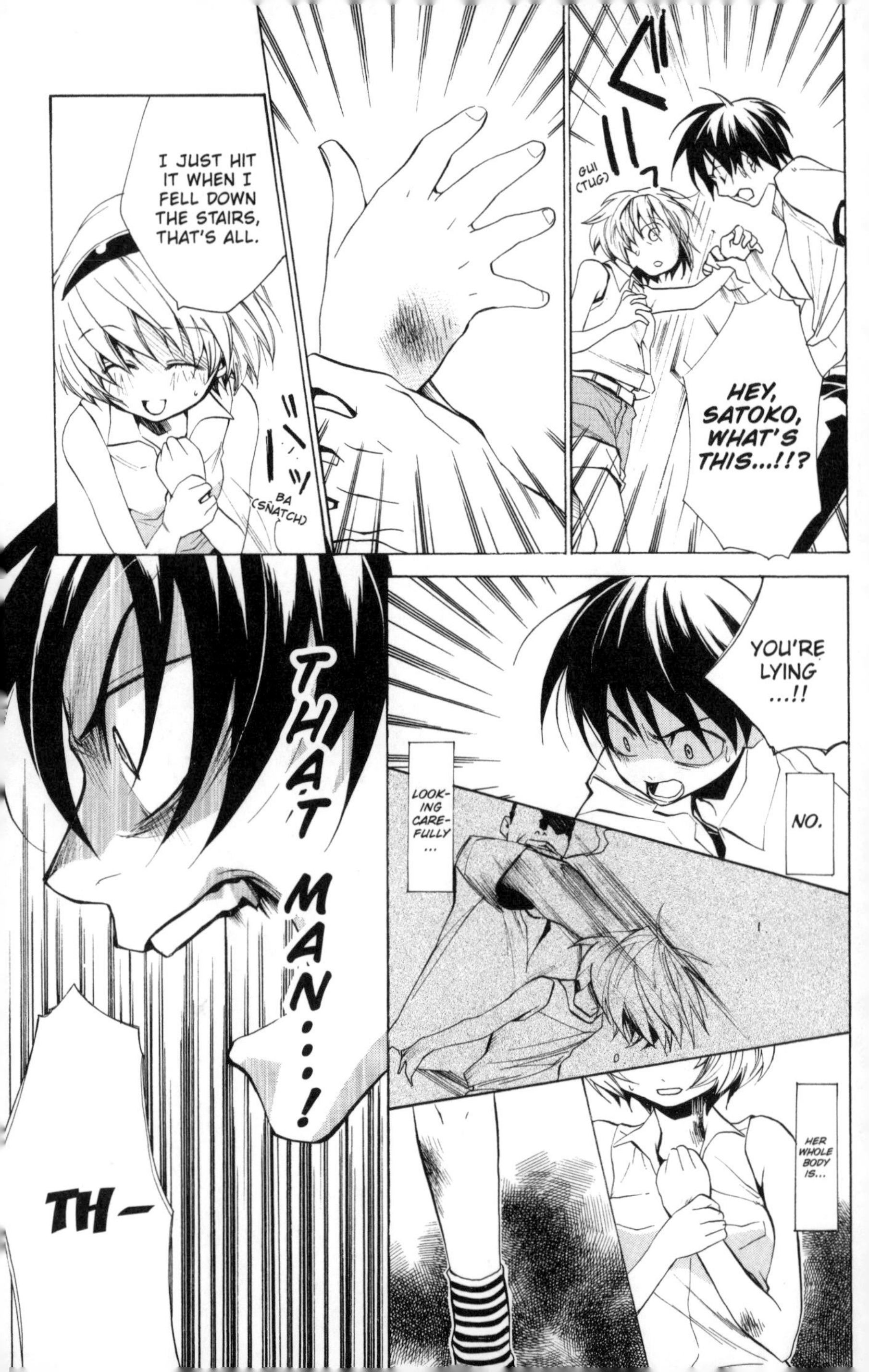
GUI (TUG)
HEY, SATOKO, WHAT'S THIS...!!?
BA (SNATCH)
I JUST HIT IT WHEN I FELL DOWN THE STAIRS, THAT'S ALL.
YOU'RE LYING ...!!
NO.
LOOKING CAREFULLY ...
HER WHOLE BODY IS...
THAT MAN...!
TH-

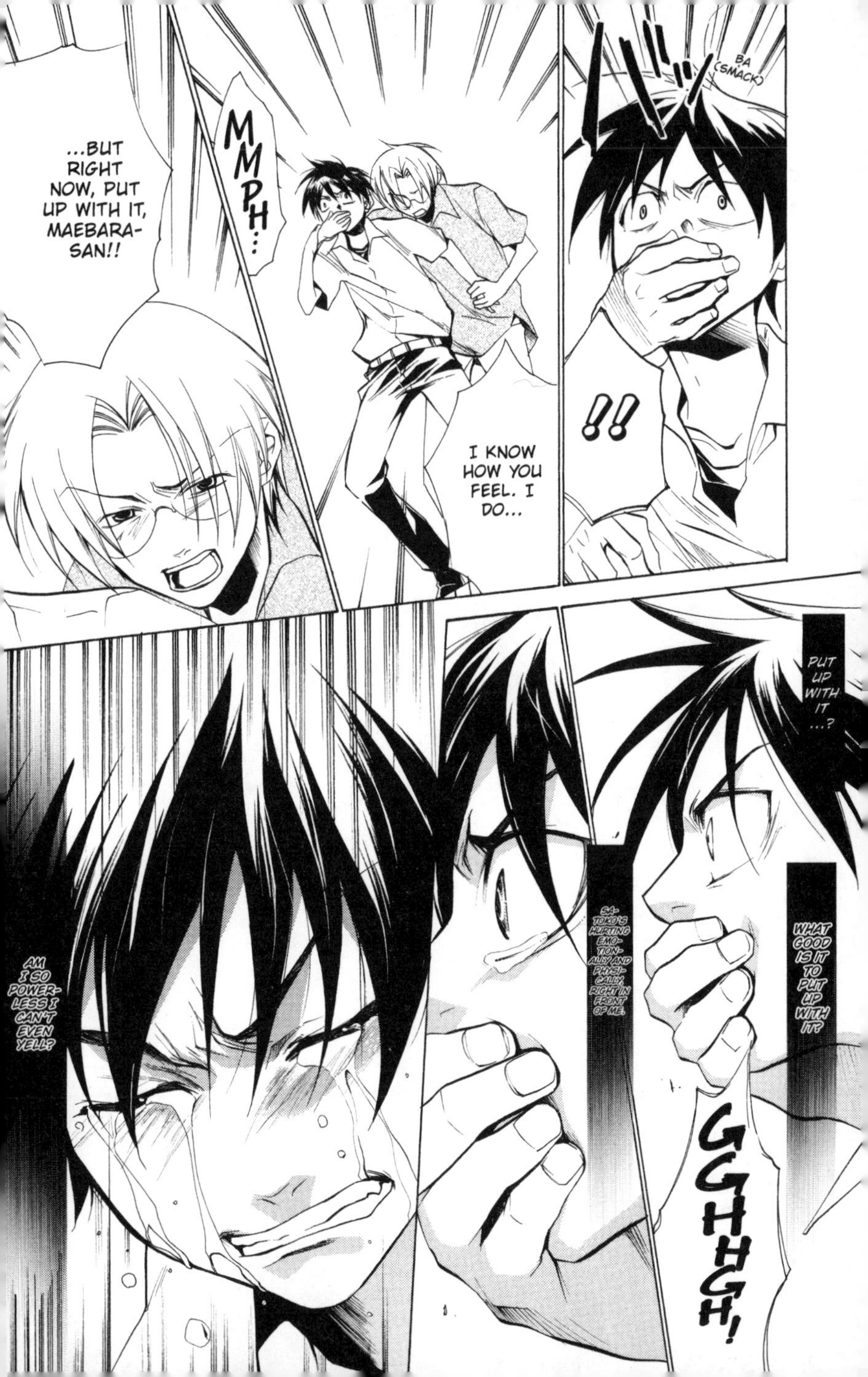
BA (SMACK)
!!
MMPH...
I KNOW HOW YOU FEEL. I DO...
...BUT RIGHT NOW, PUT UP WITH IT, MAEBARA-SAN!!
PUT UP WITH IT...?
WHAT GOOD IS IT TO PUT UP WITH IT?
GGHHGH!
SATOKO'S HURTING EMOTIONALLY AND PHYSICALLY RIGHT IN FRONT OF ME.
AM I SO POWERLESS I CAN'T EVEN YELL?

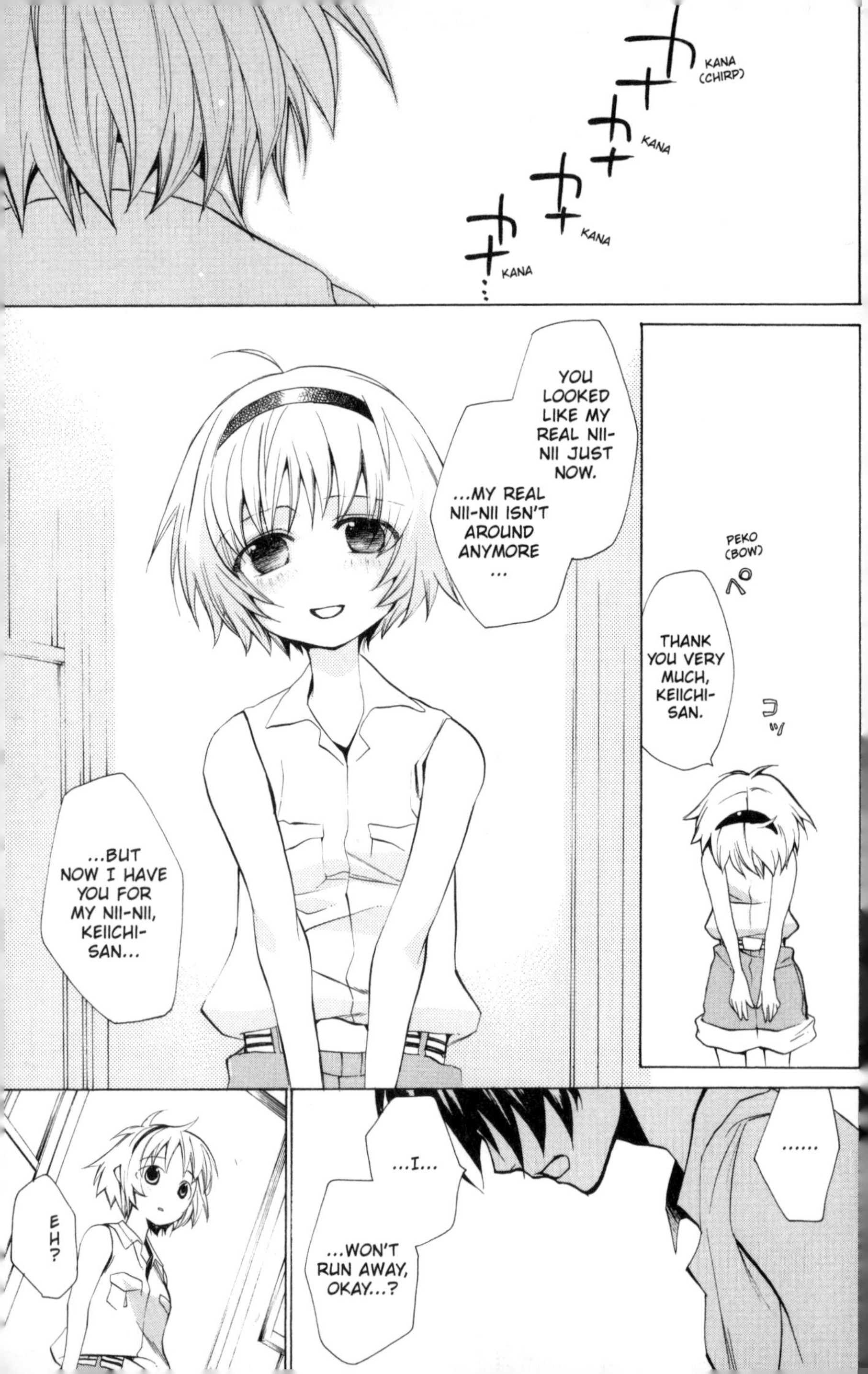
KANA (CHIRP)
KANA
KANA
KANA
PEKO (BOW)
THANK YOU VERY MUCH, KEIICHI-SAN.
YOU LOOKED LIKE MY REAL NII-NII JUST NOW.
...MY REAL NII-NII ISN'T AROUND ANYMORE ...
...BUT NOW I HAVE YOU FOR MY NII-NII, KEIICHI-SAN...
......
...I...
...WON'T RUN AWAY, OKAY...?
EH?

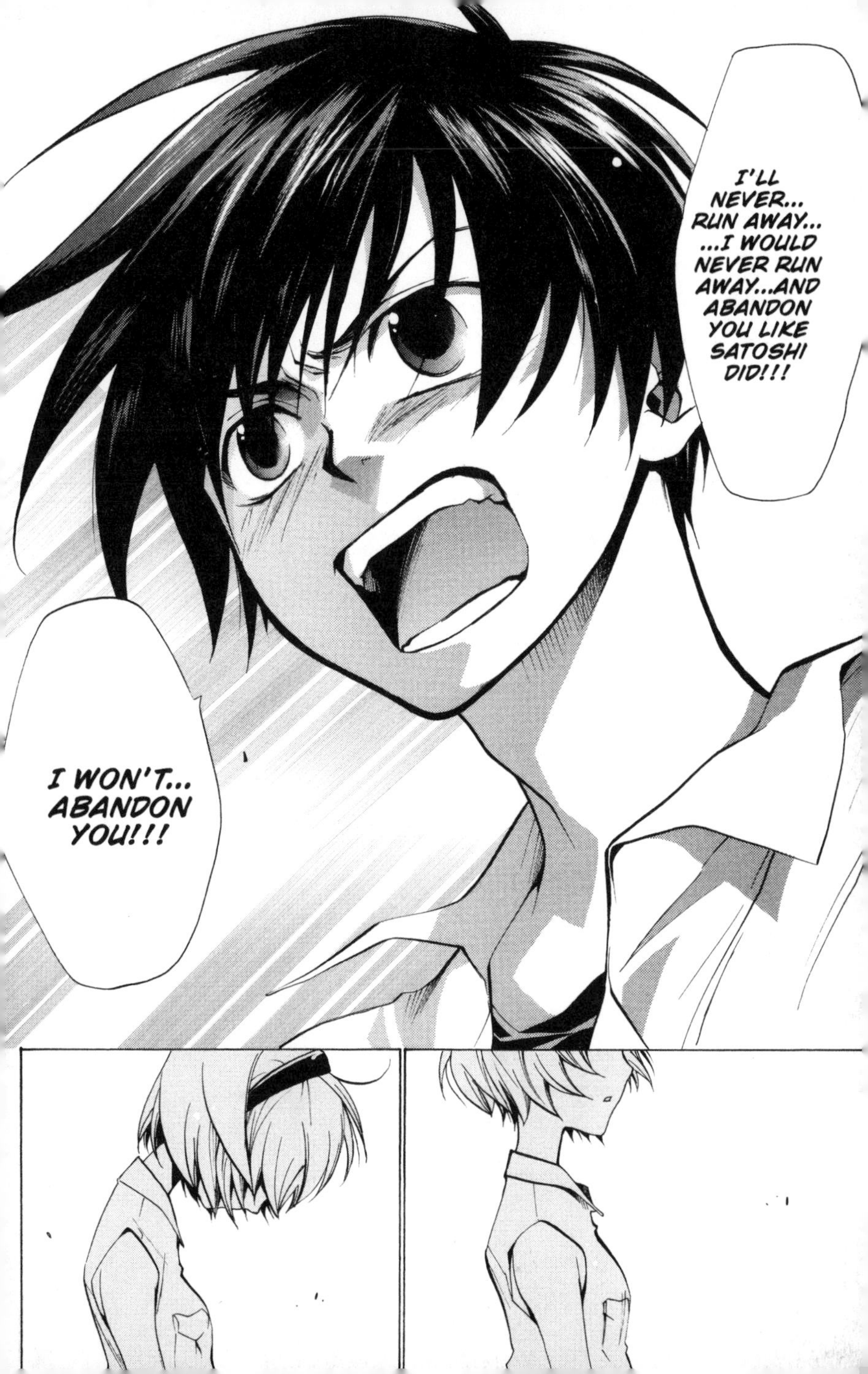
I'LL NEVER... RUN AWAY... ...I WOULD NEVER RUN AWAY...AND ABANDON YOU LIKE SATOSHI DID!!!
I WON'T... ABANDON YOU!!!

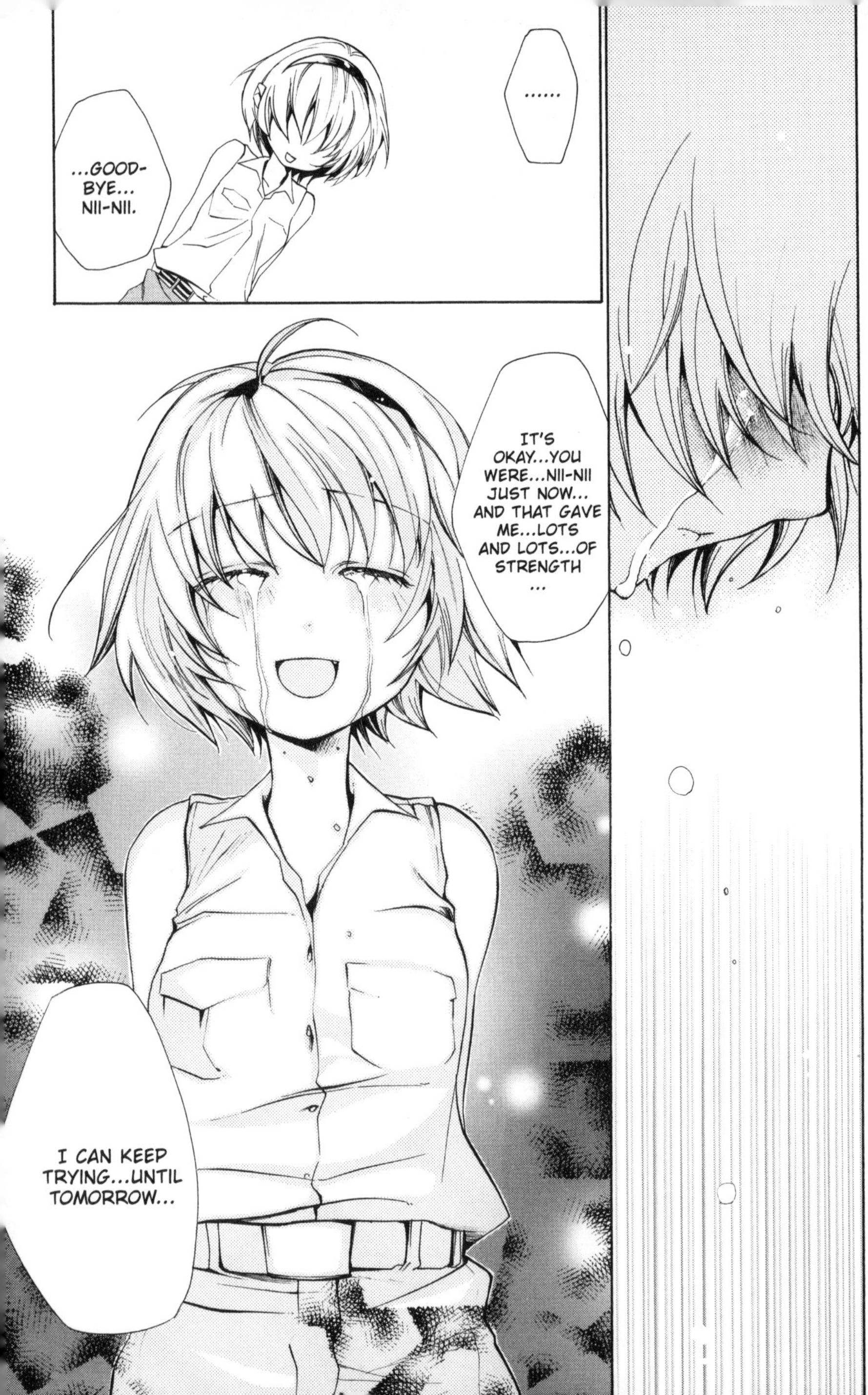
......
...GOOD-BYE... NII-NII.
IT'S OKAY...YOU WERE...NII-NII JUST NOW... AND THAT GAVE ME...LOTS AND LOTS...OF STRENGTH ...
I CAN KEEP TRYING...UNTIL TOMORROW...

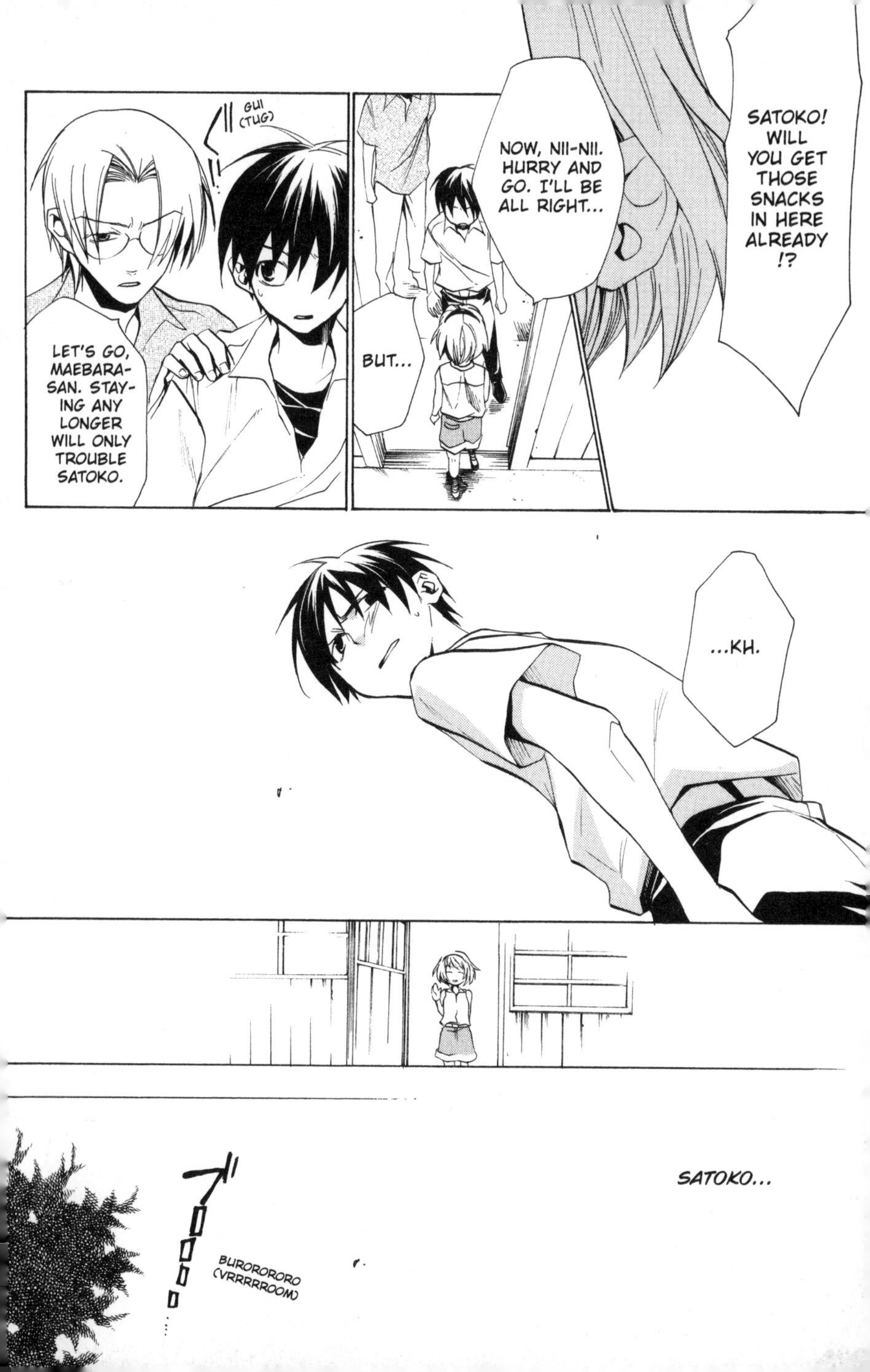
SATOKO! WILL YOU GET THOSE SNACKS IN HERE ALREADY!?
NOW, NII-NII. HURRY AND GO. I'LL BE ALL RIGHT...
BUT...
GUI (TUG)
LET'S GO, MAEBARA-SAN. STAYING ANY LONGER WILL ONLY TROUBLE SATOKO.
...KH.
SATOKO...
BURORORORO (VRRRRROOM)

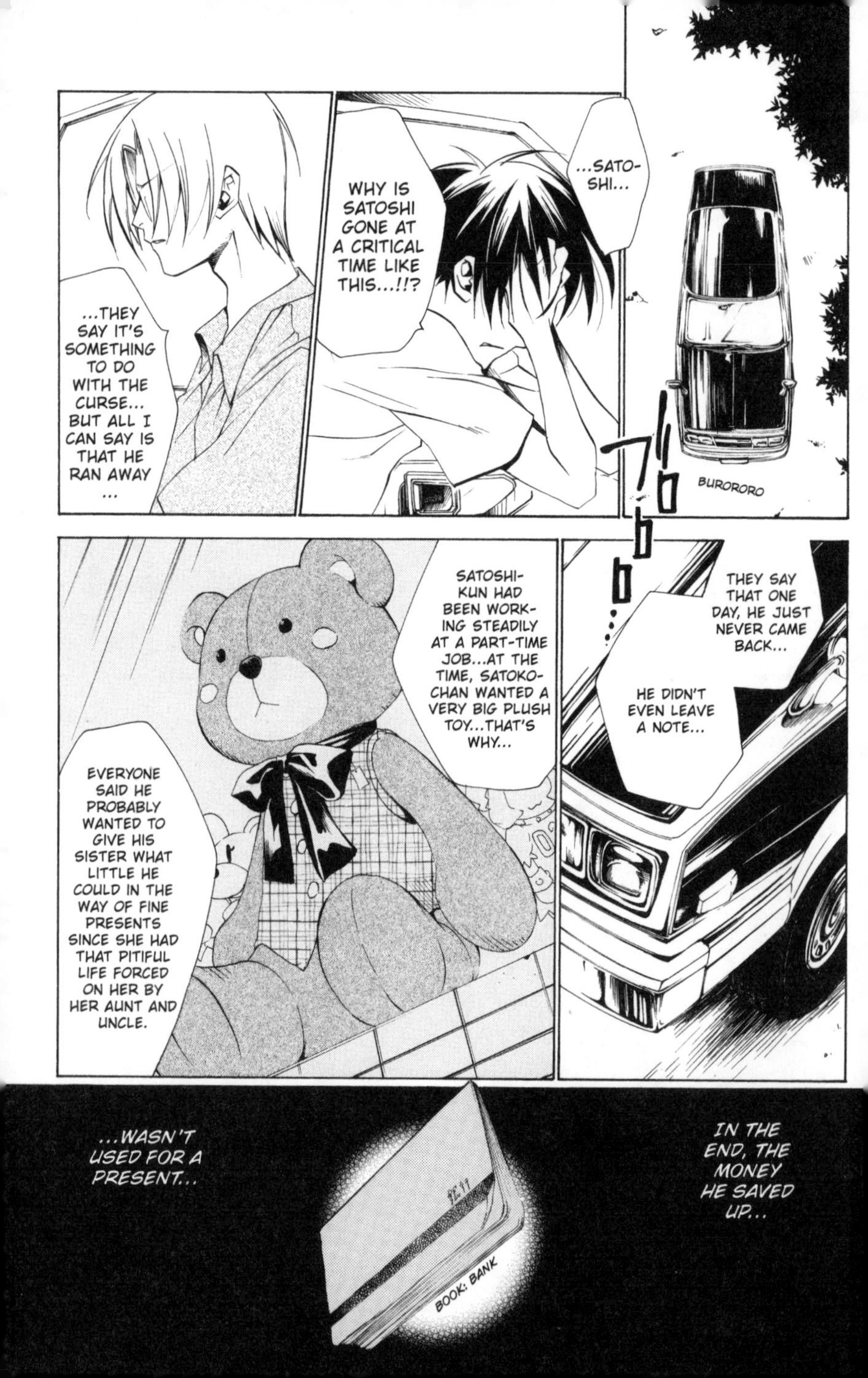
BURORORO
...SATO-SHI...
WHY IS SATOSHI GONE AT A CRITICAL TIME LIKE THIS...!!?
...THEY SAY IT'S SOMETHING TO DO WITH THE CURSE... BUT ALL I CAN SAY IS THAT HE RAN AWAY ...
THEY SAY THAT ONE DAY, HE JUST NEVER CAME BACK...
HE DIDN'T EVEN LEAVE A NOTE...
SATOSHI-KUN HAD BEEN WORKING STEADILY AT A PART-TIME JOB...AT THE TIME, SATOKO-CHAN WANTED A VERY BIG PLUSH TOY...THAT'S WHY...
EVERYONE SAID HE PROBABLY WANTED TO GIVE HIS SISTER WHAT LITTLE HE COULD IN THE WAY OF FINE PRESENTS SINCE SHE HAD THAT PITIFUL LIFE FORCED ON HER BY HER AUNT AND UNCLE.
IN THE END, THE MONEY HE SAVED UP...
...WASN'T USED FOR A PRESENT...
BOOK: BANK

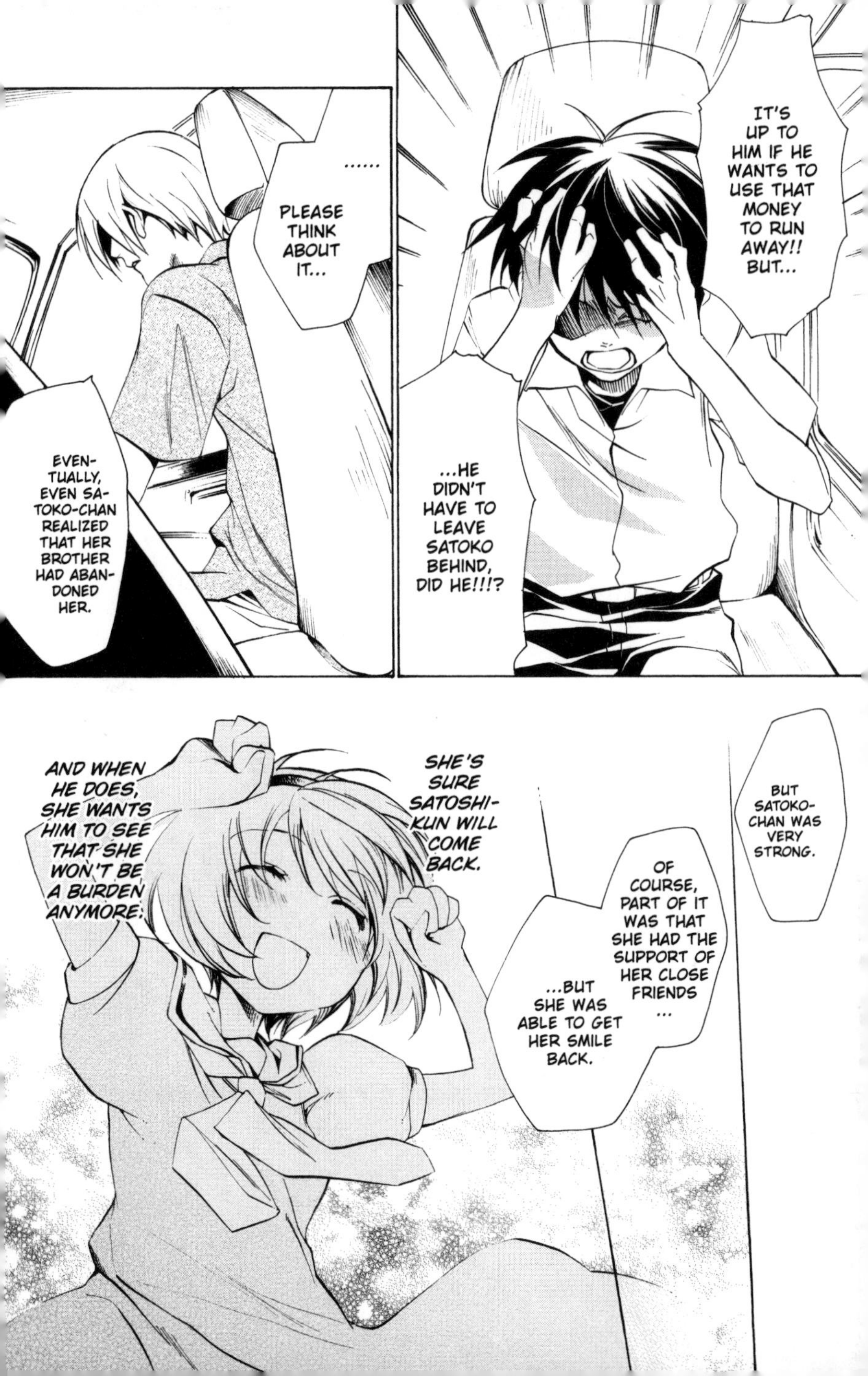
IT'S UP TO HIM IF HE WANTS TO USE THAT MONEY TO RUN AWAY!! BUT...
...HE DIDN'T HAVE TO LEAVE SATOKO BEHIND, DID HE!!!?
......
PLEASE THINK ABOUT IT...
EVEN-TUALLY, EVEN SA-TOKO-CHAN REALIZED THAT HER BROTHER HAD ABAN-DONED HER.
BUT SATOKO-CHAN WAS VERY STRONG.
OF COURSE, PART OF IT WAS THAT SHE HAD THE SUPPORT OF HER CLOSE FRIENDS ...
...BUT SHE WAS ABLE TO GET HER SMILE BACK.
SHE'S SURE SATOSHI-KUN WILL COME BACK.
AND WHEN HE DOES, SHE WANTS HIM TO SEE THAT SHE WON'T BE A BURDEN ANYMORE.

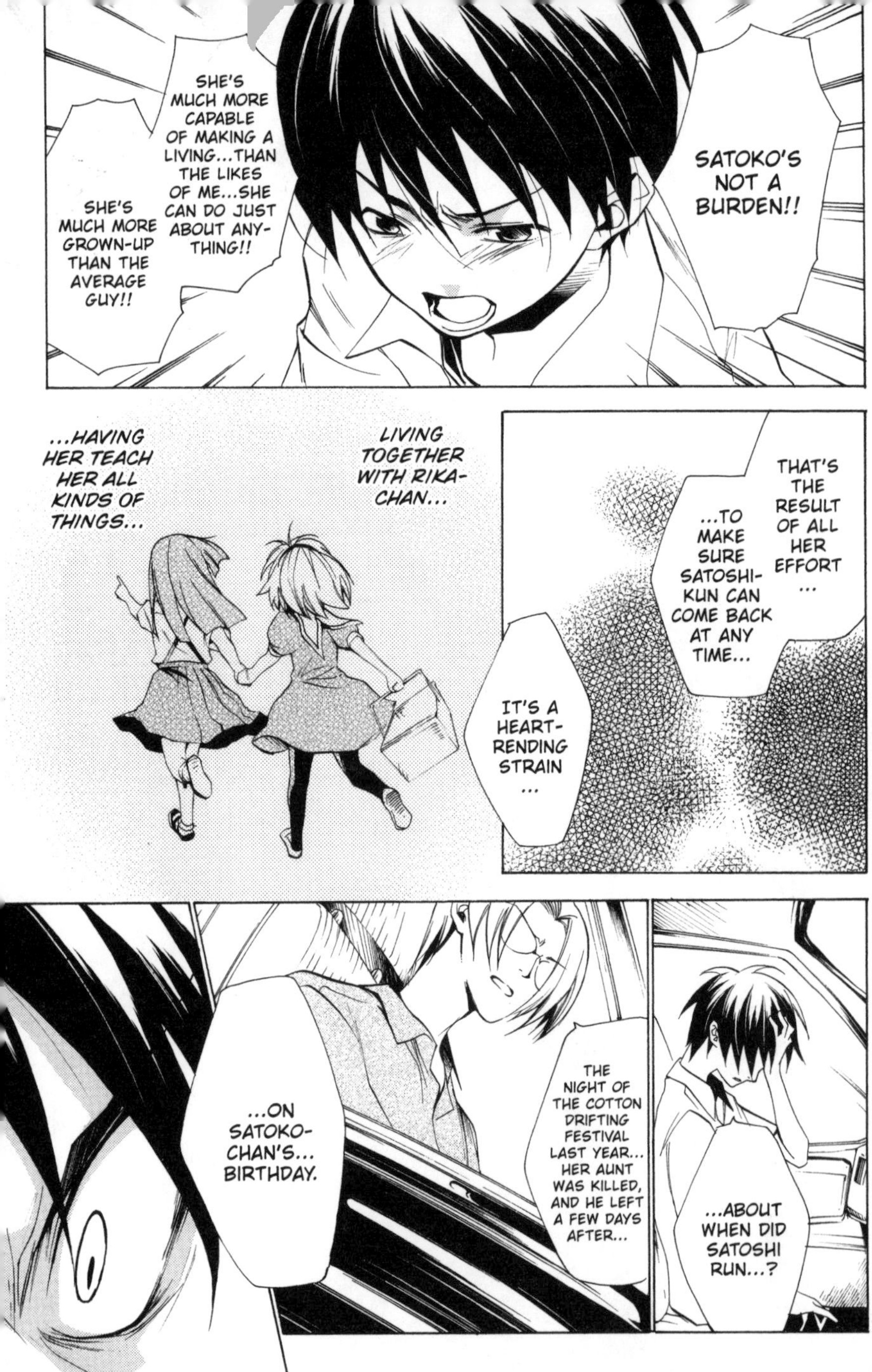
SATOKO'S NOT A BURDEN!!
SHE'S MUCH MORE CAPABLE OF MAKING A LIVING...THAN THE LIKES OF ME...SHE CAN DO JUST ABOUT ANYTHING!!
SHE'S MUCH MORE GROWN-UP THAN THE AVERAGE GUY!!
THAT'S THE RESULT OF ALL HER EFFORT...
...TO MAKE SURE SATOSHI-KUN CAN COME BACK AT ANY TIME...
IT'S A HEART-RENDING STRAIN...
LIVING TOGETHER WITH RIKA-CHAN...
...HAVING HER TEACH HER ALL KINDS OF THINGS...
...ABOUT WHEN DID SATOSHI RUN...?
THE NIGHT OF THE COTTON DRIFTING FESTIVAL LAST YEAR... HER AUNT WAS KILLED, AND HE LEFT A FEW DAYS AFTER...
...ON SATOKO-CHAN'S... BIRTHDAY.

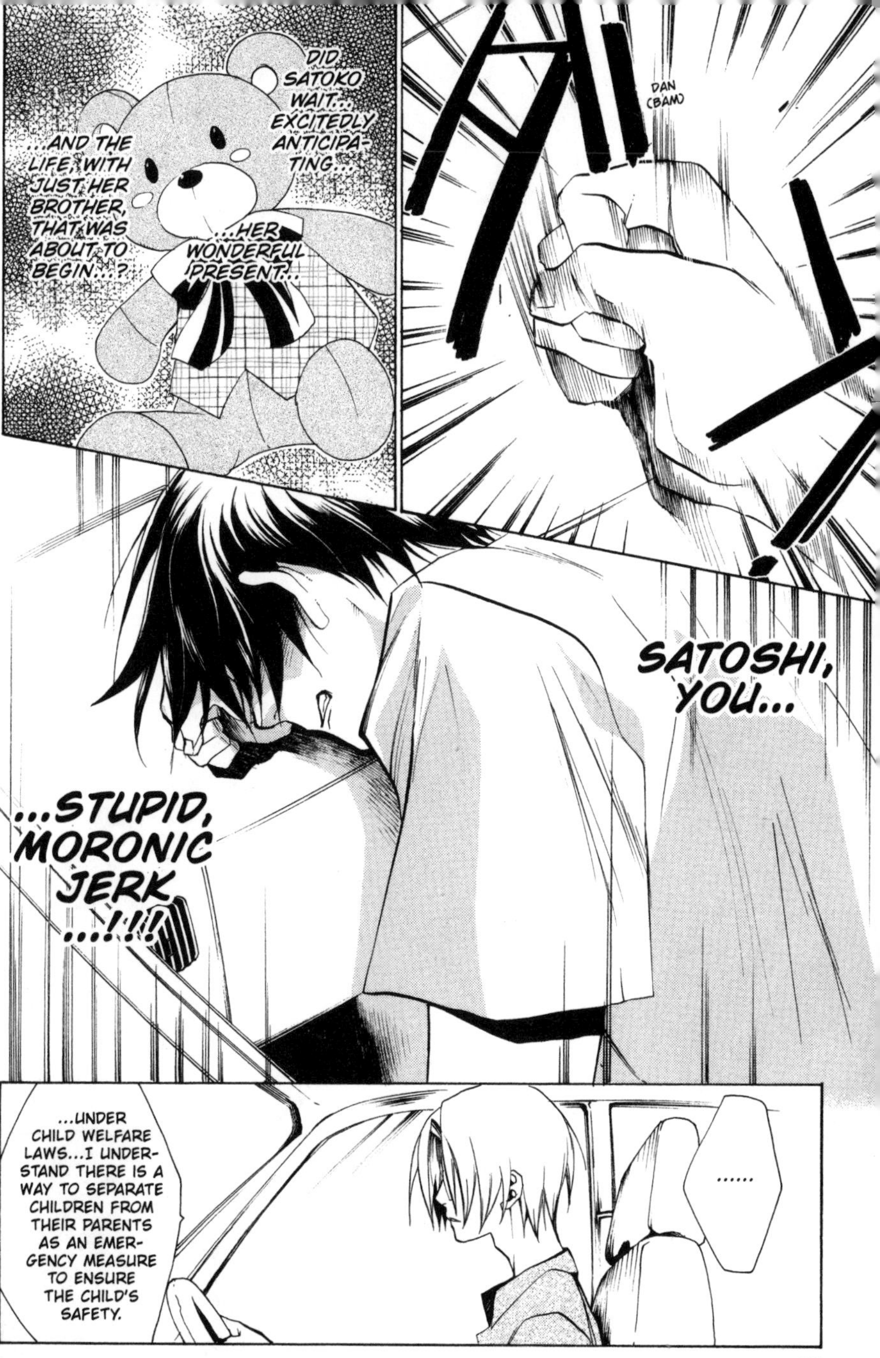
DAN (BAM)
DID SATOKO WAIT... EXCITEDLY ANTICIPA-TING...
...HER WONDERFUL PRESENT...
...AND THE LIFE, WITH JUST HER BROTHER, THAT WAS ABOUT TO BEGIN...?
SATOSHI, YOU...
...STUPID, MORONIC JERK...!!!
......
...UNDER CHILD WELFARE LAWS...I UNDER-STAND THERE IS A WAY TO SEPARATE CHILDREN FROM THEIR PARENTS AS AN EMER-GENCY MEASURE TO ENSURE THE CHILD'S SAFETY.

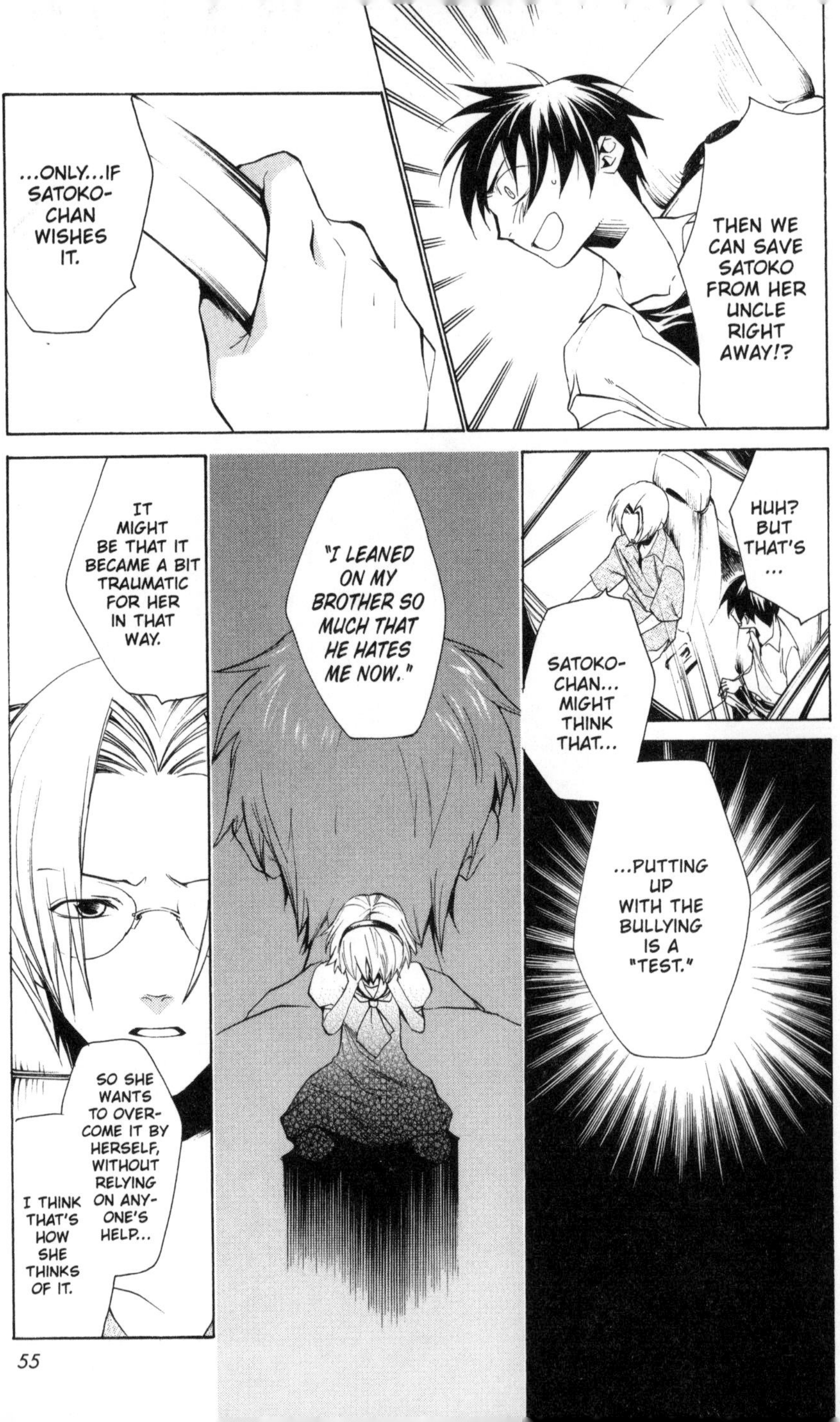
THEN WE CAN SAVE SATOKO FROM HER UNCLE RIGHT AWAY!?
...ONLY...IF SATOKO-CHAN WISHES IT.
HUH? BUT THAT'S ...
SATOKO-CHAN... MIGHT THINK THAT...
...PUTTING UP WITH THE BULLYING IS A "TEST."
"I LEANED ON MY BROTHER SO MUCH THAT HE HATES ME NOW."
IT MIGHT BE THAT IT BECAME A BIT TRAUMATIC FOR HER IN THAT WAY.
SO SHE WANTS TO OVER-COME IT BY HERSELF, WITHOUT RELYING ON ANY-ONE'S HELP...
I THINK THAT'S HOW SHE THINKS OF IT.

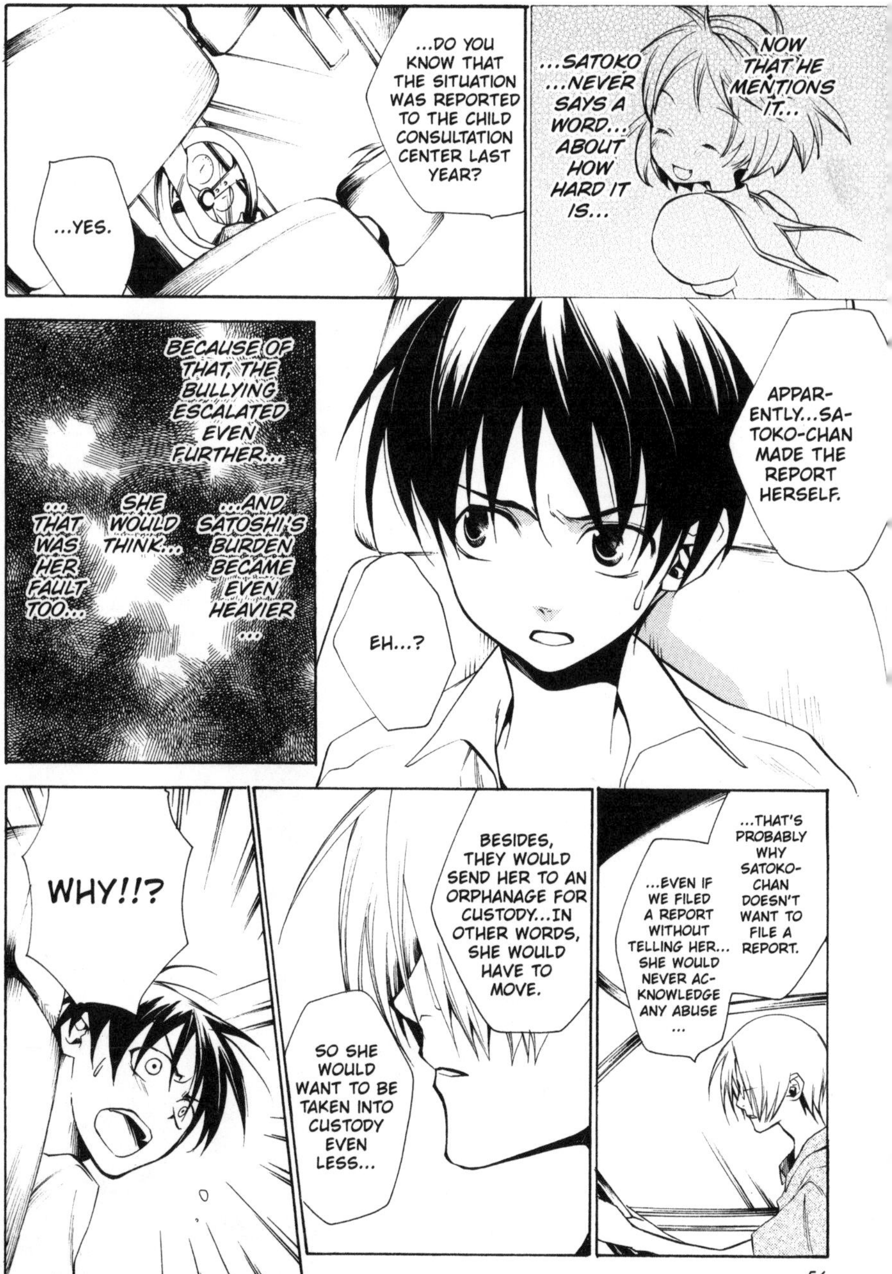
NOW THAT HE MENTIONS IT...
...SATOKO ...NEVER SAYS A WORD... ABOUT HOW HARD IT IS...
...DO YOU KNOW THAT THE SITUATION WAS REPORTED TO THE CHILD CONSULTATION CENTER LAST YEAR?
...YES.
APPAR-ENTLY...SA-TOKO-CHAN MADE THE REPORT HERSELF.
EH...?
BECAUSE OF THAT, THE BULLYING ESCALATED EVEN FURTHER...
...AND SATOSHI'S BURDEN BECAME EVEN HEAVIER...
SHE WOULD THINK...
...THAT WAS HER FAULT TOO...
...THAT'S PROBABLY WHY SATOKO-CHAN DOESN'T WANT TO FILE A REPORT.
...EVEN IF WE FILED A REPORT WITHOUT TELLING HER... SHE WOULD NEVER AC-KNOWLEDGE ANY ABUSE...
BESIDES, THEY WOULD SEND HER TO AN ORPHANAGE FOR CUSTODY...IN OTHER WORDS, SHE WOULD HAVE TO MOVE.
SO SHE WOULD WANT TO BE TAKEN INTO CUSTODY EVEN LESS...
WHY!!?

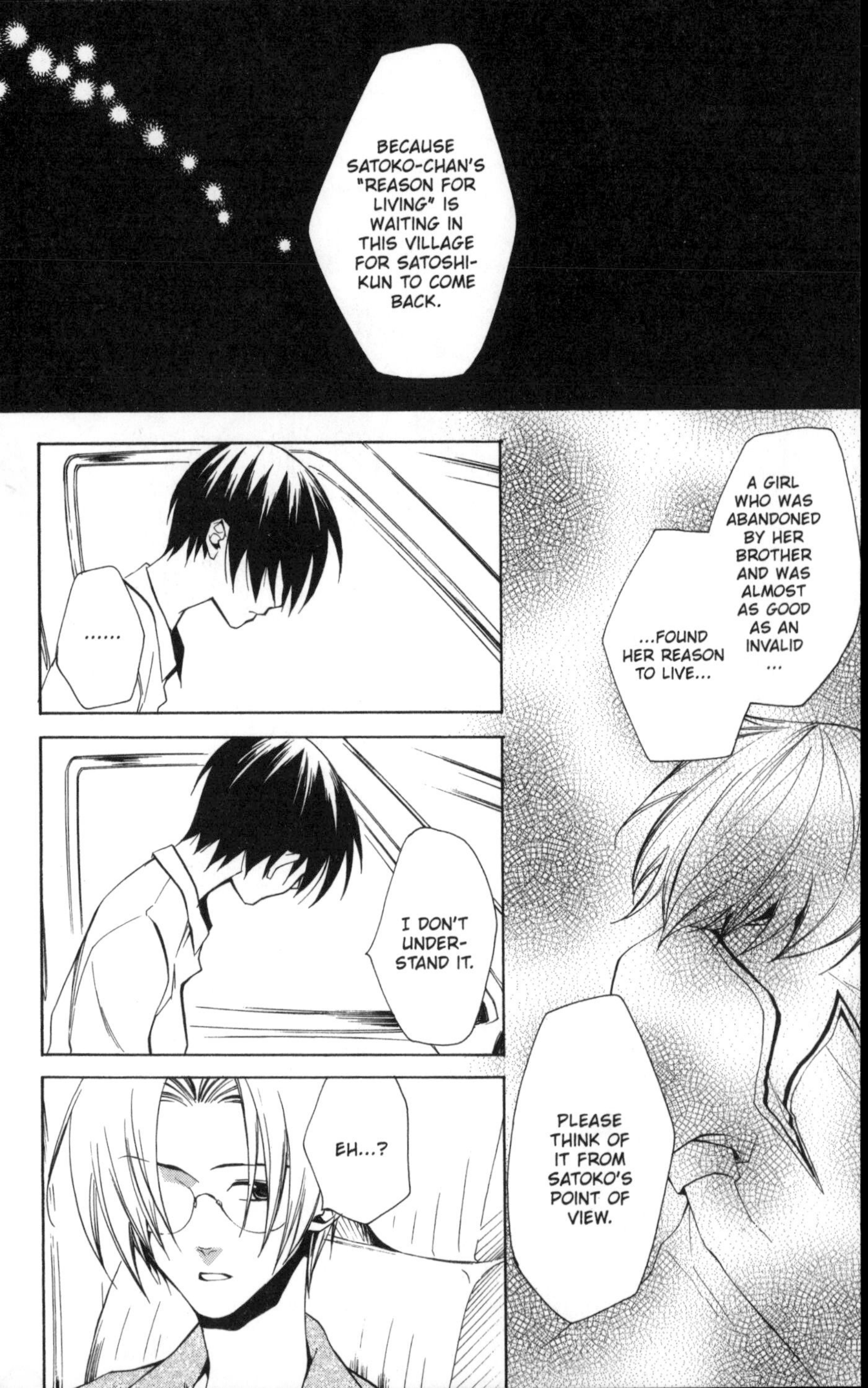
BECAUSE SATOKO-CHAN'S "REASON FOR LIVING" IS WAITING IN THIS VILLAGE FOR SATOSHI-KUN TO COME BACK.
A GIRL WHO WAS ABANDONED BY HER BROTHER AND WAS ALMOST AS GOOD AS AN INVALID ...
...FOUND HER REASON TO LIVE...
PLEASE THINK OF IT FROM SATOKO'S POINT OF VIEW.
......
I DON'T UNDER-STAND IT.
EH...?

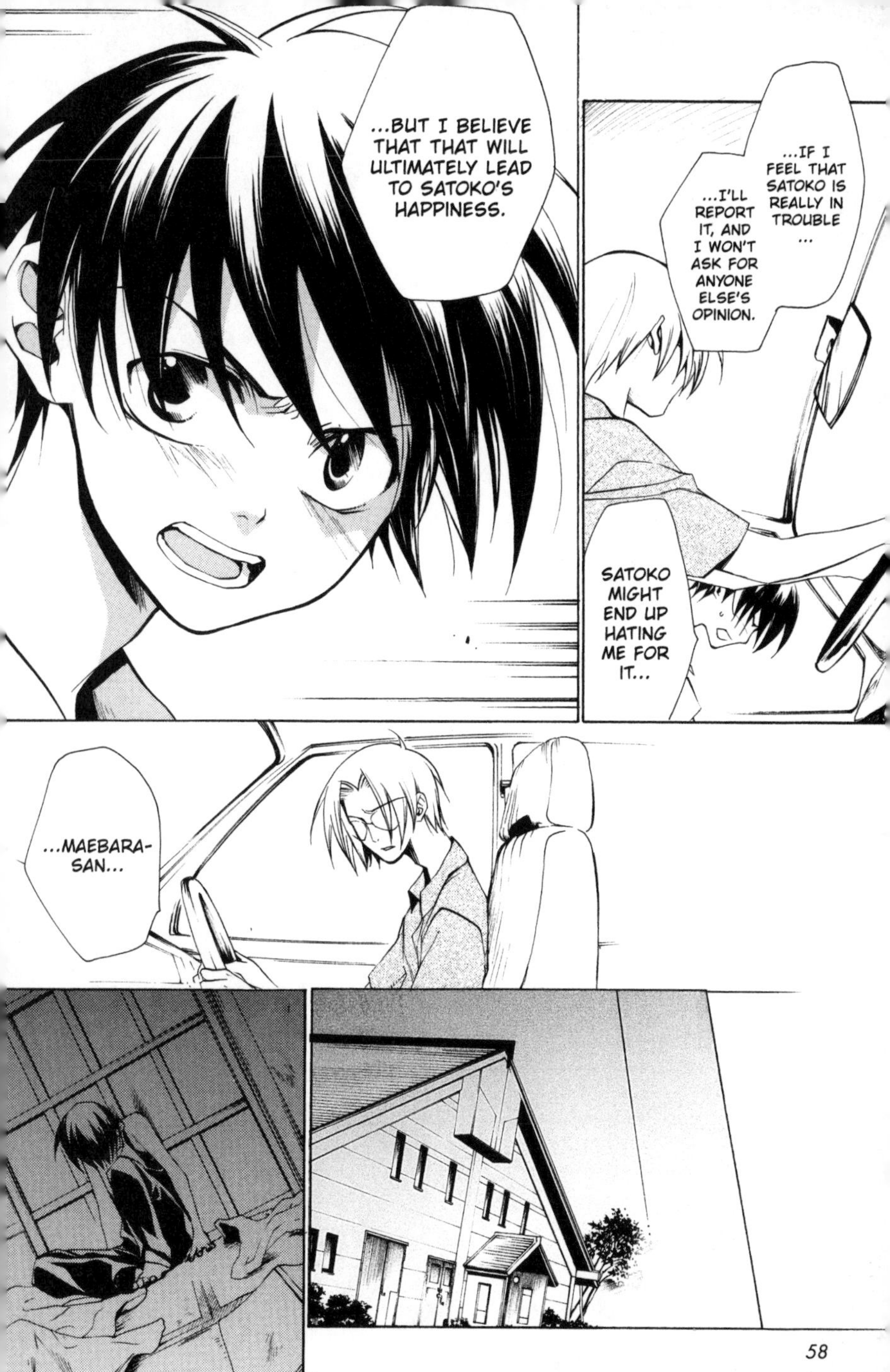
...IF I FEEL THAT SATOKO IS REALLY IN TROUBLE ...
...I'LL REPORT IT, AND I WON'T ASK FOR ANYONE ELSE'S OPINION.
SATOKO MIGHT END UP HATING ME FOR IT...
...BUT I BELIEVE THAT THAT WILL ULTIMATELY LEAD TO SATOKO'S HAPPINESS.
...MAEBARA-SAN...

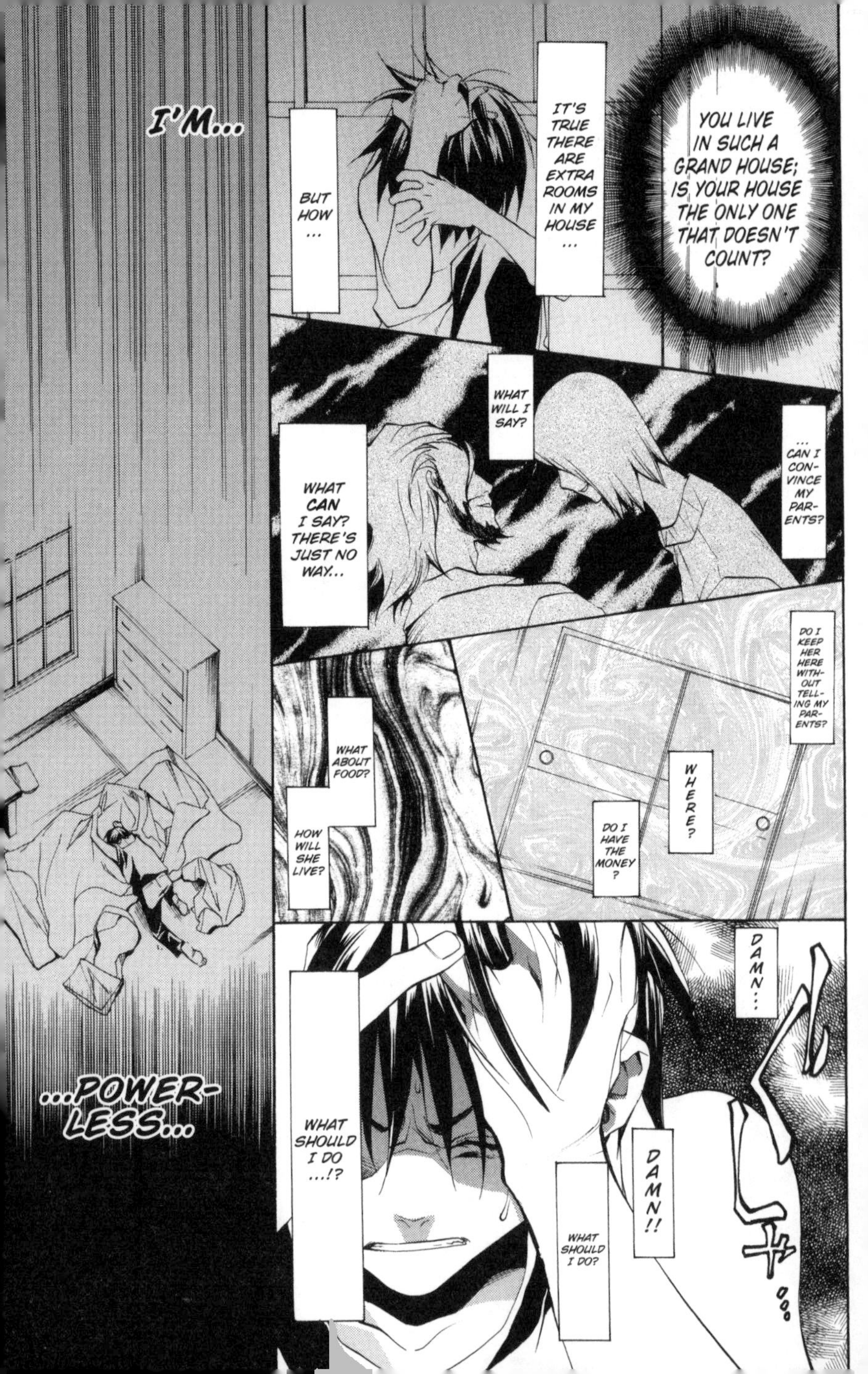
YOU LIVE IN SUCH A GRAND HOUSE; IS YOUR HOUSE THE ONLY ONE THAT DOESN'T COUNT?
IT'S TRUE THERE ARE EXTRA ROOMS IN MY HOUSE ...
BUT HOW ...
... CAN I CON-VINCE MY PAR-ENTS?
WHAT WILL I SAY?
WHAT CAN I SAY? THERE'S JUST NO WAY...
DO I KEEP HER HERE WITH-OUT TELL-ING MY PAR-ENTS?
WHERE?
DO I HAVE THE MONEY ?
WHAT ABOUT FOOD?
HOW WILL SHE LIVE?
DAMN...
DAMN!!
WHAT SHOULD I DO?
WHAT SHOULD I DO ...!?
I'M...
...POWER-LESS...

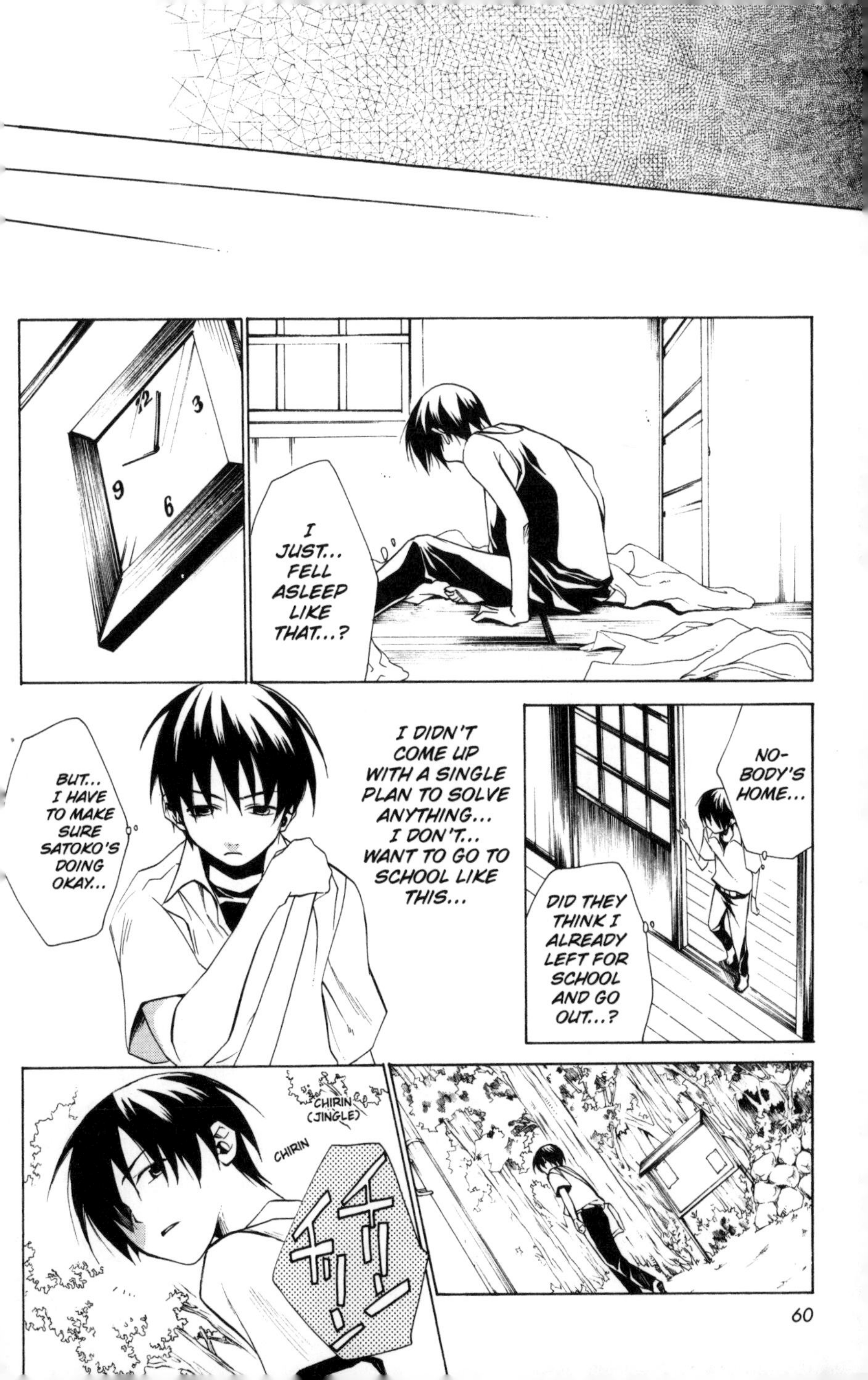
I JUST... FELL ASLEEP LIKE THAT...?
NO-BODY'S HOME...
DID THEY THINK I ALREADY LEFT FOR SCHOOL AND GO OUT...?
I DIDN'T COME UP WITH A SINGLE PLAN TO SOLVE ANYTHING... I DON'T... WANT TO GO TO SCHOOL LIKE THIS...
BUT... I HAVE TO MAKE SURE SATOKO'S DOING OKAY...
CHIRIN (JINGLE)
CHIRIN

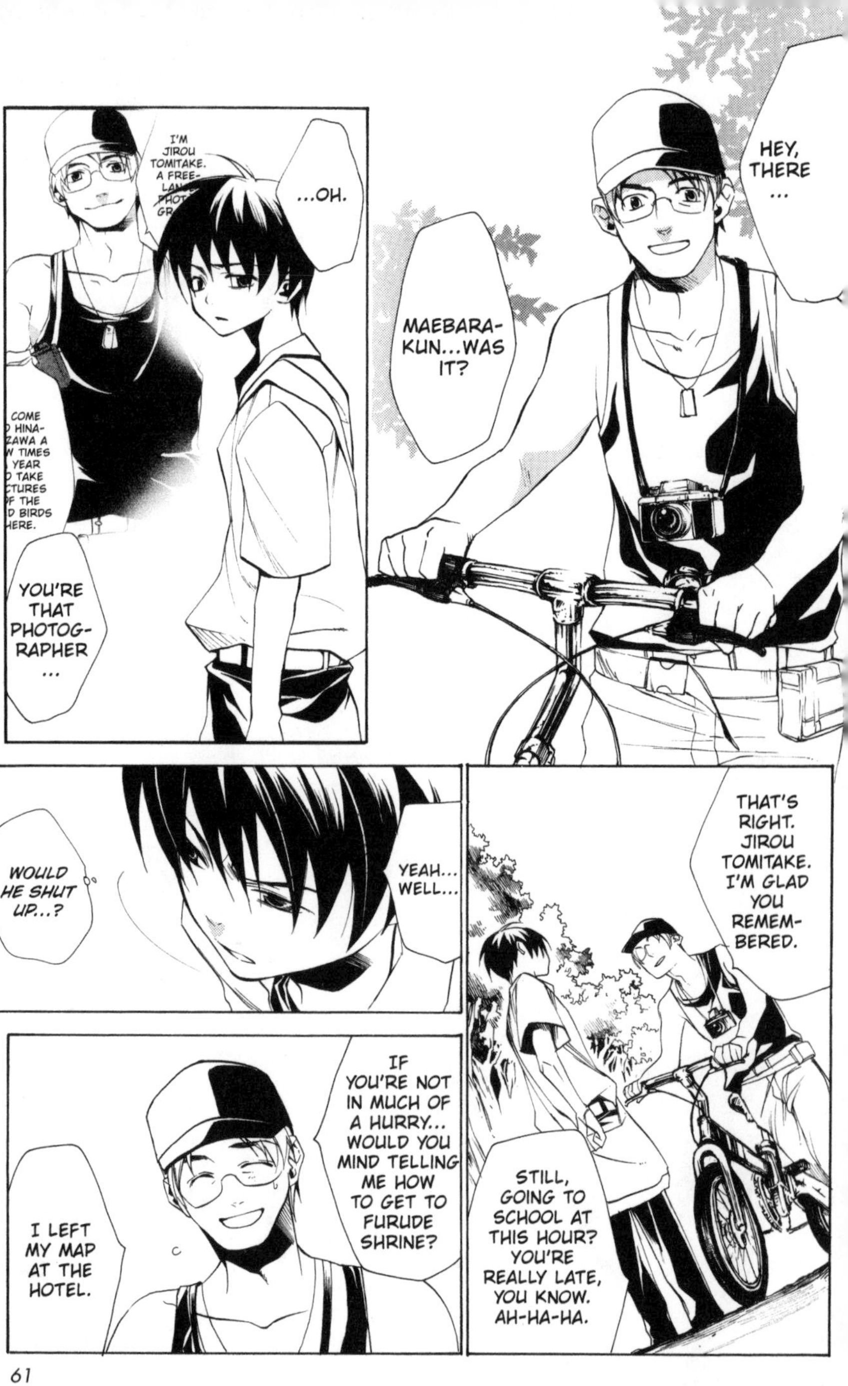
HEY, THERE ...
MAEBARA-KUN...WAS IT?
...OH.
I'M JIROU TOMITAKE. A FREE-
YOU'RE THAT PHOTOGRAPHER ...
THAT'S RIGHT. JIROU TOMITAKE. I'M GLAD YOU REMEMBERED.
STILL, GOING TO SCHOOL AT THIS HOUR? YOU'RE REALLY LATE, YOU KNOW. AH-HA-HA.
YEAH... WELL...
WOULD HE SHUT UP...?
IF YOU'RE NOT IN MUCH OF A HURRY... WOULD YOU MIND TELLING ME HOW TO GET TO FURUDE SHRINE?
I LEFT MY MAP AT THE HOTEL.

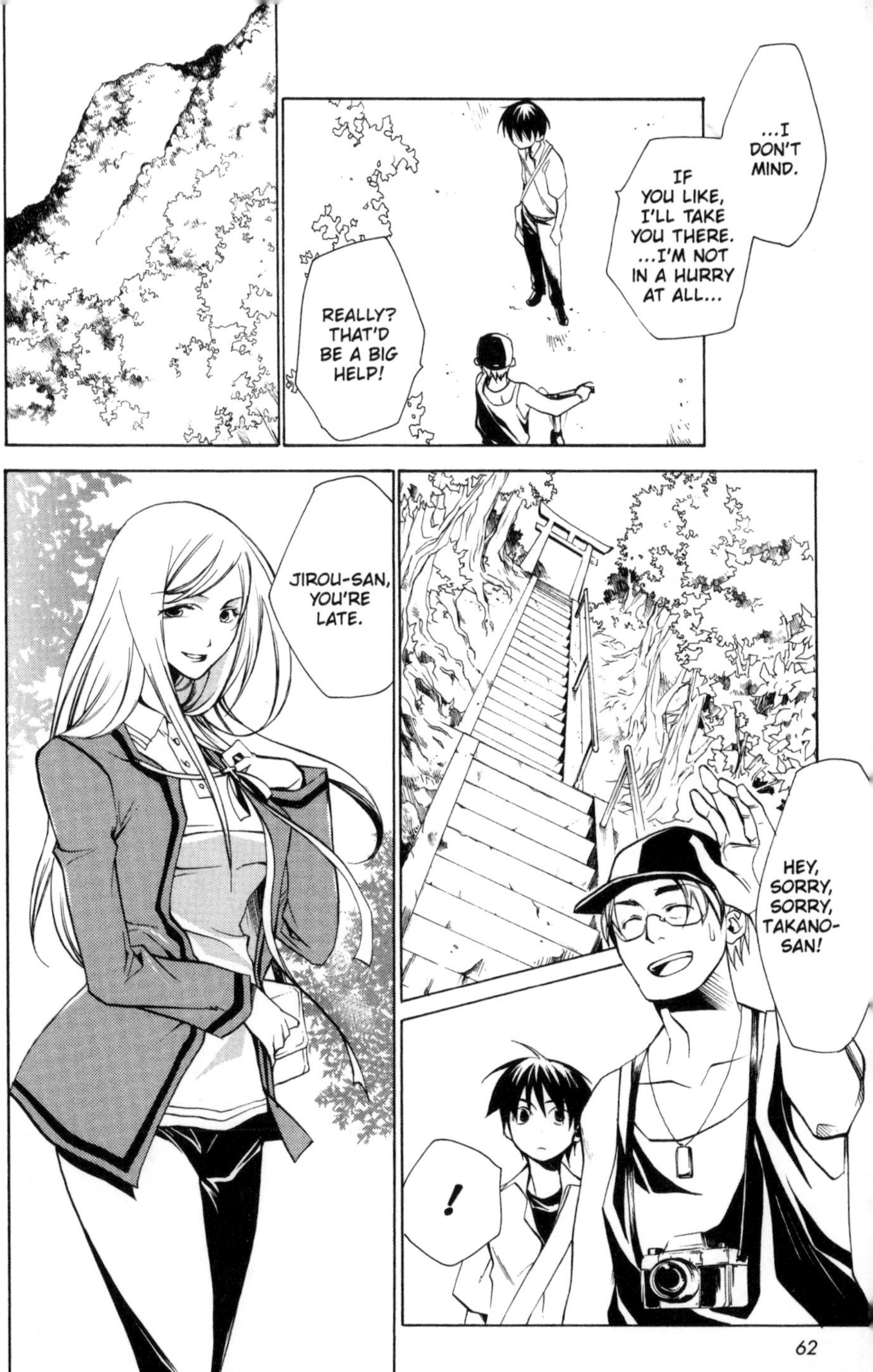
...I DON'T MIND.
IF YOU LIKE, I'LL TAKE YOU THERE. ...I'M NOT IN A HURRY AT ALL...
REALLY? THAT'D BE A BIG HELP!
HEY, SORRY, SORRY, TAKANO-SAN!
!
JIROU-SAN, YOU'RE LATE.

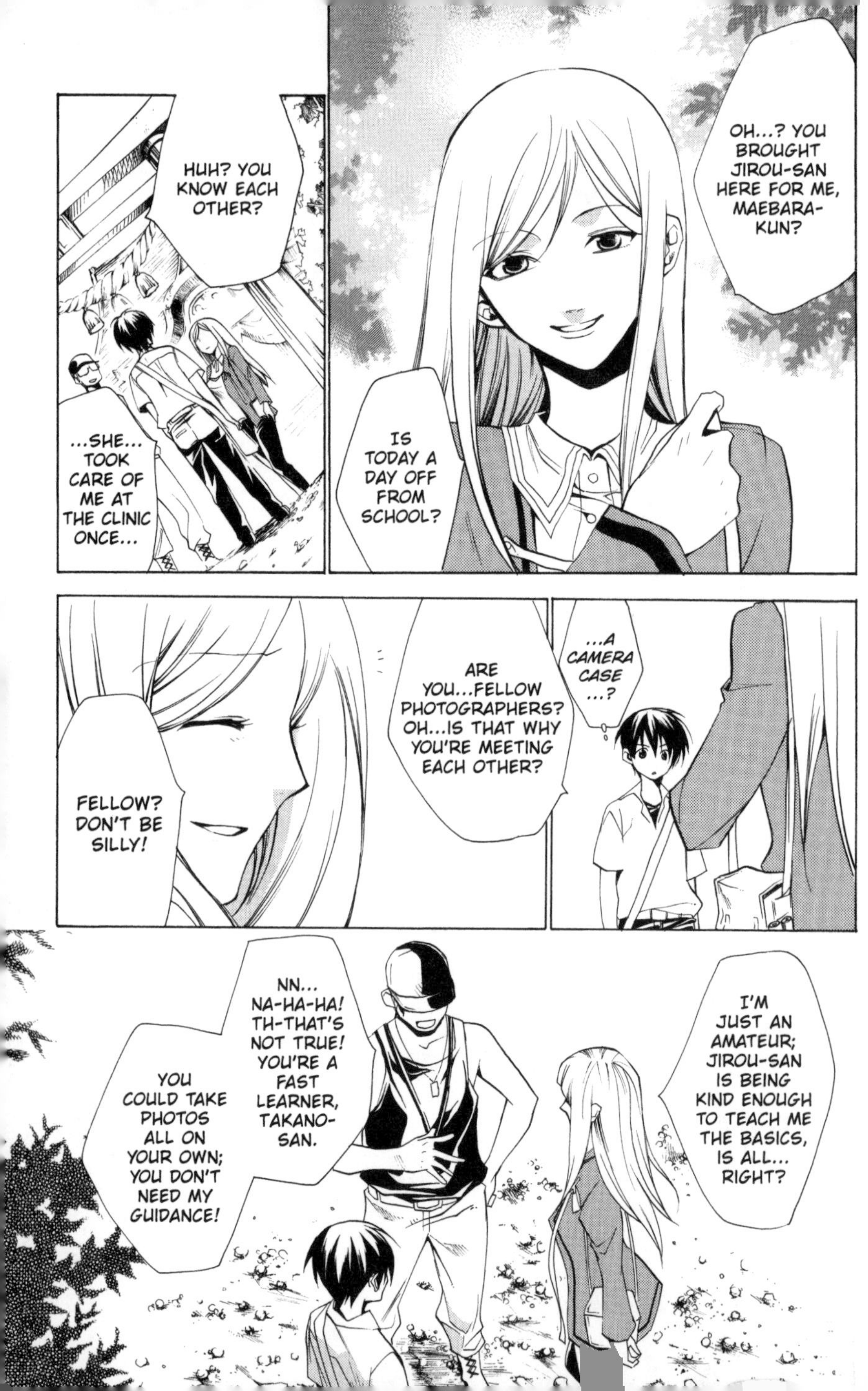
OH...? YOU BROUGHT JIROU-SAN HERE FOR ME, MAEBARA-KUN?
IS TODAY A DAY OFF FROM SCHOOL?
HUH? YOU KNOW EACH OTHER?
...SHE... TOOK CARE OF ME AT THE CLINIC ONCE...
...A CAMERA CASE ...?
ARE YOU...FELLOW PHOTOGRAPHERS? OH...IS THAT WHY YOU'RE MEETING EACH OTHER?
FELLOW? DON'T BE SILLY!
I'M JUST AN AMATEUR; JIROU-SAN IS BEING KIND ENOUGH TO TEACH ME THE BASICS, IS ALL... RIGHT?
NN... NA-HA-HA! TH-THAT'S NOT TRUE! YOU'RE A FAST LEARNER, TAKANO-SAN.
YOU COULD TAKE PHOTOS ALL ON YOUR OWN; YOU DON'T NEED MY GUIDANCE!

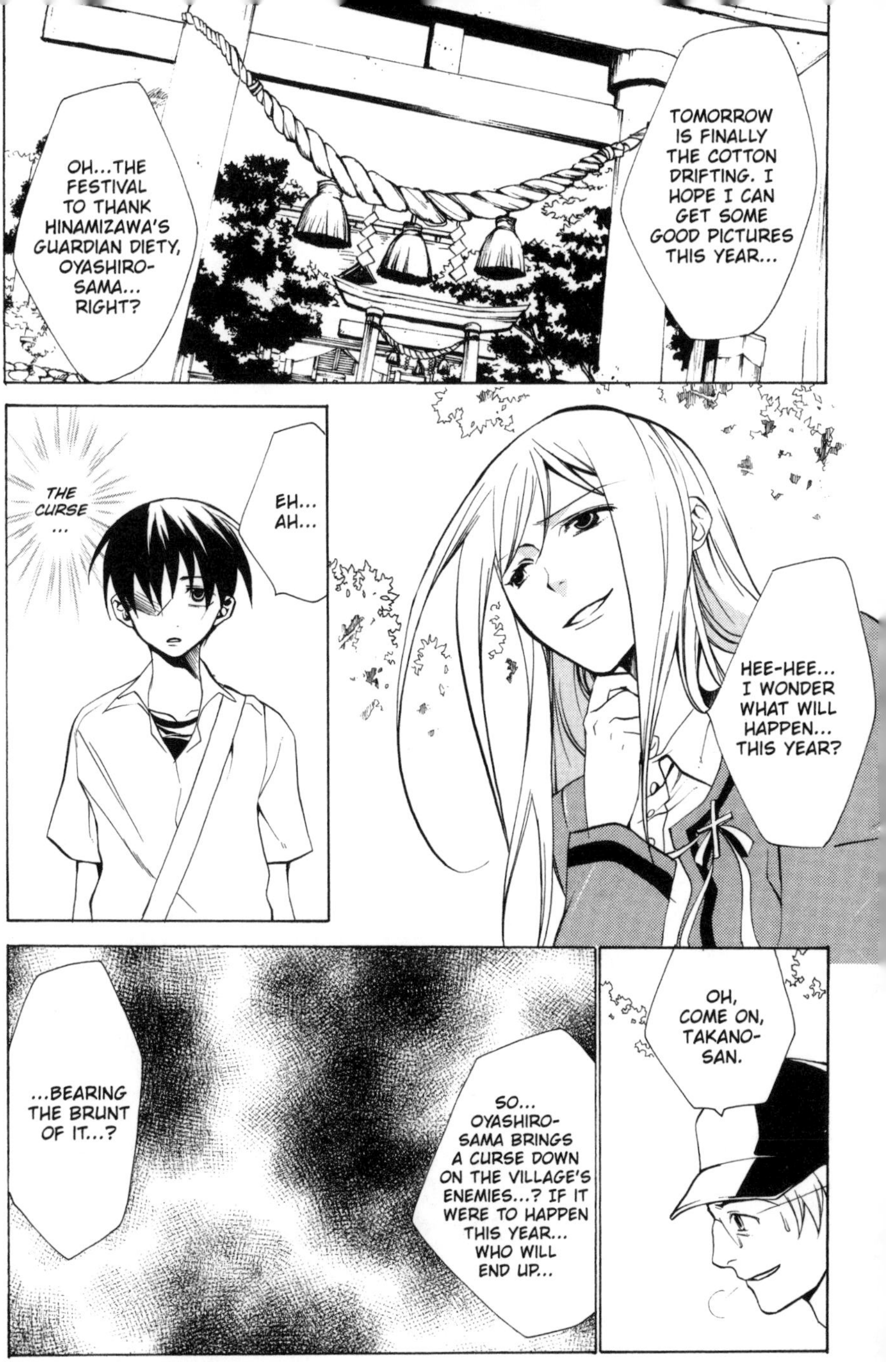
TOMORROW IS FINALLY THE COTTON DRIFTING. I HOPE I CAN GET SOME GOOD PICTURES THIS YEAR...
OH...THE FESTIVAL TO THANK HINAMIZAWA'S GUARDIAN DIETY, OYASHIRO-SAMA... RIGHT?
HEE-HEE... I WONDER WHAT WILL HAPPEN... THIS YEAR?
EH... AH...
THE CURSE ...
OH, COME ON, TAKANO-SAN.
SO... OYASHIRO-SAMA BRINGS A CURSE DOWN ON THE VILLAGE'S ENEMIES...? IF IT WERE TO HAPPEN THIS YEAR... WHO WILL END UP...
...BEARING THE BRUNT OF IT...?

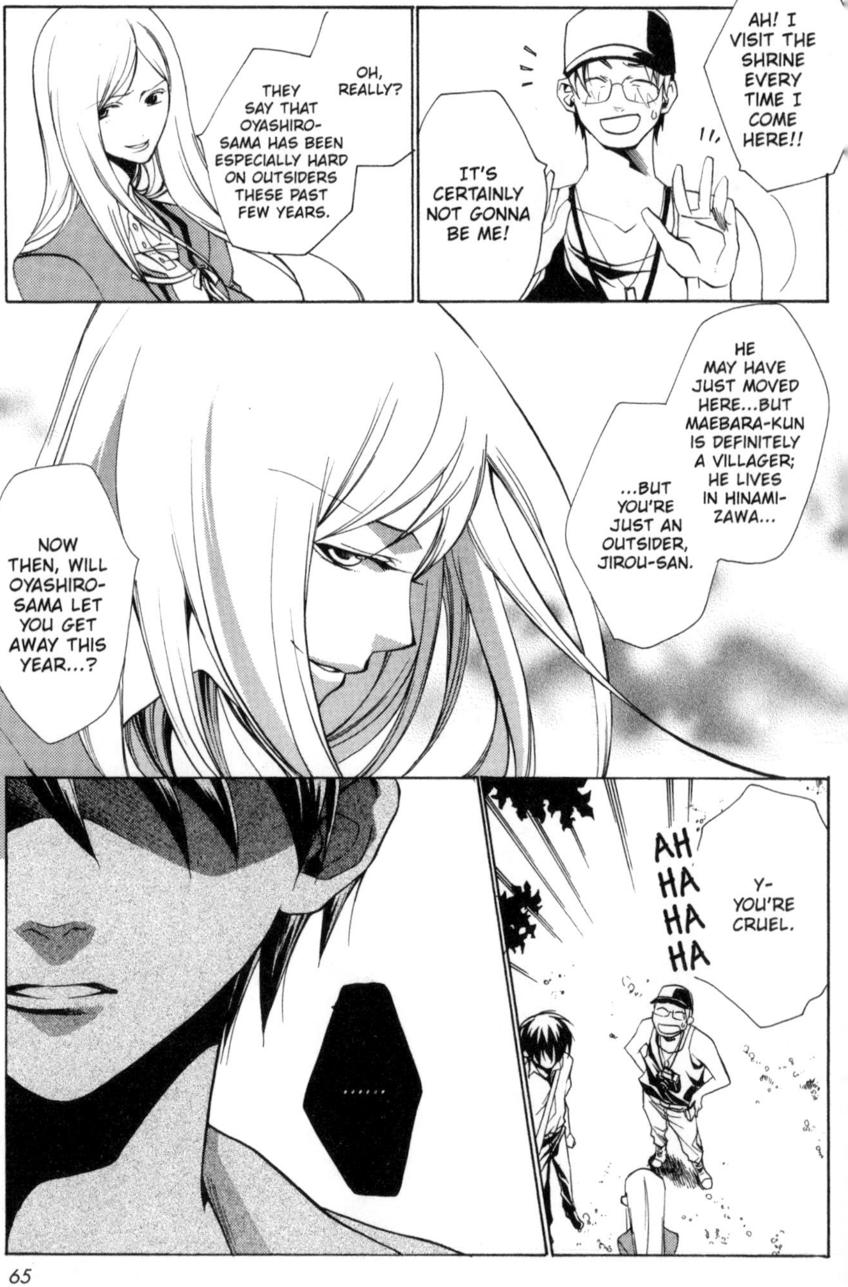
AH! I VISIT THE SHRINE EVERY TIME I COME HERE!!
IT'S CERTAINLY NOT GONNA BE ME!
OH, REALLY?
THEY SAY THAT OYASHIRO-SAMA HAS BEEN ESPECIALLY HARD ON OUTSIDERS THESE PAST FEW YEARS.
HE MAY HAVE JUST MOVED HERE...BUT MAEBARA-KUN IS DEFINITELY A VILLAGER; HE LIVES IN HINAMIZAWA...
...BUT YOU'RE JUST AN OUTSIDER, JIROU-SAN.
NOW THEN, WILL OYASHIRO-SAMA LET YOU GET AWAY THIS YEAR...?
Y-YOU'RE CRUEL.
AH HA HA HA HA
......

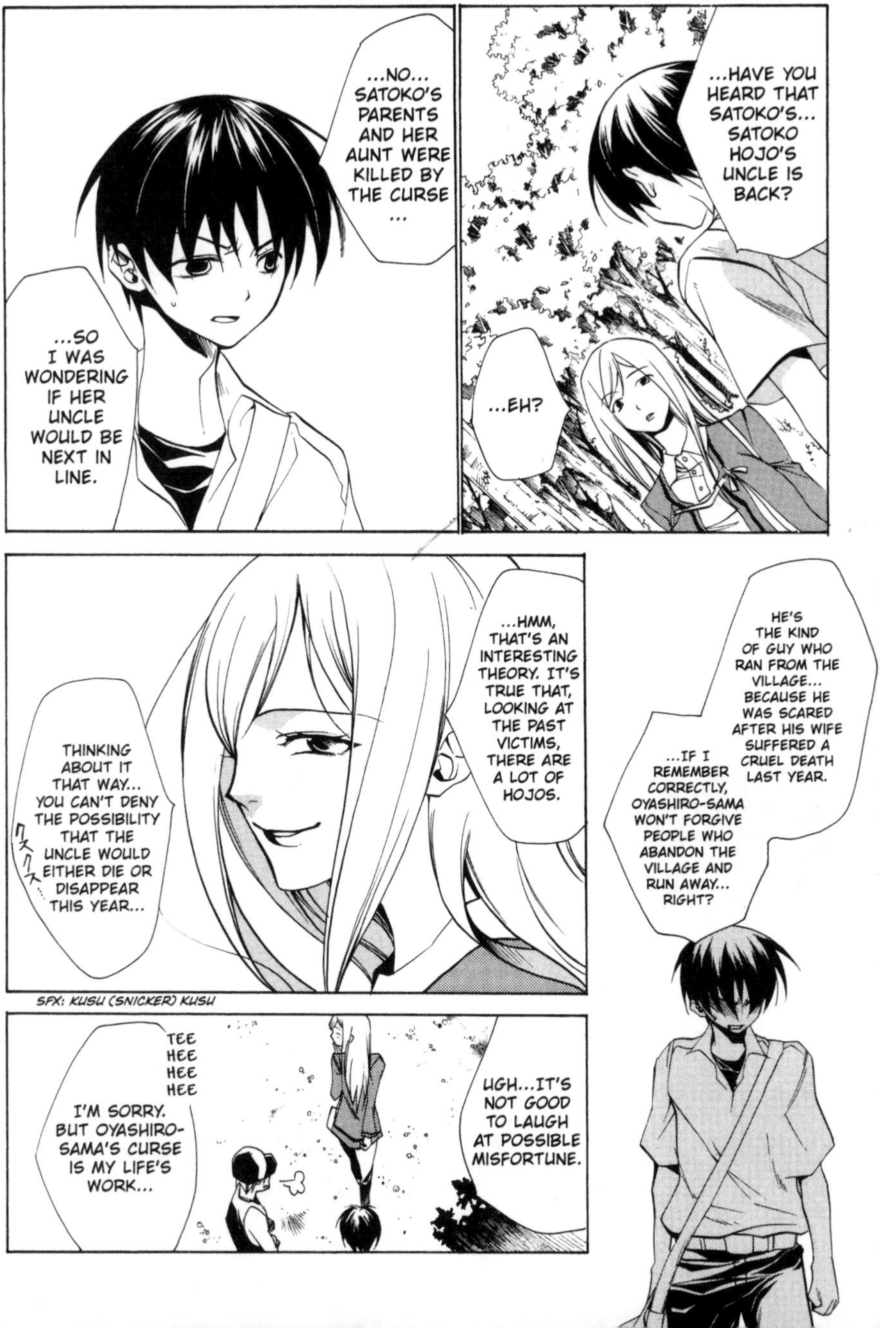
...HAVE YOU HEARD THAT SATOKO'S... SATOKO HOJO'S UNCLE IS BACK?
...EH?
...NO... SATOKO'S PARENTS AND HER AUNT WERE KILLED BY THE CURSE ...
...SO I WAS WONDERING IF HER UNCLE WOULD BE NEXT IN LINE.
HE'S THE KIND OF GUY WHO RAN FROM THE VILLAGE... BECAUSE HE WAS SCARED AFTER HIS WIFE SUFFERED A CRUEL DEATH LAST YEAR.
...IF I REMEMBER CORRECTLY, OYASHIRO-SAMA WON'T FORGIVE PEOPLE WHO ABANDON THE VILLAGE AND RUN AWAY... RIGHT?
...HMM, THAT'S AN INTERESTING THEORY. IT'S TRUE THAT, LOOKING AT THE PAST VICTIMS, THERE ARE A LOT OF HOJOS.
THINKING ABOUT IT THAT WAY... YOU CAN'T DENY THE POSSIBILITY THAT THE UNCLE WOULD EITHER DIE OR DISAPPEAR THIS YEAR...
クスクス…
SFX: KUSU (SNICKER) KUSU
UGH...IT'S NOT GOOD TO LAUGH AT POSSIBLE MISFORTUNE.
TEE HEE HEE HEE
I'M SORRY. BUT OYASHIRO-SAMA'S CURSE IS MY LIFE'S WORK...

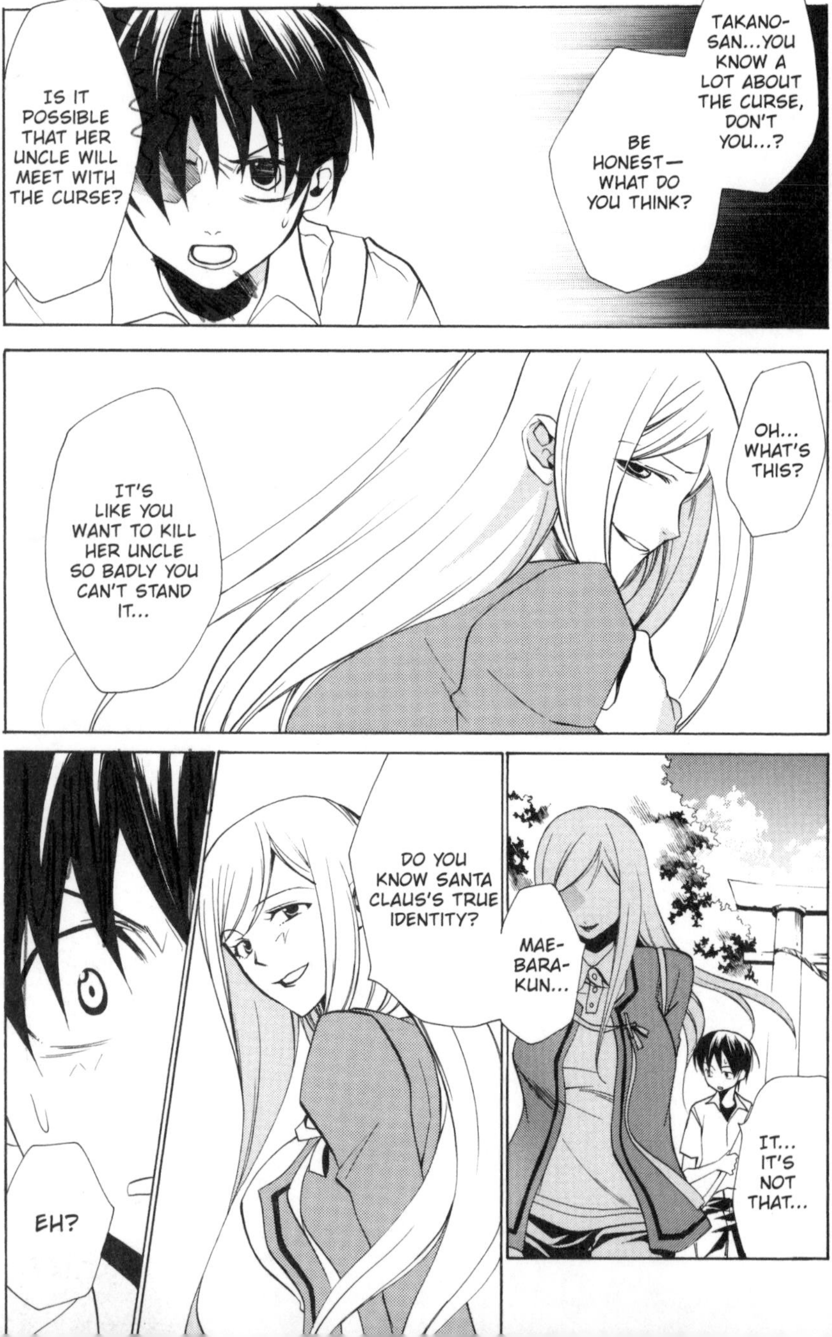
TAKANO-SAN...YOU KNOW A LOT ABOUT THE CURSE, DON'T YOU...?
BE HONEST—WHAT DO YOU THINK?
IS IT POSSIBLE THAT HER UNCLE WILL MEET WITH THE CURSE?
OH... WHAT'S THIS?
IT'S LIKE YOU WANT TO KILL HER UNCLE SO BADLY YOU CAN'T STAND IT...
MAE-BARA-KUN...
IT... IT'S NOT THAT...
DO YOU KNOW SANTA CLAUS'S TRUE IDENTITY?
EH?

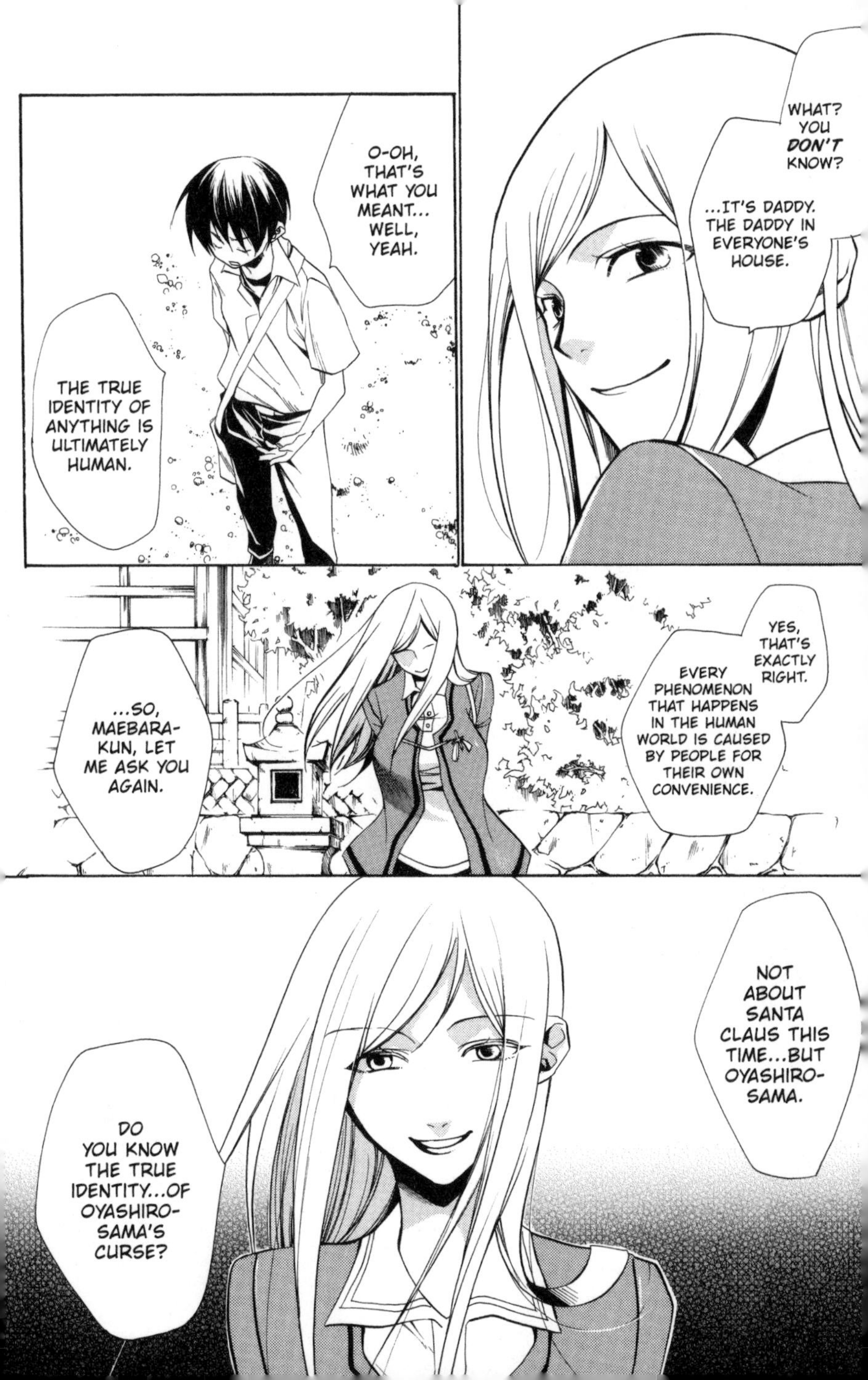

WHAT? YOU *DON'T* KNOW?
...IT'S DADDY. THE DADDY IN EVERYONE'S HOUSE.
O-OH, THAT'S WHAT YOU MEANT... WELL, YEAH.
THE TRUE IDENTITY OF ANYTHING IS ULTIMATELY HUMAN.
YES, THAT'S EXACTLY RIGHT.
EVERY PHENOMENON THAT HAPPENS IN THE HUMAN WORLD IS CAUSED BY PEOPLE FOR THEIR OWN CONVENIENCE.
...SO, MAEBARA-KUN, LET ME ASK YOU AGAIN.
NOT ABOUT SANTA CLAUS THIS TIME...BUT OYASHIRO-SAMA.
DO YOU KNOW THE TRUE IDENTITY...OF OYASHIRO-SAMA'S CURSE?

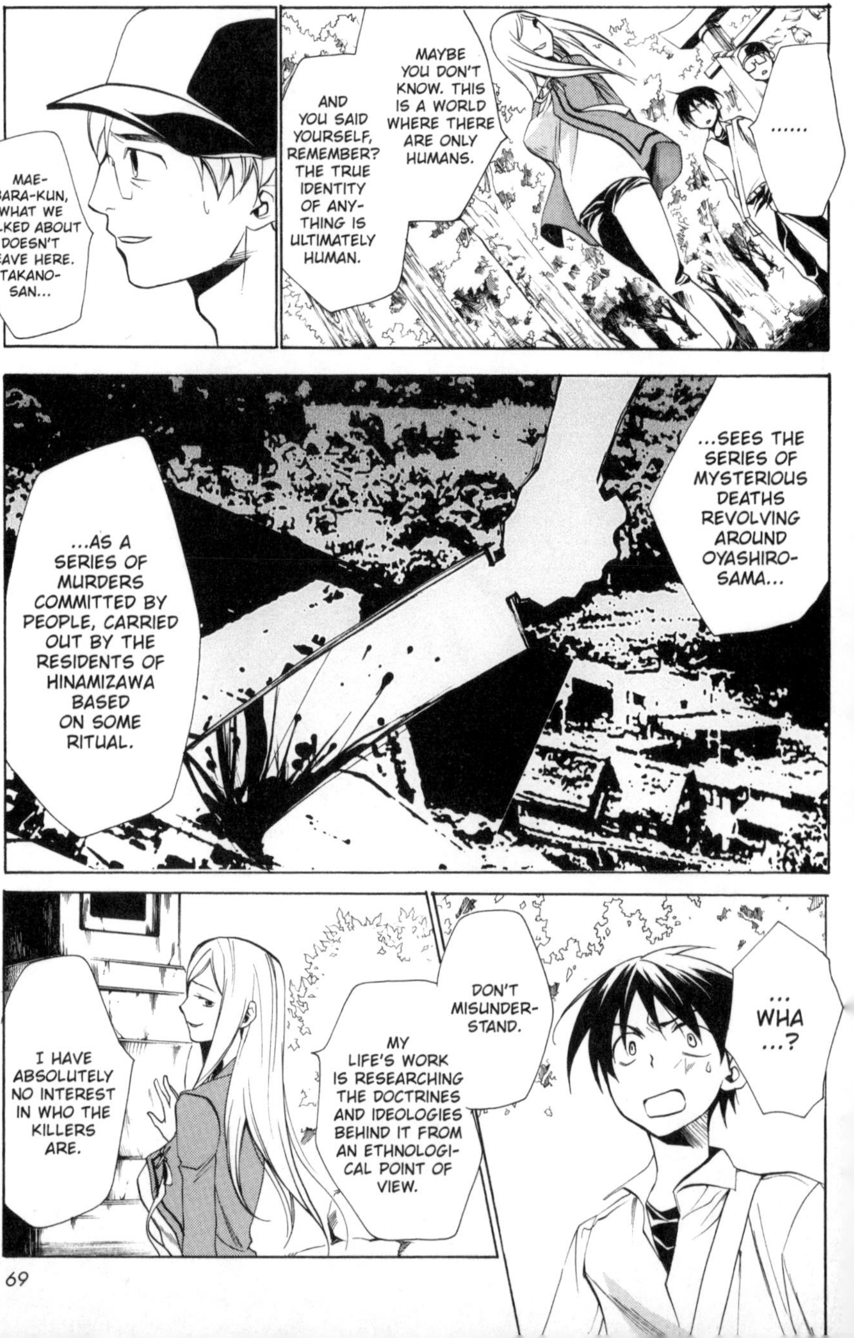
......
MAYBE YOU DON'T KNOW. THIS IS A WORLD WHERE THERE ARE ONLY HUMANS.
AND YOU SAID YOURSELF, REMEMBER? THE TRUE IDENTITY OF ANYTHING IS ULTIMATELY HUMAN.
MAE-BARA-KUN, WHAT WE TALKED ABOUT DOESN'T LEAVE HERE. TAKANO-SAN...
...SEES THE SERIES OF MYSTERIOUS DEATHS REVOLVING AROUND OYASHIRO-SAMA...
...AS A SERIES OF MURDERS COMMITTED BY PEOPLE, CARRIED OUT BY THE RESIDENTS OF HINAMIZAWA BASED ON SOME RITUAL.
... WHA ...?
DON'T MISUNDER-STAND.
MY LIFE'S WORK IS RESEARCHING THE DOCTRINES AND IDEOLOGIES BEHIND IT FROM AN ETHNOLOGI-CAL POINT OF VIEW.
I HAVE ABSOLUTELY NO INTEREST IN WHO THE KILLERS ARE.

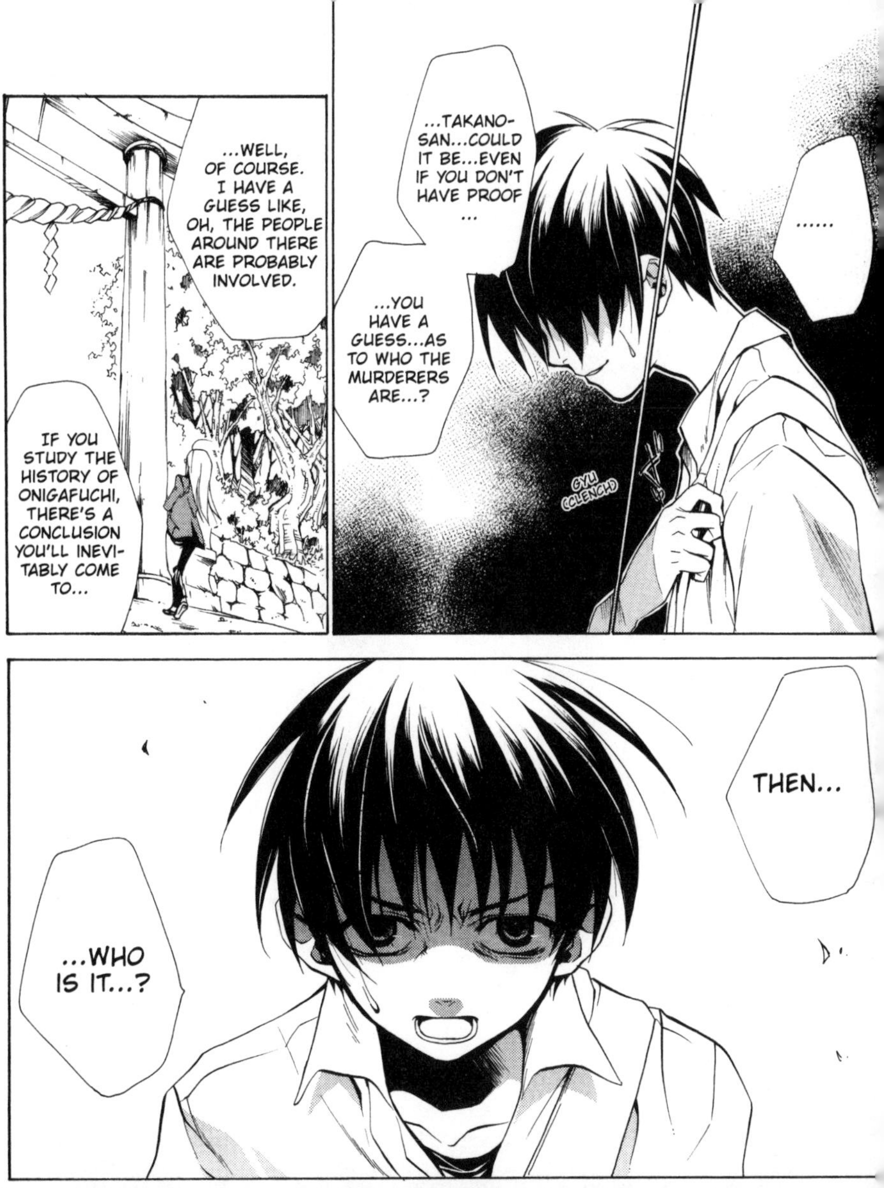
...TAKANO-SAN...COULD IT BE...EVEN IF YOU DON'T HAVE PROOF...
......
...YOU HAVE A GUESS...AS TO WHO THE MURDERERS ARE...?
GYU (CLENCH)
...WELL, OF COURSE. I HAVE A GUESS LIKE, OH, THE PEOPLE AROUND THERE ARE PROBABLY INVOLVED.
IF YOU STUDY THE HISTORY OF ONIGAFUCHI, THERE'S A CONCLUSION YOU'LL INEVITABLY COME TO...
THEN...
...WHO IS IT...?

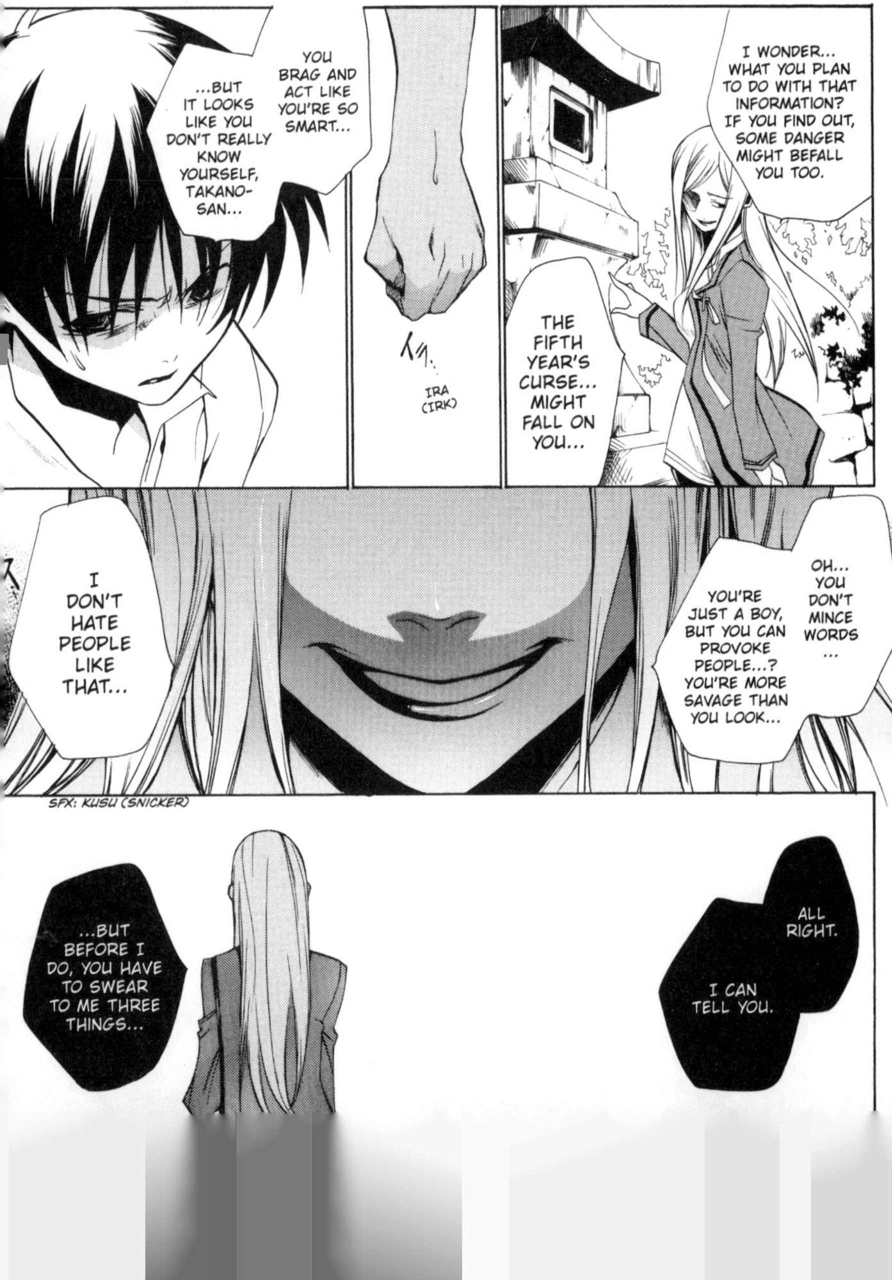
I WONDER... WHAT YOU PLAN TO DO WITH THAT INFORMATION? IF YOU FIND OUT, SOME DANGER MIGHT BEFALL YOU TOO.
THE FIFTH YEAR'S CURSE... MIGHT FALL ON YOU...
YOU BRAG AND ACT LIKE YOU'RE SO SMART...
IRA (IRK)
...BUT IT LOOKS LIKE YOU DON'T REALLY KNOW YOURSELF, TAKANO-SAN...
OH... YOU DON'T MINCE WORDS...
YOU'RE JUST A BOY, BUT YOU CAN PROVOKE PEOPLE...? YOU'RE MORE SAVAGE THAN YOU LOOK...
I DON'T HATE PEOPLE LIKE THAT...
SFX: KUSU (SNICKER)
ALL RIGHT.
I CAN TELL YOU.
...BUT BEFORE I DO, YOU HAVE TO SWEAR TO ME THREE THINGS...

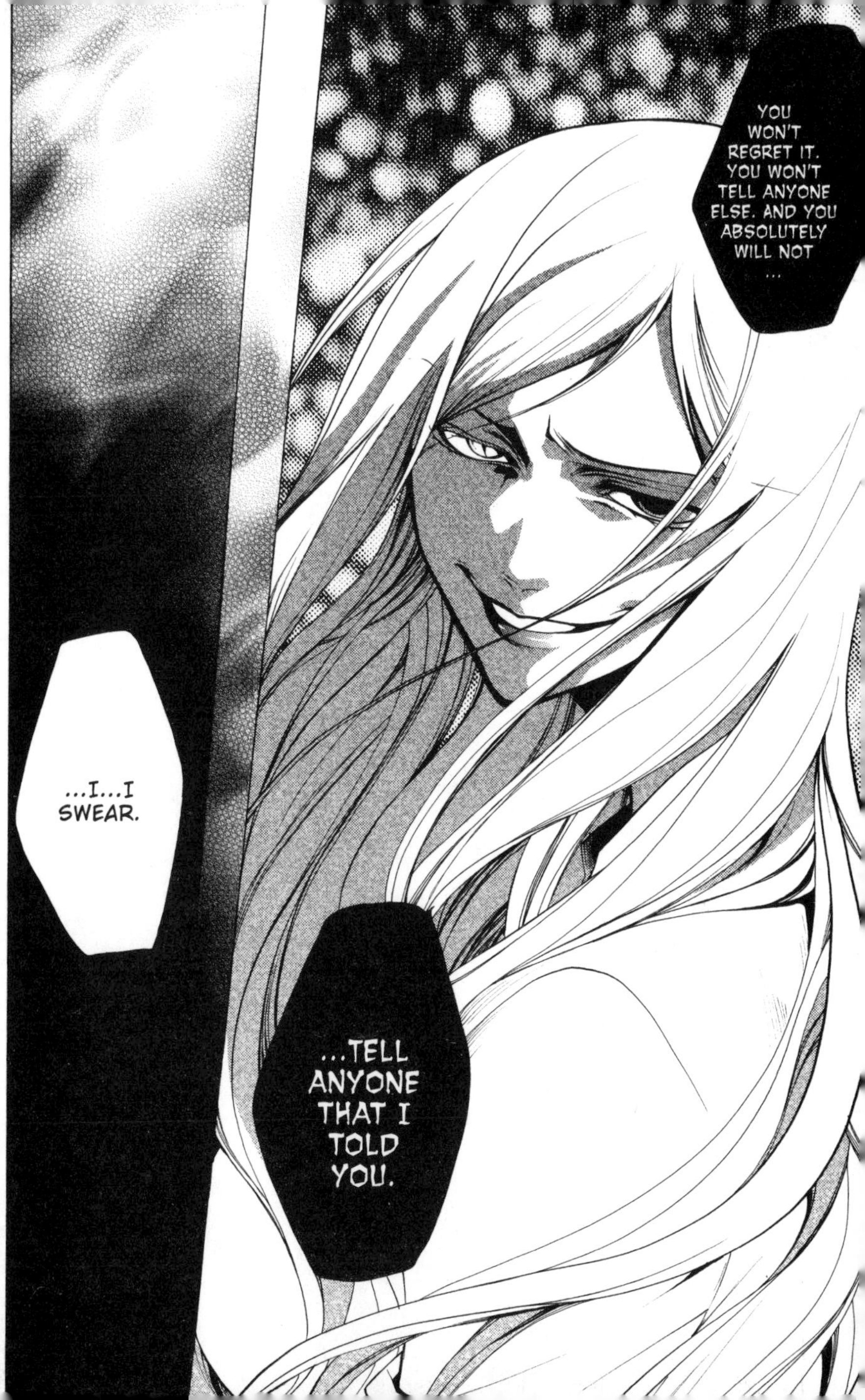
YOU WON'T REGRET IT. YOU WON'T TELL ANYONE ELSE. AND YOU ABSOLUTELY WILL NOT ...
...TELL ANYONE THAT I TOLD YOU.
...I...I SWEAR.

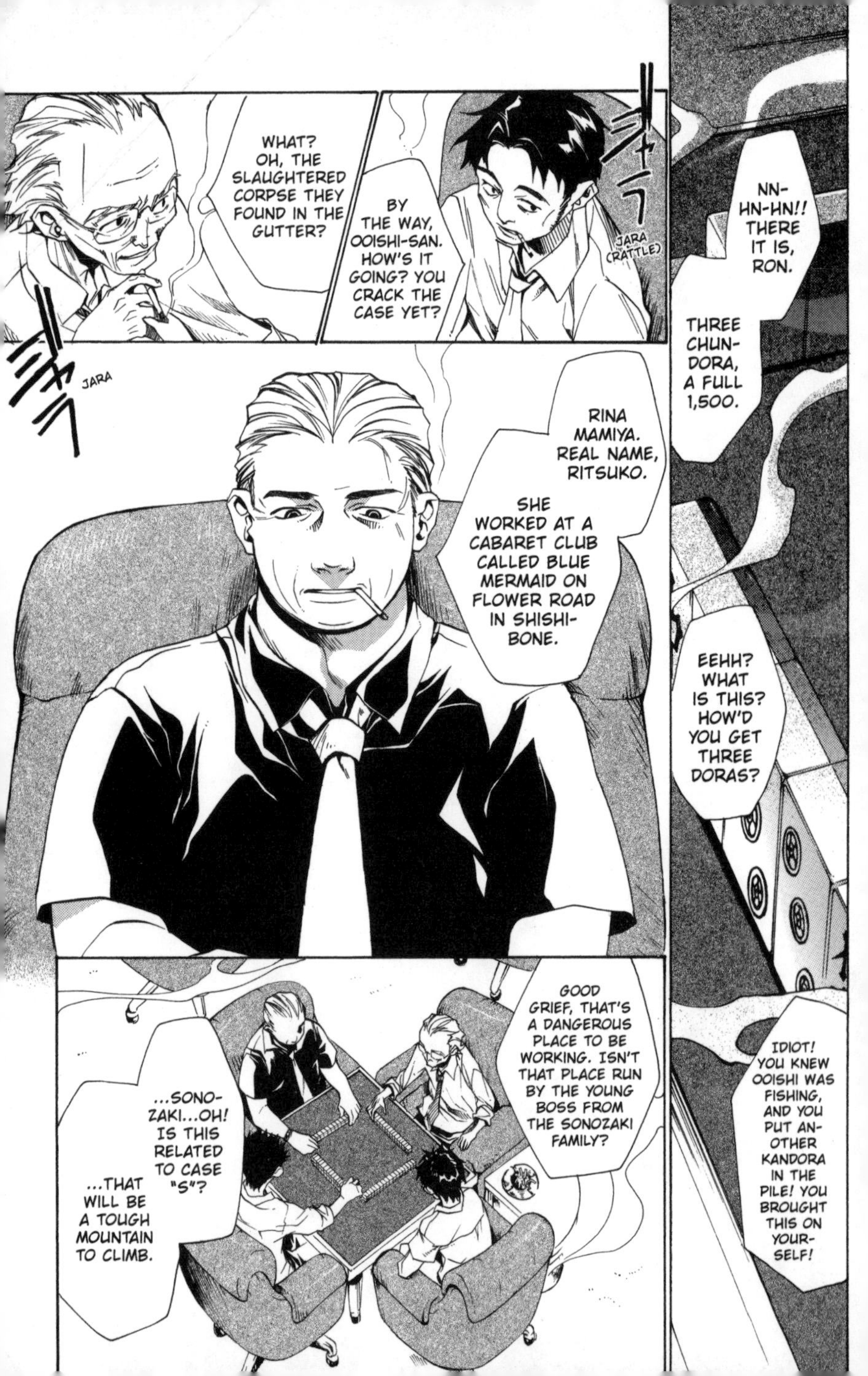
NN-HN-HN!! THERE IT IS, RON.
THREE CHUN-DORA, A FULL 1,500.
EEHH? WHAT IS THIS? HOW'D YOU GET THREE DORAS?
IDIOT! YOU KNEW OOISHI WAS FISHING, AND YOU PUT AN-OTHER KANDORA IN THE PILE! YOU BROUGHT THIS ON YOUR-SELF!
JARA (RATTLE)
BY THE WAY, OOISHI-SAN. HOW'S IT GOING? YOU CRACK THE CASE YET?
WHAT? OH, THE SLAUGHTERED CORPSE THEY FOUND IN THE GUTTER?
JARA
RINA MAMIYA. REAL NAME, RITSUKO.
SHE WORKED AT A CABARET CLUB CALLED BLUE MERMAID ON FLOWER ROAD IN SHISHI-BONE.
GOOD GRIEF, THAT'S A DANGEROUS PLACE TO BE WORKING. ISN'T THAT PLACE RUN BY THE YOUNG BOSS FROM THE SONOZAKI FAMILY?
...SONO-ZAKI...OH! IS THIS RELATED TO CASE "S"?
...THAT WILL BE A TOUGH MOUNTAIN TO CLIMB.

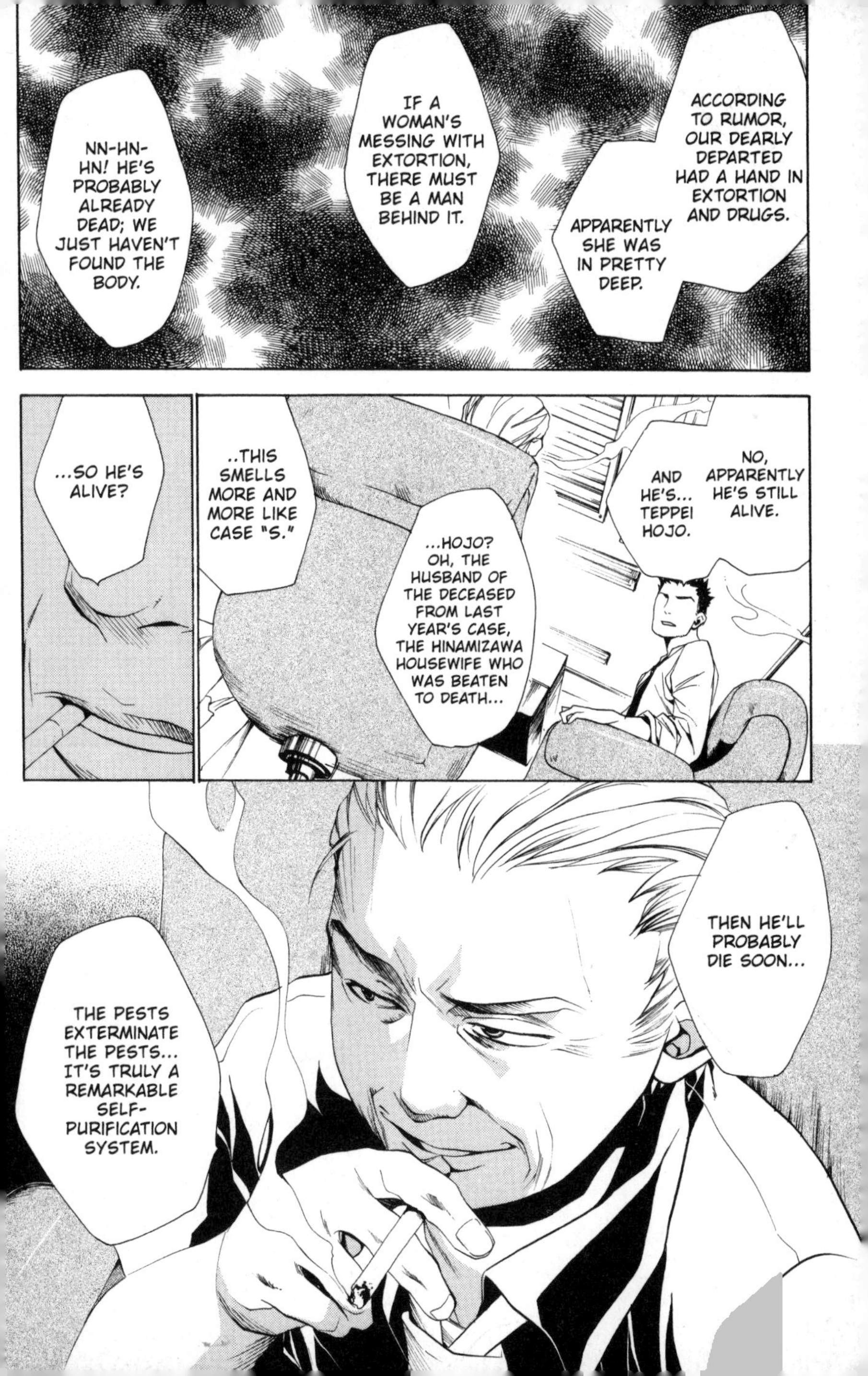
ACCORDING TO RUMOR, OUR DEARLY DEPARTED HAD A HAND IN EXTORTION AND DRUGS.
APPARENTLY SHE WAS IN PRETTY DEEP.
IF A WOMAN'S MESSING WITH EXTORTION, THERE MUST BE A MAN BEHIND IT.
NN-HN-HN! HE'S PROBABLY ALREADY DEAD; WE JUST HAVEN'T FOUND THE BODY.
NO, APPARENTLY HE'S STILL ALIVE.
AND HE'S... TEPPEI HOJO.
...HOJO? OH, THE HUSBAND OF THE DECEASED FROM LAST YEAR'S CASE, THE HINAMIZAWA HOUSEWIFE WHO WAS BEATEN TO DEATH...
..THIS SMELLS MORE AND MORE LIKE CASE "S."
...SO HE'S ALIVE?
THEN HE'LL PROBABLY DIE SOON...
THE PESTS EXTERMINATE THE PESTS... IT'S TRULY A REMARKABLE SELF-PURIFICATION SYSTEM.

CHAPTER 8

IT STINKS, I WAS TOLD.

THE FOOD STINKS, I WAS TOLD.

IT STINKS BECAUSE I STINK,

I WAS TOLD.

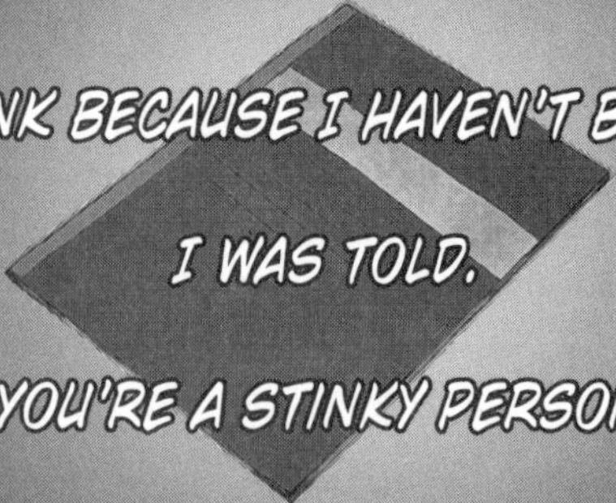

I STINK BECAUSE I HAVEN'T BATHED,

I WAS TOLD.

YOU'RE A STINKY PERSON,

SO TAKE A BATH THREE TIMES A DAY, I WAS TOLD.

AND WHEN I TAKE ONE BATH, I HAVE TO STAY IN

A LONG, LONG TIME, I WAS TOLD.

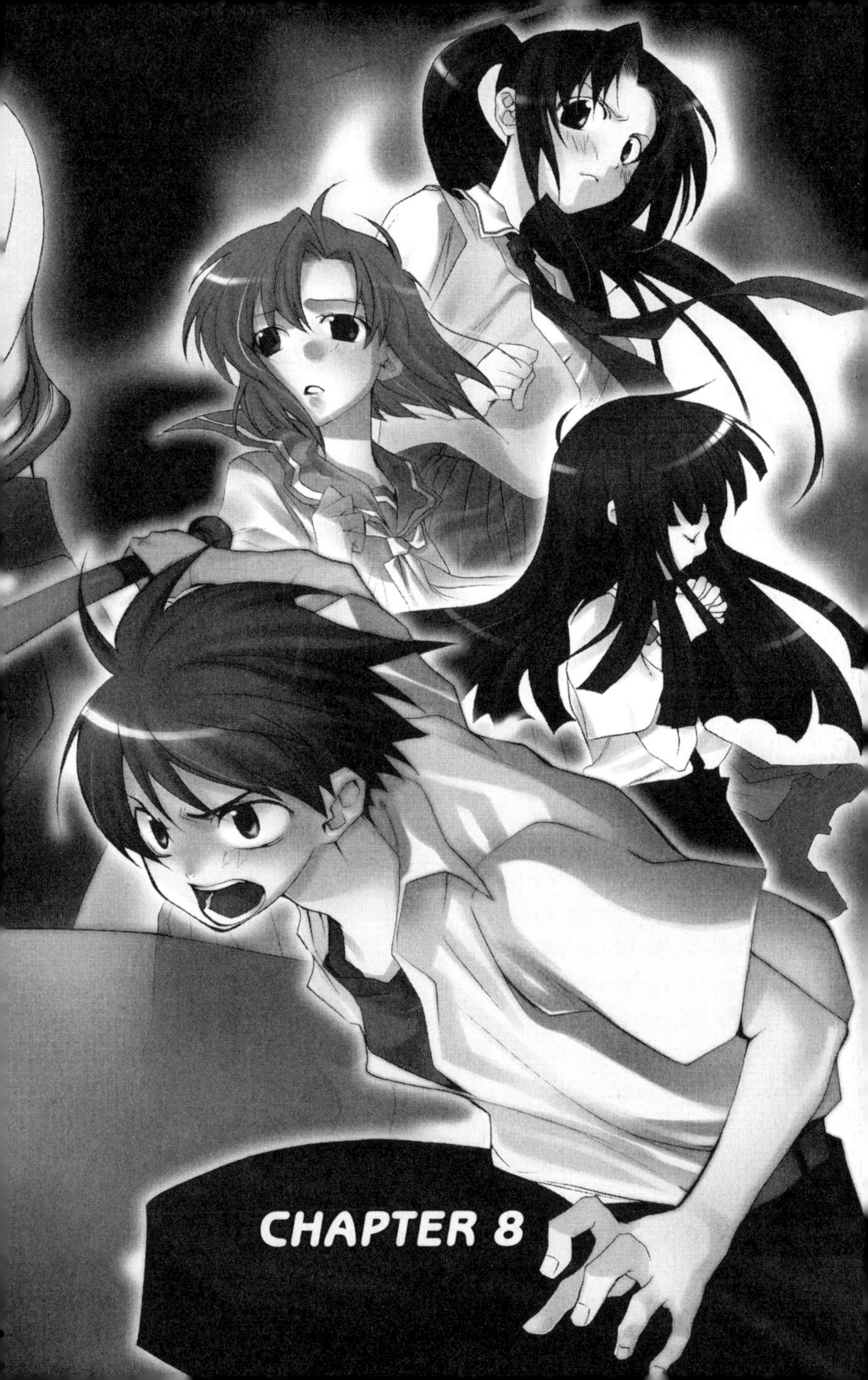
CHAPTER 8

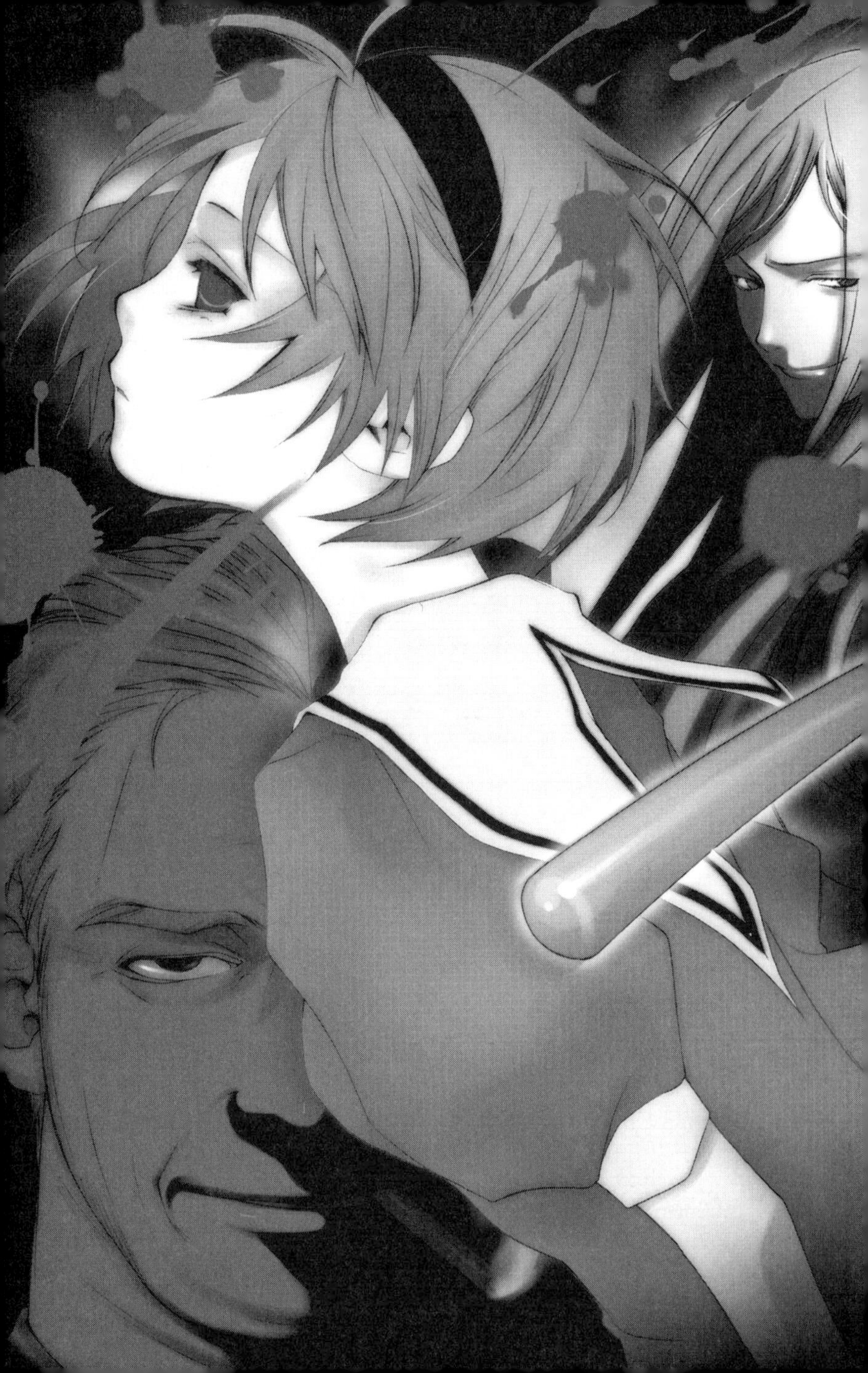

MAHJONG NOTES

Pg. 42, 44, 73
Mahjong is played with a set of illustrated tiles. There are three suits ranked from one to nine—stones, bamboo, and characters—as well as two sets of honor tiles—the four wind directions and three dragon tiles. Similar to rummy, the object is to arrange one's "hand" of tiles with sets of matching tiles or numeric sequences. For example, Ooishi's **chundora** means he's collected three chundora, or red dragon, tiles. On a player's turn, he or she draws one tile and adds it to their hand, then discards on tile. He or she may choose to draw either from the wall of tiles (like the deck in cards) or they may choose the most recently discarded tile. If a player gets a winning hand by drawing his last tile from the wall, it's **tsumo**. If the final winning tile was drawn from the previously discarded tile, it's called **ron**. **Riichi** means a player only needed one more tile to win.

NOTE: VILLAGE CHIEF, NUMBER TWO

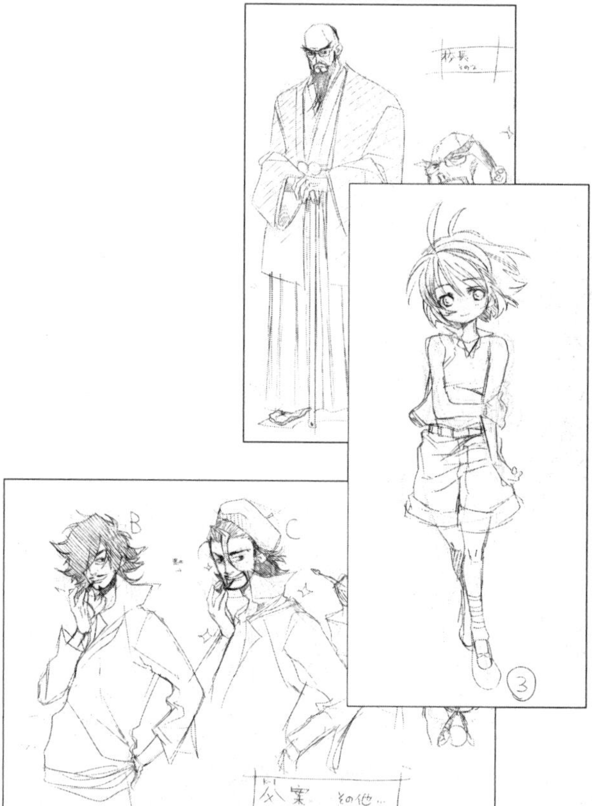
B
C

NOTE: BLACK *NOTE: FATHER ROUGH, OTHERS*

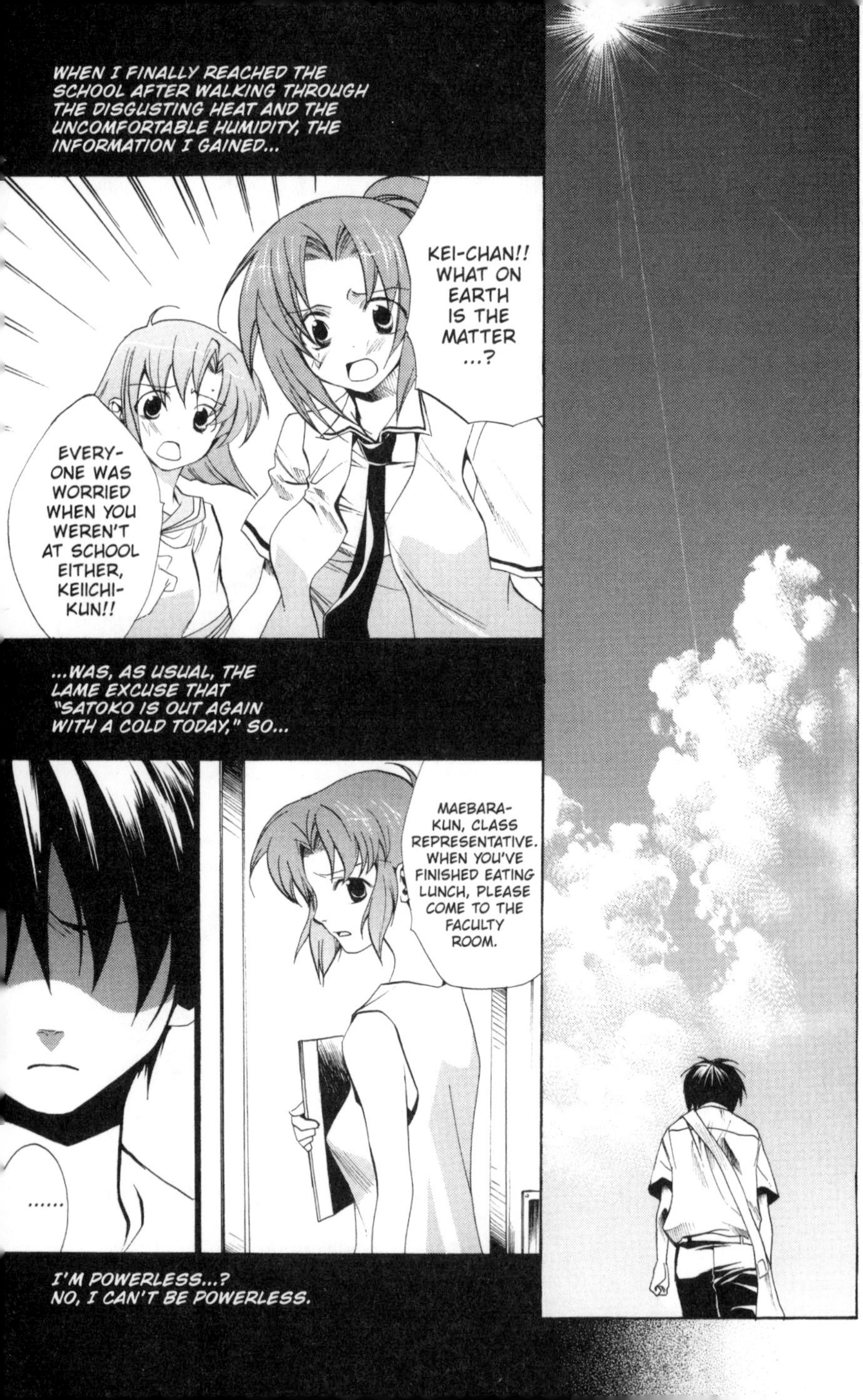
WHEN I FINALLY REACHED THE SCHOOL AFTER WALKING THROUGH THE DISGUSTING HEAT AND THE UNCOMFORTABLE HUMIDITY, THE INFORMATION I GAINED...
KEI-CHAN!! WHAT ON EARTH IS THE MATTER ...?
EVERY-ONE WAS WORRIED WHEN YOU WEREN'T AT SCHOOL EITHER, KEIICHI-KUN!!
...WAS, AS USUAL, THE LAME EXCUSE THAT "SATOKO IS OUT AGAIN WITH A COLD TODAY," SO...
MAEBARA-KUN, CLASS REPRESENTATIVE. WHEN YOU'VE FINISHED EATING LUNCH, PLEASE COME TO THE FACULTY ROOM.
......
I'M POWERLESS...? NO, I CAN'T BE POWERLESS.

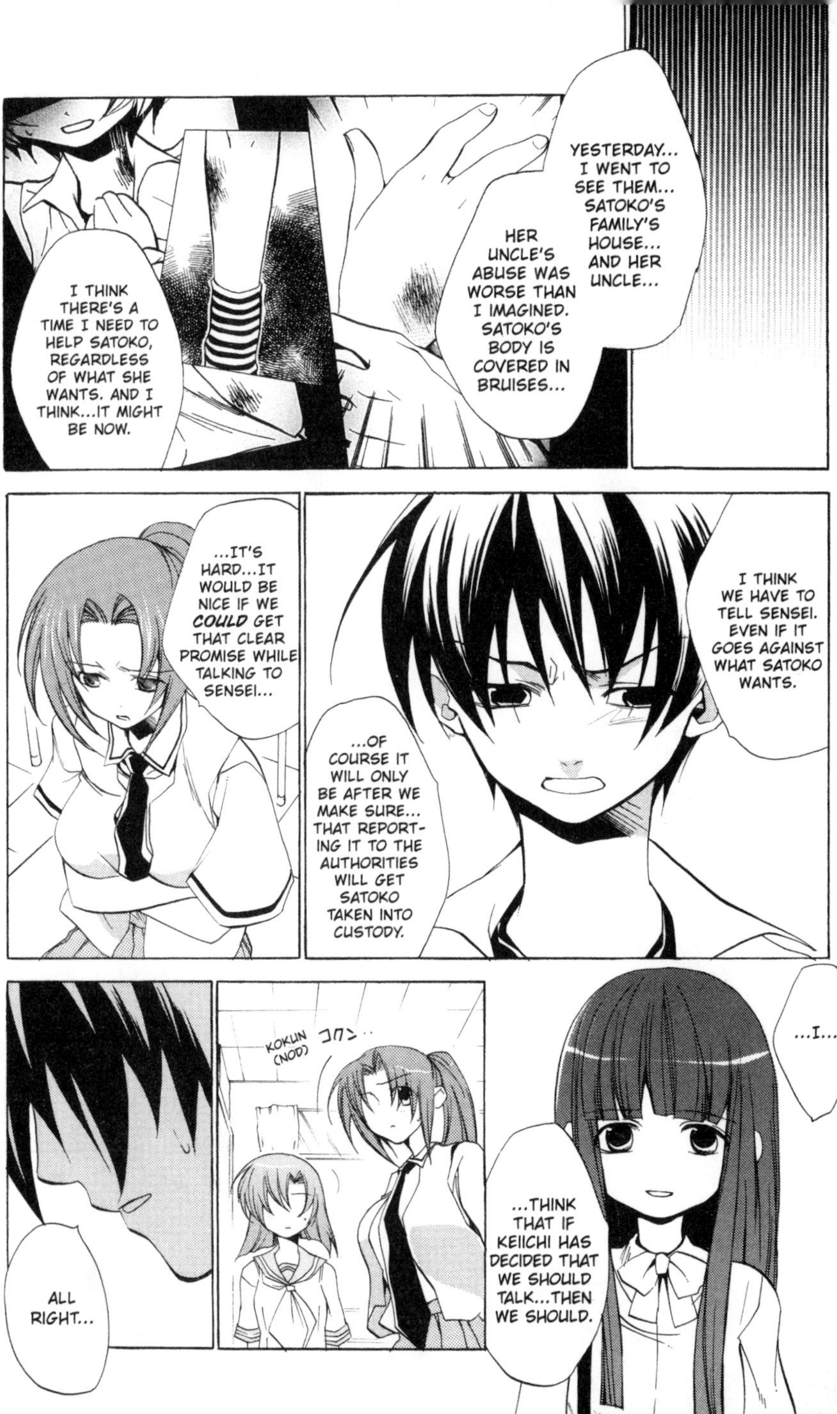
YESTERDAY... I WENT TO SEE THEM... SATOKO'S FAMILY'S HOUSE... AND HER UNCLE...
HER UNCLE'S ABUSE WAS WORSE THAN I IMAGINED. SATOKO'S BODY IS COVERED IN BRUISES...
I THINK THERE'S A TIME I NEED TO HELP SATOKO, REGARDLESS OF WHAT SHE WANTS. AND I THINK...IT MIGHT BE NOW.
I THINK WE HAVE TO TELL SENSEI. EVEN IF IT GOES AGAINST WHAT SATOKO WANTS.
...OF COURSE IT WILL ONLY BE AFTER WE MAKE SURE... THAT REPORTING IT TO THE AUTHORITIES WILL GET SATOKO TAKEN INTO CUSTODY.
...IT'S HARD...IT WOULD BE NICE IF WE *COULD* GET THAT CLEAR PROMISE WHILE TALKING TO SENSEI...
...I...
...THINK THAT IF KEIICHI HAS DECIDED THAT WE SHOULD TALK...THEN WE SHOULD.
KOKUN (NOD) コクン‥
ALL RIGHT...

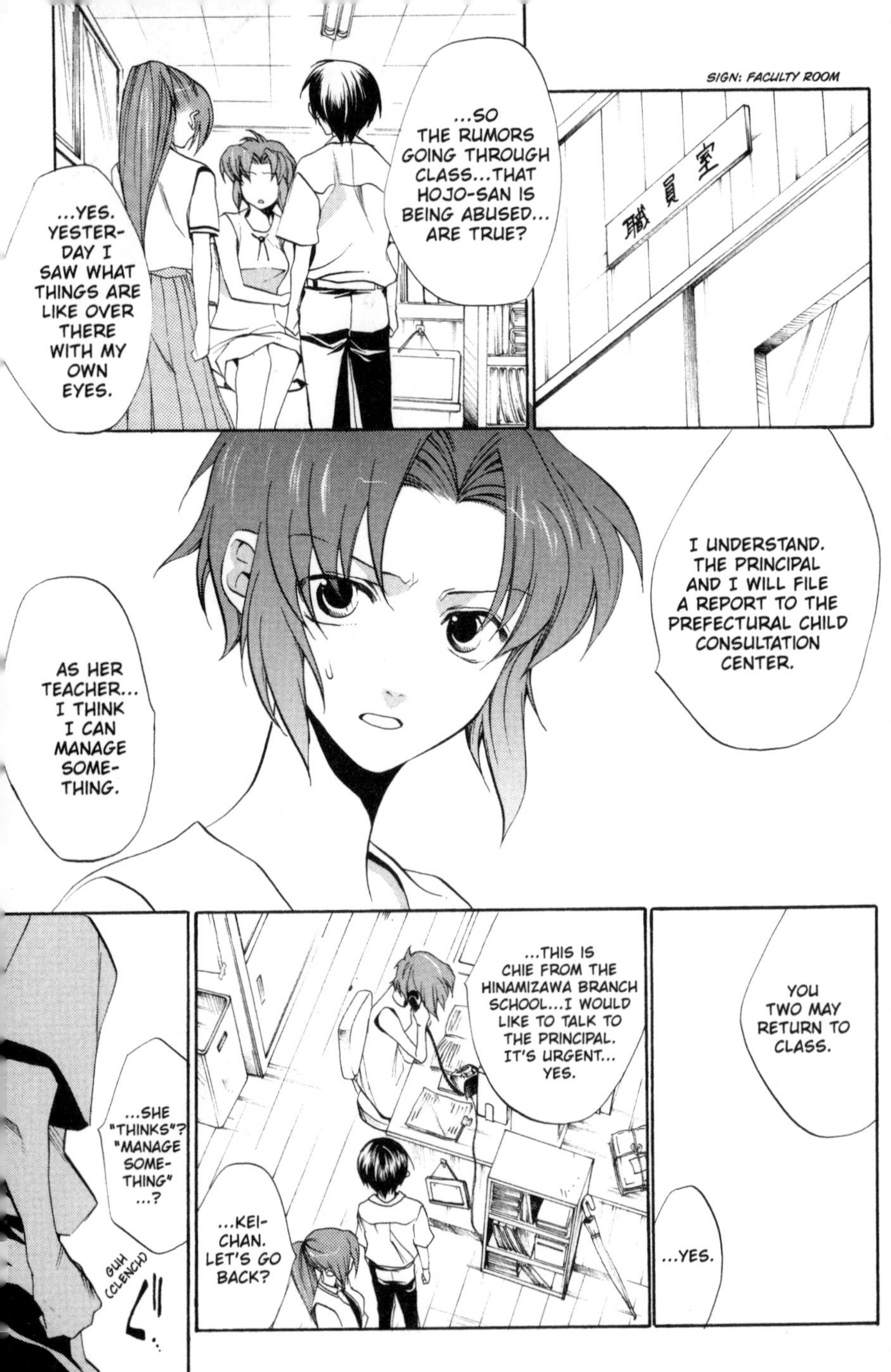

SIGN: FACULTY ROOM
職員室
...SO THE RUMORS GOING THROUGH CLASS...THAT HOJO-SAN IS BEING ABUSED... ARE TRUE?
...YES. YESTER-DAY I SAW WHAT THINGS ARE LIKE OVER THERE WITH MY OWN EYES.
I UNDERSTAND. THE PRINCIPAL AND I WILL FILE A REPORT TO THE PREFECTURAL CHILD CONSULTATION CENTER.
AS HER TEACHER... I THINK I CAN MANAGE SOME-THING.
YOU TWO MAY RETURN TO CLASS.
...YES.
...THIS IS CHIE FROM THE HINAMIZAWA BRANCH SCHOOL...I WOULD LIKE TO TALK TO THE PRINCIPAL. IT'S URGENT... YES.
...KEI-CHAN. LET'S GO BACK?
...SHE "THINKS"? "MANAGE SOME-THING" ...?
GUH (CLENCH)

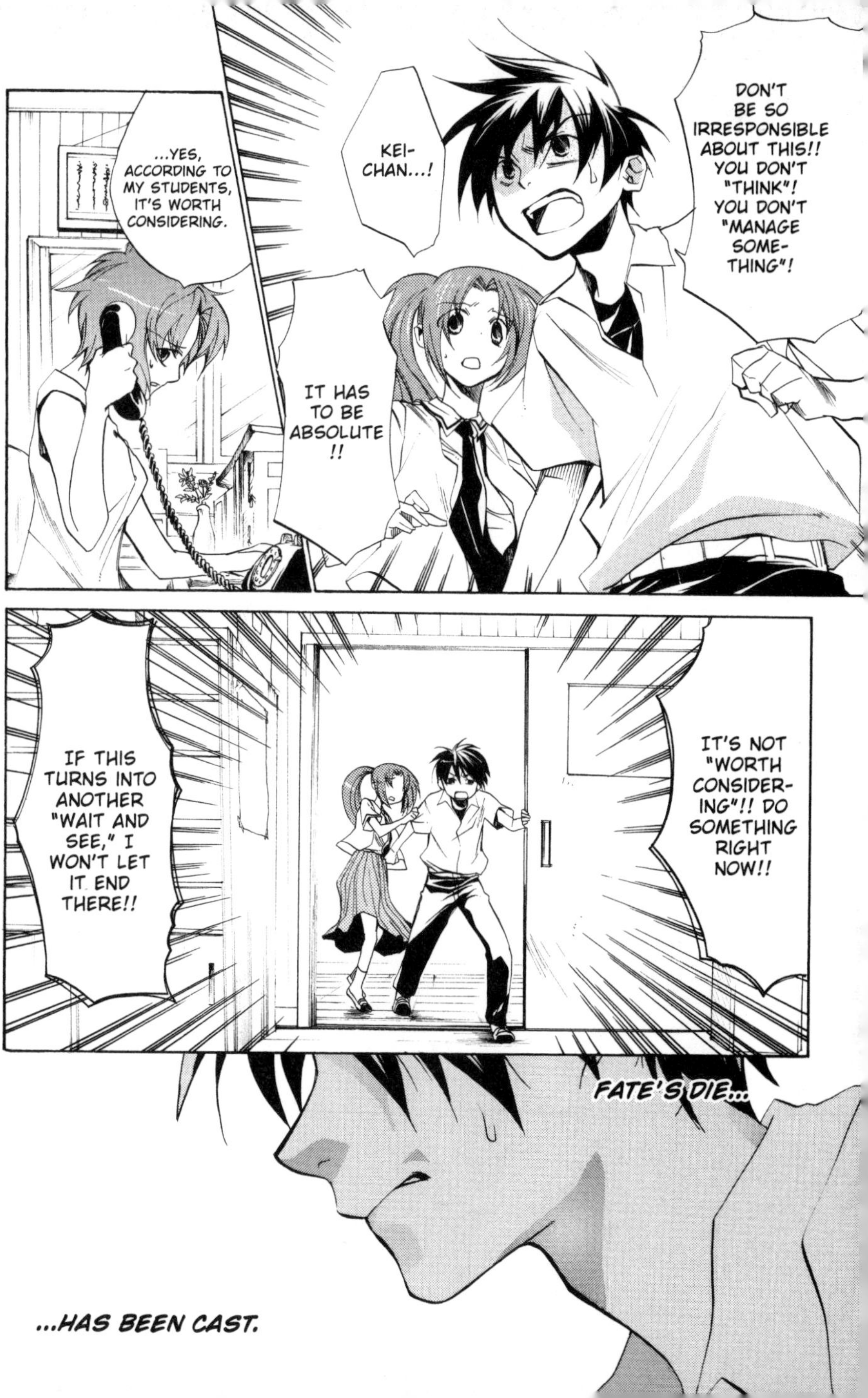
DON'T BE SO IRRESPONSIBLE ABOUT THIS!! YOU DON'T "THINK"! YOU DON'T "MANAGE SOME-THING"!
KEI-CHAN...!
...YES, ACCORDING TO MY STUDENTS, IT'S WORTH CONSIDERING.
IT HAS TO BE ABSOLUTE!!
IT'S NOT "WORTH CONSIDER-ING"!! DO SOMETHING RIGHT NOW!!
IF THIS TURNS INTO ANOTHER "WAIT AND SEE," I WON'T LET IT END THERE!!
FATE'S DIE...
...HAS BEEN CAST.

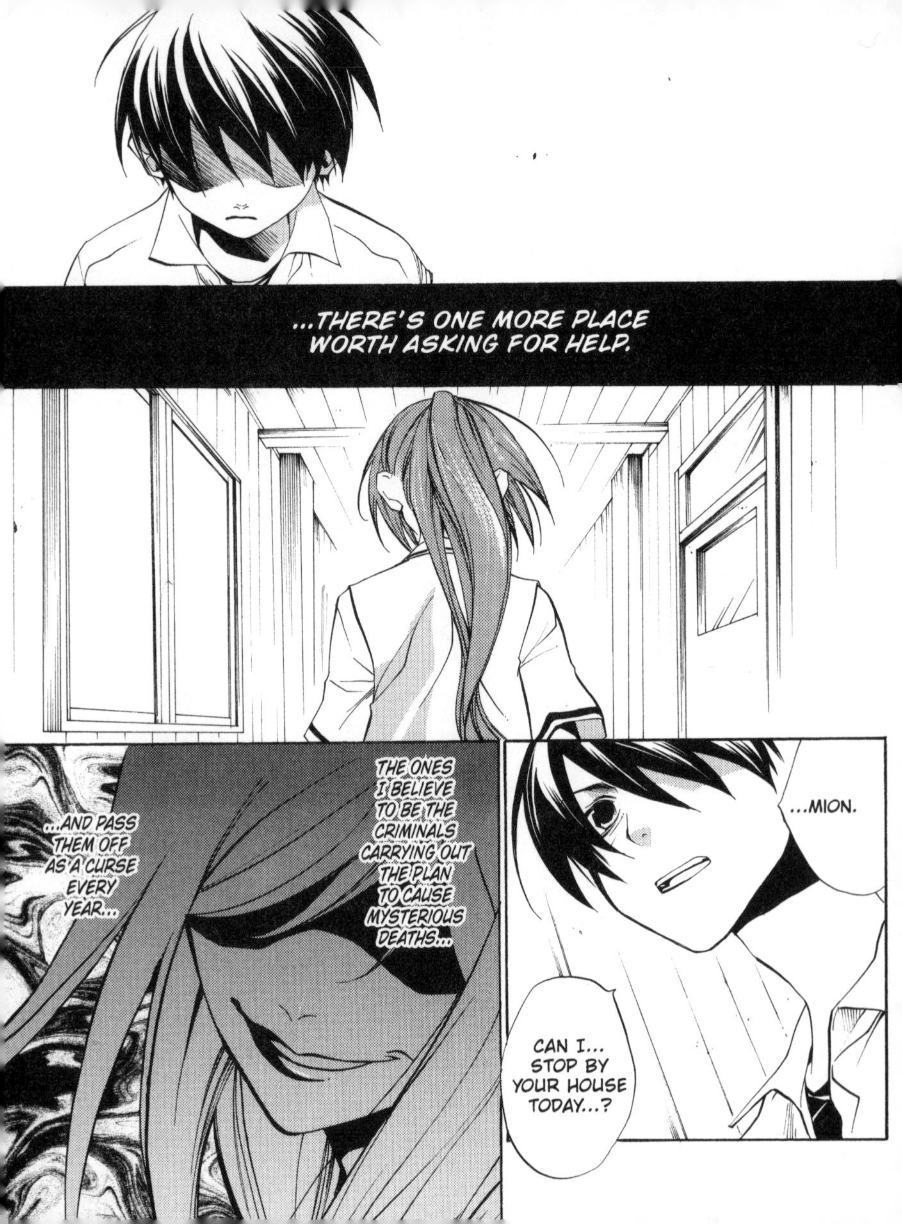
...THERE'S ONE MORE PLACE WORTH ASKING FOR HELP.
...MION.
CAN I... STOP BY YOUR HOUSE TODAY...?
THE ONES I BELIEVE TO BE THE CRIMINALS CARRYING OUT THE PLAN TO CAUSE MYSTERIOUS DEATHS...
...AND PASS THEM OFF AS A CURSE EVERY YEAR...

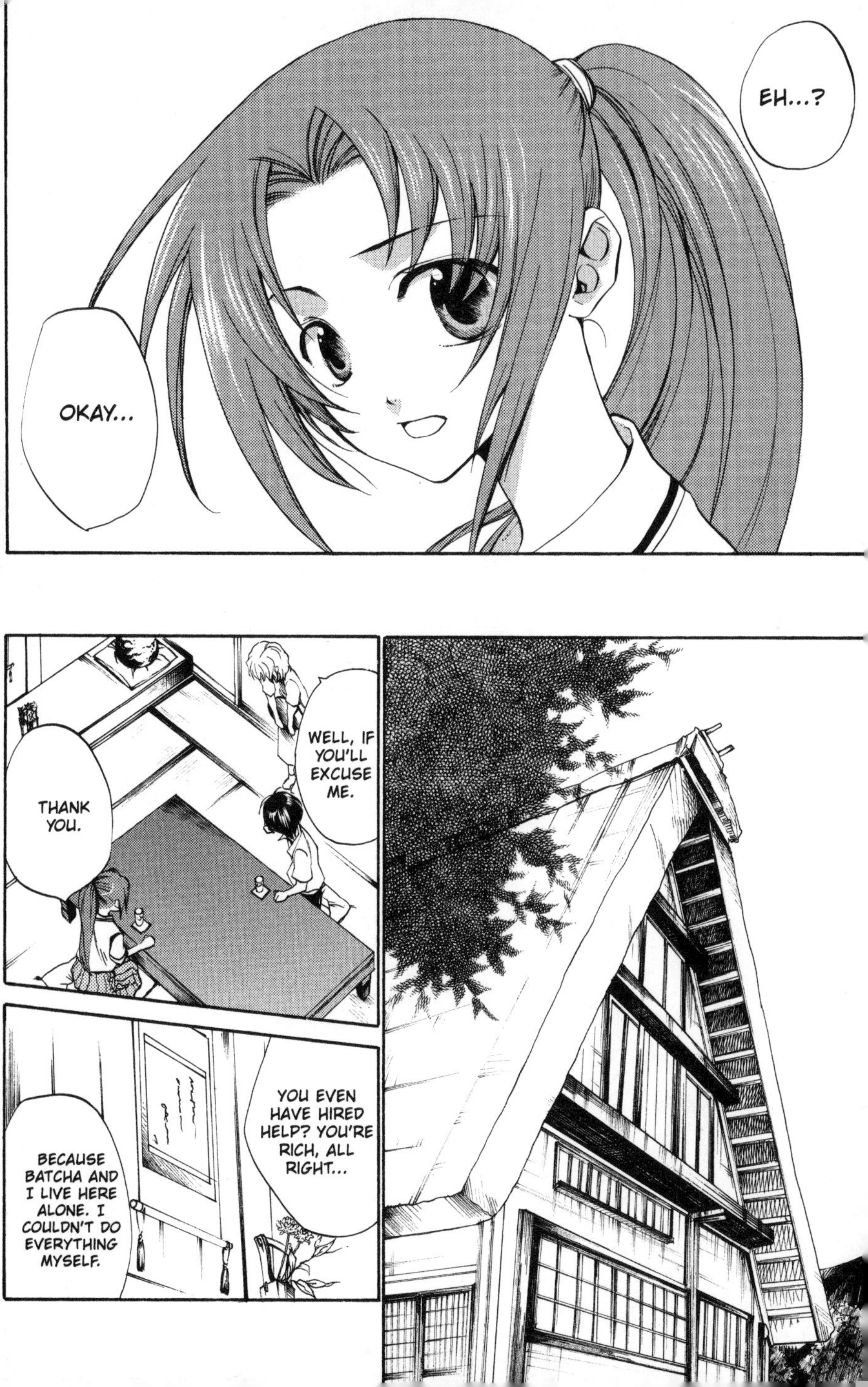
EH...?
OKAY...
WELL, IF YOU'LL EXCUSE ME.
THANK YOU.
YOU EVEN HAVE HIRED HELP? YOU'RE RICH, ALL RIGHT...
BECAUSE BATCHA AND I LIVE HERE ALONE. I COULDN'T DO EVERYTHING MYSELF.

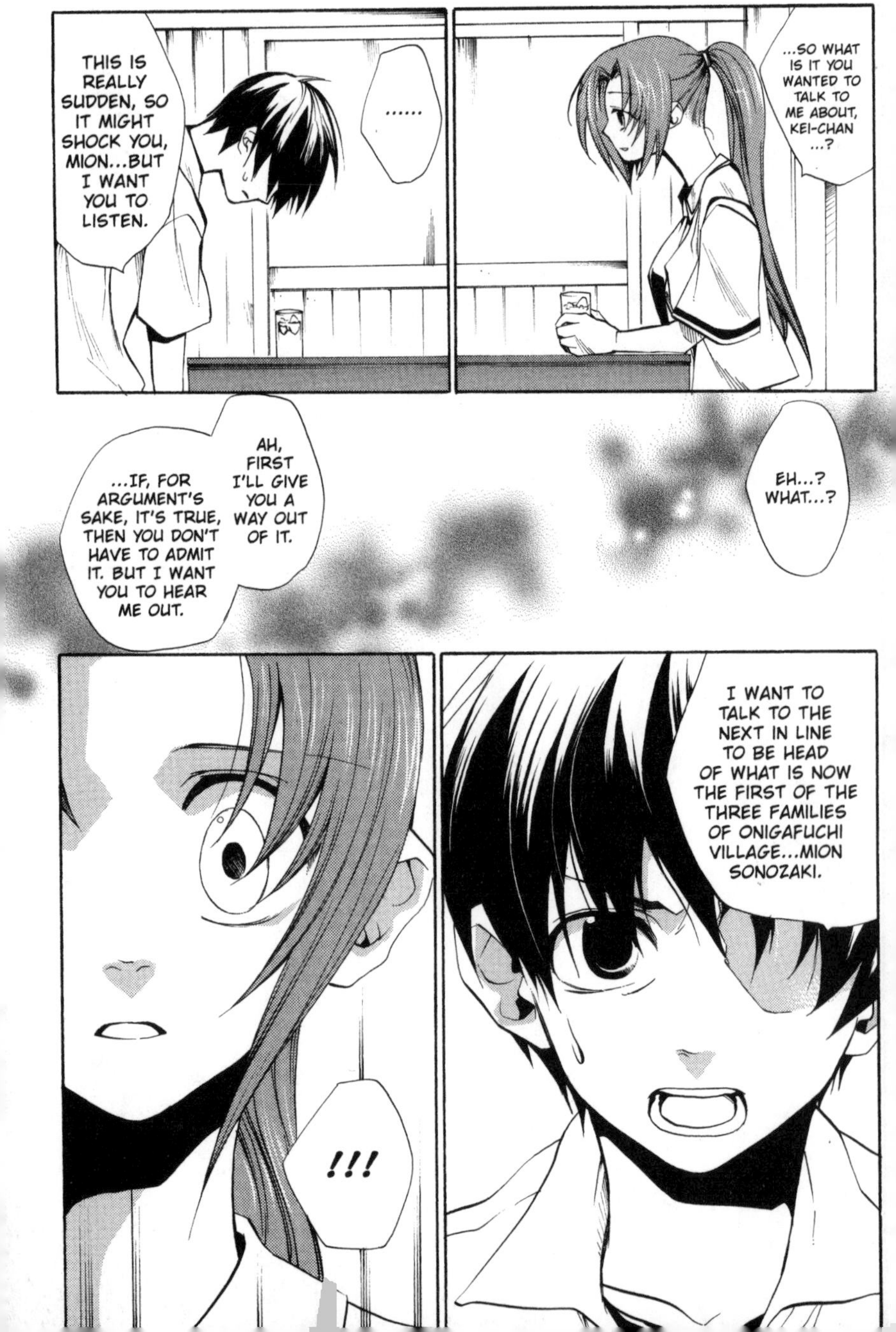
...SO WHAT IS IT YOU WANTED TO TALK TO ME ABOUT, KEI-CHAN ...?
......
THIS IS REALLY SUDDEN, SO IT MIGHT SHOCK YOU, MION...BUT I WANT YOU TO LISTEN.
EH...? WHAT...?
AH, FIRST I'LL GIVE YOU A WAY OUT OF IT.
...IF, FOR ARGUMENT'S SAKE, IT'S TRUE, THEN YOU DON'T HAVE TO ADMIT IT. BUT I WANT YOU TO HEAR ME OUT.
I WANT TO TALK TO THE NEXT IN LINE TO BE HEAD OF WHAT IS NOW THE FIRST OF THE THREE FAMILIES OF ONIGAFUCHI VILLAGE...MION SONOZAKI.
!!!

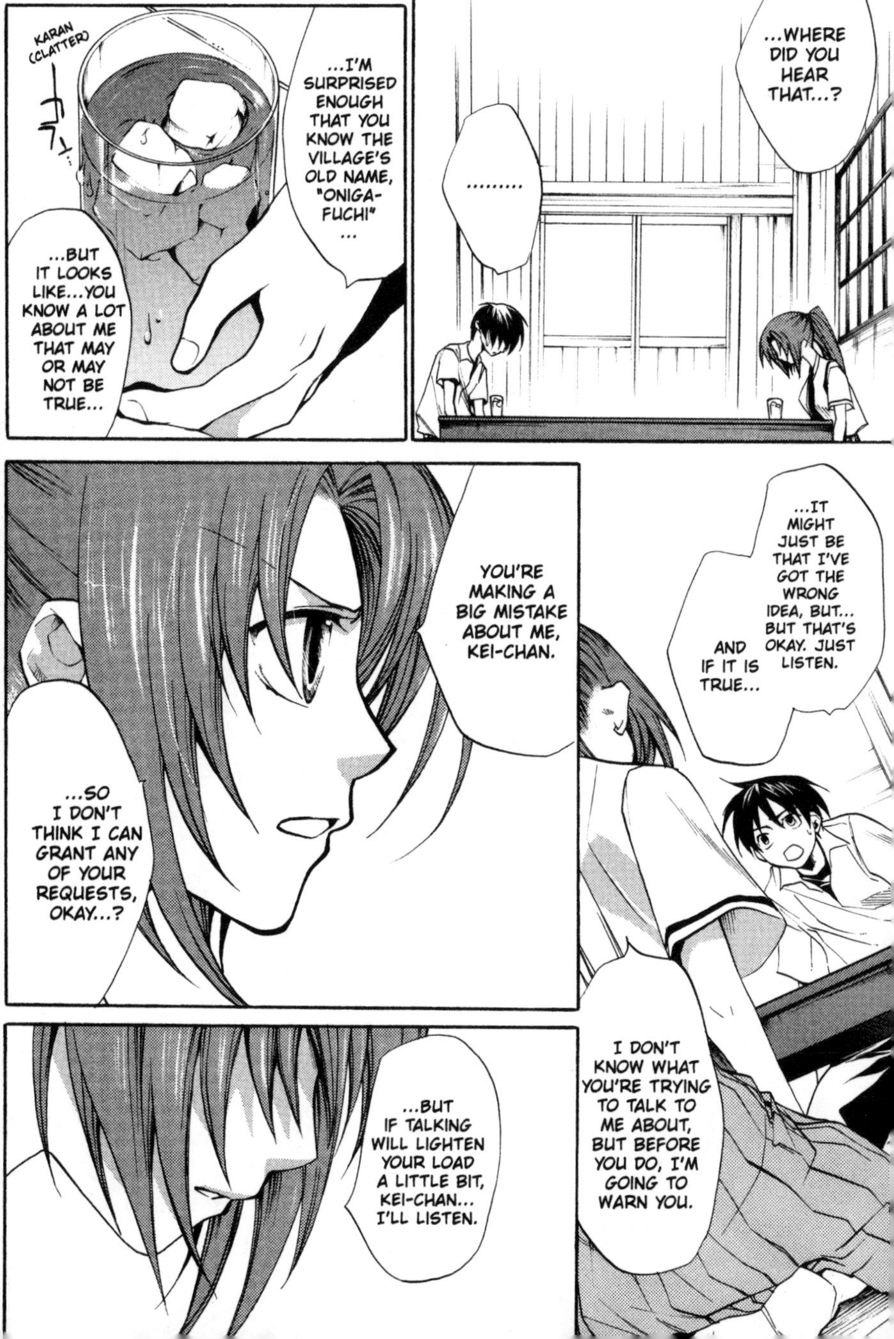
...WHERE DID YOU HEAR THAT...?
....
...I'M SURPRISED ENOUGH THAT YOU KNOW THE VILLAGE'S OLD NAME, "ONIGA-FUCHI" ...
KARAN (CLATTER)
...BUT IT LOOKS LIKE...YOU KNOW A LOT ABOUT ME THAT MAY OR MAY NOT BE TRUE...
...IT MIGHT JUST BE THAT I'VE GOT THE WRONG IDEA, BUT... BUT THAT'S OKAY. JUST LISTEN.
AND IF IT IS TRUE...
YOU'RE MAKING A BIG MISTAKE ABOUT ME, KEI-CHAN.
...SO I DON'T THINK I CAN GRANT ANY OF YOUR REQUESTS, OKAY...?
I DON'T KNOW WHAT YOU'RE TRYING TO TALK TO ME ABOUT, BUT BEFORE YOU DO, I'M GOING TO WARN YOU.
...BUT IF TALKING WILL LIGHTEN YOUR LOAD A LITTLE BIT, KEI-CHAN... I'LL LISTEN.

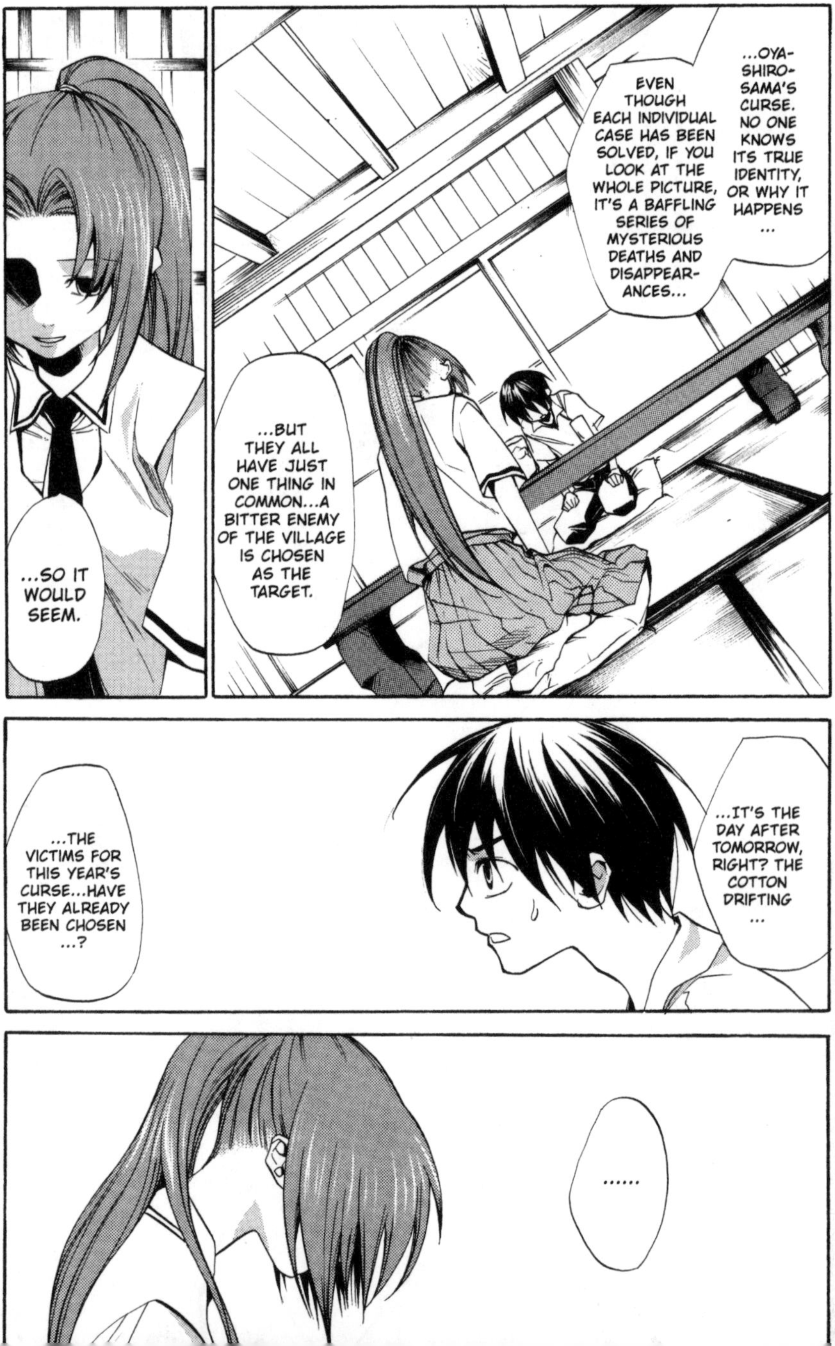
...OYA-SHIRO-SAMA'S CURSE. NO ONE KNOWS ITS TRUE IDENTITY, OR WHY IT HAPPENS...
EVEN THOUGH EACH INDIVIDUAL CASE HAS BEEN SOLVED, IF YOU LOOK AT THE WHOLE PICTURE, IT'S A BAFFLING SERIES OF MYSTERIOUS DEATHS AND DISAPPEAR-ANCES...
...BUT THEY ALL HAVE JUST ONE THING IN COMMON...A BITTER ENEMY OF THE VILLAGE IS CHOSEN AS THE TARGET.
...SO IT WOULD SEEM.
...IT'S THE DAY AFTER TOMORROW, RIGHT? THE COTTON DRIFTING...
...THE VICTIMS FOR THIS YEAR'S CURSE...HAVE THEY ALREADY BEEN CHOSEN...?
......

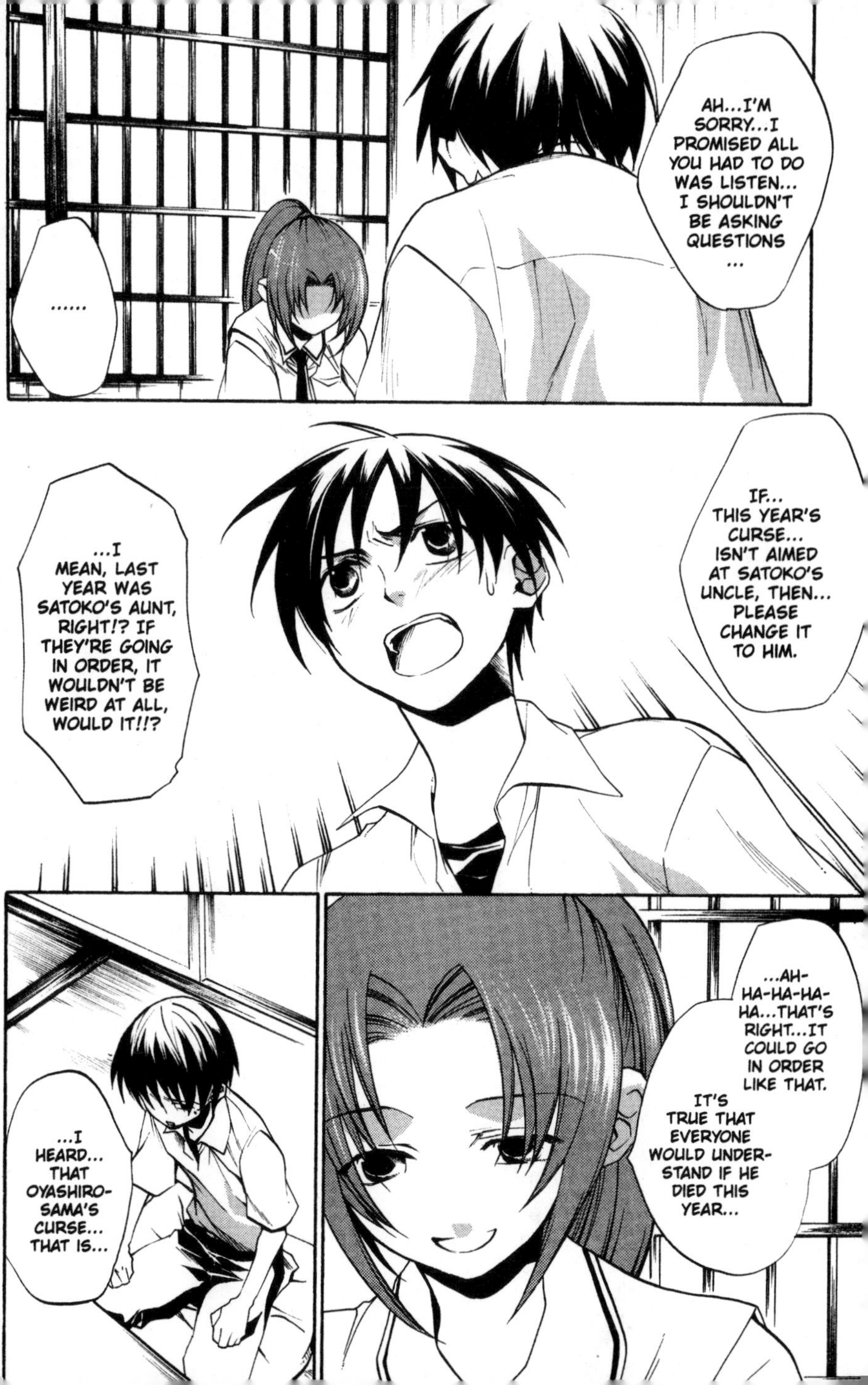
AH...I'M SORRY...I PROMISED ALL YOU HAD TO DO WAS LISTEN... I SHOULDN'T BE ASKING QUESTIONS ...
......
IF... THIS YEAR'S CURSE... ISN'T AIMED AT SATOKO'S UNCLE, THEN... PLEASE CHANGE IT TO HIM.
...I MEAN, LAST YEAR WAS SATOKO'S AUNT, RIGHT!? IF THEY'RE GOING IN ORDER, IT WOULDN'T BE WEIRD AT ALL, WOULD IT!!?
...AH-HA-HA-HA-HA...THAT'S RIGHT...IT COULD GO IN ORDER LIKE THAT.
IT'S TRUE THAT EVERYONE WOULD UNDER-STAND IF HE DIED THIS YEAR...
...I HEARD... THAT OYASHIRO-SAMA'S CURSE... THAT IS...

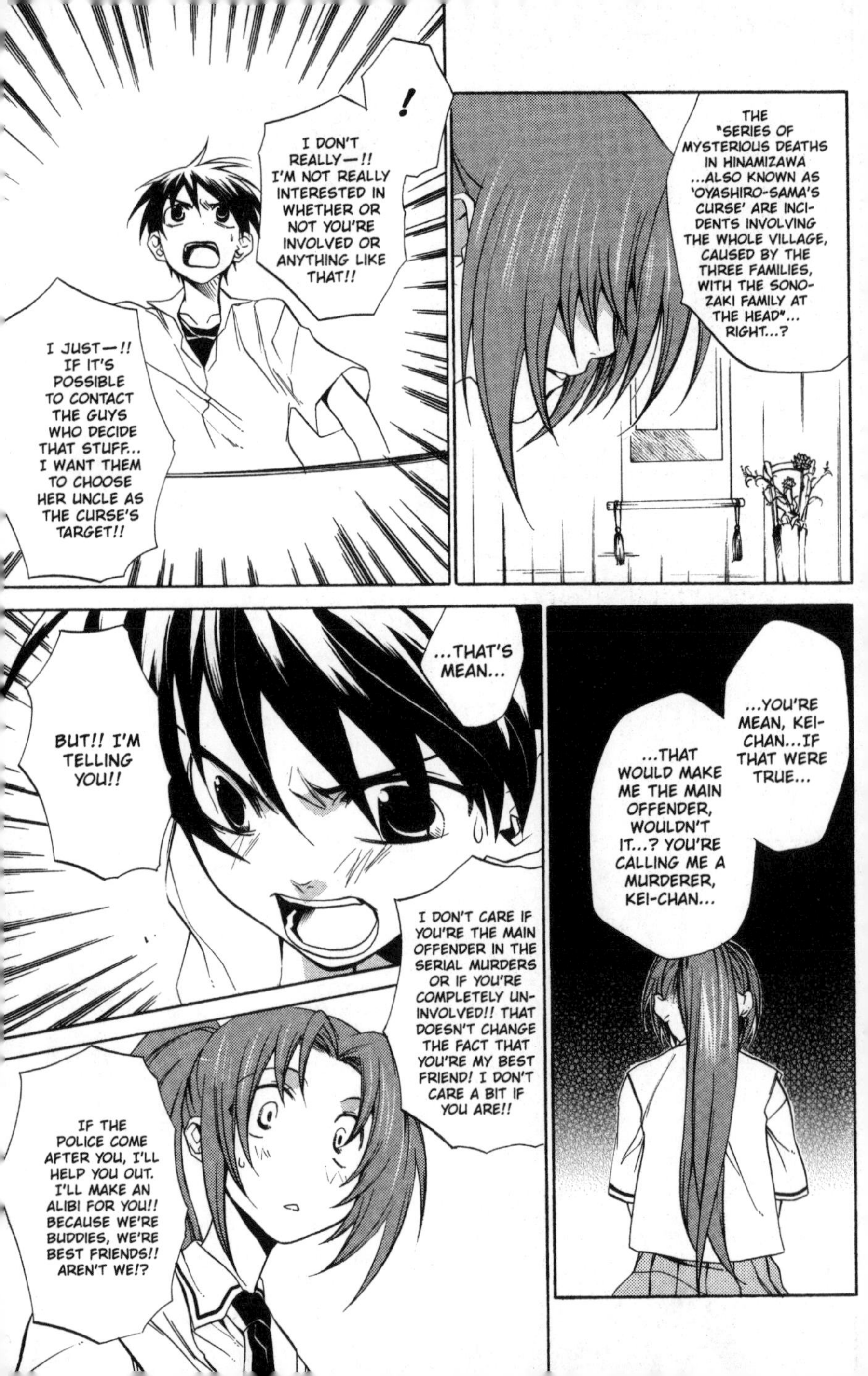
THE "SERIES OF MYSTERIOUS DEATHS IN HINAMIZAWA ...ALSO KNOWN AS 'OYASHIRO-SAMA'S CURSE' ARE INCIDENTS INVOLVING THE WHOLE VILLAGE, CAUSED BY THE THREE FAMILIES, WITH THE SONOZAKI FAMILY AT THE HEAD"... RIGHT...?
!
I DON'T REALLY—!! I'M NOT REALLY INTERESTED IN WHETHER OR NOT YOU'RE INVOLVED OR ANYTHING LIKE THAT!!
I JUST—!! IF IT'S POSSIBLE TO CONTACT THE GUYS WHO DECIDE THAT STUFF... I WANT THEM TO CHOOSE HER UNCLE AS THE CURSE'S TARGET!!
...YOU'RE MEAN, KEI-CHAN...IF THAT WERE TRUE...
...THAT WOULD MAKE ME THE MAIN OFFENDER, WOULDN'T IT...? YOU'RE CALLING ME A MURDERER, KEI-CHAN...
...THAT'S MEAN...
BUT!! I'M TELLING YOU!!
I DON'T CARE IF YOU'RE THE MAIN OFFENDER IN THE SERIAL MURDERS OR IF YOU'RE COMPLETELY UNINVOLVED!! THAT DOESN'T CHANGE THE FACT THAT YOU'RE MY BEST FRIEND! I DON'T CARE A BIT IF YOU ARE!!
IF THE POLICE COME AFTER YOU, I'LL HELP YOU OUT. I'LL MAKE AN ALIBI FOR YOU!! BECAUSE WE'RE BUDDIES, WE'RE BEST FRIENDS!! AREN'T WE!?

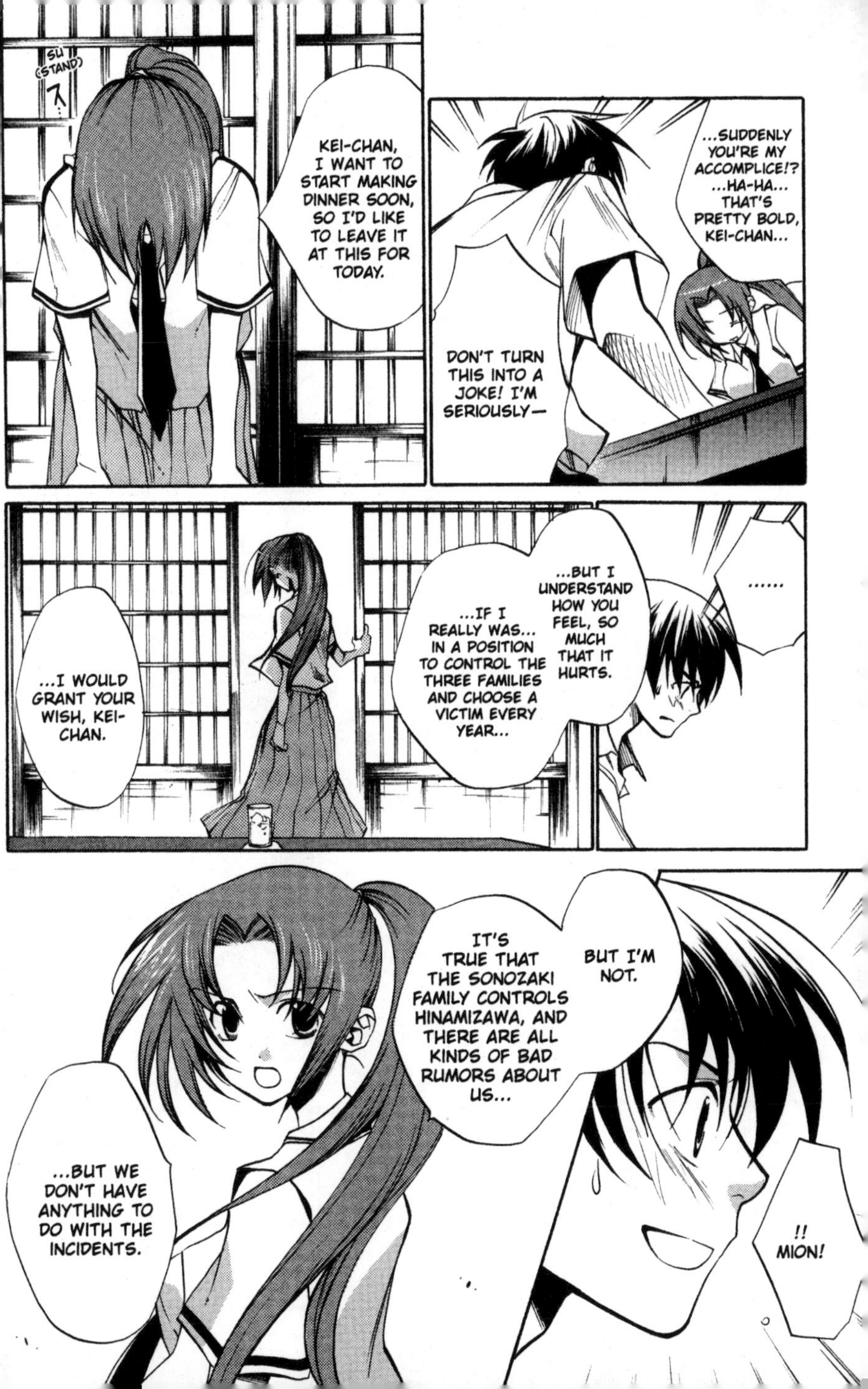

...SUDDENLY YOU'RE MY ACCOMPLICE!? ...HA-HA... THAT'S PRETTY BOLD, KEI-CHAN...
DON'T TURN THIS INTO A JOKE! I'M SERIOUSLY—
SU (STAND)
KEI-CHAN, I WANT TO START MAKING DINNER SOON, SO I'D LIKE TO LEAVE IT AT THIS FOR TODAY.
......
...BUT I UNDERSTAND HOW YOU FEEL, SO MUCH THAT IT HURTS.
...IF I REALLY WAS... IN A POSITION TO CONTROL THE THREE FAMILIES AND CHOOSE A VICTIM EVERY YEAR...
...I WOULD GRANT YOUR WISH, KEI-CHAN.
BUT I'M NOT.
IT'S TRUE THAT THE SONOZAKI FAMILY CONTROLS HINAMIZAWA, AND THERE ARE ALL KINDS OF BAD RUMORS ABOUT US...
...BUT WE DON'T HAVE ANYTHING TO DO WITH THE INCIDENTS.
!! MION!

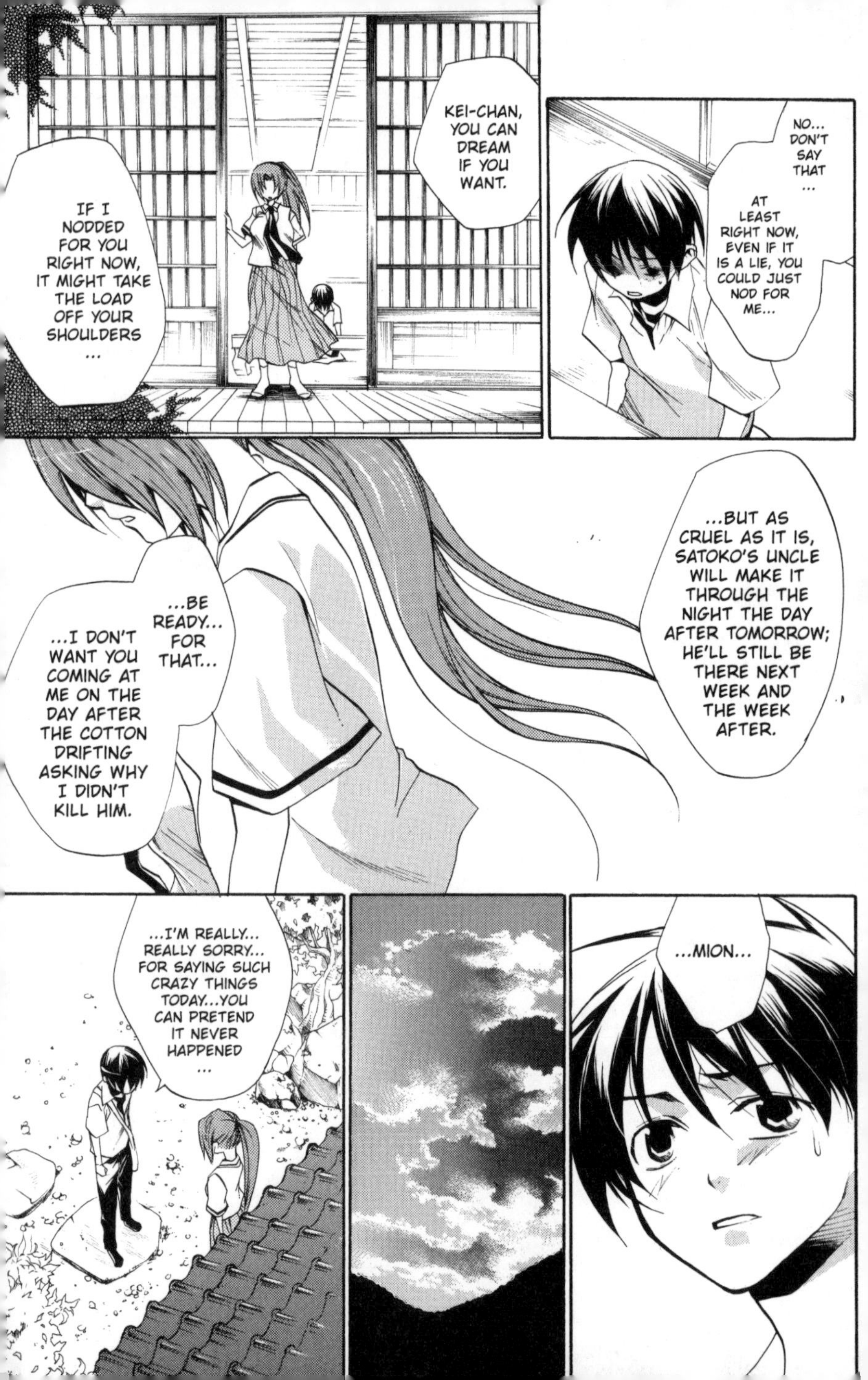
NO... DON'T SAY THAT...
AT LEAST RIGHT NOW, EVEN IF IT IS A LIE, YOU COULD JUST NOD FOR ME...
KEI-CHAN, YOU CAN DREAM IF YOU WANT.
IF I NODDED FOR YOU RIGHT NOW, IT MIGHT TAKE THE LOAD OFF YOUR SHOULDERS...
...BUT AS CRUEL AS IT IS, SATOKO'S UNCLE WILL MAKE IT THROUGH THE NIGHT THE DAY AFTER TOMORROW; HE'LL STILL BE THERE NEXT WEEK AND THE WEEK AFTER.
...BE READY... FOR THAT...
...I DON'T WANT YOU COMING AT ME ON THE DAY AFTER THE COTTON DRIFTING ASKING WHY I DIDN'T KILL HIM.
...MION...
...I'M REALLY... REALLY SORRY... FOR SAYING SUCH CRAZY THINGS TODAY...YOU CAN PRETEND IT NEVER HAPPENED...

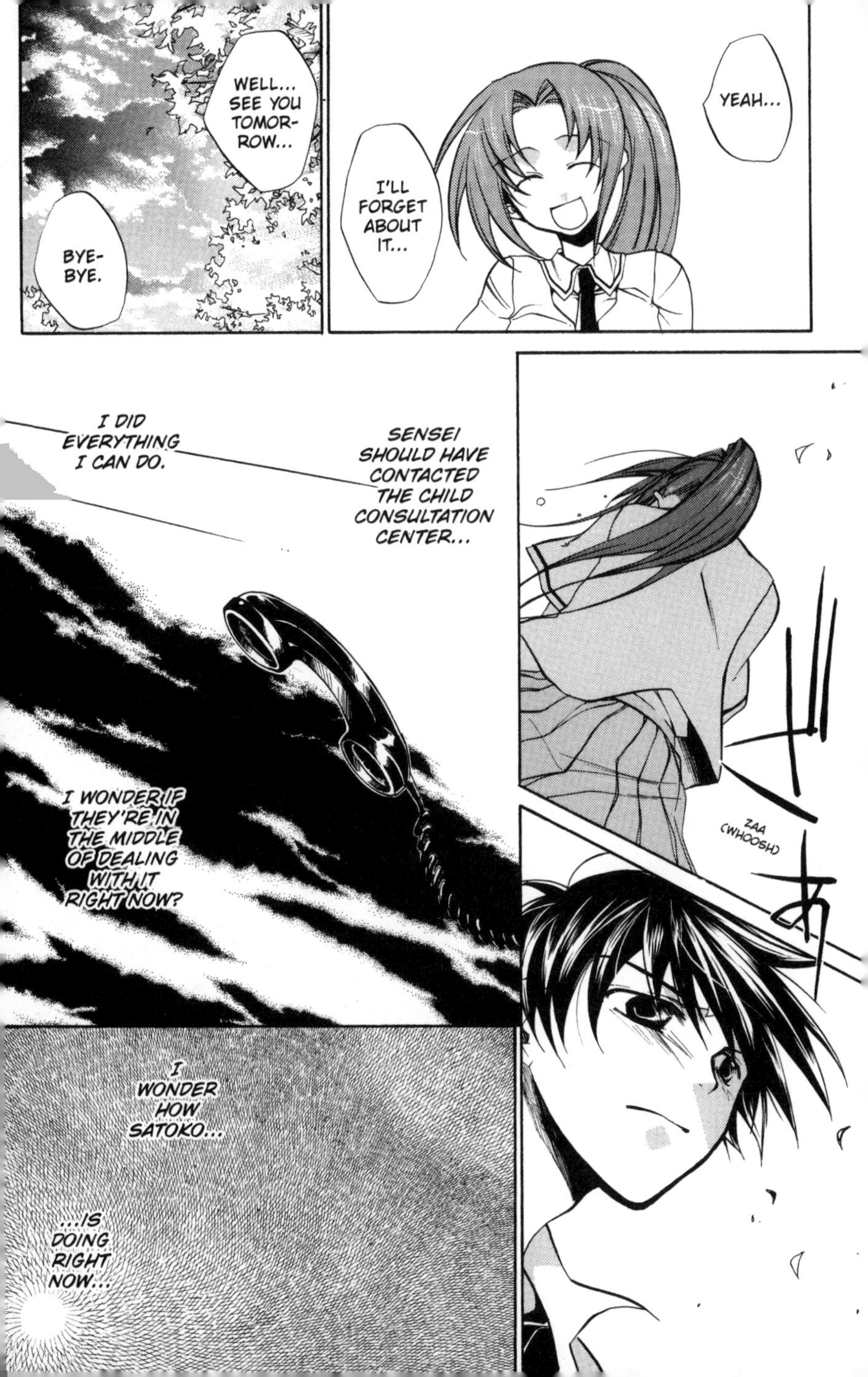
YEAH...
I'LL FORGET ABOUT IT...
WELL... SEE YOU TOMOR-ROW...
BYE-BYE.
ZAA (WHOOSH)
SENSEI SHOULD HAVE CONTACTED THE CHILD CONSULTATION CENTER...
I DID EVERYTHING I CAN DO.
I WONDER IF THEY'RE IN THE MIDDLE OF DEALING WITH IT RIGHT NOW?
I WONDER HOW SATOKO...
...IS DOING RIGHT NOW...

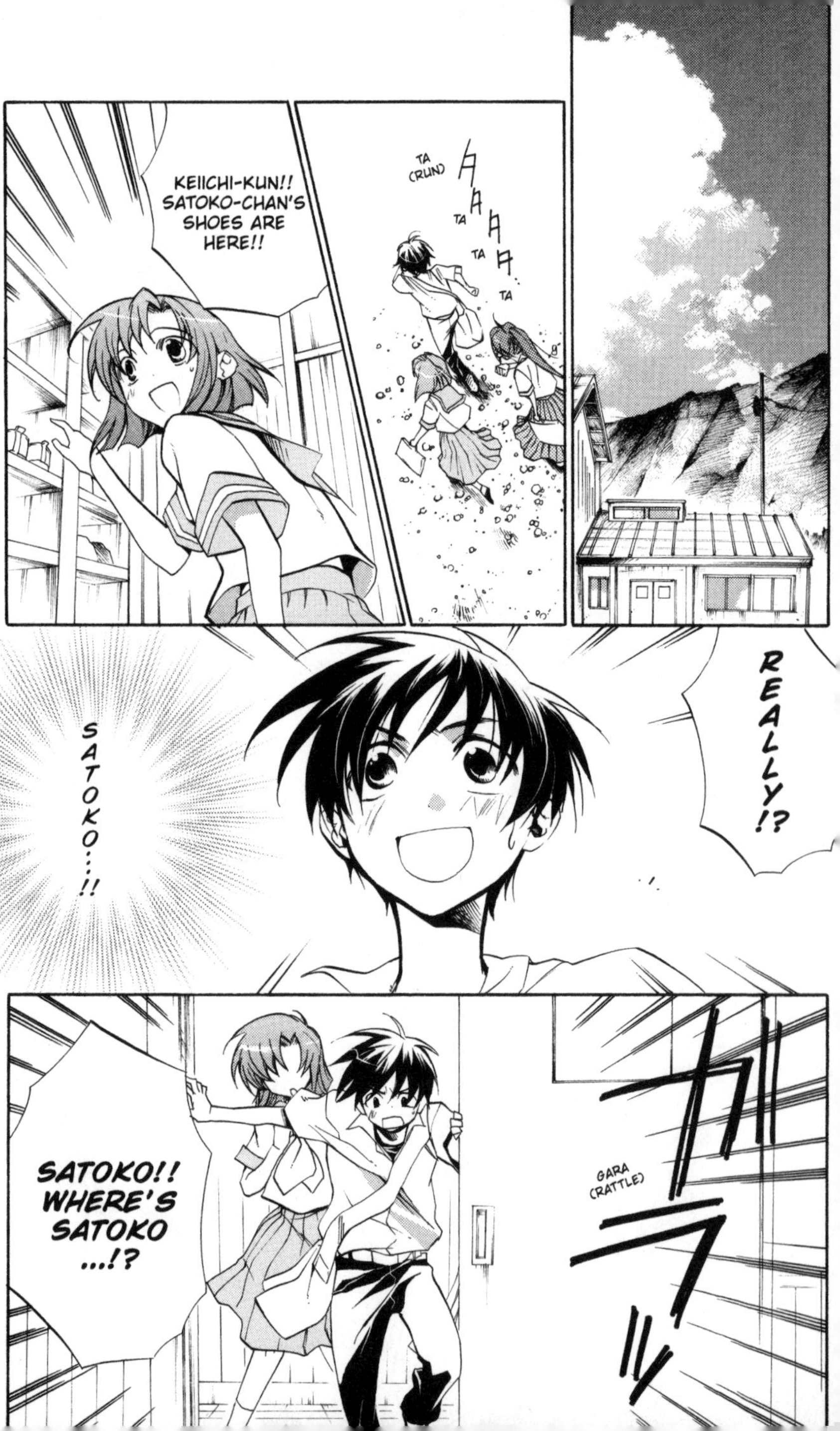
TA (RUN)
TA
TA
TA
KEIICHI-KUN!! SATOKO-CHAN'S SHOES ARE HERE!!
REALLY!?
SATOKO...!!
GARA (RATTLE)
SATOKO!! WHERE'S SATOKO ...!?

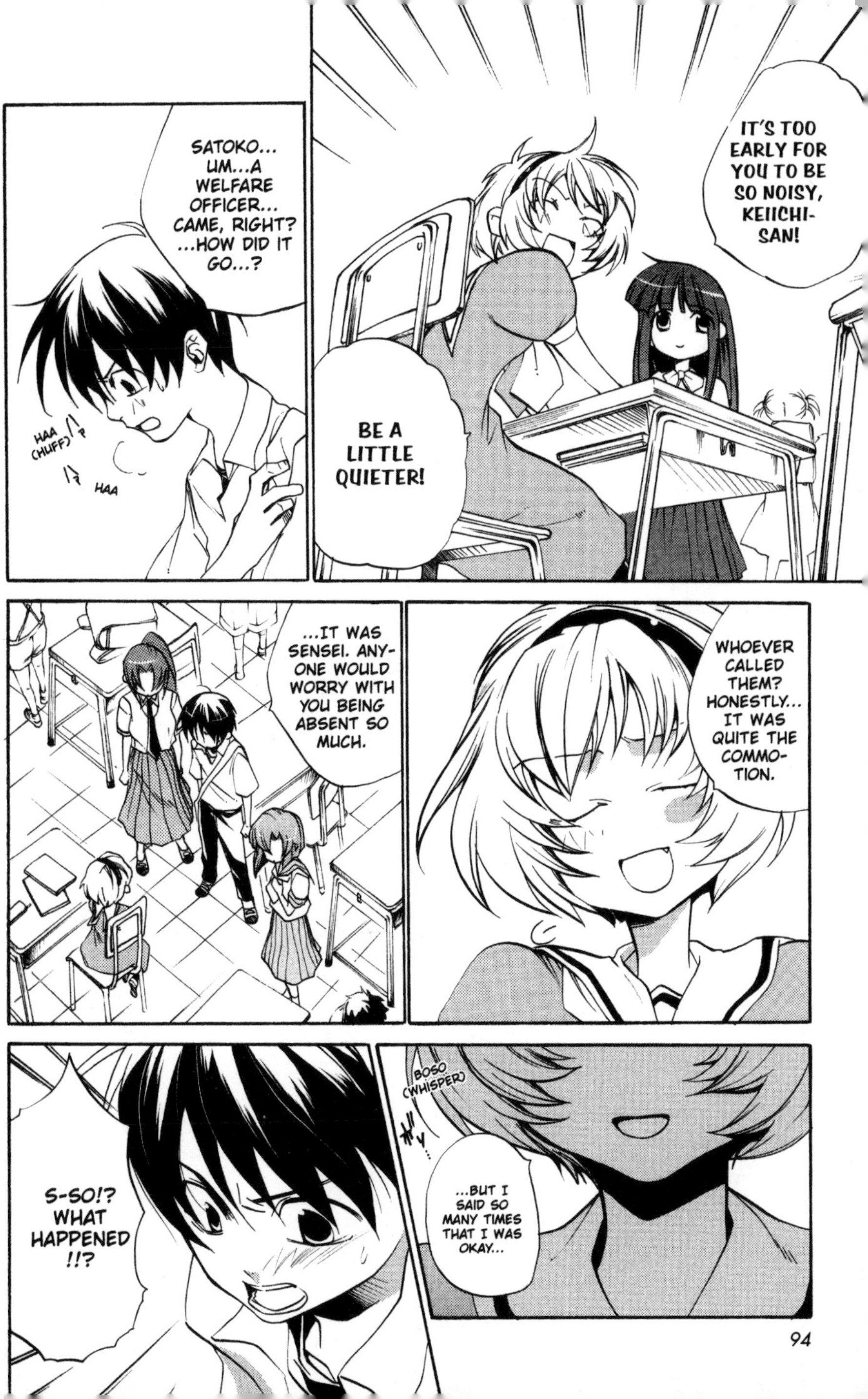
IT'S TOO EARLY FOR YOU TO BE SO NOISY, KEIICHI-SAN!
BE A LITTLE QUIETER!
SATOKO... UM...A WELFARE OFFICER... CAME, RIGHT? ...HOW DID IT GO...?
HAA (HUFF)
HAA
WHOEVER CALLED THEM? HONESTLY... IT WAS QUITE THE COMMOTION.
...IT WAS SENSEI. ANYONE WOULD WORRY WITH YOU BEING ABSENT SO MUCH.
BOSO (WHISPER)
...BUT I SAID SO MANY TIMES THAT I WAS OKAY...
S-SO!? WHAT HAPPENED !!?

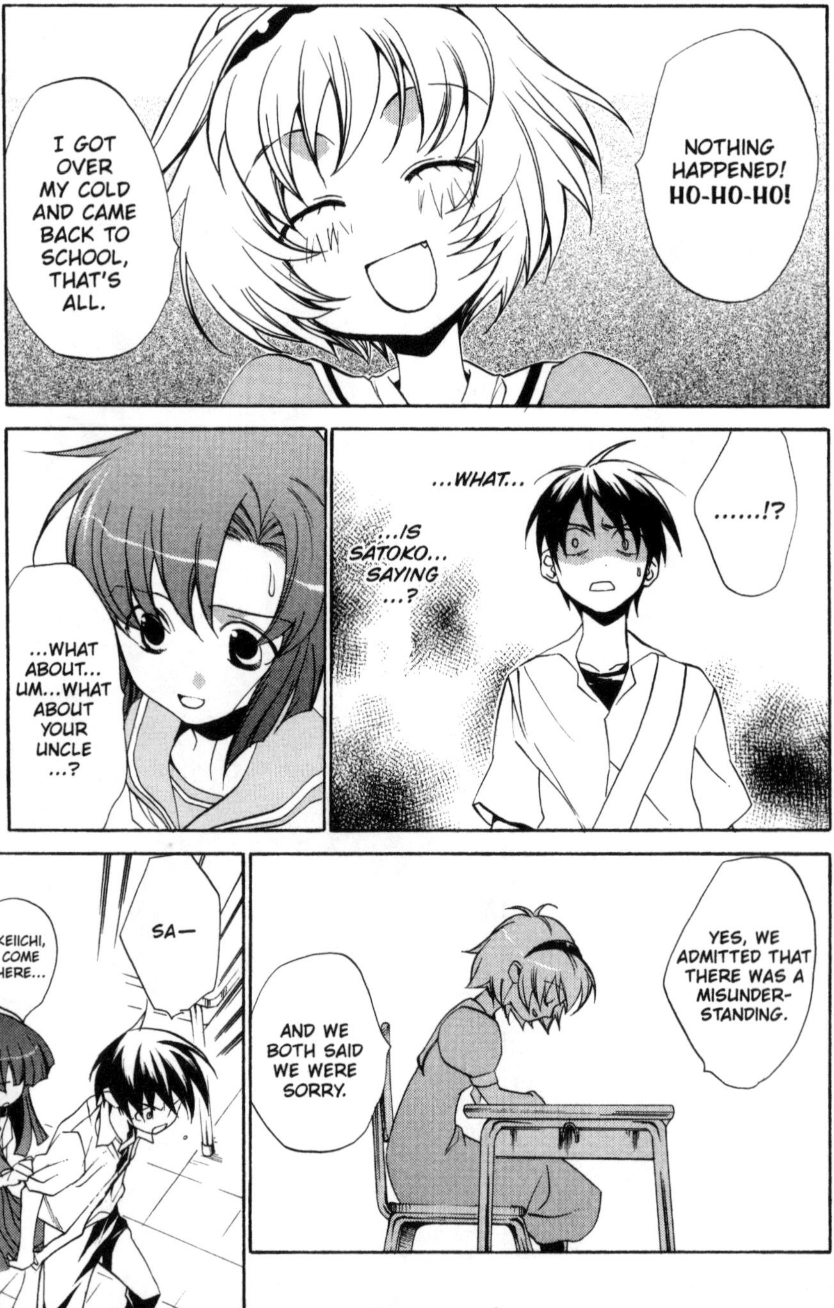
NOTHING HAPPENED! HO-HO-HO!
I GOT OVER MY COLD AND CAME BACK TO SCHOOL, THAT'S ALL.
......!?
...WHAT...
...IS SATOKO... SAYING ...?
...WHAT ABOUT... UM...WHAT ABOUT YOUR UNCLE ...?
YES, WE ADMITTED THAT THERE WAS A MISUNDER-STANDING.
AND WE BOTH SAID WE WERE SORRY.
SA—
KEIICHI, COME HERE...

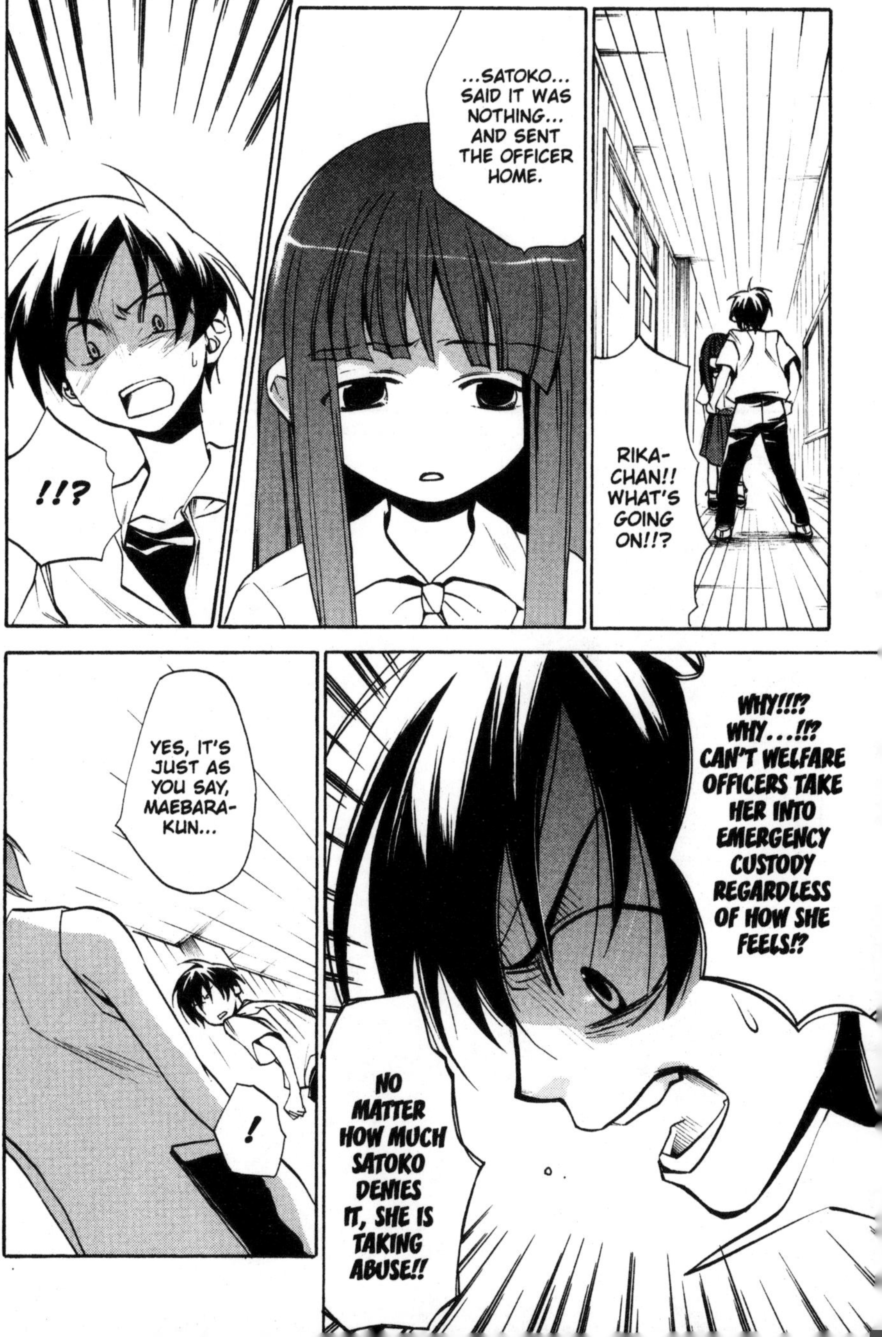
RIKA-CHAN!! WHAT'S GOING ON!!?
...SATOKO... SAID IT WAS NOTHING... AND SENT THE OFFICER HOME.
!!?
WHY!!!? WHY...!!? CAN'T WELFARE OFFICERS TAKE HER INTO EMERGENCY CUSTODY REGARDLESS OF HOW SHE FEELS!?
NO MATTER HOW MUCH SATOKO DENIES IT, SHE IS TAKING ABUSE!!
YES, IT'S JUST AS YOU SAY, MAEBARA-KUN...
!

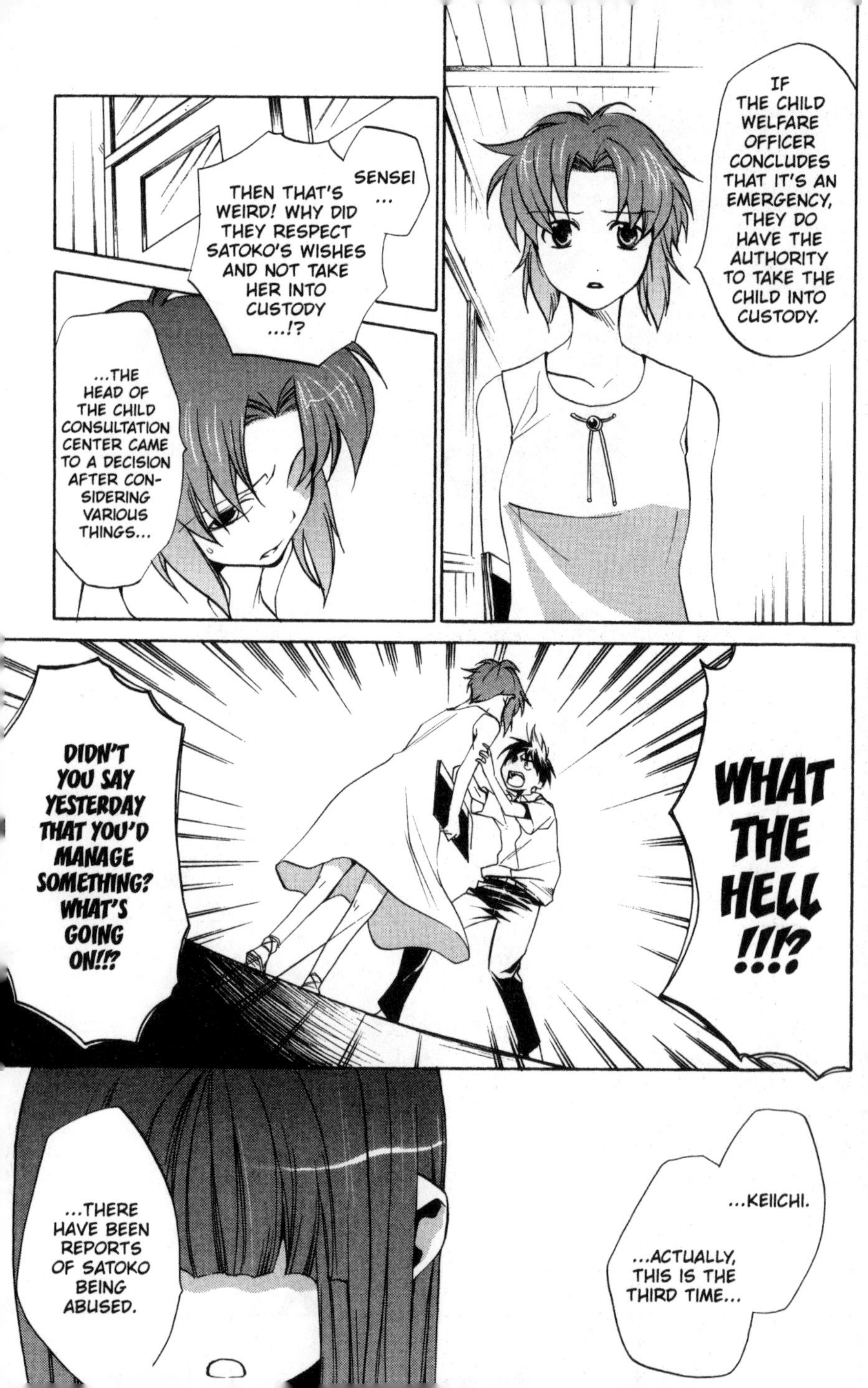
IF THE CHILD WELFARE OFFICER CONCLUDES THAT IT'S AN EMERGENCY, THEY DO HAVE THE AUTHORITY TO TAKE THE CHILD INTO CUSTODY.
SENSEI...
THEN THAT'S WEIRD! WHY DID THEY RESPECT SATOKO'S WISHES AND NOT TAKE HER INTO CUSTODY...!?
...THE HEAD OF THE CHILD CONSULTATION CENTER CAME TO A DECISION AFTER CON-SIDERING VARIOUS THINGS...
WHAT THE HELL!!!?
DIDN'T YOU SAY YESTERDAY THAT YOU'D MANAGE SOMETHING? WHAT'S GOING ON!!?
...KEIICHI.
...ACTUALLY, THIS IS THE THIRD TIME...
...THERE HAVE BEEN REPORTS OF SATOKO BEING ABUSED.

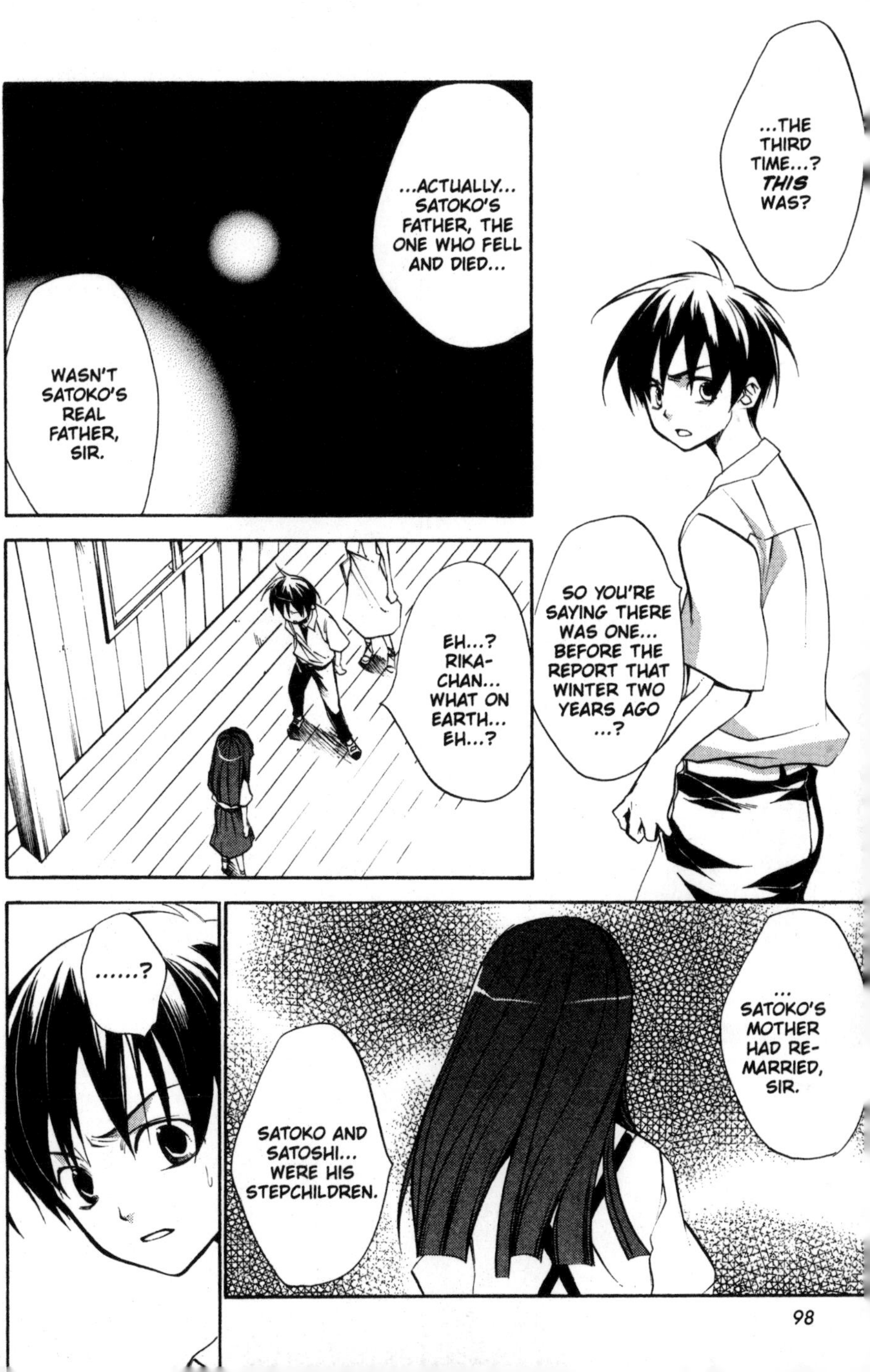
...THE THIRD TIME...? *THIS* WAS?
SO YOU'RE SAYING THERE WAS ONE... BEFORE THE REPORT THAT WINTER TWO YEARS AGO ...?
...ACTUALLY... SATOKO'S FATHER, THE ONE WHO FELL AND DIED...
WASN'T SATOKO'S REAL FATHER, SIR.
EH...? RIKA-CHAN... WHAT ON EARTH... EH...?
... SATOKO'S MOTHER HAD RE-MARRIED, SIR.
SATOKO AND SATOSHI... WERE HIS STEPCHILDREN.
......?

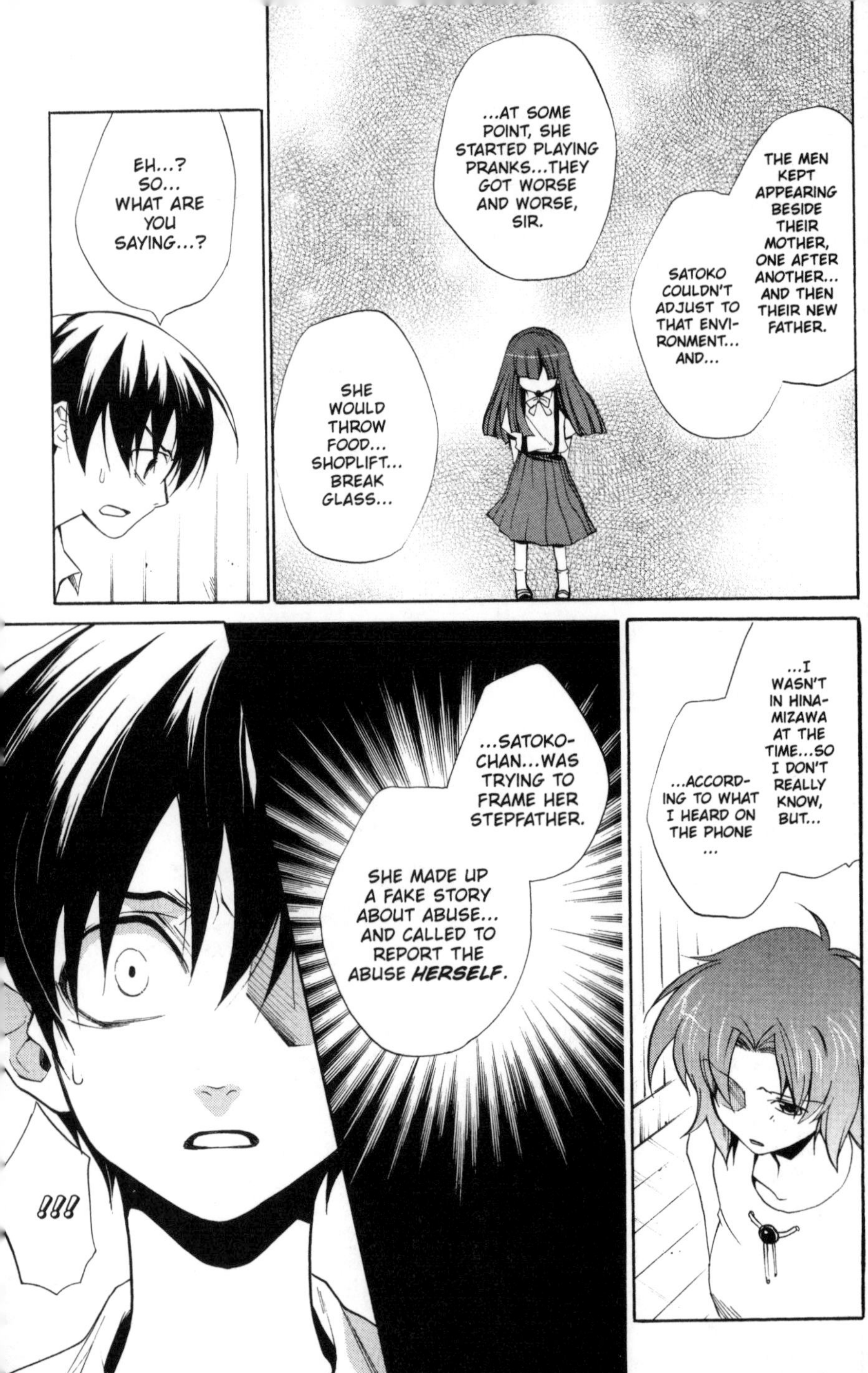
THE MEN KEPT APPEARING BESIDE THEIR MOTHER, ONE AFTER ANOTHER... AND THEN THEIR NEW FATHER.
SATOKO COULDN'T ADJUST TO THAT ENVIRONMENT... AND...
...AT SOME POINT, SHE STARTED PLAYING PRANKS...THEY GOT WORSE AND WORSE, SIR.
SHE WOULD THROW FOOD... SHOPLIFT... BREAK GLASS...
EH...? SO... WHAT ARE YOU SAYING...?
...I WASN'T IN HINAMIZAWA AT THE TIME...SO I DON'T REALLY KNOW, BUT...
...ACCORDING TO WHAT I HEARD ON THE PHONE...
...SATOKO-CHAN...WAS TRYING TO FRAME HER STEPFATHER.
SHE MADE UP A FAKE STORY ABOUT ABUSE... AND CALLED TO REPORT THE ABUSE ***HERSELF***.
!!!

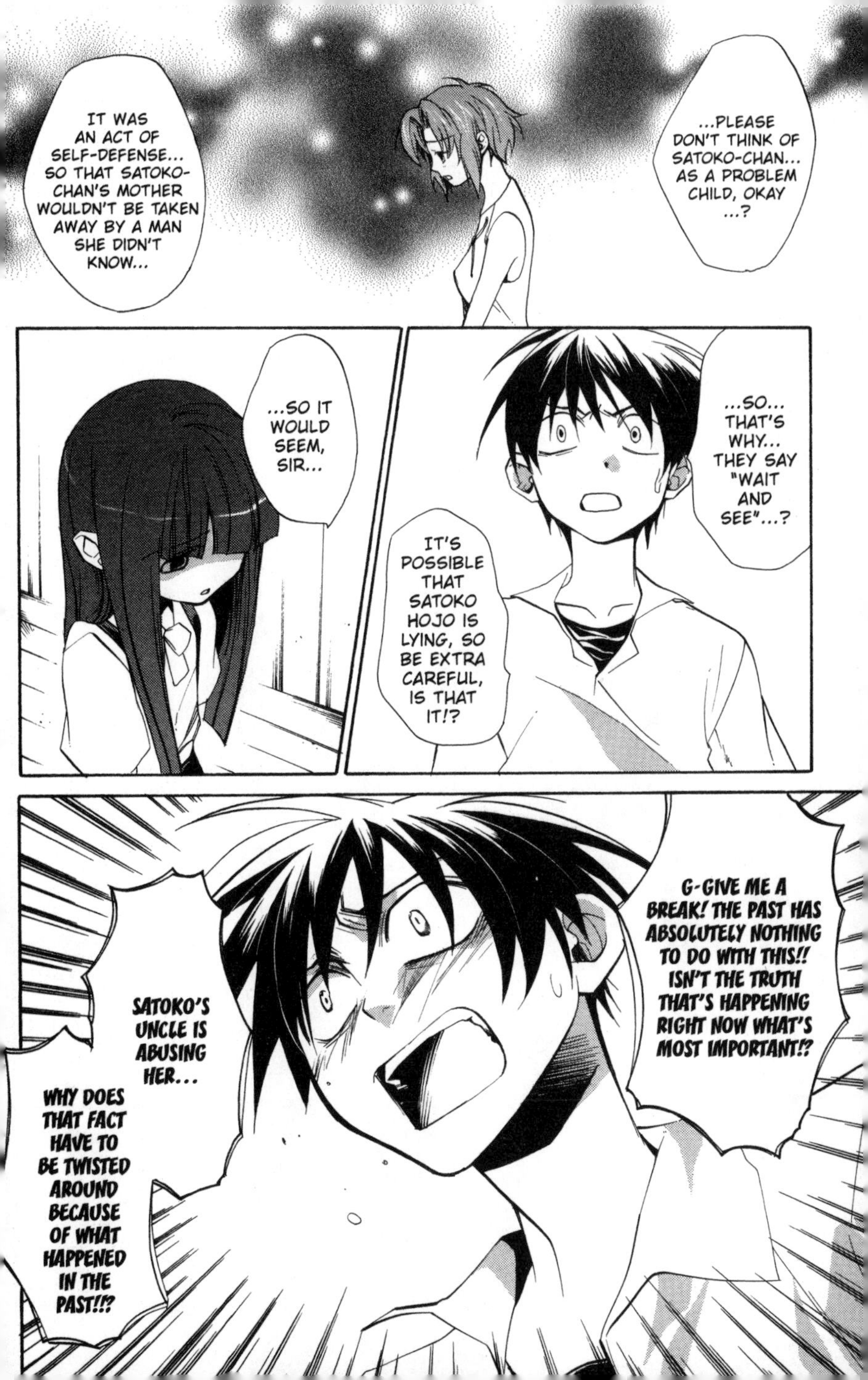
...PLEASE DON'T THINK OF SATOKO-CHAN... AS A PROBLEM CHILD, OKAY ...?
IT WAS AN ACT OF SELF-DEFENSE... SO THAT SATOKO-CHAN'S MOTHER WOULDN'T BE TAKEN AWAY BY A MAN SHE DIDN'T KNOW...
...SO... THAT'S WHY... THEY SAY "WAIT AND SEE"...?
IT'S POSSIBLE THAT SATOKO HOJO IS LYING, SO BE EXTRA CAREFUL, IS THAT IT!?
...SO IT WOULD SEEM, SIR...
G-GIVE ME A BREAK! THE PAST HAS ABSOLUTELY NOTHING TO DO WITH THIS!! ISN'T THE TRUTH THAT'S HAPPENING RIGHT NOW WHAT'S MOST IMPORTANT!?
SATOKO'S UNCLE IS ABUSING HER...
WHY DOES THAT FACT HAVE TO BE TWISTED AROUND BECAUSE OF WHAT HAPPENED IN THE PAST!!?

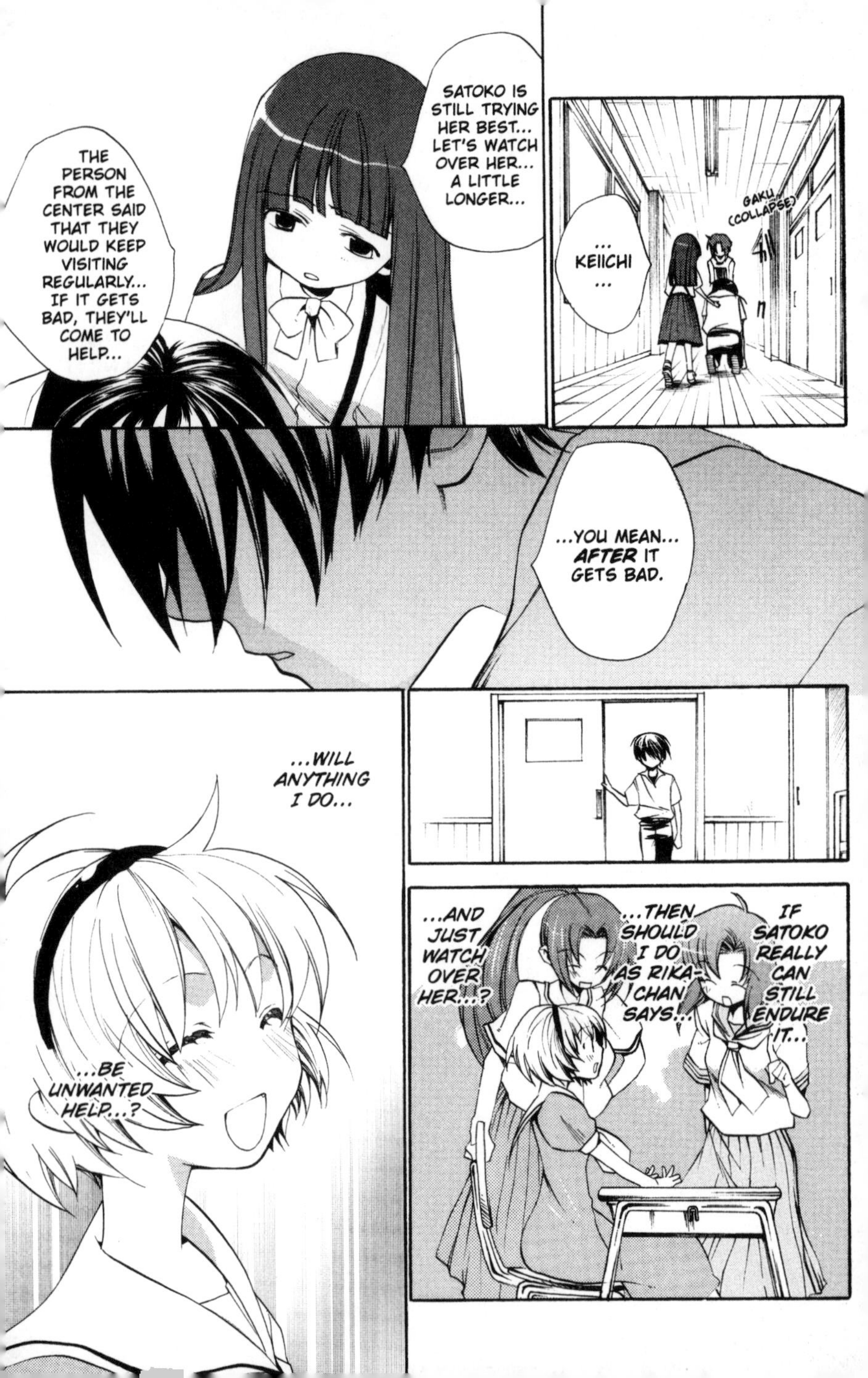
GAKU (COLLAPSE)
... KEIICHI ...
SATOKO IS STILL TRYING HER BEST... LET'S WATCH OVER HER... A LITTLE LONGER...
THE PERSON FROM THE CENTER SAID THAT THEY WOULD KEEP VISITING REGULARLY... IF IT GETS BAD, THEY'LL COME TO HELP...
...YOU MEAN... **AFTER** IT GETS BAD.
IF SATOKO REALLY CAN STILL ENDURE IT...
...THEN SHOULD I DO AS RIKA-CHAN SAYS...
...AND JUST WATCH OVER HER...?
...WILL ANYTHING I DO...
...BE UNWANTED HELP...?

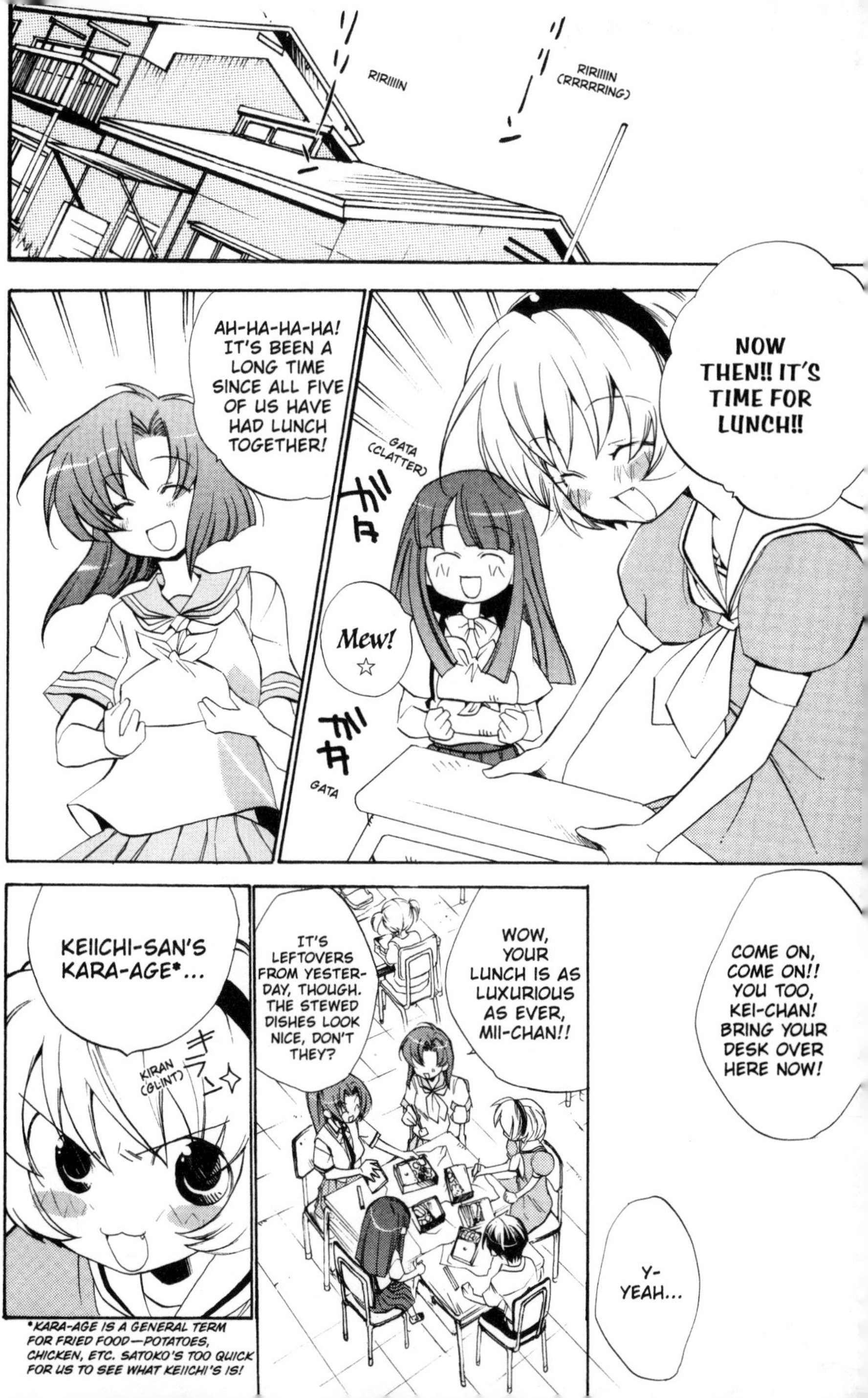
RIRIIIIN (RRRRRING)
RIRIIIN
NOW THEN!! IT'S TIME FOR LUNCH!!
GATA (CLATTER)
Mew! ☆
GATA
AH-HA-HA-HA! IT'S BEEN A LONG TIME SINCE ALL FIVE OF US HAVE HAD LUNCH TOGETHER!
COME ON, COME ON!! YOU TOO, KEI-CHAN! BRING YOUR DESK OVER HERE NOW!
Y-YEAH...
WOW, YOUR LUNCH IS AS LUXURIOUS AS EVER, MII-CHAN!!
IT'S LEFTOVERS FROM YESTER-DAY, THOUGH. THE STEWED DISHES LOOK NICE, DON'T THEY?
KEIICHI-SAN'S KARA-AGE*...
KIRAN (GLINT)

*KARA-AGE IS A GENERAL TERM FOR FRIED FOOD—POTATOES, CHICKEN, ETC. SATOKO'S TOO QUICK FOR US TO SEE WHAT KEIICHI'S IS!

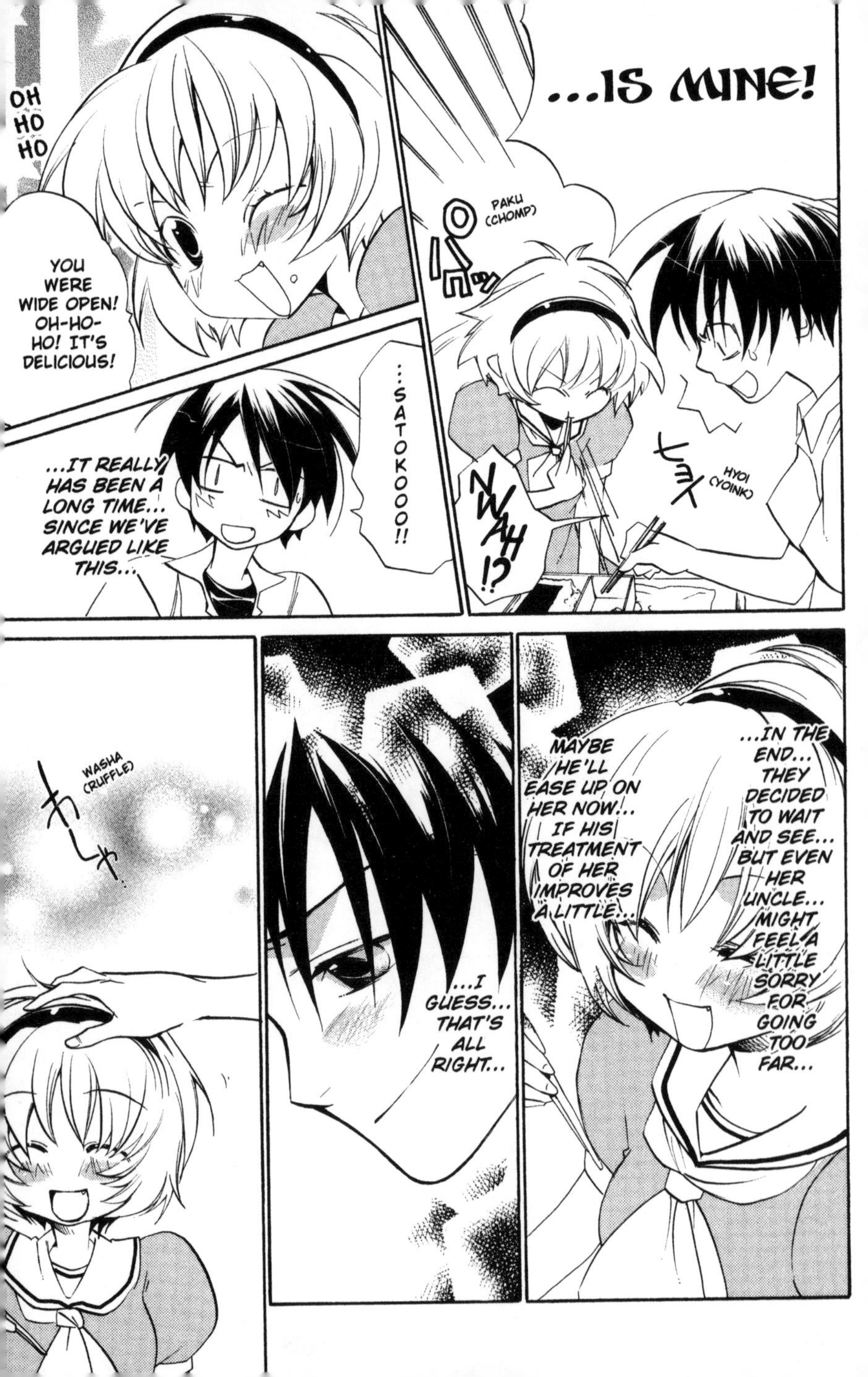
...IS MINE!
PAKU (CHOMP)
HYOI (YOINK)
NWAH!?
OH HO HO
YOU WERE WIDE OPEN! OH-HO-HO! IT'S DELICIOUS!
...SATOKOOOO!!
...IT REALLY HAS BEEN A LONG TIME... SINCE WE'VE ARGUED LIKE THIS...
...IN THE END... THEY DECIDED TO WAIT AND SEE... BUT EVEN HER UNCLE... MIGHT FEEL A LITTLE SORRY FOR GOING TOO FAR...
MAYBE HE'LL EASE UP ON HER NOW... IF HIS TREATMENT OF HER IMPROVES A LITTLE...
...I GUESS... THAT'S ALL RIGHT...
WASHA (RUFFLE)

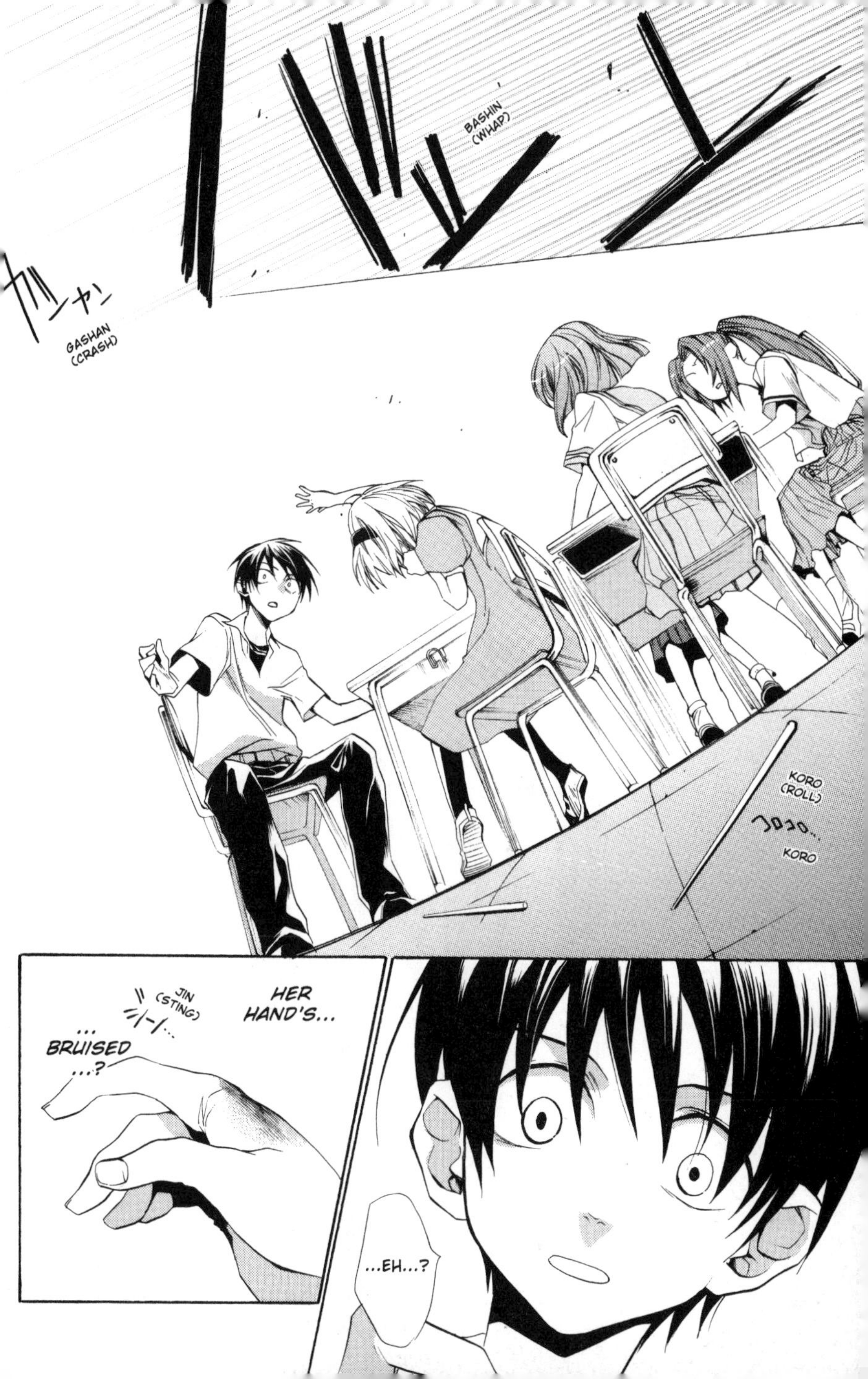
BASHIN (WHAP)
GASHAN (CRASH)
KORO (ROLL)
KORO
...EH...?
HER HAND'S...
JIN (STING)
...BRUISED...?

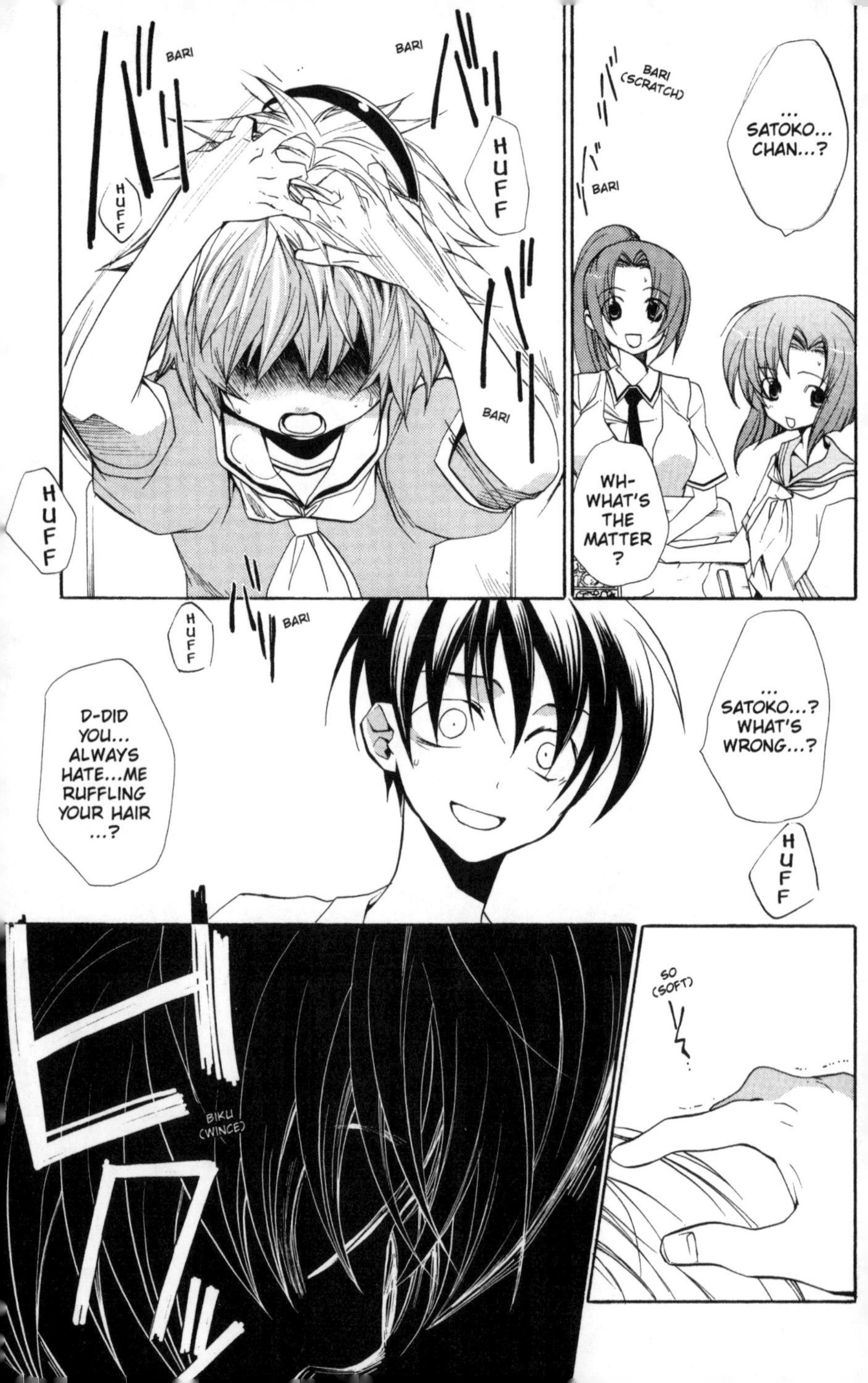

BARI (SCRATCH)
BARI
... SATOKO... CHAN...?
WH- WHAT'S THE MATTER?
BARI
BARI
HUFF
HUFF
BARI
HUFF
... SATOKO...? WHAT'S WRONG...?
HUFF
BARI
HUFF
D-DID YOU... ALWAYS HATE...ME RUFFLING YOUR HAIR ...?
SO (SOFT)
......
BIKU (WINCE)

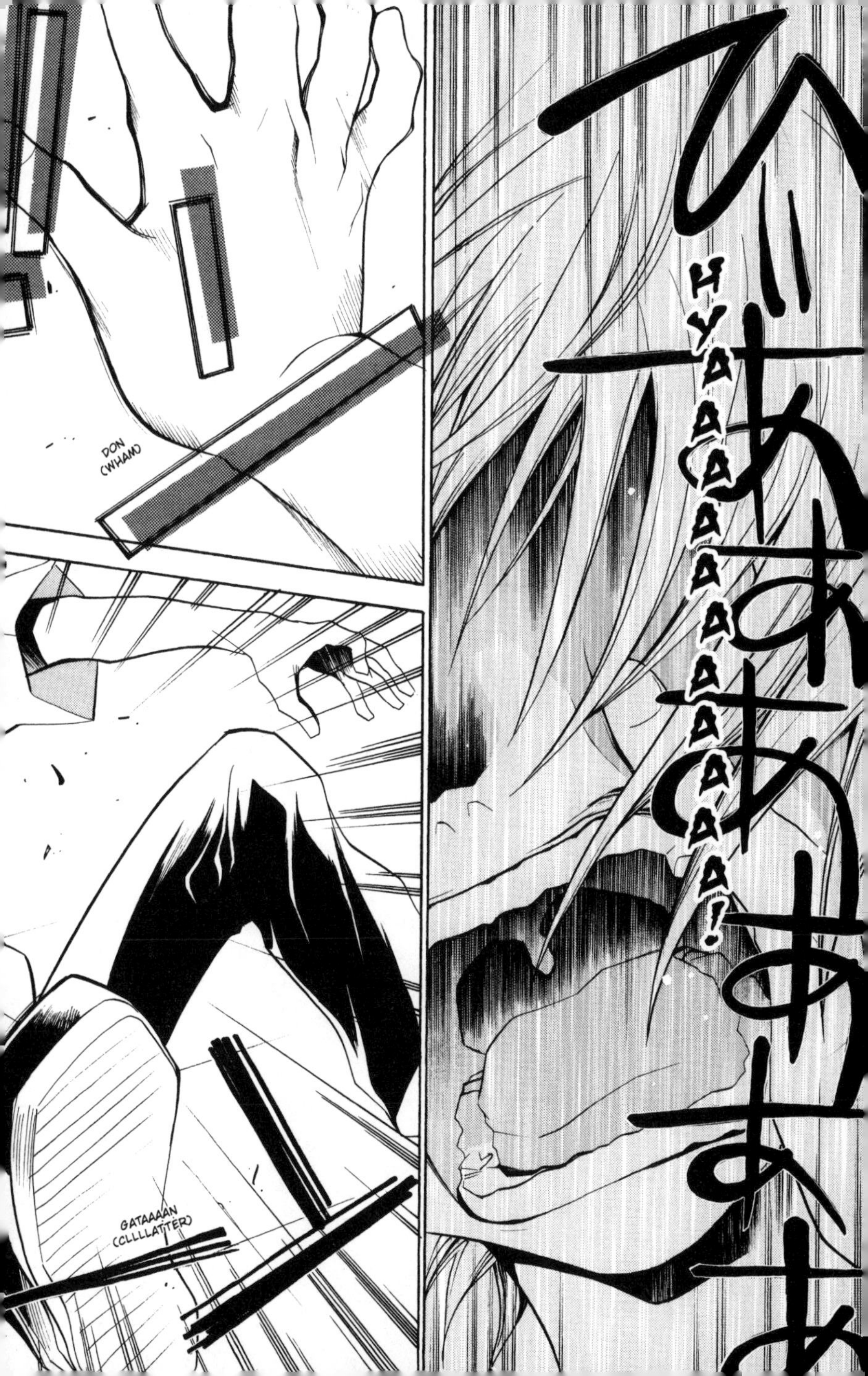

ひあああああ
HYAAAAAAAAAA!
DON (WHAM)
GATAAAAN (CLLLLATTER)

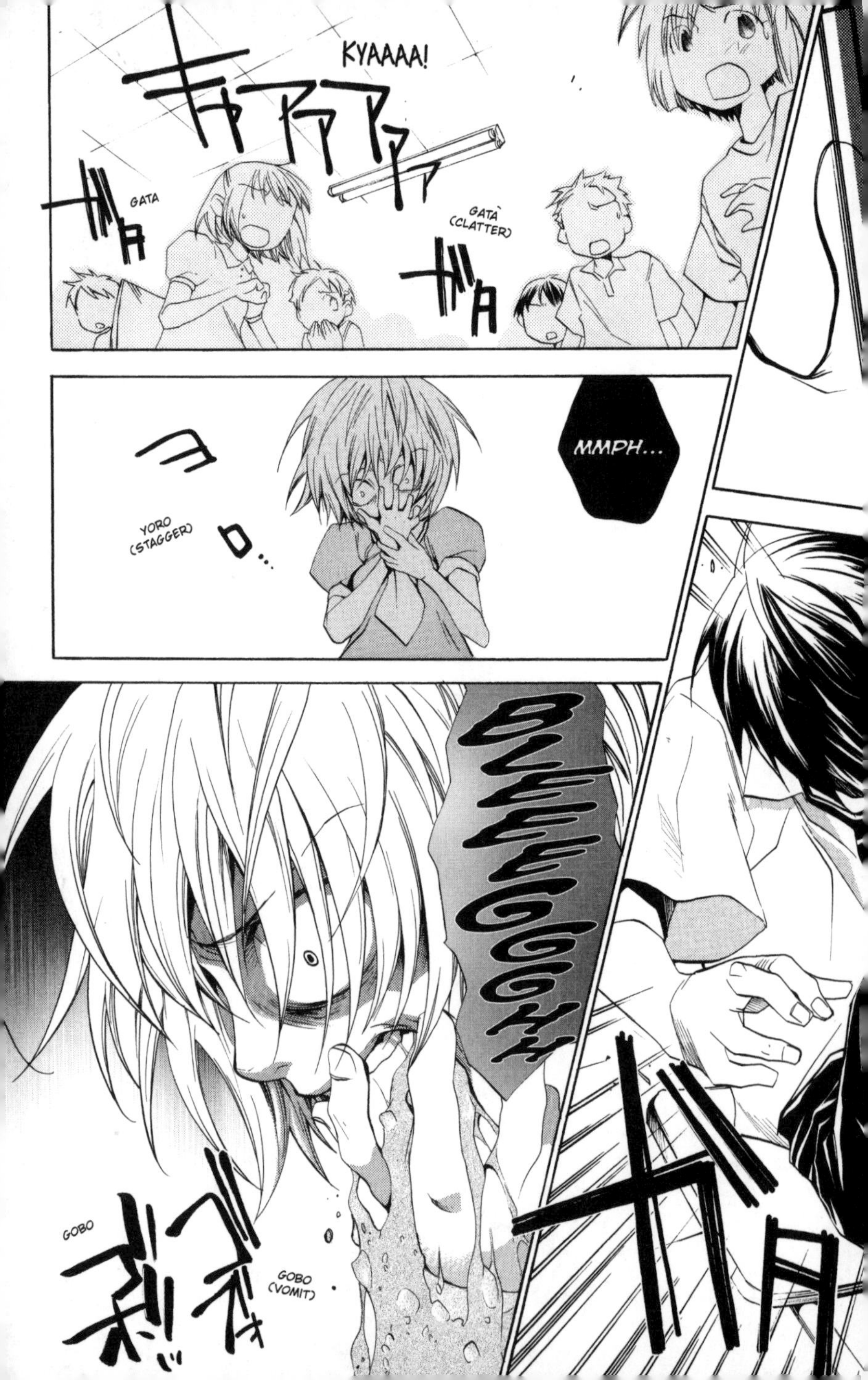
KYAAAA!
GATA
(CLATTER)
GATA
MMPH...
YORO
(STAGGER)
BLEEEOOGH
GOBO
(VOMIT)
GOBO

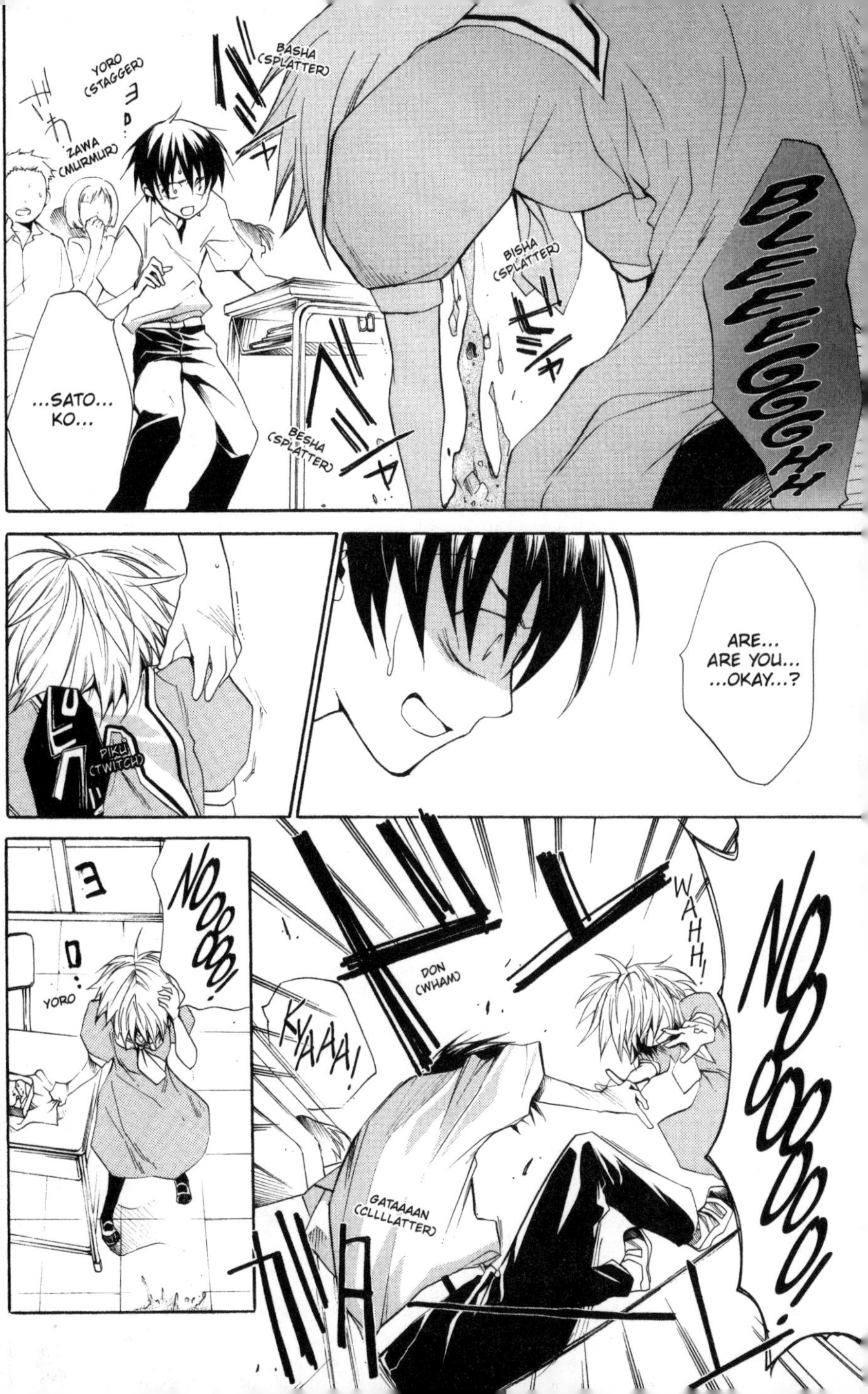
BLEEEGGGHH
BASHA (SPLATTER)
BISHA (SPLATTER)
YORO (STAGGER)
ZAWA (MURMUR)
BESHA (SPLATTER)
...SATO... KO...
ARE... ARE YOU... ...OKAY...?
PIKU (TWITCH)
NOOOOOOOOO!
WAHH!
DON (WHAM)
KYAAA!
GATAAAAN (CLLLLATTER)
NOOOOO!
YORO

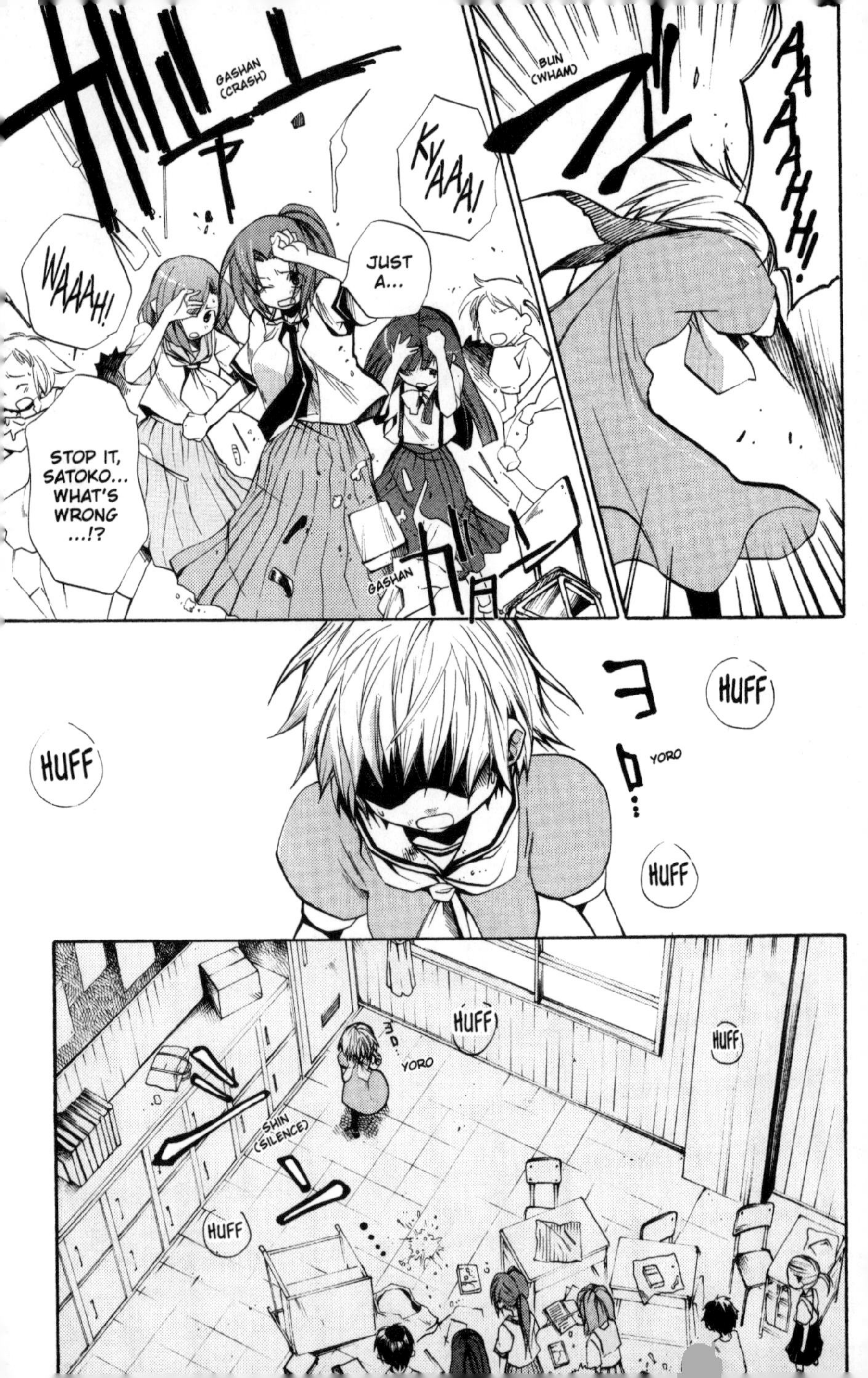
AAAAHH!
BUN (WHAM)
KYAAA!
GASHAN (CRASH)
JUST A...
WAAAH!
STOP IT, SATOKO... WHAT'S WRONG ...!?
GASHAN
HUFF
YORO
HUFF
HUFF
HUFF
HUFF
YORO
SHIN (SILENCE)
HUFF

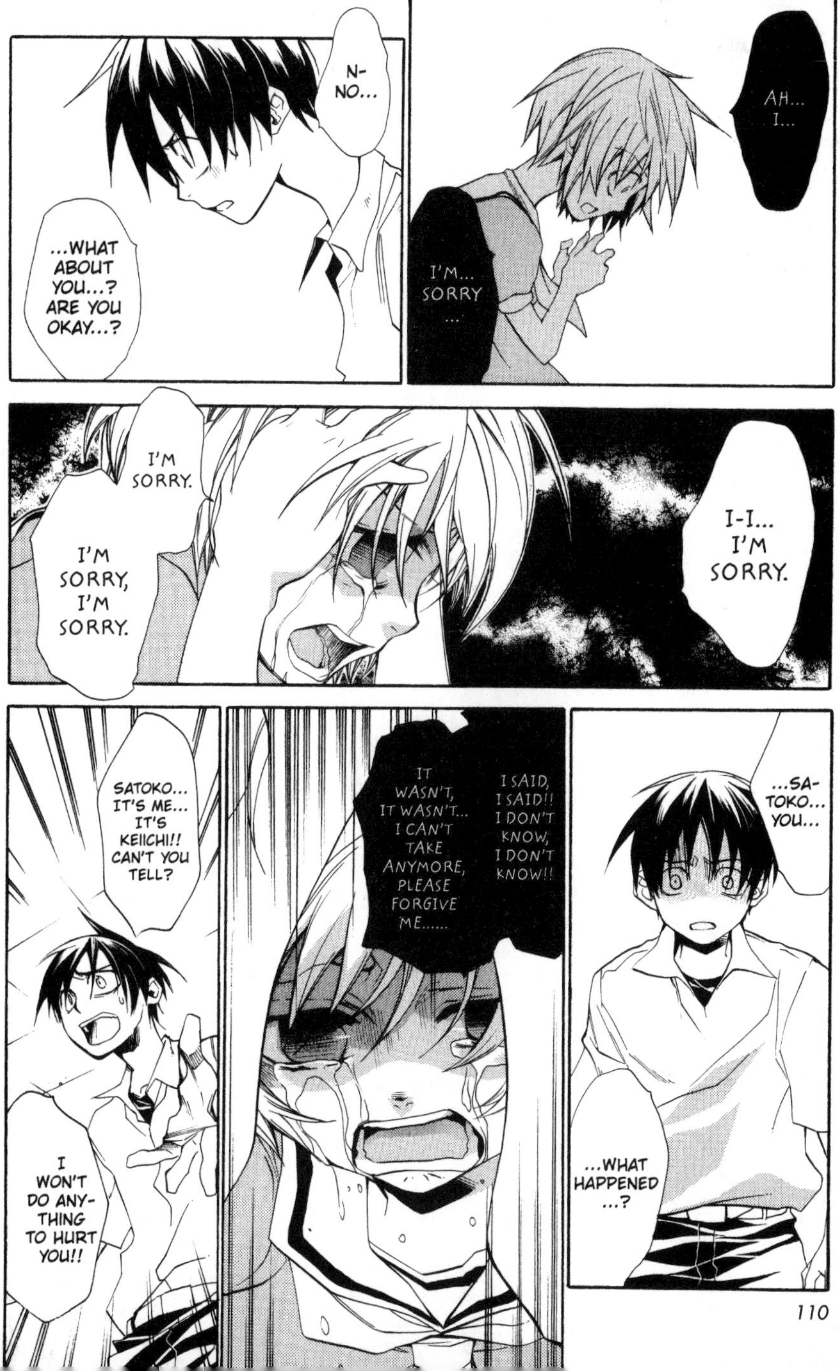
AH... I...
I'M... SORRY ...
N- NO...
...WHAT ABOUT YOU...? ARE YOU OKAY...?
I-I... I'M SORRY.
I'M SORRY.
I'M SORRY, I'M SORRY.
...SA- TOKO... YOU...
...WHAT HAPPENED ...?
I SAID, I SAID!! I DON'T KNOW, I DON'T KNOW!!
IT WASN'T, IT WASN'T... I CAN'T TAKE ANYMORE, PLEASE FORGIVE ME......
SATOKO... IT'S ME... IT'S KEIICHI!! CAN'T YOU TELL?
I WON'T DO ANY- THING TO HURT YOU!!

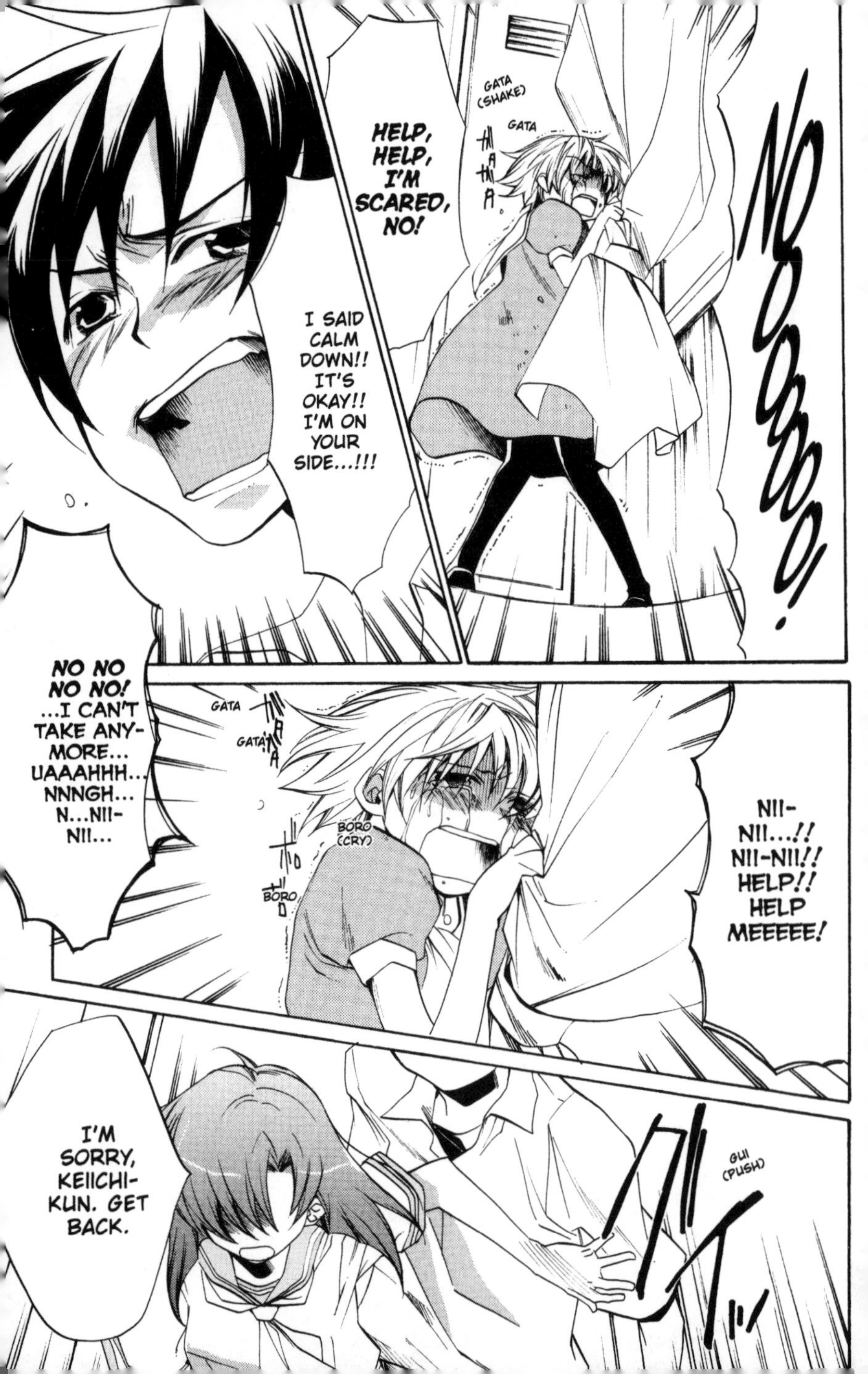
NOOOOOO!!
GATA (SHAKE)
GATA
HELP, HELP, I'M SCARED, NO!
I SAID CALM DOWN!! IT'S OKAY!! I'M ON YOUR SIDE...!!!
NII-NII...!! NII-NII!! HELP!! HELP MEEEEE!
BORO (CRY)
BORO
GATA
GATA
NO NO NO NO! ...I CAN'T TAKE ANYMORE... UAAAHHH... NNNGH... N...NII-NII...
GUI (PUSH)
I'M SORRY, KEIICHI-KUN. GET BACK.

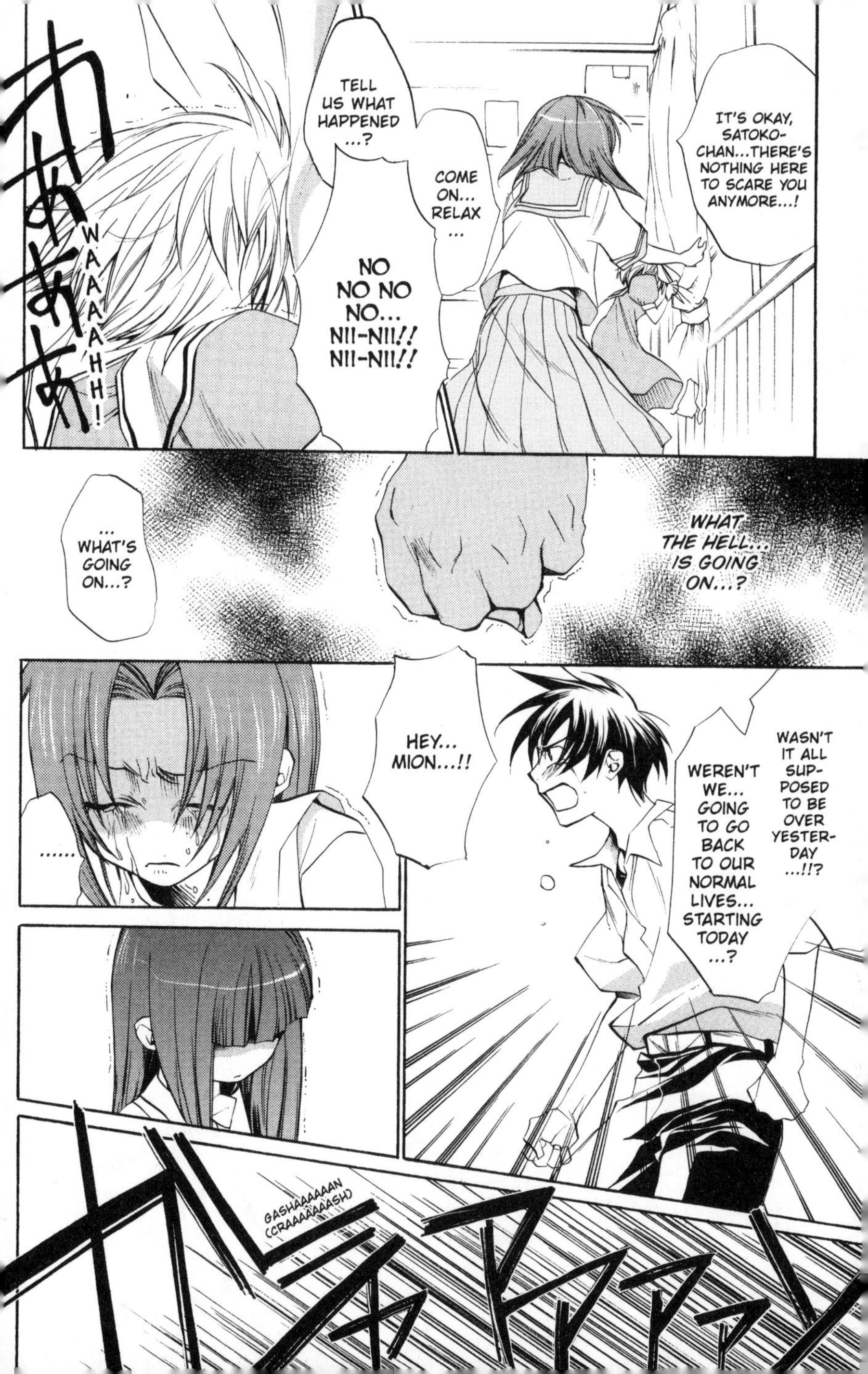

IT'S OKAY, SATOKO-CHAN...THERE'S NOTHING HERE TO SCARE YOU ANYMORE...!
TELL US WHAT HAPPENED ...?
COME ON... RELAX ...
NO NO NO NO... NII-NII!! NII-NII!!
WAAAAAHH!
WHAT THE HELL... IS GOING ON...?
... WHAT'S GOING ON...?
WASN'T IT ALL SUPPOSED TO BE OVER YESTERDAY ...!!?
WEREN'T WE... GOING TO GO BACK TO OUR NORMAL LIVES... STARTING TODAY ...?
HEY... MION...!!
......
GASHAAAAAAN (CRAAAAAAASH)

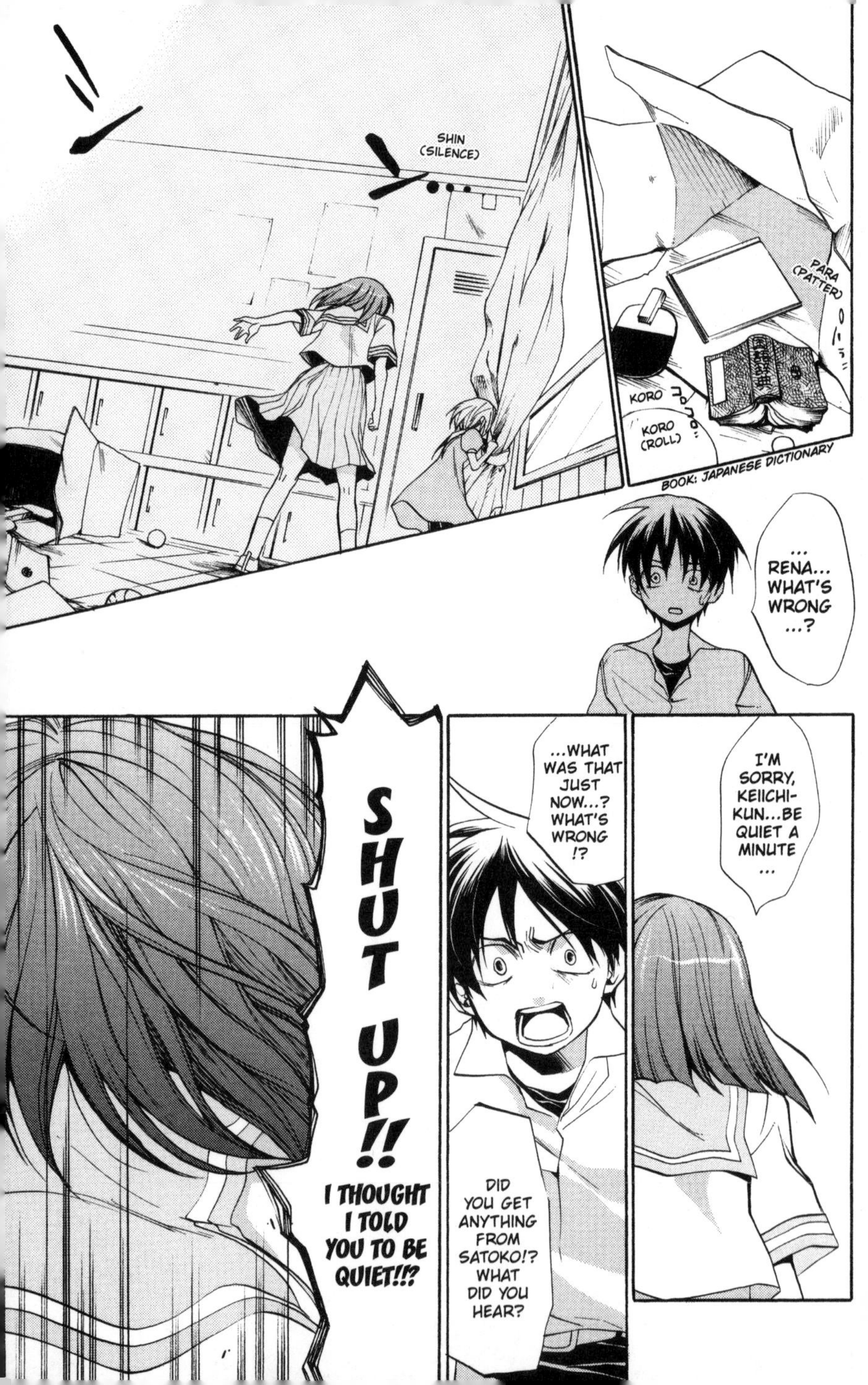
PARA (PATTER)
KORO
KORO (ROLL)
BOOK: JAPANESE DICTIONARY
SHIN (SILENCE)
... RENA... WHAT'S WRONG ...?
I'M SORRY, KEIICHI-KUN...BE QUIET A MINUTE ...
...WHAT WAS THAT JUST NOW...? WHAT'S WRONG !?
DID YOU GET ANYTHING FROM SATOKO!? WHAT DID YOU HEAR?
SHUT UP!!
I THOUGHT I TOLD YOU TO BE QUIET!!?

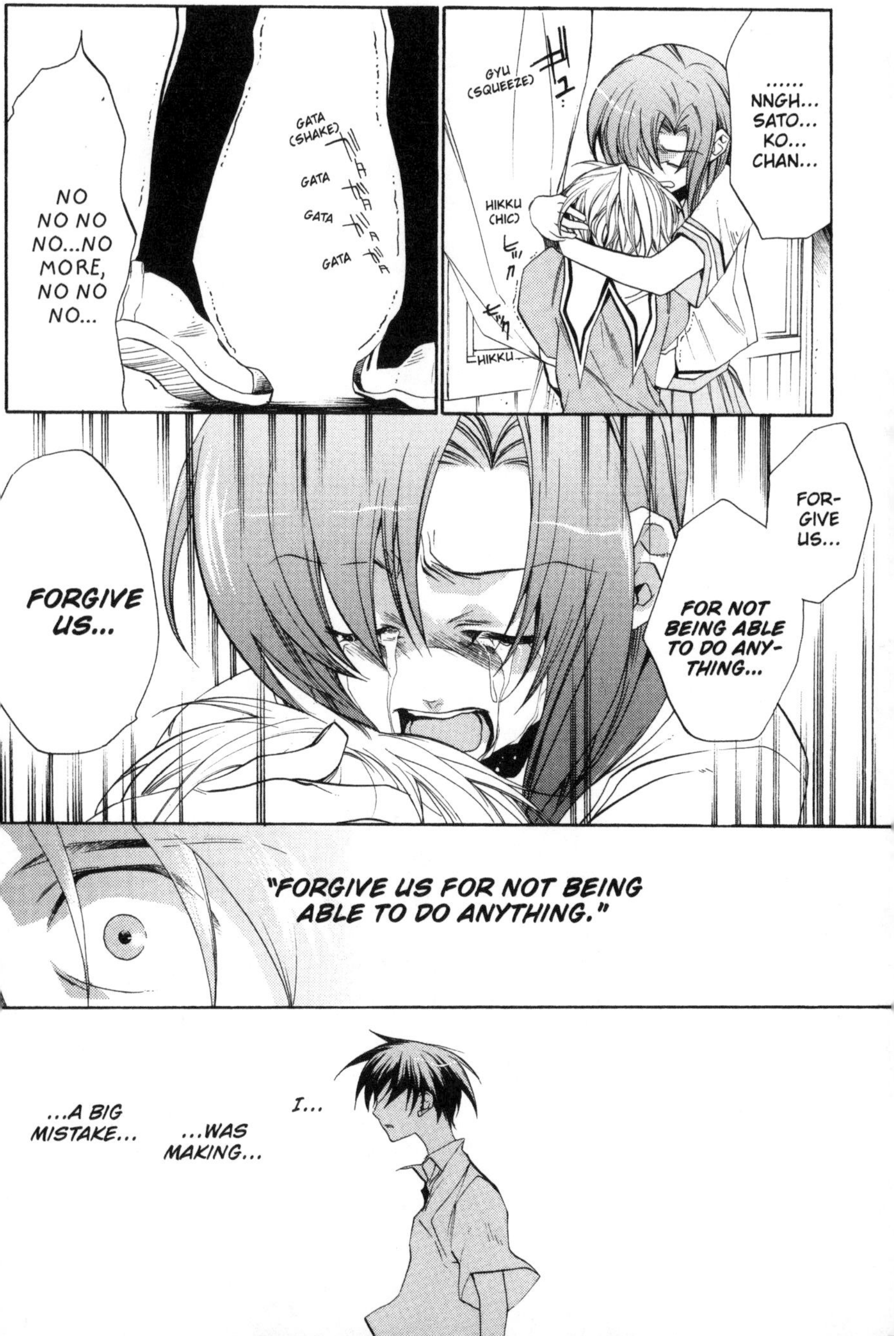

GYU (SQUEEZE)
...... NNGH... SATO... KO... CHAN...
HIKKU (HIC)
HIKKU
GATA (SHAKE)
GATA
GATA
GATA
NO NO NO NO...NO MORE, NO NO NO...
FOR-GIVE US...
FOR NOT BEING ABLE TO DO ANY-THING...
FORGIVE US...
"FORGIVE US FOR NOT BEING ABLE TO DO ANYTHING."
I...
...WAS MAKING...
...A BIG MISTAKE...

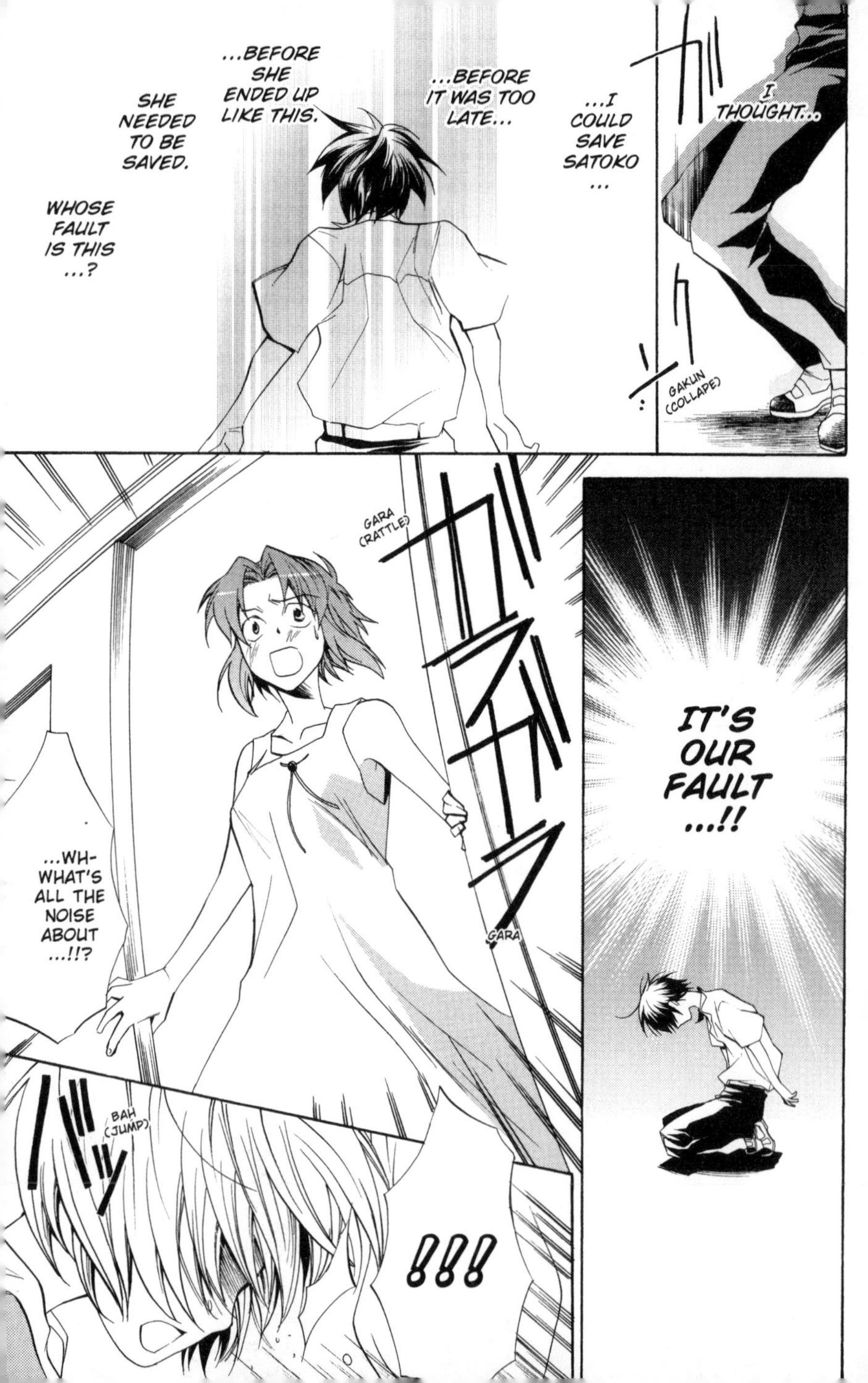
I THOUGHT...
GAKUN (COLLAPSE)
...I COULD SAVE SATOKO...
...BEFORE IT WAS TOO LATE...
...BEFORE SHE ENDED UP LIKE THIS.
SHE NEEDED TO BE SAVED.
WHOSE FAULT IS THIS...?
IT'S OUR FAULT...!!
GARA (RATTLE)
GARA
...WH-WHAT'S ALL THE NOISE ABOUT...!!?
!!!
BAH (JUMP)

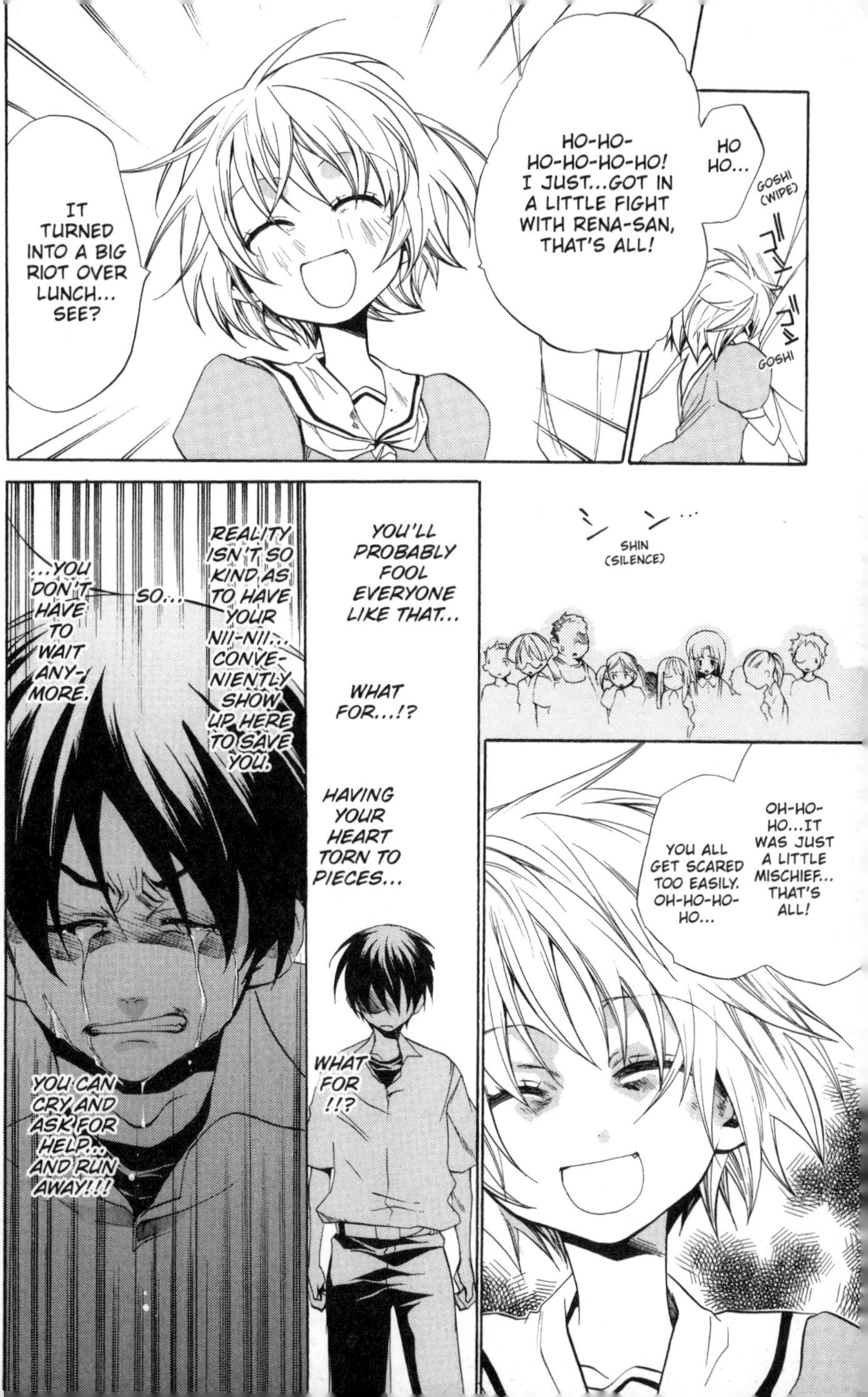
HO HO...
GOSHI (WIPE)
GOSHI
HO-HO-HO-HO-HO-HO-HO! I JUST...GOT IN A LITTLE FIGHT WITH RENA-SAN, THAT'S ALL!
IT TURNED INTO A BIG RIOT OVER LUNCH... SEE?
SHIN (SILENCE)
OH-HO-HO...IT WAS JUST A LITTLE MISCHIEF... THAT'S ALL!
YOU ALL GET SCARED TOO EASILY. OH-HO-HO-HO...
YOU'LL PROBABLY FOOL EVERYONE LIKE THAT...
WHAT FOR...!?
HAVING YOUR HEART TORN TO PIECES...
WHAT FOR !!?
REALITY ISN'T SO KIND AS TO HAVE YOUR NII-NII... CONVENIENTLY SHOW UP HERE TO SAVE YOU.
SO...
...YOU DON'T HAVE TO WAIT ANYMORE.
YOU CAN CRY AND ASK FOR HELP... AND RUN AWAY!!!

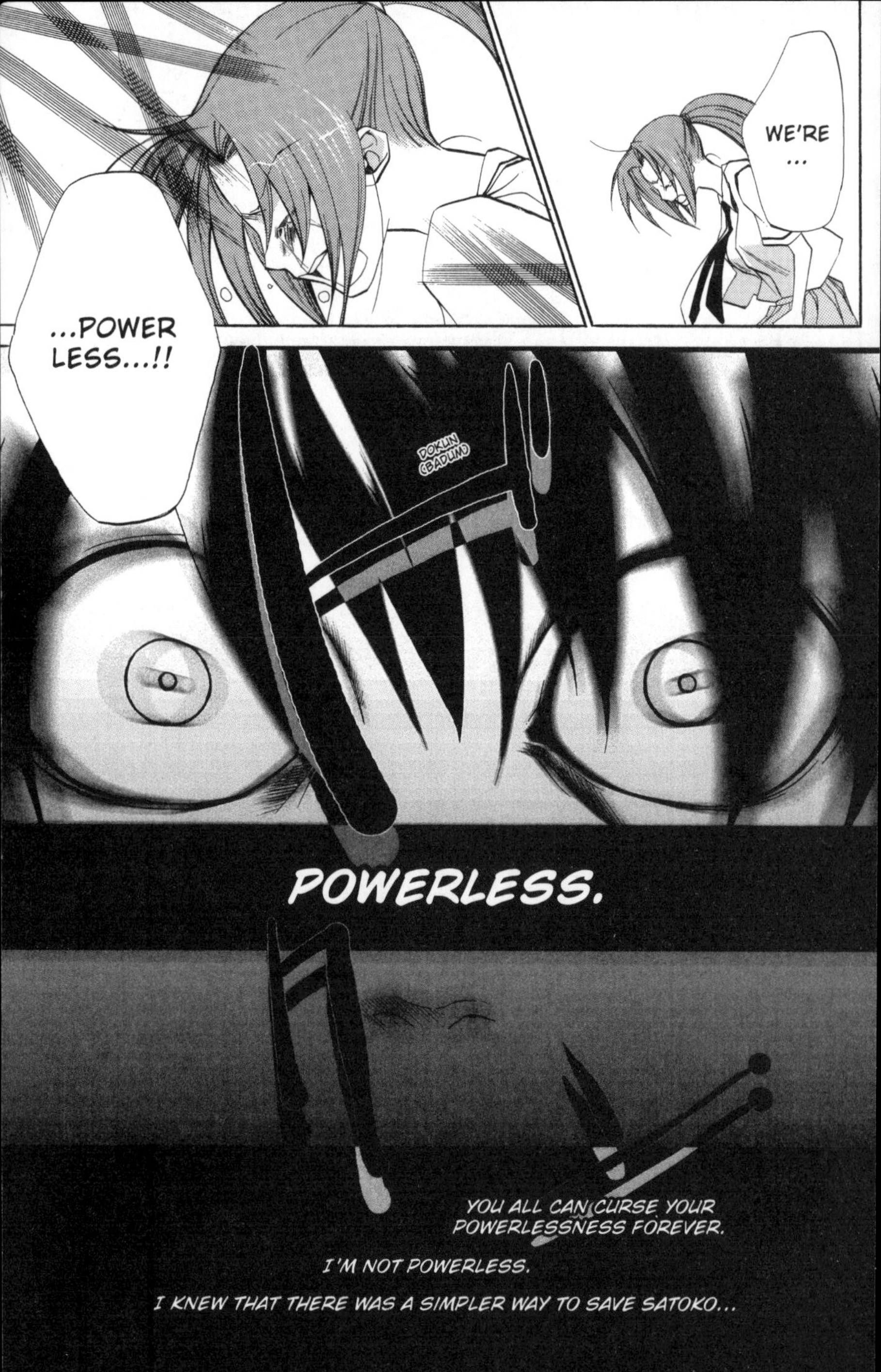
WE'RE ...
...POWER LESS...!!
DOKUN (BADUM)
POWERLESS.
YOU ALL CAN CURSE YOUR POWERLESSNESS FOREVER.
I'M NOT POWERLESS.
I KNEW THAT THERE WAS A SIMPLER WAY TO SAVE SATOKO...

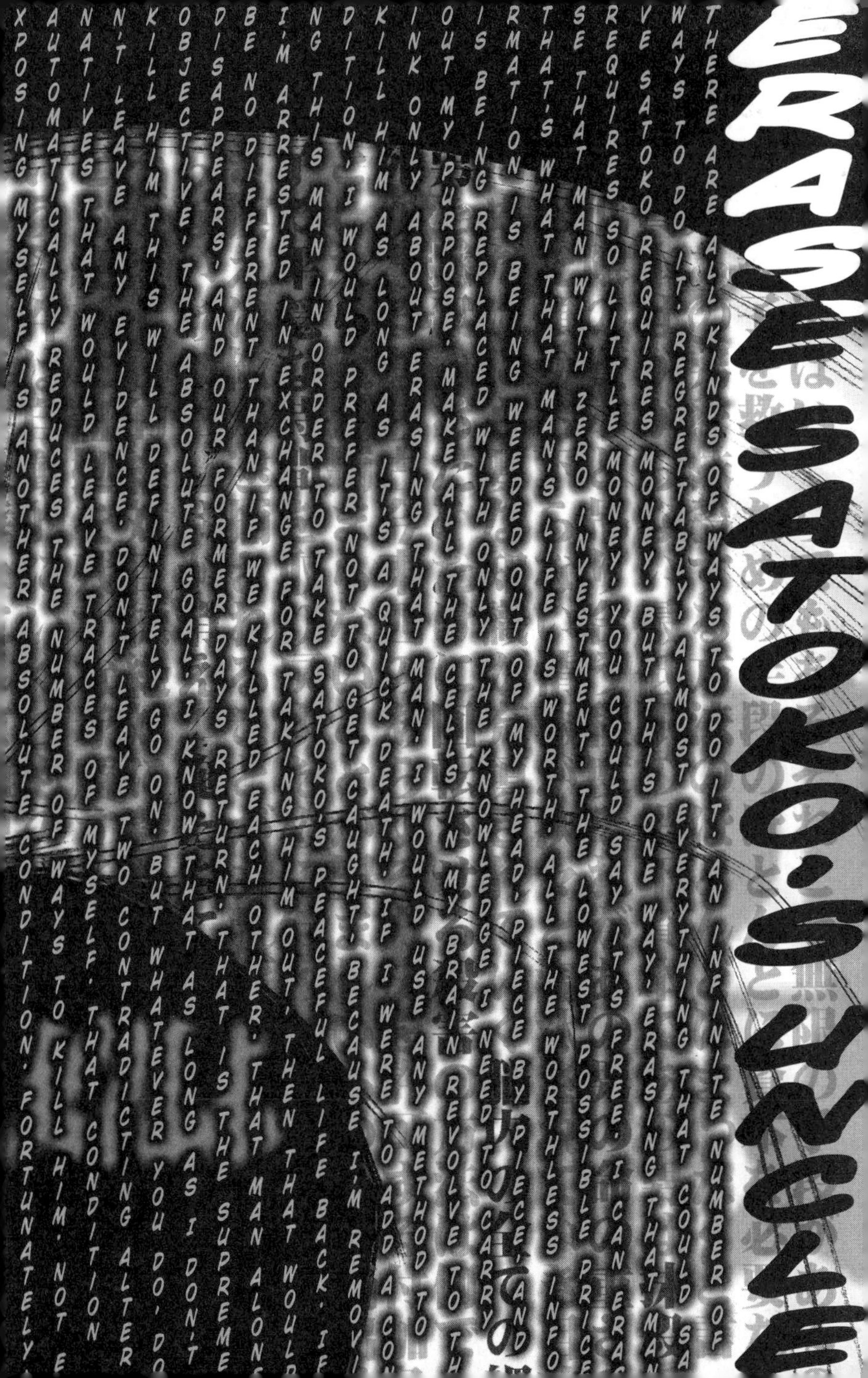
ERASE SATOKO'S UNCLE
THERE ARE ALL KINDS OF WAYS TO DO IT. AN INFINITE NUMBER OF WAYS TO DO IT. REGRETTABLY, ALMOST EVERYTHING THAT COULD SAVE SATOKO REQUIRES MONEY. BUT THIS ONE WAY, ERASING THAT MAN, REQUIRES SO LITTLE MONEY, YOU COULD SAY IT'S FREE. I CAN ERASE THAT MAN WITH ZERO INVESTMENT. THE LOWEST POSSIBLE PRICE THAT'S WHAT THAT MAN'S LIFE IS WORTH. ALL THE WORTHLESS INFORMATION IS BEING WEEDED OUT OF MY HEAD, PIECE BY PIECE, AND IS BEING REPLACED WITH ONLY THE KNOWLEDGE I NEED TO CARRY OUT MY PURPOSE. MAKE ALL THE CELLS IN MY BRAIN REVOLVE TO THINK ONLY ABOUT ERASING THAT MAN. I WOULD USE ANY METHOD TO KILL HIM AS LONG AS IT'S A QUICK DEATH. IF I WERE TO ADD A CONDITION, I WOULD PREFER NOT TO GET CAUGHT, BECAUSE I'M REMOVING THIS MAN IN ORDER TO TAKE SATOKO'S PEACEFUL LIFE BACK. IF I'M ARRESTED IN EXCHANGE FOR TAKING HIM OUT, THEN THAT WOULD BE NO DIFFERENT THAN IF WE KILLED EACH OTHER. THAT MAN ALONG DISAPPEARS, AND OUR FORMER DAYS RETURN. THAT IS THE SUPREME OBJECTIVE, THE ABSOLUTE GOAL. I KNOW THAT AS LONG AS I DON'T KILL HIM THIS WILL DEFINITELY GO ON. BUT WHATEVER YOU DO, DON'T LEAVE ANY EVIDENCE. DON'T LEAVE TWO CONTRADICTING ALTERNATIVES THAT WOULD LEAVE TRACES OF MYSELF. THAT CONDITION AUTOMATICALLY REDUCES THE NUMBER OF WAYS TO KILL HIM. NOT EXPOSING MYSELF IS ANOTHER ABSOLUTE CONDITION. FORTUNATELY

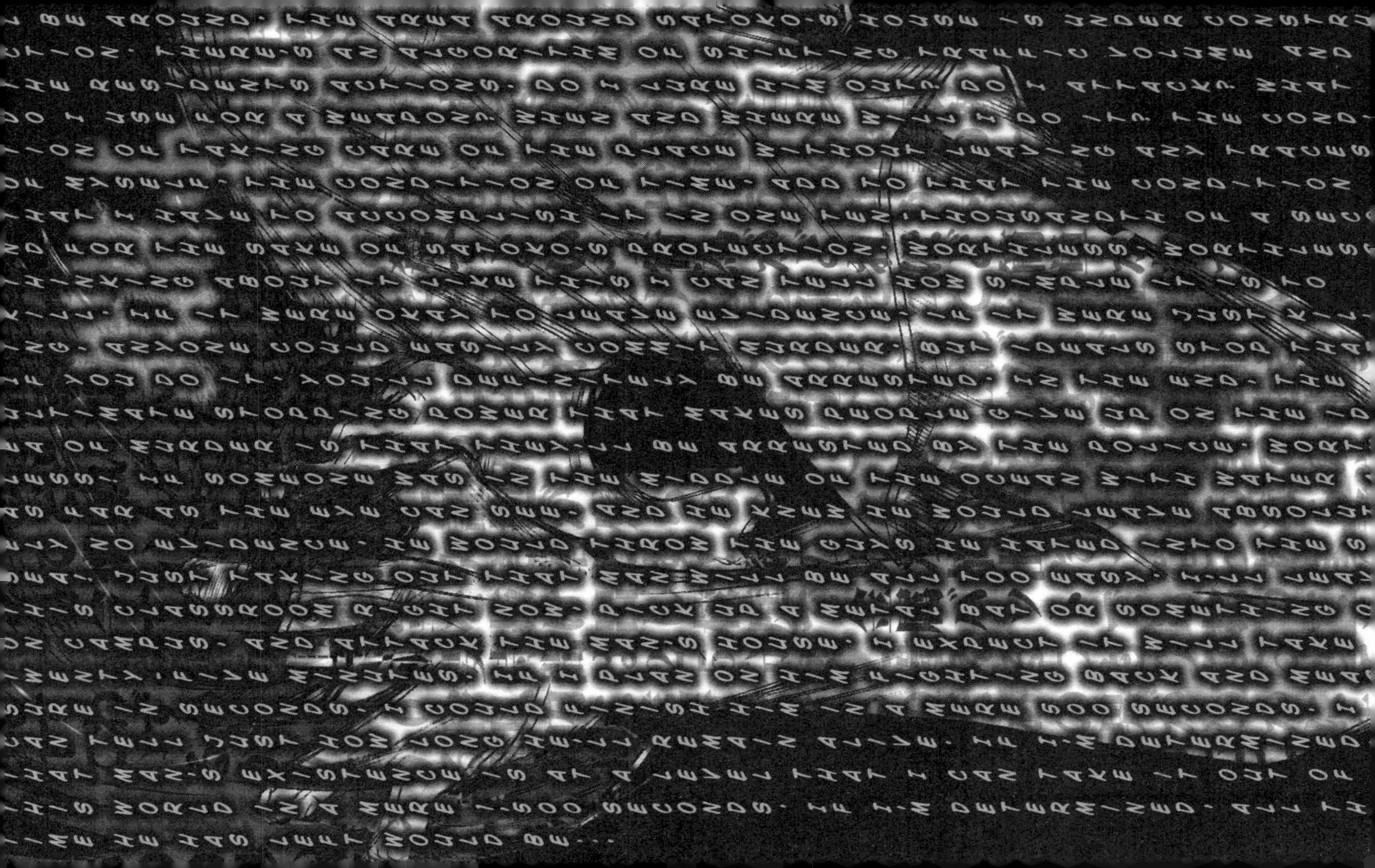
L BE AROUND. THE AREA AROUND SATOKO'S HOUSE IS UNDER CONSTRU
CTION. THERE'S AN ALGORITHM OF SHIFTING TRAFFIC VOLUME AND
THE RESIDENTS' ACTIONS. DO I LURE HIM OUT? DO I ATTACK? WHAT
DO I USE FOR A WEAPON? WHEN AND WHERE WILL I DO IT? THE COND
TION OF TAKING CARE OF THE PLACE WITHOUT LEAVING ANY TRACES
OF MYSELF, THE CONDITION OF TIME, ADD TO THAT THE CONDITION
THAT I HAVE TO ACCOMPLISH IT IN ONE TEN-THOUSANDTH OF A SEC
ND FOR THE SAKE OF SATOKO'S PROTECTION. WORTHLESS. WORTHLESS
THINKING ABOUT IT LIKE THIS I CAN TELL HOW SIMPLE IT IS TO
KILL. IF IT WERE OKAY TO LEAVE EVIDENCE, IF IT WERE JUST KIL
ING, ANYONE COULD EASILY COMMIT MURDER. BUT IDEALS STOP THA
IF YOU DO IT, YOU'LL DEFINITELY BE ARRESTED. IN THE END, THE
ULTIMATE STOPPING POWER THAT MAKES PEOPLE GIVE UP ON THE ID
EA OF MURDER IS THAT THEY'LL BE ARRESTED BY THE POLICE. WORT
LESS! IF SOMEONE WAS IN THE MIDDLE OF THE OCEAN WITH WATER
AS FAR AS THE EYE CAN SEE, AND HE KNEW HE WOULD LEAVE ABSOLUT
ELY NO EVIDENCE, HE WOULD THROW THE GUYS HE HATED INTO THE S
SEA! JUST TAKING OUT THAT MAN WILL BE ALL TOO EASY. I'LL LEAV
THIS CLASSROOM RIGHT NOW, PICK UP A METAL BAT OR SOMETHING O
ON CAMPUS, AND ATTACK THE MAN'S HOUSE. I EXPECT IT WILL TAKE
TWENTY-FIVE MINUTES. IF I PLAN ON HIM FIGHTING BACK AND MEA
SURE IN SECONDS, I COULD FINISH HIM IN A MERE 500 SECONDS. I
CAN TELL JUST HOW LONG HE'LL REMAIN ALIVE. IF I'M DETERMINED
THAT MAN'S EXISTENCE IS AT A LEVEL THAT I CAN TAKE IT OUT OF
THIS WORLD IN A MERE 1,500 SECONDS. IF I'M DETERMINED, ALL TH
TIME HE HAS LEFT WOULD BE...

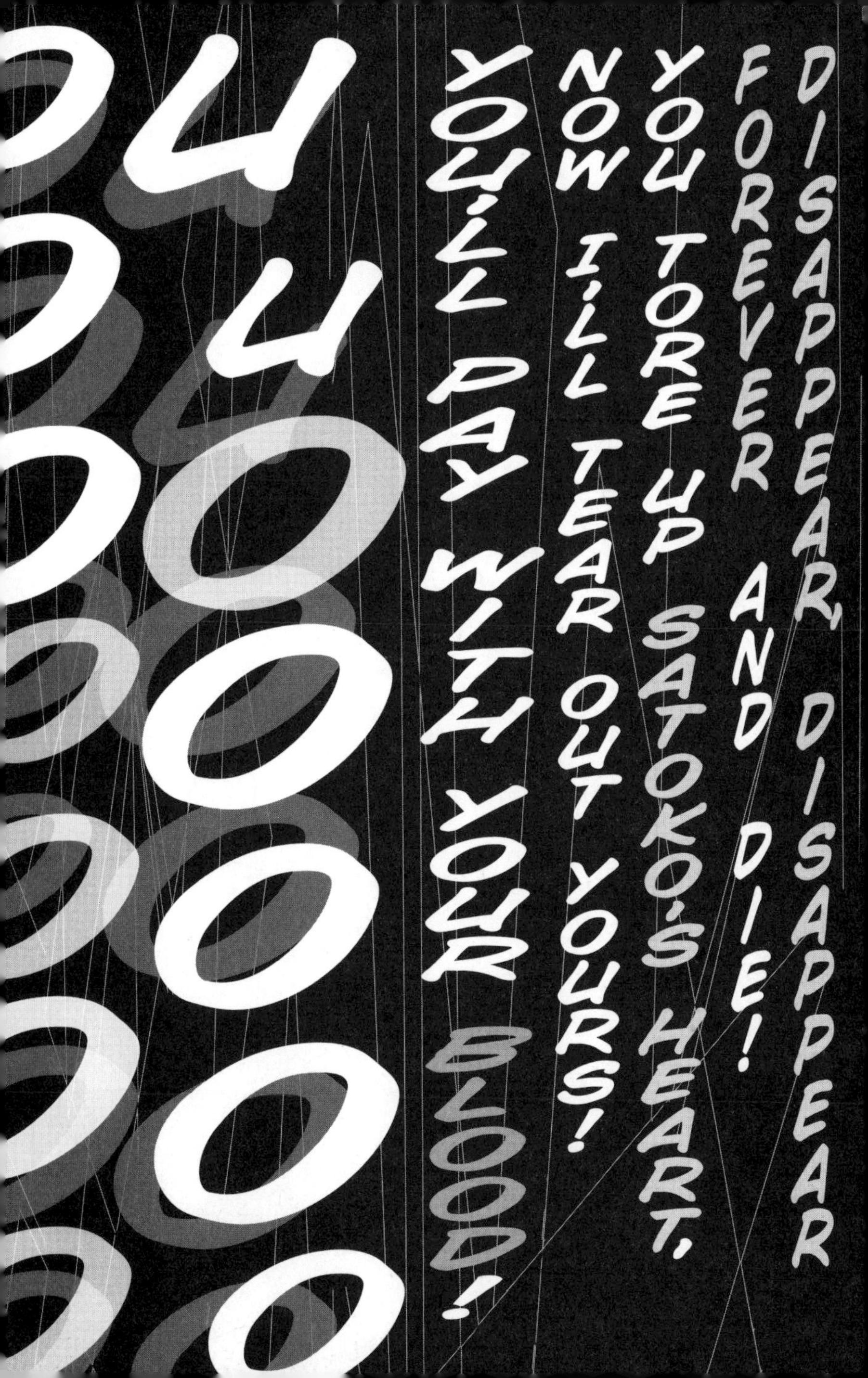
DISAPPEAR, DISAPPEAR
FOREVER AND DIE!
YOU TORE UP SATOKO'S HEART,
NOW I'LL TEAR OUT YOURS!
YOU'LL PAY WITH YOUR BLOOD!
UUOOOOO

CHAPTER 9

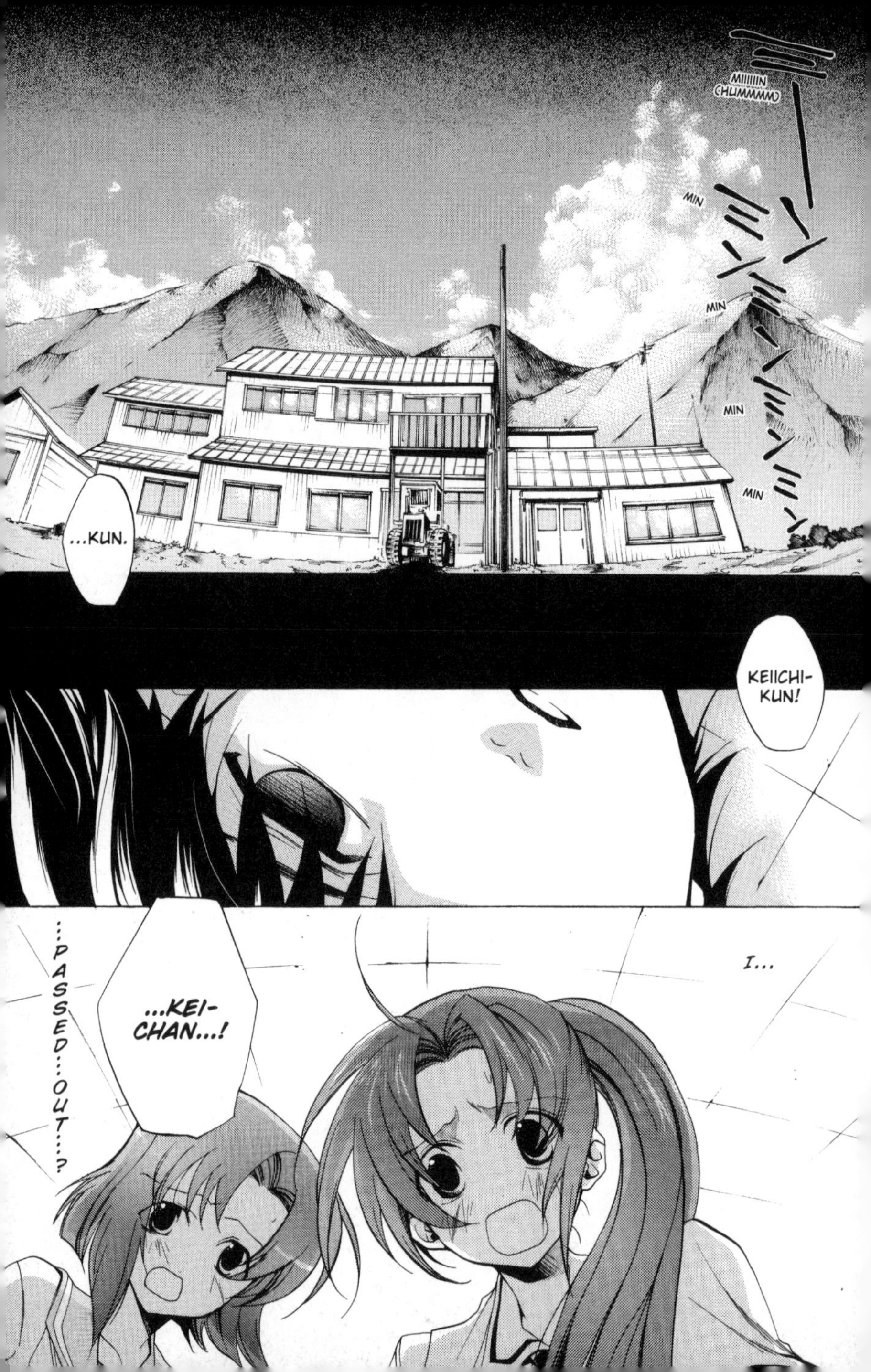
MIIIIIIN
(HUMMMMM)
MIN
MIN
MIN
MIN
...KUN.
KEIICHI-KUN!
I...
...KEI-CHAN...!
...PASSED...OUT...?

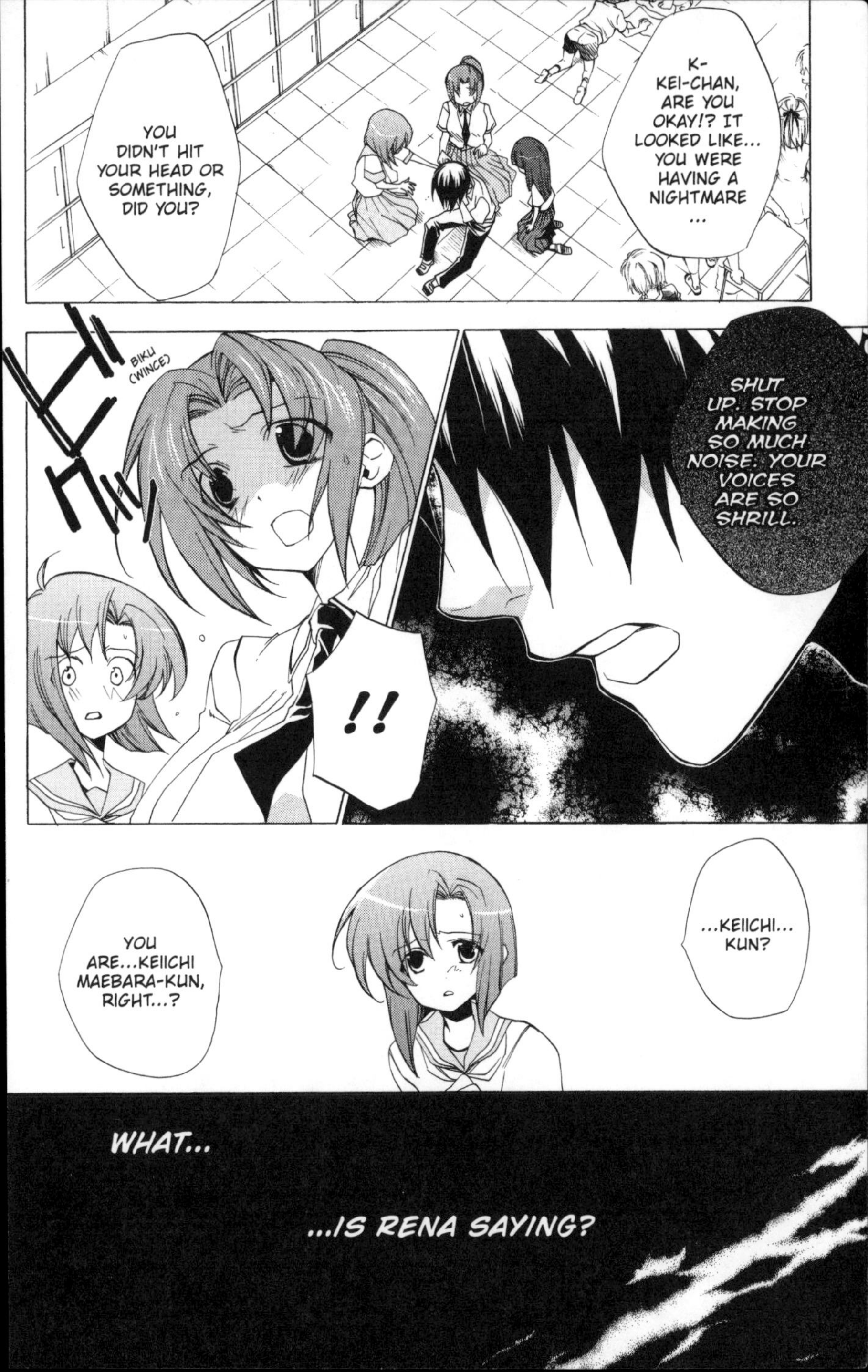
K-KEI-CHAN, ARE YOU OKAY!? IT LOOKED LIKE... YOU WERE HAVING A NIGHTMARE...
YOU DIDN'T HIT YOUR HEAD OR SOMETHING, DID YOU?
SHUT UP. STOP MAKING SO MUCH NOISE. YOUR VOICES ARE SO SHRILL.
BIKU (WINCE)
!!
...KEIICHI... KUN?
YOU ARE...KEIICHI MAEBARA-KUN, RIGHT...?
WHAT...
...IS RENA SAYING?

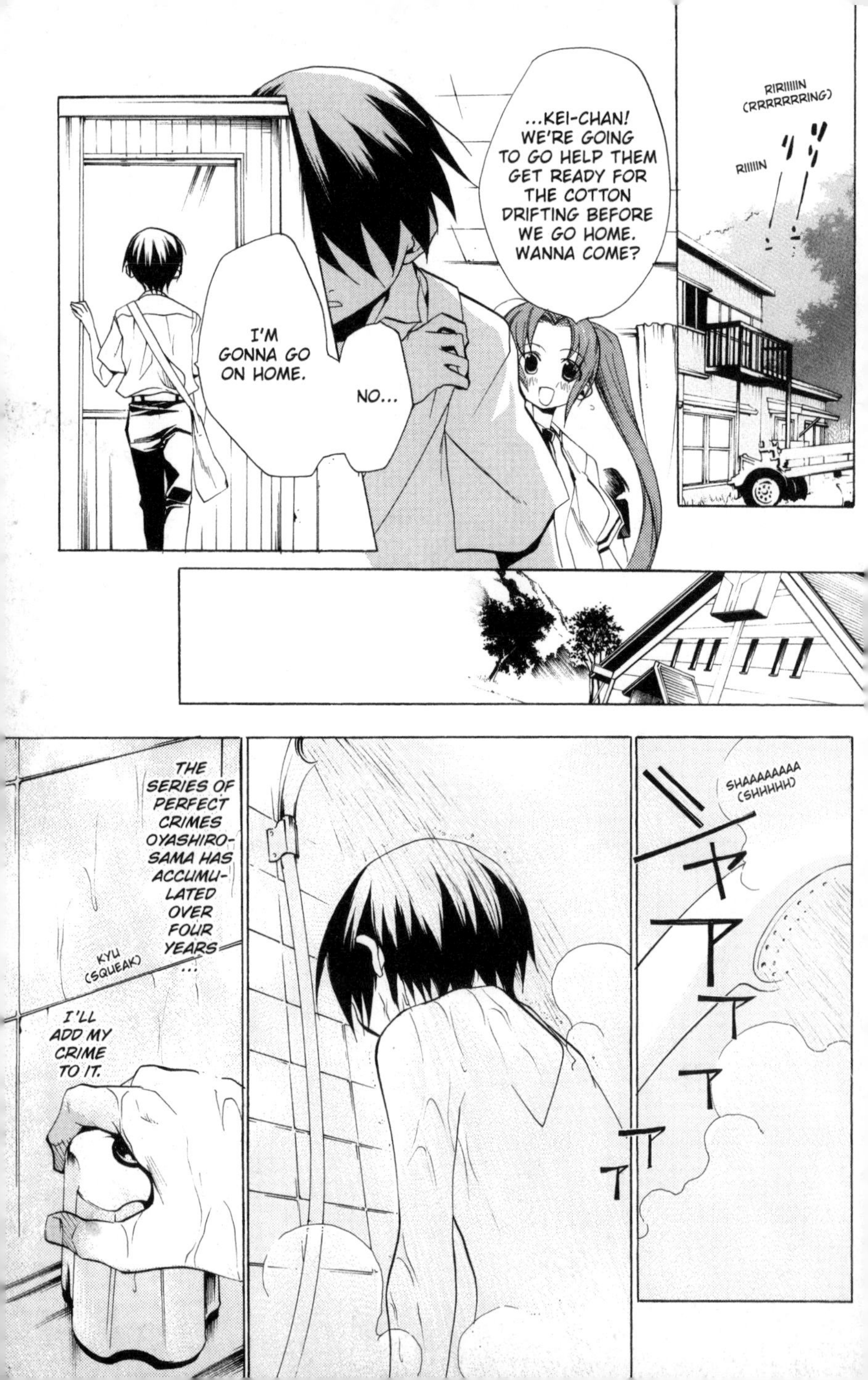
RIRIIIIIN (RRRRRRRRING)
RIIIIIN
...KEI-CHAN! WE'RE GOING TO GO HELP THEM GET READY FOR THE COTTON DRIFTING BEFORE WE GO HOME. WANNA COME?
NO...
I'M GONNA GO ON HOME.
SHAAAAAAAA (SHHHHH)
シャアアアアア
THE SERIES OF PERFECT CRIMES OYASHIRO-SAMA HAS ACCUMULATED OVER FOUR YEARS...
KYU (SQUEAK)
I'LL ADD MY CRIME TO IT.

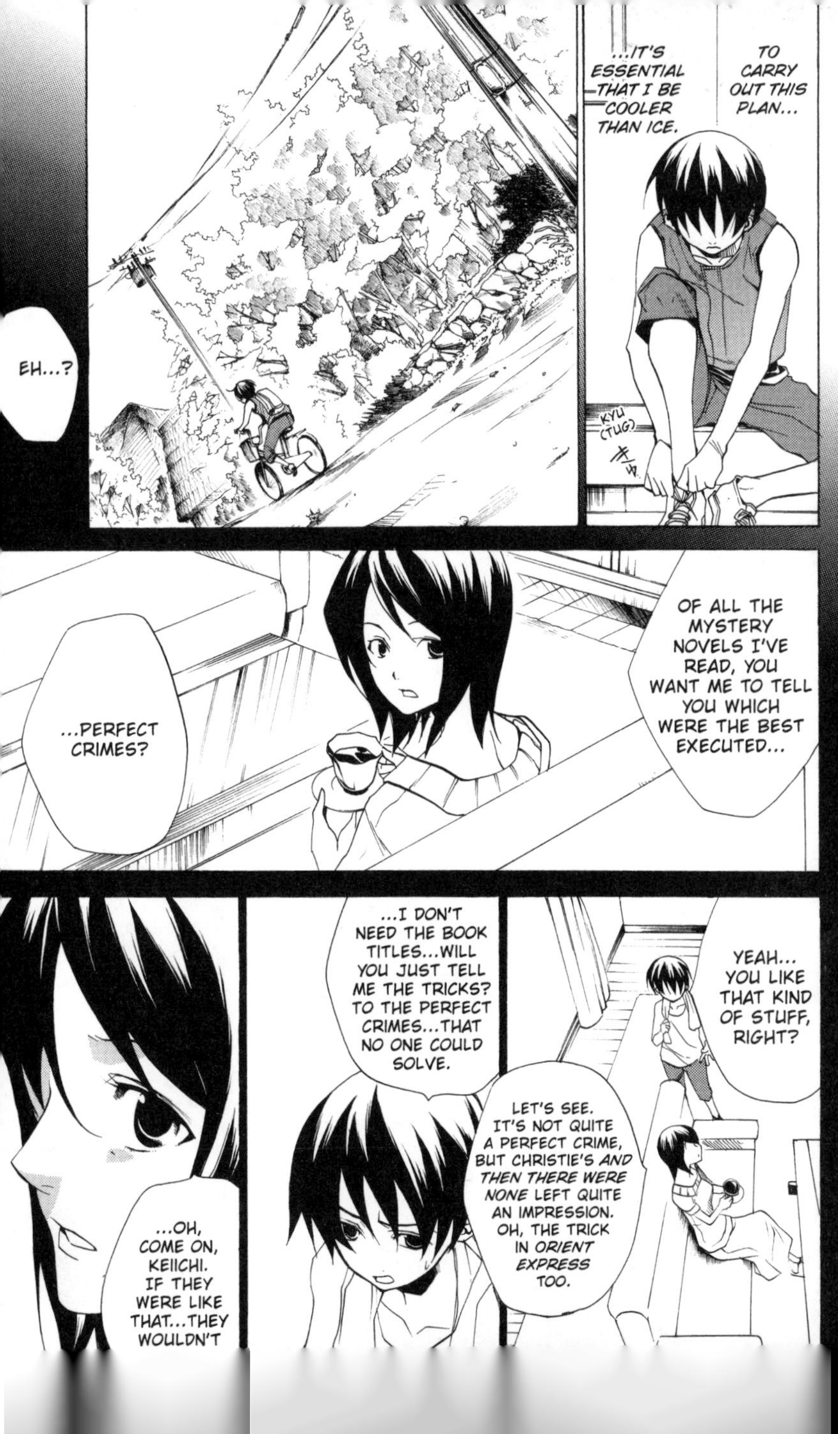
TO CARRY OUT THIS PLAN...
...IT'S ESSENTIAL THAT I BE COOLER THAN ICE.
KYU (TUG)
EH...?
OF ALL THE MYSTERY NOVELS I'VE READ, YOU WANT ME TO TELL YOU WHICH WERE THE BEST EXECUTED...
...PERFECT CRIMES?
YEAH... YOU LIKE THAT KIND OF STUFF, RIGHT?
LET'S SEE. IT'S NOT QUITE A PERFECT CRIME, BUT CHRISTIE'S *AND THEN THERE WERE NONE* LEFT QUITE AN IMPRESSION. OH, THE TRICK IN *ORIENT EXPRESS* TOO.
...I DON'T NEED THE BOOK TITLES...WILL YOU JUST TELL ME THE TRICKS? TO THE PERFECT CRIMES...THAT NO ONE COULD SOLVE.
...OH, COME ON, KEIICHI. IF THEY WERE LIKE THAT...THEY WOULDN'T

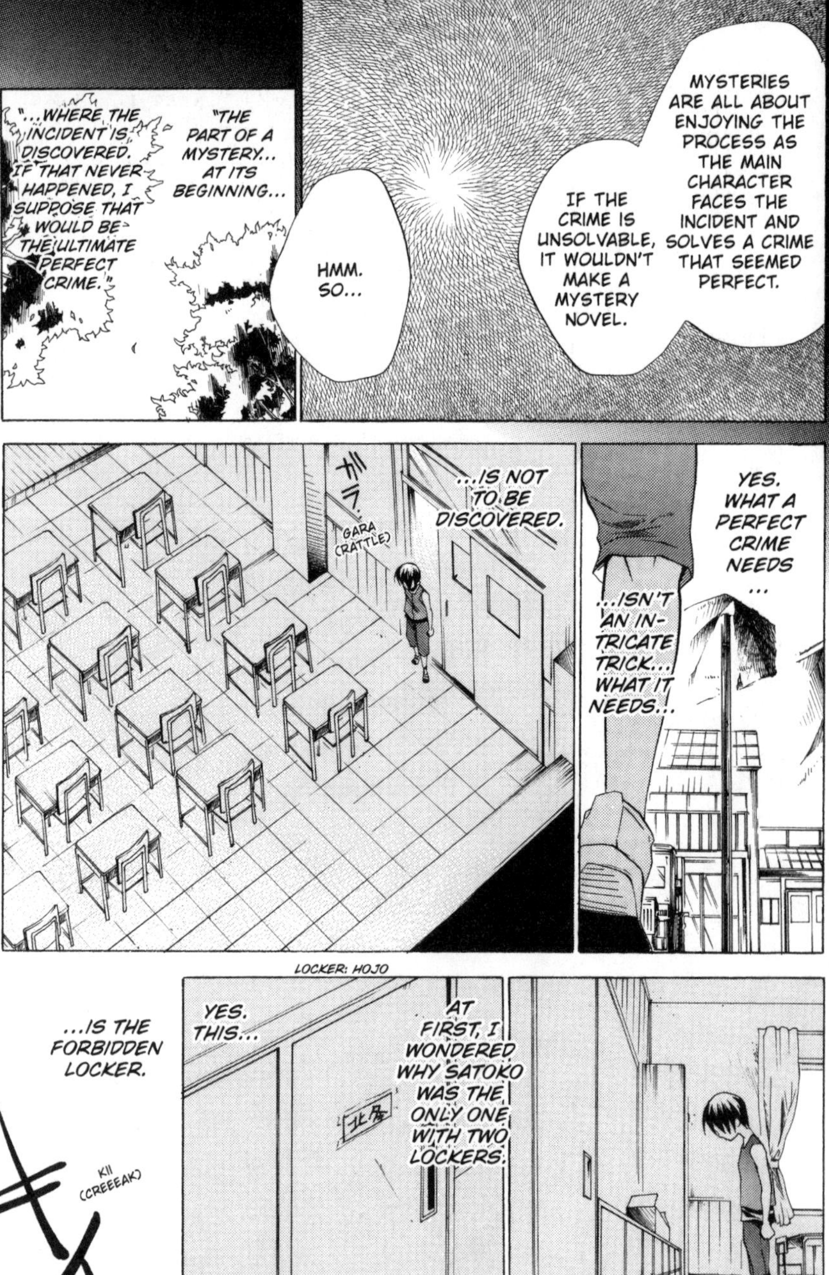
MYSTERIES ARE ALL ABOUT ENJOYING THE PROCESS AS THE MAIN CHARACTER FACES THE INCIDENT AND SOLVES A CRIME THAT SEEMED PERFECT.
IF THE CRIME IS UNSOLVABLE, IT WOULDN'T MAKE A MYSTERY NOVEL.
HMM. SO...
"THE PART OF A MYSTERY... AT ITS BEGINNING...
"...WHERE THE INCIDENT IS DISCOVERED. IF THAT NEVER HAPPENED, I SUPPOSE THAT WOULD BE THE ULTIMATE PERFECT CRIME."
YES. WHAT A PERFECT CRIME NEEDS...
...ISN'T AN INTRICATE TRICK... WHAT IT NEEDS...
...IS NOT TO BE DISCOVERED.
GARA (RATTLE)
LOCKER: HOJO
AT FIRST, I WONDERED WHY SATOKO WAS THE ONLY ONE WITH TWO LOCKERS.
YES. THIS...
...IS THE FORBIDDEN LOCKER.
KII (CREEEAK)

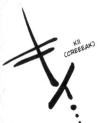

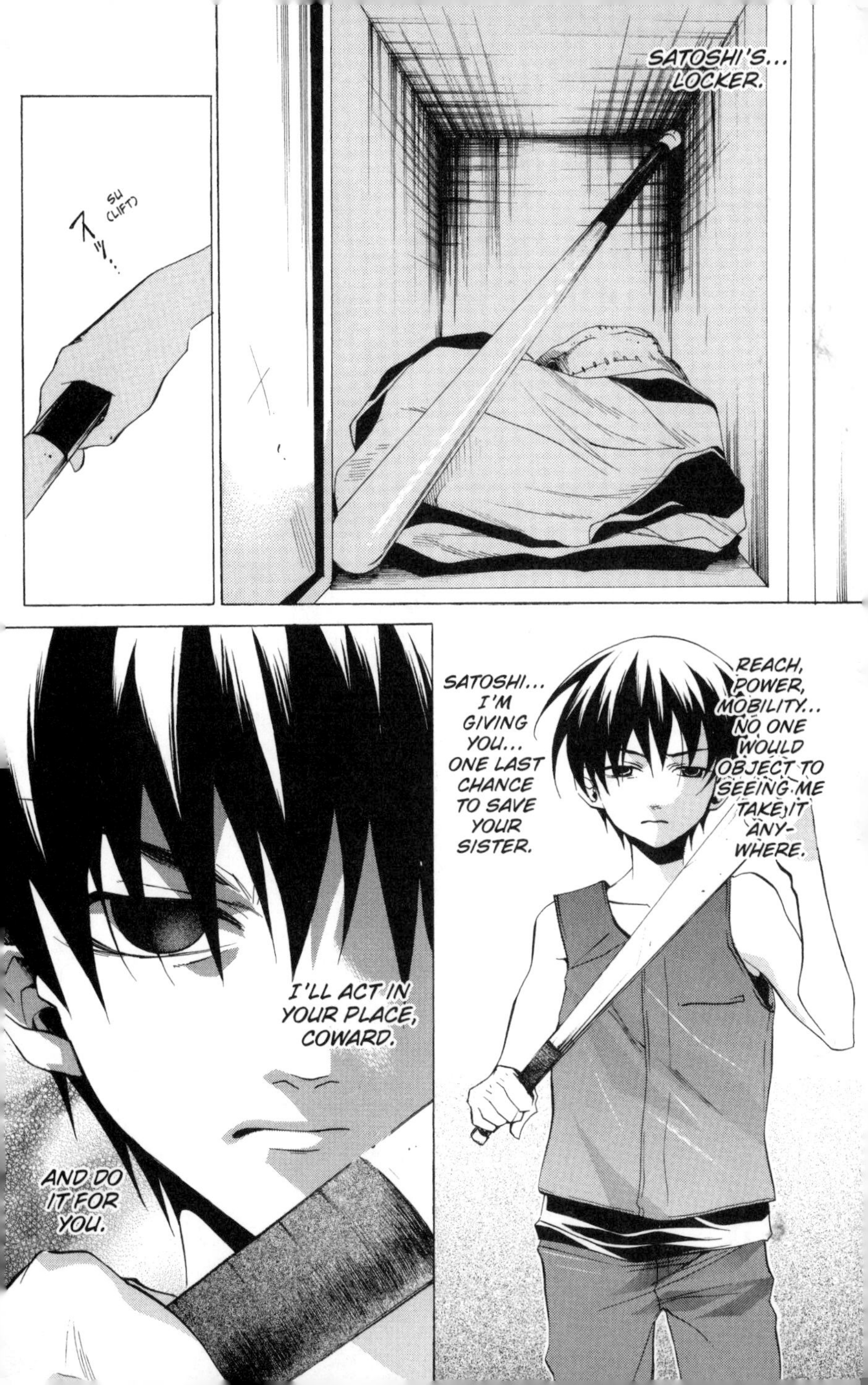
SATOSHI'S... LOCKER.
スッ…
SU (LIFT)
REACH, POWER, MOBILITY... NO ONE WOULD OBJECT TO SEEING ME TAKE IT ANYWHERE.
SATOSHI... I'M GIVING YOU... ONE LAST CHANCE TO SAVE YOUR SISTER.
I'LL ACT IN YOUR PLACE, COWARD.
AND DO IT FOR YOU.

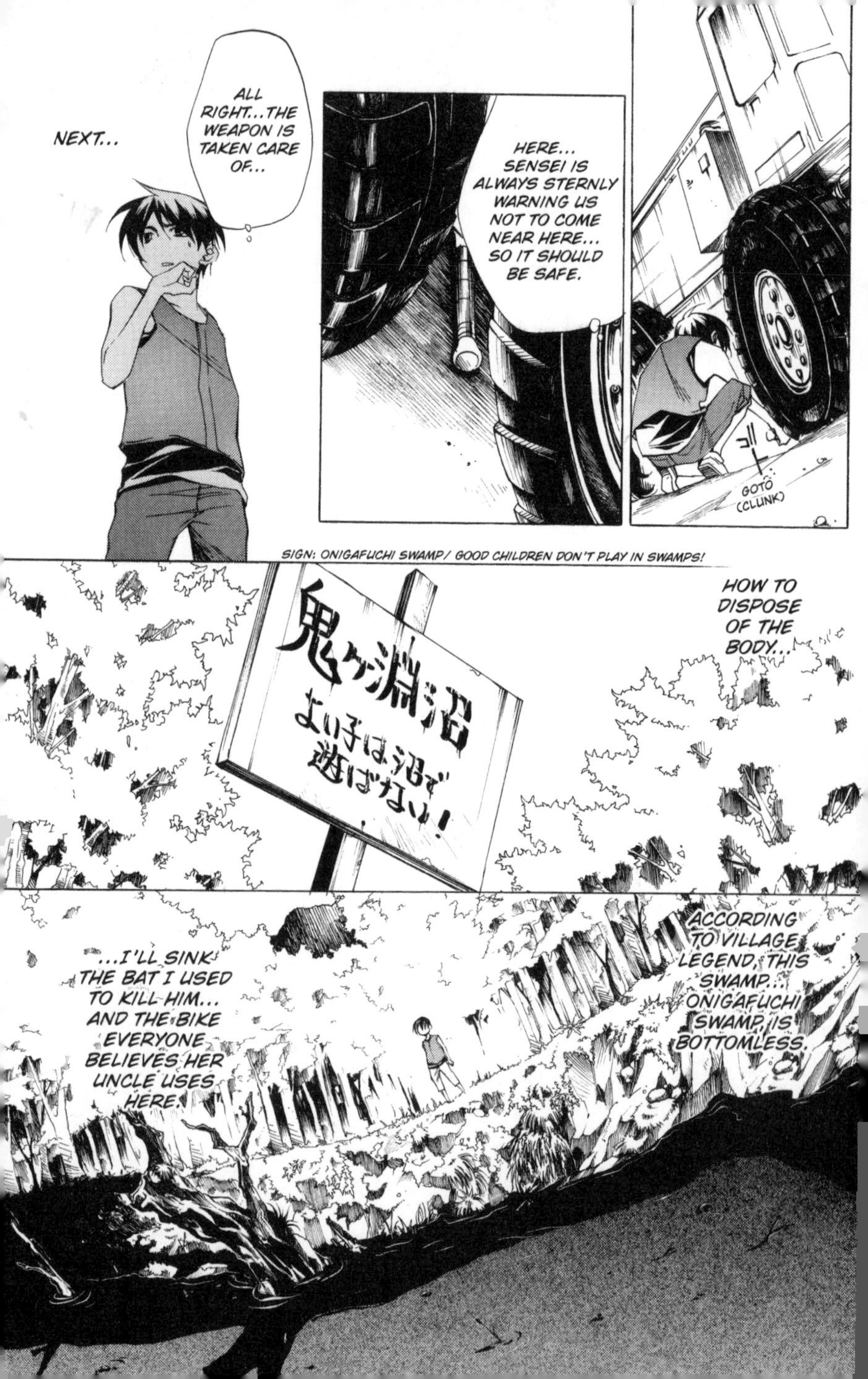
GOTO (CLUNK)
HERE... SENSEI IS ALWAYS STERNLY WARNING US NOT TO COME NEAR HERE... SO IT SHOULD BE SAFE.
ALL RIGHT...THE WEAPON IS TAKEN CARE OF...
NEXT...
HOW TO DISPOSE OF THE BODY...
鬼ヶ淵沼
よい子は沼で遊ばない!
SIGN: ONIGAFUCHI SWAMP/ GOOD CHILDREN DON'T PLAY IN SWAMPS!
ACCORDING TO VILLAGE LEGEND, THIS SWAMP... ONIGAFUCHI SWAMP, IS BOTTOMLESS.
...I'LL SINK THE BAT I USED TO KILL HIM... AND THE BIKE EVERYONE BELIEVES HER UNCLE USES HERE.

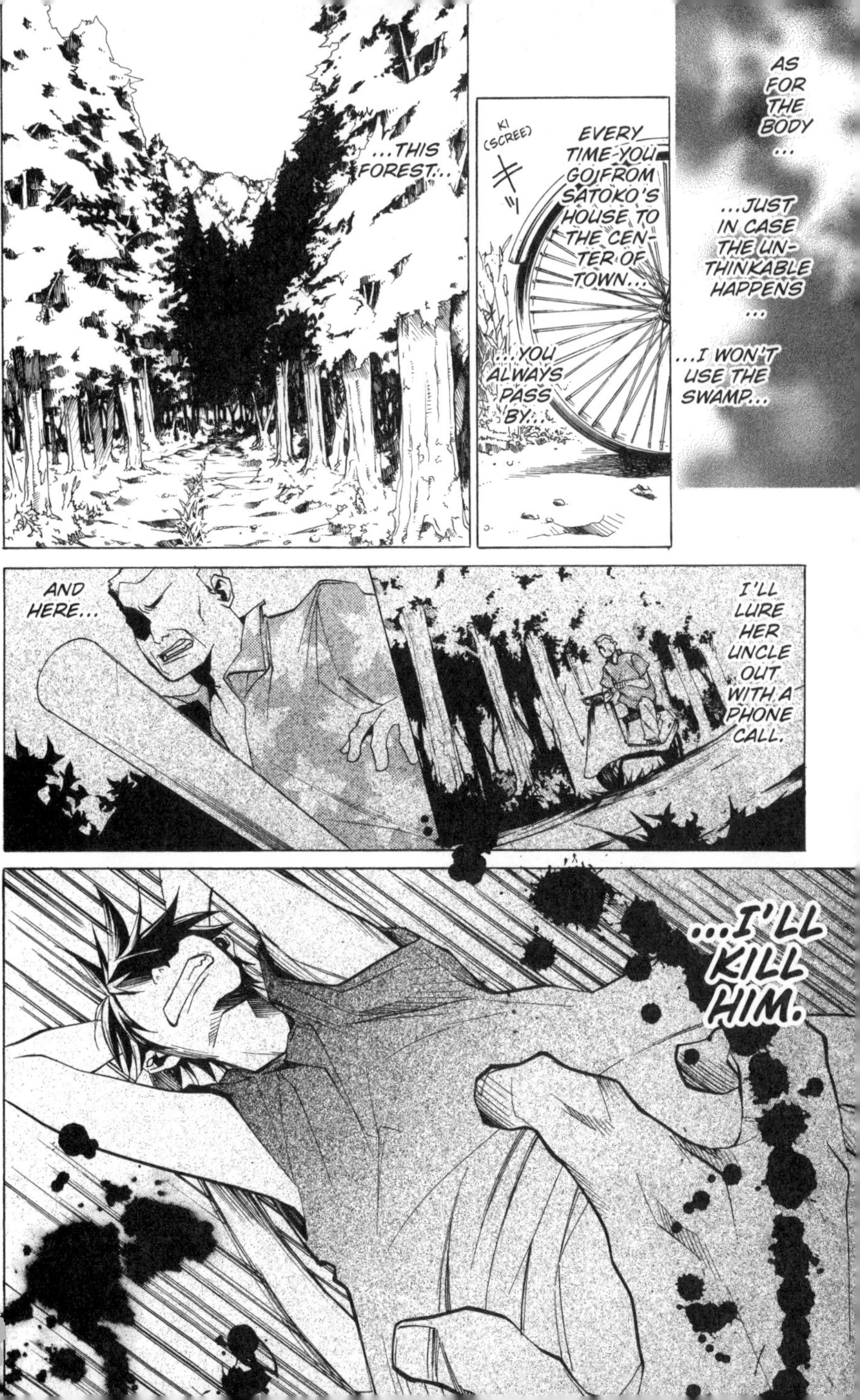
AS FOR THE BODY...
...JUST IN CASE THE UNTHINKABLE HAPPENS...
...I WON'T USE THE SWAMP...
KI (SCREE)
EVERY TIME YOU GO FROM SATOKO'S HOUSE TO THE CENTER OF TOWN...
...YOU ALWAYS PASS BY...
...THIS FOREST...
AND HERE...
I'LL LURE HER UNCLE OUT WITH A PHONE CALL.
...I'LL KILL HIM.

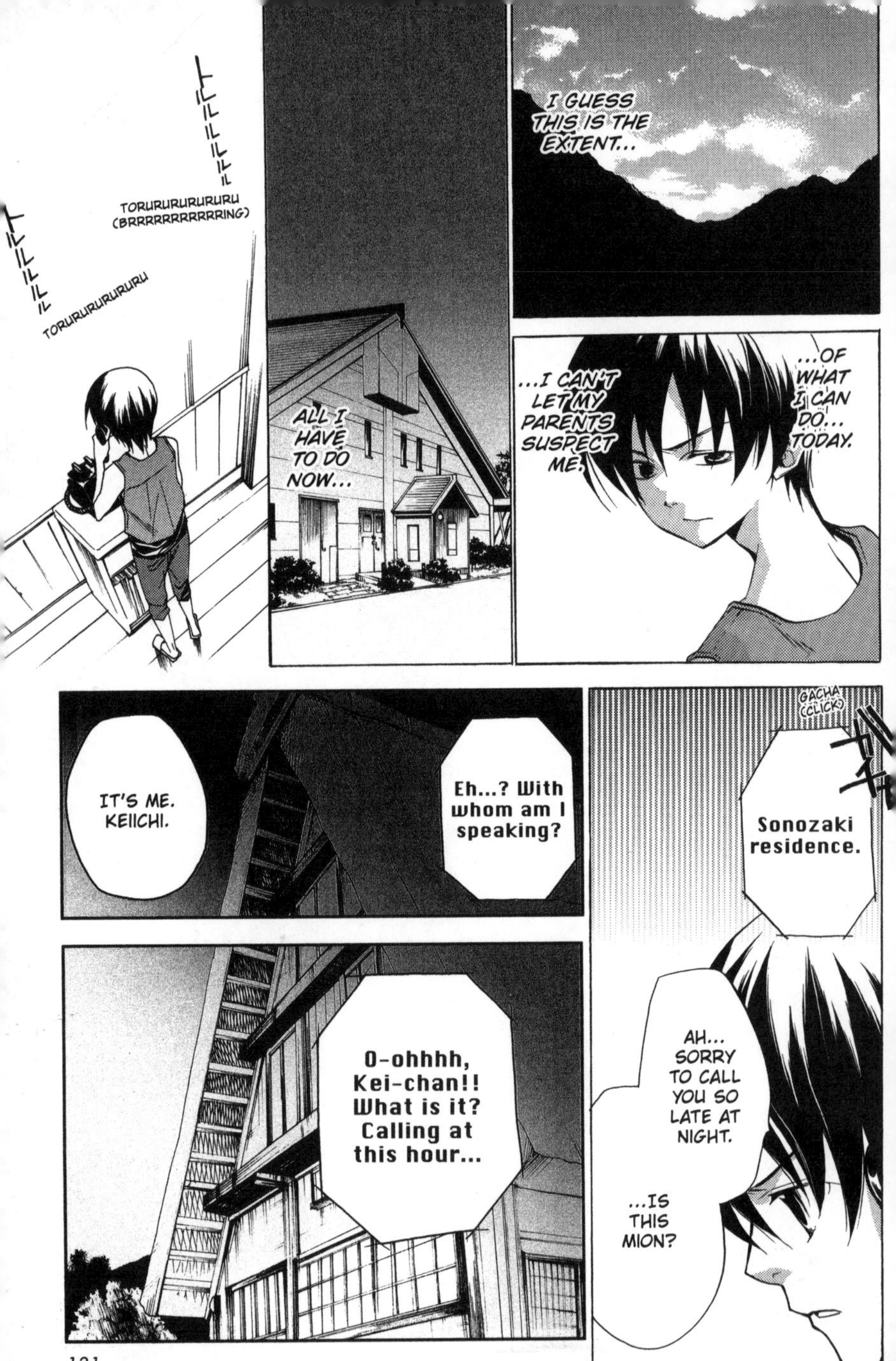
I GUESS THIS IS THE EXTENT...
...OF WHAT I CAN DO... TODAY.
...I CAN'T LET MY PARENTS SUSPECT ME.
ALL I HAVE TO DO NOW...
TORURURURURURU (BRRRRRRRRRRRING)
TORURURURURU
GACHA (CLICK)
Sonozaki residence.
AH... SORRY TO CALL YOU SO LATE AT NIGHT.
...IS THIS MION?
Eh...? With whom am I speaking?
IT'S ME. KEIICHI.
O-ohhhh, Kei-chan!! What is it? Calling at this hour...

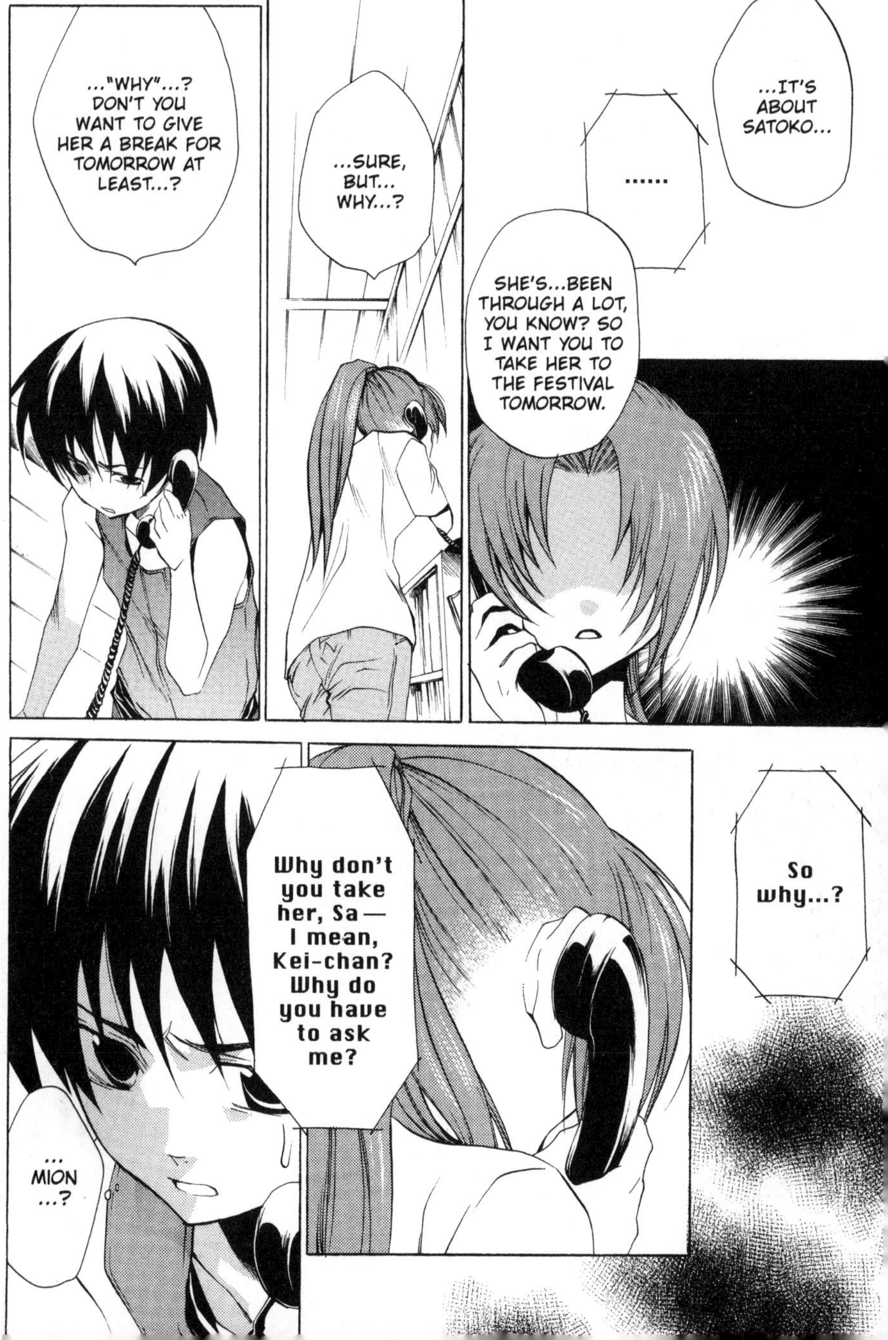
...IT'S ABOUT SATOKO...
......
SHE'S...BEEN THROUGH A LOT, YOU KNOW? SO I WANT YOU TO TAKE HER TO THE FESTIVAL TOMORROW.
...SURE, BUT... WHY...?
..."WHY"...? DON'T YOU WANT TO GIVE HER A BREAK FOR TOMORROW AT LEAST...?
So why...?
Why don't you take her, Sa— I mean, Kei-chan? Why do you have to ask me?
... MION ...?

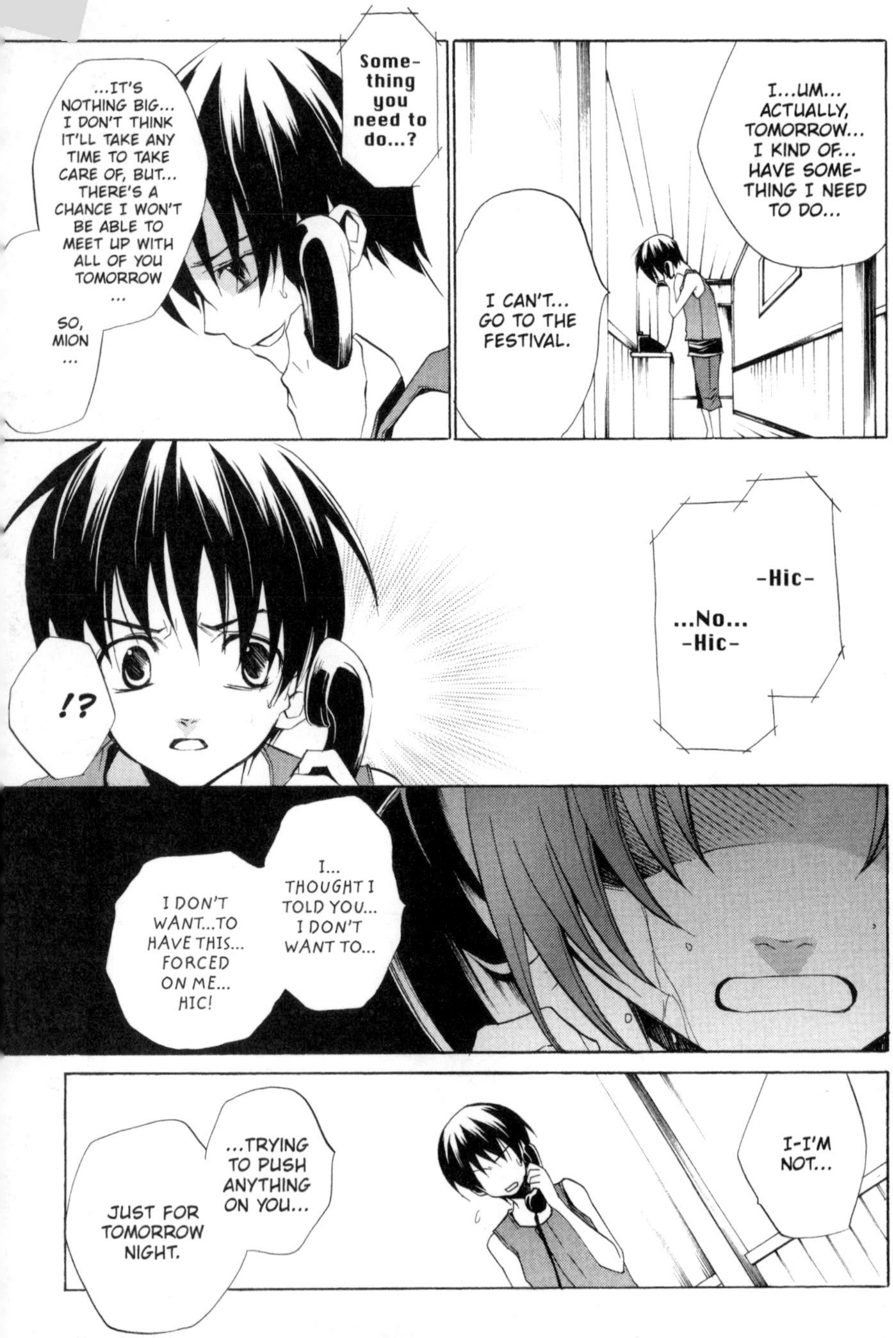
I...UM... ACTUALLY, TOMORROW... I KIND OF... HAVE SOME-THING I NEED TO DO...
I CAN'T... GO TO THE FESTIVAL.
Some-thing you need to do...?
...IT'S NOTHING BIG... I DON'T THINK IT'LL TAKE ANY TIME TO TAKE CARE OF, BUT... THERE'S A CHANCE I WON'T BE ABLE TO MEET UP WITH ALL OF YOU TOMORROW ...
SO, MION ...
-Hic- ...No... -Hic-
!?
I... THOUGHT I TOLD YOU... I DON'T WANT TO...
I DON'T WANT...TO HAVE THIS... FORCED ON ME... HIC!
I-I'M NOT...
...TRYING TO PUSH ANYTHING ON YOU...
JUST FOR TOMORROW NIGHT.

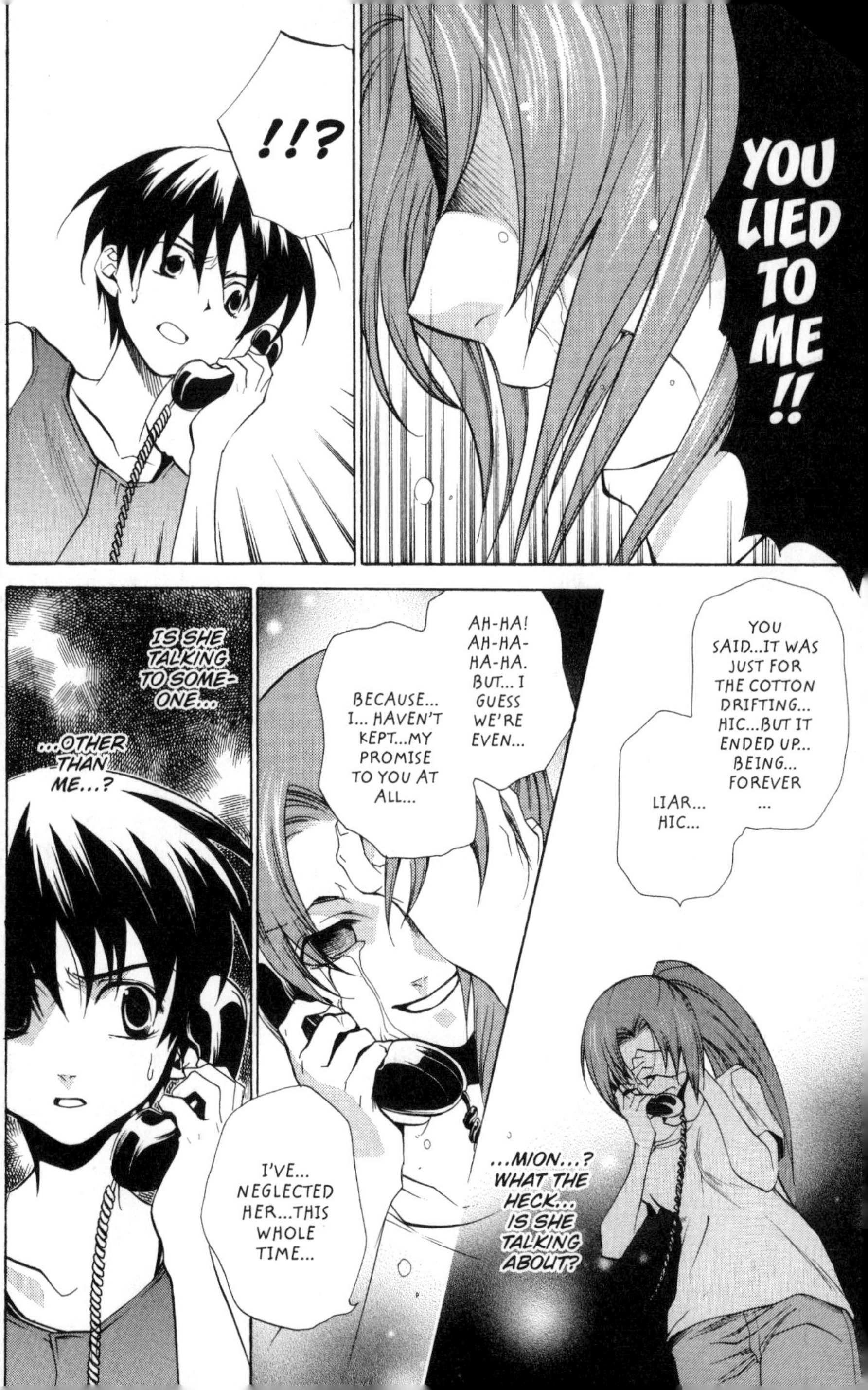
YOU LIED TO ME!!
!!?
YOU SAID...IT WAS JUST FOR THE COTTON DRIFTING... HIC...BUT IT ENDED UP... BEING... FOREVER ...
LIAR... HIC...
...MION...? WHAT THE HECK... IS SHE TALKING ABOUT?
AH-HA! AH-HA-HA-HA. BUT... I GUESS WE'RE EVEN...
BECAUSE... I... HAVEN'T KEPT...MY PROMISE TO YOU AT ALL...
I'VE... NEGLECTED HER...THIS WHOLE TIME...
IS SHE TALKING TO SOME-ONE...
...OTHER THAN ME...?

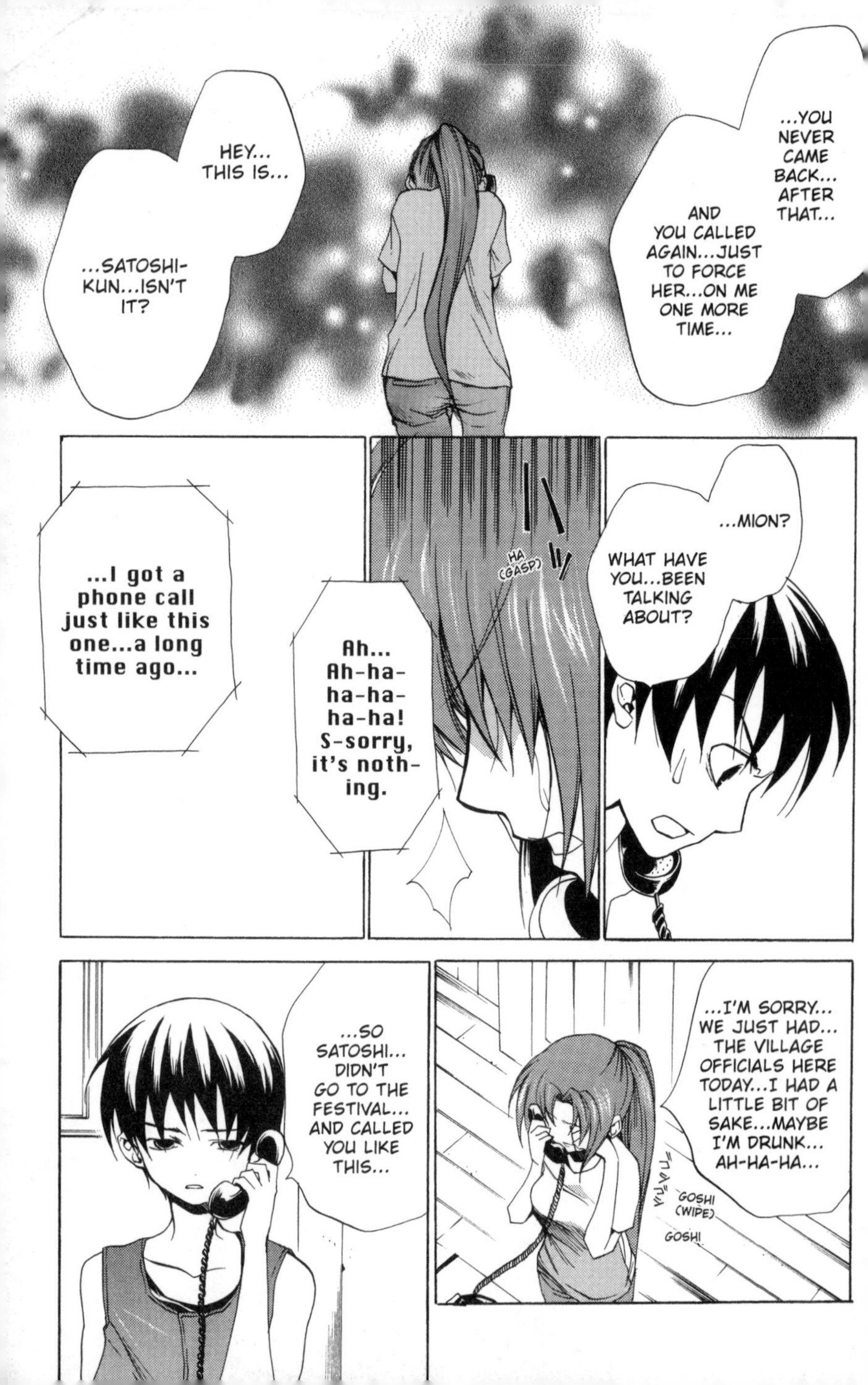
...YOU NEVER CAME BACK... AFTER THAT...
AND YOU CALLED AGAIN...JUST TO FORCE HER...ON ME ONE MORE TIME...
HEY... THIS IS...
...SATOSHI-KUN...ISN'T IT?
...MION?
WHAT HAVE YOU...BEEN TALKING ABOUT?
HA (GASP)
Ah... Ah-ha-ha-ha-ha-ha! S-sorry, it's nothing.
...I got a phone call just like this one...a long time ago...
...I'M SORRY... WE JUST HAD... THE VILLAGE OFFICIALS HERE TODAY...I HAD A LITTLE BIT OF SAKE...MAYBE I'M DRUNK... AH-HA-HA...
GOSHI (WIPE)
GOSHI
...SO SATOSHI... DIDN'T GO TO THE FESTIVAL... AND CALLED YOU LIKE THIS...

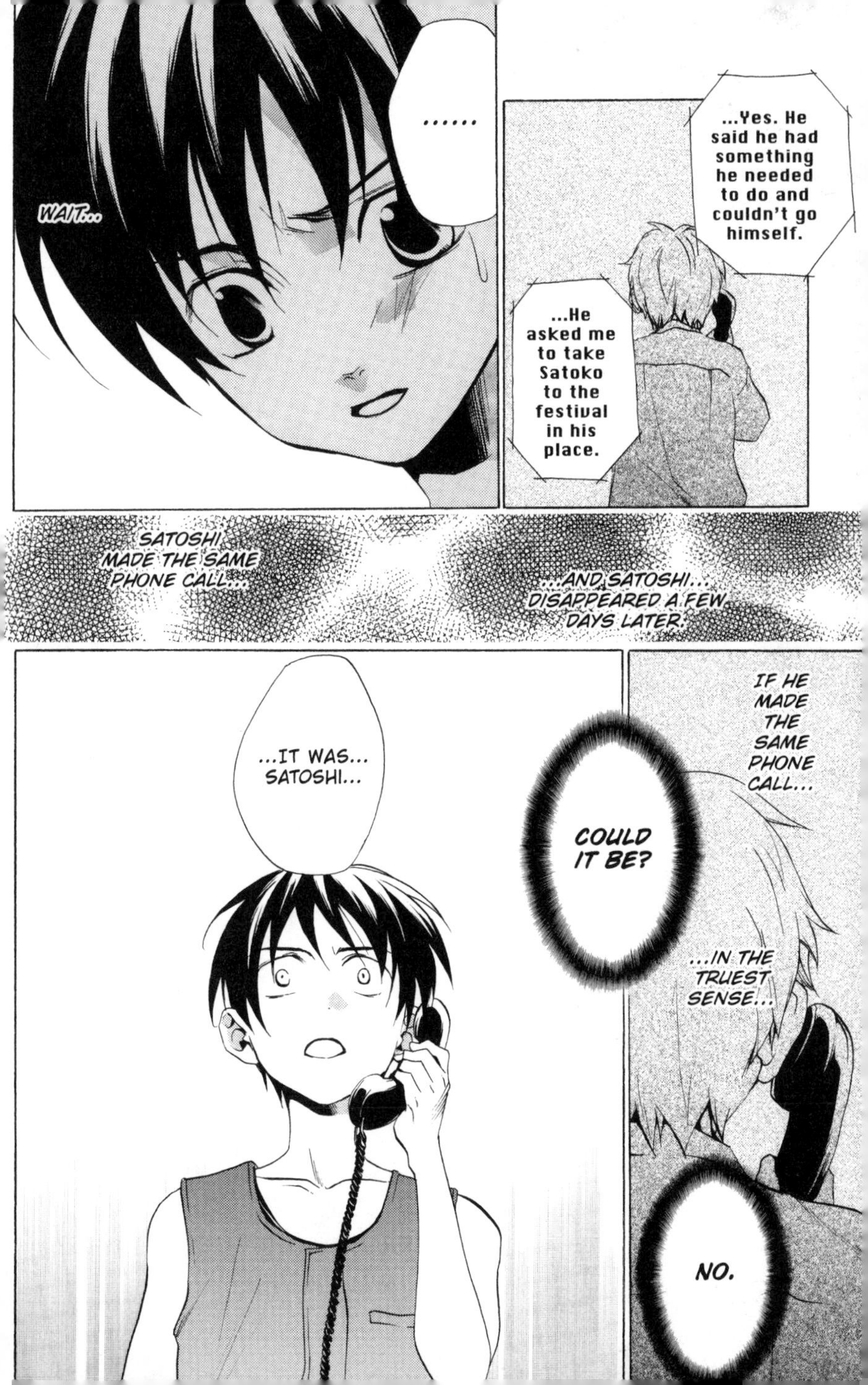
...Yes. He said he had something he needed to do and couldn't go himself.
...He asked me to take Satoko to the festival in his place.
......
WAIT...
SATOSHI MADE THE SAME PHONE CALL...
...AND SATOSHI... DISAPPEARED A FEW DAYS LATER.
IF HE MADE THE SAME PHONE CALL...
COULD IT BE?
...IN THE TRUEST SENSE...
NO.
...IT WAS... SATOSHI...

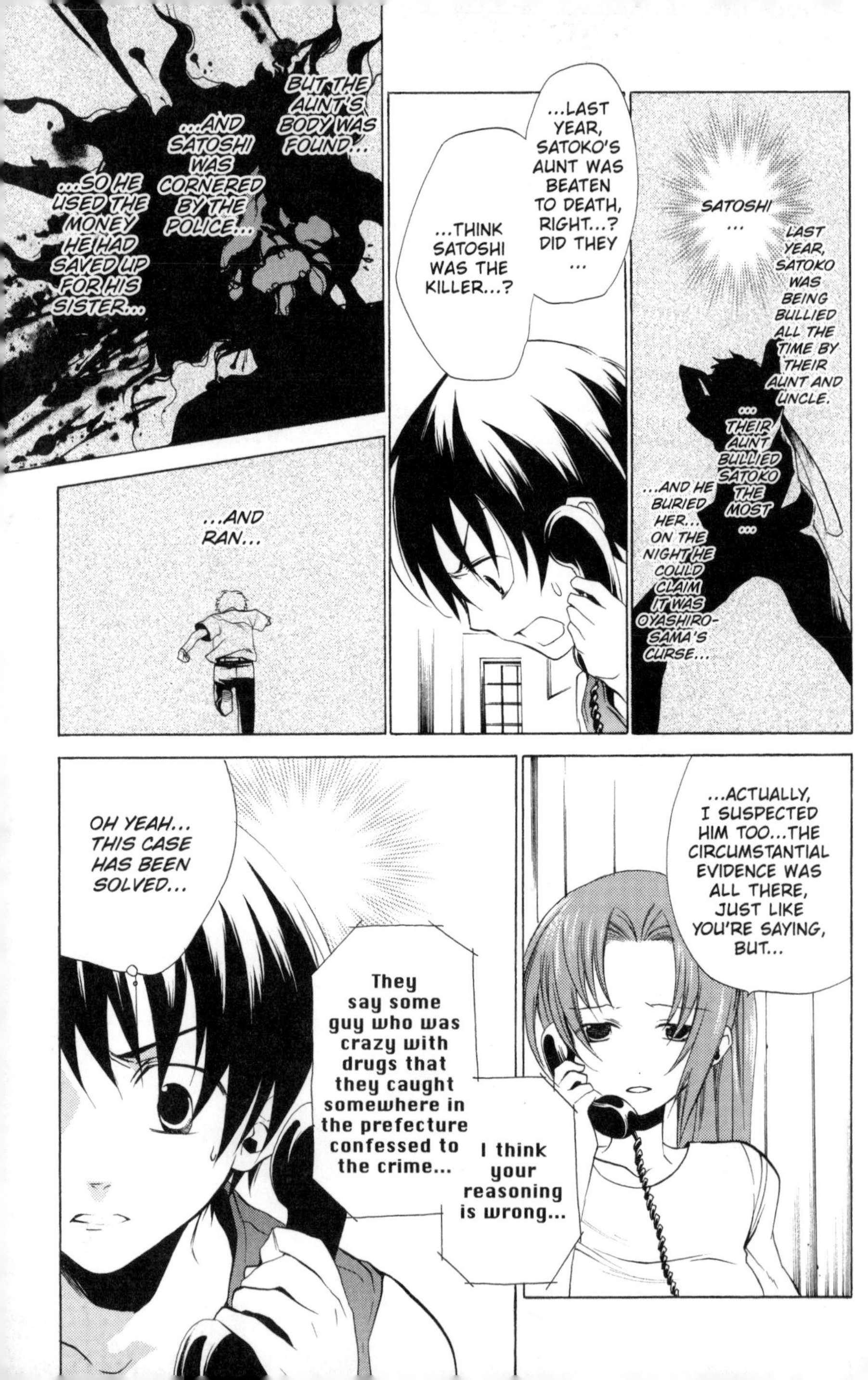
SATOSHI ...
LAST YEAR, SATOKO WAS BEING BULLIED ALL THE TIME BY THEIR AUNT AND UNCLE.
...THEIR AUNT BULLIED SATOKO THE MOST ...
...AND HE BURIED HER... ON THE NIGHT HE COULD CLAIM IT WAS OYASHIRO-SAMA'S CURSE...
...LAST YEAR, SATOKO'S AUNT WAS BEATEN TO DEATH, RIGHT...? DID THEY ...
...THINK SATOSHI WAS THE KILLER...?
BUT THE AUNT'S BODY WAS FOUND...
...AND SATOSHI WAS CORNERED BY THE POLICE...
...SO HE USED THE MONEY HE HAD SAVED UP FOR HIS SISTER...
...AND RAN...
...ACTUALLY, I SUSPECTED HIM TOO...THE CIRCUMSTANTIAL EVIDENCE WAS ALL THERE, JUST LIKE YOU'RE SAYING, BUT...
I think your reasoning is wrong...
They say some guy who was crazy with drugs that they caught somewhere in the prefecture confessed to the crime...
OH YEAH... THIS CASE HAS BEEN SOLVED...

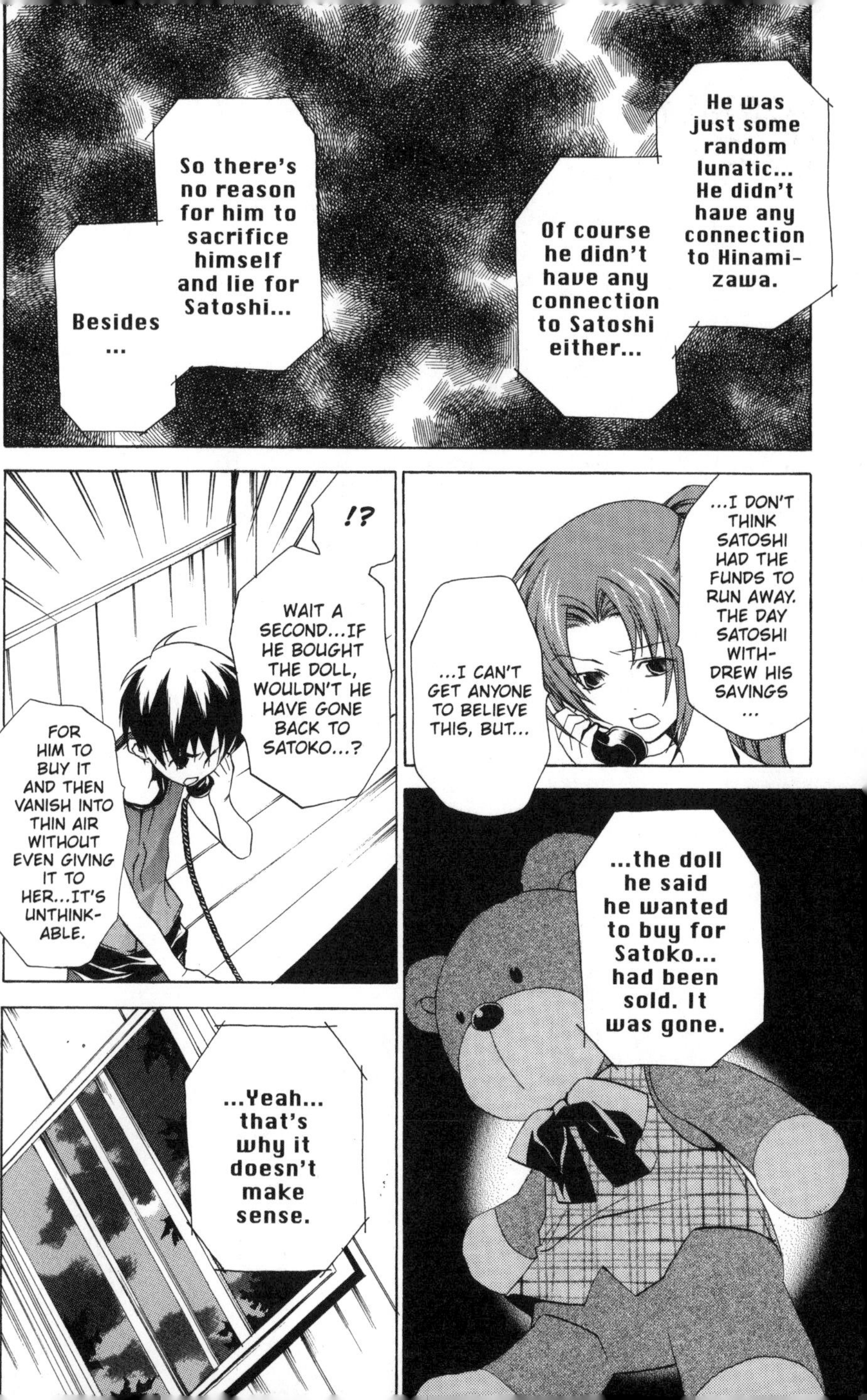
He was just some random lunatic... He didn't have any connection to Hinami-zawa.
Of course he didn't have any connection to Satoshi either...
So there's no reason for him to sacrifice himself and lie for Satoshi...
Besides...
...I DON'T THINK SATOSHI HAD THE FUNDS TO RUN AWAY. THE DAY SATOSHI WITH-DREW HIS SAVINGS...
...I CAN'T GET ANYONE TO BELIEVE THIS, BUT...
...the doll he said he wanted to buy for Satoko... had been sold. It was gone.
!?
WAIT A SECOND...IF HE BOUGHT THE DOLL, WOULDN'T HE HAVE GONE BACK TO SATOKO...?
FOR HIM TO BUY IT AND THEN VANISH INTO THIN AIR WITHOUT EVEN GIVING IT TO HER...IT'S UNTHINK-ABLE.
...Yeah... that's why it doesn't make sense.

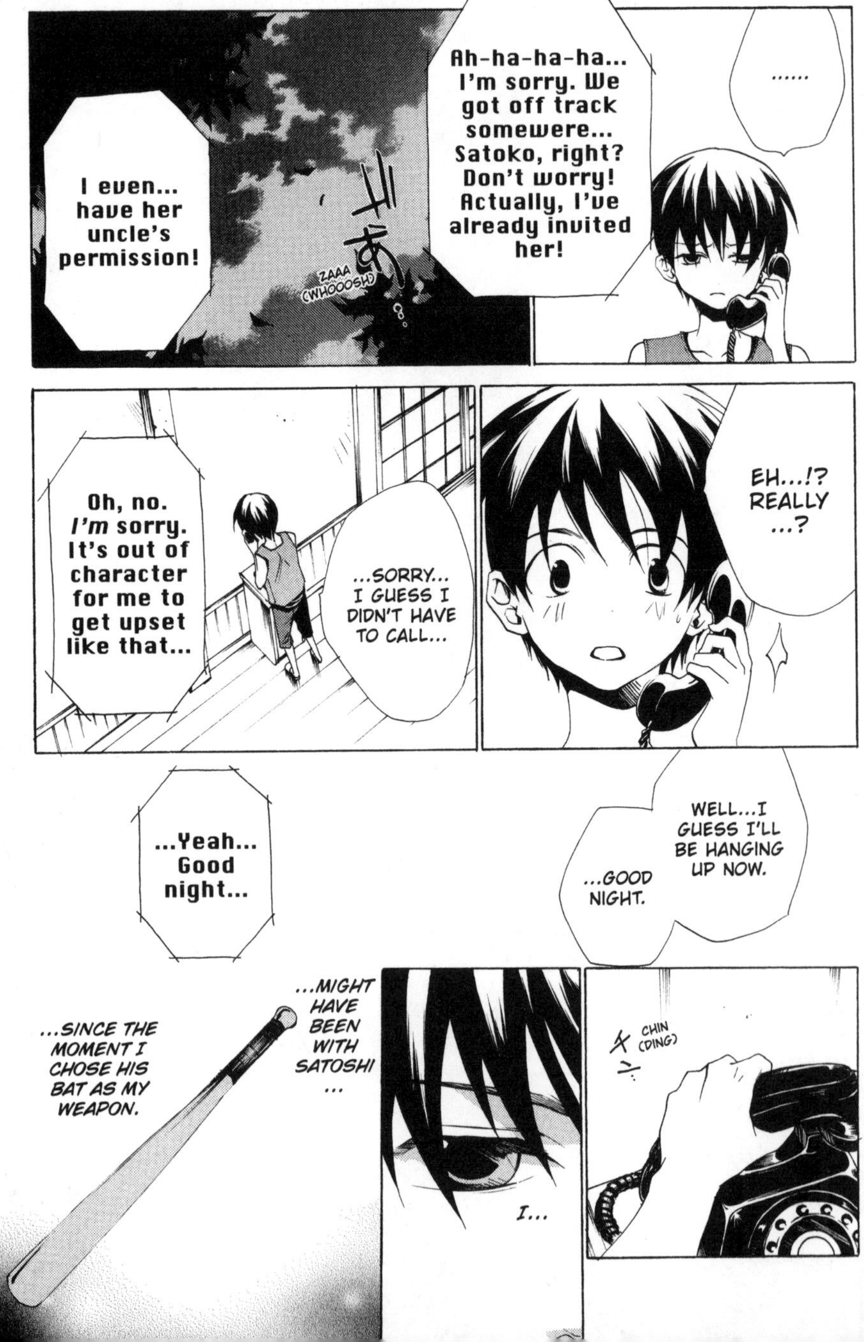
......
Ah-ha-ha-ha... I'm sorry. We got off track somewere... Satoko, right? Don't worry! Actually, I've already invited her!
I even... have her uncle's permission!
ZAAA (WHOOOSH)
EH...!? REALLY ...?
...SORRY... I GUESS I DIDN'T HAVE TO CALL...
Oh, no. *I'm* sorry. It's out of character for me to get upset like that...
WELL...I GUESS I'LL BE HANGING UP NOW.
...GOOD NIGHT.
...Yeah... Good night...
CHIN (DING)
I...
...MIGHT HAVE BEEN WITH SATOSHI ...
...SINCE THE MOMENT I CHOSE HIS BAT AS MY WEAPON.

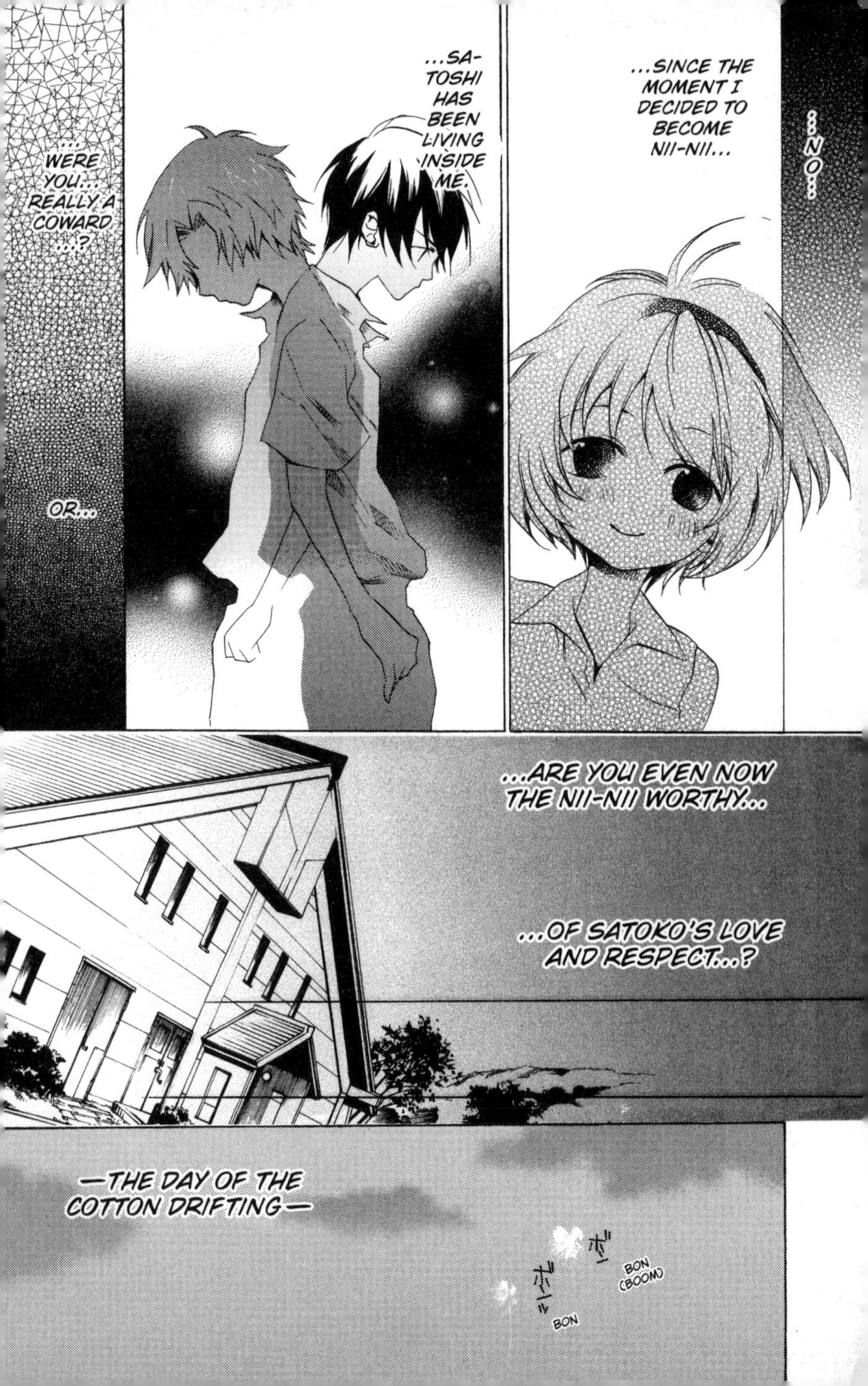
...NO...
...SINCE THE MOMENT I DECIDED TO BECOME NII-NII...
...SA-TOSHI HAS BEEN LIVING INSIDE ME.
...WERE YOU... REALLY A COWARD ...?
OR...
...ARE YOU EVEN NOW THE NII-NII WORTHY...
...OF SATOKO'S LOVE AND RESPECT...?
—THE DAY OF THE COTTON DRIFTING—
BON (BOOM)
BON

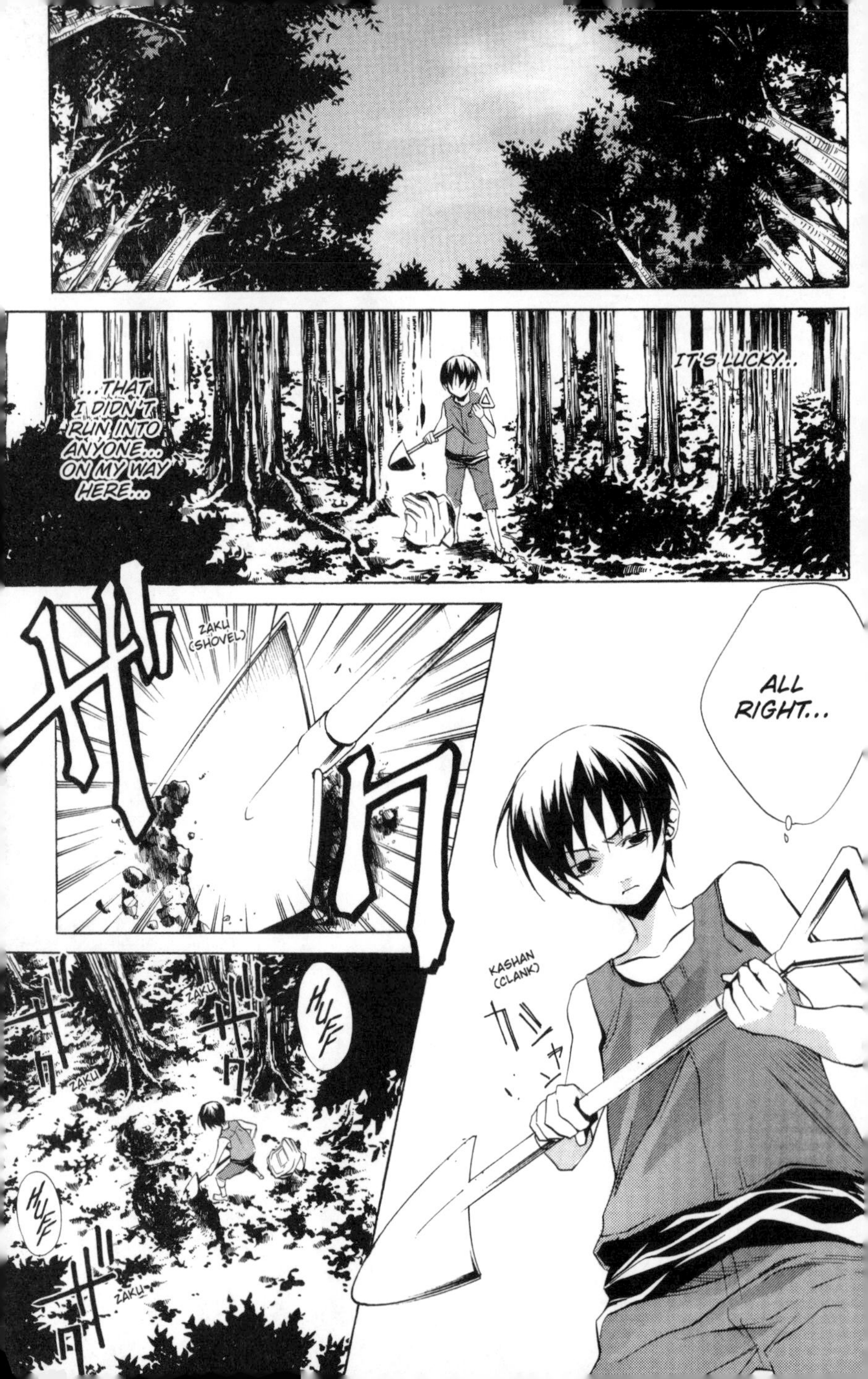
IT'S LUCKY...
...THAT I DIDN'T RUN INTO ANYONE... ON MY WAY HERE...
ALL RIGHT...
KASHAN (CLANK)
ZAKU (SHOVEL)
HUFF
ZAKU
ZAKU
HUFF
ZAKU

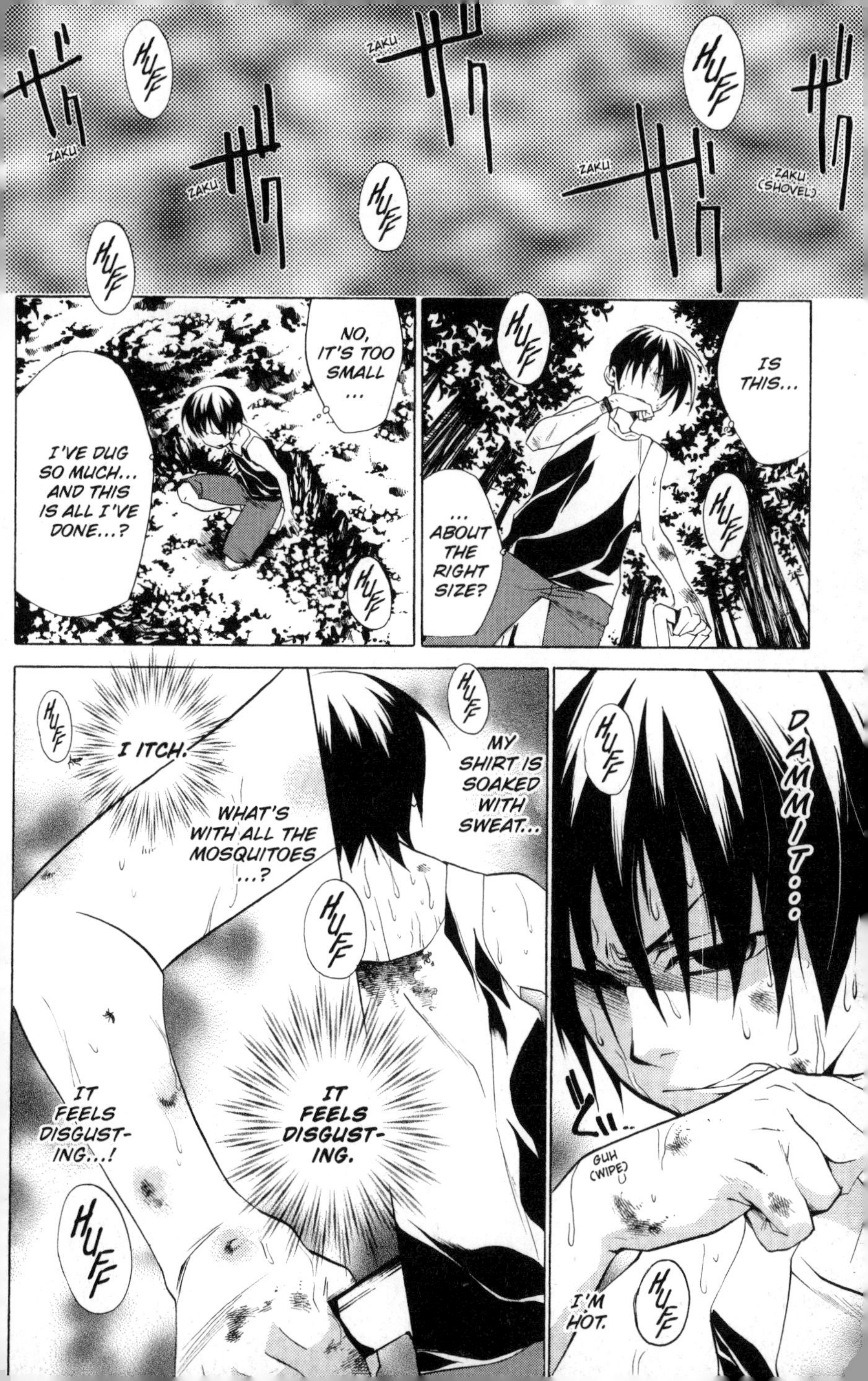
ZAKU (SHOVEL)
HUFF
ZAKU
ZAKU
HUFF
HUFF
ZAKU
ZAKU
HUFF
HUFF
IS THIS...
... ABOUT THE RIGHT SIZE?
HUFF
NO, IT'S TOO SMALL ...
I'VE DUG SO MUCH... AND THIS IS ALL I'VE DONE...?
HUFF
DAMMITOOO
HUFF
GUH (WIPE)
HUFF
I'M HOT.
HUFF
MY SHIRT IS SOAKED WITH SWEAT...
I ITCH.
HUFF
WHAT'S WITH ALL THE MOSQUITOES ...?
HUFF
IT FEELS DISGUSTING.
IT FEELS DISGUSTING...!
HUFF

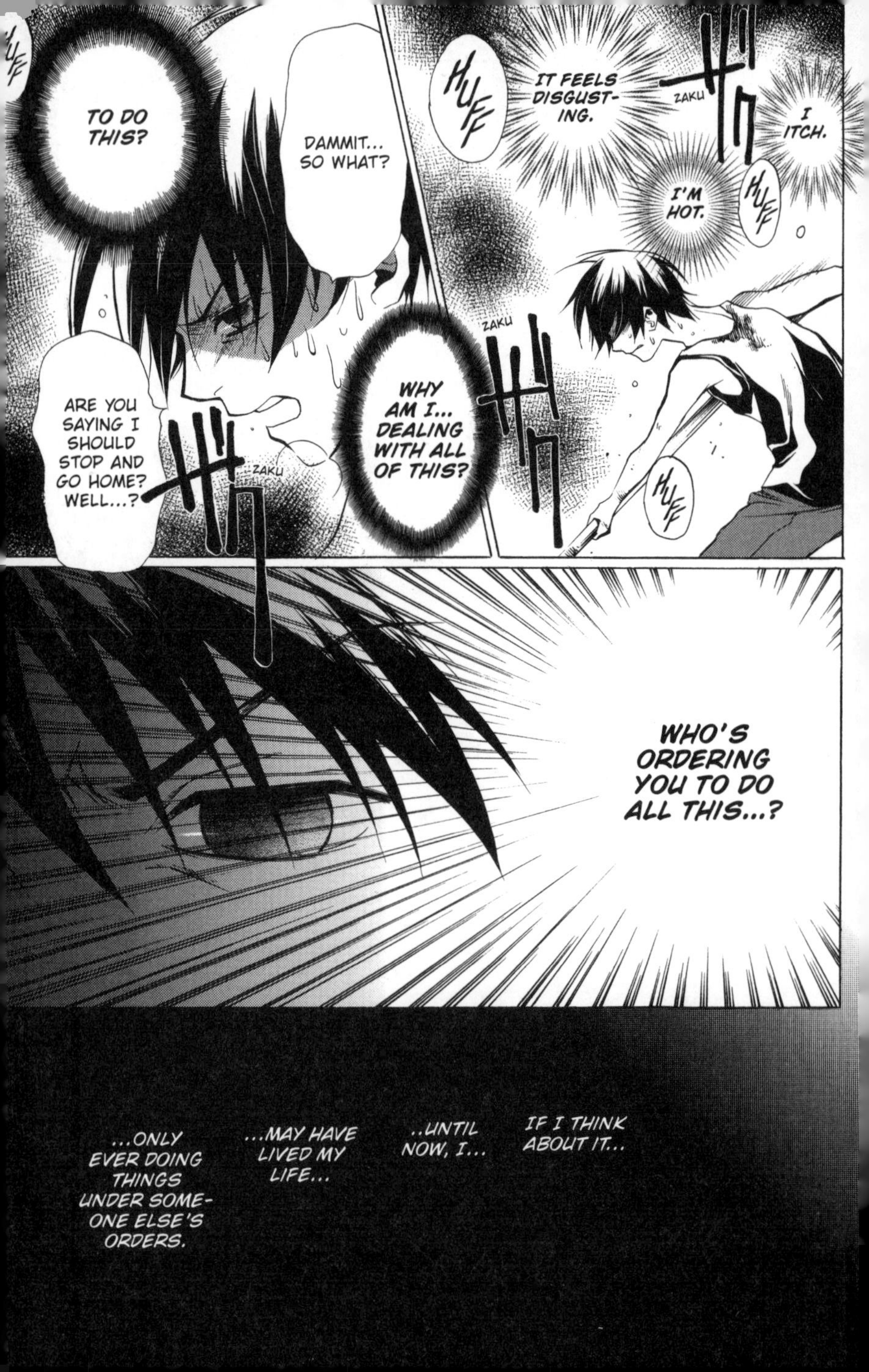
I ITCH.
ZAKU
IT FEELS DISGUST-ING.
HUFF
I'M HOT.
HUFF
ZAKU
HUFF
WHY AM I... DEALING WITH ALL OF THIS?
DAMMIT... SO WHAT?
TO DO THIS?
HUFF
ARE YOU SAYING I SHOULD STOP AND GO HOME? WELL...?
ZAKU
WHO'S ORDERING YOU TO DO ALL THIS...?
IF I THINK ABOUT IT...
..UNTIL NOW, I...
...MAY HAVE LIVED MY LIFE...
...ONLY EVER DOING THINGS UNDER SOME-ONE ELSE'S ORDERS.

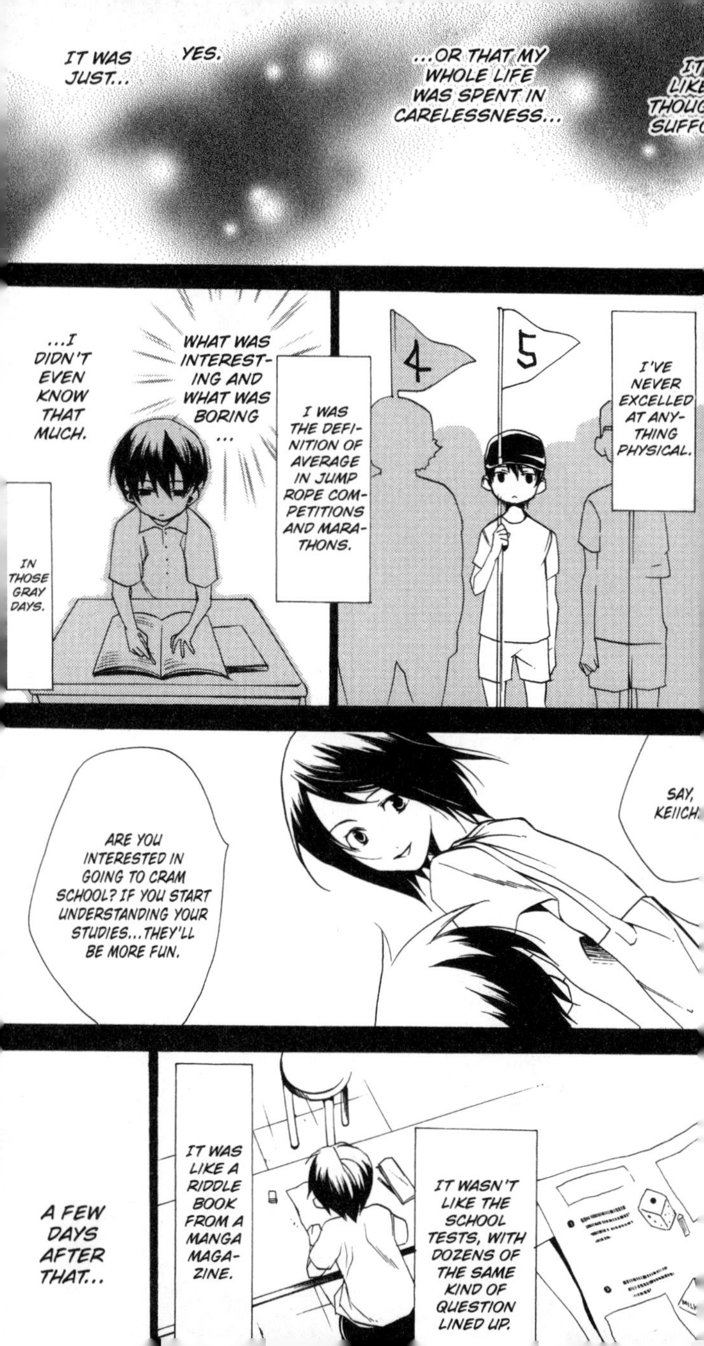

...OR THAT MY WHOLE LIFE WAS SPENT IN CARELESSNESS...
YES.
IT WAS JUST...
I'VE NEVER EXCELLED AT ANYTHING PHYSICAL.
I WAS THE DEFINITION OF AVERAGE IN JUMP ROPE COMPETITIONS AND MARATHONS.
WHAT WAS INTERESTING AND WHAT WAS BORING...
...I DIDN'T EVEN KNOW THAT MUCH.
IN THOSE GRAY DAYS.
SAY,
ARE YOU INTERESTED IN GOING TO CRAM SCHOOL? IF YOU START UNDERSTANDING YOUR STUDIES...THEY'LL BE MORE FUN.
IT WASN'T LIKE THE SCHOOL TESTS, WITH DOZENS OF THE SAME KIND OF QUESTION LINED UP.
IT WAS LIKE A RIDDLE BOOK FROM A MANGA MAGAZINE.
A FEW DAYS AFTER THAT...

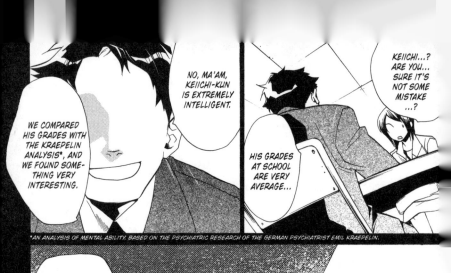

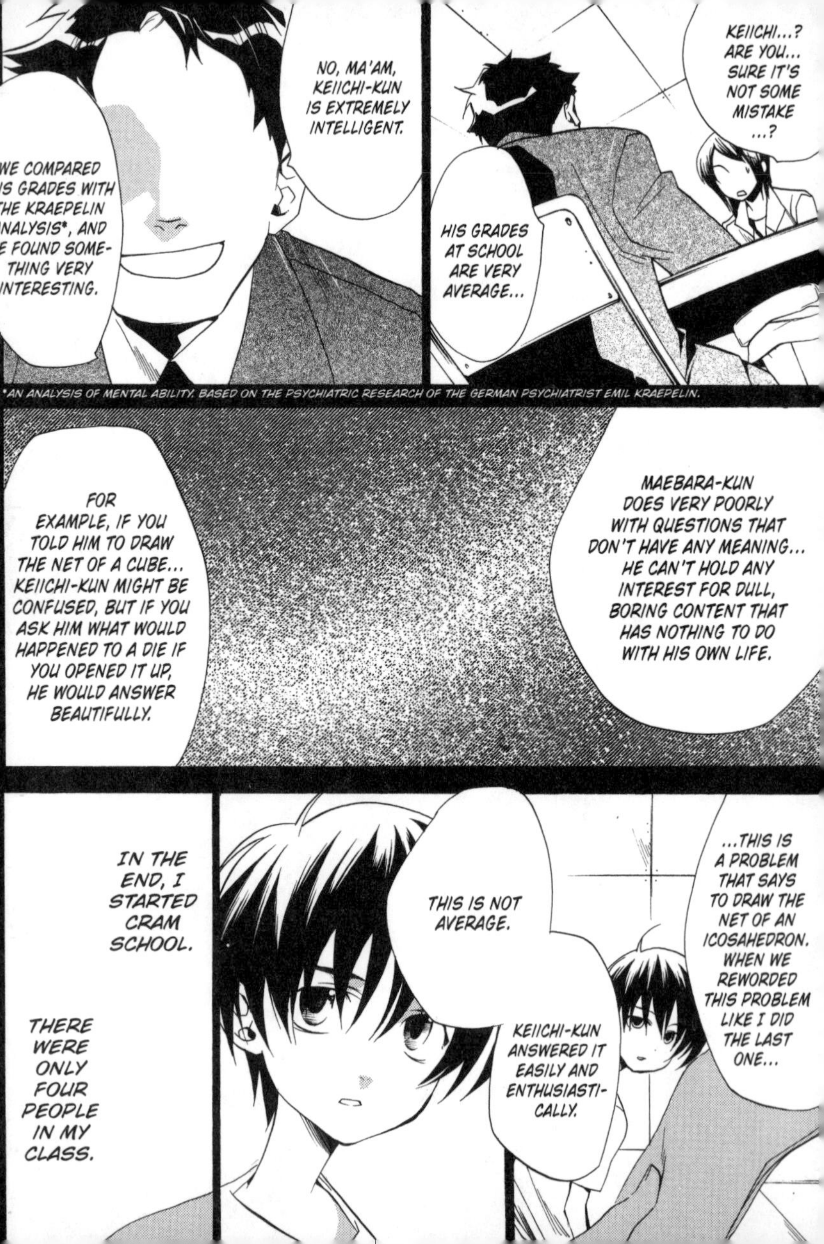
KEIICHI...? ARE YOU... SURE IT'S NOT SOME MISTAKE ...?
HIS GRADES AT SCHOOL ARE VERY AVERAGE...
NO, MA'AM, KEIICHI-KUN IS EXTREMELY INTELLIGENT.
WE COMPARED HIS GRADES WITH THE KRAEPELIN ANALYSIS*, AND WE FOUND SOME-THING VERY INTERESTING.
MAEBARA-KUN DOES VERY POORLY WITH QUESTIONS THAT DON'T HAVE ANY MEANING... HE CAN'T HOLD ANY INTEREST FOR DULL, BORING CONTENT THAT HAS NOTHING TO DO WITH HIS OWN LIFE.
FOR EXAMPLE, IF YOU TOLD HIM TO DRAW THE NET OF A CUBE... KEIICHI-KUN MIGHT BE CONFUSED, BUT IF YOU ASK HIM WHAT WOULD HAPPENED TO A DIE IF YOU OPENED IT UP, HE WOULD ANSWER BEAUTIFULLY.
...THIS IS A PROBLEM THAT SAYS TO DRAW THE NET OF AN ICOSAHEDRON. WHEN WE REWORDED THIS PROBLEM LIKE I DID THE LAST ONE...
KEIICHI-KUN ANSWERED IT EASILY AND ENTHUSIASTI-CALLY.
THIS IS NOT AVERAGE.
IN THE END, I STARTED CRAM SCHOOL.
THERE WERE ONLY FOUR PEOPLE IN MY CLASS.

*AN ANALYSIS OF MENTAL ABILITY. BASED ON THE PSYCHIATRIC RESEARCH OF THE GERMAN PSYCHIATRIST EMIL KRAEPELIN.

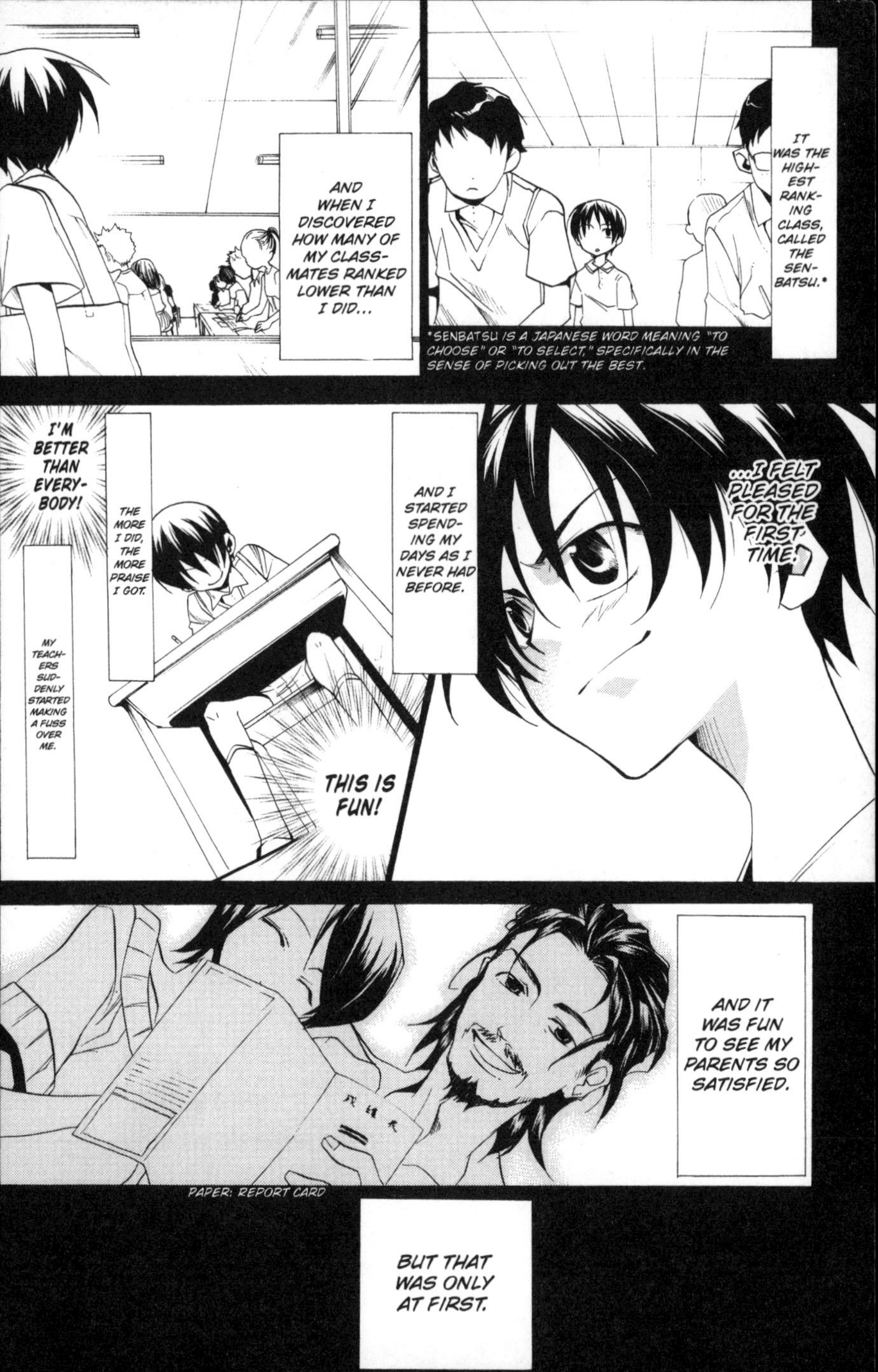
IT WAS THE HIGHEST RANKING CLASS, CALLED THE SENBATSU.*
*SENBATSU IS A JAPANESE WORD MEANING "TO CHOOSE" OR "TO SELECT," SPECIFICALLY IN THE SENSE OF PICKING OUT THE BEST.
AND WHEN I DISCOVERED HOW MANY OF MY CLASSMATES RANKED LOWER THAN I DID...
...I FELT PLEASED FOR THE FIRST TIME!
AND I STARTED SPENDING MY DAYS AS I NEVER HAD BEFORE.
THE MORE I DID, THE MORE PRAISE I GOT.
I'M BETTER THAN EVERYBODY!
MY TEACHERS SUDDENLY STARTED MAKING A FUSS OVER ME.
THIS IS FUN!
AND IT WAS FUN TO SEE MY PARENTS SO SATISFIED.
PAPER: REPORT CARD
BUT THAT WAS ONLY AT FIRST.

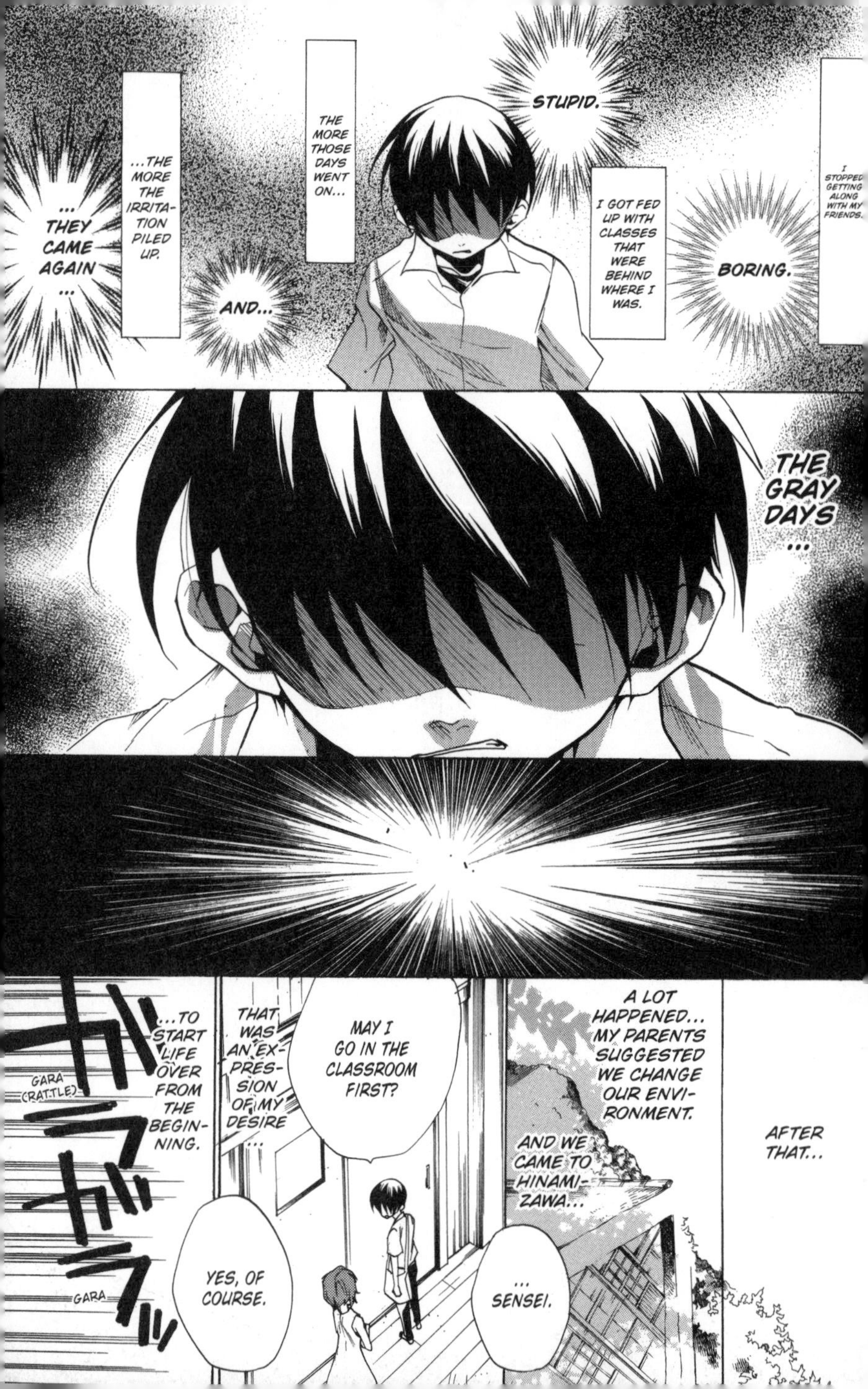
I STOPPED GETTING ALONG WITH MY FRIENDS.
BORING.
I GOT FED UP WITH CLASSES THAT WERE BEHIND WHERE I WAS.
STUPID.
THE MORE THOSE DAYS WENT ON...
AND...
...THE MORE THE IRRITATION PILED UP.
...THEY CAME AGAIN...
THE GRAY DAYS...
AFTER THAT...
A LOT HAPPENED... MY PARENTS SUGGESTED WE CHANGE OUR ENVIRONMENT.
AND WE CAME TO HINAMIZAWA...
...SENSEI.
MAY I GO IN THE CLASSROOM FIRST?
YES, OF COURSE.
THAT WAS AN EXPRESSION OF MY DESIRE...
...TO START LIFE OVER FROM THE BEGINNING.
GARA (RATTLE)
GARA

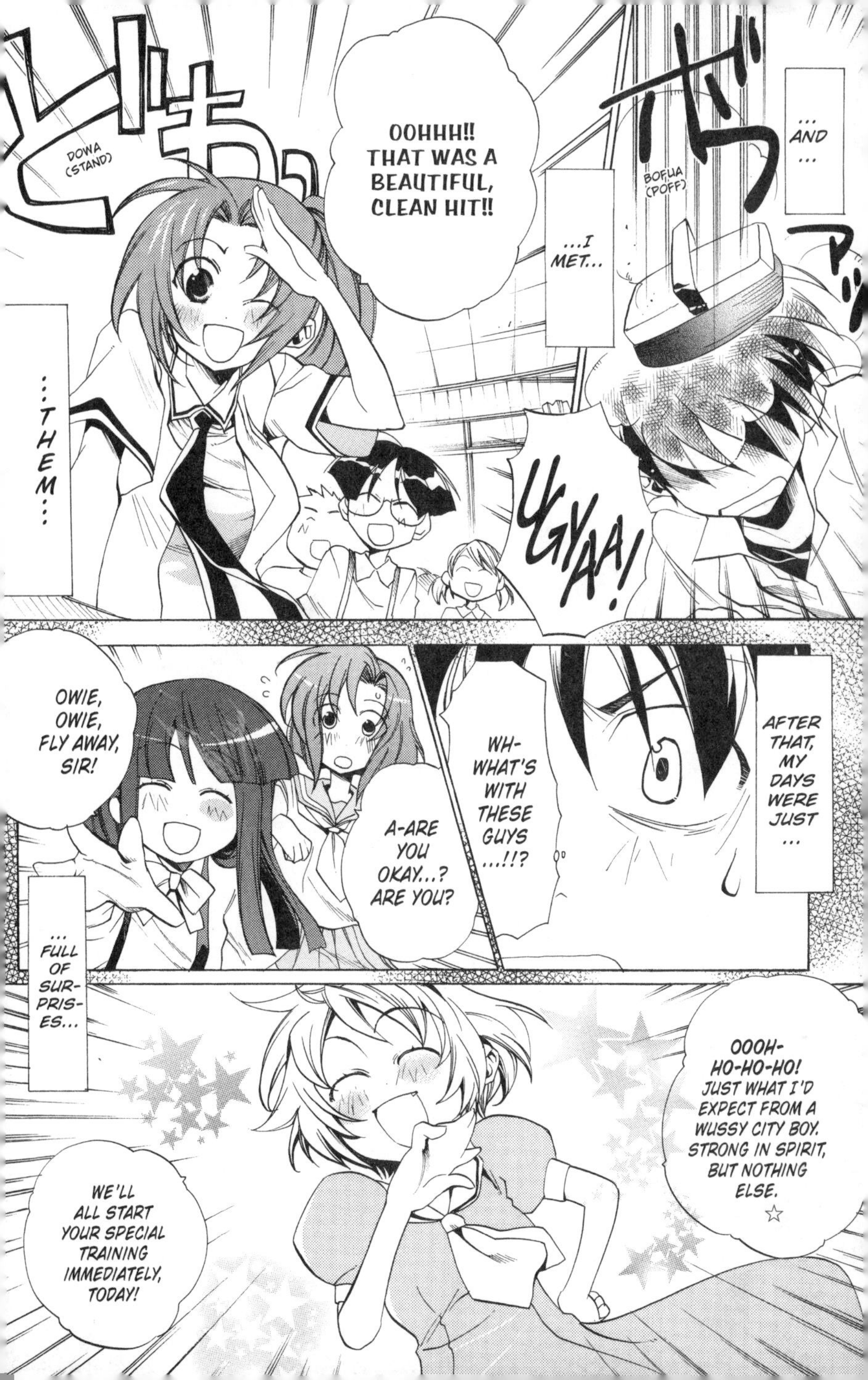
...AND...
BOFUA (POFF)
...I MET...
OOHHH!! THAT WAS A BEAUTIFUL, CLEAN HIT!!
DOWA (STAND)
UGYAA!
...THEM...
AFTER THAT, MY DAYS WERE JUST ...
WH-WHAT'S WITH THESE GUYS ...!!?
A-ARE YOU OKAY...? ARE YOU?
OWIE, OWIE, FLY AWAY, SIR!
... FULL OF SURPRISES...
OOOH-HO-HO-HO! JUST WHAT I'D EXPECT FROM A WUSSY CITY BOY. STRONG IN SPIRIT, BUT NOTHING ELSE. ☆
WE'LL ALL START YOUR SPECIAL TRAINING IMMEDIATELY, TODAY!

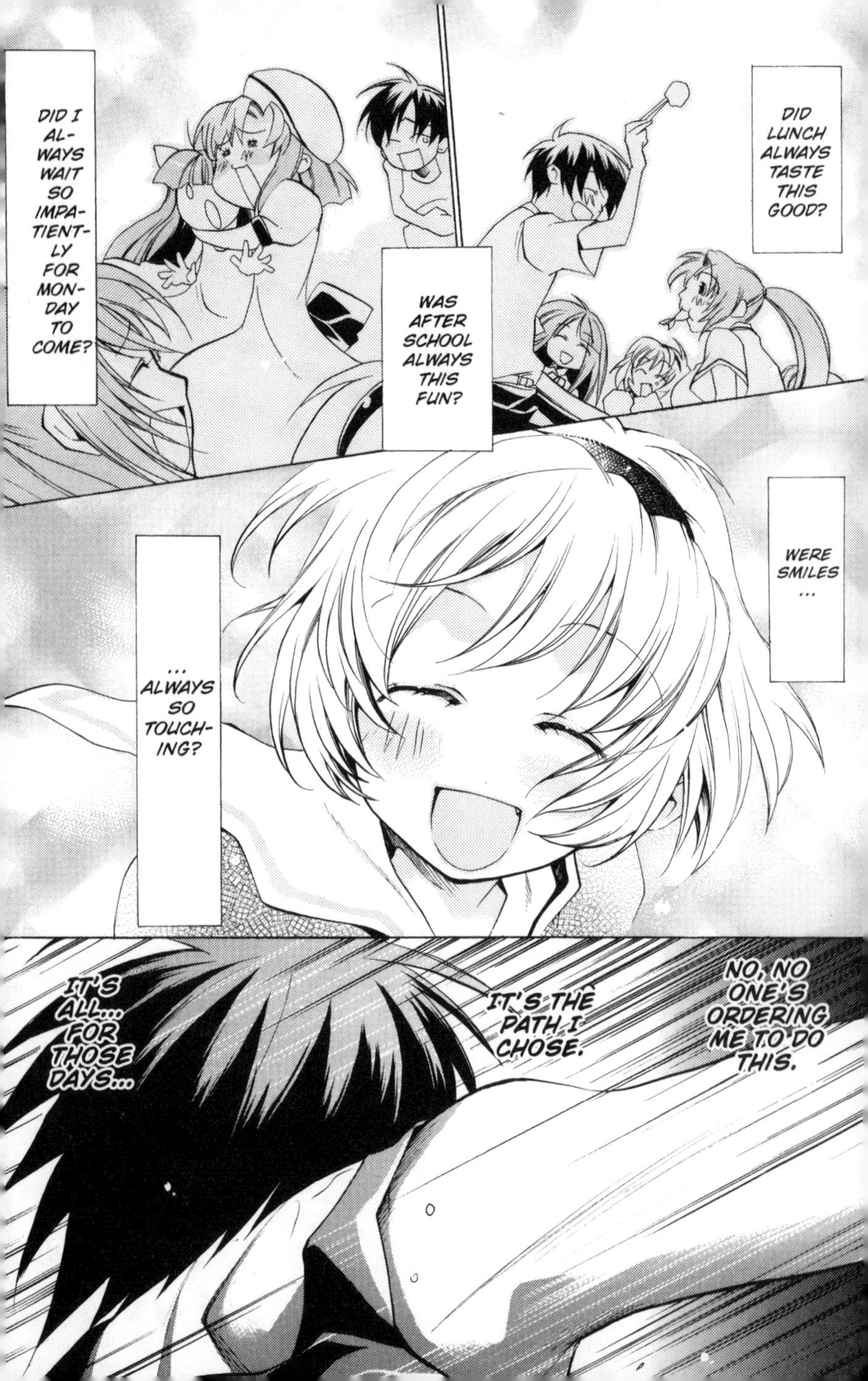
DID LUNCH ALWAYS TASTE THIS GOOD?
WAS AFTER SCHOOL ALWAYS THIS FUN?
DID I ALWAYS WAIT SO IMPATIENTLY FOR MONDAY TO COME?
WERE SMILES ...
... ALWAYS SO TOUCHING?
NO, NO ONE'S ORDERING ME TO DO THIS.
IT'S THE PATH I CHOSE.
IT'S ALL... FOR THOSE DAYS...

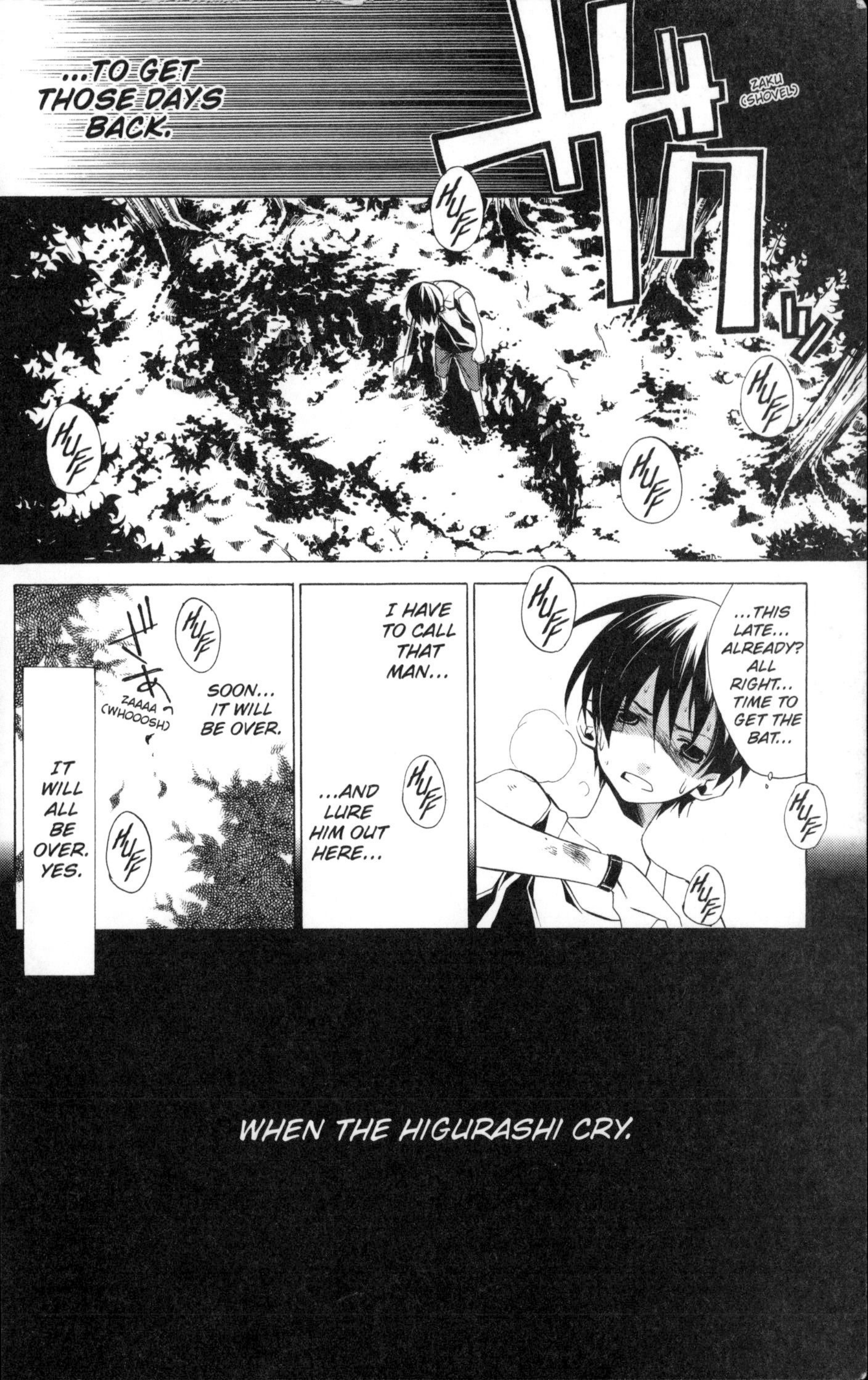
...TO GET THOSE DAYS BACK.
ZAKU (SHOVEL)
HUFF
HUFF
HUFF
HUFF
HUFF
...THIS LATE... ALREADY? ALL RIGHT... TIME TO GET THE BAT...
HUFF
HUFF
I HAVE TO CALL THAT MAN...
HUFF
...AND LURE HIM OUT HERE...
HUFF
ZAAAA (WHOOOSH)
SOON... IT WILL BE OVER.
IT WILL ALL BE OVER. YES.
HUFF
WHEN THE HIGURASHI CRY.

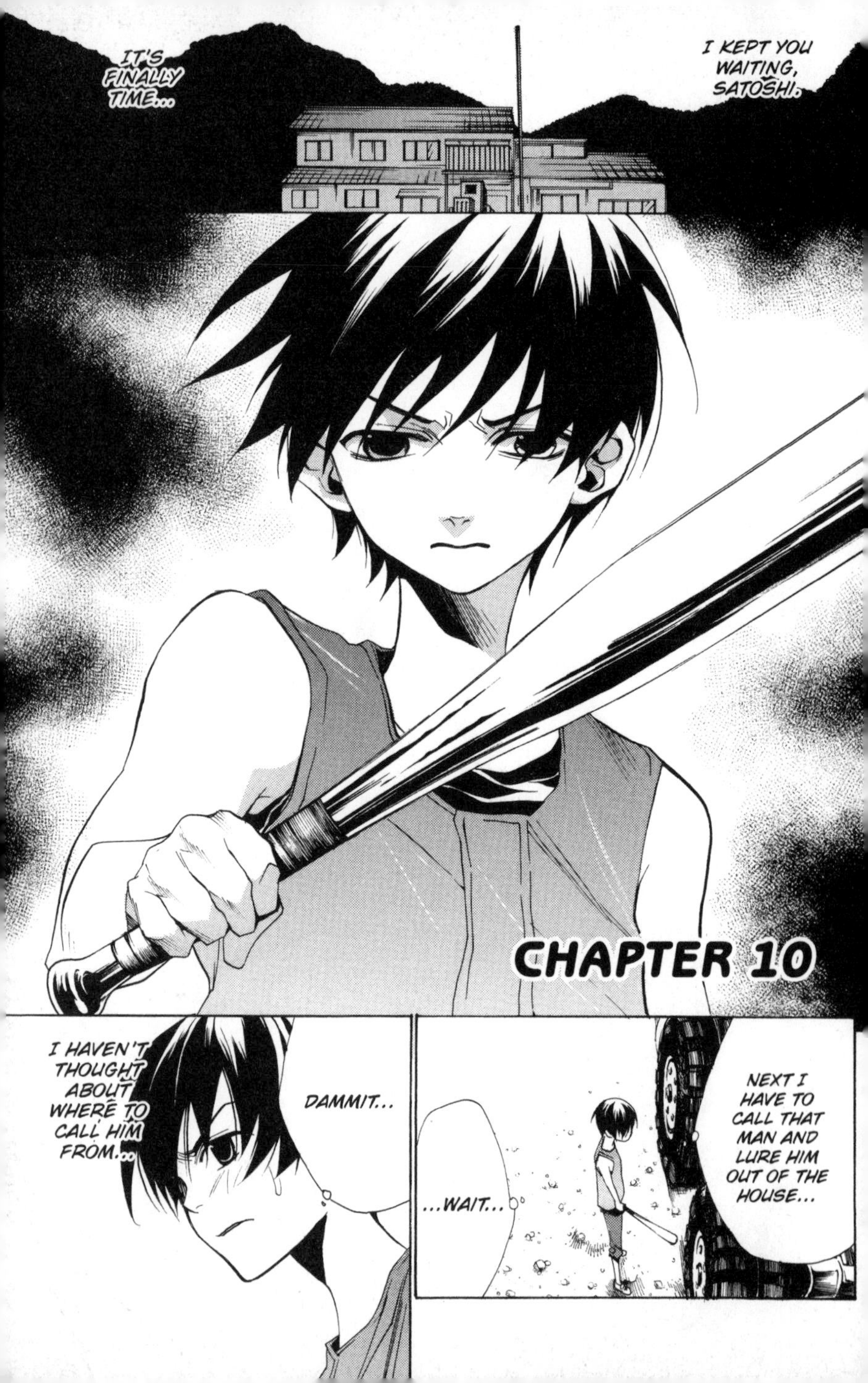
I KEPT YOU WAITING, SATOSHI.
IT'S FINALLY TIME...
CHAPTER 10
NEXT I HAVE TO CALL THAT MAN AND LURE HIM OUT OF THE HOUSE...
...WAIT...
DAMMIT...
I HAVEN'T THOUGHT ABOUT WHERE TO CALL HIM FROM...

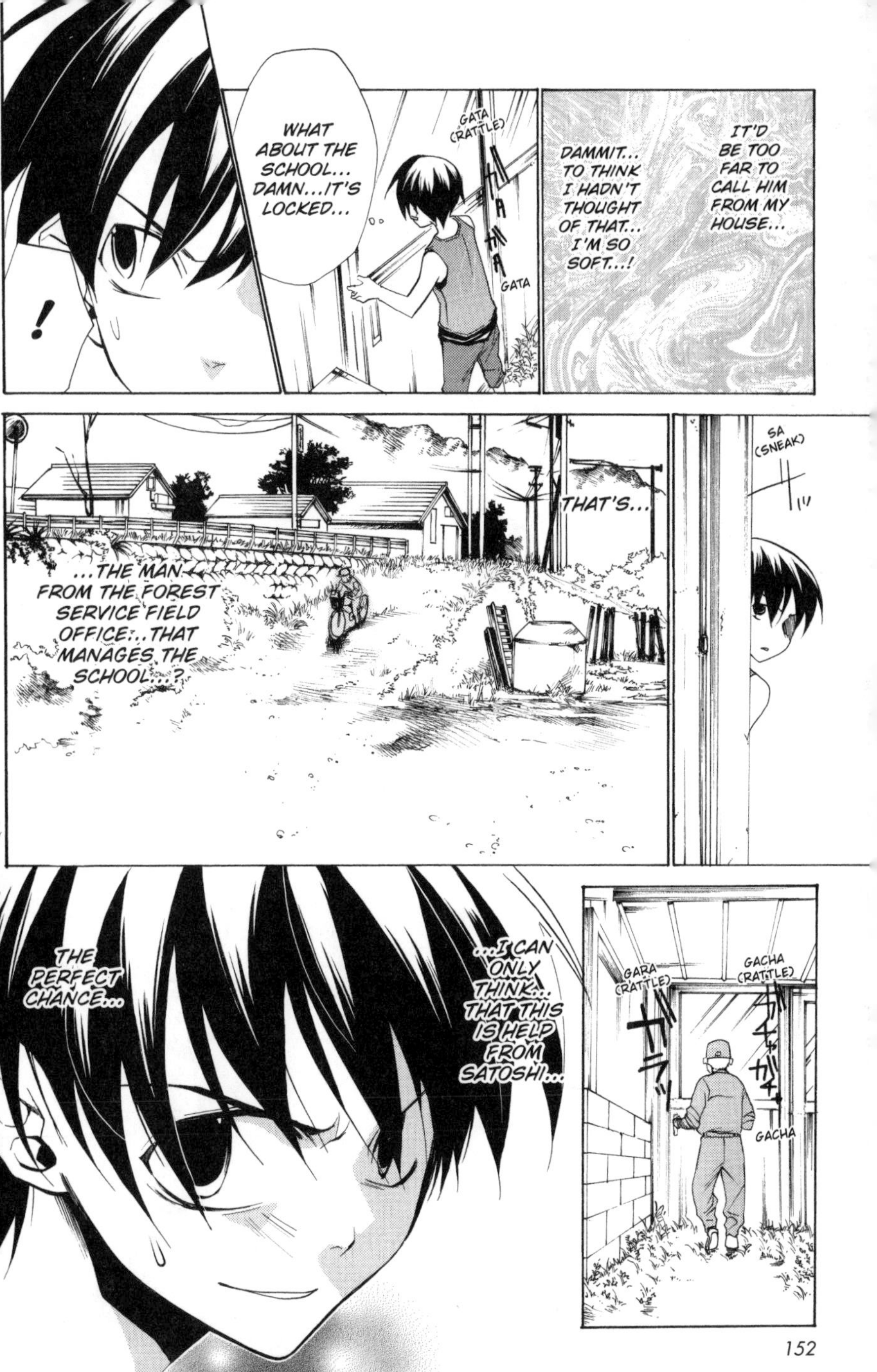
IT'D BE TOO FAR TO CALL HIM FROM MY HOUSE...
DAMMIT... TO THINK I HADN'T THOUGHT OF THAT... I'M SO SOFT...!
GATA (RATTLE)
WHAT ABOUT THE SCHOOL... DAMN...IT'S LOCKED...
GATA
!
SA (SNEAK)
THAT'S...
...THE MAN FROM THE FOREST SERVICE FIELD OFFICE...THAT MANAGES THE SCHOOL...?
GACHA (RATTLE)
GACHA
GARA (RATTLE)
...I CAN ONLY THINK... THAT THIS IS HELP FROM SATOSHI...
THE PERFECT CHANCE...

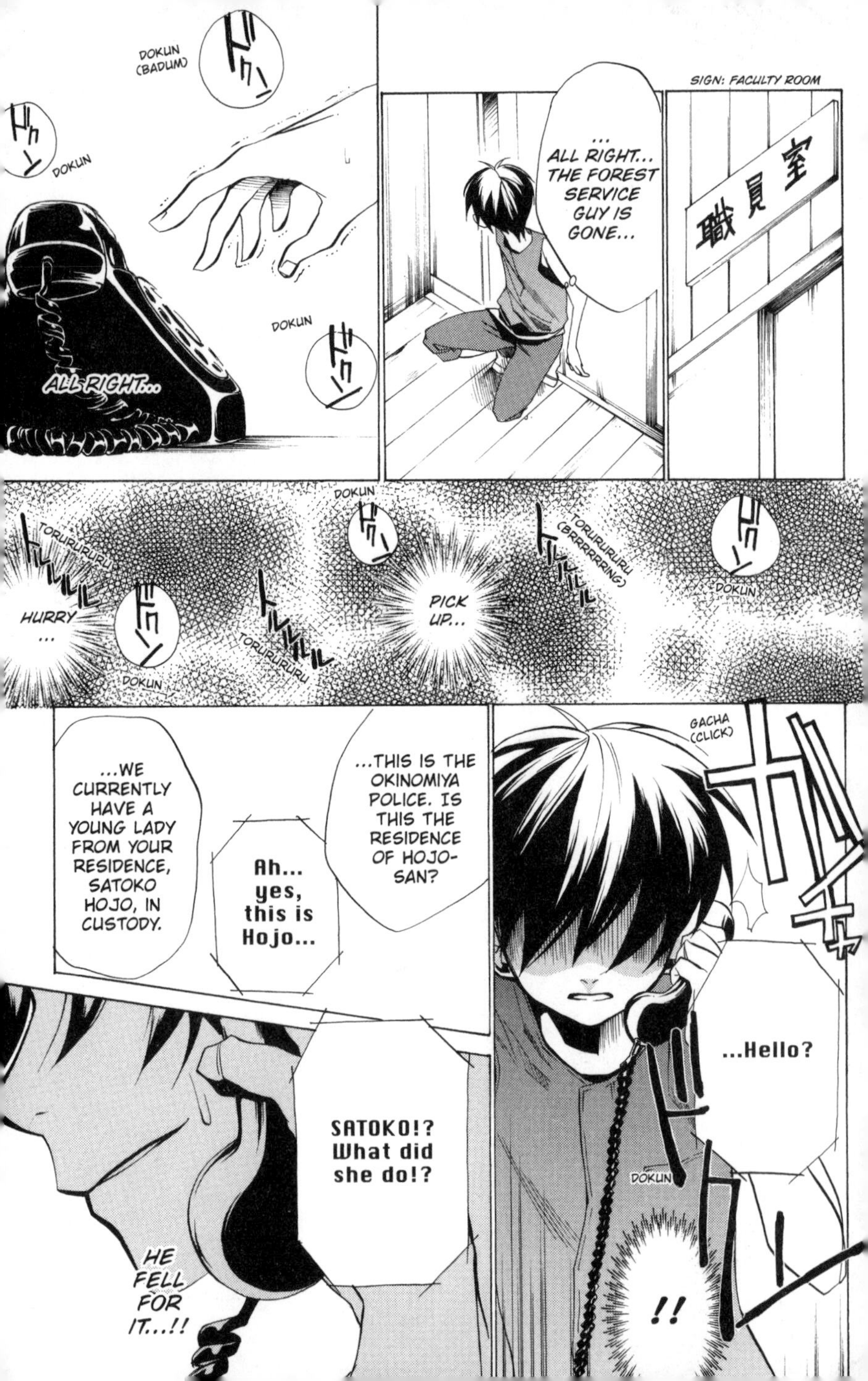

SIGN: FACULTY ROOM
職員室
... ALL RIGHT... THE FOREST SERVICE GUY IS GONE...
DOKUN (BADUM)
DOKUN
DOKUN
ALL RIGHT...
DOKUN
TORURURURU (BRRRRRRING)
PICK UP...
DOKUN
TORURURURU
DOKUN
HURRY ...
TORURURURU
GACHA (CLICK)
...Hello?
DOKUN
!!
...THIS IS THE OKINOMIYA POLICE. IS THIS THE RESIDENCE OF HOJO-SAN?
Ah... yes, this is Hojo...
...WE CURRENTLY HAVE A YOUNG LADY FROM YOUR RESIDENCE, SATOKO HOJO, IN CUSTODY.
SATOKO!? What did she do!?
HE FELL FOR IT...!!

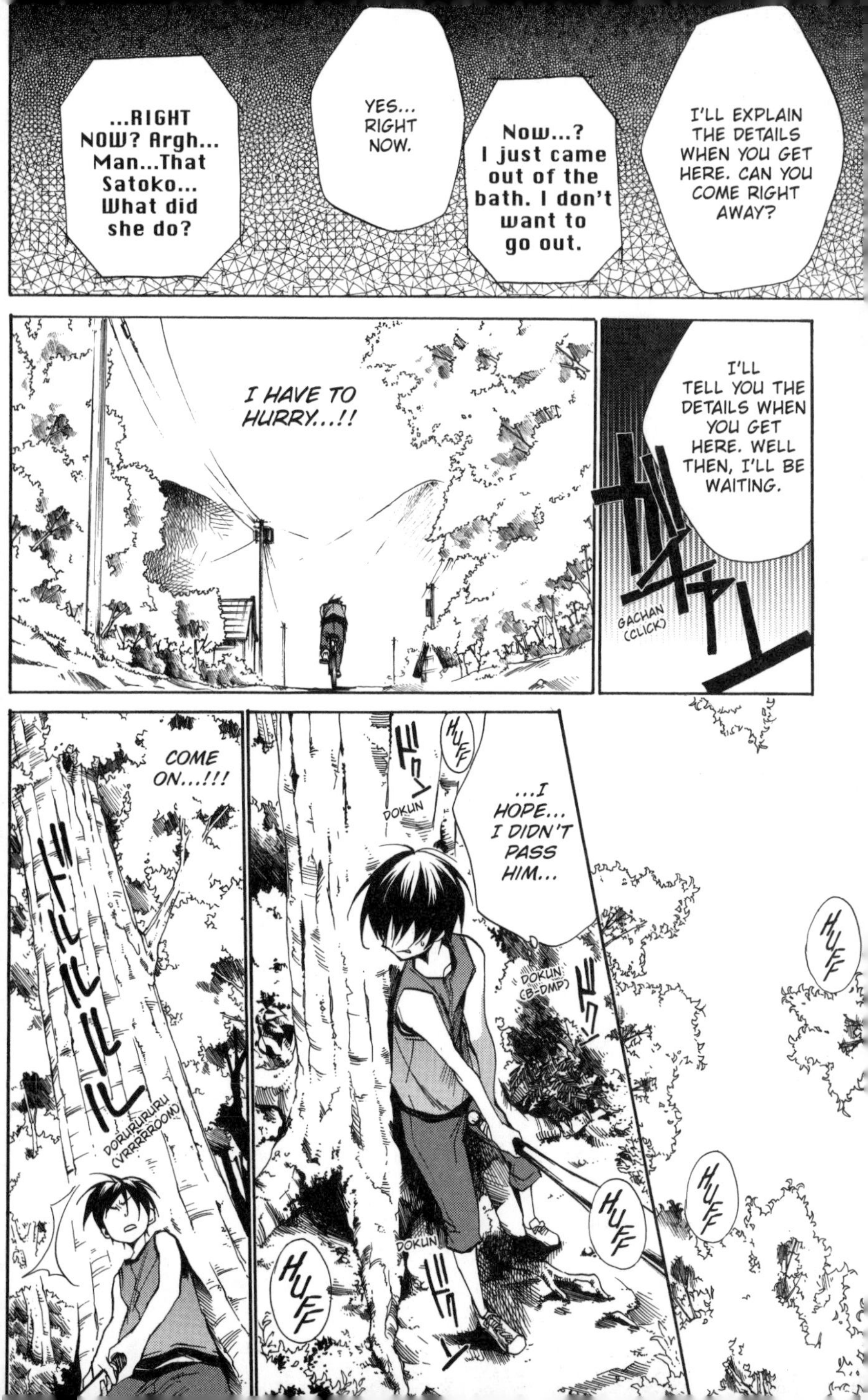
I'LL EXPLAIN THE DETAILS WHEN YOU GET HERE. CAN YOU COME RIGHT AWAY?
Now...? I just came out of the bath. I don't want to go out.
YES... RIGHT NOW.
...RIGHT NOW? Argh... Man...That Satoko... What did she do?
I'LL TELL YOU THE DETAILS WHEN YOU GET HERE. WELL THEN, I'LL BE WAITING.
GACHAN (CLICK)
I HAVE TO HURRY...!!
HUFF
DOKUN
...I HOPE... I DIDN'T PASS HIM...
DOKUN (B-DMP)
HUFF
HUFF
HUFF
DOKUN
HUFF
COME ON...!!!
DORURURURU (VRRRRROOM)

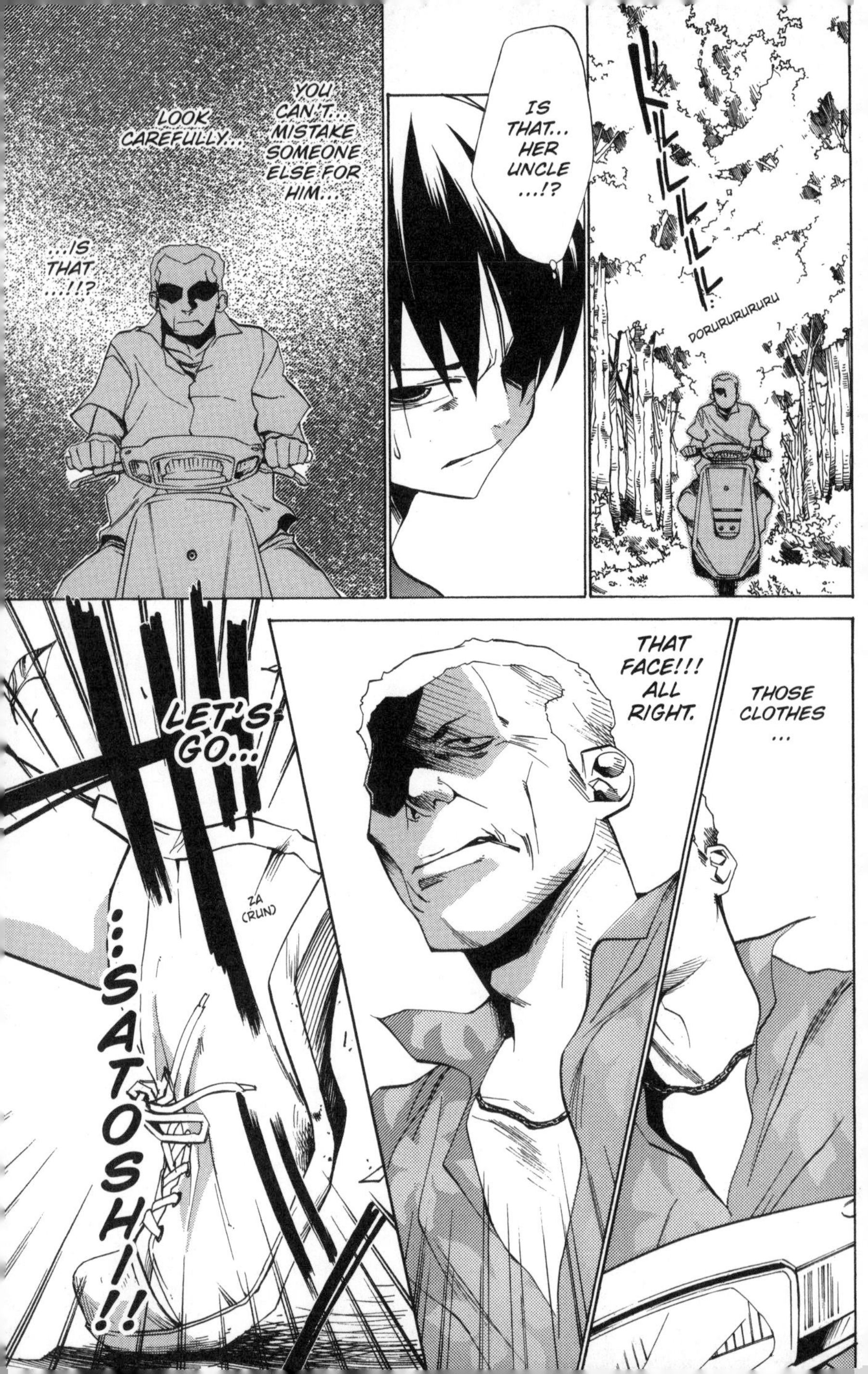
DORURURURURU
IS THAT... HER UNCLE ...!?
YOU CAN'T... MISTAKE SOMEONE ELSE FOR HIM...
LOOK CAREFULLY...
...IS THAT ...!!?
THOSE CLOTHES ...
THAT FACE!!! ALL RIGHT.
LET'S GO...
ZA (RUN)
...SATOSHI!!

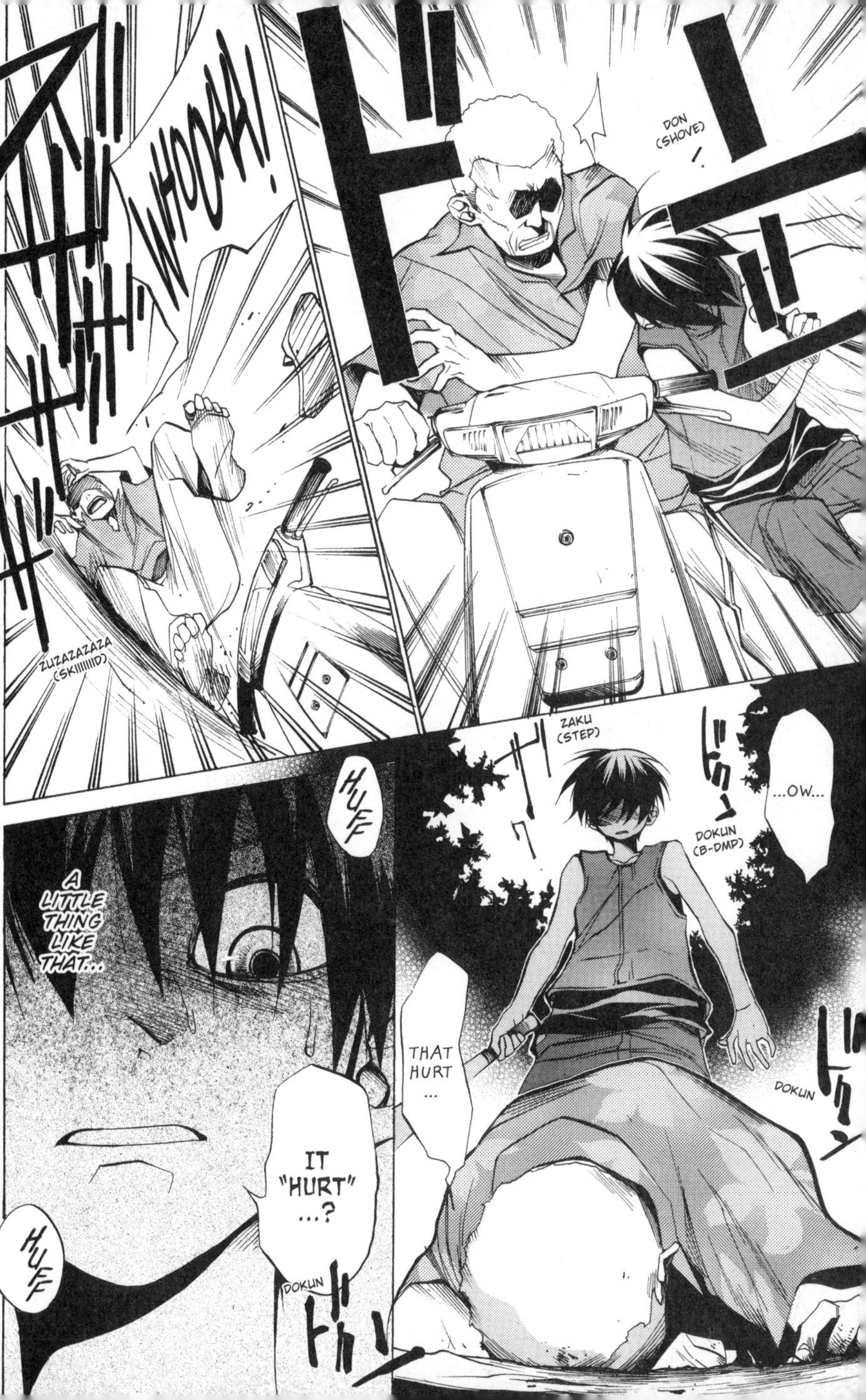
DON (SHOVE)
WHOOA!
ZUZAZAZAZA (SKIIIIIID)
ZAKU (STEP)
...OW...
DOKUN (B-DMP)
THAT HURT ...
DOKUN
HUFF
A LITTLE THING LIKE THAT...
IT "HURT" ...?
HUFF
DOKUN

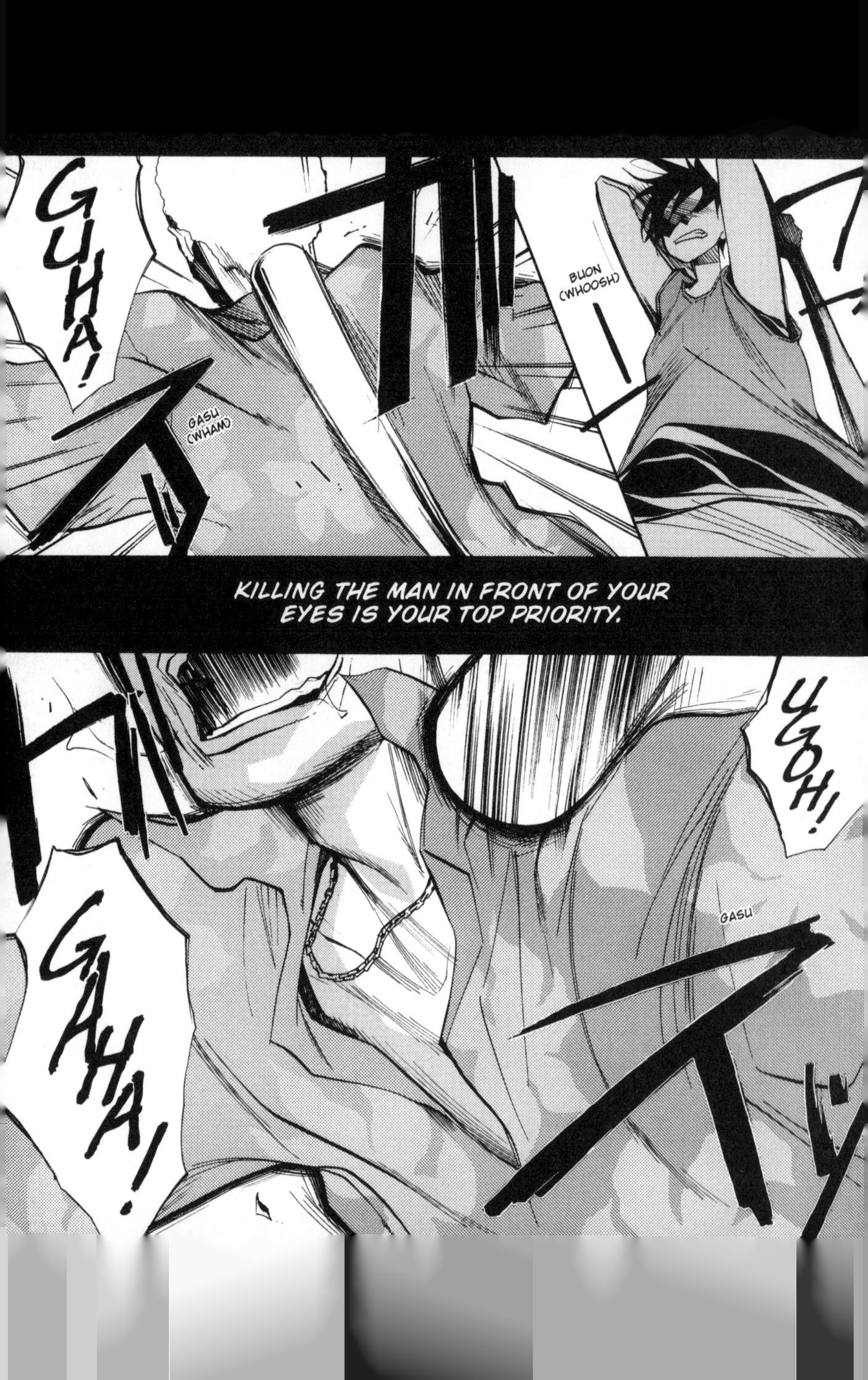
BUON (WHOOSH)
GUHA!
GASU (WHAM)
KILLING THE MAN IN FRONT OF YOUR EYES IS YOUR TOP PRIORITY.
UGOH!
GASU
GAHA!

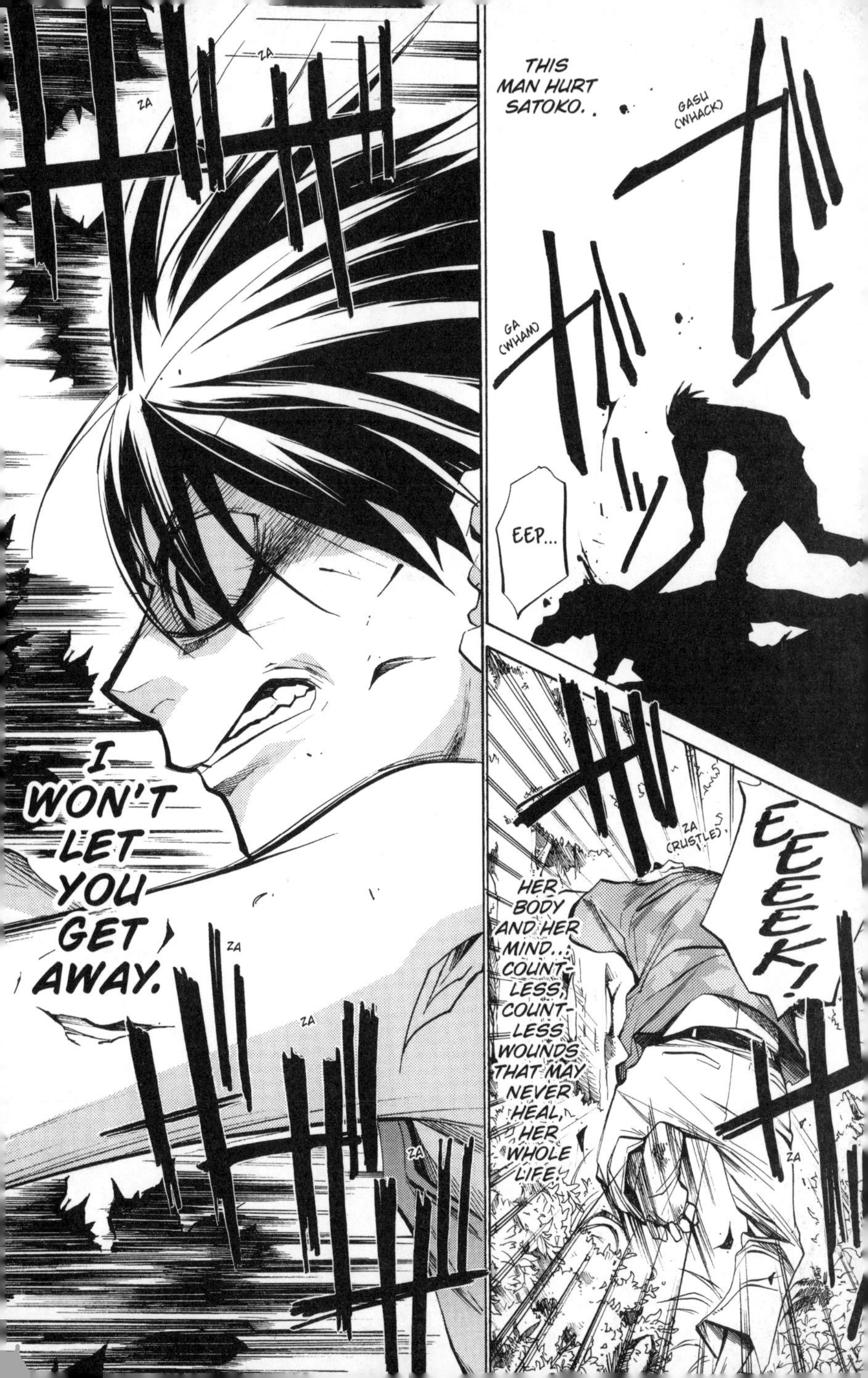
THIS MAN HURT SATOKO..
GASU (WHACK)
GA (WHAM)
EEP...
ZA (RUSTLE)
EEEEK!
HER BODY AND HER MIND... COUNTLESS, COUNTLESS WOUNDS THAT MAY NEVER HEAL, HER WHOLE LIFE.
ZA
ZA
ZA
I WON'T LET YOU GET AWAY.
ZA
ZA
ZA

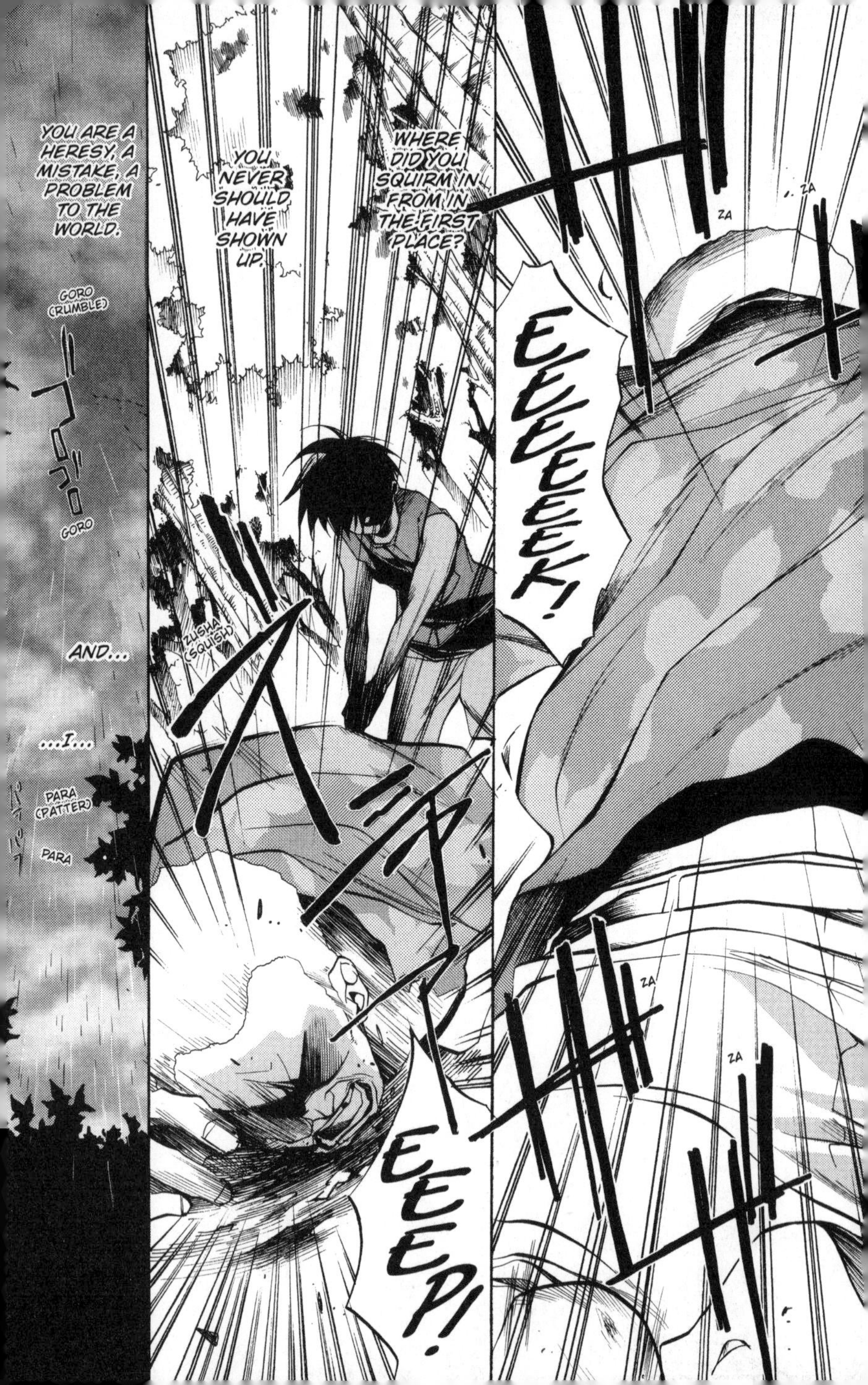
ZA
ZA
EEEEEEEEK!
ZA
ZA
WHERE DID YOU SQUIRM IN FROM IN THE FIRST PLACE?
YOU NEVER SHOULD HAVE SHOWN UP.
ZLISHA (SQUISH)
...
EEEP!
YOU ARE A HERESY, A MISTAKE, A PROBLEM TO THE WORLD.
GORO (RUMBLE)
GORO
AND...
...I...
PARA (PATTER)
PARA

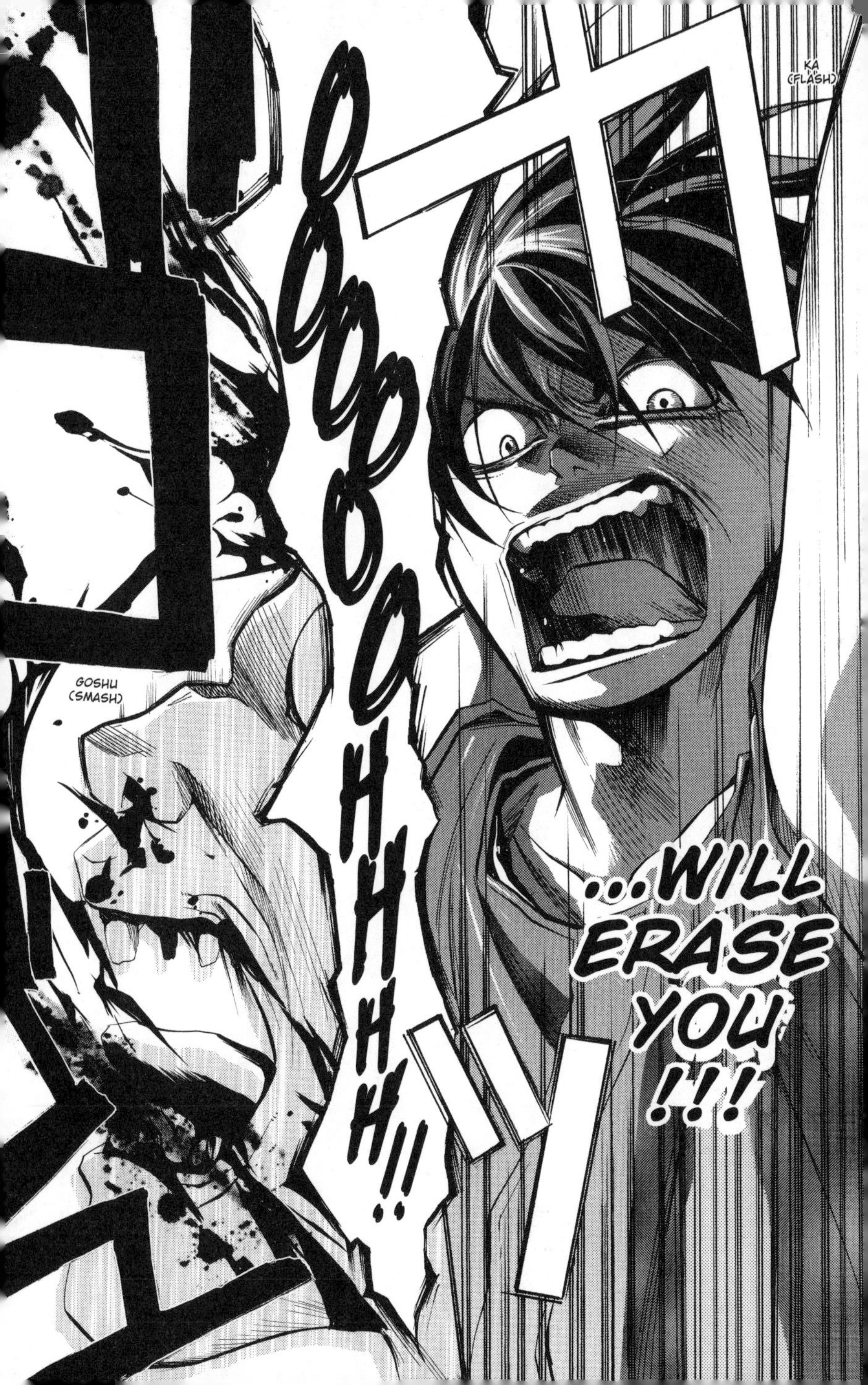
KA (FLASH)
...WILL ERASE YOU !!!
OOOOOOOOOOOHHHHHH!!
GOSHU (SMASH)

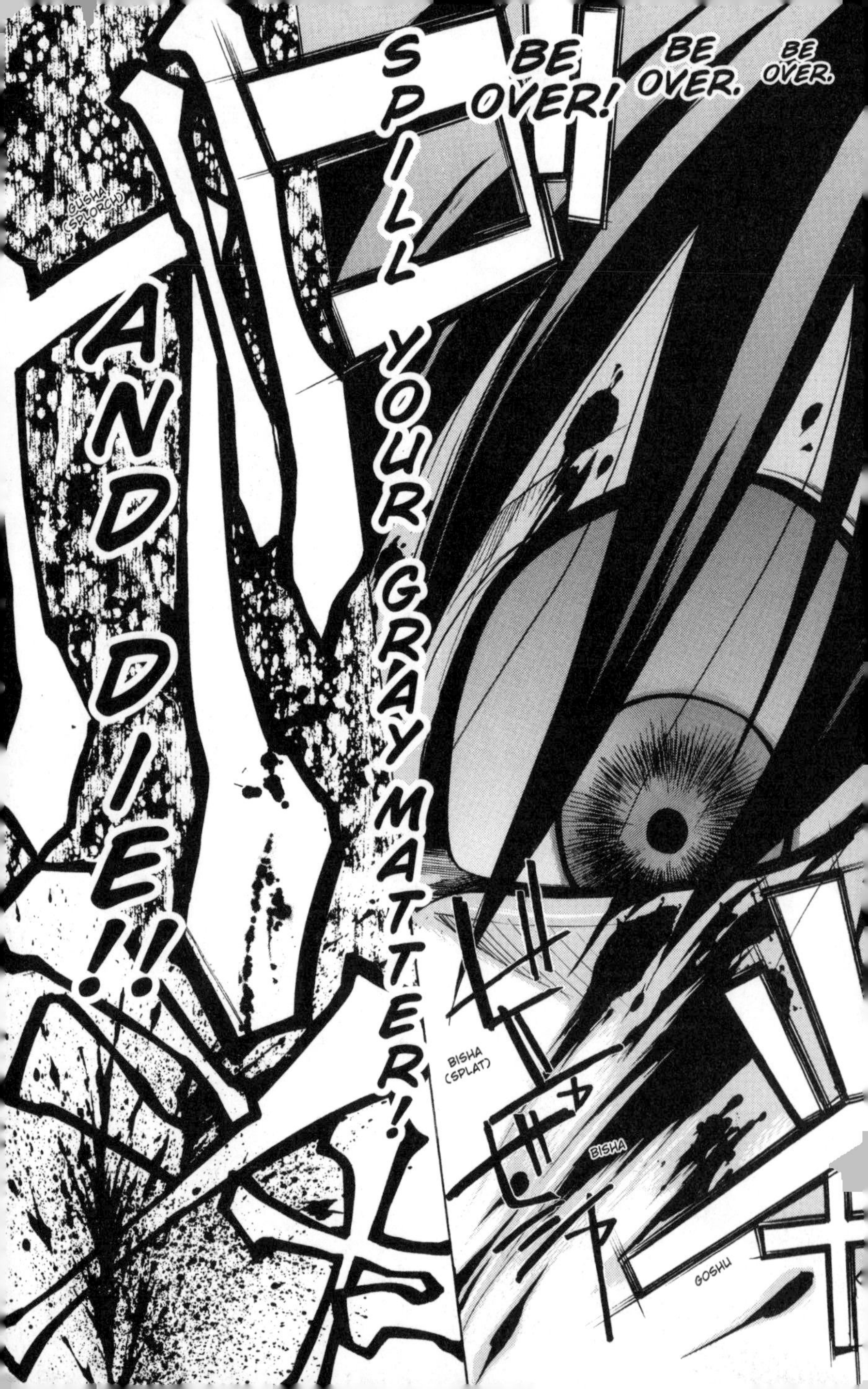
BE OVER.
BE OVER.
BE OVER!
SPILL YOUR GRAY MATTER!
GUSHA (SPLORCH)
AND DIE!!
GOSHU
BISHA
BISHA (SPLAT)

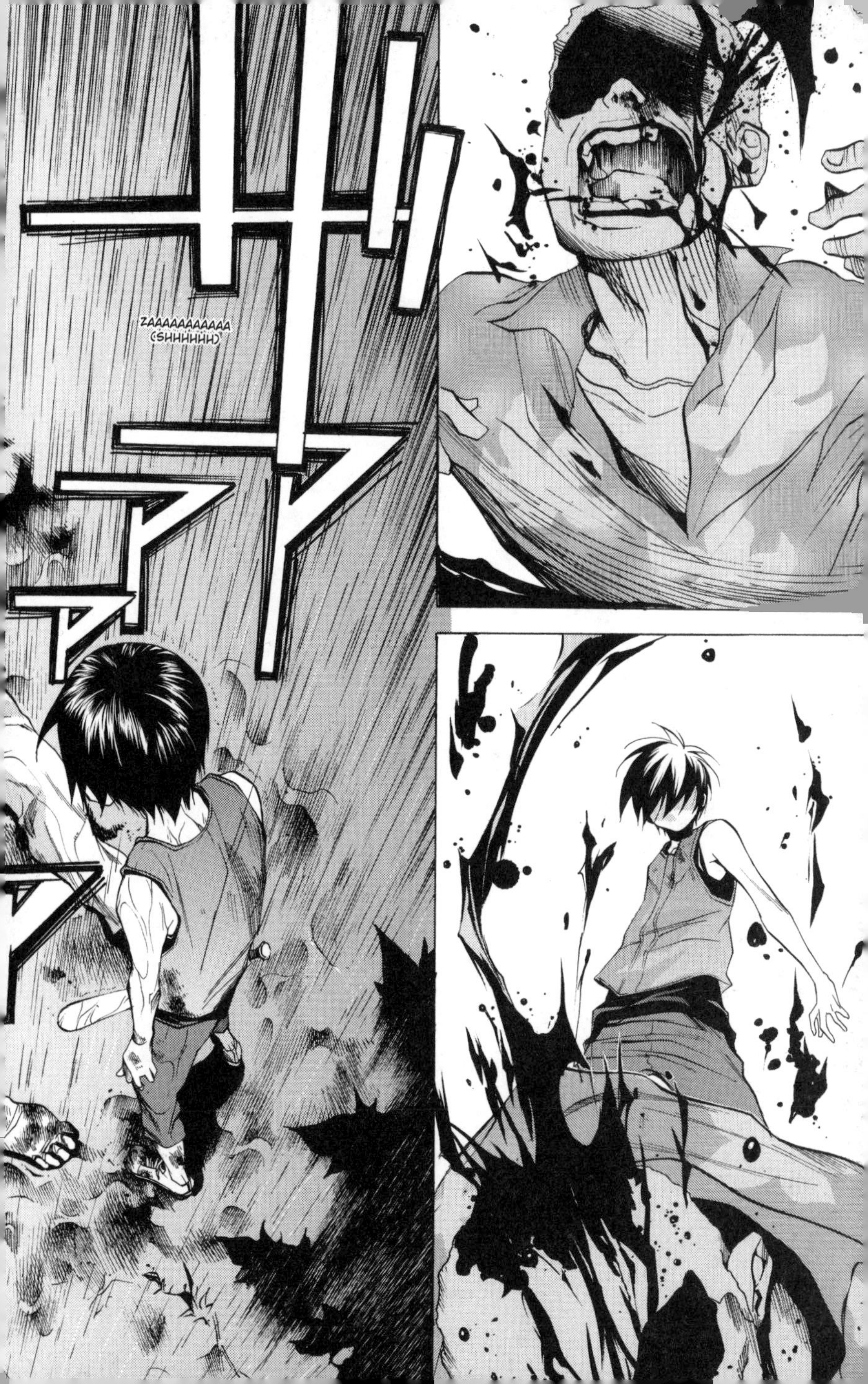
ZAAAAAAAAAAAA
(SHHHHHH)

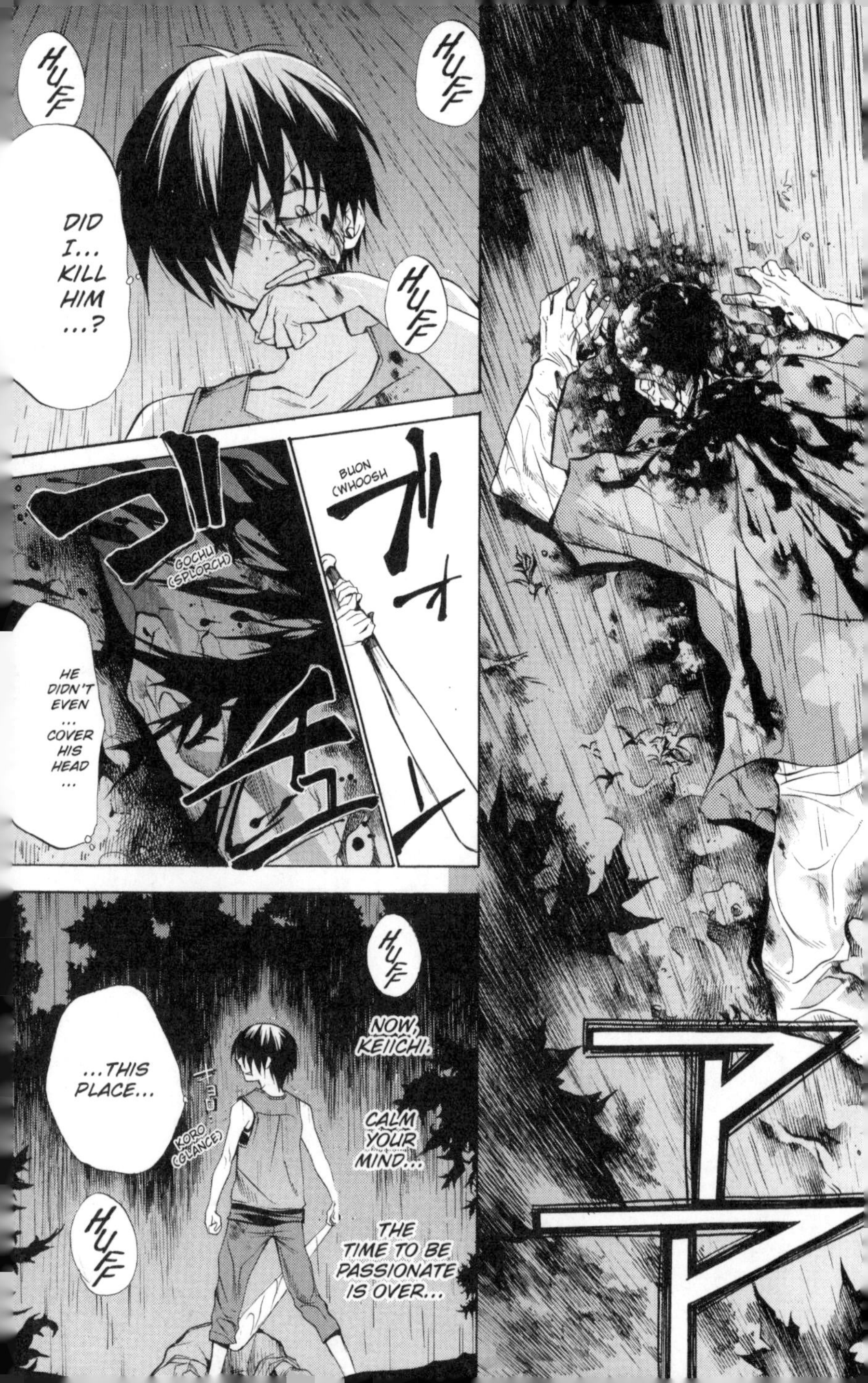
HUFF
HUFF
DID I... KILL HIM ...?
HUFF
BUON (WHOOSH
GOCHU (SPLORCH)
HE DIDN'T EVEN ... COVER HIS HEAD ...
HUFF
NOW, KEIICHI.
CALM YOUR MIND...
THE TIME TO BE PASSIONATE IS OVER...
KORO (GLANCE)
...THIS PLACE...
HUFF

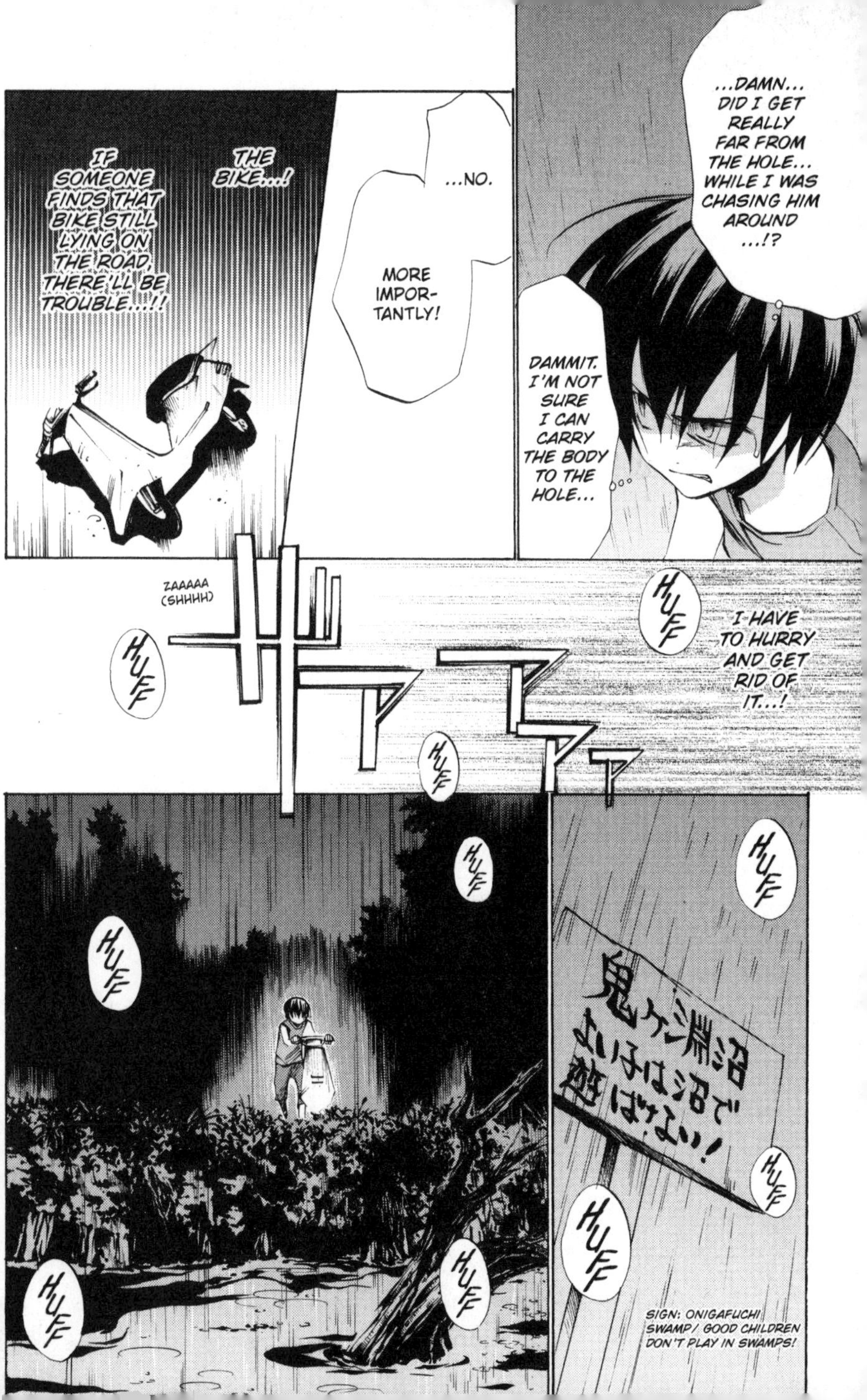
...DAMN... DID I GET REALLY FAR FROM THE HOLE... WHILE I WAS CHASING HIM AROUND ...!?
DAMMIT. I'M NOT SURE I CAN CARRY THE BODY TO THE HOLE...
...NO.
MORE IMPOR-TANTLY!
THE BIKE...!
IF SOMEONE FINDS THAT BIKE STILL LYING ON THE ROAD, THERE'LL BE TROUBLE...!!
HUFF
I HAVE TO HURRY AND GET RID OF IT...!
HUFF
ZAAAAA (SHHHH)
HUFF
HUFF
鬼ヶ淵沼
よい子は沼で遊ばない!
HUFF
HUFF
SIGN: ONIGAFUCHI SWAMP/ GOOD CHILDREN DON'T PLAY IN SWAMPS!
HUFF
HUFF
HUFF
HUFF

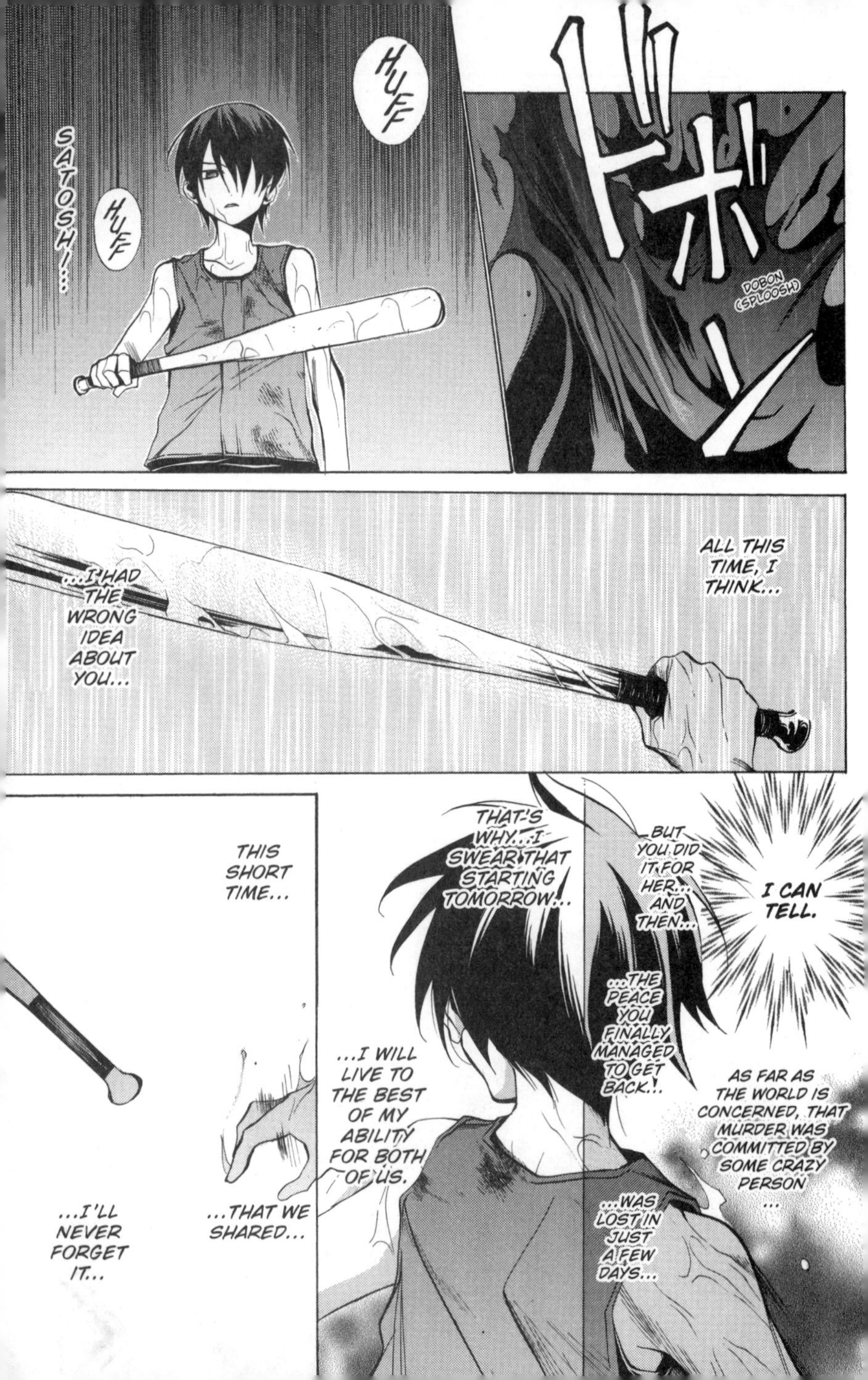
ドボン
DOBON (SPLOOSH)
HUFF
HUFF
SATOSHI!...
ALL THIS TIME, I THINK...
...I HAD THE WRONG IDEA ABOUT YOU...
I CAN TELL.
BUT YOU DID IT FOR HER... AND THEN...
...THE PEACE YOU FINALLY MANAGED TO GET BACK...
AS FAR AS THE WORLD IS CONCERNED, THAT MURDER WAS COMMITTED BY SOME CRAZY PERSON...
...WAS LOST IN JUST A FEW DAYS...
THAT'S WHY... I SWEAR THAT STARTING TOMORROW...
...I WILL LIVE TO THE BEST OF MY ABILITY FOR BOTH OF US.
THIS SHORT TIME...
...THAT WE SHARED...
...I'LL NEVER FORGET IT...

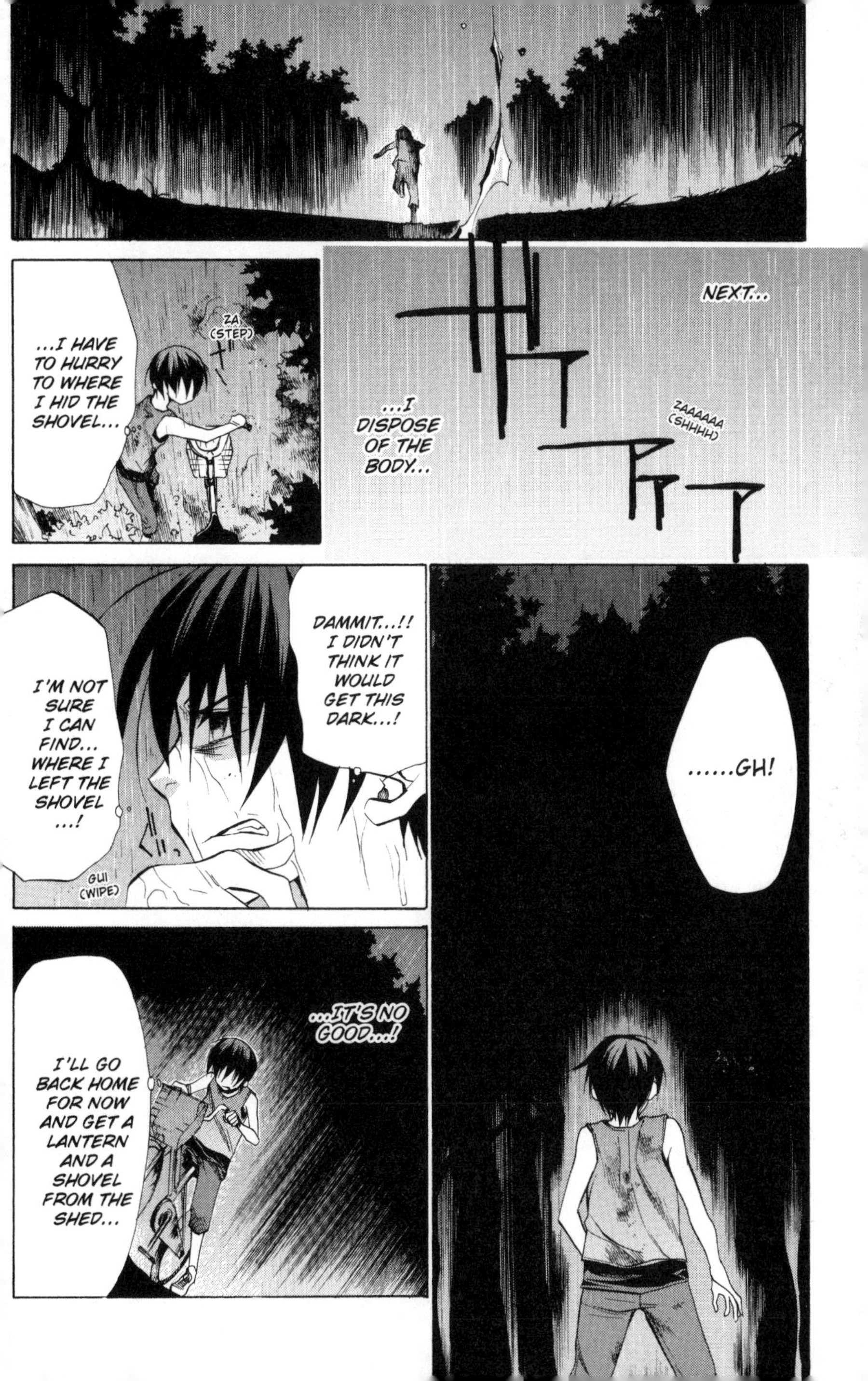
NEXT...
...I DISPOSE OF THE BODY...
ZAAAAAA (SHHHH)
...I HAVE TO HURRY TO WHERE I HID THE SHOVEL...
ZA (STEP)
......GH!
DAMMIT...!! I DIDN'T THINK IT WOULD GET THIS DARK...!
I'M NOT SURE I CAN FIND... WHERE I LEFT THE SHOVEL...!
GUI (WIPE)
...IT'S NO GOOD...!
I'LL GO BACK HOME FOR NOW AND GET A LANTERN AND A SHOVEL FROM THE SHED...

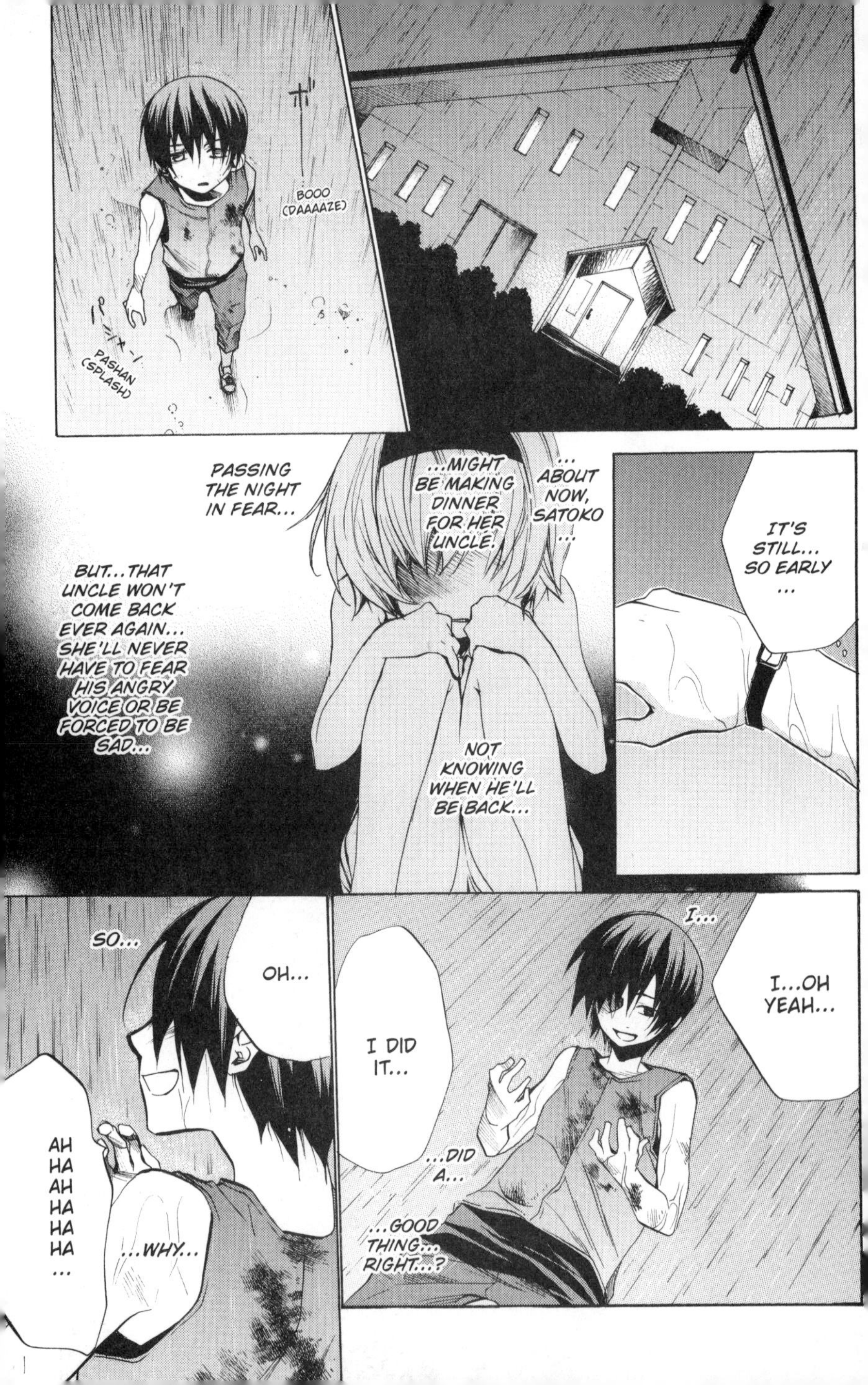
BOOO (DAAAAZE)
PASHAN (SPLASH)
IT'S STILL... SO EARLY...
...ABOUT NOW, SATOKO...
...MIGHT BE MAKING DINNER FOR HER UNCLE.
PASSING THE NIGHT IN FEAR...
NOT KNOWING WHEN HE'LL BE BACK...
BUT...THAT UNCLE WON'T COME BACK EVER AGAIN... SHE'LL NEVER HAVE TO FEAR HIS ANGRY VOICE OR BE FORCED TO BE SAD...
I...
I...OH YEAH...
I DID IT...
...DID A...
...GOOD THING... RIGHT...?
SO...
OH...
AH HA AH HA HA HA...
...WHY...

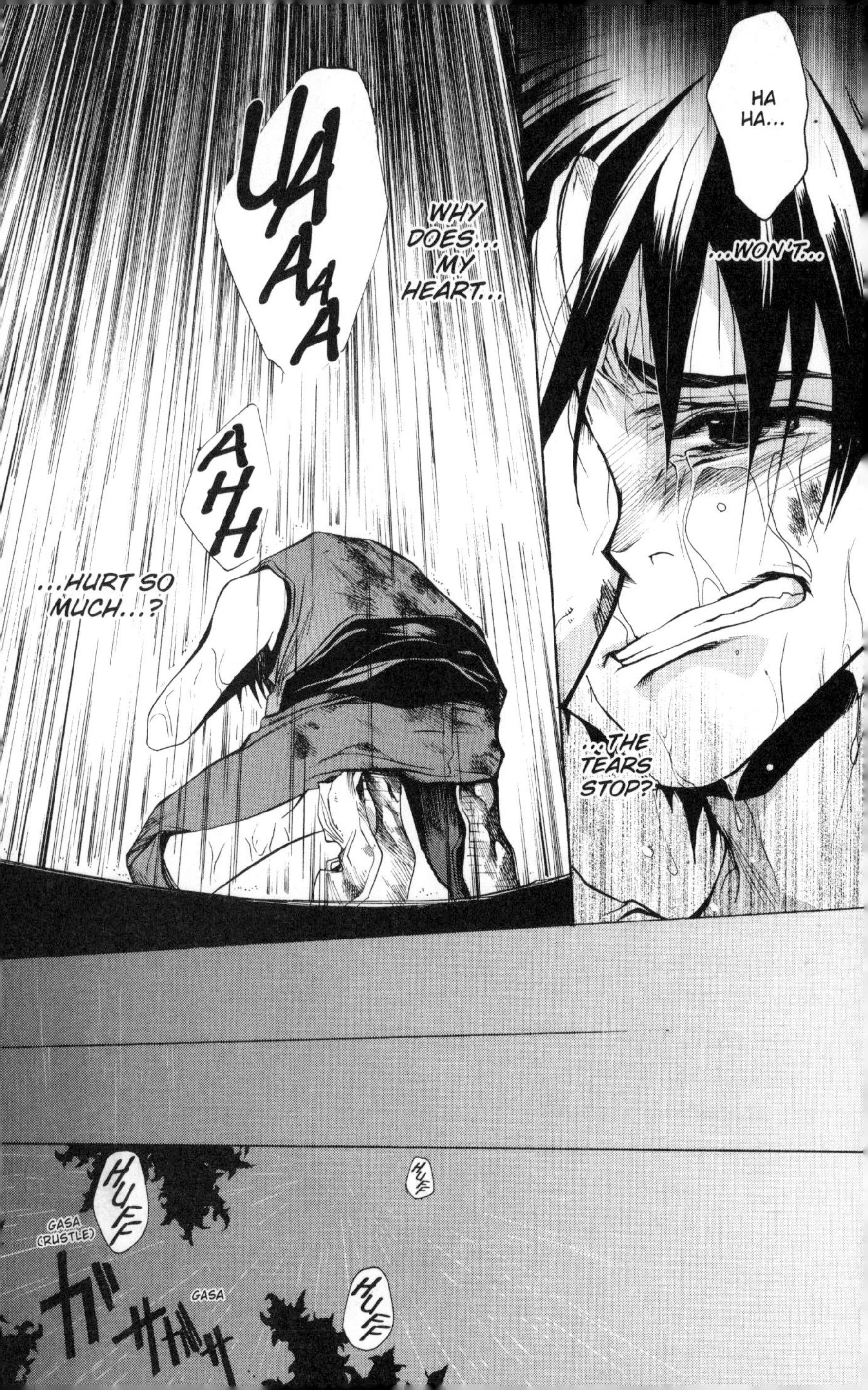
HA HA...
...WON'T...
...THE TEARS STOP?
UAAAA
WHY DOES... MY HEART...
AHH
...HURT SO MUCH...?
HUFF
HUFF
GASA (RUSTLE)
HUFF
GASA

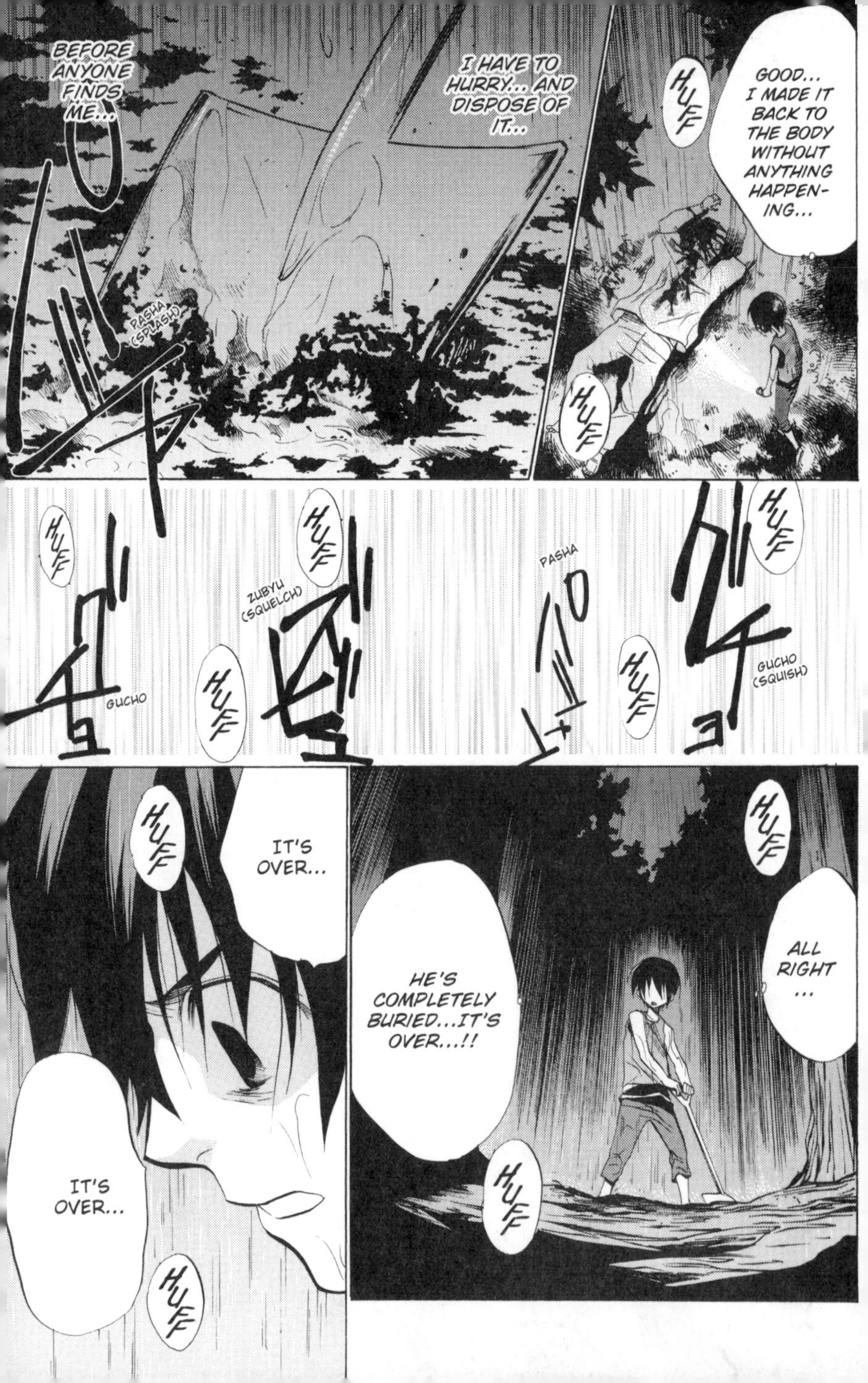
HUFF
GOOD... I MADE IT BACK TO THE BODY WITHOUT ANYTHING HAPPENING...
HUFF
I HAVE TO HURRY... AND DISPOSE OF IT...
BEFORE ANYONE FINDS ME...
PASHA (SPLASH)
HUFF
GUCHO (SQUISH)
HUFF
PASHA
HUFF
ZUBYU (SQUELCH)
HUFF
GUCHO
HUFF
HUFF
ALL RIGHT...
HE'S COMPLETELY BURIED...IT'S OVER...!!
HUFF
HUFF
IT'S OVER...
IT'S OVER...
HUFF

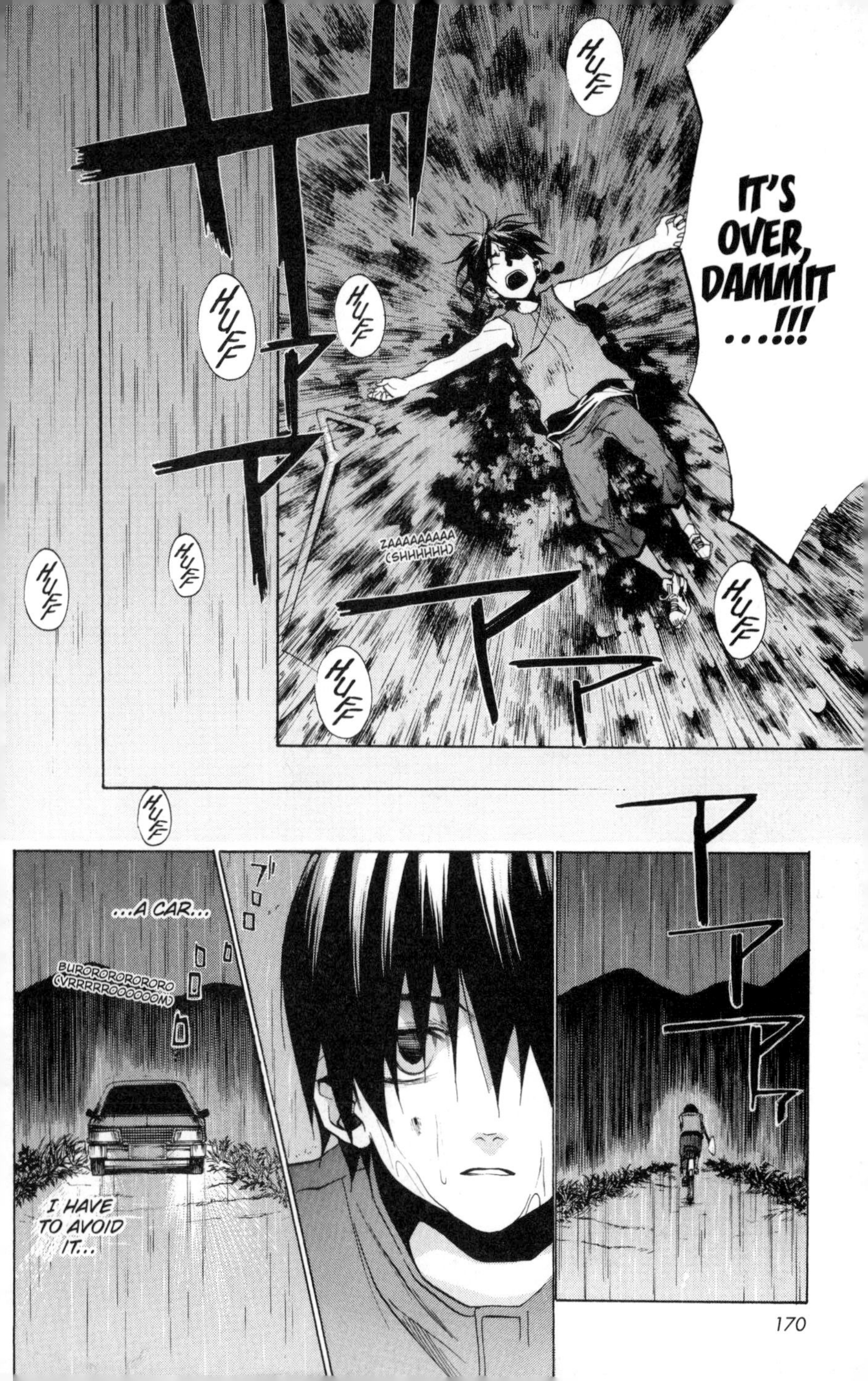
IT'S OVER, DAMMIT ....!!!
HUFF
HUFF
HUFF
HUFF
ZAAAAAAAAA (SHHHHHHH)
HUFF
HUFF
HUFF
HUFF
...A CAR...
BURORORORORORO (VRRRRROOOOOOM)
I HAVE TO AVOID IT...

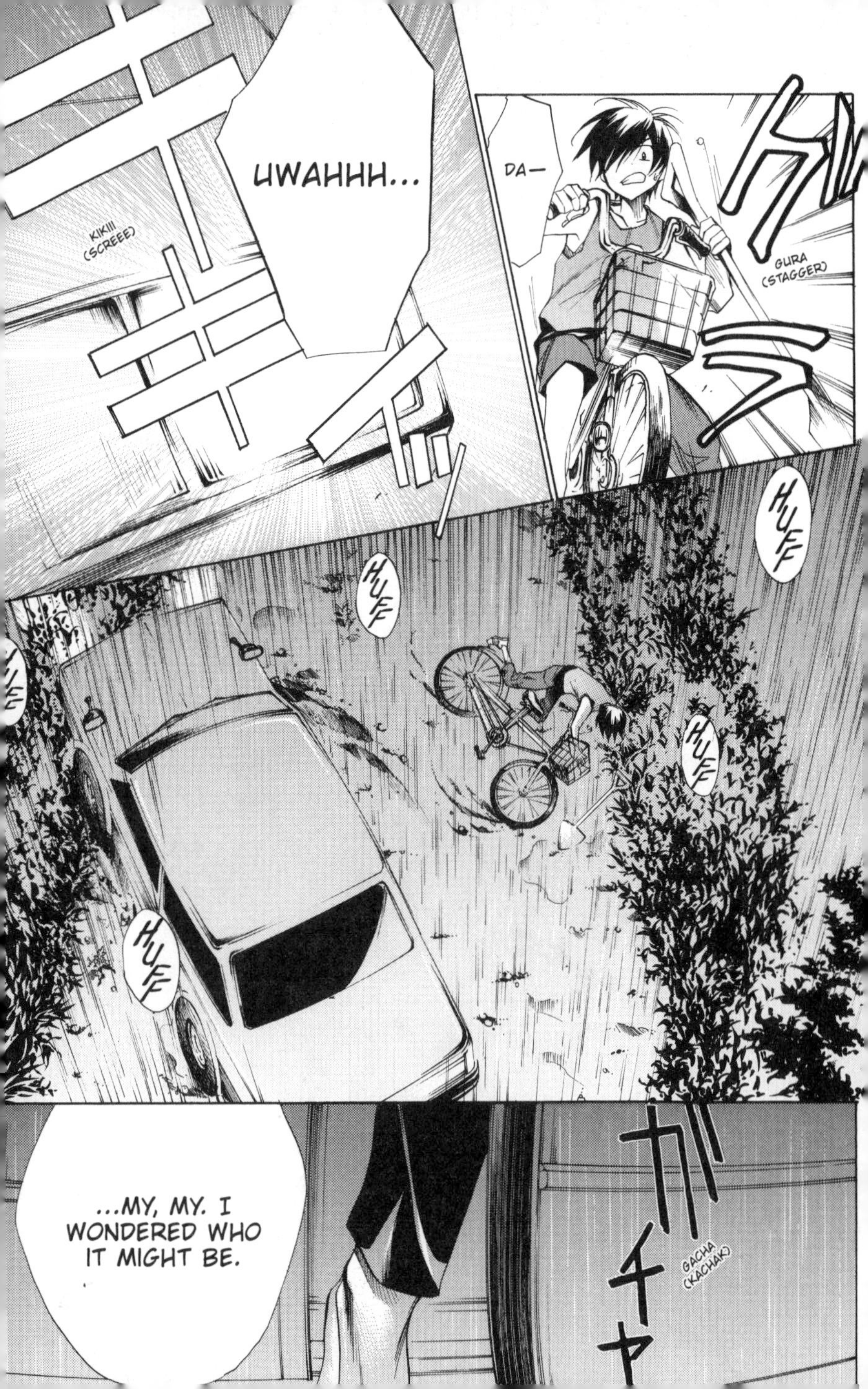
DA—
GURA (STAGGER)
UWAHHH...
KIKIII (SCREEE)
HUFF
HUFF
HUFF
HUFF
GACHA (KACHAK)
...MY, MY. I WONDERED WHO IT MIGHT BE.

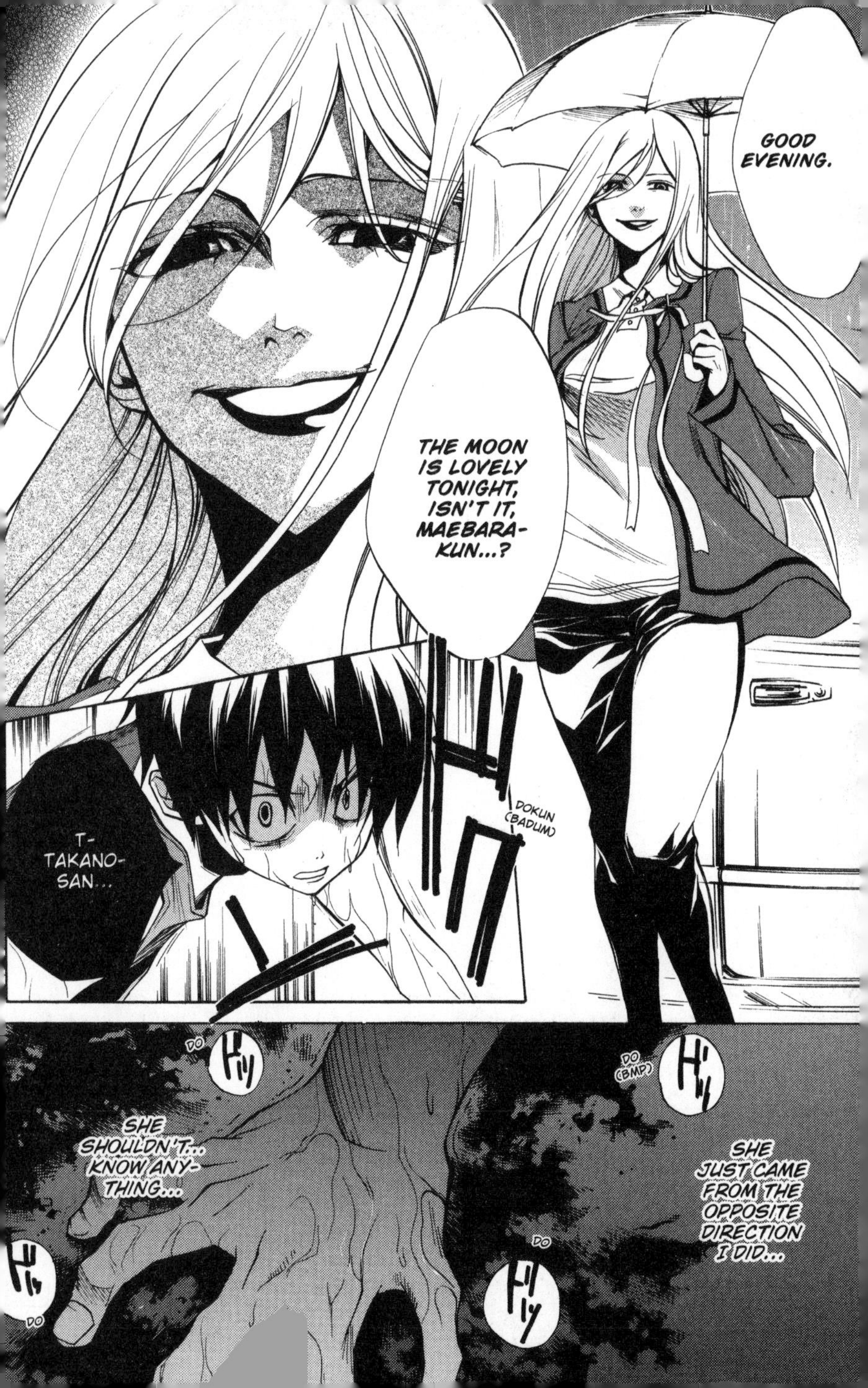
GOOD EVENING.
THE MOON IS LOVELY TONIGHT, ISN'T IT, MAEBARA-KUN...?
DOKUN (BADUM)
T-TAKANO-SAN...
DO (BMP)
DO
SHE JUST CAME FROM THE OPPOSITE DIRECTION I DID...
SHE SHOULDN'T... KNOW ANY-THING...
DO
DO

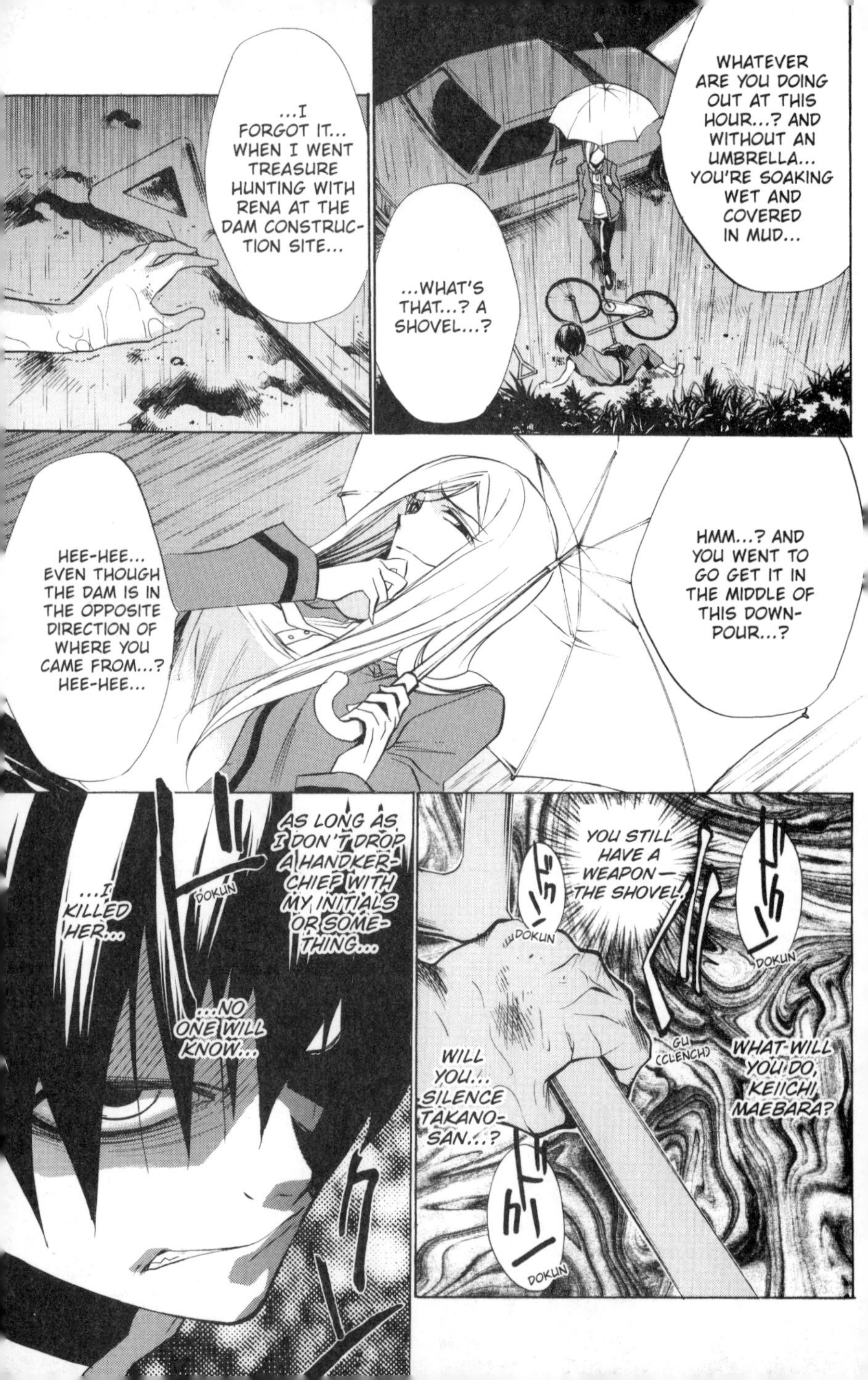
WHATEVER ARE YOU DOING OUT AT THIS HOUR...? AND WITHOUT AN UMBRELLA... YOU'RE SOAKING WET AND COVERED IN MUD...
...WHAT'S THAT...? A SHOVEL...?
...I FORGOT IT... WHEN I WENT TREASURE HUNTING WITH RENA AT THE DAM CONSTRUCTION SITE...
HMM...? AND YOU WENT TO GO GET IT IN THE MIDDLE OF THIS DOWNPOUR...?
HEE-HEE... EVEN THOUGH THE DAM IS IN THE OPPOSITE DIRECTION OF WHERE YOU CAME FROM...? HEE-HEE...
DOKUN
YOU STILL HAVE A WEAPON—THE SHOVEL!
DOKUN
DOKUN
WHAT WILL YOU DO, KEIICHI MAEBARA?
GU (CLENCH)
WILL YOU... SILENCE TAKANO-SAN...?
DOKUN
AS LONG AS I DON'T DROP A HANDKERCHIEF WITH MY INITIALS OR SOMETHING...
DOKUN
...I KILLED HER...
...NO ONE WILL KNOW...

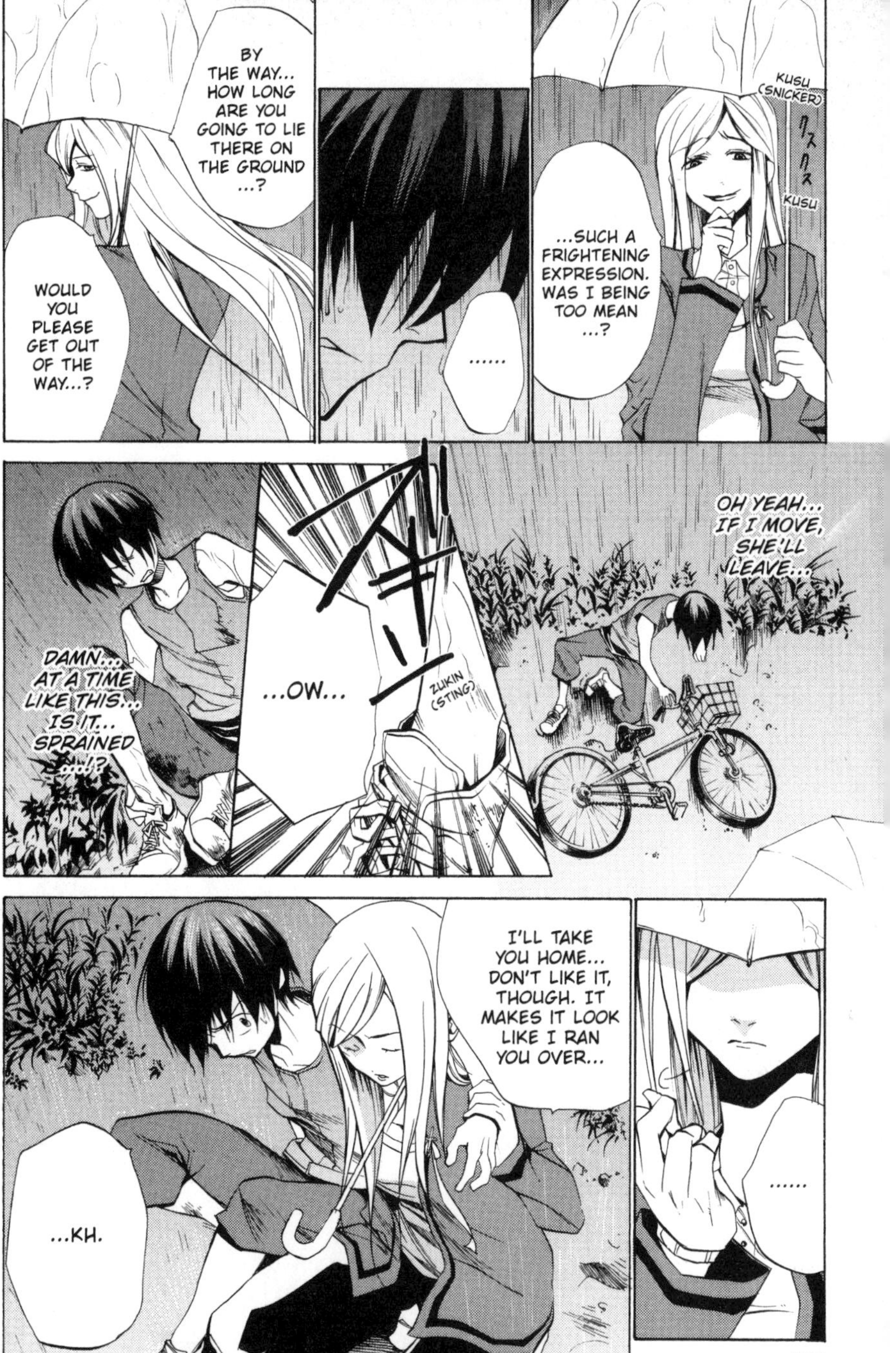
KUSU (SNICKER)
クスクス
KUSU
...SUCH A FRIGHTENING EXPRESSION. WAS I BEING TOO MEAN ...?
......
BY THE WAY... HOW LONG ARE YOU GOING TO LIE THERE ON THE GROUND ...?
WOULD YOU PLEASE GET OUT OF THE WAY...?
OH YEAH... IF I MOVE, SHE'LL LEAVE...
ZUKIN (STING)
...OW...
DAMN... AT A TIME LIKE THIS... IS IT... SPRAINED ...!?
......
I'LL TAKE YOU HOME... DON'T LIKE IT, THOUGH. IT MAKES IT LOOK LIKE I RAN YOU OVER...
...KH.

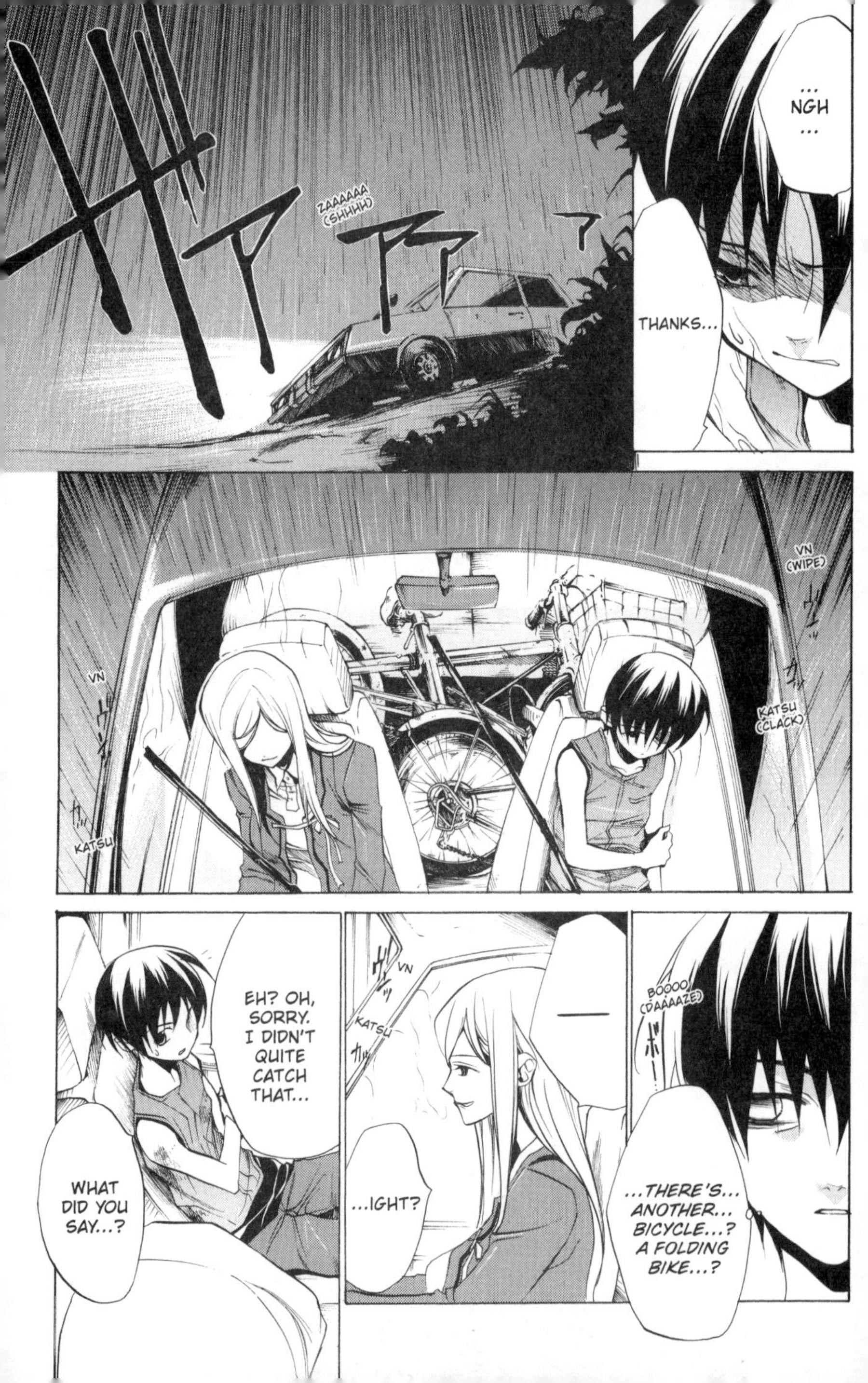

... NGH ...
THANKS...
ZAAAAAA (SHHHH)
VN (WIPE)
KATSU (CLACK)
VN
KATSU
BOOOO (DAAAAZE)
...THERE'S... ANOTHER... BICYCLE...? A FOLDING BIKE...?
—
VN
KATSU
...IGHT?
EH? OH, SORRY. I DIDN'T QUITE CATCH THAT...
WHAT DID YOU SAY...?

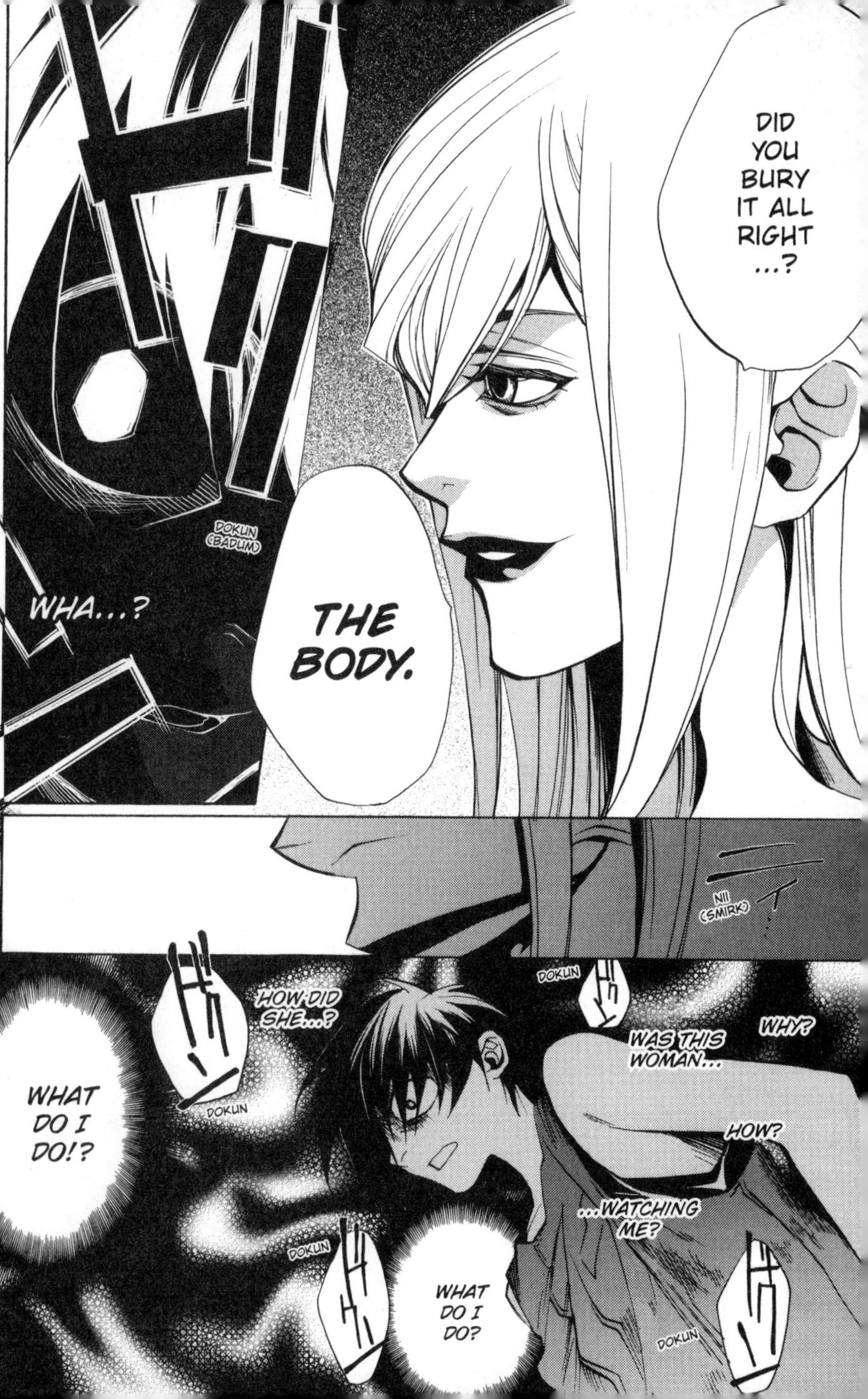
DID YOU BURY IT ALL RIGHT ...?
THE BODY.
DOKUN (BADUM)
WHA...?
NII (SMIRK)
WHY?
WAS THIS WOMAN...
DOKUN
HOW DID SHE...?
HOW?
...WATCHING ME?
DOKUN
WHAT DO I DO?
DOKUN
DOKUN
WHAT DO I DO!?
DOKUN

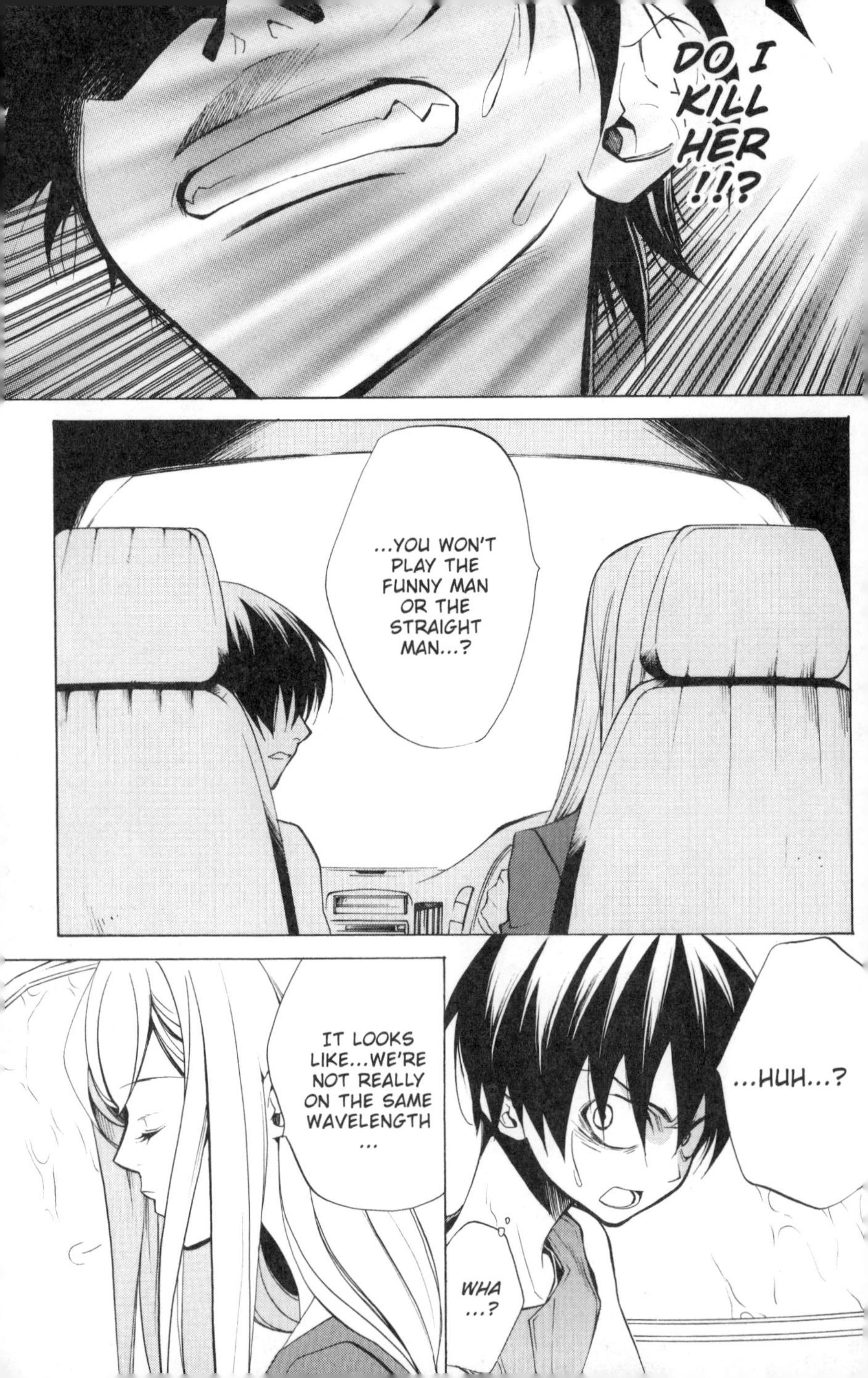
DO I KILL HER!!?
...YOU WON'T PLAY THE FUNNY MAN OR THE STRAIGHT MAN...?
...HUH...?
WHA...?
IT LOOKS LIKE...WE'RE NOT REALLY ON THE SAME WAVELENGTH...

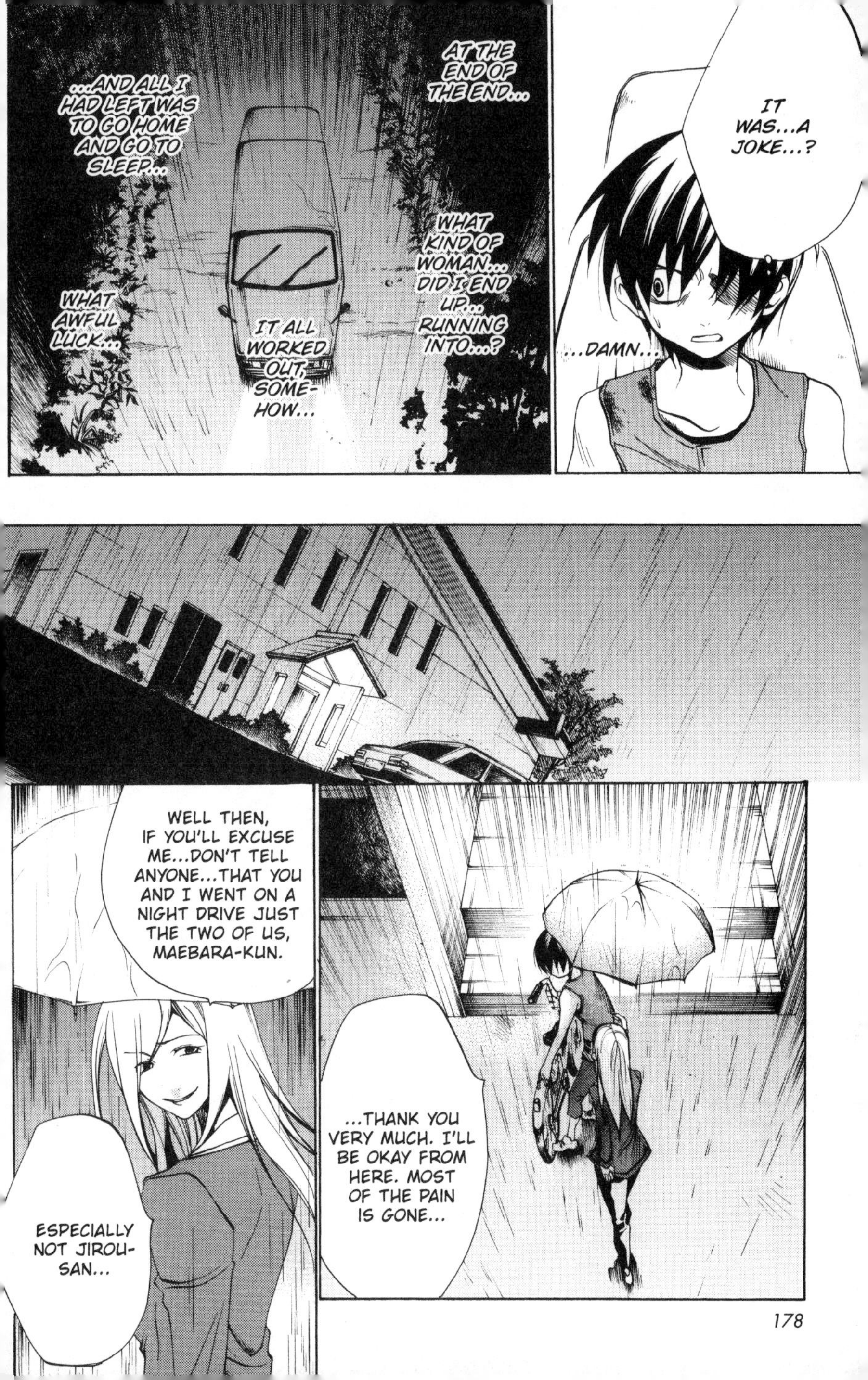
IT WAS...A JOKE...?
...DAMN...
AT THE END OF THE END...
...AND ALL I HAD LEFT WAS TO GO HOME AND GO TO SLEEP...
WHAT KIND OF WOMAN... DID I END UP... RUNNING INTO...?
IT ALL WORKED OUT, SOME-HOW...
WHAT AWFUL LUCK...
...THANK YOU VERY MUCH. I'LL BE OKAY FROM HERE. MOST OF THE PAIN IS GONE...
WELL THEN, IF YOU'LL EXCUSE ME...DON'T TELL ANYONE...THAT YOU AND I WENT ON A NIGHT DRIVE JUST THE TWO OF US, MAEBARA-KUN.
ESPECIALLY NOT JIROU-SAN...

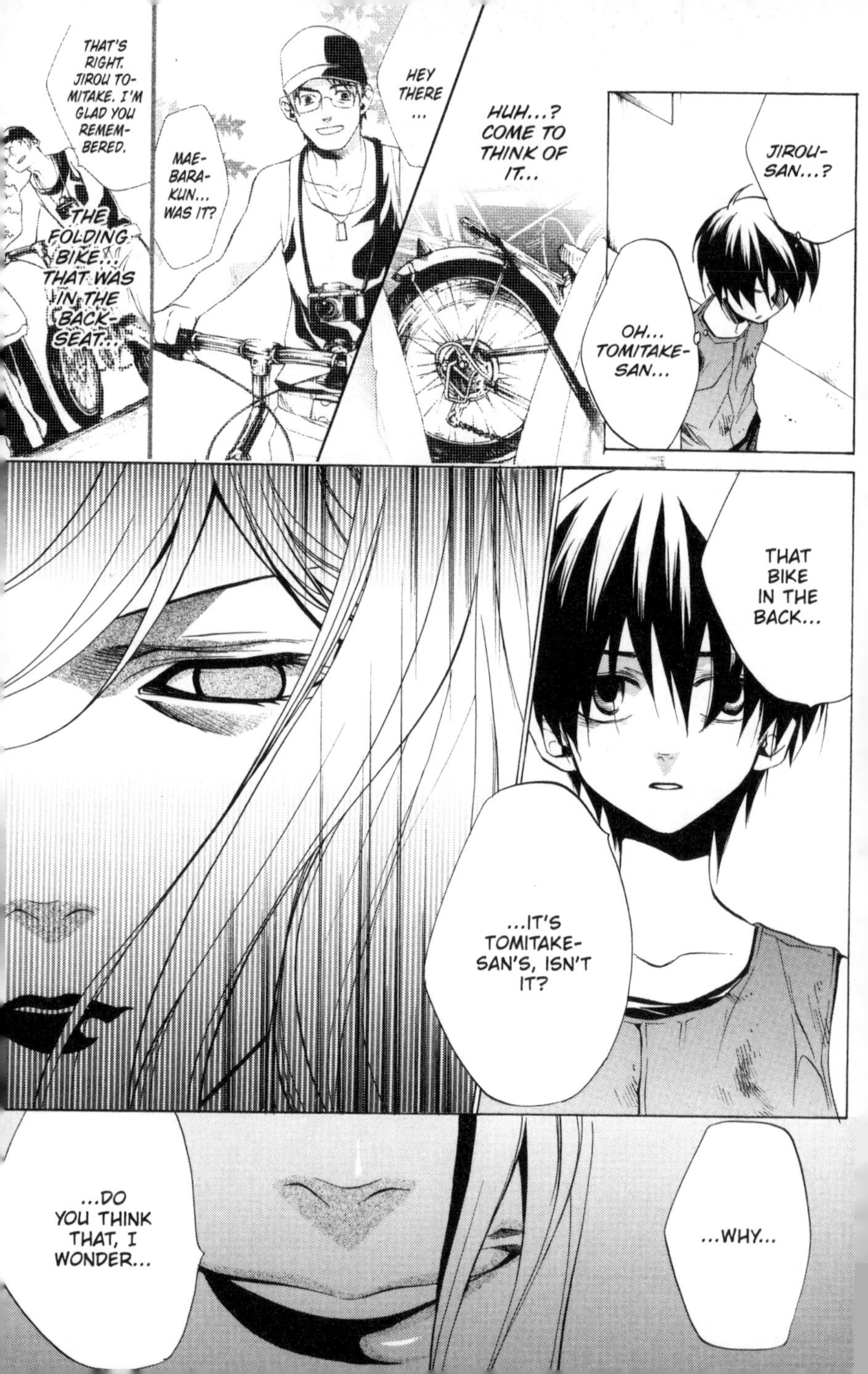
JIROU-SAN...?
OH... TOMITAKE-SAN...
HUH...? COME TO THINK OF IT...
HEY THERE...
MAE-BARA-KUN... WAS IT?
THAT'S RIGHT. JIROU TO-MITAKE. I'M GLAD YOU REMEM-BERED.
THE FOLDING BIKE... THAT WAS IN THE BACK-SEAT...
THAT BIKE IN THE BACK...
...IT'S TOMITAKE-SAN'S, ISN'T IT?
...WHY...
...DO YOU THINK THAT, I WONDER...

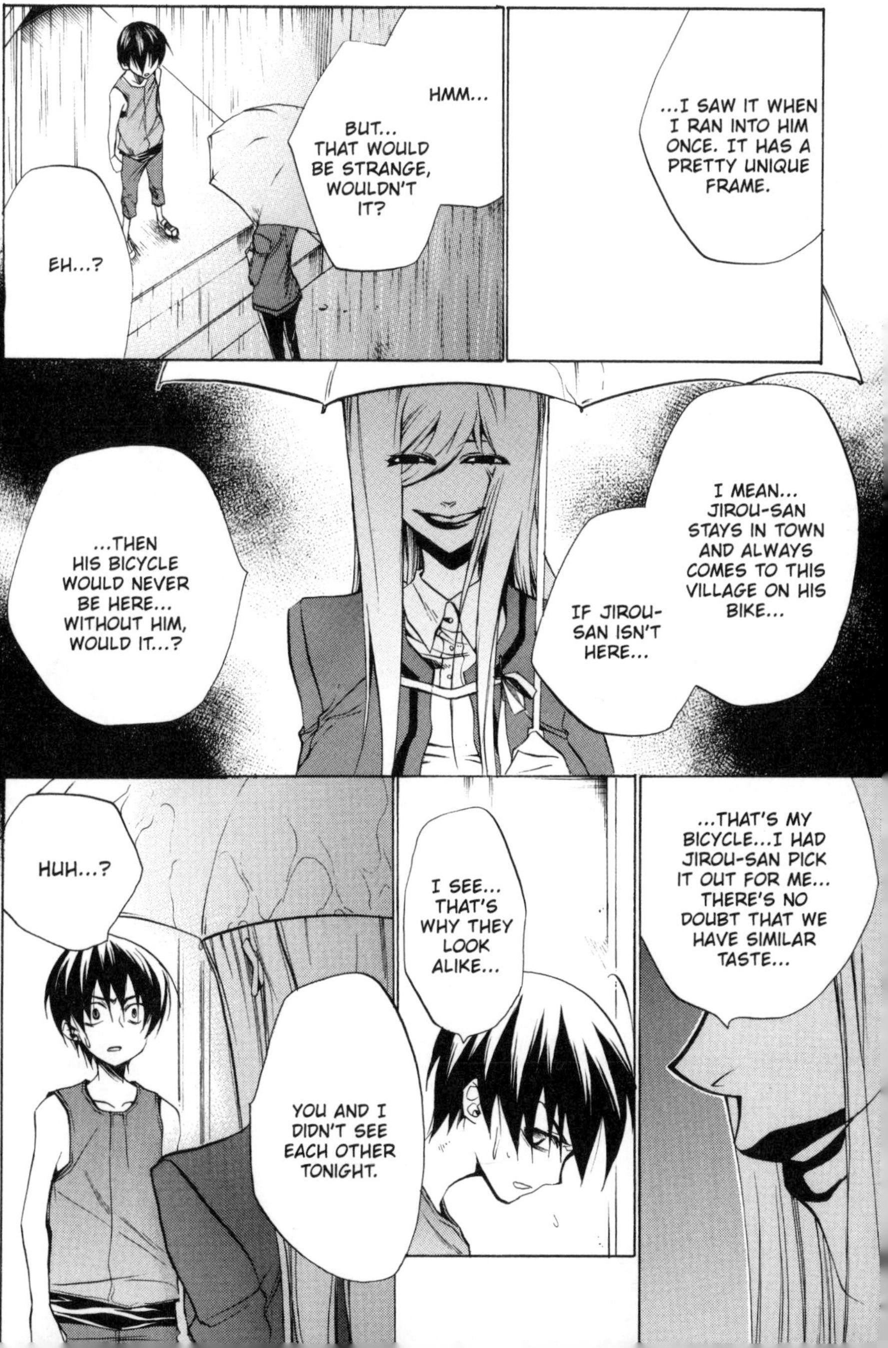

...I SAW IT WHEN I RAN INTO HIM ONCE. IT HAS A PRETTY UNIQUE FRAME.
HMM...
BUT... THAT WOULD BE STRANGE, WOULDN'T IT?
EH...?
I MEAN... JIROU-SAN STAYS IN TOWN AND ALWAYS COMES TO THIS VILLAGE ON HIS BIKE...
IF JIROU-SAN ISN'T HERE...
...THEN HIS BICYCLE WOULD NEVER BE HERE... WITHOUT HIM, WOULD IT...?
...THAT'S MY BICYCLE...I HAD JIROU-SAN PICK IT OUT FOR ME... THERE'S NO DOUBT THAT WE HAVE SIMILAR TASTE...
I SEE... THAT'S WHY THEY LOOK ALIKE...
HUH...?
YOU AND I DIDN'T SEE EACH OTHER TONIGHT.

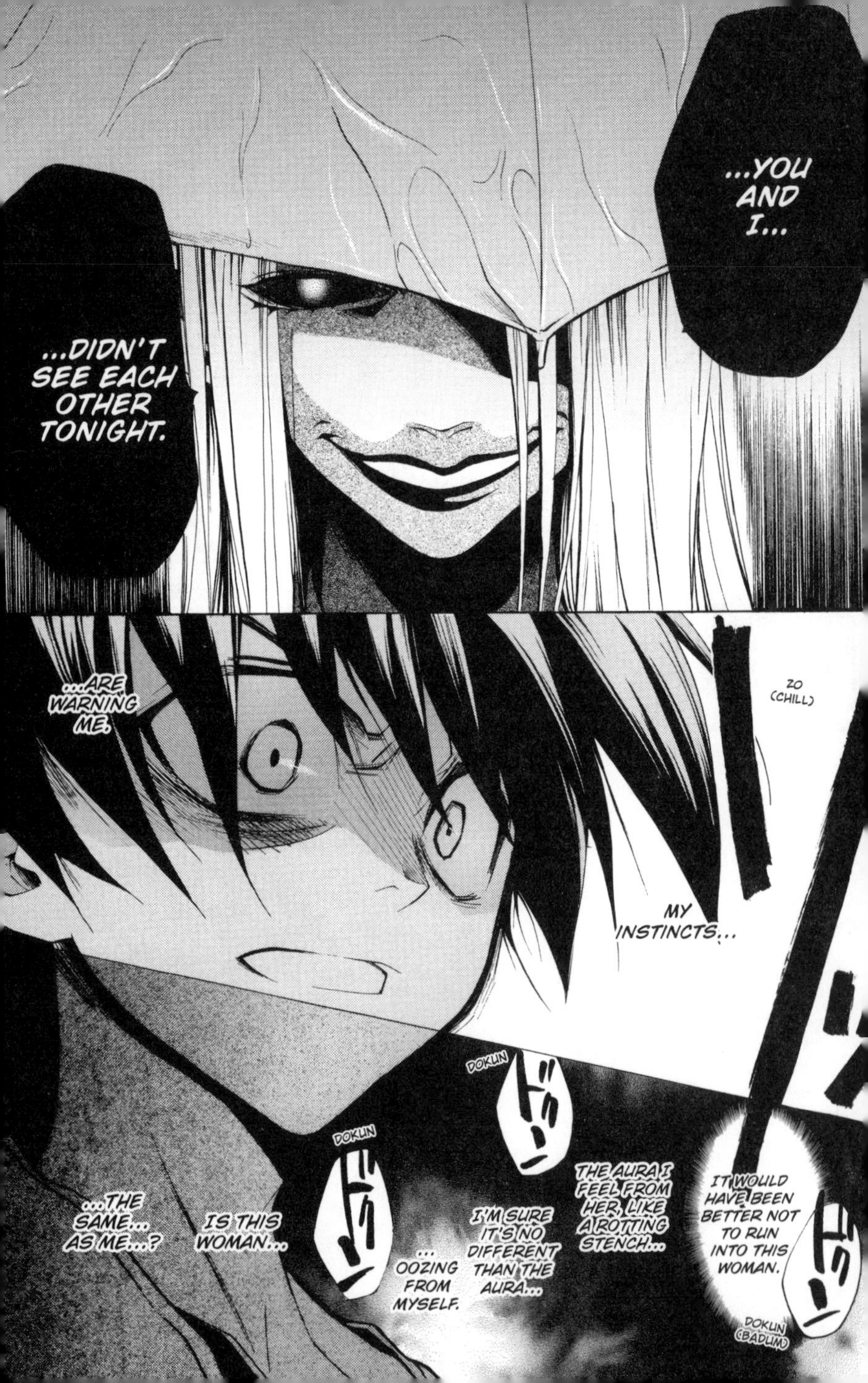
...YOU AND I...
...DIDN'T SEE EACH OTHER TONIGHT.
ZO (CHILL)
MY INSTINCTS...
...ARE WARNING ME.
DOKUN
IT WOULD HAVE BEEN BETTER NOT TO RUN INTO THIS WOMAN.
DOKUN (BADUM)
THE AURA I FEEL FROM HER, LIKE A ROTTING STENCH...
I'M SURE IT'S NO DIFFERENT THAN THE AURA...
...OOZING FROM MYSELF.
DOKUN
IS THIS WOMAN...
...THE SAME... AS ME...?

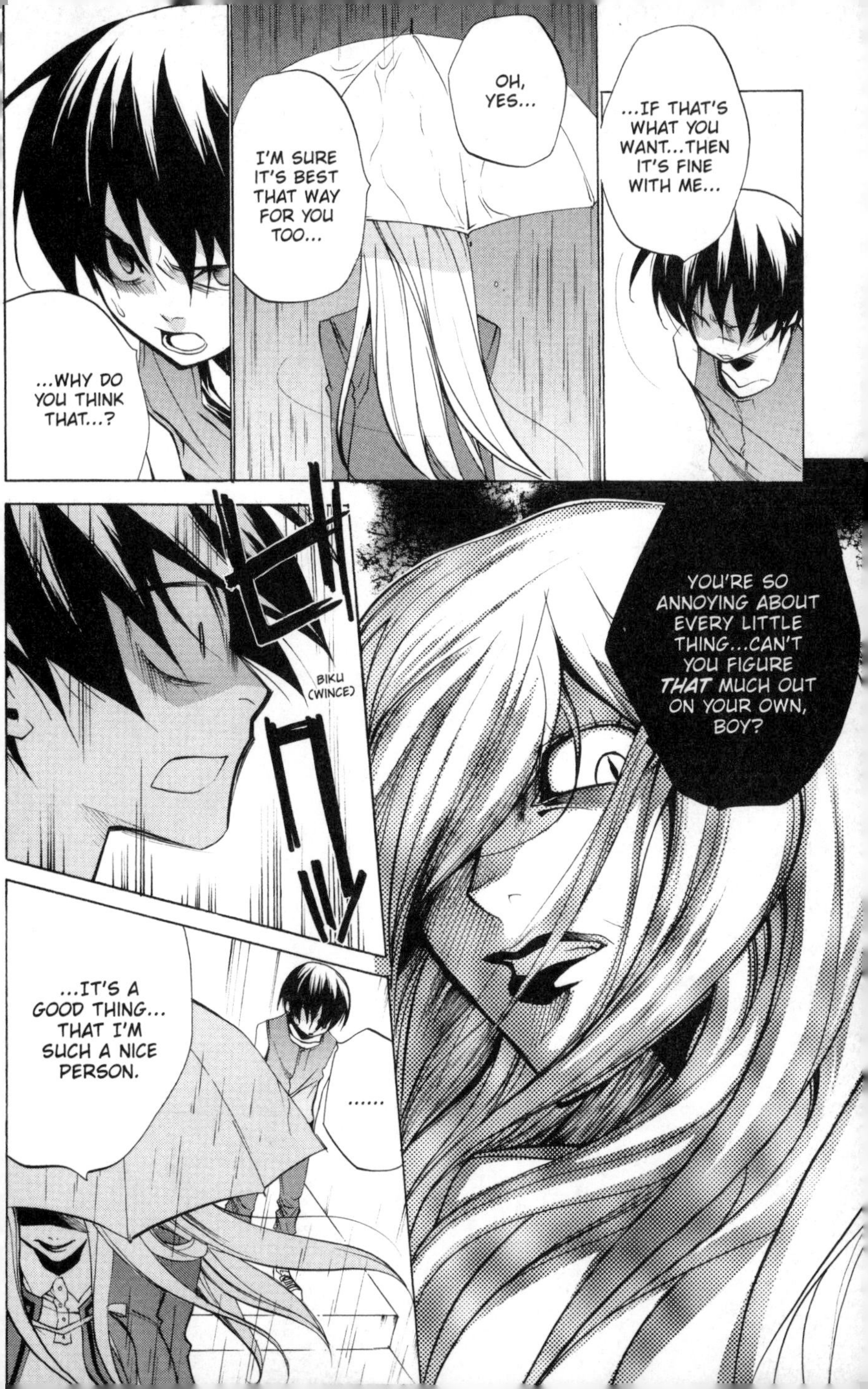
...IF THAT'S WHAT YOU WANT...THEN IT'S FINE WITH ME...
OH, YES...
I'M SURE IT'S BEST THAT WAY FOR YOU TOO...
...WHY DO YOU THINK THAT...?
YOU'RE SO ANNOYING ABOUT EVERY LITTLE THING...CAN'T YOU FIGURE *THAT* MUCH OUT ON YOUR OWN, BOY?
BIKU (WINCE)
......
...IT'S A GOOD THING... THAT I'M SUCH A NICE PERSON.

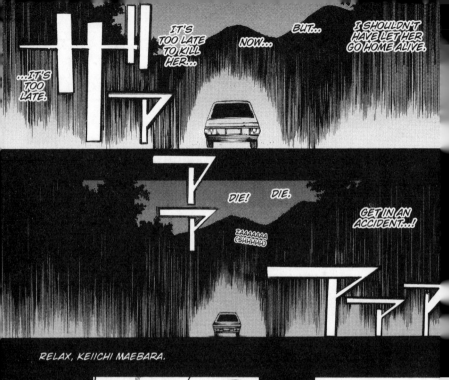

I SHOULDN'T HAVE LET HER GO HOME ALIVE.
BUT...
NOW...
IT'S TOO LATE TO KILL HER...
...IT'S TOO LATE.
GET IN AN ACCIDENT...!
DIE.
DIE!
ZAAAAAAA (SHHHHH)
RELAX, KEIICHI MAEBARA.
YORO (STAGGER)
THAT WOMAN...
...WILL DIE.
GUSHA (SQUISH)
GUSHA
A CRUEL END...
...BEFITTING HER.
GUSHA

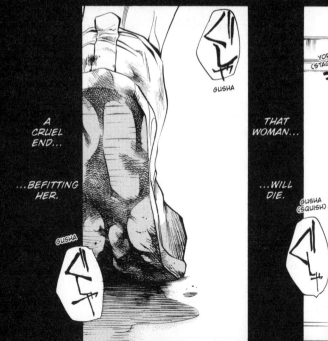

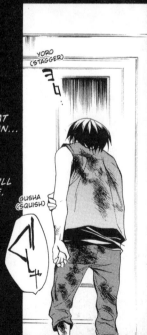

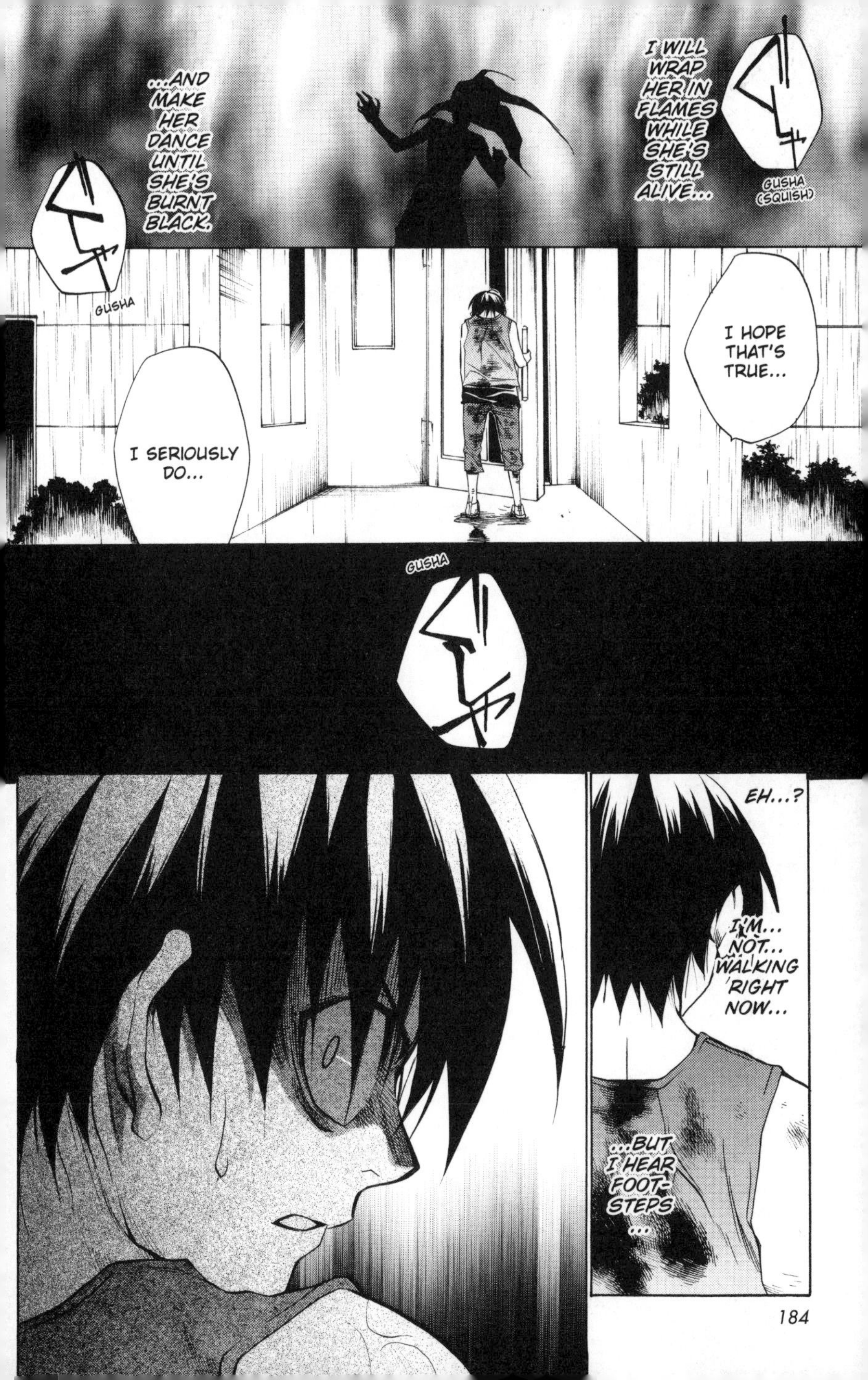
I WILL WRAP HER IN FLAMES WHILE SHE'S STILL ALIVE...
GUSHA (SQUISH)
...AND MAKE HER DANCE UNTIL SHE'S BURNT BLACK.
GUSHA
I HOPE THAT'S TRUE...
I SERIOUSLY DO...
GUSHA
EH...?
I'M... NOT... WALKING RIGHT NOW...
...BUT I HEAR FOOT-STEPS...

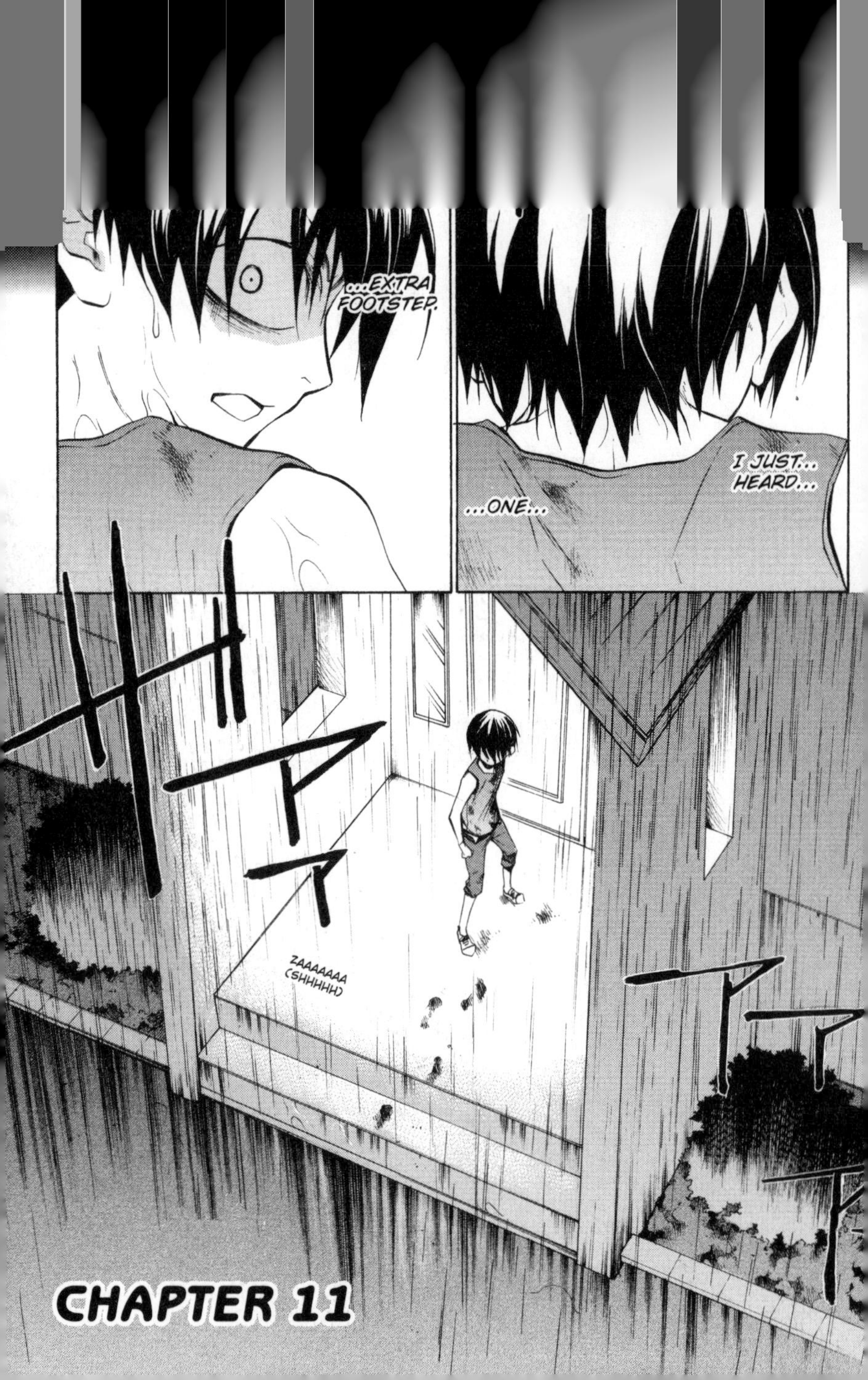
I JUST... HEARD...
...ONE...
...EXTRA FOOTSTEP.
ZAAAAAAA (SHHHHH)
CHAPTER 11

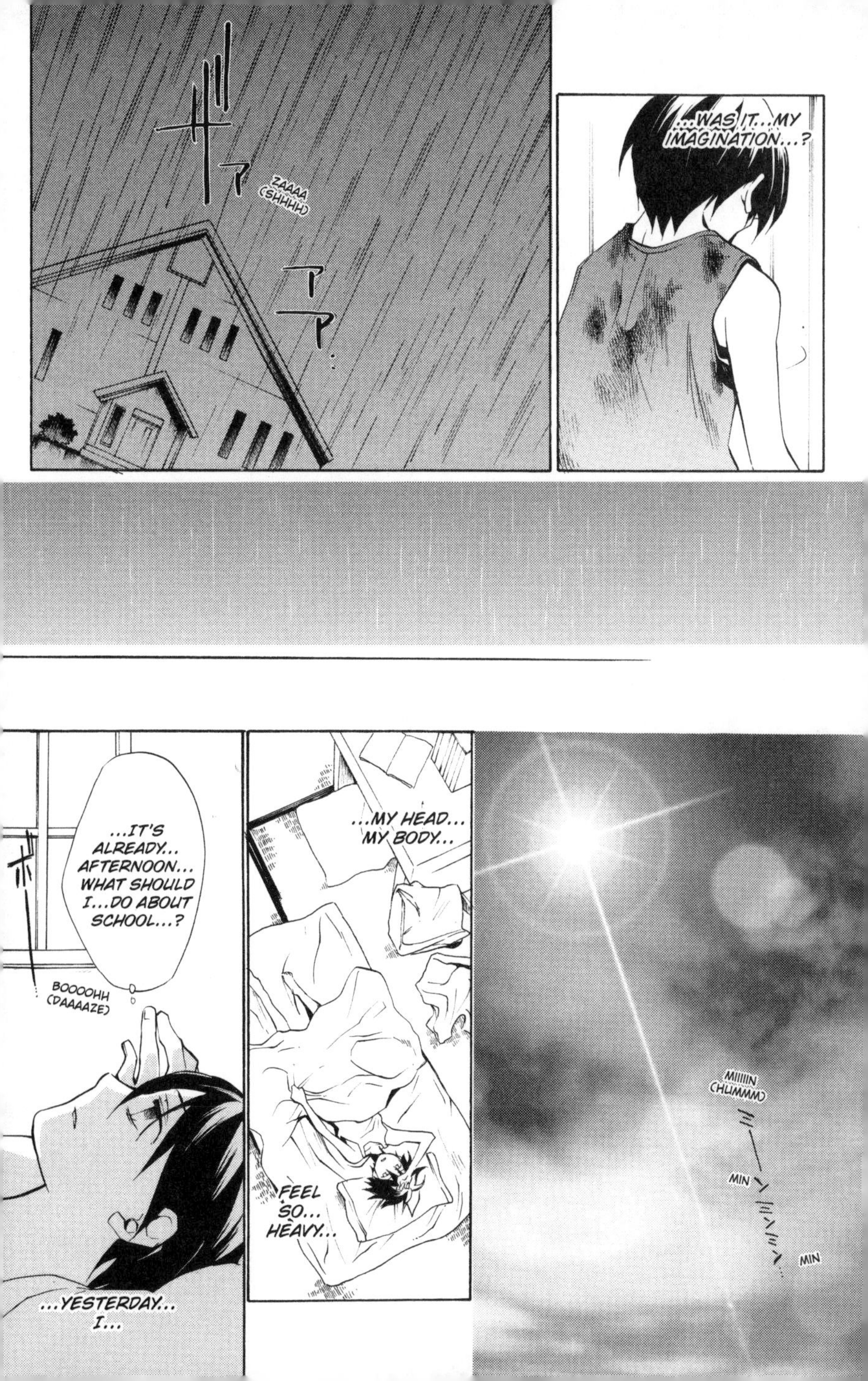
...WAS IT...MY IMAGINATION...?
ZAAAA (SHHHH)
MIIIIN (HUMMM)
MIN
MIN
...MY HEAD... MY BODY...
FEEL SO... HEAVY...
...IT'S ALREADY... AFTERNOON... WHAT SHOULD I...DO ABOUT SCHOOL...?
BOOOOHH (DAAAAZE)
...YESTERDAY... I...

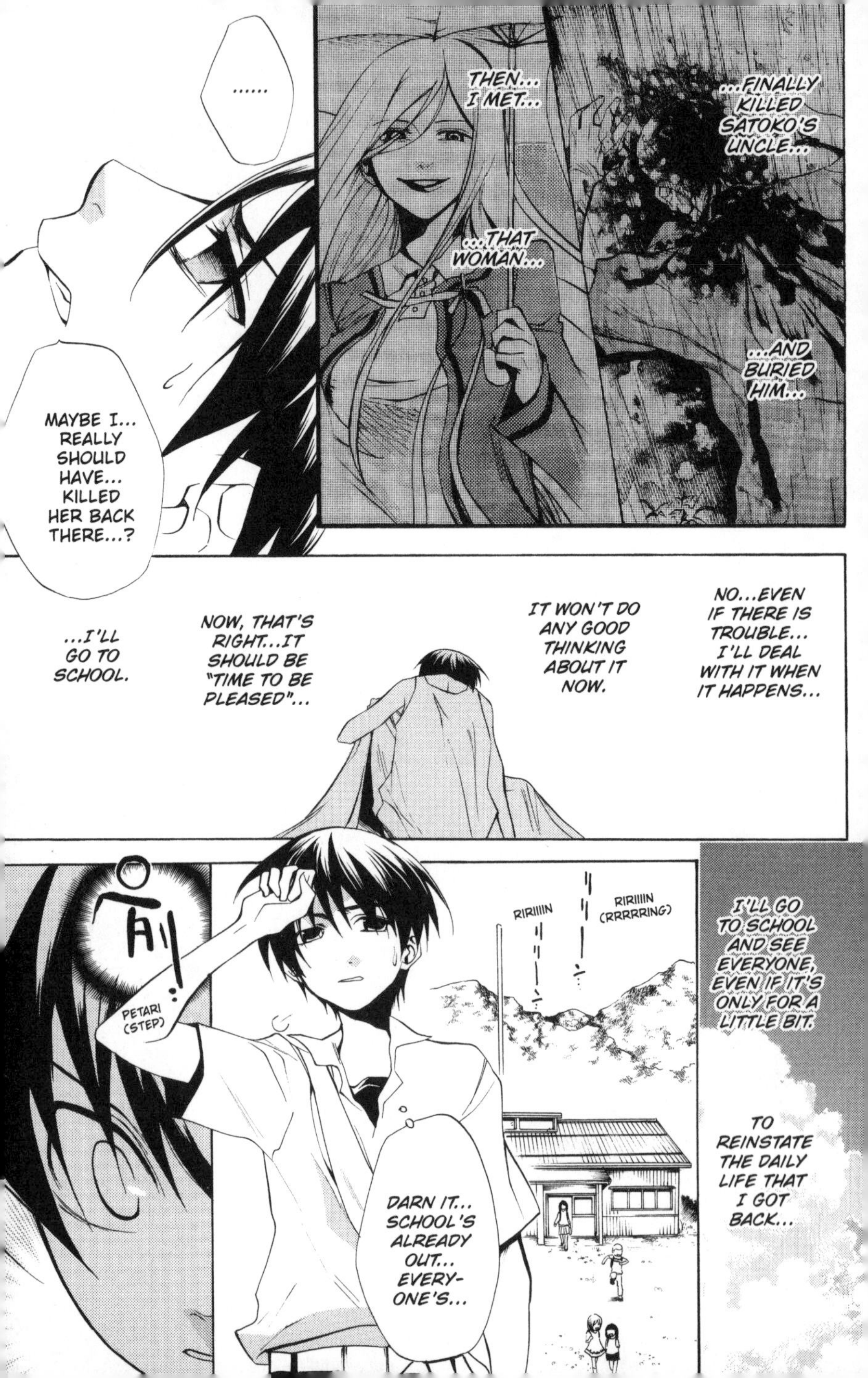
...FINALLY KILLED SATOKO'S UNCLE...
...AND BURIED HIM...
THEN... I MET...
...THAT WOMAN...
......
MAYBE I... REALLY SHOULD HAVE... KILLED HER BACK THERE...?
NO...EVEN IF THERE IS TROUBLE... I'LL DEAL WITH IT WHEN IT HAPPENS...
IT WON'T DO ANY GOOD THINKING ABOUT IT NOW.
NOW, THAT'S RIGHT...IT SHOULD BE "TIME TO BE PLEASED"...
...I'LL GO TO SCHOOL.
I'LL GO TO SCHOOL AND SEE EVERYONE, EVEN IF IT'S ONLY FOR A LITTLE BIT.
TO REINSTATE THE DAILY LIFE THAT I GOT BACK...
RIRIIIIN (RRRRRING)
RIRIIIIN
DARN IT... SCHOOL'S ALREADY OUT... EVERY-ONE'S...
PETARI (STEP)

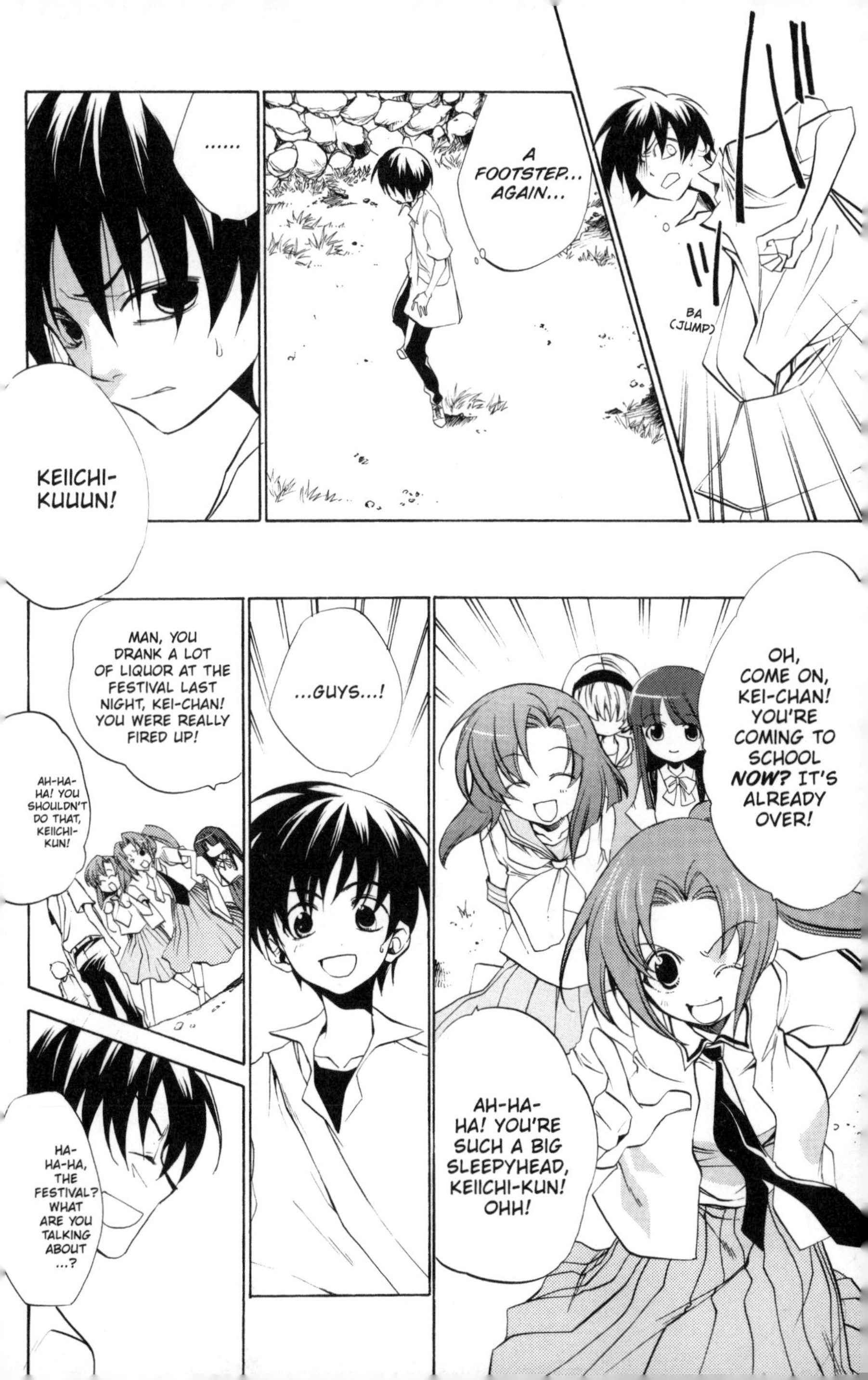
BA (JUMP)
A FOOTSTEP... AGAIN...
......
KEIICHI-KUUUN!
OH, COME ON, KEI-CHAN! YOU'RE COMING TO SCHOOL **NOW?** IT'S ALREADY OVER!
AH-HA-HA! YOU'RE SUCH A BIG SLEEPYHEAD, KEIICHI-KUN! OHH!
...GUYS...!
MAN, YOU DRANK A LOT OF LIQUOR AT THE FESTIVAL LAST NIGHT, KEI-CHAN! YOU WERE REALLY FIRED UP!
AH-HA-HA! YOU SHOULDN'T DO THAT, KEIICHI-KUN!
HA-HA-HA, THE FESTIVAL? WHAT ARE YOU TALKING ABOUT ...?

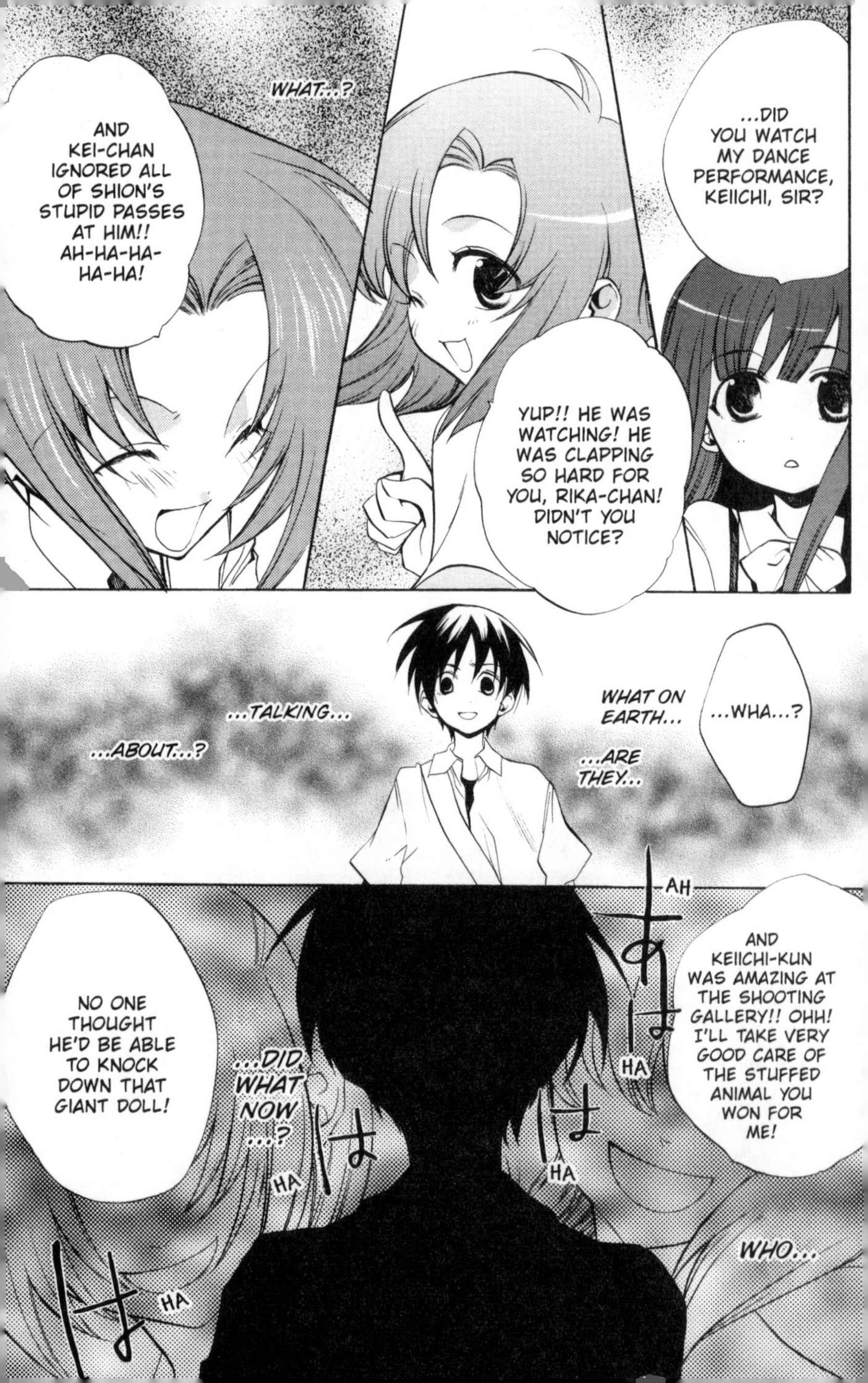
...DID YOU WATCH MY DANCE PERFORMANCE, KEIICHI, SIR?
YUP!! HE WAS WATCHING! HE WAS CLAPPING SO HARD FOR YOU, RIKA-CHAN! DIDN'T YOU NOTICE?
WHAT...?
AND KEI-CHAN IGNORED ALL OF SHION'S STUPID PASSES AT HIM!! AH-HA-HA-HA-HA!
...WHA...?
WHAT ON EARTH...
...ARE THEY...
...TALKING...
...ABOUT...?
AH
AND KEIICHI-KUN WAS AMAZING AT THE SHOOTING GALLERY!! OHH! I'LL TAKE VERY GOOD CARE OF THE STUFFED ANIMAL YOU WON FOR ME!
HA
HA
WHO...
...DID WHAT NOW...?
HA
NO ONE THOUGHT HE'D BE ABLE TO KNOCK DOWN THAT GIANT DOLL!
HA

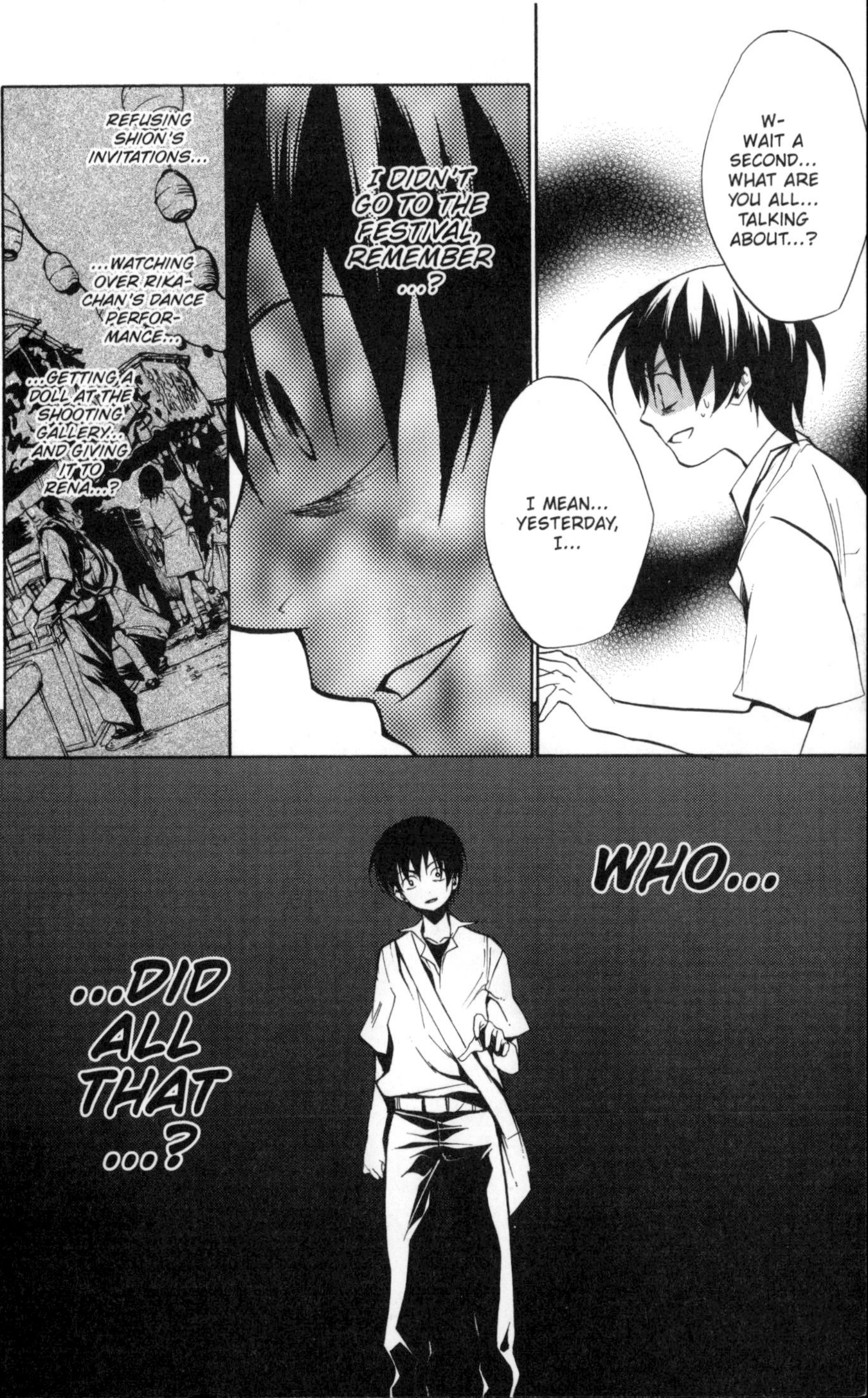
W-WAIT A SECOND... WHAT ARE YOU ALL... TALKING ABOUT...?
I MEAN... YESTERDAY, I...
I DIDN'T GO TO THE FESTIVAL, REMEMBER...?
REFUSING SHION'S INVITATIONS...
...WATCHING OVER RIKA-CHAN'S DANCE PERFORMANCE...
...GETTING A DOLL AT THE SHOOTING GALLERY... AND GIVING IT TO RENA...?
WHO...
...DID ALL THAT...?

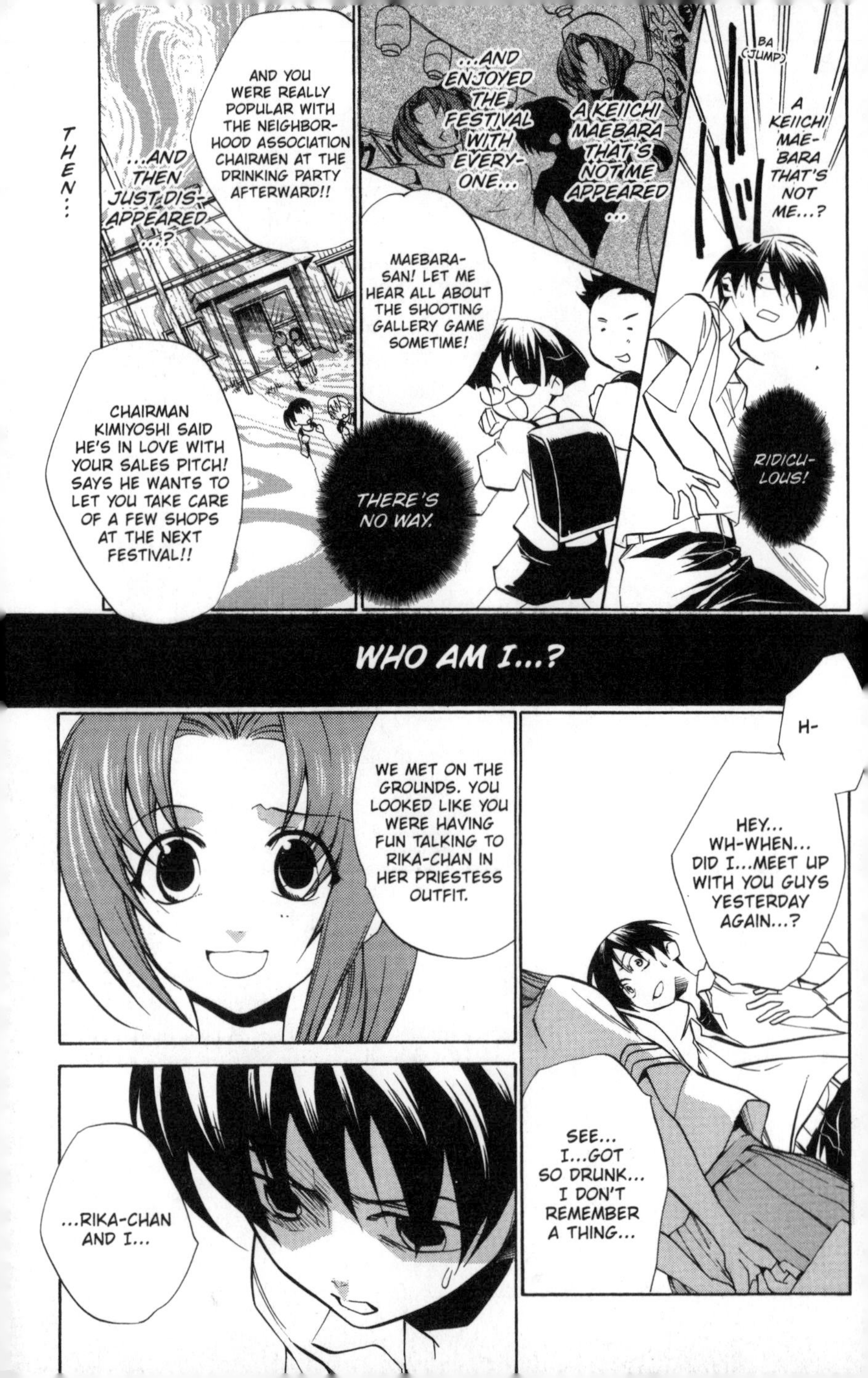
BA (JUMP)
A KEIICHI MAE-BARA THAT'S NOT ME...?
RIDICU-LOUS!
...AND ENJOYED THE FESTIVAL WITH EVERY-ONE...
A KEIICHI MAEBARA THAT'S NOT ME APPEARED...
MAEBARA-SAN! LET ME HEAR ALL ABOUT THE SHOOTING GALLERY GAME SOMETIME!
THERE'S NO WAY.
AND YOU WERE REALLY POPULAR WITH THE NEIGHBOR-HOOD ASSOCIATION CHAIRMEN AT THE DRINKING PARTY AFTERWARD!!
THEN...
...AND THEN JUST DIS-APPEARED...?
CHAIRMAN KIMIYOSHI SAID HE'S IN LOVE WITH YOUR SALES PITCH! SAYS HE WANTS TO LET YOU TAKE CARE OF A FEW SHOPS AT THE NEXT FESTIVAL!!
WHO AM I...?
H-
HEY... WH-WHEN... DID I...MEET UP WITH YOU GUYS YESTERDAY AGAIN...?
SEE... I...GOT SO DRUNK... I DON'T REMEMBER A THING...
WE MET ON THE GROUNDS. YOU LOOKED LIKE YOU WERE HAVING FUN TALKING TO RIKA-CHAN IN HER PRIESTESS OUTFIT.
...RIKA-CHAN AND I...

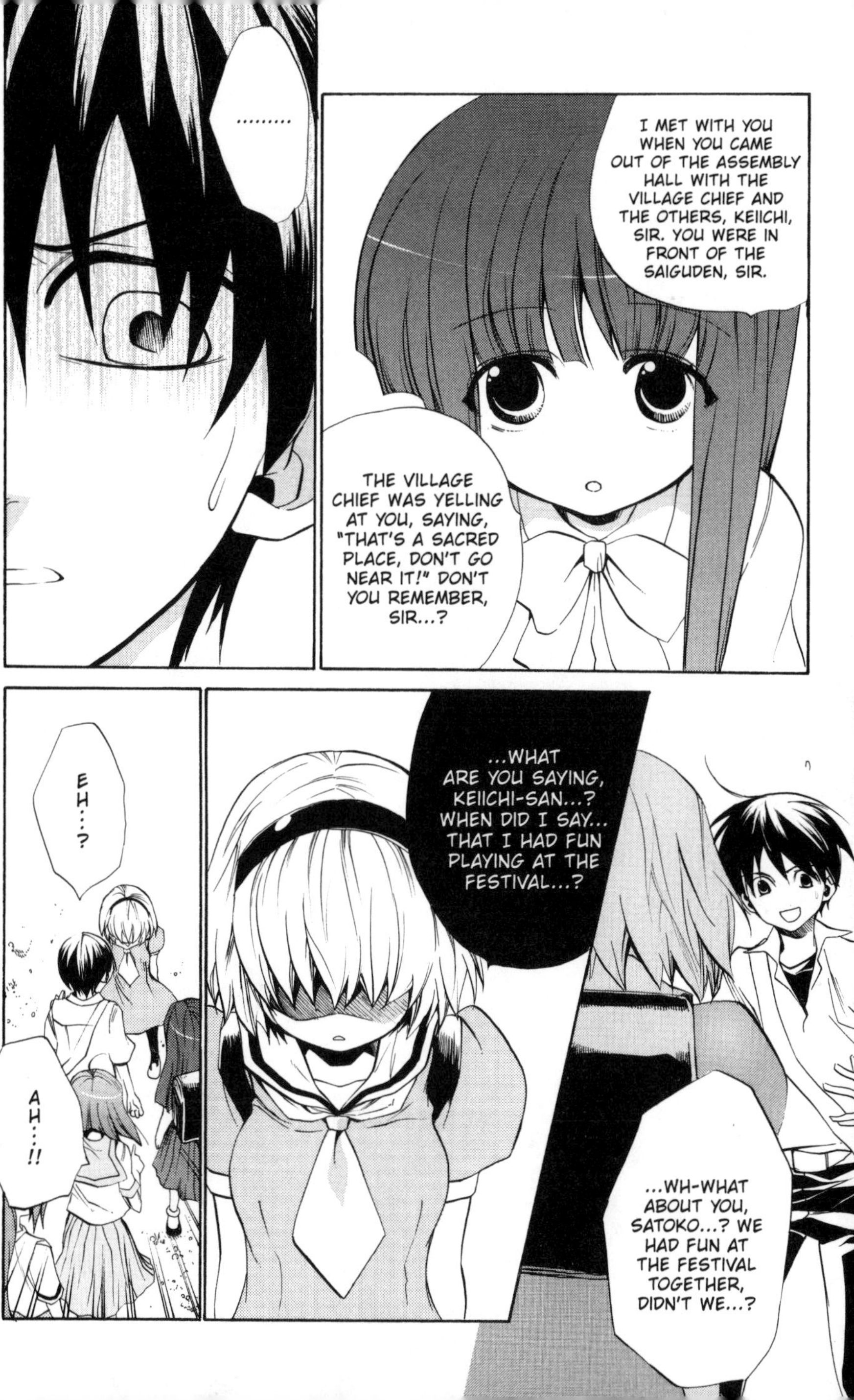
I MET WITH YOU WHEN YOU CAME OUT OF THE ASSEMBLY HALL WITH THE VILLAGE CHIEF AND THE OTHERS, KEIICHI, SIR. YOU WERE IN FRONT OF THE SAIGUDEN, SIR.
THE VILLAGE CHIEF WAS YELLING AT YOU, SAYING, "THAT'S A SACRED PLACE, DON'T GO NEAR IT!" DON'T YOU REMEMBER, SIR...?
....
...WHAT ARE YOU SAYING, KEIICHI-SAN...? WHEN DID I SAY... THAT I HAD FUN PLAYING AT THE FESTIVAL...?
...WH-WHAT ABOUT YOU, SATOKO...? WE HAD FUN AT THE FESTIVAL TOGETHER, DIDN'T WE...?
EH...?
AH...!!

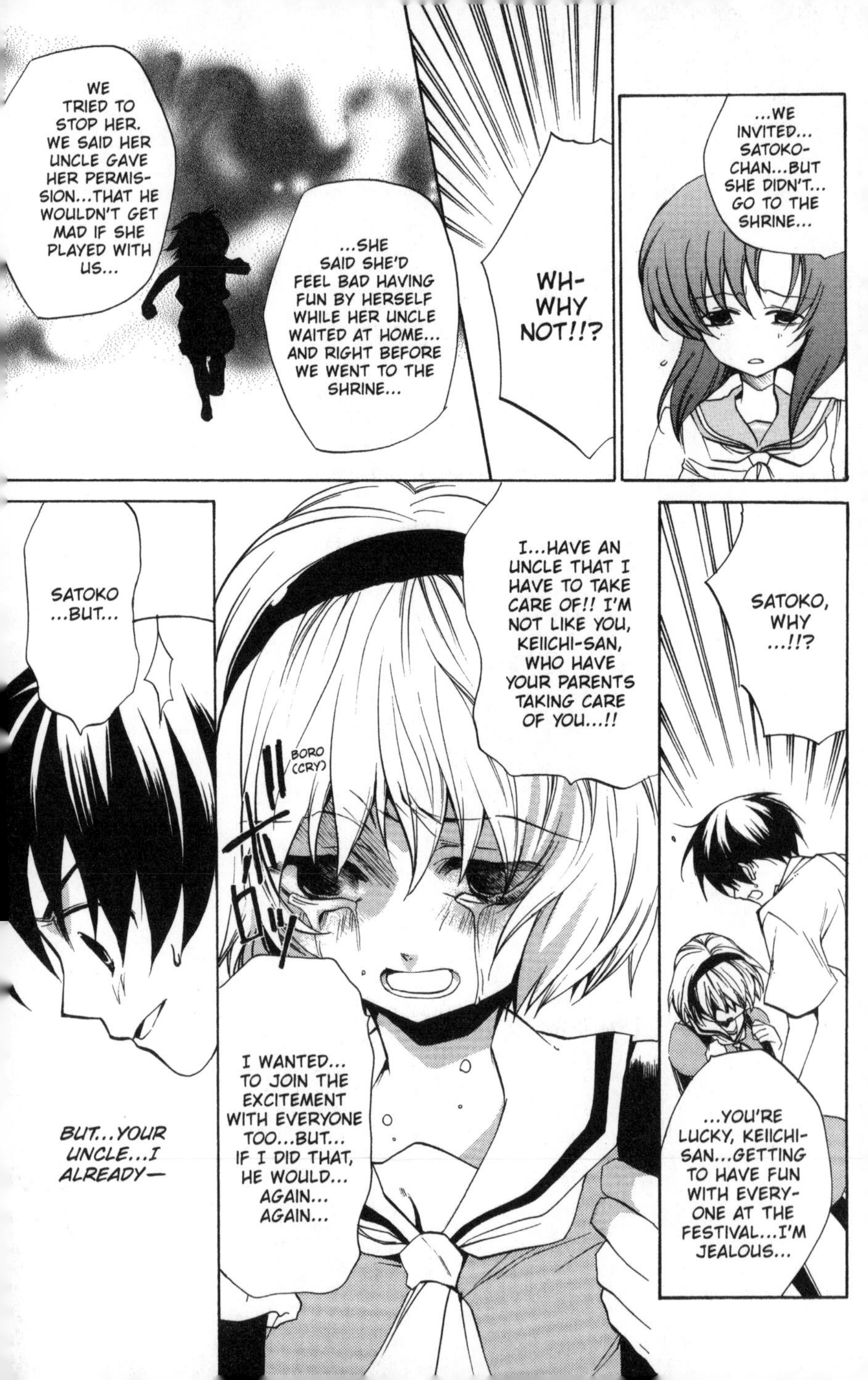
...WE INVITED... SATOKO-CHAN...BUT SHE DIDN'T... GO TO THE SHRINE...
WH-WHY NOT!!?
...SHE SAID SHE'D FEEL BAD HAVING FUN BY HERSELF WHILE HER UNCLE WAITED AT HOME... AND RIGHT BEFORE WE WENT TO THE SHRINE...
WE TRIED TO STOP HER. WE SAID HER UNCLE GAVE HER PERMISSION...THAT HE WOULDN'T GET MAD IF SHE PLAYED WITH US...
SATOKO, WHY ...!!?
...YOU'RE LUCKY, KEIICHI-SAN...GETTING TO HAVE FUN WITH EVERYONE AT THE FESTIVAL...I'M JEALOUS...
I...HAVE AN UNCLE THAT I HAVE TO TAKE CARE OF!! I'M NOT LIKE YOU, KEIICHI-SAN, WHO HAVE YOUR PARENTS TAKING CARE OF YOU...!!
BORO (CRY)
I WANTED... TO JOIN THE EXCITEMENT WITH EVERYONE TOO...BUT... IF I DID THAT, HE WOULD... AGAIN... AGAIN...
SATOKO ...BUT...
BUT...YOUR UNCLE...I ALREADY—

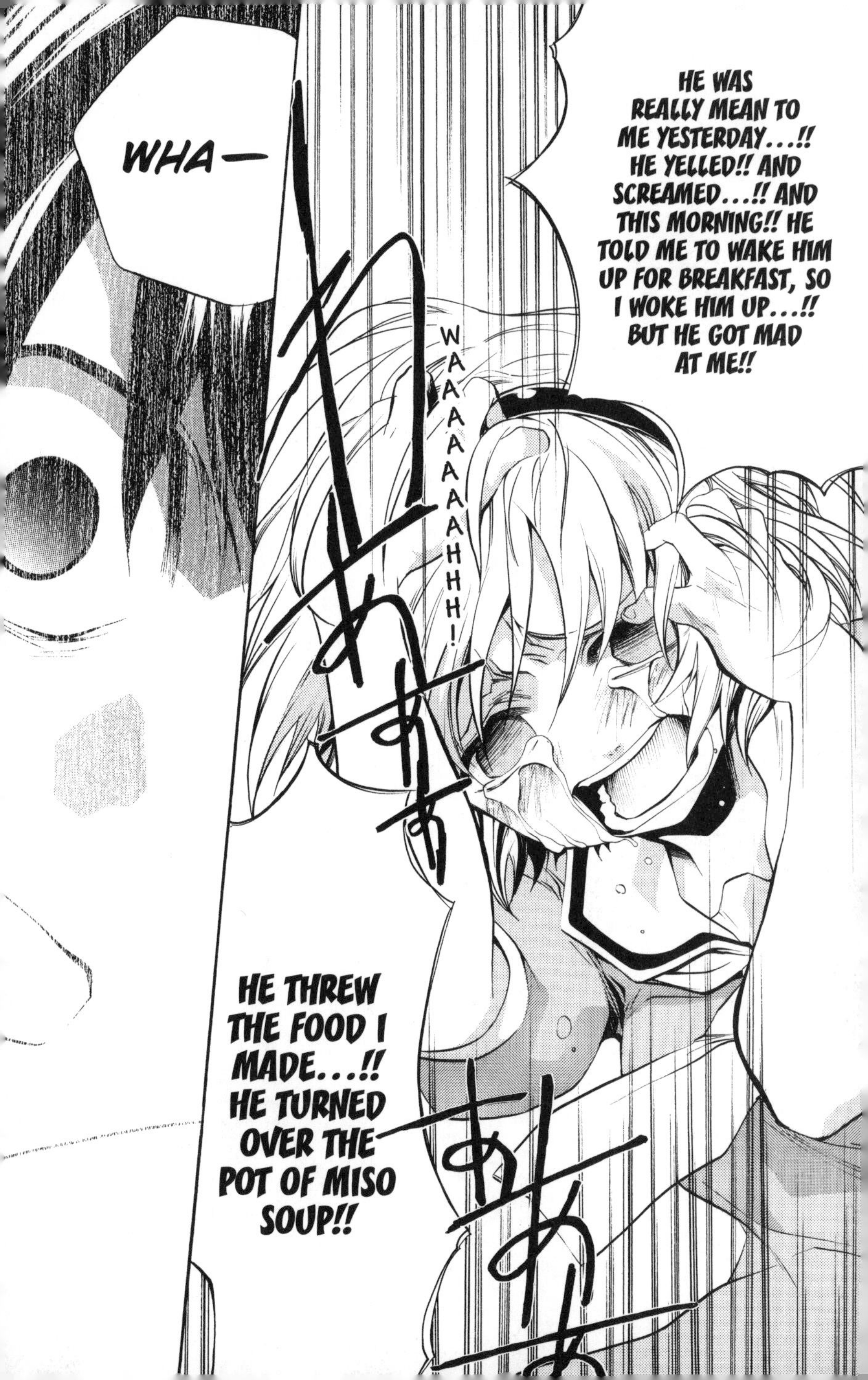
HE WAS REALLY MEAN TO ME YESTERDAY...!! HE YELLED!! AND SCREAMED...!! AND THIS MORNING!! HE TOLD ME TO WAKE HIM UP FOR BREAKFAST, SO I WOKE HIM UP...!! BUT HE GOT MAD AT ME!!
WAAAAAAAHHH!
HE THREW THE FOOD I MADE...!! HE TURNED OVER THE POT OF MISO SOUP!!
WHA—

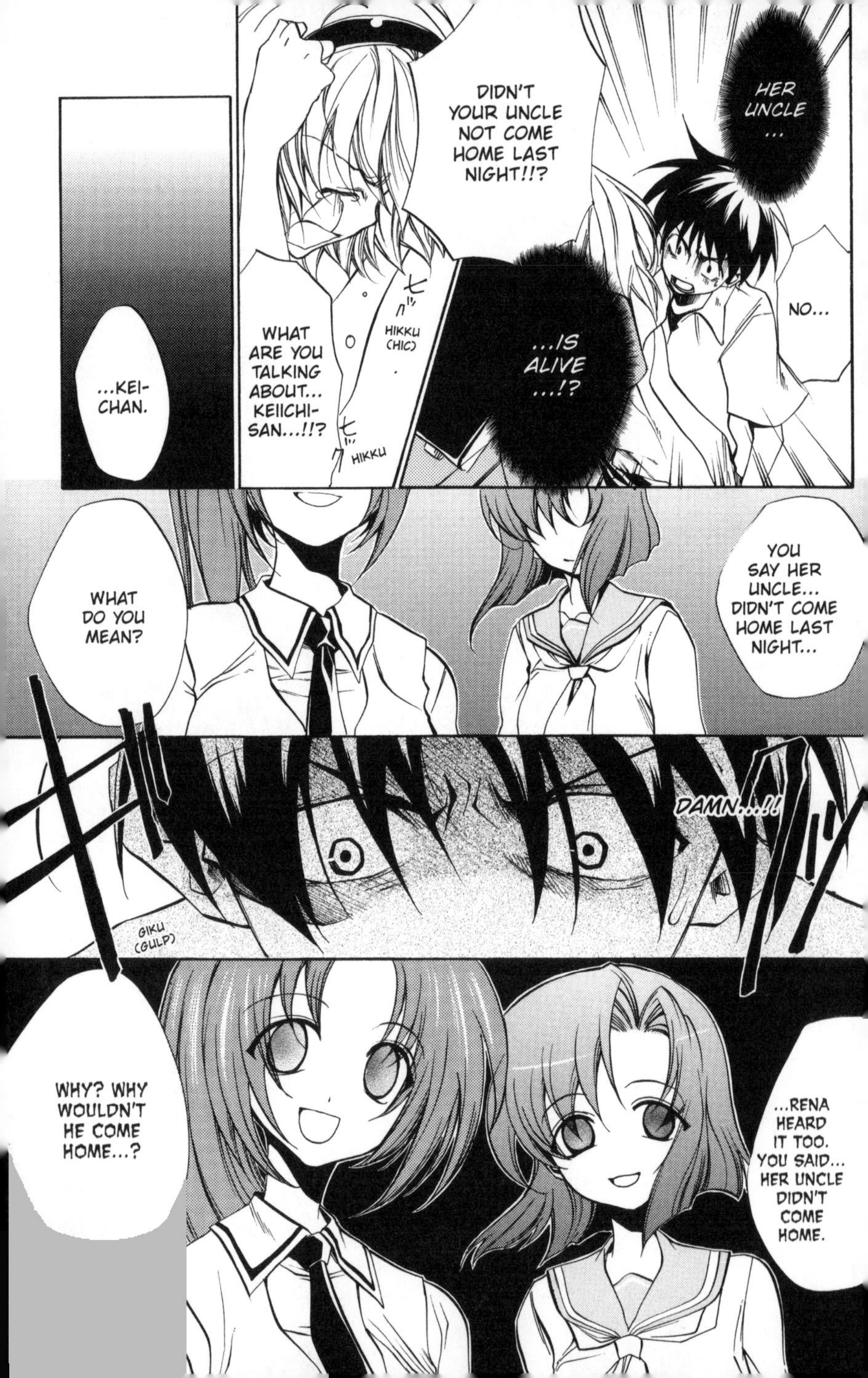
HER UNCLE ...
DIDN'T YOUR UNCLE NOT COME HOME LAST NIGHT!!?
NO...
...IS ALIVE ...!?
HIKKU (HIC)
WHAT ARE YOU TALKING ABOUT... KEIICHI-SAN...!!?
HIKKU
...KEI-CHAN.
YOU SAY HER UNCLE... DIDN'T COME HOME LAST NIGHT...
WHAT DO YOU MEAN?
DAMN...!!
GIKU (GULP)
...RENA HEARD IT TOO. YOU SAID... HER UNCLE DIDN'T COME HOME.
WHY? WHY WOULDN'T HE COME HOME...?

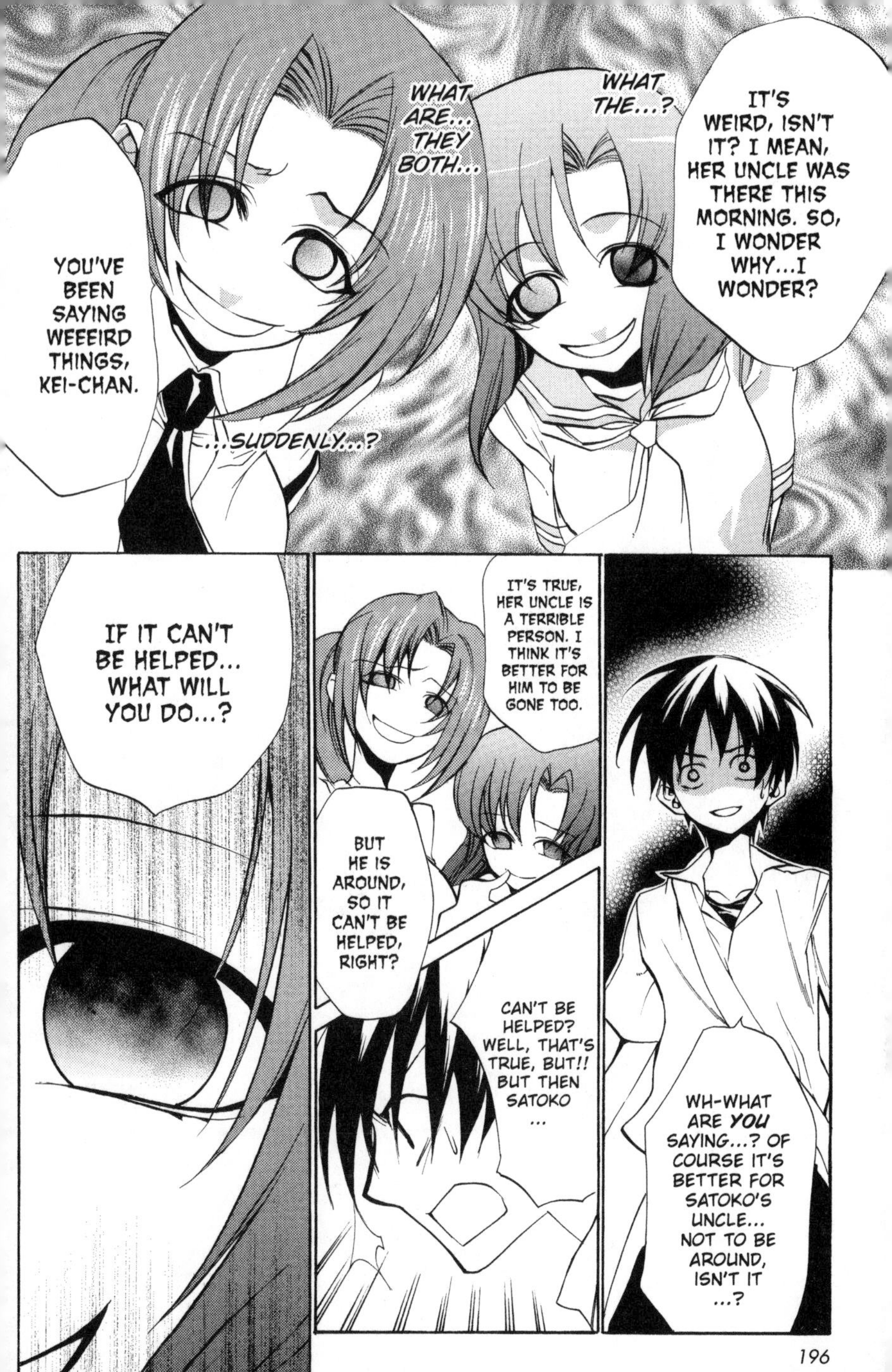
IT'S WEIRD, ISN'T IT? I MEAN, HER UNCLE WAS THERE THIS MORNING. SO, I WONDER WHY...I WONDER?
WHAT THE...?
WHAT ARE... THEY BOTH...
YOU'VE BEEN SAYING WEEEIRD THINGS, KEI-CHAN.
...SUDDENLY...?
WH-WHAT ARE *YOU* SAYING...? OF COURSE IT'S BETTER FOR SATOKO'S UNCLE... NOT TO BE AROUND, ISN'T IT ...?
IT'S TRUE, HER UNCLE IS A TERRIBLE PERSON. I THINK IT'S BETTER FOR HIM TO BE GONE TOO.
BUT HE IS AROUND, SO IT CAN'T BE HELPED, RIGHT?
CAN'T BE HELPED? WELL, THAT'S TRUE, BUT!! BUT THEN SATOKO ...
IF IT CAN'T BE HELPED... WHAT WILL YOU DO...?

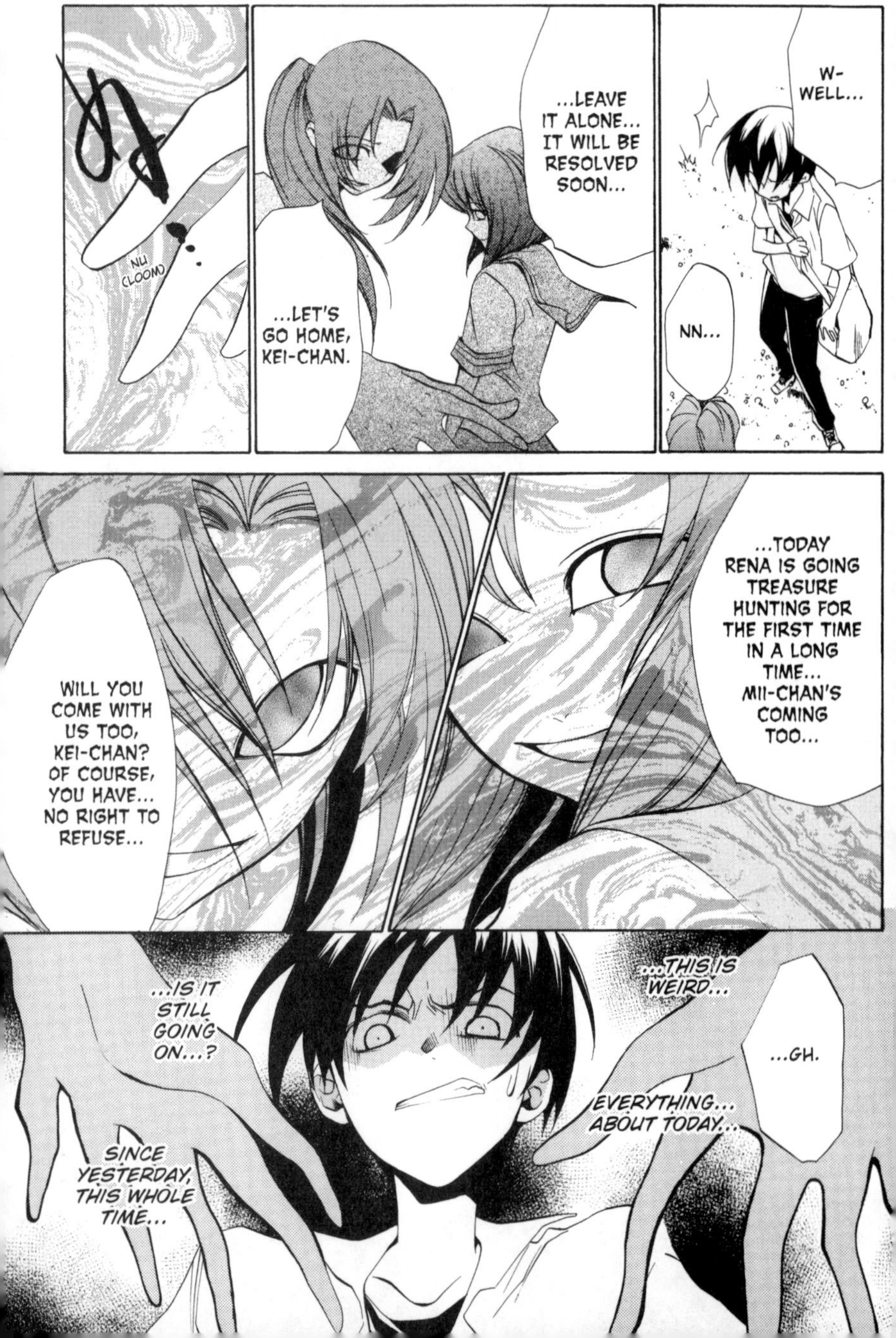
W- WELL...
NN...
...LEAVE IT ALONE... IT WILL BE RESOLVED SOON...
...LET'S GO HOME, KEI-CHAN.
NU (LOOM)
...TODAY RENA IS GOING TREASURE HUNTING FOR THE FIRST TIME IN A LONG TIME... MII-CHAN'S COMING TOO...
WILL YOU COME WITH US TOO, KEI-CHAN? OF COURSE, YOU HAVE... NO RIGHT TO REFUSE...
...THIS IS WEIRD...
...GH.
EVERYTHING... ABOUT TODAY...
...IS IT STILL GOING ON...?
SINCE YESTERDAY, THIS WHOLE TIME...

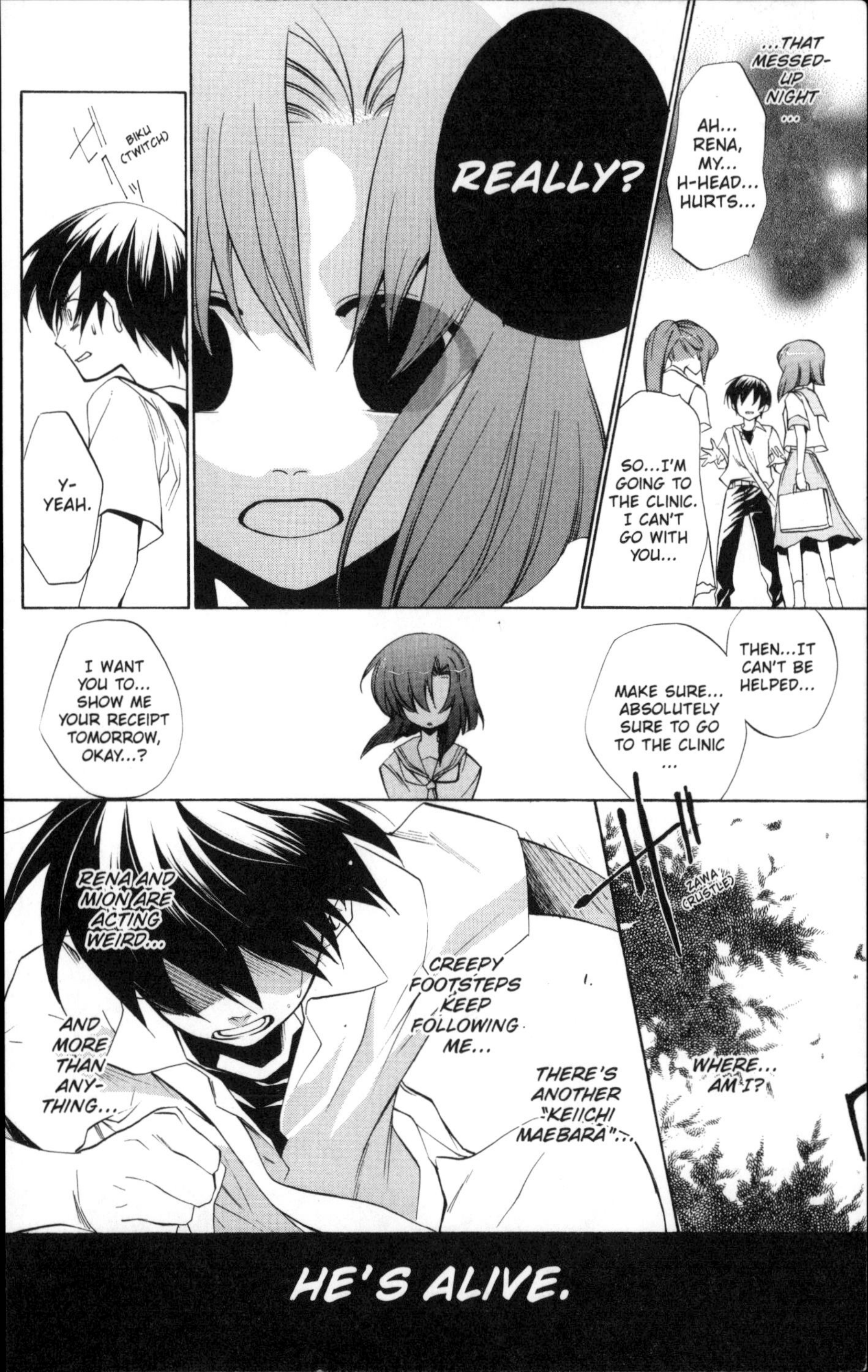
...THAT MESSED-UP NIGHT ...
AH... RENA, MY... H-HEAD... HURTS...
SO...I'M GOING TO THE CLINIC. I CAN'T GO WITH YOU...
REALLY?
BIKU (TWITCH)
Y-YEAH.
THEN...IT CAN'T BE HELPED...
MAKE SURE... ABSOLUTELY SURE TO GO TO THE CLINIC ...
I WANT YOU TO... SHOW ME YOUR RECEIPT TOMORROW, OKAY...?
ZAWA (RUSTLE)
WHERE... AM I?
RENA AND MION ARE ACTING WEIRD...
CREEPY FOOTSTEPS KEEP FOLLOWING ME...
AND MORE THAN ANY-THING...
THERE'S ANOTHER "KEIICHI MAEBARA"...
HE'S ALIVE.

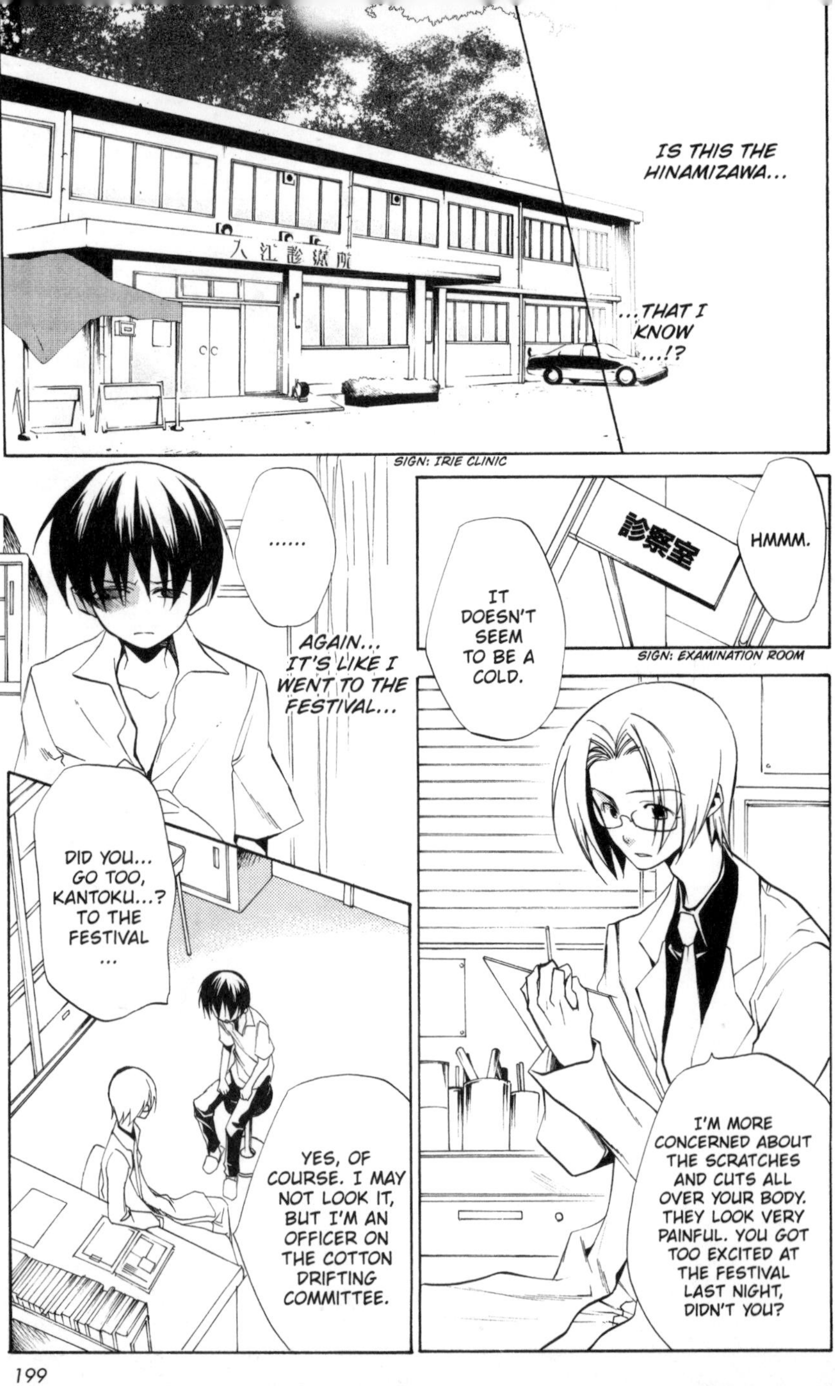

IS THIS THE HINAMIZAWA...
...THAT I KNOW ...!?
入江診療所
SIGN: IRIE CLINIC
診察室
HMMM.
IT DOESN'T SEEM TO BE A COLD.
SIGN: EXAMINATION ROOM
......
AGAIN... IT'S LIKE I WENT TO THE FESTIVAL...
I'M MORE CONCERNED ABOUT THE SCRATCHES AND CUTS ALL OVER YOUR BODY. THEY LOOK VERY PAINFUL. YOU GOT TOO EXCITED AT THE FESTIVAL LAST NIGHT, DIDN'T YOU?
DID YOU... GO TOO, KANTOKU...? TO THE FESTIVAL ...
YES, OF COURSE. I MAY NOT LOOK IT, BUT I'M AN OFFICER ON THE COTTON DRIFTING COMMITTEE.

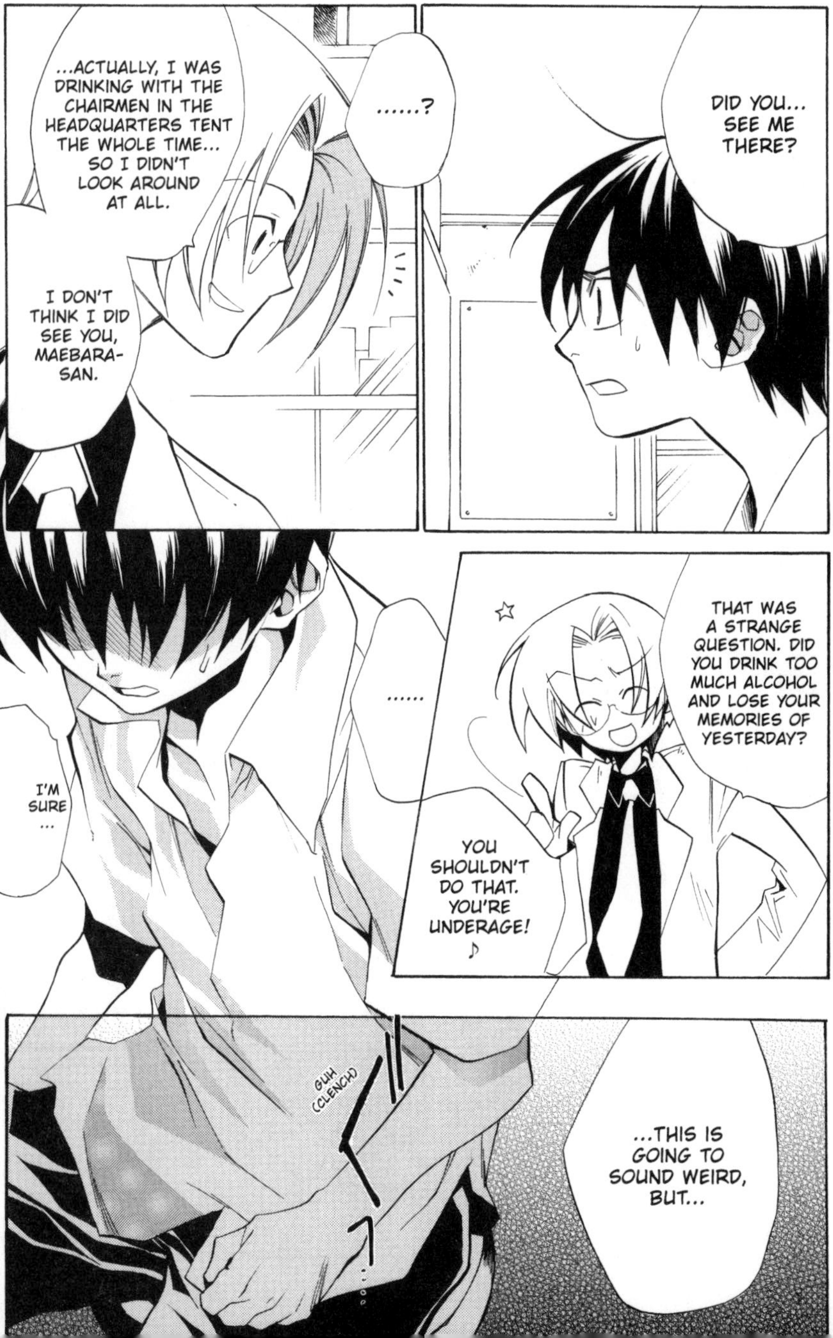
DID YOU... SEE ME THERE?
......?
...ACTUALLY, I WAS DRINKING WITH THE CHAIRMEN IN THE HEADQUARTERS TENT THE WHOLE TIME... SO I DIDN'T LOOK AROUND AT ALL.
I DON'T THINK I DID SEE YOU, MAEBARA-SAN.
THAT WAS A STRANGE QUESTION. DID YOU DRINK TOO MUCH ALCOHOL AND LOSE YOUR MEMORIES OF YESTERDAY?
YOU SHOULDN'T DO THAT. YOU'RE UNDERAGE! ♪
......
I'M SURE ...
...THIS IS GOING TO SOUND WEIRD, BUT...
GUH (CLENCH)

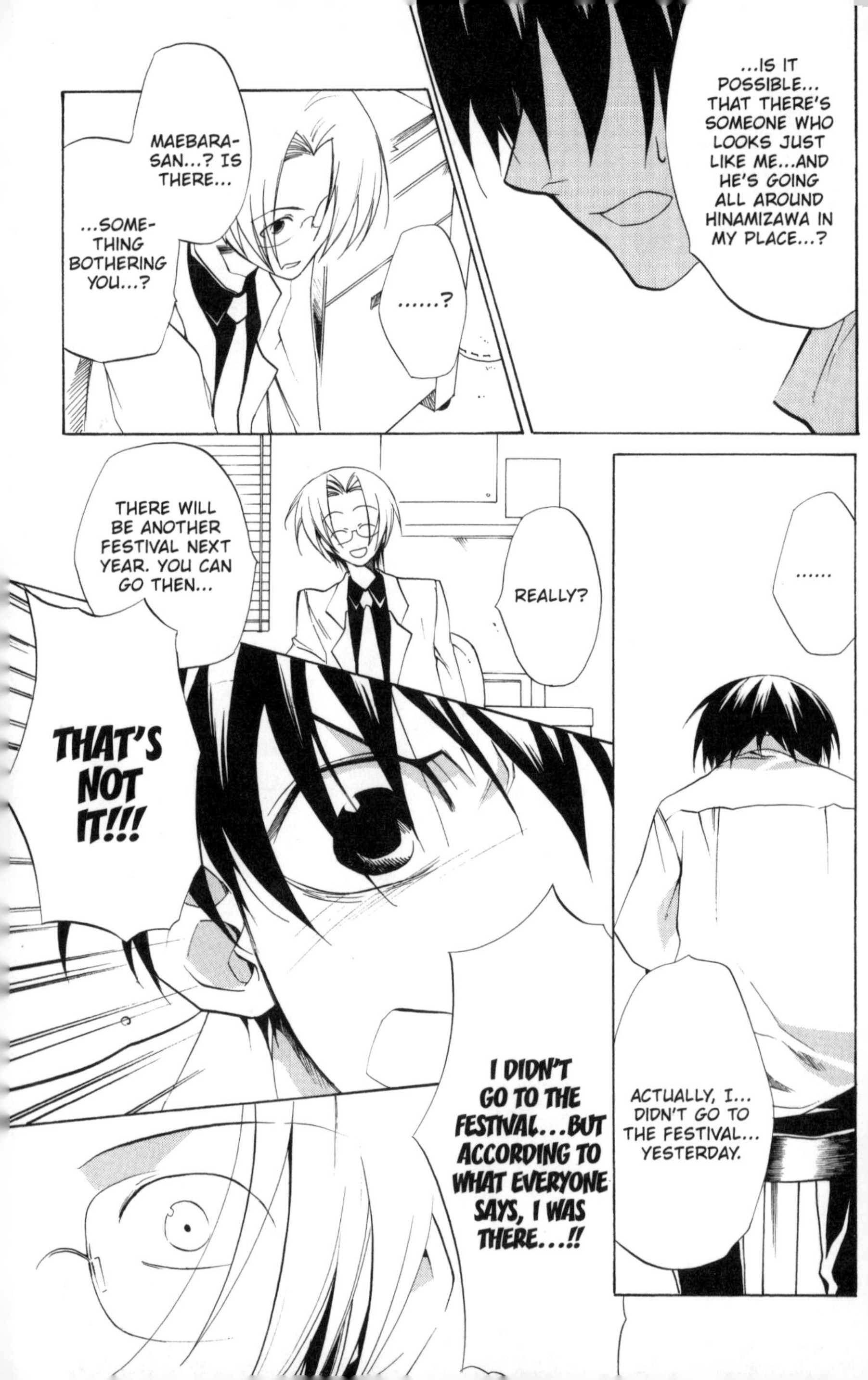
...IS IT POSSIBLE... THAT THERE'S SOMEONE WHO LOOKS JUST LIKE ME...AND HE'S GOING ALL AROUND HINAMIZAWA IN MY PLACE...?
MAEBARA-SAN...? IS THERE...
...SOMETHING BOTHERING YOU...?
......?
......
ACTUALLY, I... DIDN'T GO TO THE FESTIVAL... YESTERDAY.
REALLY?
THERE WILL BE ANOTHER FESTIVAL NEXT YEAR. YOU CAN GO THEN...
THAT'S NOT IT!!!
I DIDN'T GO TO THE FESTIVAL...BUT ACCORDING TO WHAT EVERYONE SAYS, I WAS THERE...!!

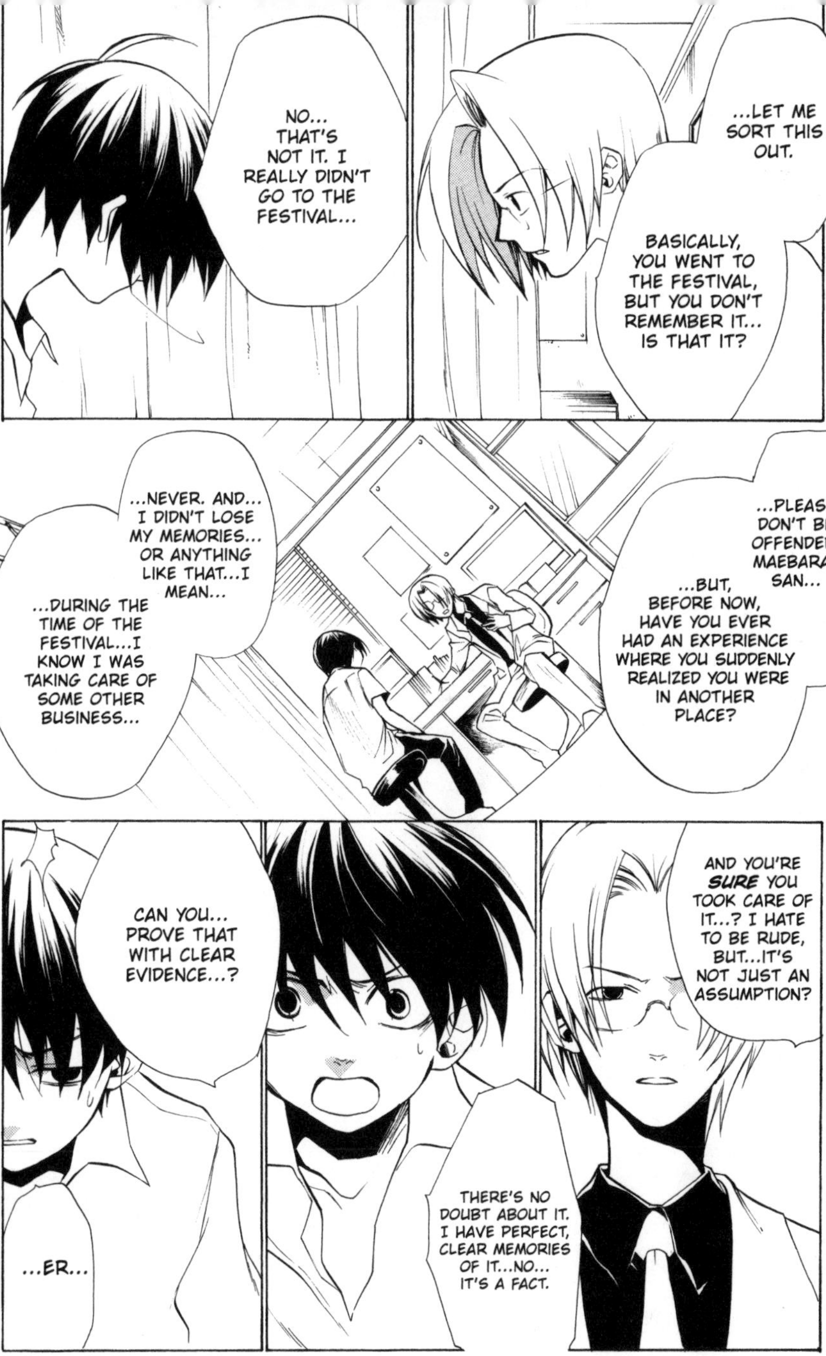
...LET ME SORT THIS OUT.
BASICALLY, YOU WENT TO THE FESTIVAL, BUT YOU DON'T REMEMBER IT... IS THAT IT?
NO... THAT'S NOT IT. I REALLY DIDN'T GO TO THE FESTIVAL...
...PLEASE DON'T BE OFFENDED, MAEBARA-SAN...
...BUT, BEFORE NOW, HAVE YOU EVER HAD AN EXPERIENCE WHERE YOU SUDDENLY REALIZED YOU WERE IN ANOTHER PLACE?
...NEVER. AND... I DIDN'T LOSE MY MEMORIES... OR ANYTHING LIKE THAT...I MEAN...
...DURING THE TIME OF THE FESTIVAL...I KNOW I WAS TAKING CARE OF SOME OTHER BUSINESS...
AND YOU'RE ***SURE*** YOU TOOK CARE OF IT...? I HATE TO BE RUDE, BUT...IT'S NOT JUST AN ASSUMPTION?
THERE'S NO DOUBT ABOUT IT. I HAVE PERFECT, CLEAR MEMORIES OF IT...NO... IT'S A FACT.
CAN YOU... PROVE THAT WITH CLEAR EVIDENCE...?
...ER...

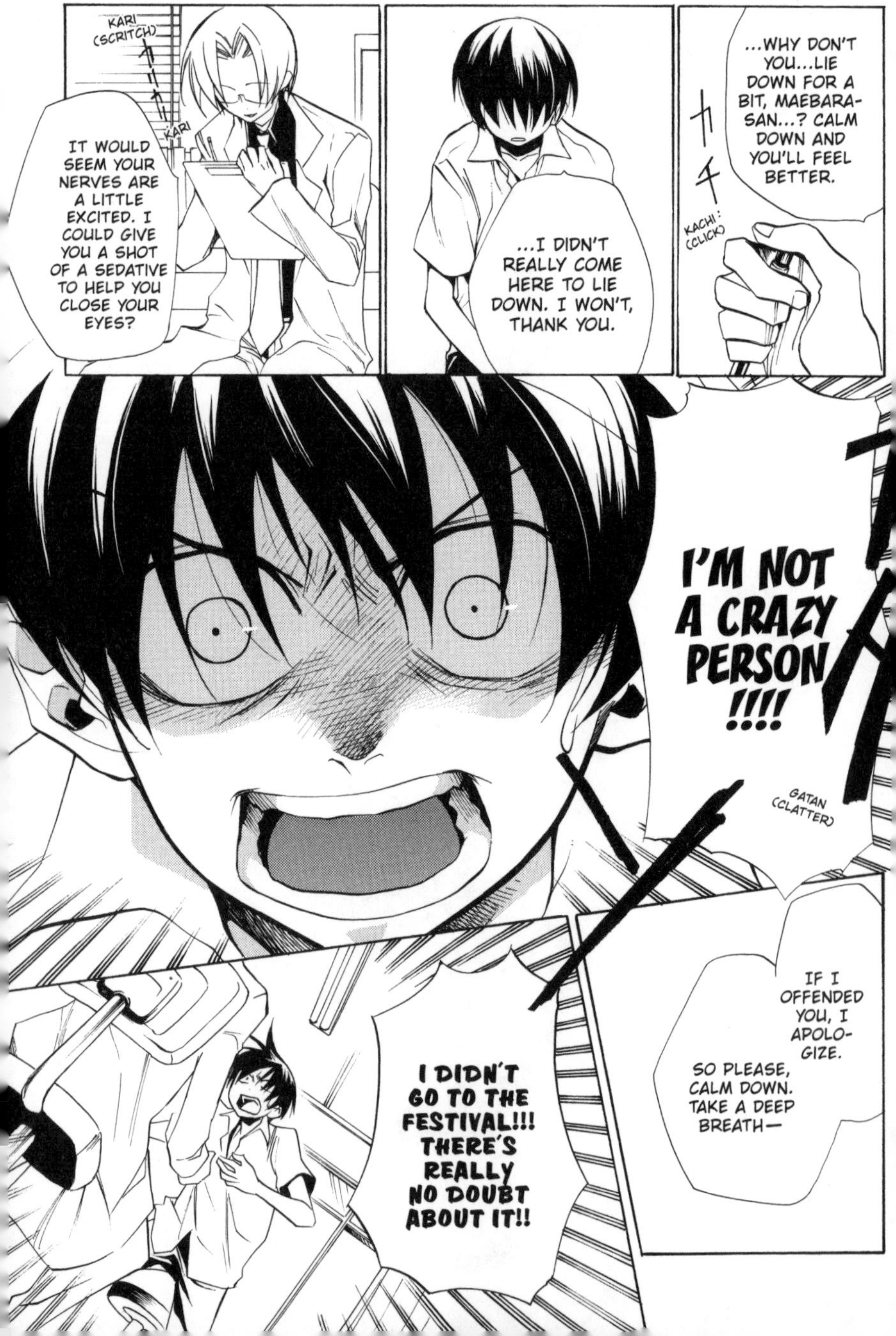
...WHY DON'T YOU...LIE DOWN FOR A BIT, MAEBARA-SAN...? CALM DOWN AND YOU'LL FEEL BETTER.
KACHI (CLICK)
...I DIDN'T REALLY COME HERE TO LIE DOWN. I WON'T, THANK YOU.
KARI (SCRITCH)
KARI
IT WOULD SEEM YOUR NERVES ARE A LITTLE EXCITED. I COULD GIVE YOU A SHOT OF A SEDATIVE TO HELP YOU CLOSE YOUR EYES?
I'M NOT A CRAZY PERSON!!!!
GATAN (CLATTER)
IF I OFFENDED YOU, I APOLOGIZE.
SO PLEASE, CALM DOWN. TAKE A DEEP BREATH—
I DIDN'T GO TO THE FESTIVAL!!! THERE'S REALLY NO DOUBT ABOUT IT!!

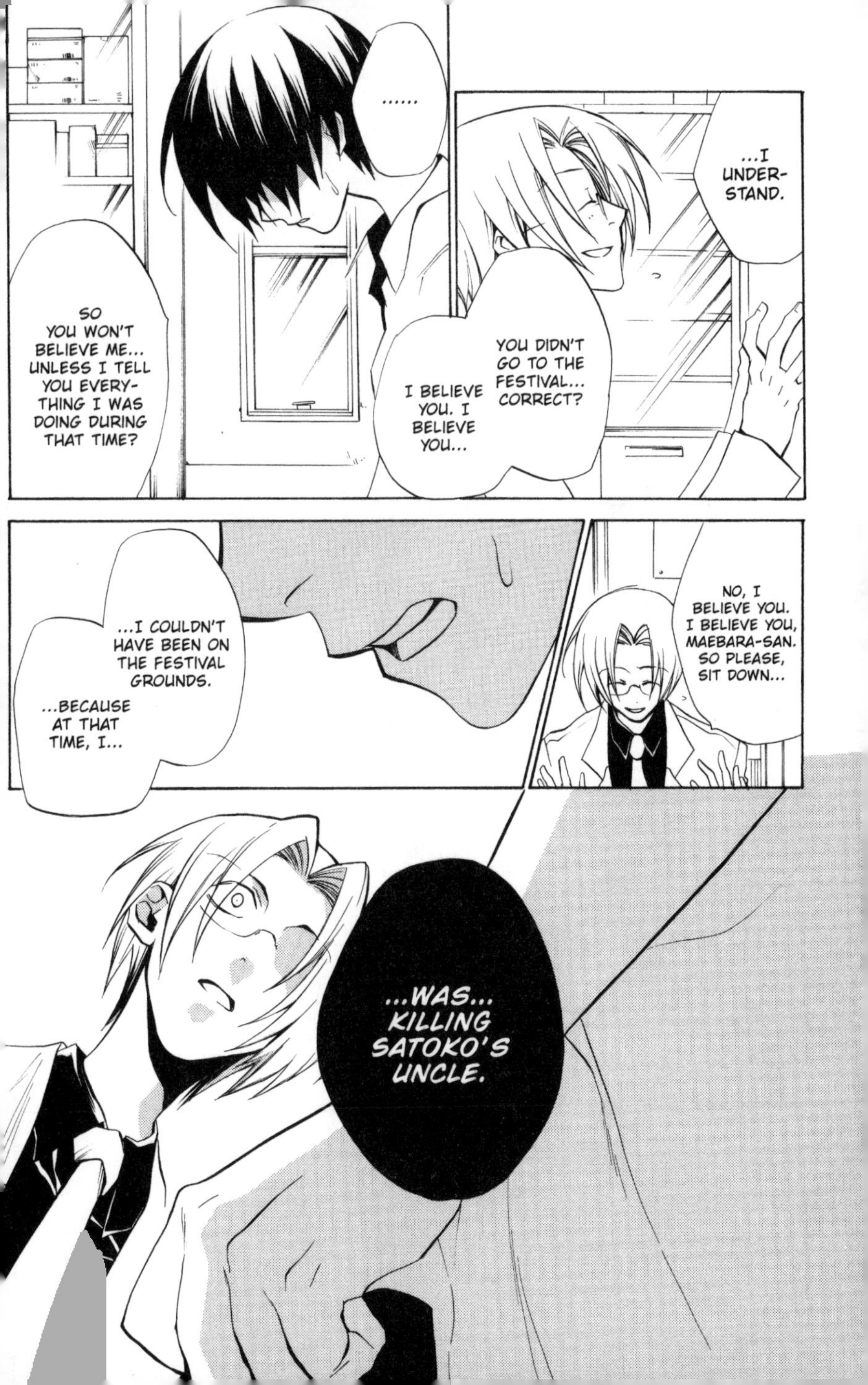
...I UNDERSTAND.
YOU DIDN'T GO TO THE FESTIVAL... CORRECT?
I BELIEVE YOU. I BELIEVE YOU...
......
SO YOU WON'T BELIEVE ME... UNLESS I TELL YOU EVERYTHING I WAS DOING DURING THAT TIME?
NO, I BELIEVE YOU. I BELIEVE YOU, MAEBARA-SAN. SO PLEASE, SIT DOWN...
...I COULDN'T HAVE BEEN ON THE FESTIVAL GROUNDS.
...BECAUSE AT THAT TIME, I...
...WAS... KILLING SATOKO'S UNCLE.

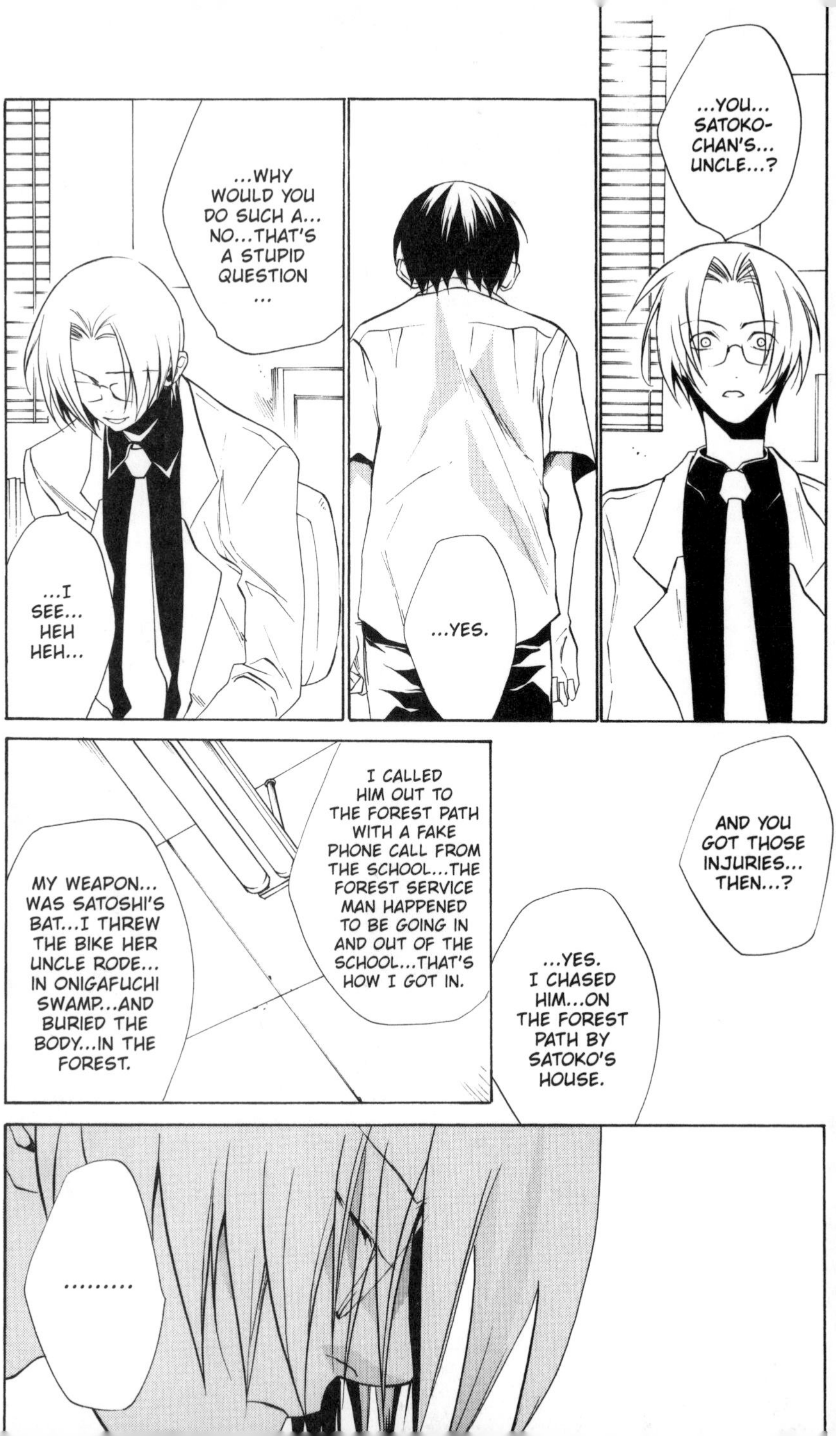
...YOU... SATOKO-CHAN'S... UNCLE...?
...YES.
...WHY WOULD YOU DO SUCH A... NO...THAT'S A STUPID QUESTION ...
...I SEE... HEH HEH...
AND YOU GOT THOSE INJURIES... THEN...?
...YES. I CHASED HIM...ON THE FOREST PATH BY SATOKO'S HOUSE.
I CALLED HIM OUT TO THE FOREST PATH WITH A FAKE PHONE CALL FROM THE SCHOOL...THE FOREST SERVICE MAN HAPPENED TO BE GOING IN AND OUT OF THE SCHOOL...THAT'S HOW I GOT IN.
MY WEAPON... WAS SATOSHI'S BAT...I THREW THE BIKE HER UNCLE RODE... IN ONIGAFUCHI SWAMP...AND BURIED THE BODY...IN THE FOREST.
....

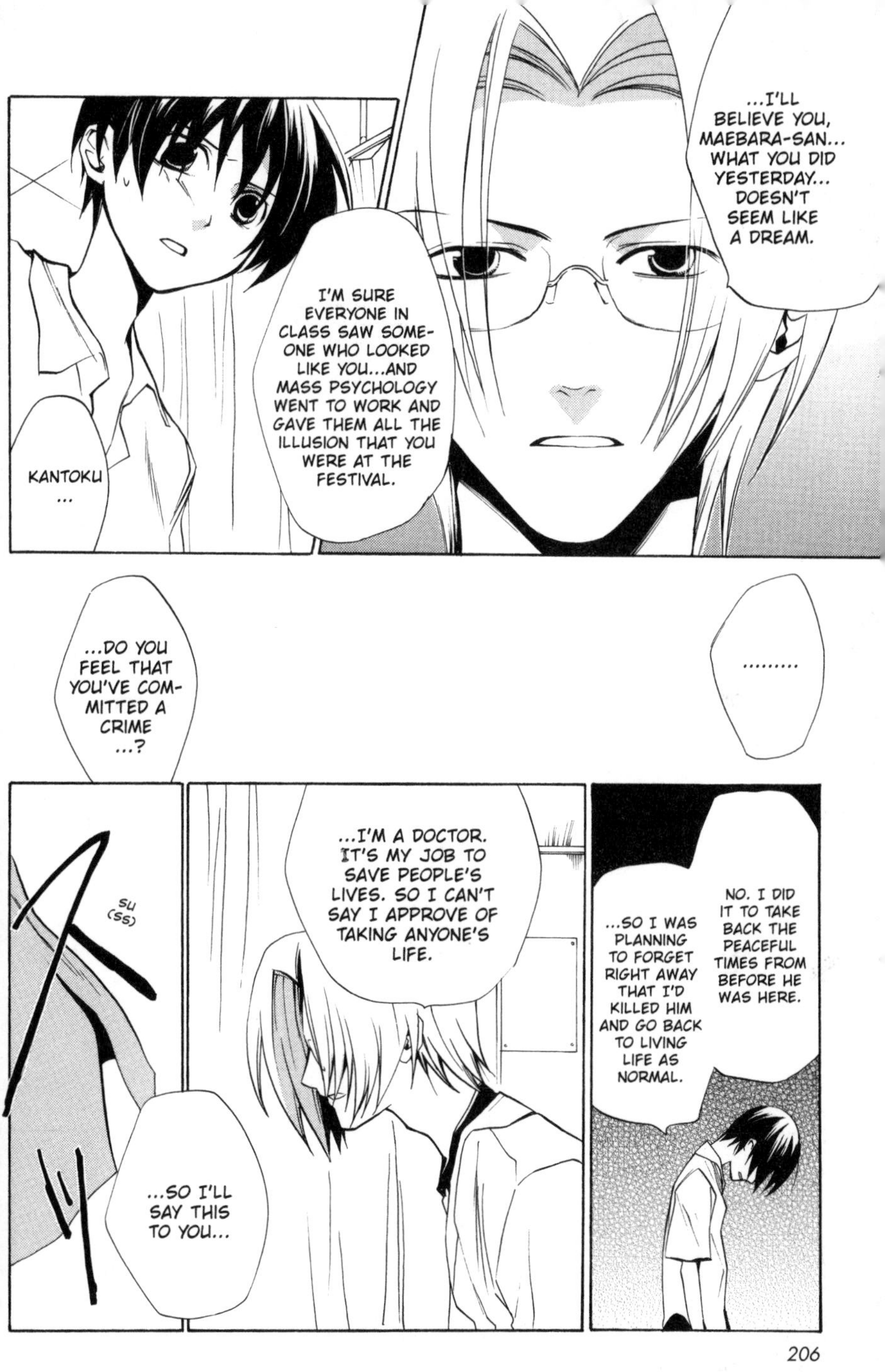
...I'LL BELIEVE YOU, MAEBARA-SAN... WHAT YOU DID YESTERDAY... DOESN'T SEEM LIKE A DREAM.
I'M SURE EVERYONE IN CLASS SAW SOME-ONE WHO LOOKED LIKE YOU...AND MASS PSYCHOLOGY WENT TO WORK AND GAVE THEM ALL THE ILLUSION THAT YOU WERE AT THE FESTIVAL.
KANTOKU ...
....
...DO YOU FEEL THAT YOU'VE COM-MITTED A CRIME ...?
NO. I DID IT TO TAKE BACK THE PEACEFUL TIMES FROM BEFORE HE WAS HERE.
...SO I WAS PLANNING TO FORGET RIGHT AWAY THAT I'D KILLED HIM AND GO BACK TO LIVING LIFE AS NORMAL.
...I'M A DOCTOR. IT'S MY JOB TO SAVE PEOPLE'S LIVES. SO I CAN'T SAY I APPROVE OF TAKING ANYONE'S LIFE.
...SO I'LL SAY THIS TO YOU...
SU (SS)

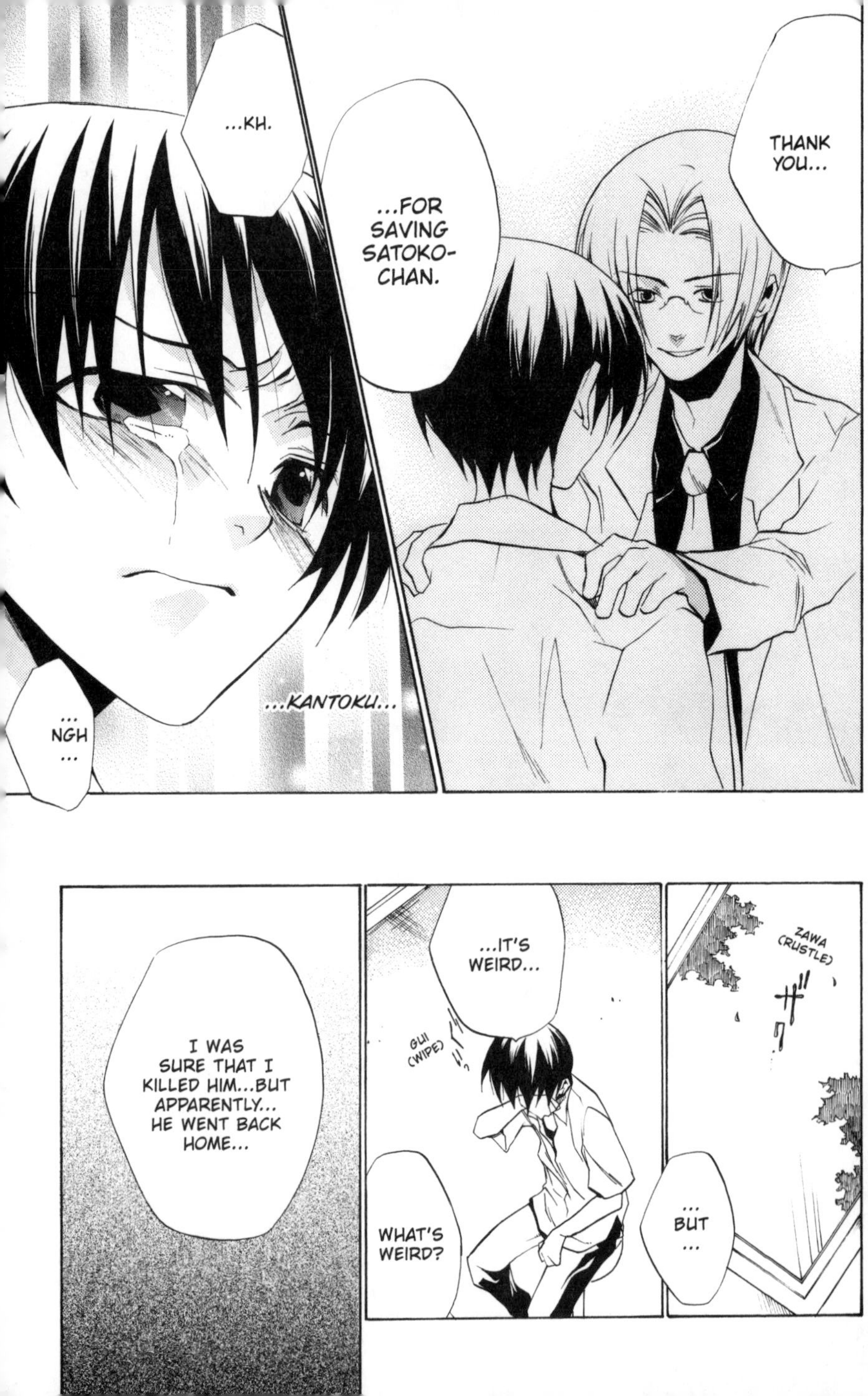
THANK YOU...
...FOR SAVING SATOKO-CHAN.
...KH.
...KANTOKU...
...NGH...
ZAWA (RUSTLE)
...BUT...
...IT'S WEIRD...
GUI (WIPE)
WHAT'S WEIRD?
I WAS SURE THAT I KILLED HIM...BUT APPARENTLY... HE WENT BACK HOME...

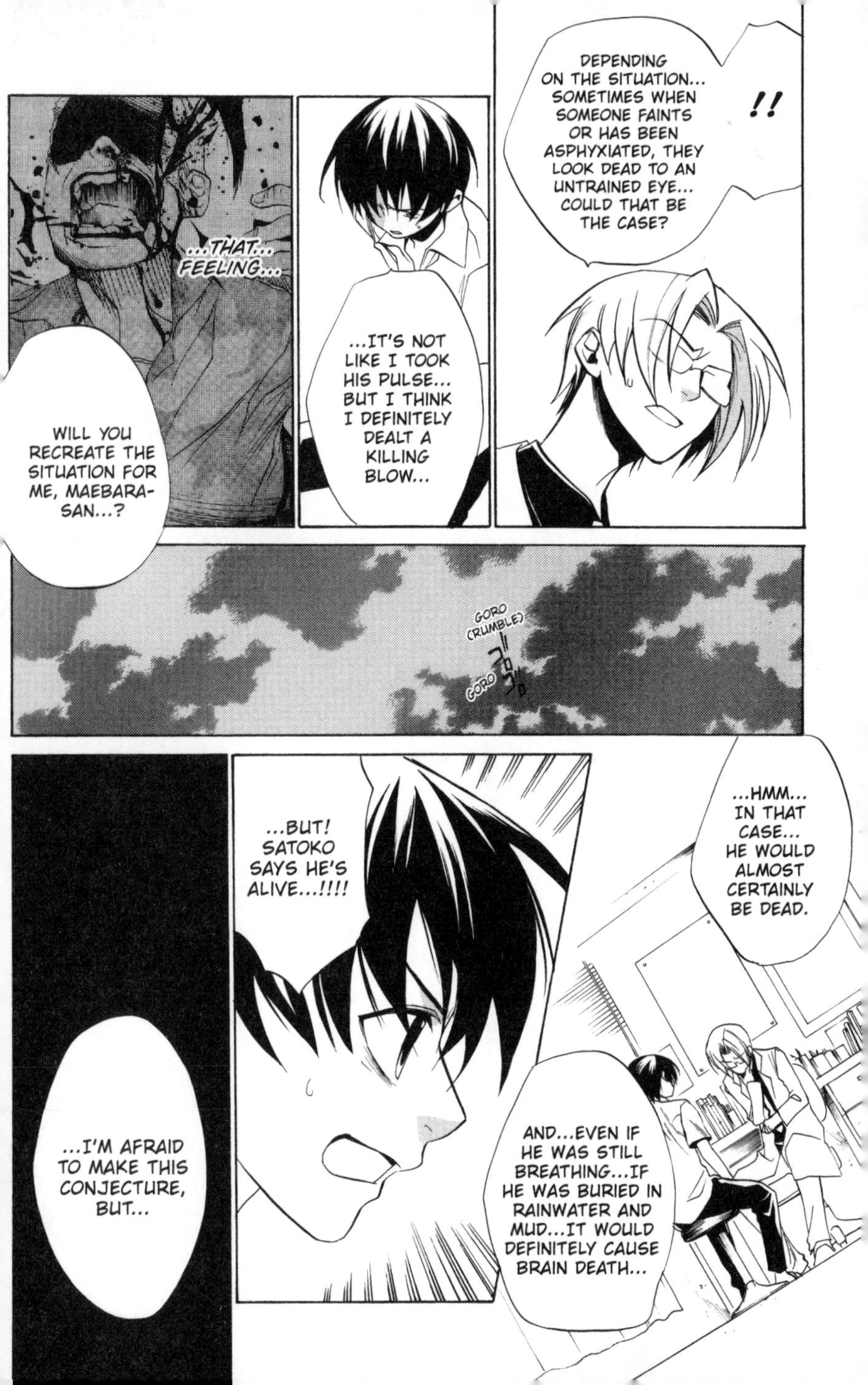
DEPENDING ON THE SITUATION... SOMETIMES WHEN SOMEONE FAINTS OR HAS BEEN ASPHYXIATED, THEY LOOK DEAD TO AN UNTRAINED EYE... COULD THAT BE THE CASE?
!!
...IT'S NOT LIKE I TOOK HIS PULSE... BUT I THINK I DEFINITELY DEALT A KILLING BLOW...
...THAT... FEELING...
WILL YOU RECREATE THE SITUATION FOR ME, MAEBARA-SAN...?
GORO (RUMBLE)
GORO
...HMM... IN THAT CASE... HE WOULD ALMOST CERTAINLY BE DEAD.
AND...EVEN IF HE WAS STILL BREATHING...IF HE WAS BURIED IN RAINWATER AND MUD...IT WOULD DEFINITELY CAUSE BRAIN DEATH...
...BUT! SATOKO SAYS HE'S ALIVE...!!!!
...I'M AFRAID TO MAKE THIS CONJECTURE, BUT...

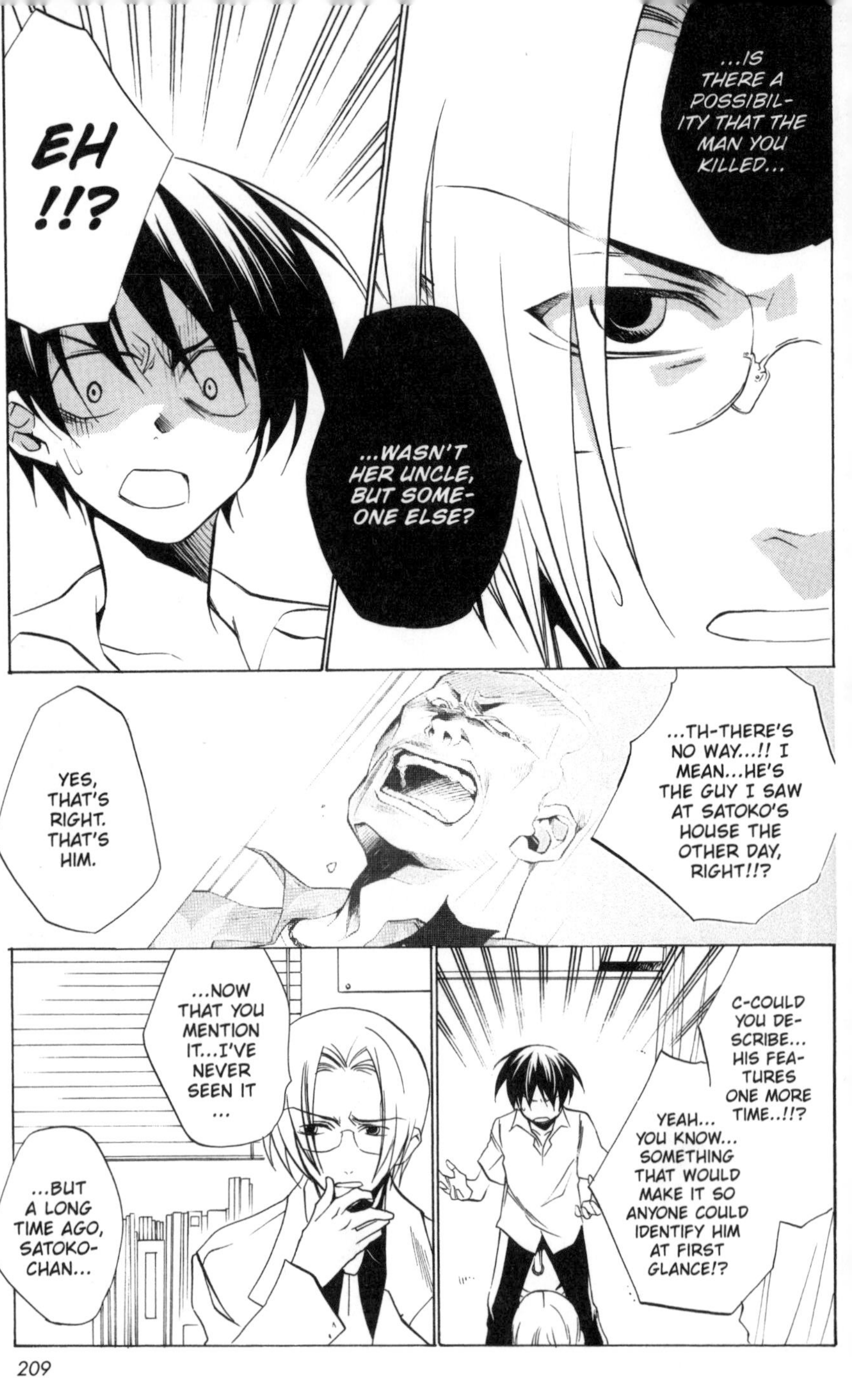
...IS THERE A POSSIBILITY THAT THE MAN YOU KILLED...
...WASN'T HER UNCLE, BUT SOME-ONE ELSE?
EH !!?
...TH-THERE'S NO WAY...!! I MEAN...HE'S THE GUY I SAW AT SATOKO'S HOUSE THE OTHER DAY, RIGHT!!?
YES, THAT'S RIGHT. THAT'S HIM.
C-COULD YOU DE-SCRIBE... HIS FEA-TURES ONE MORE TIME..!!?
YEAH... YOU KNOW... SOMETHING THAT WOULD MAKE IT SO ANYONE COULD IDENTIFY HIM AT FIRST GLANCE!?
...NOW THAT YOU MENTION IT...I'VE NEVER SEEN IT ...
...BUT A LONG TIME AGO, SATOKO-CHAN...

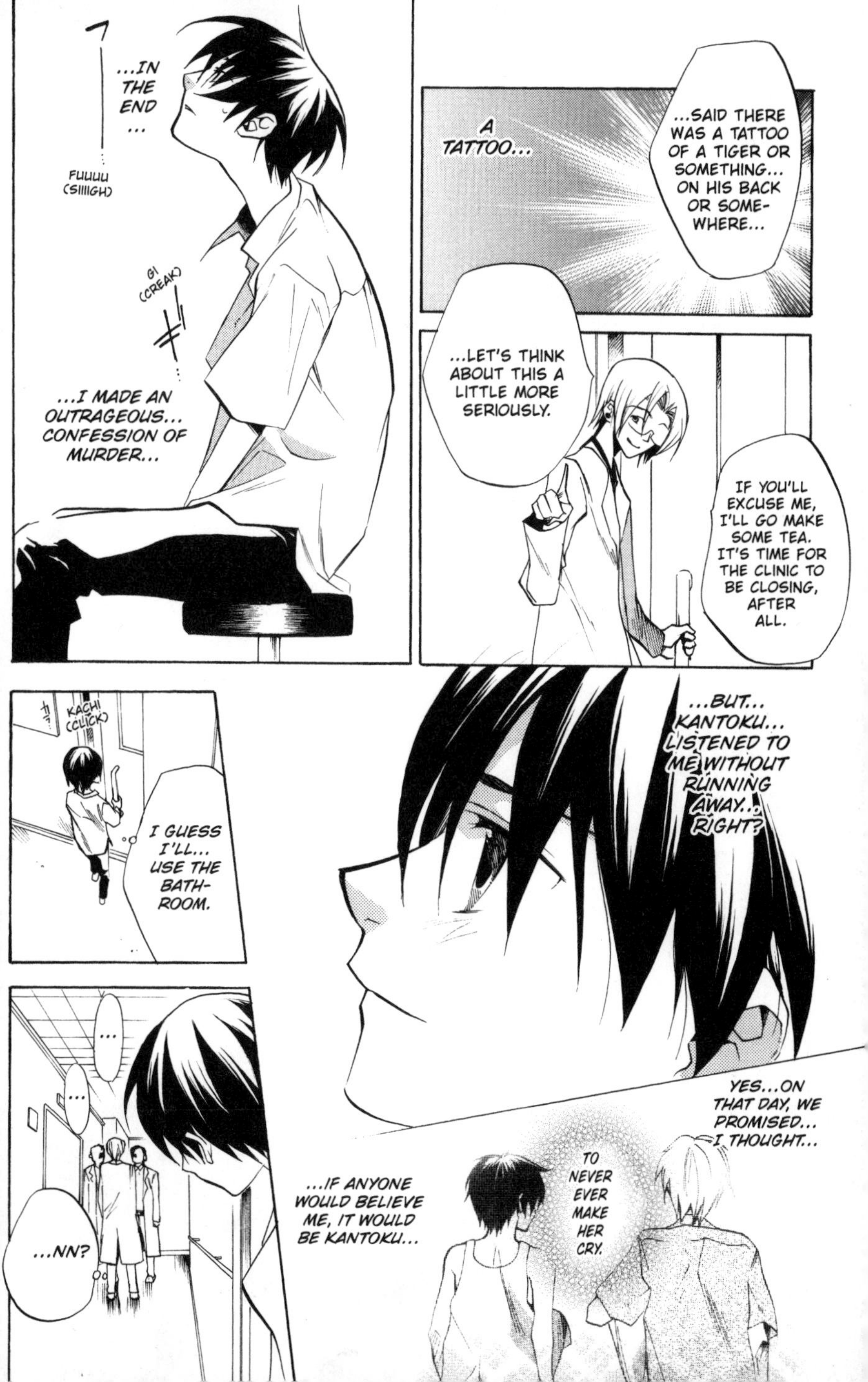
...SAID THERE WAS A TATTOO OF A TIGER OR SOMETHING... ON HIS BACK OR SOME-WHERE...
A TATTOO...
...LET'S THINK ABOUT THIS A LITTLE MORE SERIOUSLY.
IF YOU'LL EXCUSE ME, I'LL GO MAKE SOME TEA. IT'S TIME FOR THE CLINIC TO BE CLOSING, AFTER ALL.
...IN THE END...
FUUUU (SIIIIGH)
GI (CREAK)
...I MADE AN OUTRAGEOUS... CONFESSION OF MURDER...
...BUT... KANTOKU... LISTENED TO ME WITHOUT RUNNING AWAY... RIGHT?
KACHI (CLICK)
I GUESS I'LL... USE THE BATH-ROOM.
YES...ON THAT DAY, WE PROMISED... I THOUGHT...
TO NEVER EVER MAKE HER CRY.
...IF ANYONE WOULD BELIEVE ME, IT WOULD BE KANTOKU...
...
...
...NN?

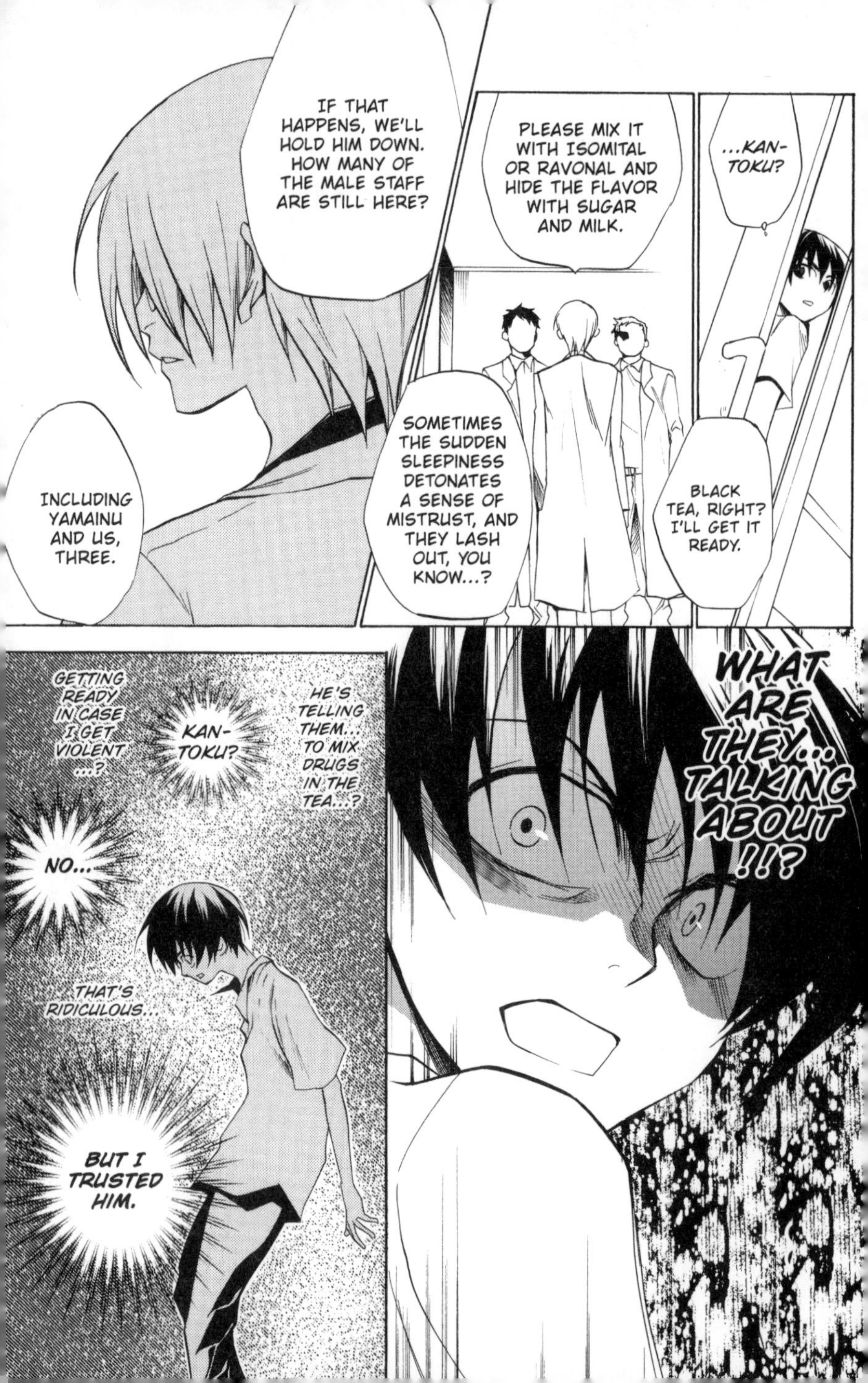
...KAN-TOKU?
BLACK TEA, RIGHT? I'LL GET IT READY.
PLEASE MIX IT WITH ISOMITAL OR RAVONAL AND HIDE THE FLAVOR WITH SUGAR AND MILK.
SOMETIMES THE SUDDEN SLEEPINESS DETONATES A SENSE OF MISTRUST, AND THEY LASH OUT, YOU KNOW...?
IF THAT HAPPENS, WE'LL HOLD HIM DOWN. HOW MANY OF THE MALE STAFF ARE STILL HERE?
INCLUDING YAMAINU AND US, THREE.
WHAT ARE THEY... TALKING ABOUT!!?
HE'S TELLING THEM... TO MIX DRUGS IN THE TEA...?
KAN-TOKU?
GETTING READY IN CASE I GET VIOLENT...?
NO...
THAT'S RIDICULOUS...
BUT I TRUSTED HIM.

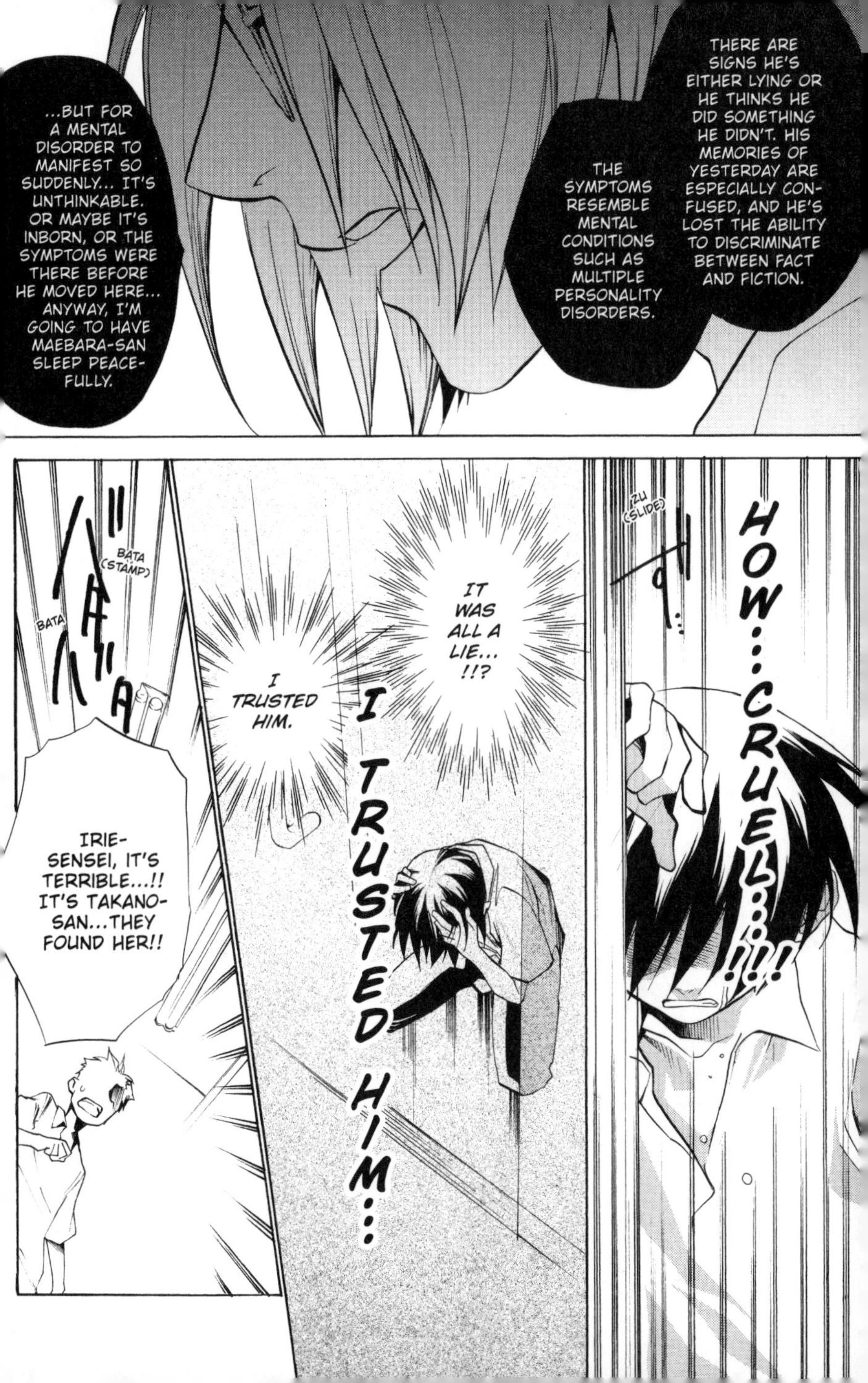
THERE ARE SIGNS HE'S EITHER LYING OR HE THINKS HE DID SOMETHING HE DIDN'T. HIS MEMORIES OF YESTERDAY ARE ESPECIALLY CON-FUSED, AND HE'S LOST THE ABILITY TO DISCRIMINATE BETWEEN FACT AND FICTION.
THE SYMPTOMS RESEMBLE MENTAL CONDITIONS SUCH AS MULTIPLE PERSONALITY DISORDERS.
...BUT FOR A MENTAL DISORDER TO MANIFEST SO SUDDENLY... IT'S UNTHINKABLE. OR MAYBE IT'S INBORN, OR THE SYMPTOMS WERE THERE BEFORE HE MOVED HERE... ANYWAY, I'M GOING TO HAVE MAEBARA-SAN SLEEP PEACE-FULLY.
ZU (SLIDE)
HOW...CRUEL...!!!
IT WAS ALL A LIE...!!?
I TRUSTED HIM.
I TRUSTED HIM...
BATA (STAMP)
BATA
IRIE-SENSEI, IT'S TERRIBLE...!! IT'S TAKANO-SAN...THEY FOUND HER!!

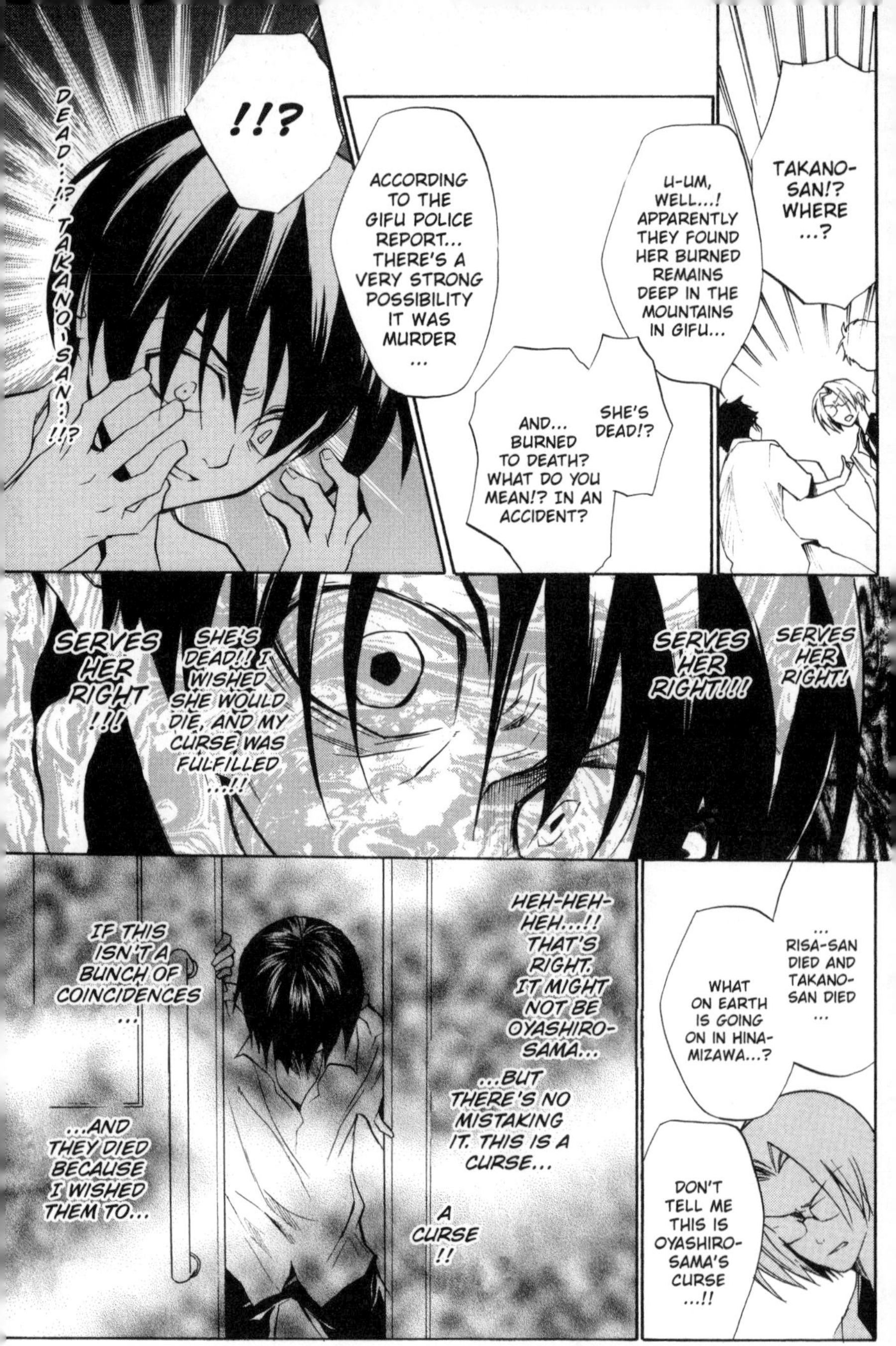

TAKANO-SAN!? WHERE ...?
U-UM, WELL...! APPARENTLY THEY FOUND HER BURNED REMAINS DEEP IN THE MOUNTAINS IN GIFU...
SHE'S DEAD!?
AND... BURNED TO DEATH? WHAT DO YOU MEAN!? IN AN ACCIDENT?
ACCORDING TO THE GIFU POLICE REPORT... THERE'S A VERY STRONG POSSIBILITY IT WAS MURDER ...
!!?
DEAD...!? TAKANO-SAN...!!?
SERVES HER RIGHT!
SERVES HER RIGHT!!!
SHE'S DEAD!! I WISHED SHE WOULD DIE, AND MY CURSE WAS FULFILLED ...!!
SERVES HER RIGHT !!!
... RISA-SAN DIED AND TAKANO-SAN DIED ...
WHAT ON EARTH IS GOING ON IN HINA-MIZAWA...?
DON'T TELL ME THIS IS OYASHIRO-SAMA'S CURSE ...!!
HEH-HEH-HEH...!! THAT'S RIGHT. IT MIGHT NOT BE OYASHIRO-SAMA...
...BUT THERE'S NO MISTAKING IT. THIS IS A CURSE...
A CURSE !!
IF THIS ISN'T A BUNCH OF COINCIDENCES ...
...AND THEY DIED BECAUSE I WISHED THEM TO...

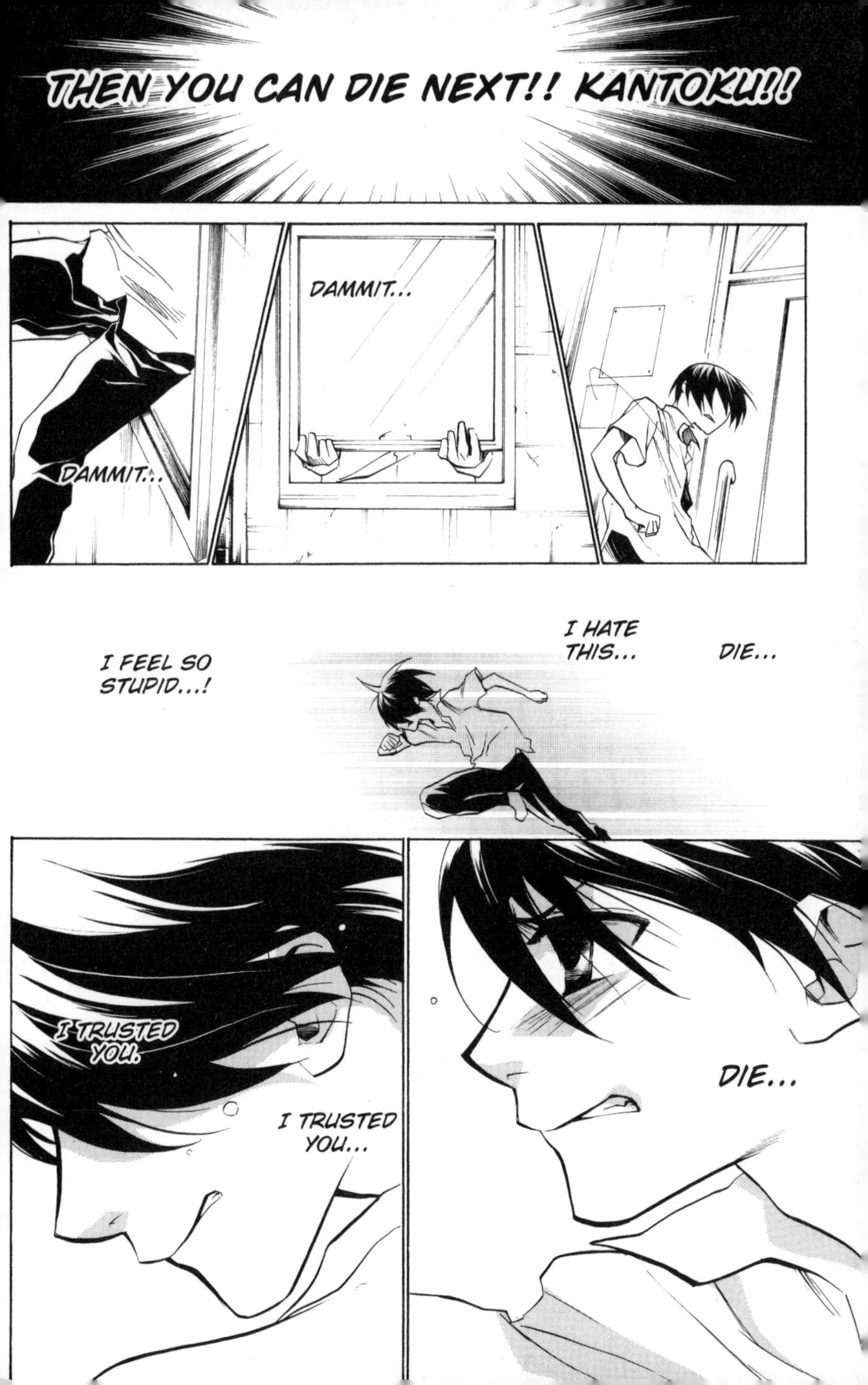
THEN YOU CAN DIE NEXT!! KANTOKU!!
DAMMIT...
DAMMIT...
DIE...
I HATE THIS...
I FEEL SO STUPID...!
DIE...
I TRUSTED YOU.
I TRUSTED YOU...

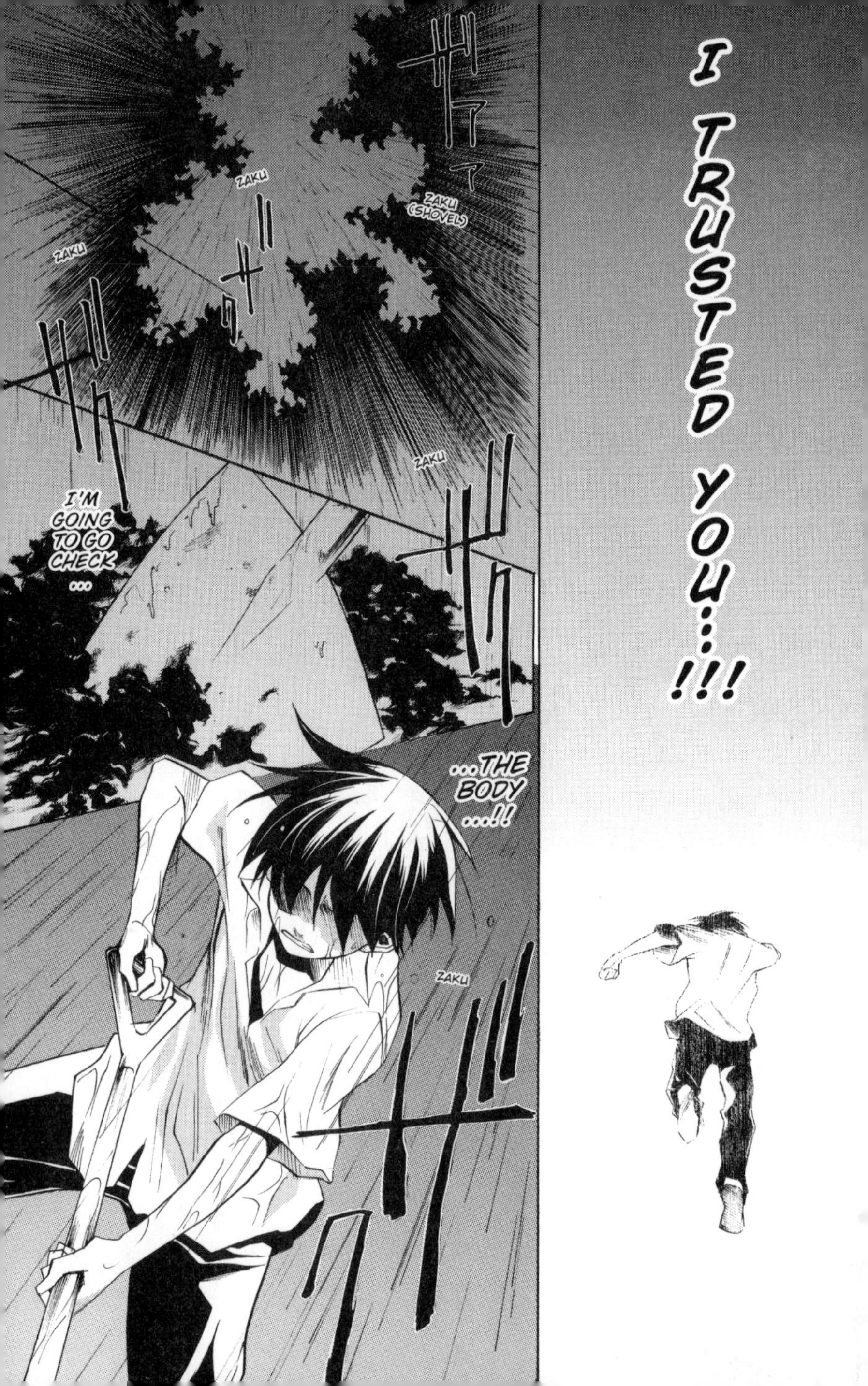
I TRUSTED YOU...!!!
ZAKU (SHOVEL)
ZAKU
ZAKU
ZAKU
I'M GOING TO GO CHECK ...
...THE BODY ...!!
ZAKU

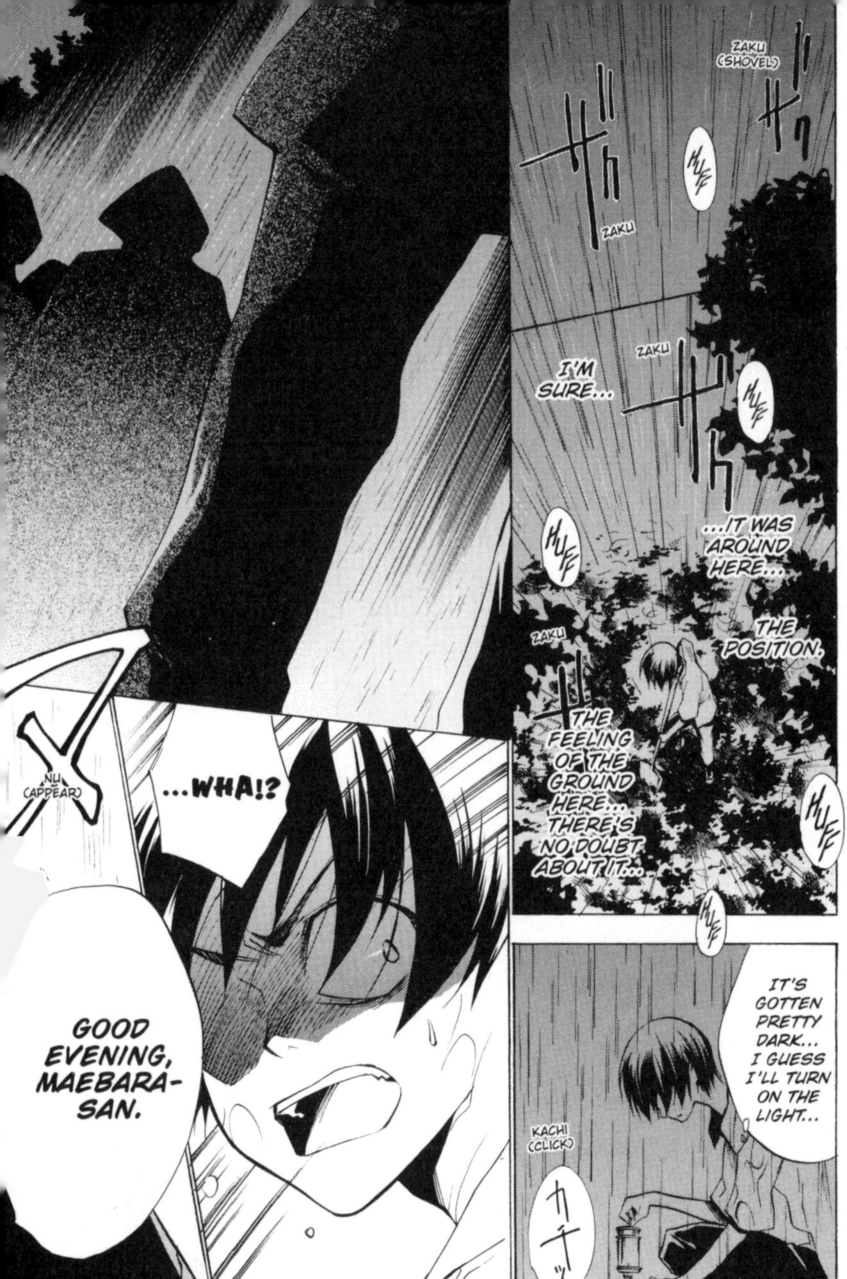
ZAKU (SHOVEL)
ザク
HUFF
ザク
ZAKU
I'M SURE...
ZAKU
ザク
HUFF
HUFF
...IT WAS AROUND HERE...
THE POSITION.
ZAKU
THE FEELING OF THE GROUND HERE... THERE'S NO DOUBT ABOUT IT...
HUFF
HUFF
IT'S GOTTEN PRETTY DARK... I GUESS I'LL TURN ON THE LIGHT...
KACHI (CLICK)
カチッ
NU (APPEAR)
...WHA!?
GOOD EVENING, MAEBARA-SAN.

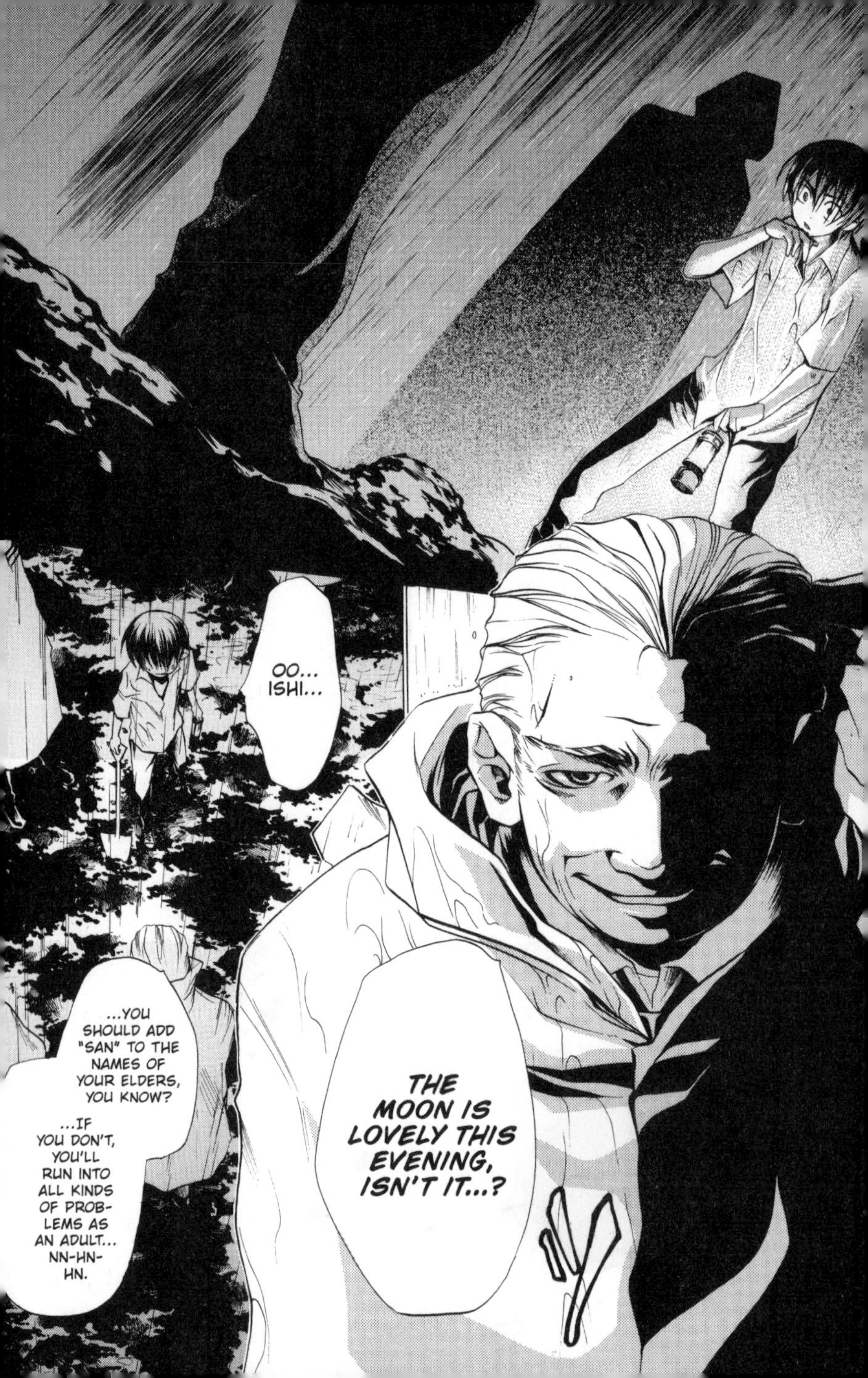
OO... ISHI...
THE MOON IS LOVELY THIS EVENING, ISN'T IT...?
...YOU SHOULD ADD "SAN" TO THE NAMES OF YOUR ELDERS, YOU KNOW?
...IF YOU DON'T, YOU'LL RUN INTO ALL KINDS OF PROB-LEMS AS AN ADULT... NN-HN-HN.

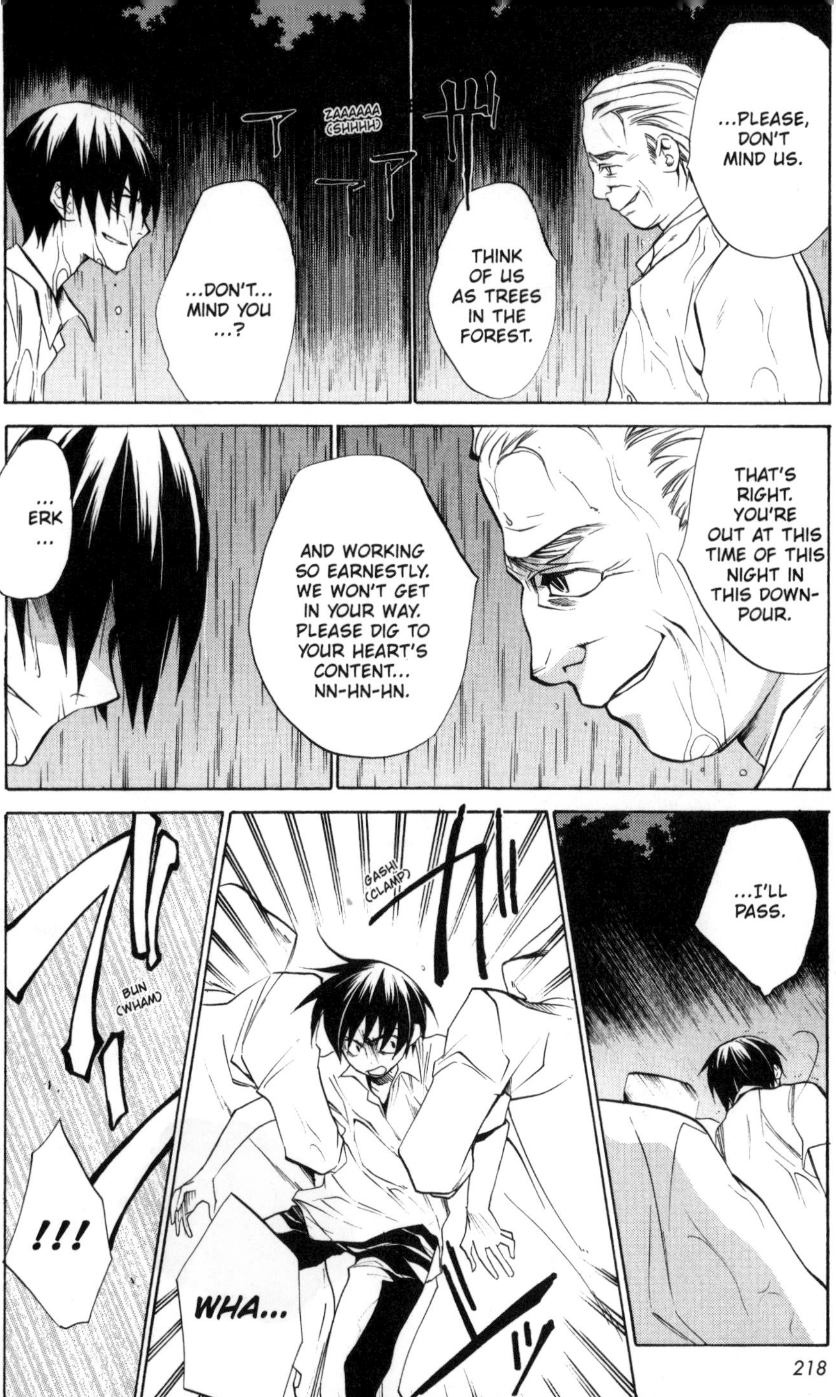
...PLEASE, DON'T MIND US.
THINK OF US AS TREES IN THE FOREST.
ZAAAAAA (SHHHH)
...DON'T... MIND YOU ...?
THAT'S RIGHT. YOU'RE OUT AT THIS TIME OF THIS NIGHT IN THIS DOWN-POUR.
AND WORKING SO EARNESTLY. WE WON'T GET IN YOUR WAY. PLEASE DIG TO YOUR HEART'S CONTENT... NN-HN-HN.
... ERK ...
...I'LL PASS.
GASHI (CLAMP)
WHA...
BUN (WHAM)
!!!

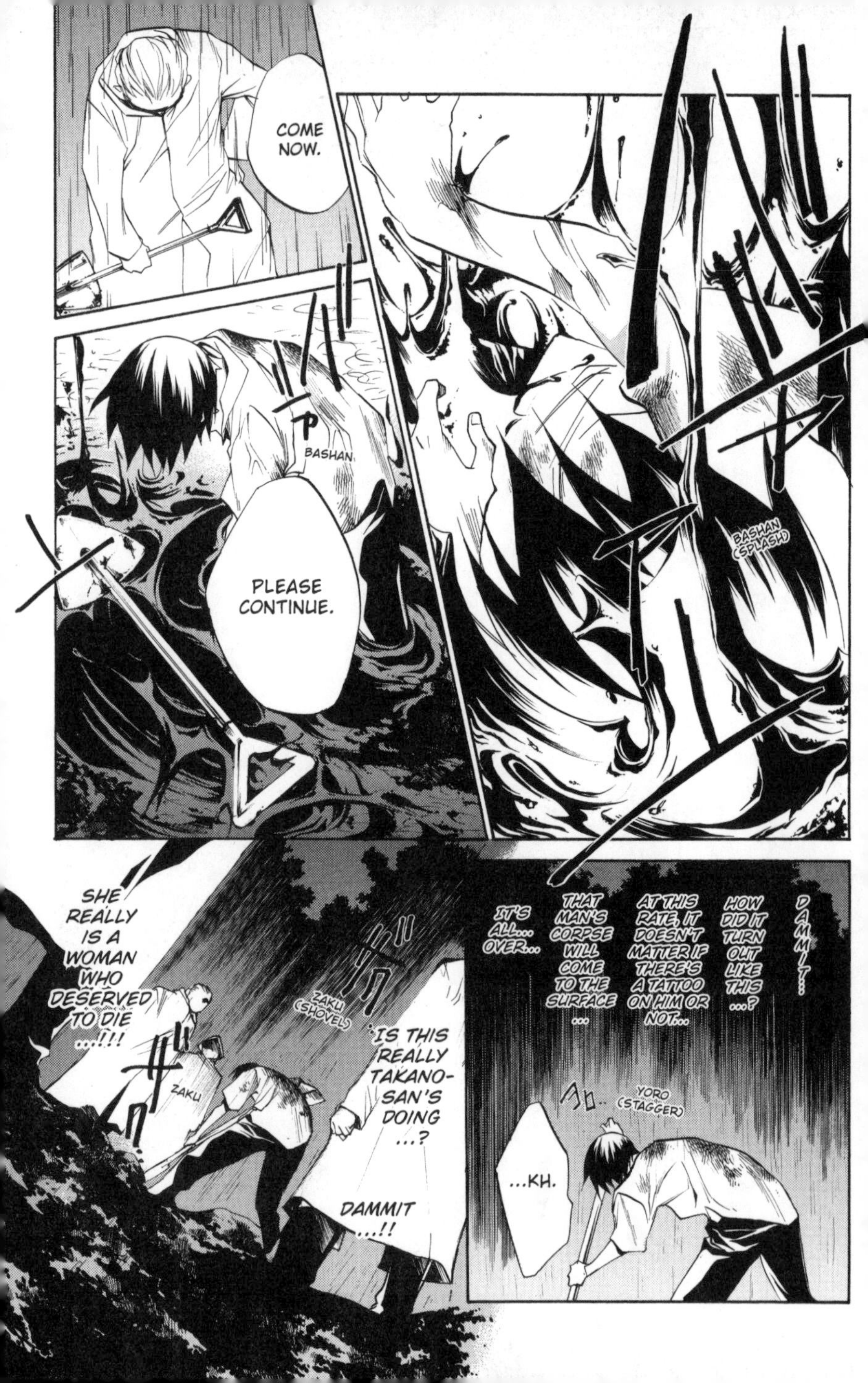
BASHAN (SPLASH)
COME NOW.
BASHAN
PLEASE CONTINUE.
DAMMIT...
HOW DID IT TURN OUT LIKE THIS ...?
AT THIS RATE, IT DOESN'T MATTER IF THERE'S A TATTOO ON HIM OR NOT...
THAT MAN'S CORPSE WILL COME TO THE SURFACE ...
IT'S ALL... OVER...
YORO (STAGGER)
...KH.
IS THIS REALLY TAKANO-SAN'S DOING ...?
ZAKU (SHOVEL)
SHE REALLY IS A WOMAN WHO DESERVED TO DIE ...!!!
ZAKU
DAMMIT ...!!

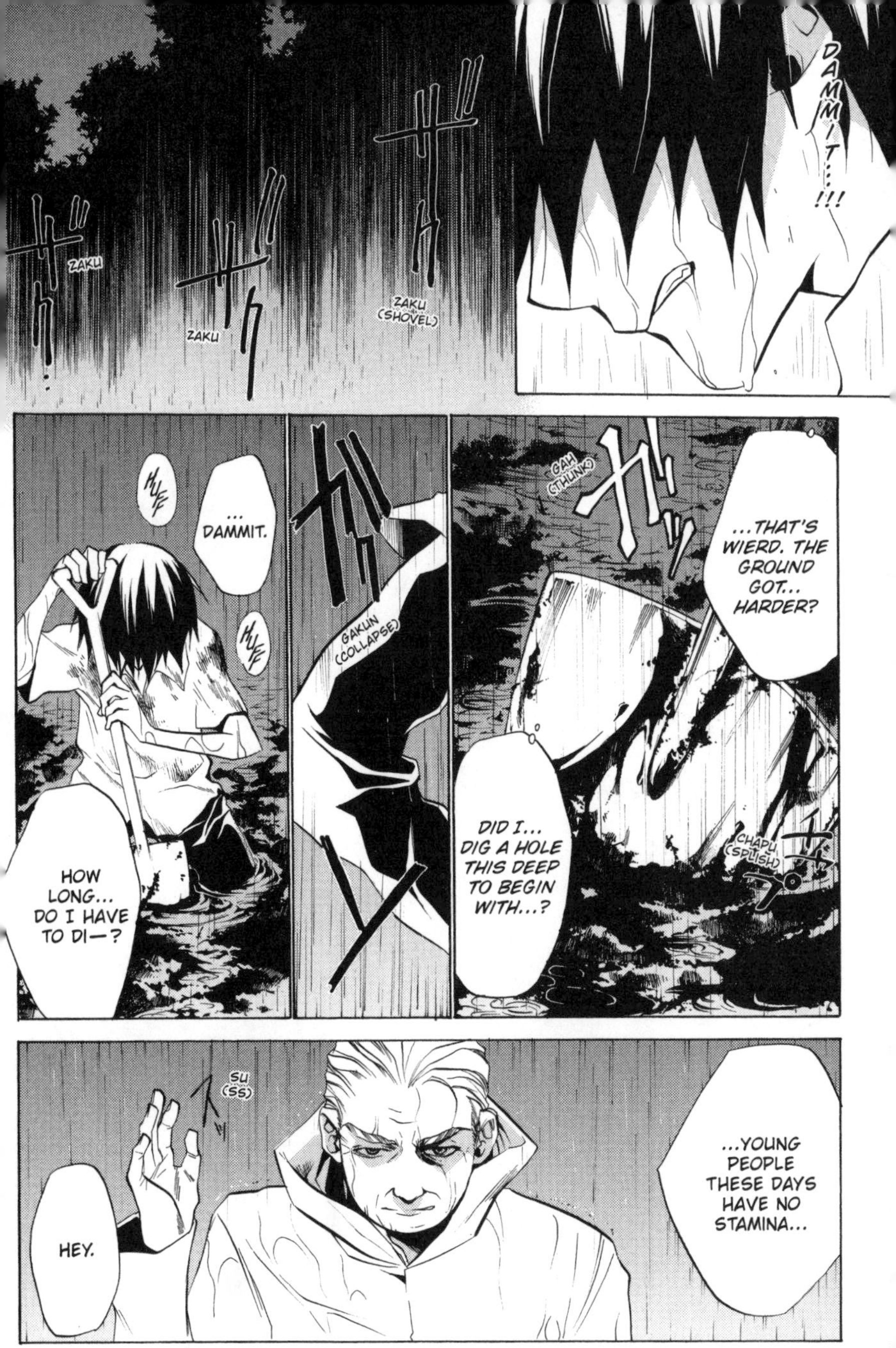
DAMMIT...!!!
ZAKU (SHOVEL)
ZAKU
ZAKU
...THAT'S WIERD. THE GROUND GOT... HARDER?
GAH (THUNK)
DID I... DIG A HOLE THIS DEEP TO BEGIN WITH...?
CHAPU (SPLISH)
GAKUN (COLLAPSE)
HUFF
...DAMMIT.
HUFF
HOW LONG... DO I HAVE TO DI—?
...YOUNG PEOPLE THESE DAYS HAVE NO STAMINA...
SU (SS)
HEY.

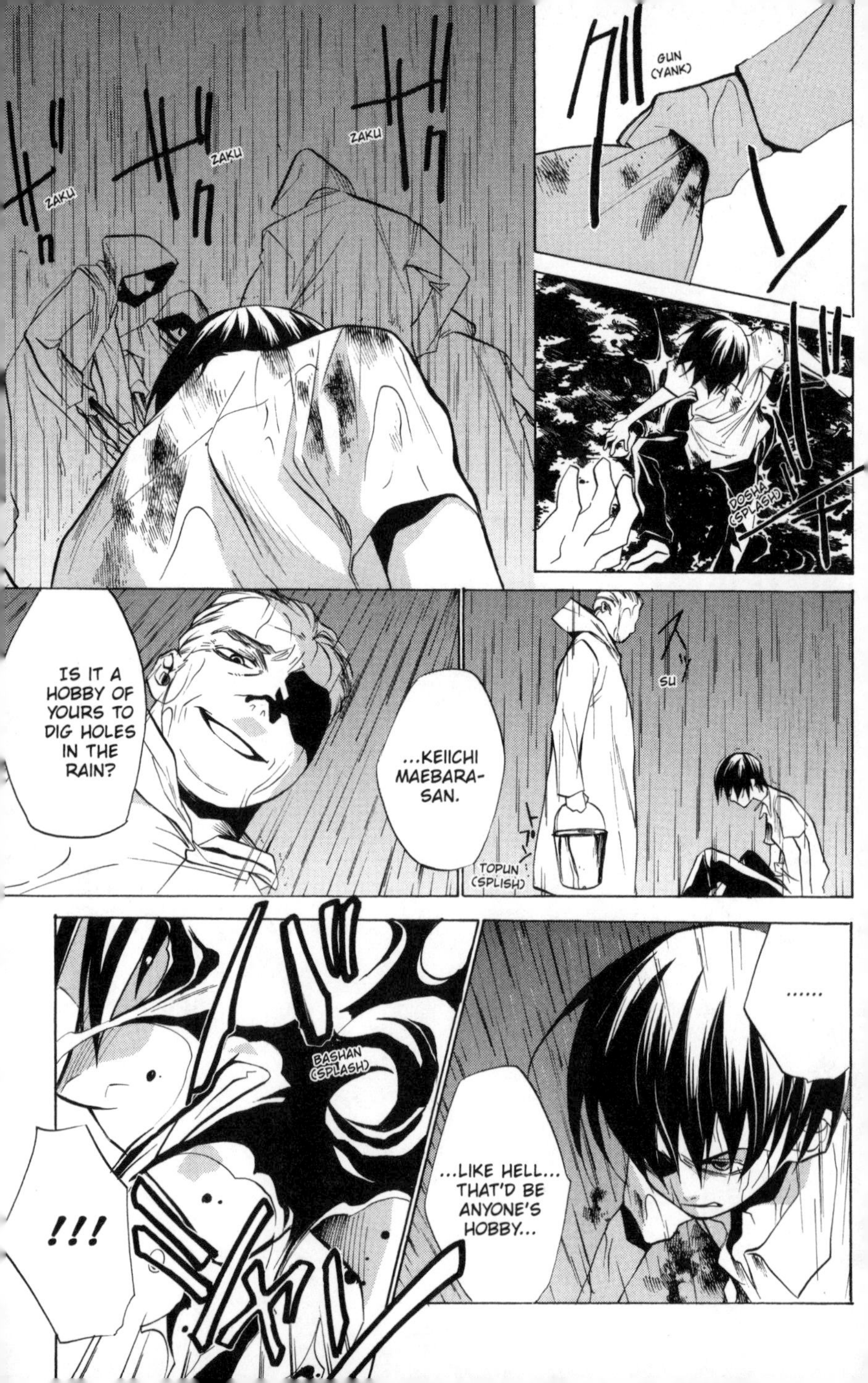
GUN (YANK)
DOSHA (SPLASH)
ZAKU
ZAKU
ZAKU
SU
TOPUN (SPLISH)
IS IT A HOBBY OF YOURS TO DIG HOLES IN THE RAIN?
...KEIICHI MAEBARA-SAN.
......
...LIKE HELL... THAT'D BE ANYONE'S HOBBY...
BASHAN (SPLASH)
!!!

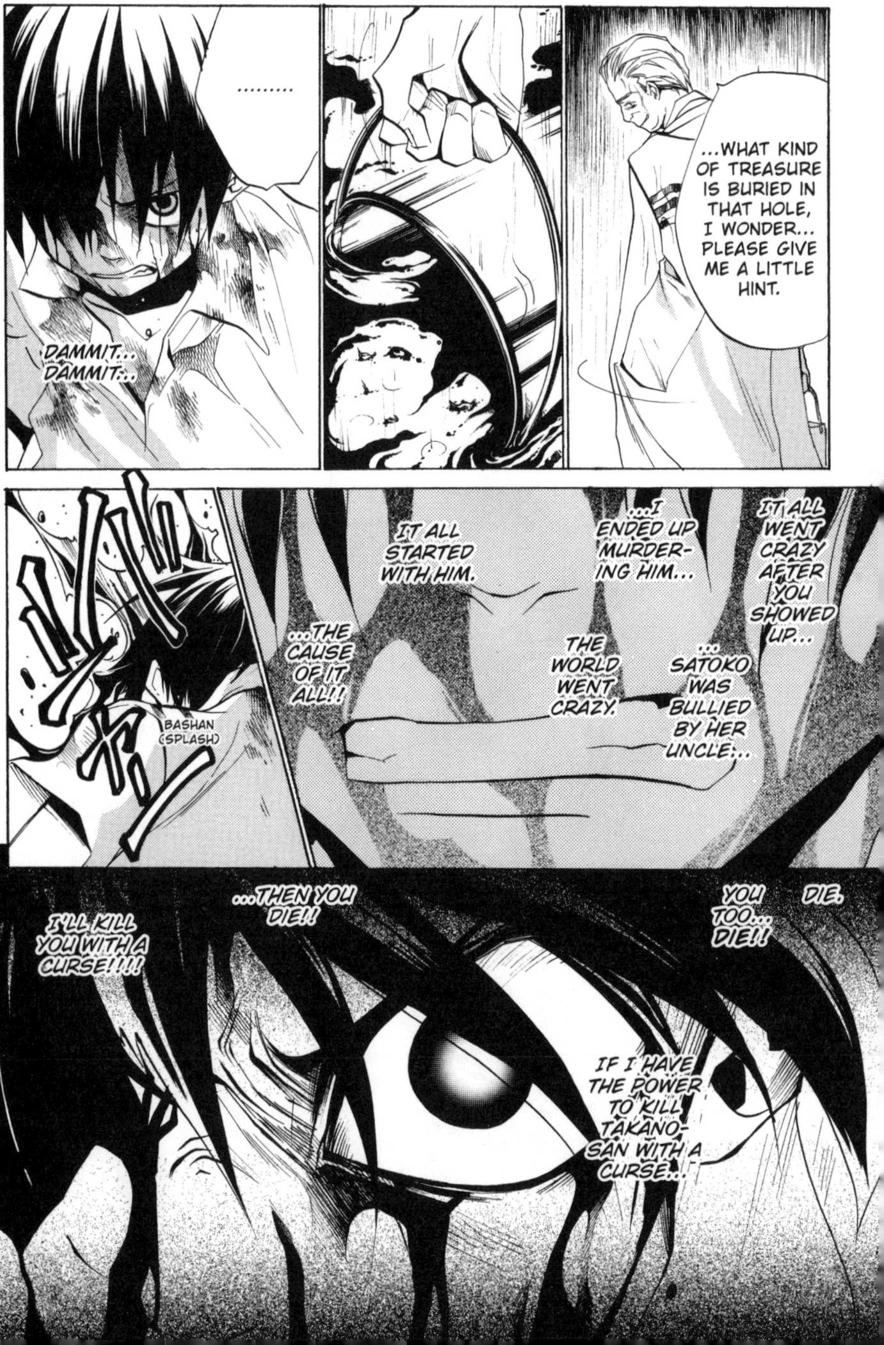
...WHAT KIND OF TREASURE IS BURIED IN THAT HOLE, I WONDER... PLEASE GIVE ME A LITTLE HINT.
....
DAMMIT... DAMMIT...
IT ALL WENT CRAZY AFTER YOU SHOWED UP...
...SATOKO WAS BULLIED BY HER UNCLE...
...I ENDED UP MURDER-ING HIM...
THE WORLD WENT CRAZY.
IT ALL STARTED WITH HIM.
...THE CAUSE OF IT ALL!!
BASHAN (SPLASH)
DIE.
YOU TOO... DIE!!
...THEN YOU DIE!!
I'LL KILL YOU WITH A CURSE!!!!
IF I HAVE THE POWER TO KILL TAKANO-SAN WITH A CURSE...

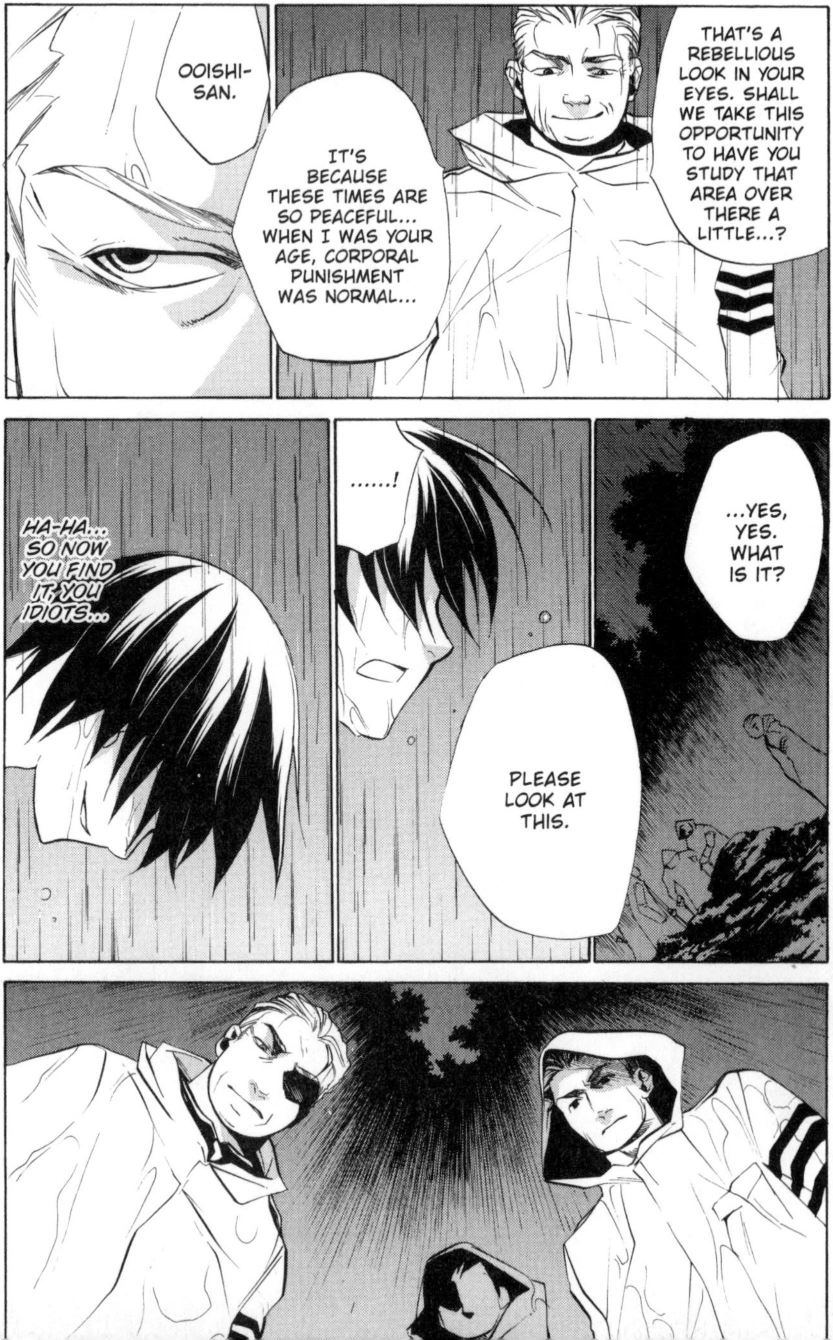
THAT'S A REBELLIOUS LOOK IN YOUR EYES. SHALL WE TAKE THIS OPPORTUNITY TO HAVE YOU STUDY THAT AREA OVER THERE A LITTLE...?
IT'S BECAUSE THESE TIMES ARE SO PEACEFUL... WHEN I WAS YOUR AGE, CORPORAL PUNISHMENT WAS NORMAL...
OOISHI-SAN.
...YES, YES. WHAT IS IT?
PLEASE LOOK AT THIS.
......!
HA-HA... SO NOW YOU FIND IT, YOU IDIOTS...

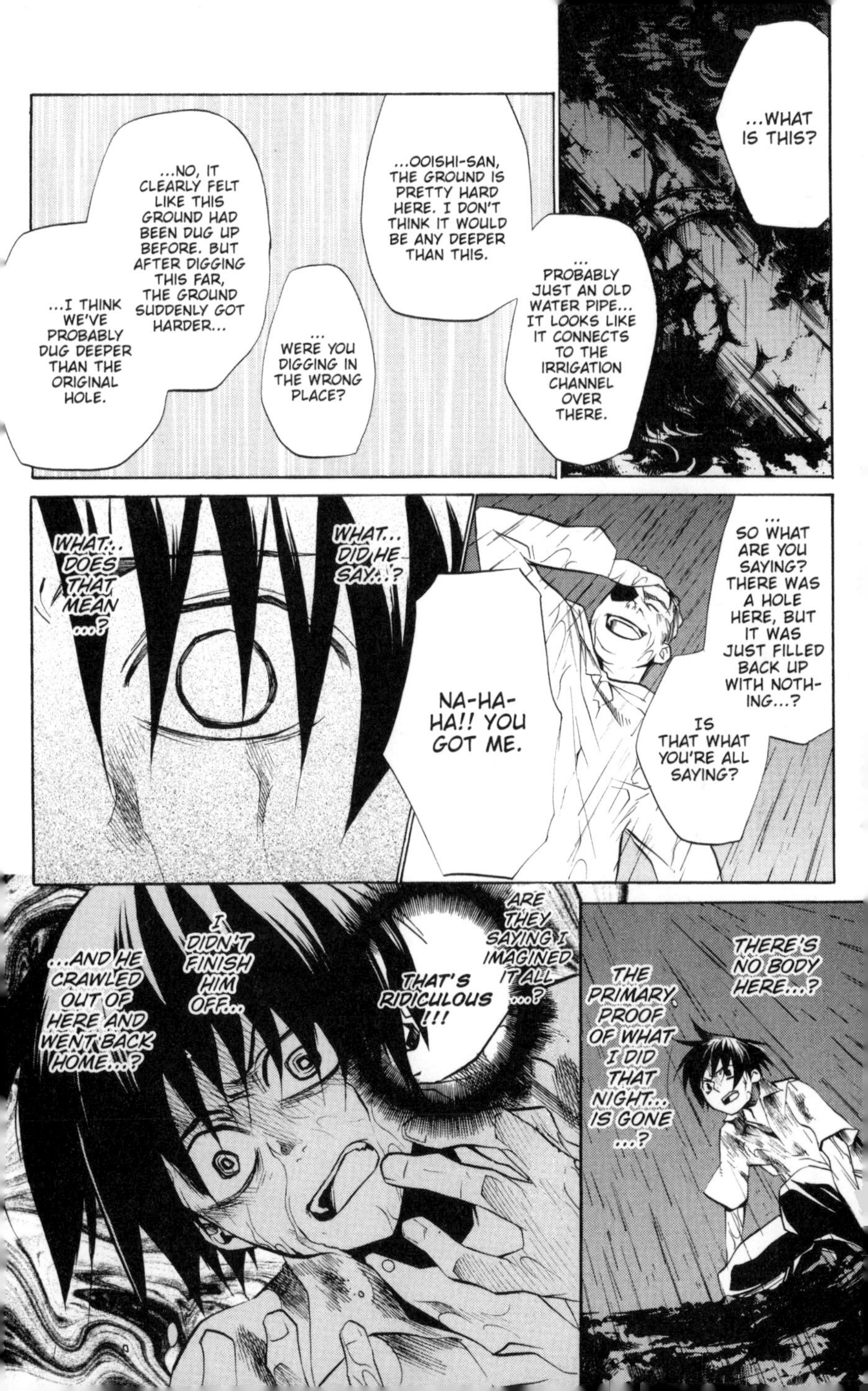
...WHAT IS THIS?
... PROBABLY JUST AN OLD WATER PIPE... IT LOOKS LIKE IT CONNECTS TO THE IRRIGATION CHANNEL OVER THERE.
...OOISHI-SAN, THE GROUND IS PRETTY HARD HERE. I DON'T THINK IT WOULD BE ANY DEEPER THAN THIS.
... WERE YOU DIGGING IN THE WRONG PLACE?
...NO, IT CLEARLY FELT LIKE THIS GROUND HAD BEEN DUG UP BEFORE. BUT AFTER DIGGING THIS FAR, THE GROUND SUDDENLY GOT HARDER...
...I THINK WE'VE PROBABLY DUG DEEPER THAN THE ORIGINAL HOLE.
... SO WHAT ARE YOU SAYING? THERE WAS A HOLE HERE, BUT IT WAS JUST FILLED BACK UP WITH NOTHING...?
IS THAT WHAT YOU'RE ALL SAYING?
NA-HA-HA!! YOU GOT ME.
WHAT... DID HE SAY...?
WHAT... DOES THAT MEAN...?
THERE'S NO BODY HERE...?
THE PRIMARY PROOF OF WHAT I DID THAT NIGHT... IS GONE...?
ARE THEY SAYING I IMAGINED IT ALL...?
THAT'S RIDICULOUS!!!
I DIDN'T FINISH HIM OFF...
...AND HE CRAWLED OUT OF HERE AND WENT BACK HOME...?

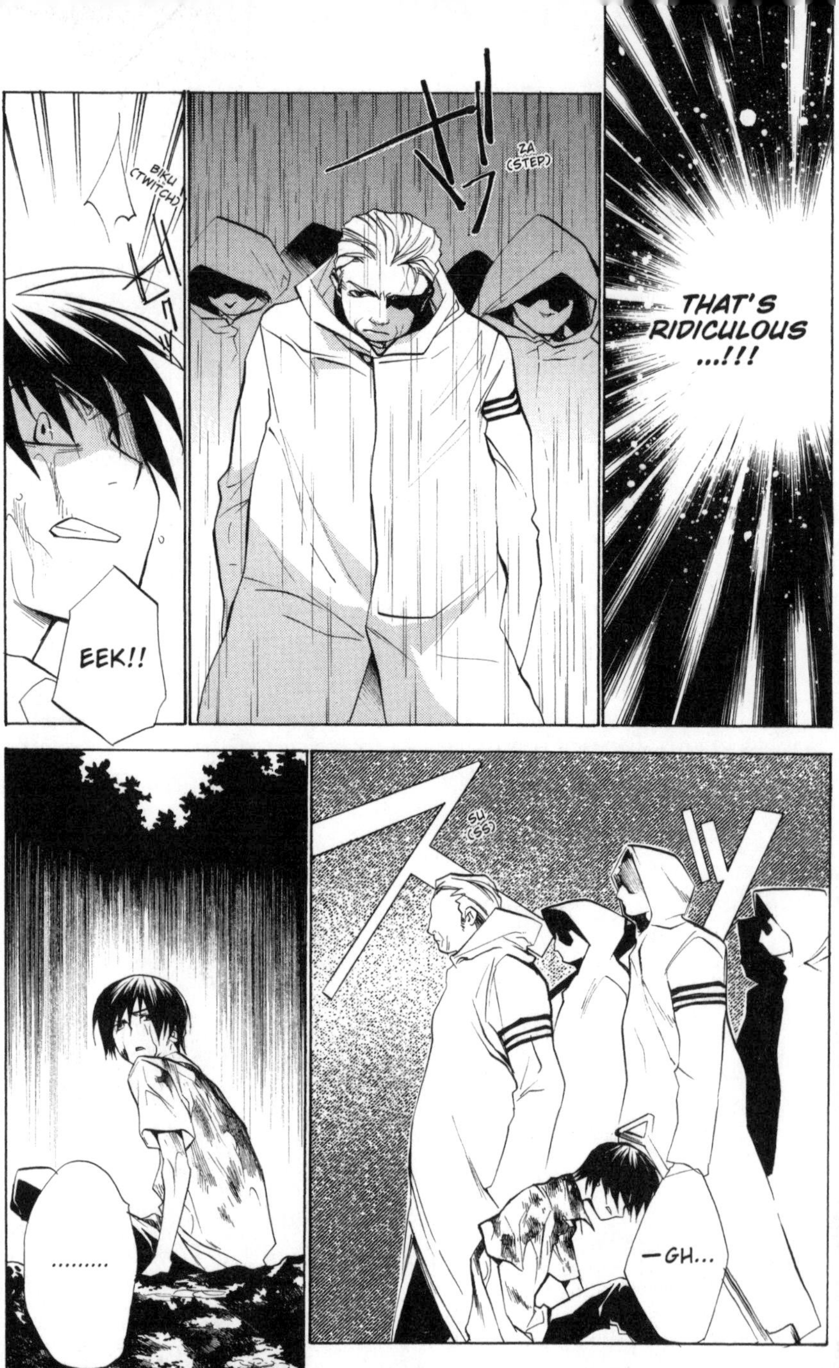
THAT'S RIDICULOUS ...!!!
ZA (STEP)
BIKU (TWITCH)
EEK!!
SU (SS)
—GH...
....

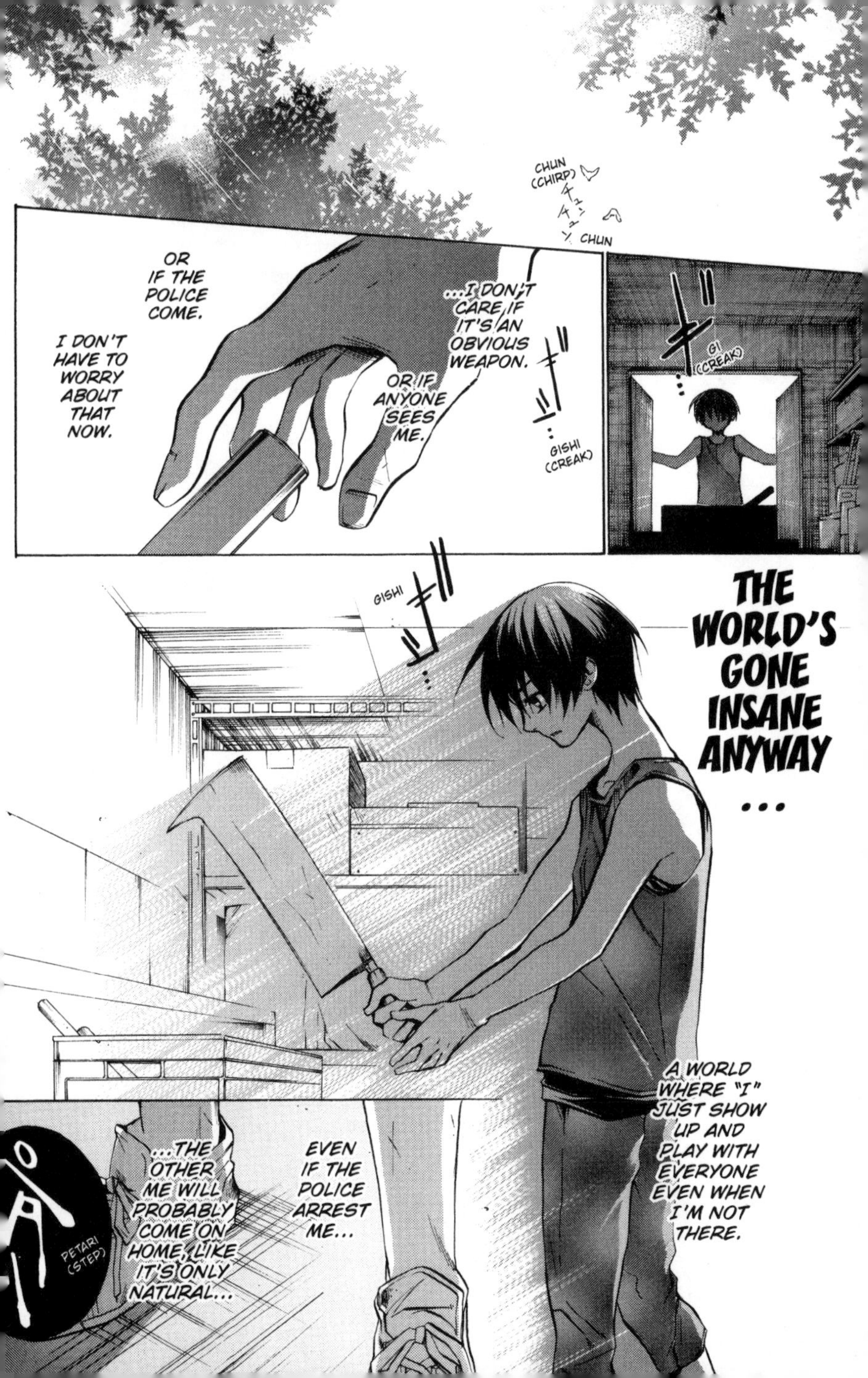
CHUN (CHIRP)
CHUN
GI (CREAK)
GISHI (CREAK)
...I DON'T CARE IF IT'S AN OBVIOUS WEAPON.
OR IF ANYONE SEES ME.
OR IF THE POLICE COME.
I DON'T HAVE TO WORRY ABOUT THAT NOW.
GISHI
THE WORLD'S GONE INSANE ANYWAY...
A WORLD WHERE "I" JUST SHOW UP AND PLAY WITH EVERYONE EVEN WHEN I'M NOT THERE.
EVEN IF THE POLICE ARREST ME...
...THE OTHER ME WILL PROBABLY COME ON HOME, LIKE IT'S ONLY NATURAL...
PETARI (STEP)

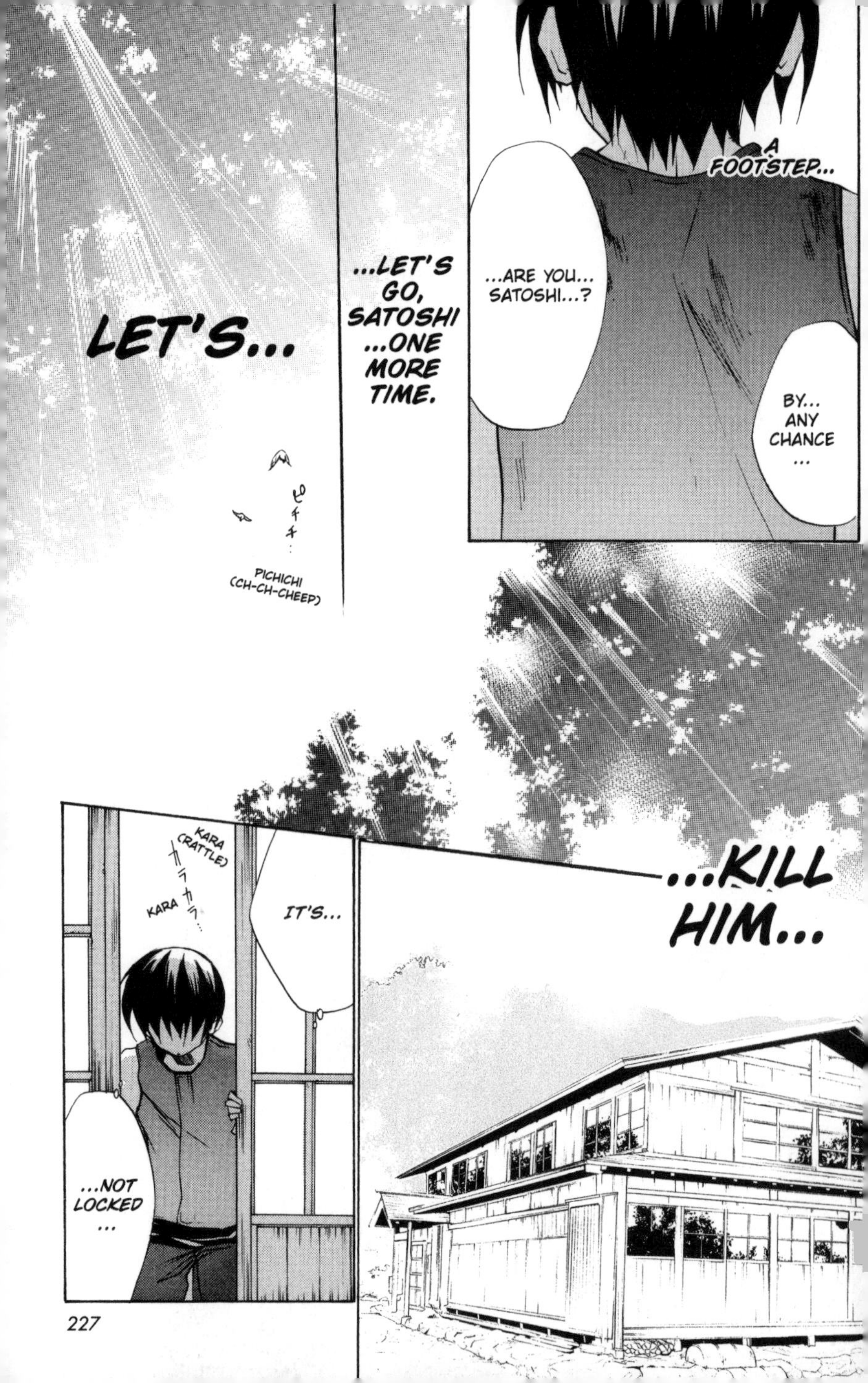
A FOOTSTEP...
...ARE YOU... SATOSHI...?
BY... ANY CHANCE ...
...LET'S GO, SATOSHI ...ONE MORE TIME.
LET'S...
ピチチ…
PICHICHI (CH-CH-CHEEP)
...KILL HIM...
カラカラ…
KARA (RATTLE) KARA
IT'S...
...NOT LOCKED ...

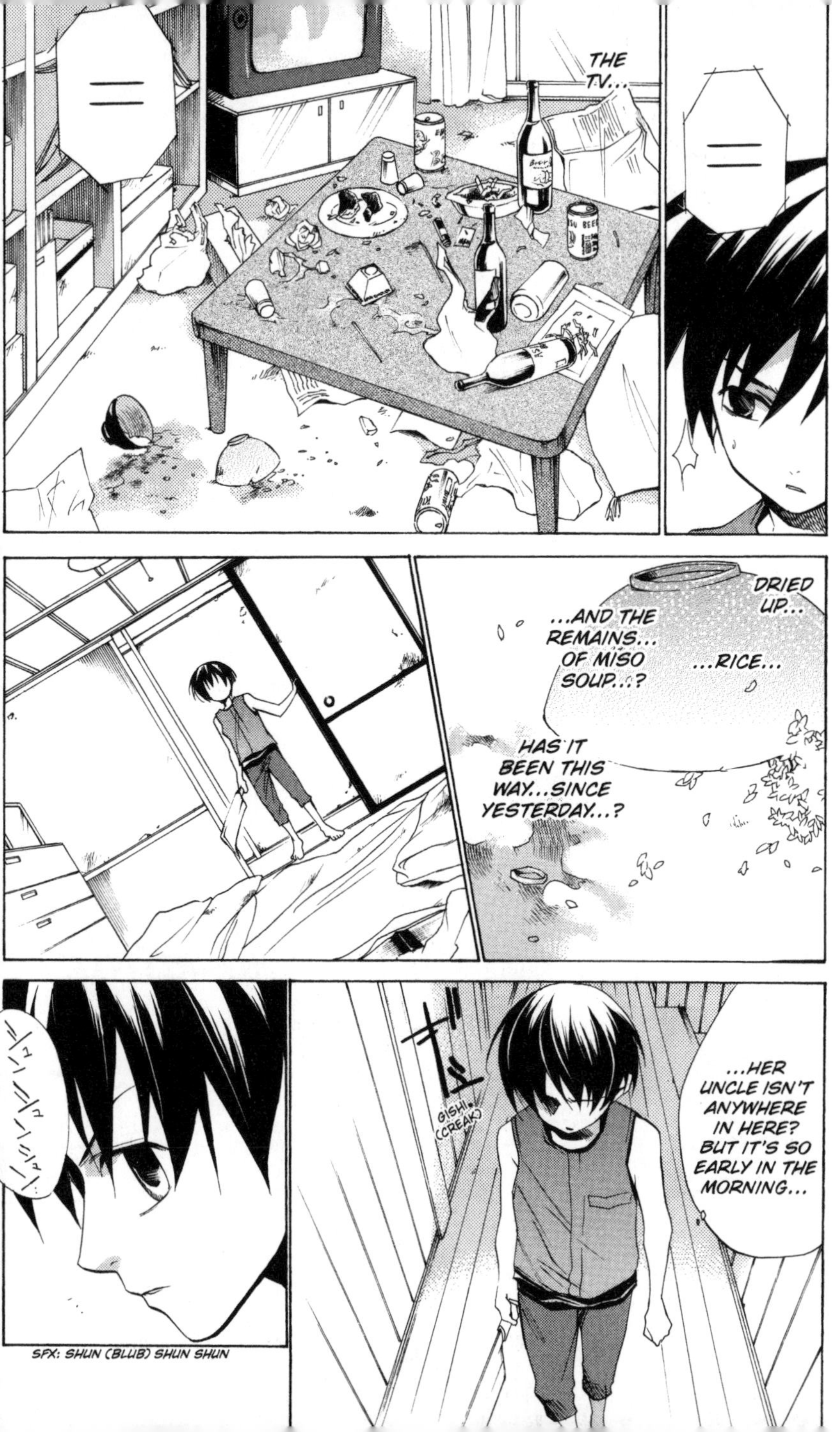
—
THE TV...
—
DRIED UP...
...RICE...
...AND THE REMAINS... OF MISO SOUP...?
HAS IT BEEN THIS WAY...SINCE YESTERDAY...?
...HER UNCLE ISN'T ANYWHERE IN HERE? BUT IT'S SO EARLY IN THE MORNING...
GISHI (CREAK)
SFX: SHUN (BLUB) SHUN SHUN

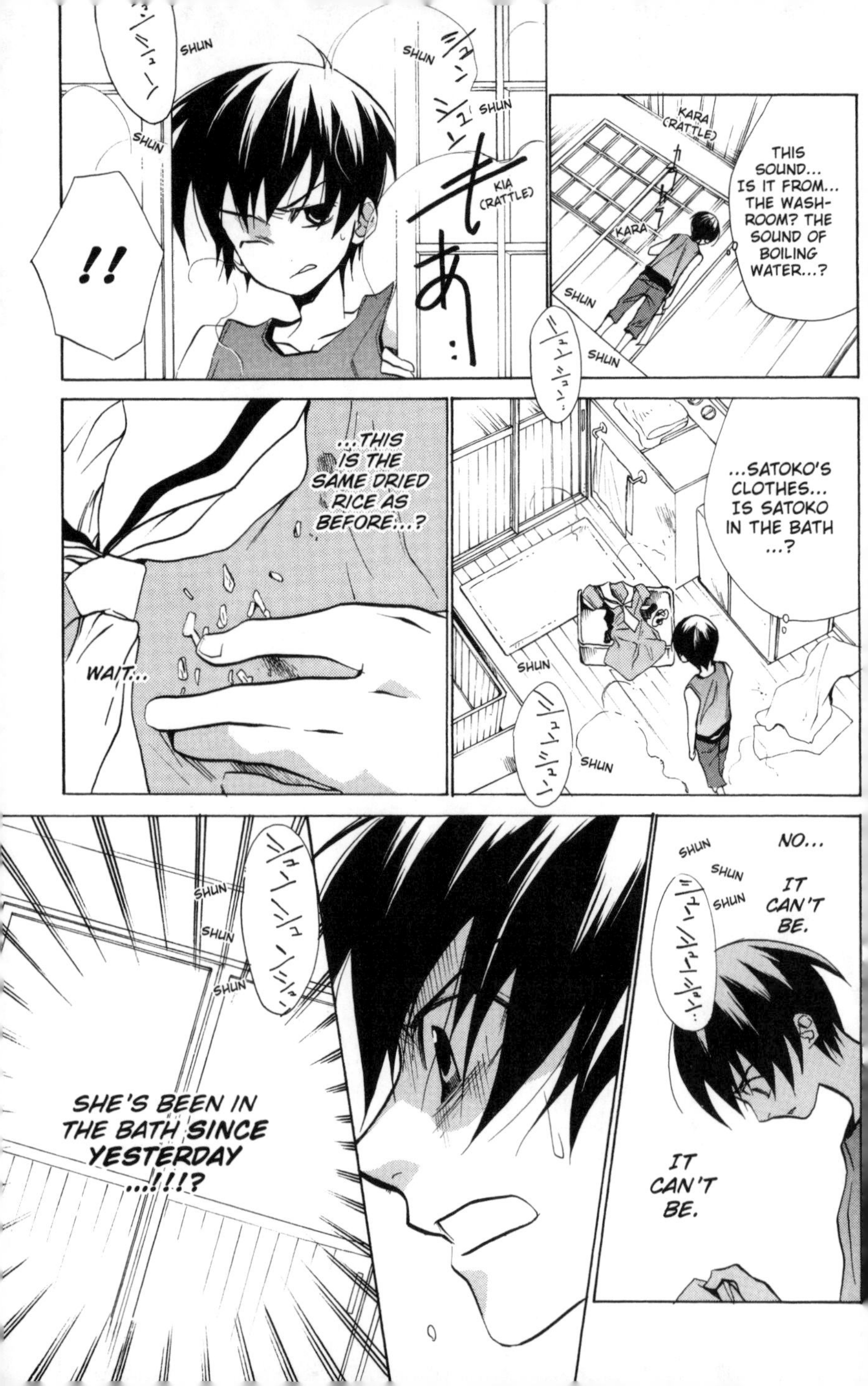
KARA (RATTLE)
THIS SOUND... IS IT FROM... THE WASH-ROOM? THE SOUND OF BOILING WATER...?
KARA
SHUN
SHUN
SHUN
SHUN
SHUN
KIA (RATTLE)
SHUN
!!
...SATOKO'S CLOTHES... IS SATOKO IN THE BATH ...?
SHUN
SHUN
...THIS IS THE SAME DRIED RICE AS BEFORE...?
WAIT...
NO...
SHUN
SHUN
SHUN
IT CAN'T BE.
IT CAN'T BE.
SHUN
SHUN
SHUN
SHE'S BEEN IN THE BATH SINCE YESTERDAY ...!!!?

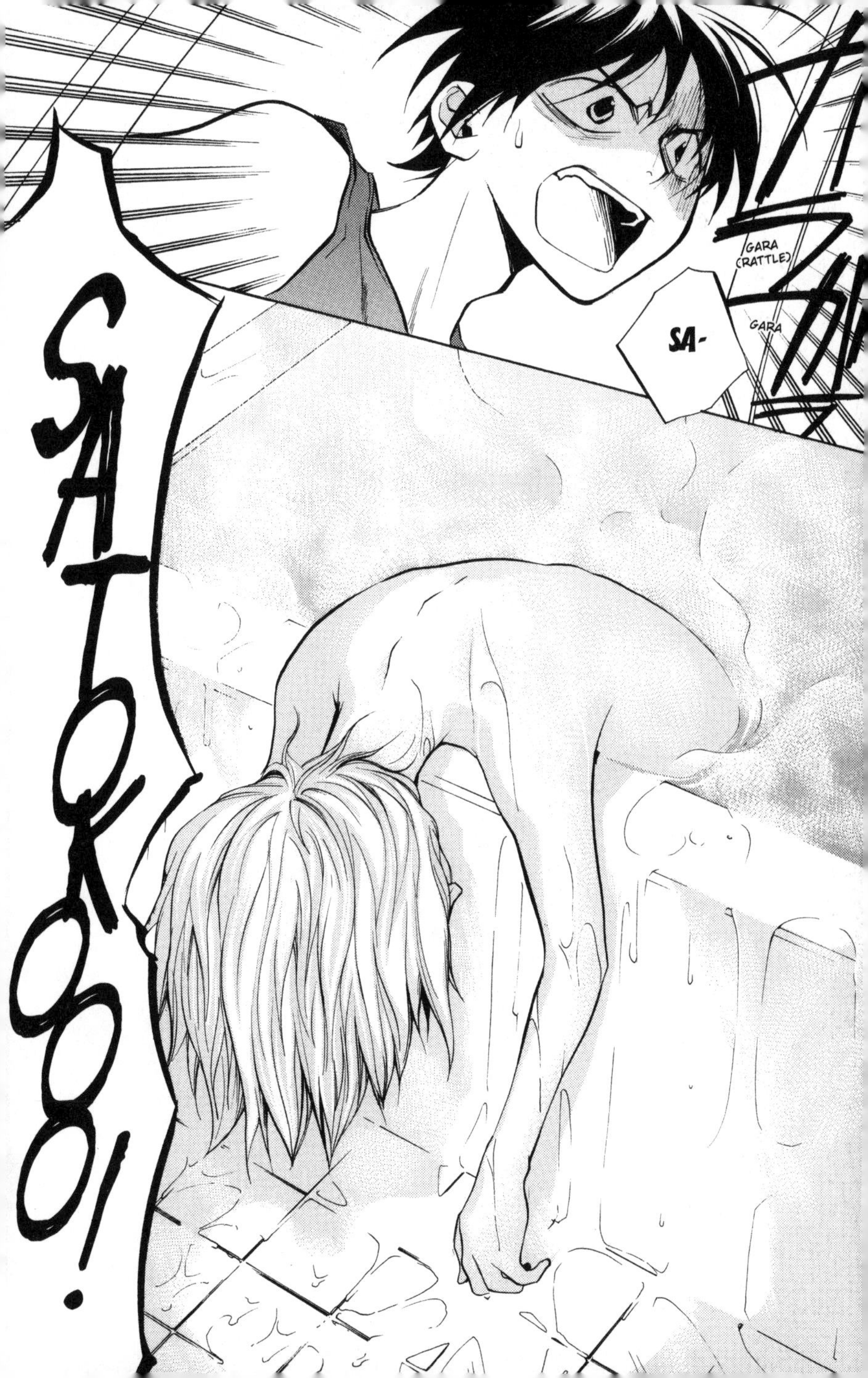
GARA (RATTLE)
GARA
SA-
SATOOOOO!

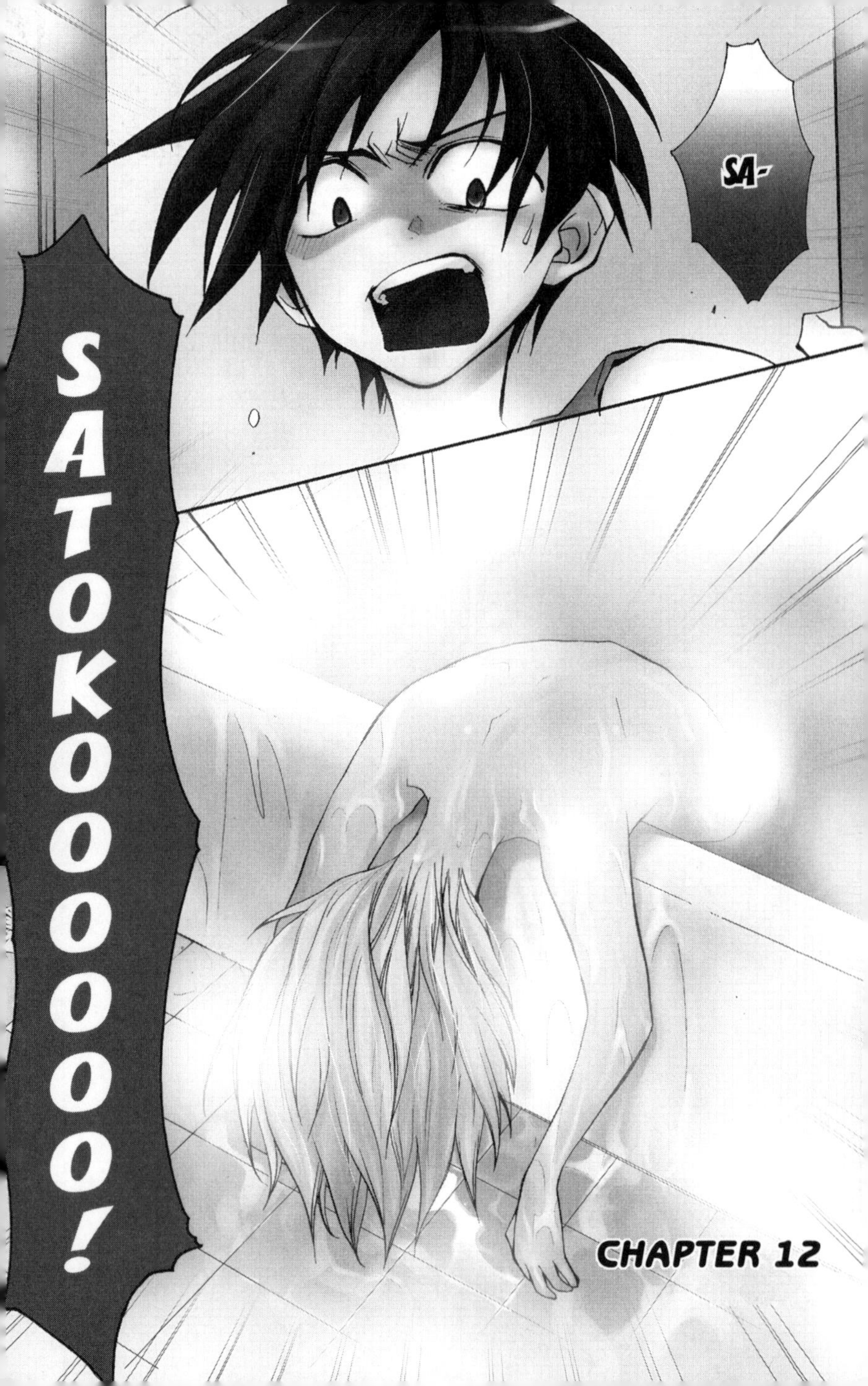
SA-
SATOKOOOOOOO!
CHAPTER 12

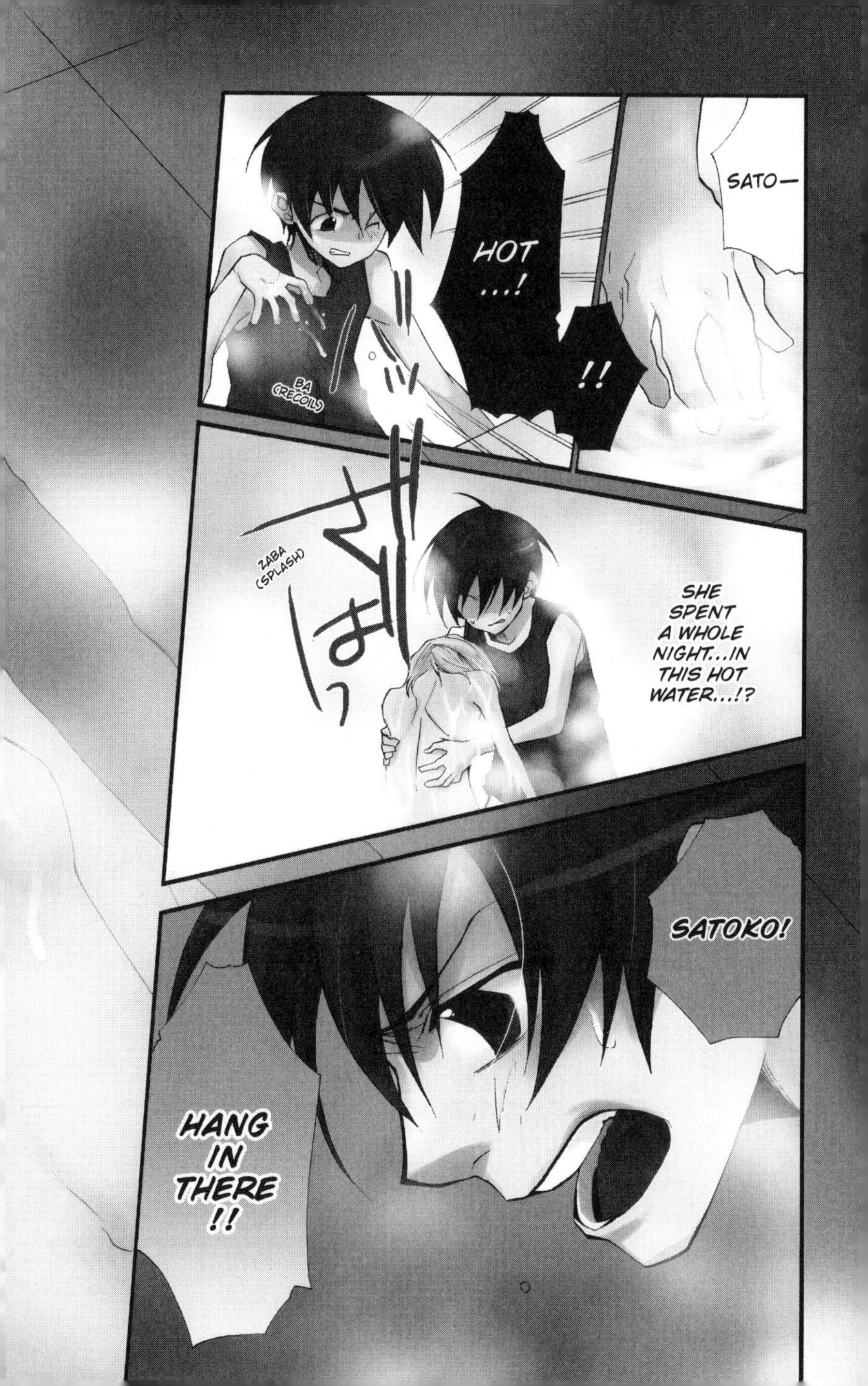
SATO—
!!
HOT ...!
BA (RECOIL)
SHE SPENT A WHOLE NIGHT...IN THIS HOT WATER...!?
ZABA (SPLASH)
SATOKO!
HANG IN THERE !!

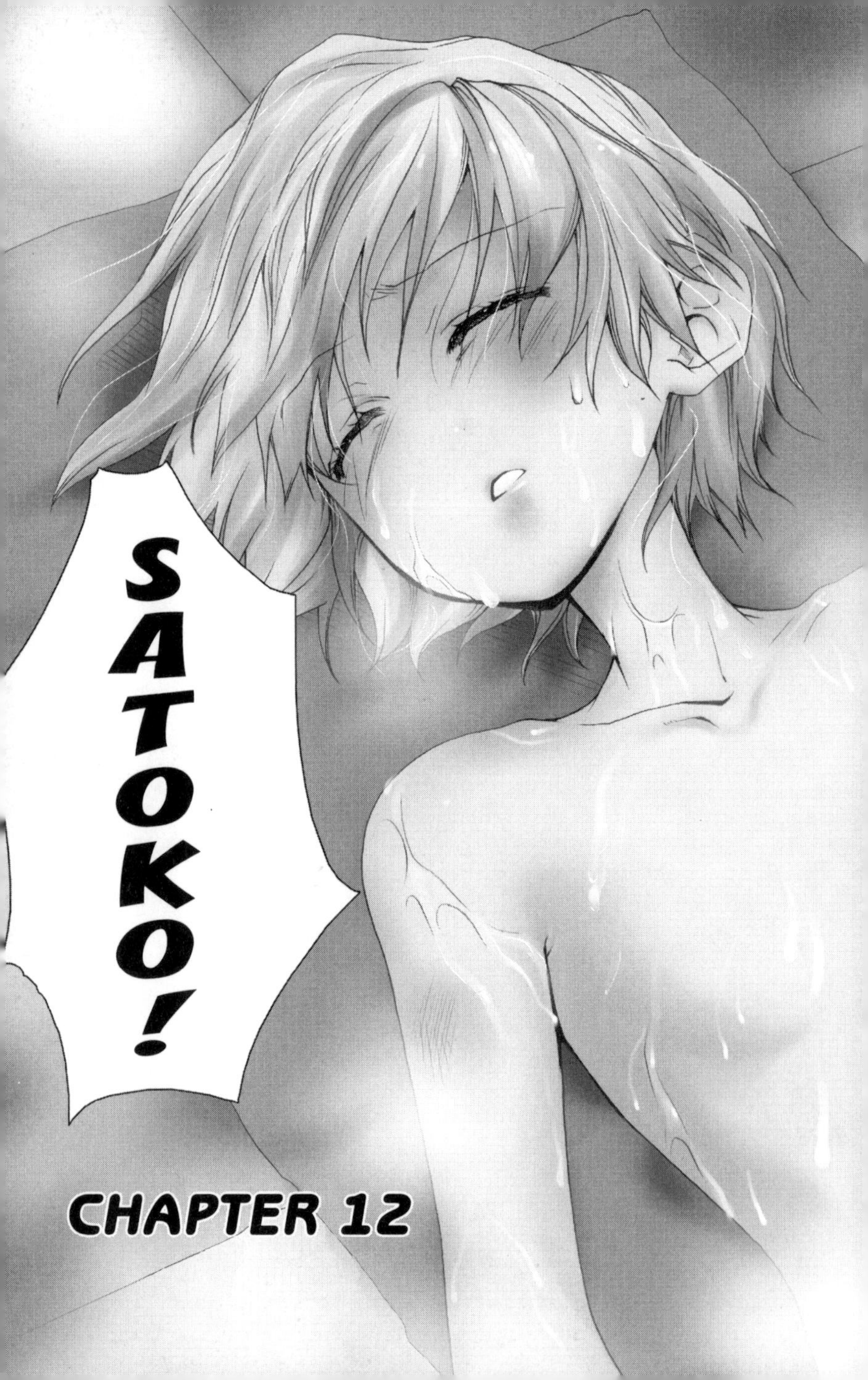
SATOKO!
CHAPTER 12

Special Thanks:

· Barusu Noda-sama

· ARIMATTY-sama

· Ayumi Shiina-sama

· My editor, Mochizuki-sama

CAPTION: TEPPEI-SAN

ARROWS: NECKLACE, HAWAIIAN

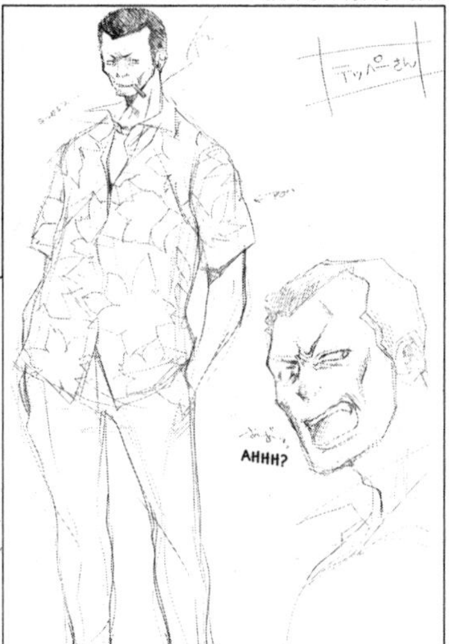
AHHH?

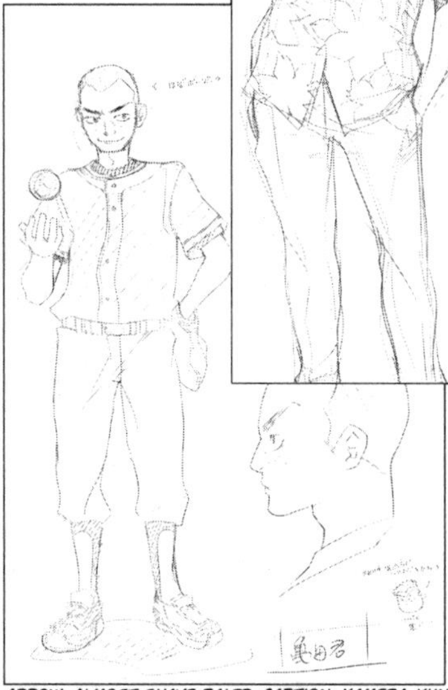

ARROW: ALMOST SHAVE BALD? CAPTION: KAMEDA-KUN

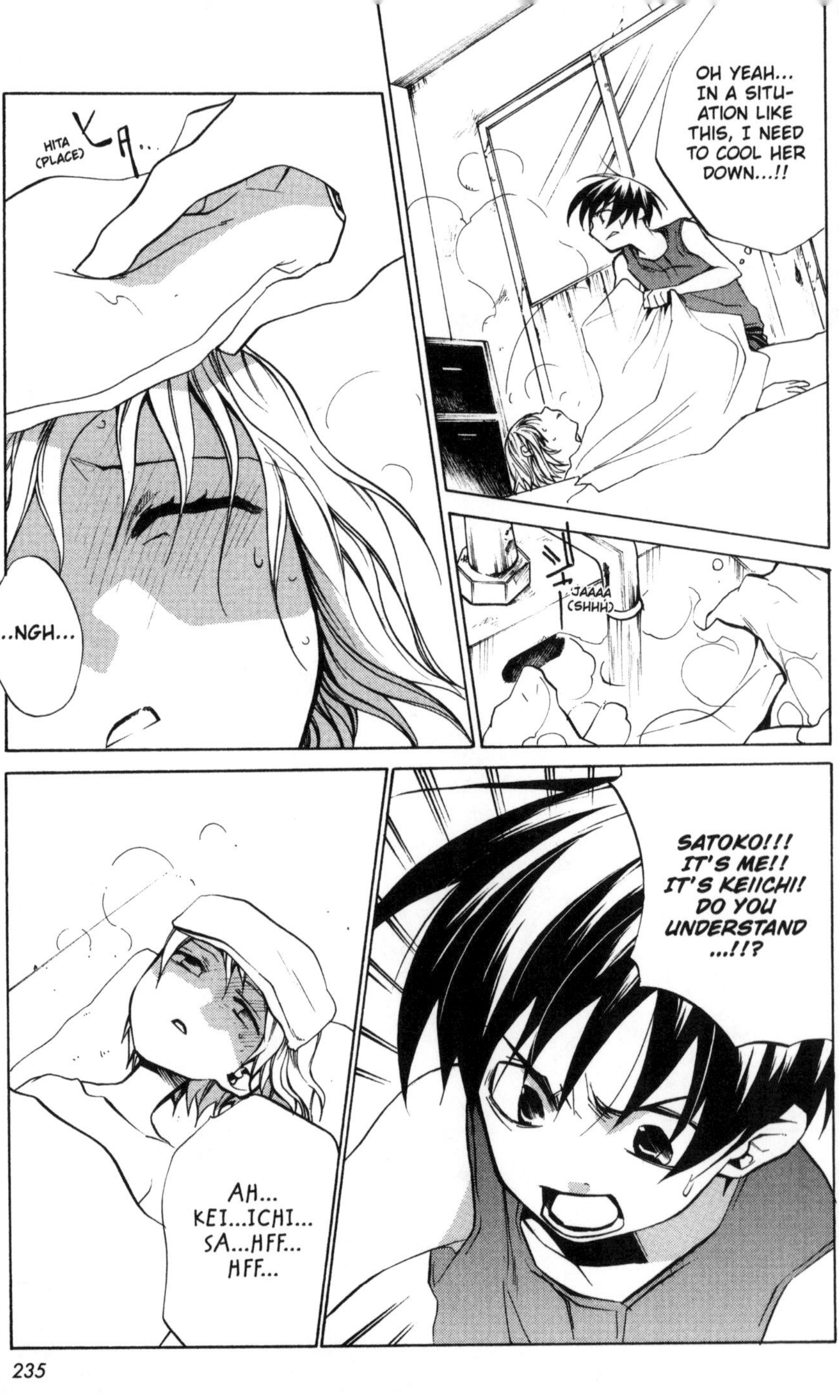
OH YEAH... IN A SITUATION LIKE THIS, I NEED TO COOL HER DOWN...!!
JAAAA (SHHH)
HITA (PLACE)
...NGH...
SATOKO!!! IT'S ME!! IT'S KEIICHI! DO YOU UNDERSTAND ...!!?
AH... KEI...ICHI... SA...HFF... HFF...

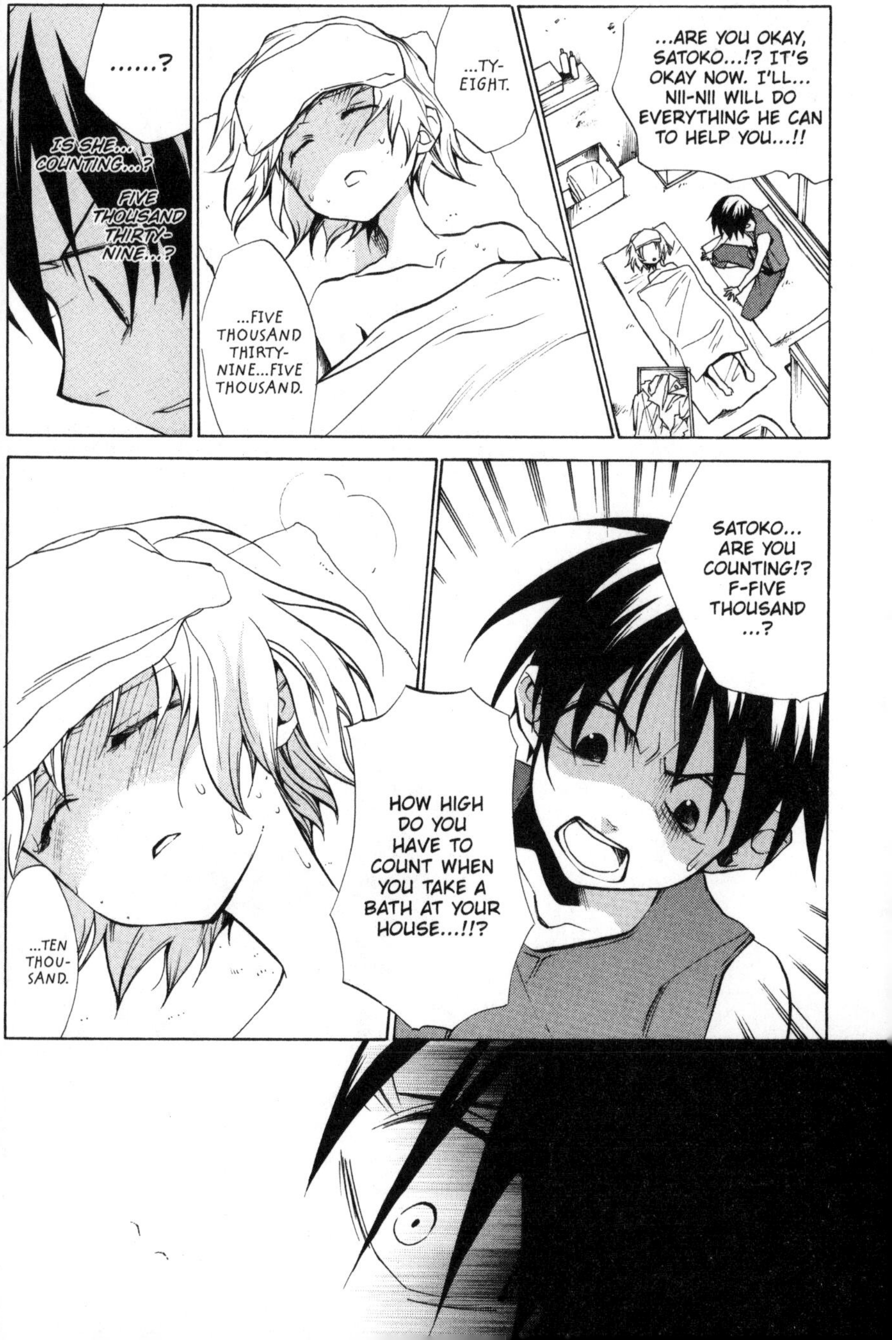
...ARE YOU OKAY, SATOKO...!? IT'S OKAY NOW. I'LL... NII-NII WILL DO EVERYTHING HE CAN TO HELP YOU...!!
...TY-EIGHT.
...FIVE THOUSAND THIRTY-NINE...FIVE THOUSAND.
......?
IS SHE... COUNTING...?
FIVE THOUSAND THIRTY-NINE...?
SATOKO... ARE YOU COUNTING!? F-FIVE THOUSAND ...?
HOW HIGH DO YOU HAVE TO COUNT WHEN YOU TAKE A BATH AT YOUR HOUSE...!!?
...TEN THOUSAND.

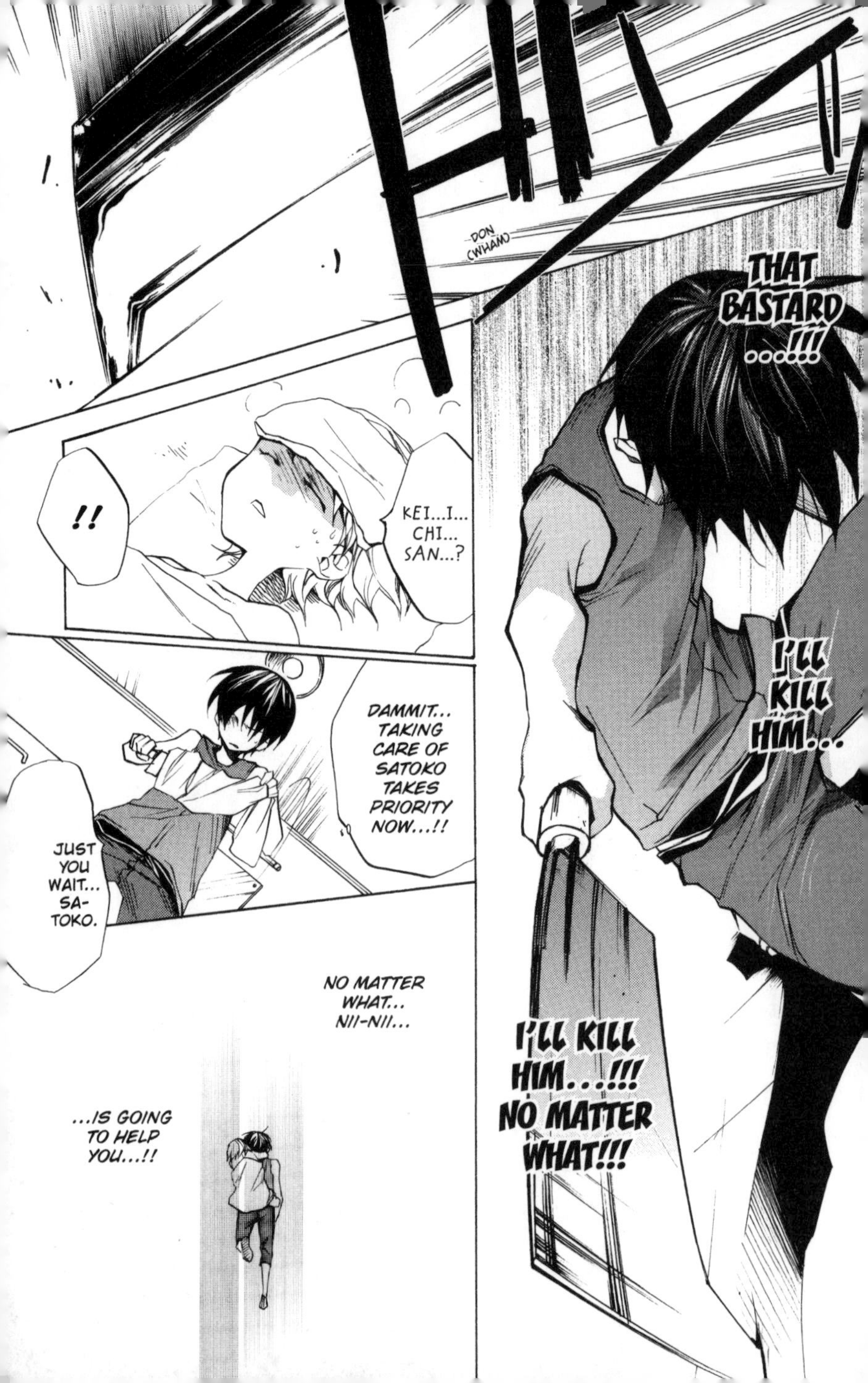
DON (WHAM)
THAT BASTARD ......!!!
I'LL KILL HIM...
I'LL KILL HIM...!!! NO MATTER WHAT!!!
KEI...I... CHI... SAN...?
!!
DAMMIT... TAKING CARE OF SATOKO TAKES PRIORITY NOW...!!
JUST YOU WAIT... SA-TOKO.
NO MATTER WHAT... NII-NII...
...IS GOING TO HELP YOU...!!

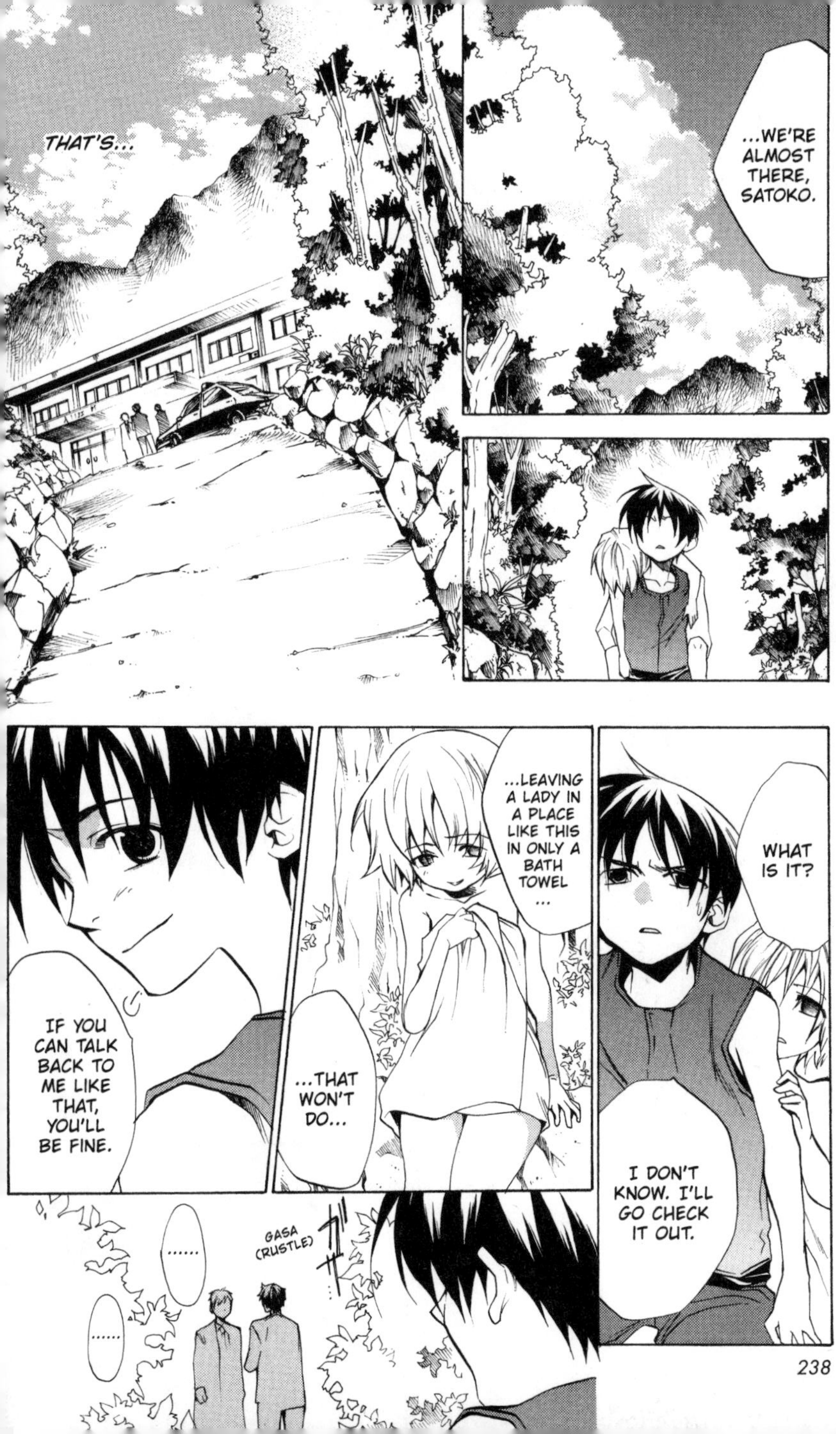
...WE'RE ALMOST THERE, SATOKO.
THAT'S...
WHAT IS IT?
I DON'T KNOW. I'LL GO CHECK IT OUT.
...LEAVING A LADY IN A PLACE LIKE THIS IN ONLY A BATH TOWEL ...
...THAT WON'T DO...
IF YOU CAN TALK BACK TO ME LIKE THAT, YOU'LL BE FINE.
GASA (RUSTLE)
......
......

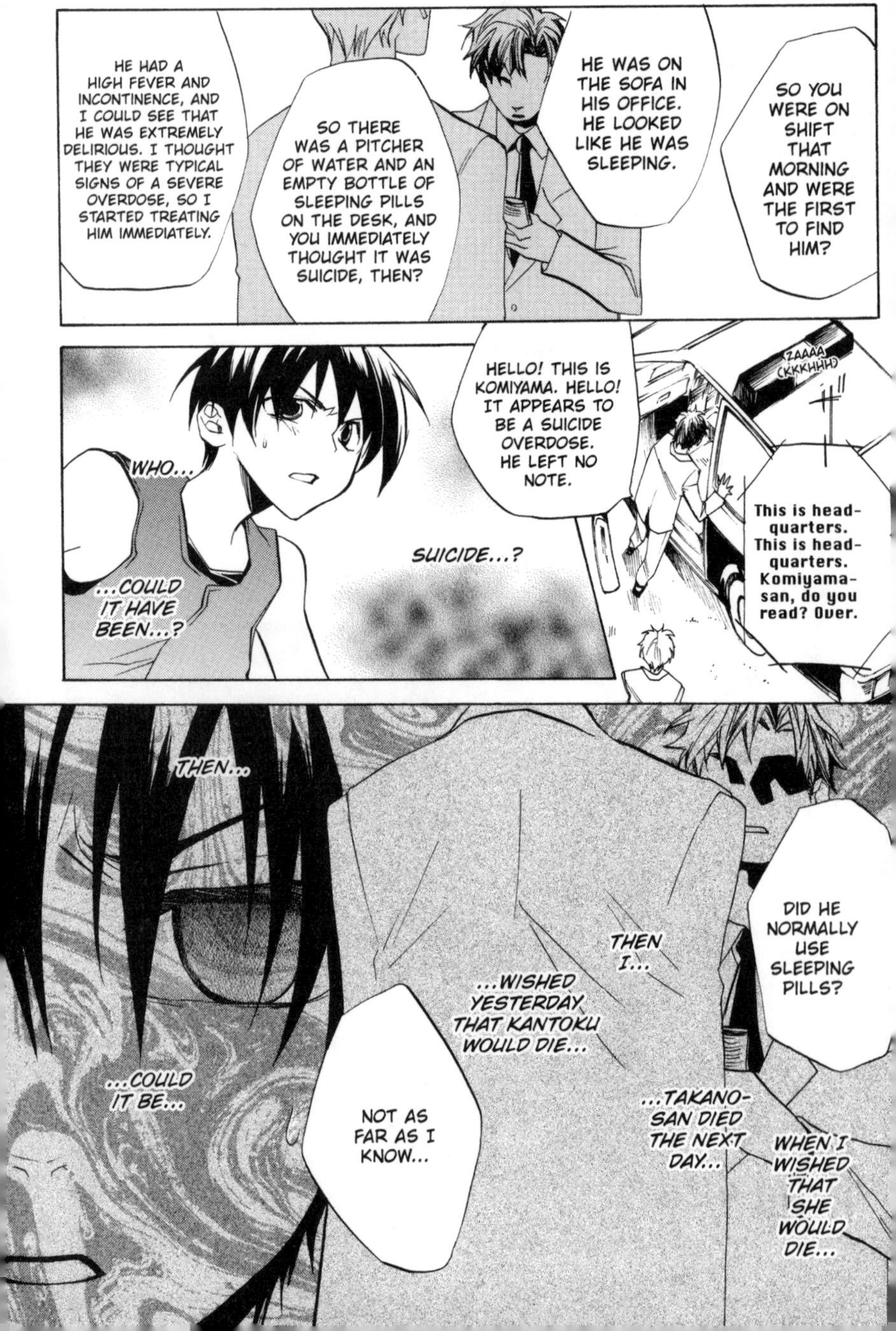
SO YOU WERE ON SHIFT THAT MORNING AND WERE THE FIRST TO FIND HIM?
HE WAS ON THE SOFA IN HIS OFFICE. HE LOOKED LIKE HE WAS SLEEPING.
SO THERE WAS A PITCHER OF WATER AND AN EMPTY BOTTLE OF SLEEPING PILLS ON THE DESK, AND YOU IMMEDIATELY THOUGHT IT WAS SUICIDE, THEN?
HE HAD A HIGH FEVER AND INCONTINENCE, AND I COULD SEE THAT HE WAS EXTREMELY DELIRIOUS. I THOUGHT THEY WERE TYPICAL SIGNS OF A SEVERE OVERDOSE, SO I STARTED TREATING HIM IMMEDIATELY.
ZAAAA (KKKHHH)
HELLO! THIS IS KOMIYAMA. HELLO! IT APPEARS TO BE A SUICIDE OVERDOSE. HE LEFT NO NOTE.
This is head-quarters. This is head-quarters. Komiyama-san, do you read? Over.
SUICIDE...?
WHO...
...COULD IT HAVE BEEN...?
DID HE NORMALLY USE SLEEPING PILLS?
WHEN I WISHED THAT SHE WOULD DIE...
...TAKANO-SAN DIED THE NEXT DAY...
THEN I...
...WISHED YESTERDAY THAT KANTOKU WOULD DIE...
NOT AS FAR AS I KNOW...
...COULD IT BE...
THEN...

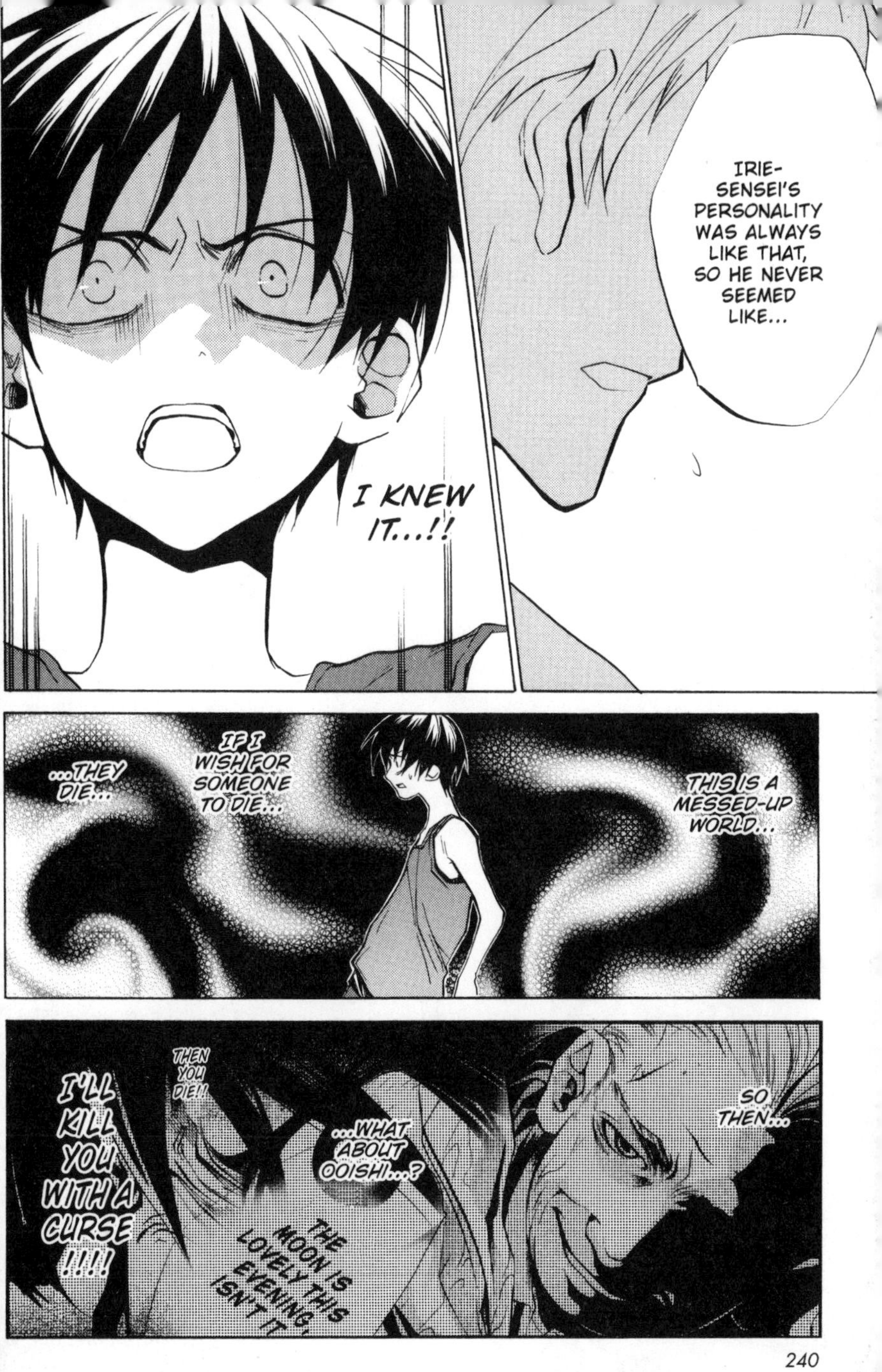
IRIE-SENSEI'S PERSONALITY WAS ALWAYS LIKE THAT, SO HE NEVER SEEMED LIKE...
I KNEW IT...!!
THIS IS A MESSED-UP WORLD...
IF I WISH FOR SOMEONE TO DIE...
...THEY DIE...
SO THEN...
...WHAT ABOUT OOISHI...?
THEN YOU DIE!!
I'LL KILL YOU WITH A CURSE!!!!
THE MOON IS LOVELY THIS EVENING, ISN'T IT

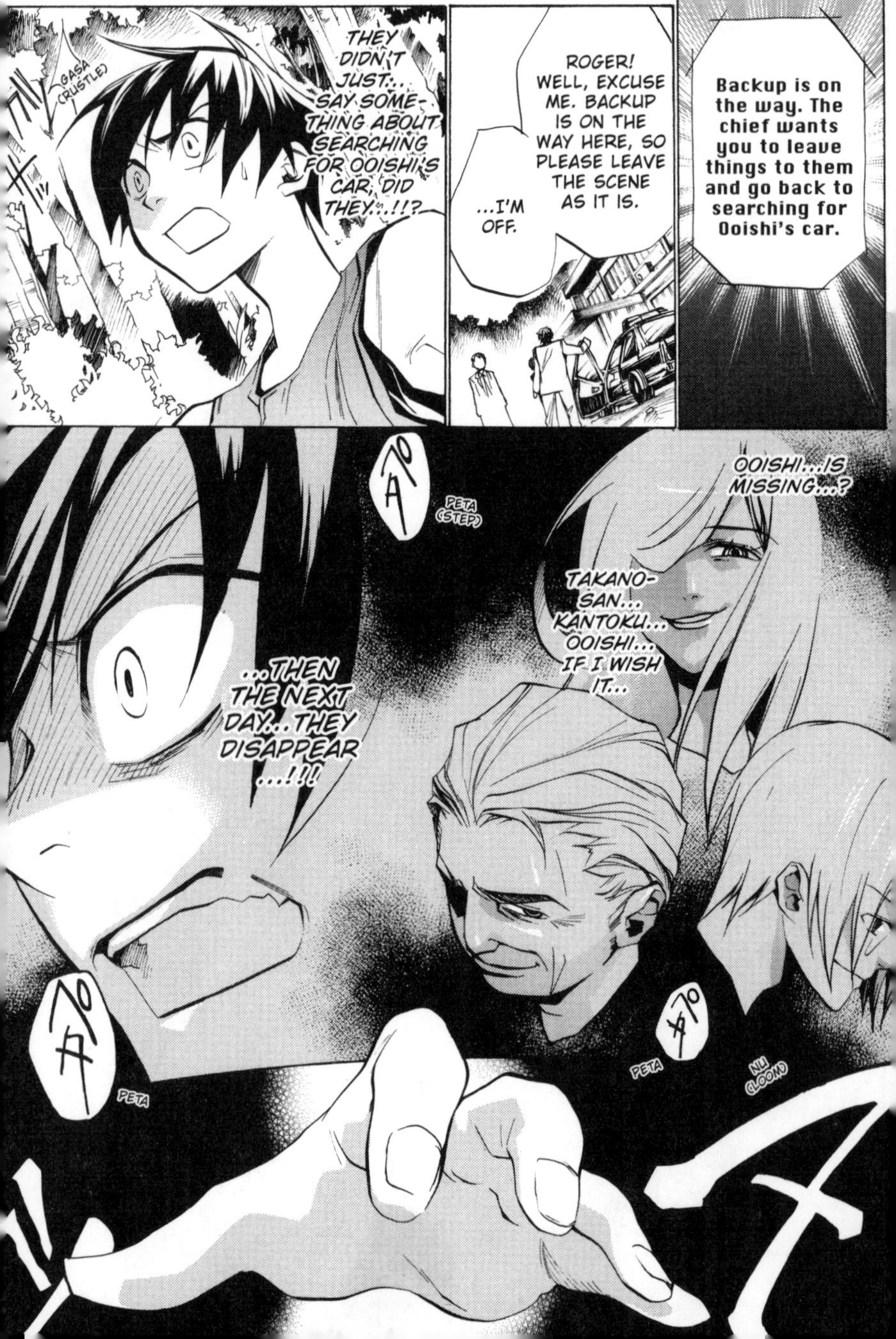
Backup is on the way. The chief wants you to leave things to them and go back to searching for Ooishi's car.
ROGER! WELL, EXCUSE ME. BACKUP IS ON THE WAY HERE, SO PLEASE LEAVE THE SCENE AS IT IS.
...I'M OFF.
THEY DIDN'T JUST... SAY SOMETHING ABOUT SEARCHING FOR OOISHI'S CAR, DID THEY...!!?
GASA (CRUSTLE)
OOISHI...IS MISSING...?
PETA (STEP)
TAKANO-SAN... KANTOKU... OOISHI... IF I WISH IT...
...THEN THE NEXT DAY...THEY DISAPPEAR ...!!!
NU (LOOM)
PETA
PETA

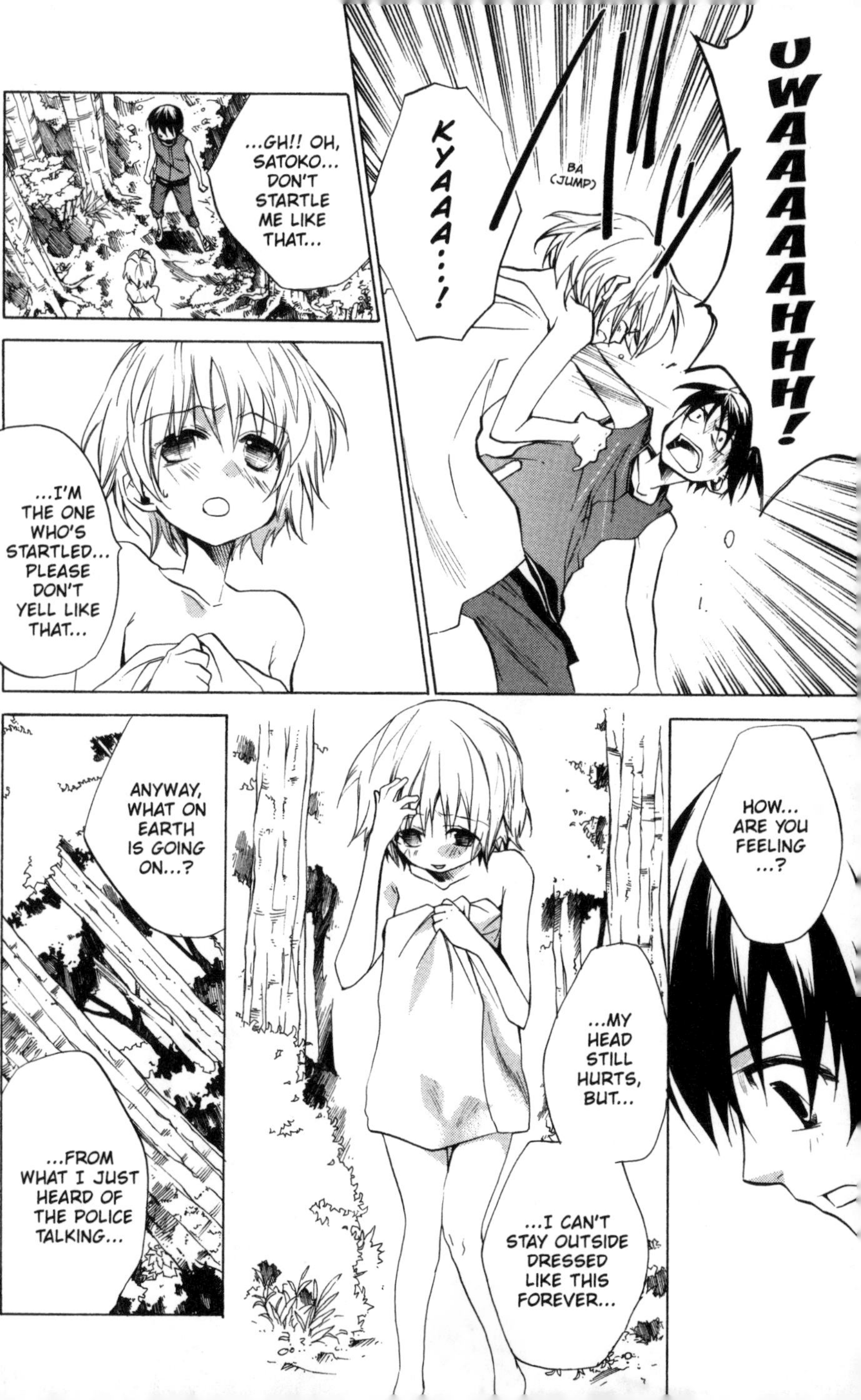
UWAAAAAAHHH!
KYAAA...!
BA (JUMP)
...GH!! OH, SATOKO... DON'T STARTLE ME LIKE THAT...
...I'M THE ONE WHO'S STARTLED... PLEASE DON'T YELL LIKE THAT...
HOW... ARE YOU FEELING ...?
...MY HEAD STILL HURTS, BUT...
...I CAN'T STAY OUTSIDE DRESSED LIKE THIS FOREVER...
ANYWAY, WHAT ON EARTH IS GOING ON...?
...FROM WHAT I JUST HEARD OF THE POLICE TALKING...

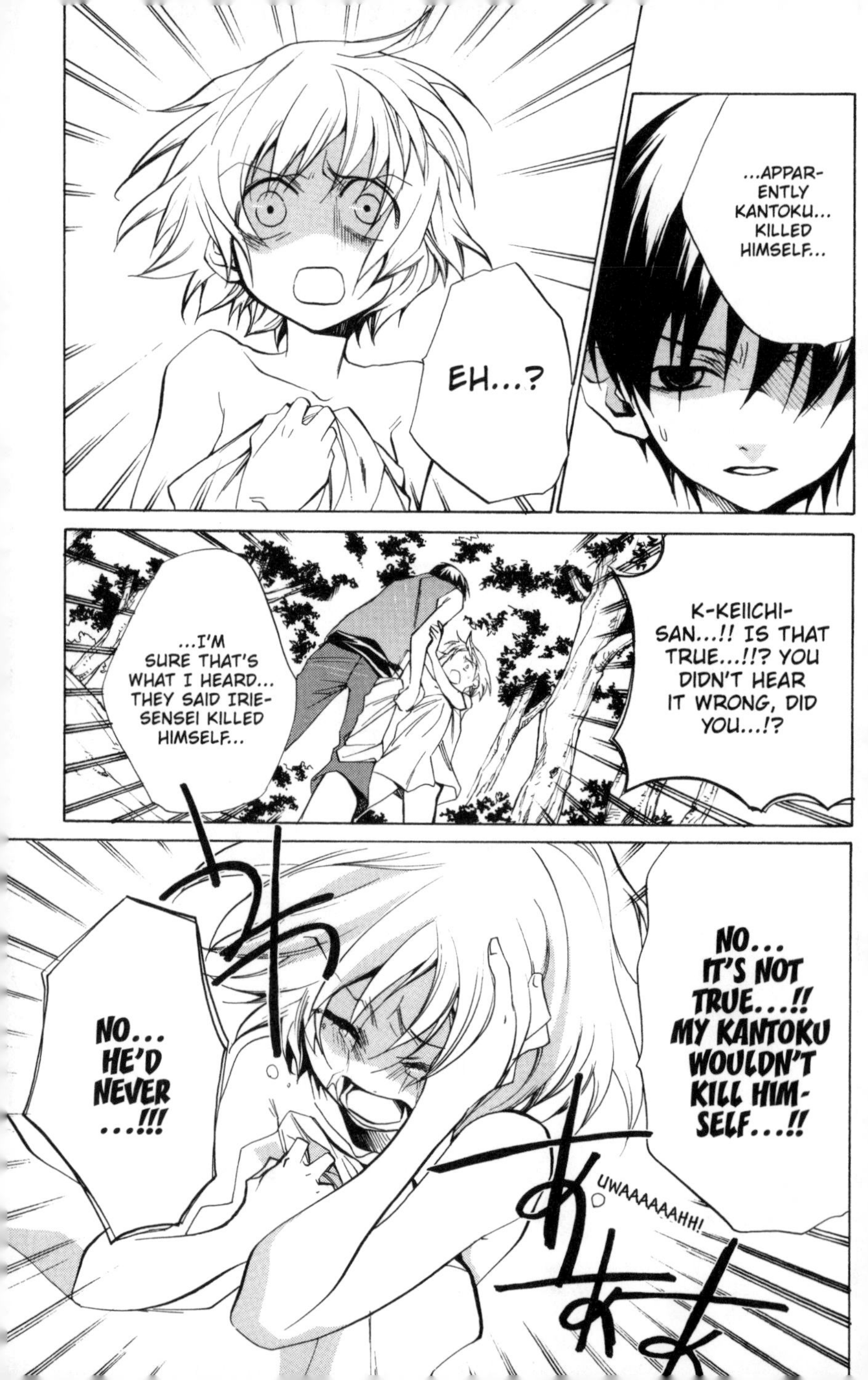
...APPAR-ENTLY KANTOKU... KILLED HIMSELF...
EH...?
K-KEIICHI-SAN...!! IS THAT TRUE...!!? YOU DIDN'T HEAR IT WRONG, DID YOU...!?
...I'M SURE THAT'S WHAT I HEARD... THEY SAID IRIE-SENSEI KILLED HIMSELF...
NO... IT'S NOT TRUE...!! MY KANTOKU WOULDN'T KILL HIM-SELF...!!
NO... HE'D NEVER ...!!!
UWAAAAAAHH!

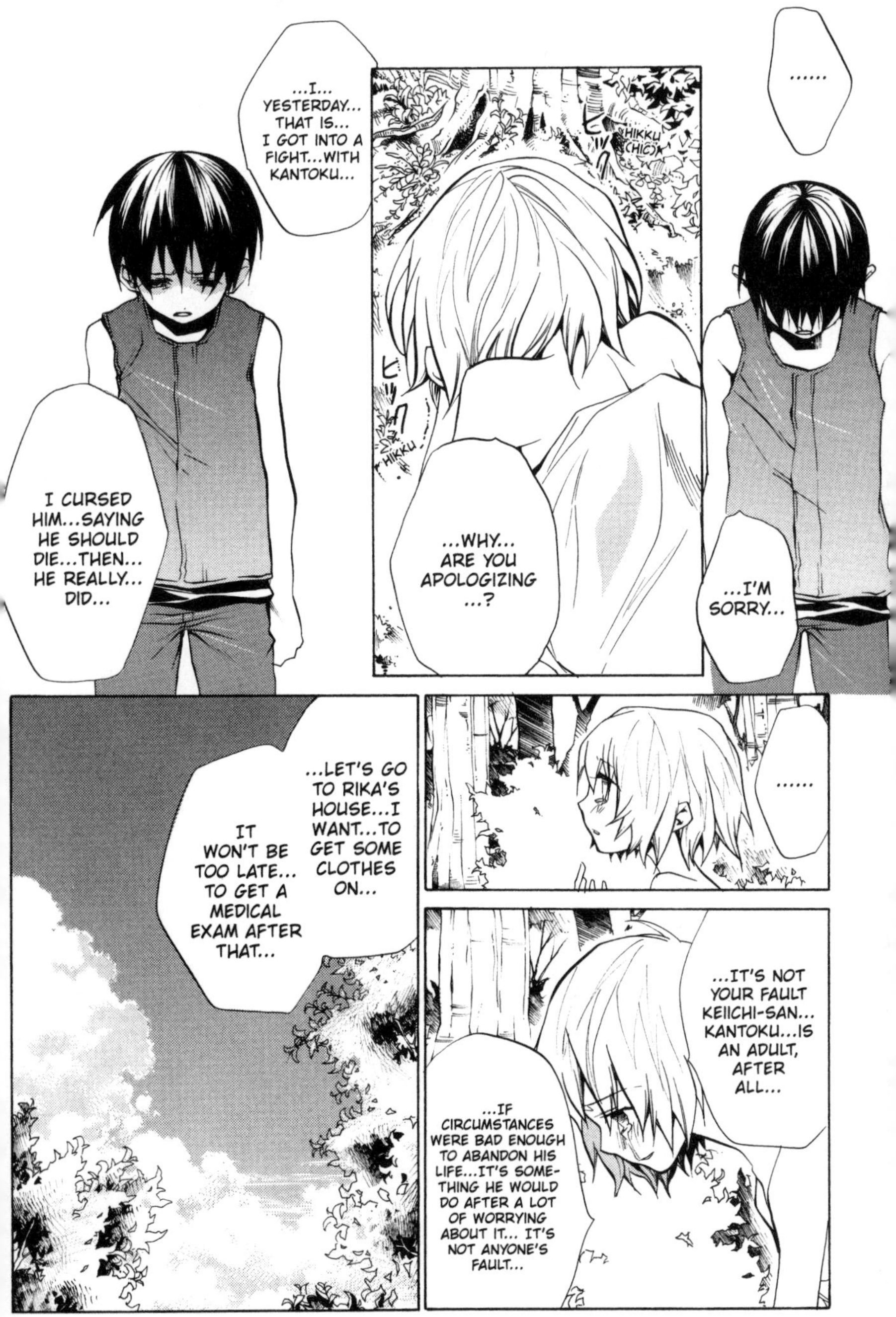
......
...I'M SORRY...
HIKKU (HIC)
...WHY... ARE YOU APOLOGIZING ...?
HIKKU
...I... YESTERDAY... THAT IS... I GOT INTO A FIGHT...WITH KANTOKU...
I CURSED HIM...SAYING HE SHOULD DIE...THEN... HE REALLY... DID...
......
...IT'S NOT YOUR FAULT KEIICHI-SAN... KANTOKU...IS AN ADULT, AFTER ALL...
...IF CIRCUMSTANCES WERE BAD ENOUGH TO ABANDON HIS LIFE...IT'S SOMETHING HE WOULD DO AFTER A LOT OF WORRYING ABOUT IT... IT'S NOT ANYONE'S FAULT...
...LET'S GO TO RIKA'S HOUSE...I WANT...TO GET SOME CLOTHES ON...
IT WON'T BE TOO LATE... TO GET A MEDICAL EXAM AFTER THAT...

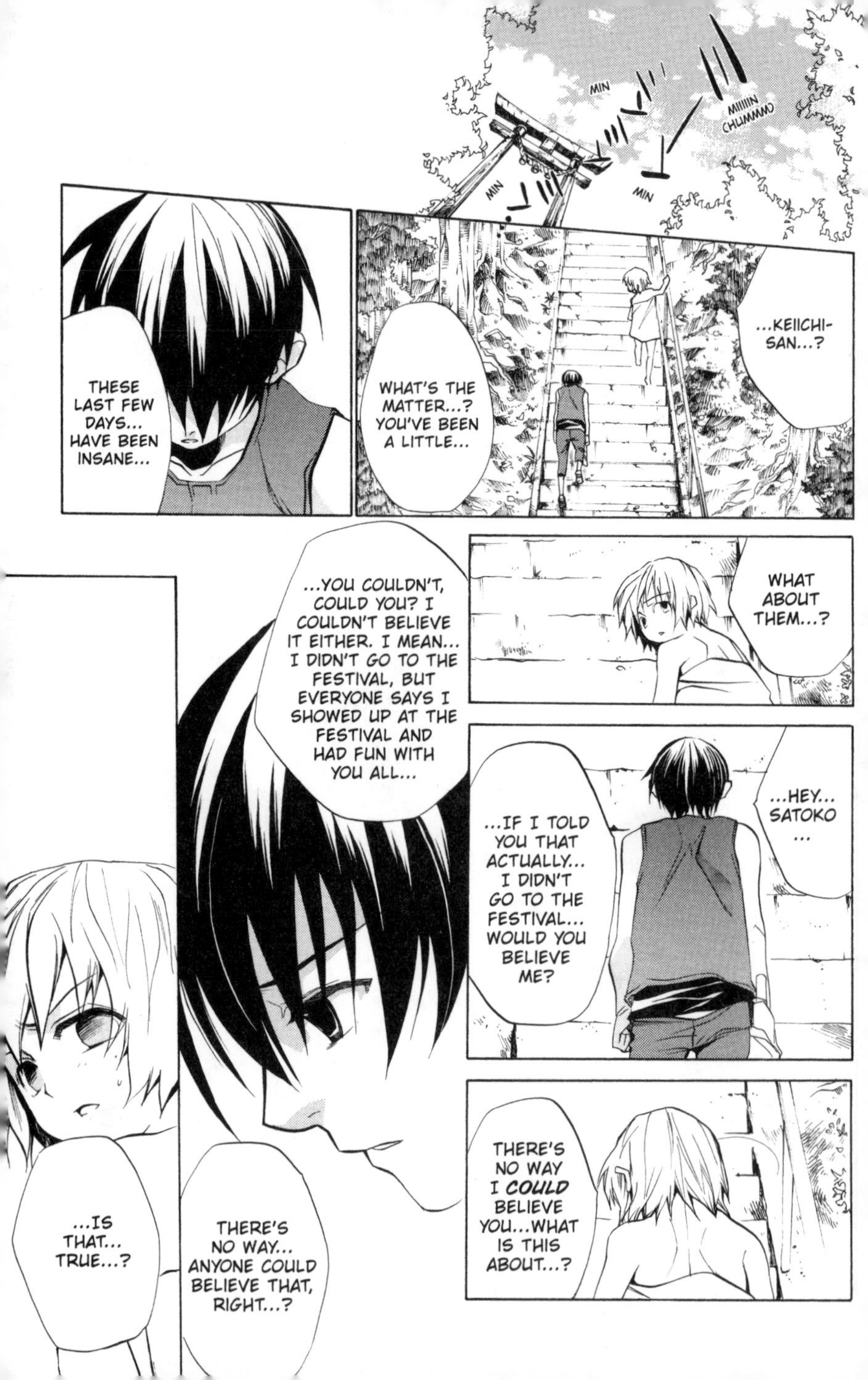
MIIIIIN (HUMMM)
MIN
MIN
MIN
...KEIICHI-SAN...?
WHAT'S THE MATTER...? YOU'VE BEEN A LITTLE...
THESE LAST FEW DAYS... HAVE BEEN INSANE...
WHAT ABOUT THEM...?
...HEY... SATOKO...
...IF I TOLD YOU THAT ACTUALLY... I DIDN'T GO TO THE FESTIVAL... WOULD YOU BELIEVE ME?
THERE'S NO WAY I *COULD* BELIEVE YOU...WHAT IS THIS ABOUT...?
...YOU COULDN'T, COULD YOU? I COULDN'T BELIEVE IT EITHER. I MEAN... I DIDN'T GO TO THE FESTIVAL, BUT EVERYONE SAYS I SHOWED UP AT THE FESTIVAL AND HAD FUN WITH YOU ALL...
THERE'S NO WAY... ANYONE COULD BELIEVE THAT, RIGHT...?
...IS THAT... TRUE...?

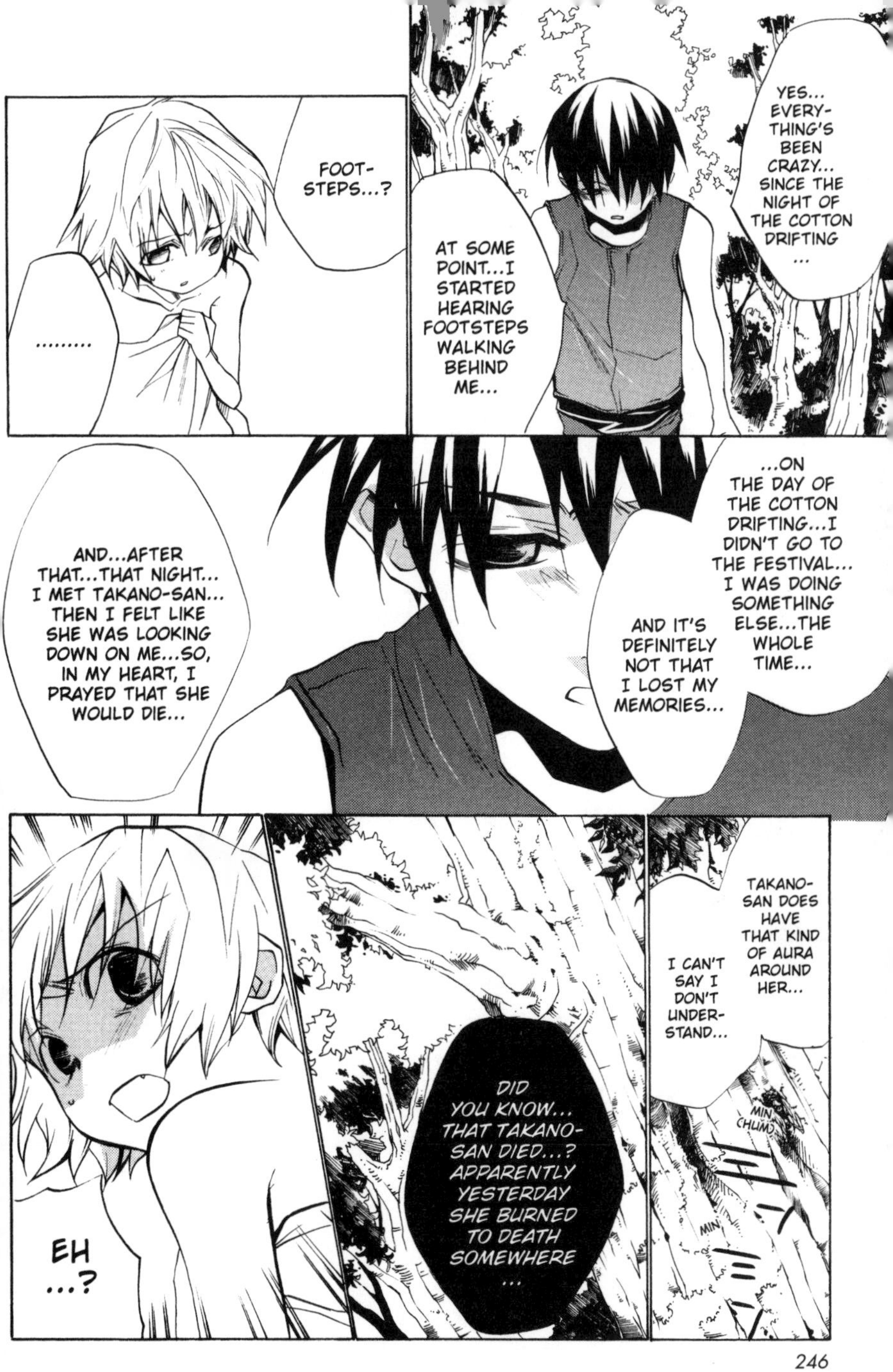
YES... EVERYTHING'S BEEN CRAZY... SINCE THE NIGHT OF THE COTTON DRIFTING...
AT SOME POINT...I STARTED HEARING FOOTSTEPS WALKING BEHIND ME...
FOOTSTEPS...?
....
...ON THE DAY OF THE COTTON DRIFTING...I DIDN'T GO TO THE FESTIVAL... I WAS DOING SOMETHING ELSE...THE WHOLE TIME...
AND IT'S DEFINITELY NOT THAT I LOST MY MEMORIES...
AND...AFTER THAT...THAT NIGHT... I MET TAKANO-SAN... THEN I FELT LIKE SHE WAS LOOKING DOWN ON ME...SO, IN MY HEART, I PRAYED THAT SHE WOULD DIE...
TAKANO-SAN DOES HAVE THAT KIND OF AURA AROUND HER...
I CAN'T SAY I DON'T UNDERSTAND...
MIN CHUMI
MIN
DID YOU KNOW... THAT TAKANO-SAN DIED...? APPARENTLY YESTERDAY SHE BURNED TO DEATH SOMEWHERE...
EH...?

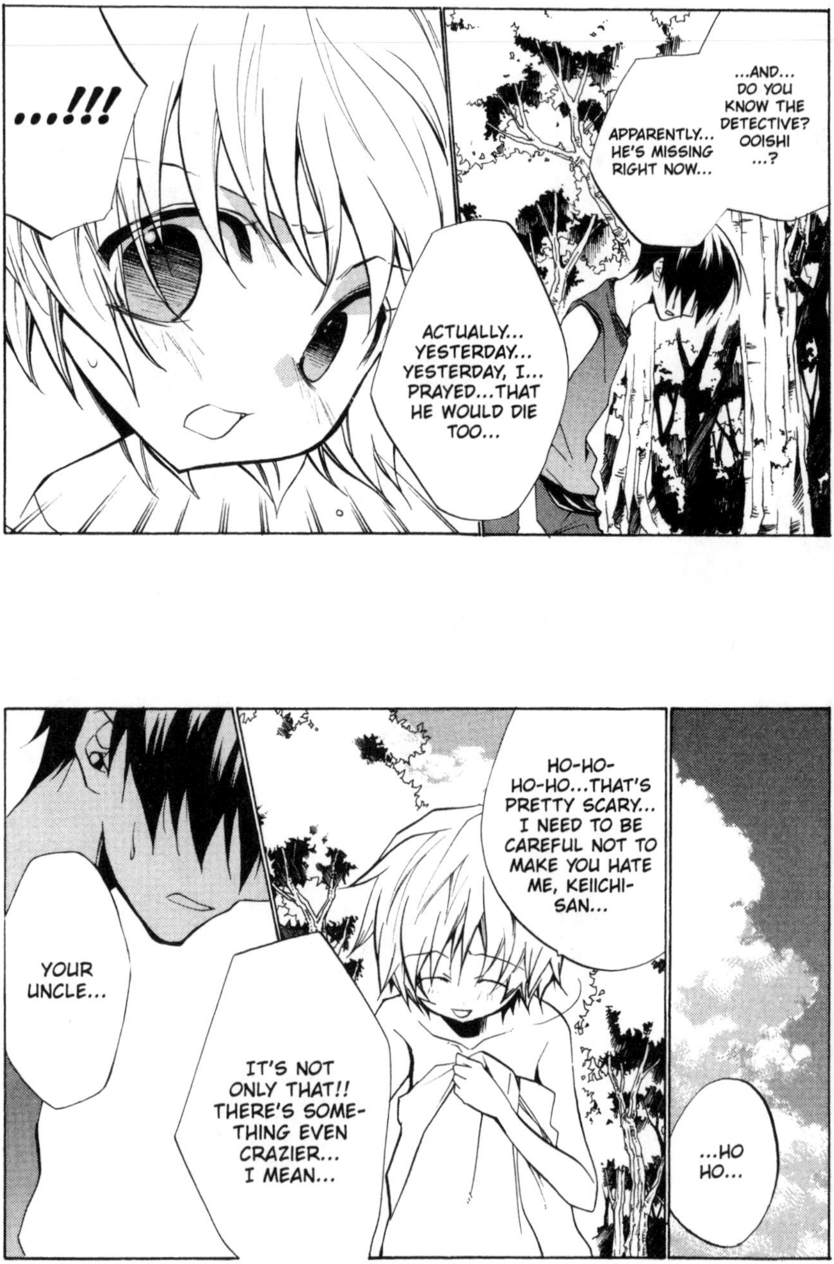
...AND... DO YOU KNOW THE DETECTIVE? OOISHI ...?
APPARENTLY... HE'S MISSING RIGHT NOW...
ACTUALLY... YESTERDAY... YESTERDAY, I... PRAYED...THAT HE WOULD DIE TOO...
...!!!
...HO HO...
HO-HO-HO-HO...THAT'S PRETTY SCARY... I NEED TO BE CAREFUL NOT TO MAKE YOU HATE ME, KEIICHI-SAN...
IT'S NOT ONLY THAT!! THERE'S SOME-THING EVEN CRAZIER... I MEAN...
YOUR UNCLE...

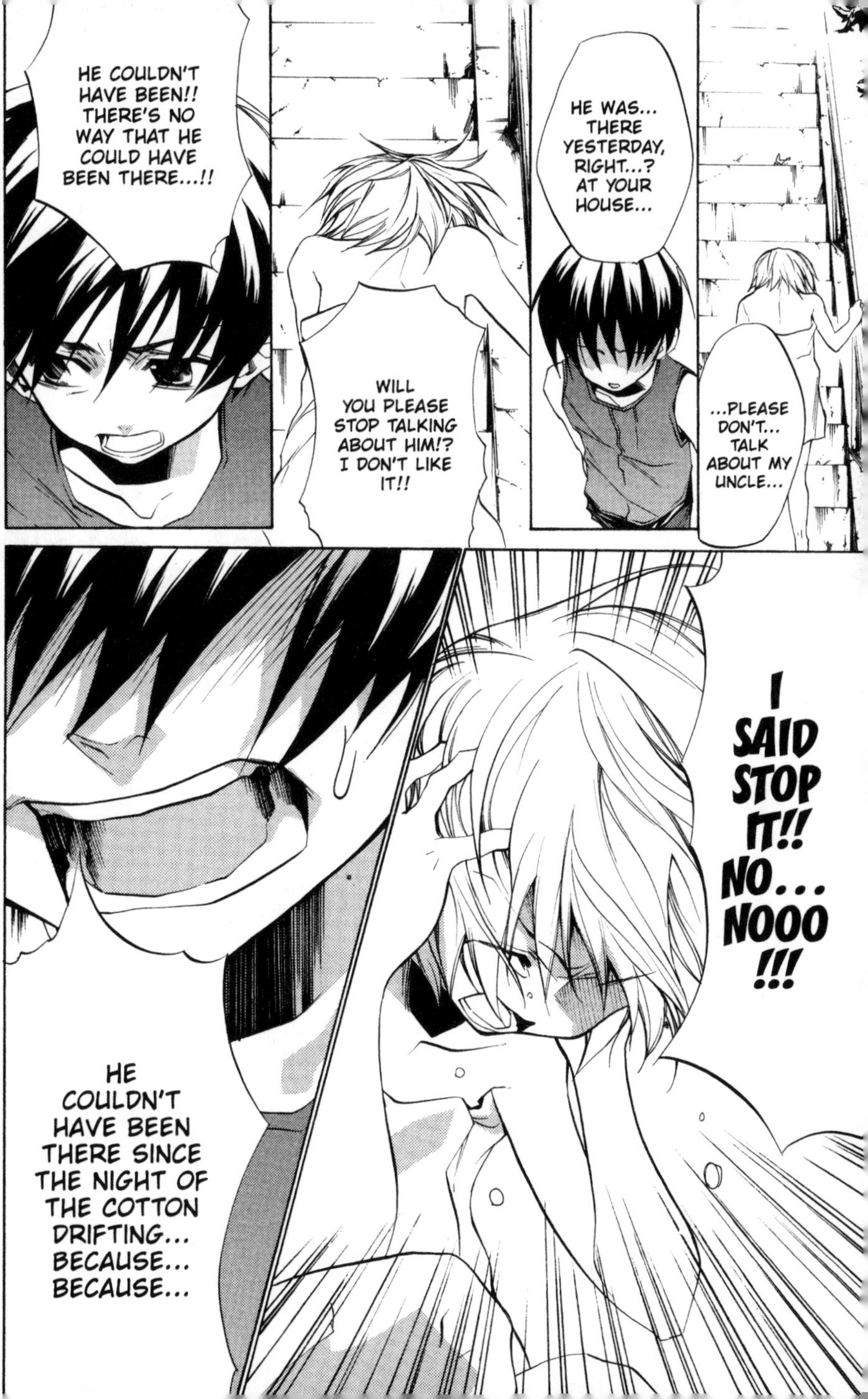
...PLEASE DON'T... TALK ABOUT MY UNCLE...
HE WAS... THERE YESTERDAY, RIGHT...? AT YOUR HOUSE...
WILL YOU PLEASE STOP TALKING ABOUT HIM!? I DON'T LIKE IT!!
HE COULDN'T HAVE BEEN!! THERE'S NO WAY THAT HE COULD HAVE BEEN THERE...!!
I SAID STOP IT!! NO... NOOO!!!
HE COULDN'T HAVE BEEN THERE SINCE THE NIGHT OF THE COTTON DRIFTING... BECAUSE... BECAUSE...

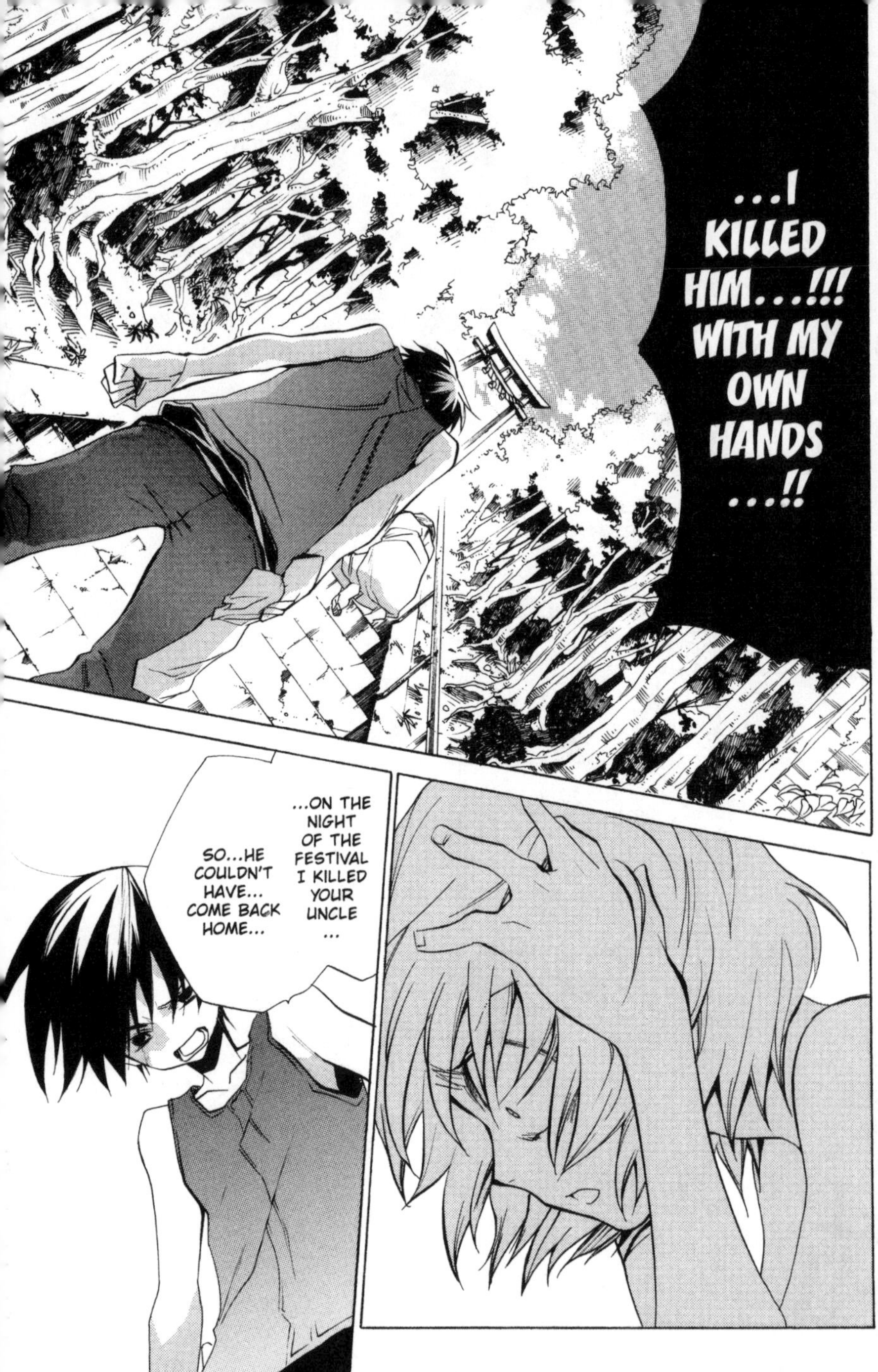
...I KILLED HIM...!!! WITH MY OWN HANDS ...!!
...ON THE NIGHT OF THE FESTIVAL I KILLED YOUR UNCLE ...
SO...HE COULDN'T HAVE... COME BACK HOME...

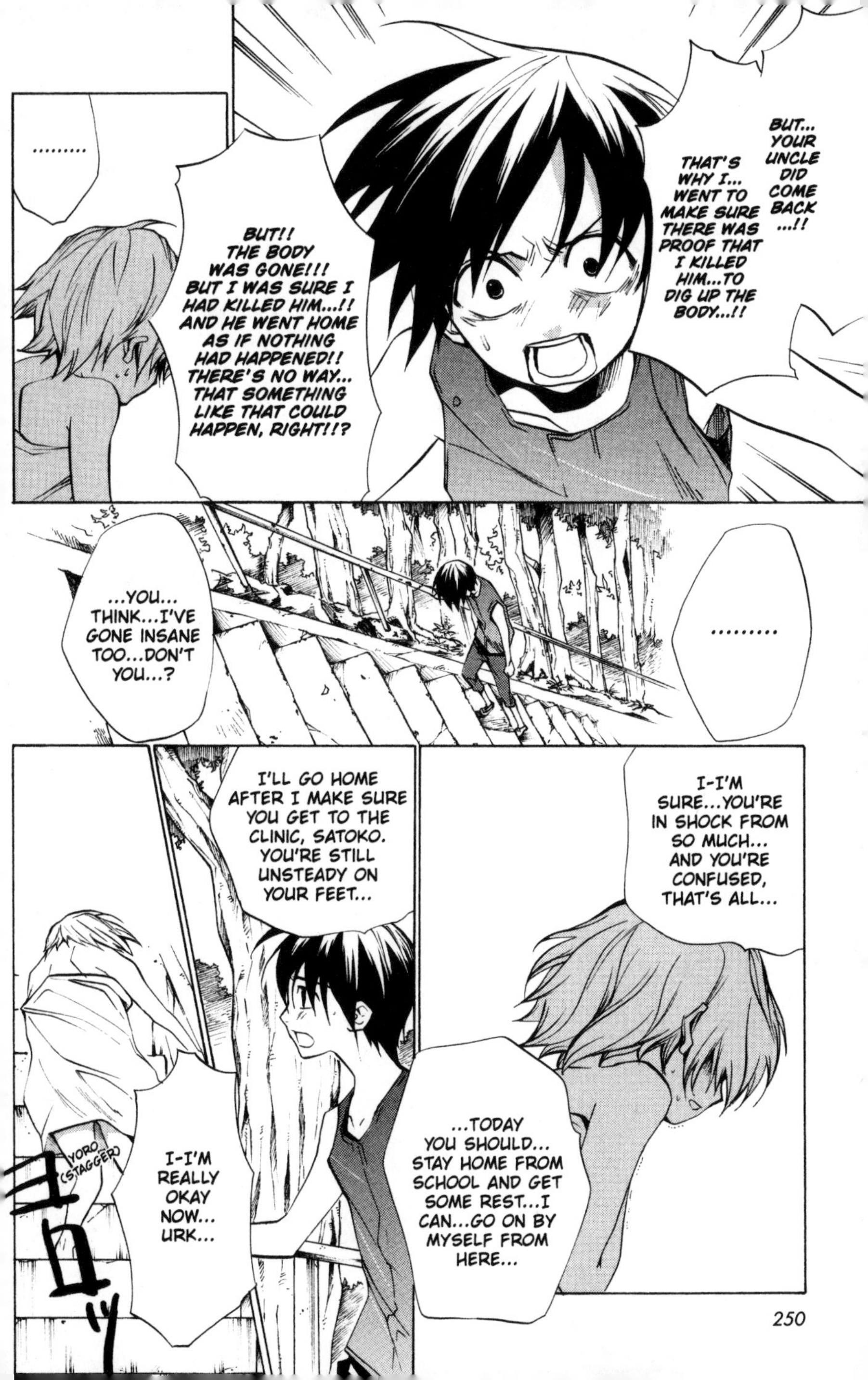
BUT... YOUR UNCLE DID COME BACK...!!
THAT'S WHY I... WENT TO MAKE SURE THERE WAS PROOF THAT I KILLED HIM...TO DIG UP THE BODY...!!
BUT!! THE BODY WAS GONE!!! BUT I WAS SURE I HAD KILLED HIM...!! AND HE WENT HOME AS IF NOTHING HAD HAPPENED!! THERE'S NO WAY... THAT SOMETHING LIKE THAT COULD HAPPEN, RIGHT!!?
....
....
...YOU... THINK...I'VE GONE INSANE TOO...DON'T YOU...?
I-I'M SURE...YOU'RE IN SHOCK FROM SO MUCH... AND YOU'RE CONFUSED, THAT'S ALL...
...TODAY YOU SHOULD... STAY HOME FROM SCHOOL AND GET SOME REST...I CAN...GO ON BY MYSELF FROM HERE...
I'LL GO HOME AFTER I MAKE SURE YOU GET TO THE CLINIC, SATOKO. YOU'RE STILL UNSTEADY ON YOUR FEET...
YORO (STAGGER)
I-I'M REALLY OKAY NOW... URK...

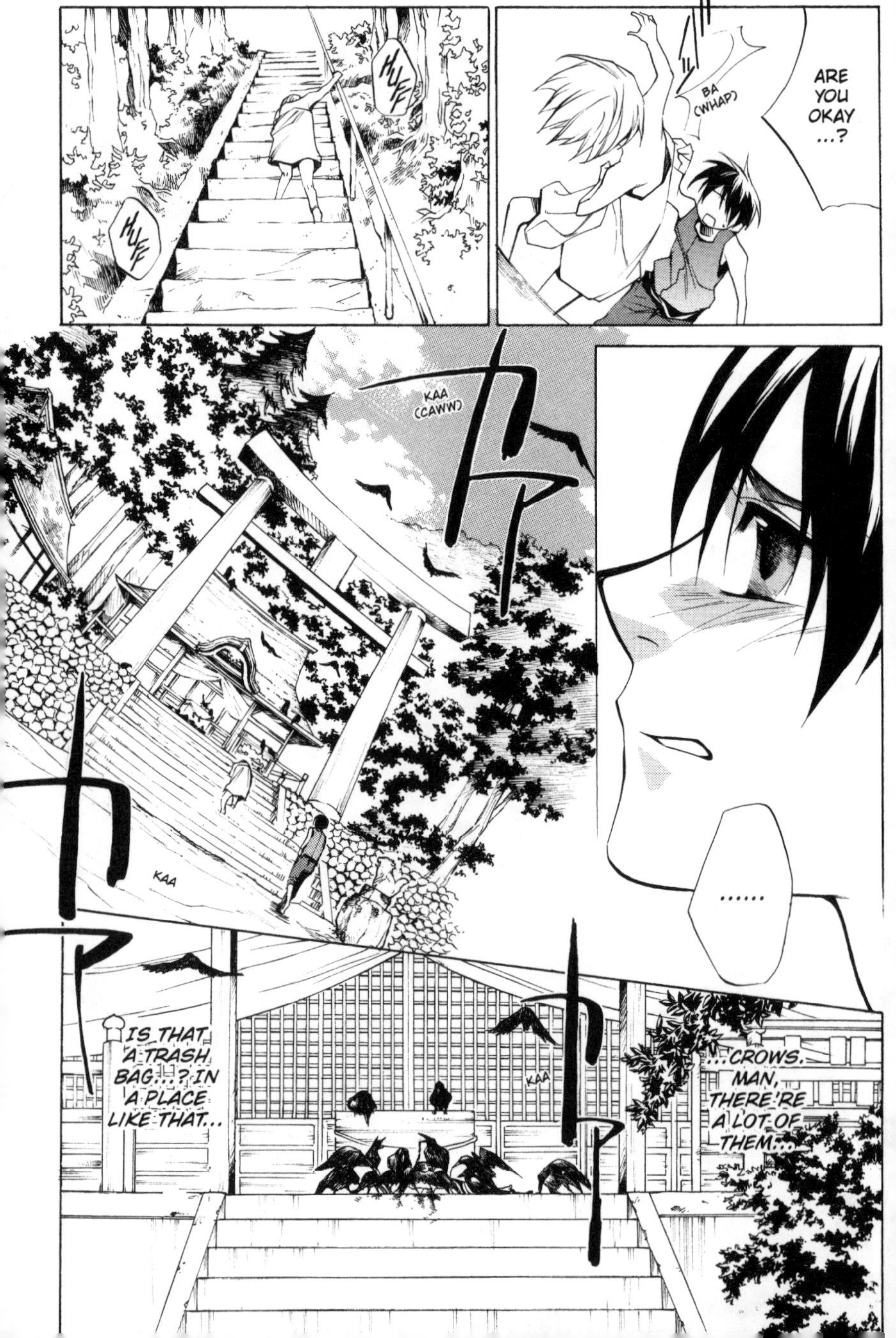
ARE YOU OKAY ...?
BA (WHAP)
HUFF
HUFF
....
KAA (CAWW)
KAA
...CROWS. MAN, THERE'RE A LOT OF THEM...
KAA
IS THAT A TRASH BAG...? IN A PLACE LIKE THAT...

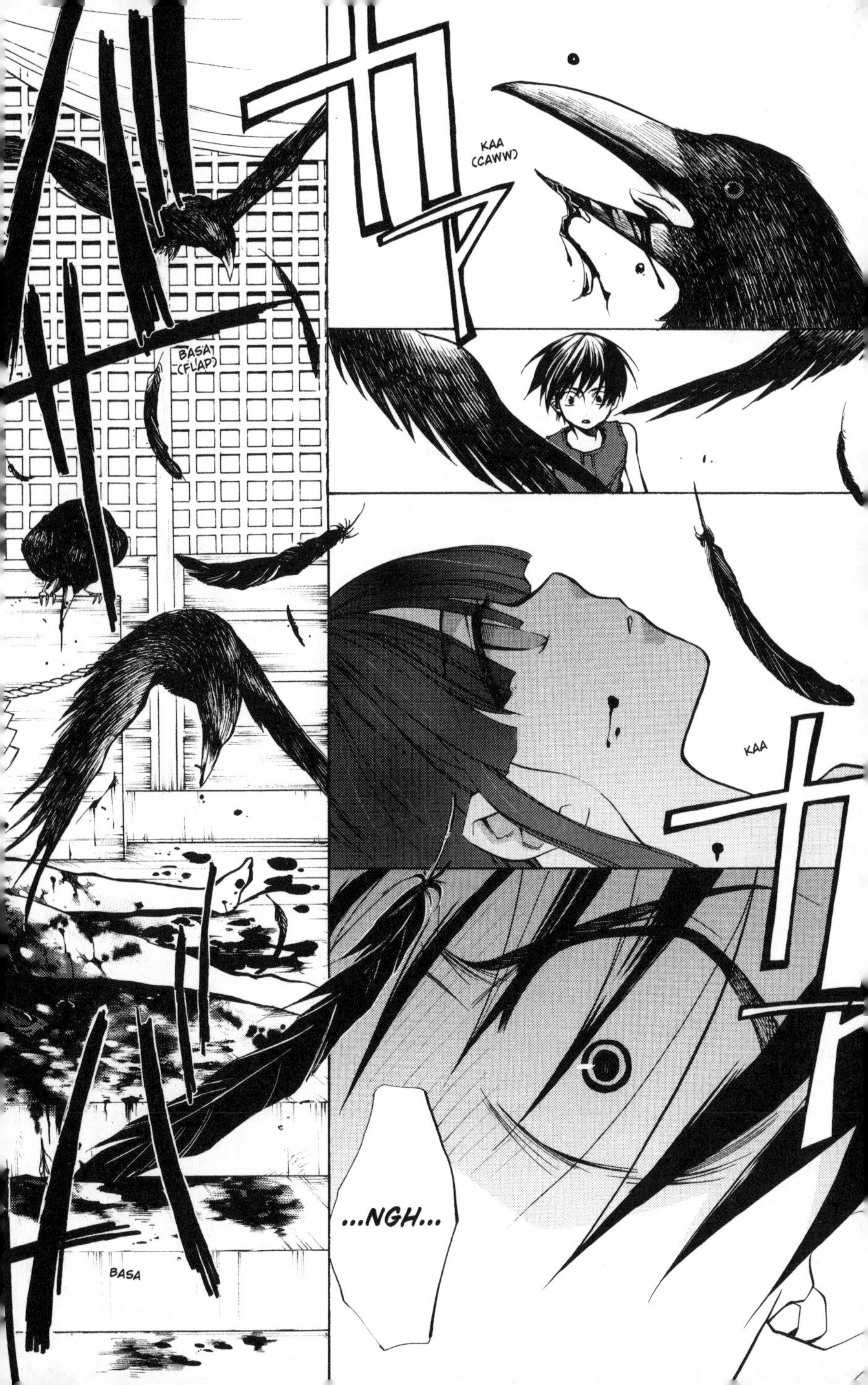
KAA (CAWW)
KAA
...NGH...
BASA (FLAP)
BASA

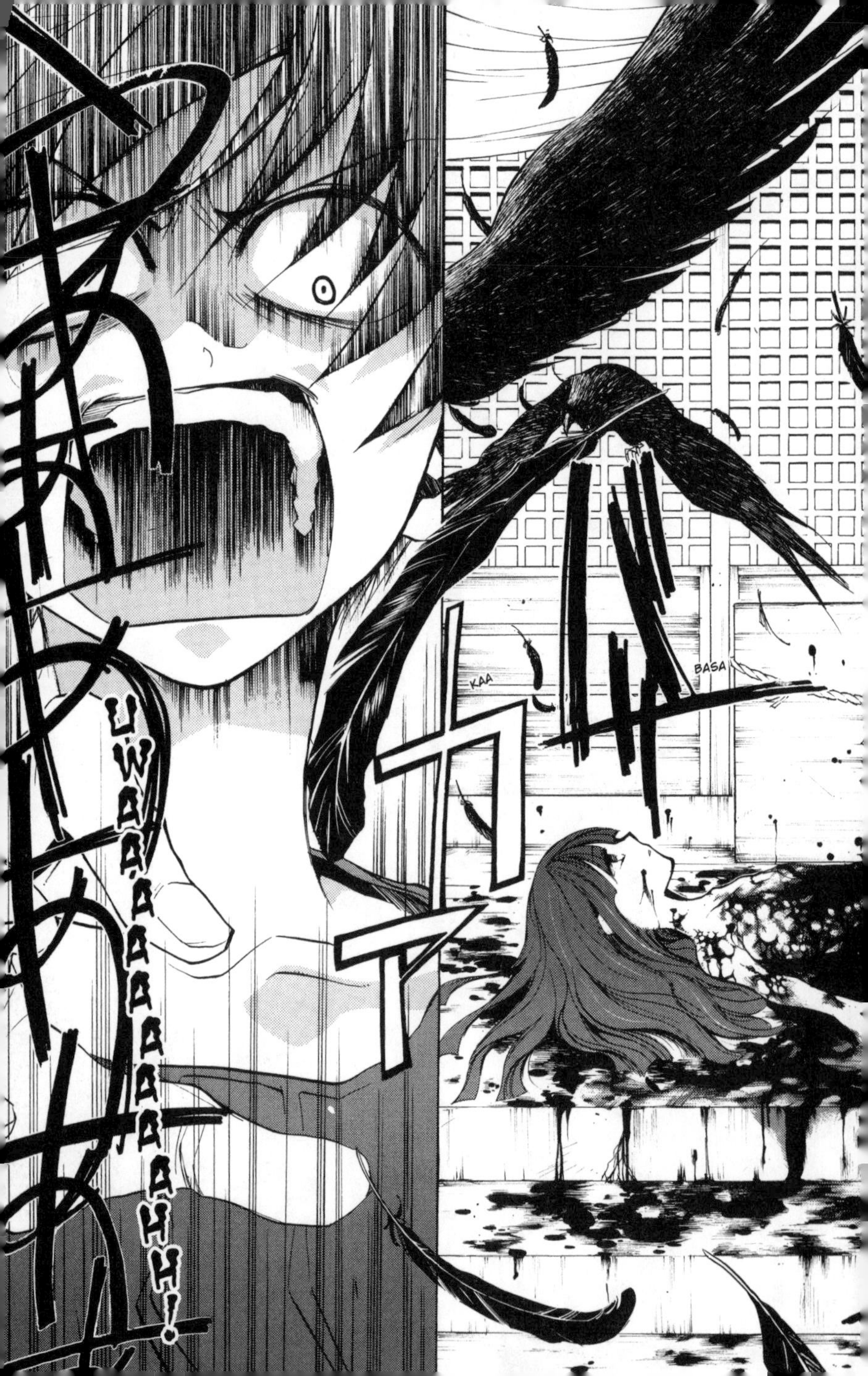
BASA
KAA
UWAAAAAAAAAHH!

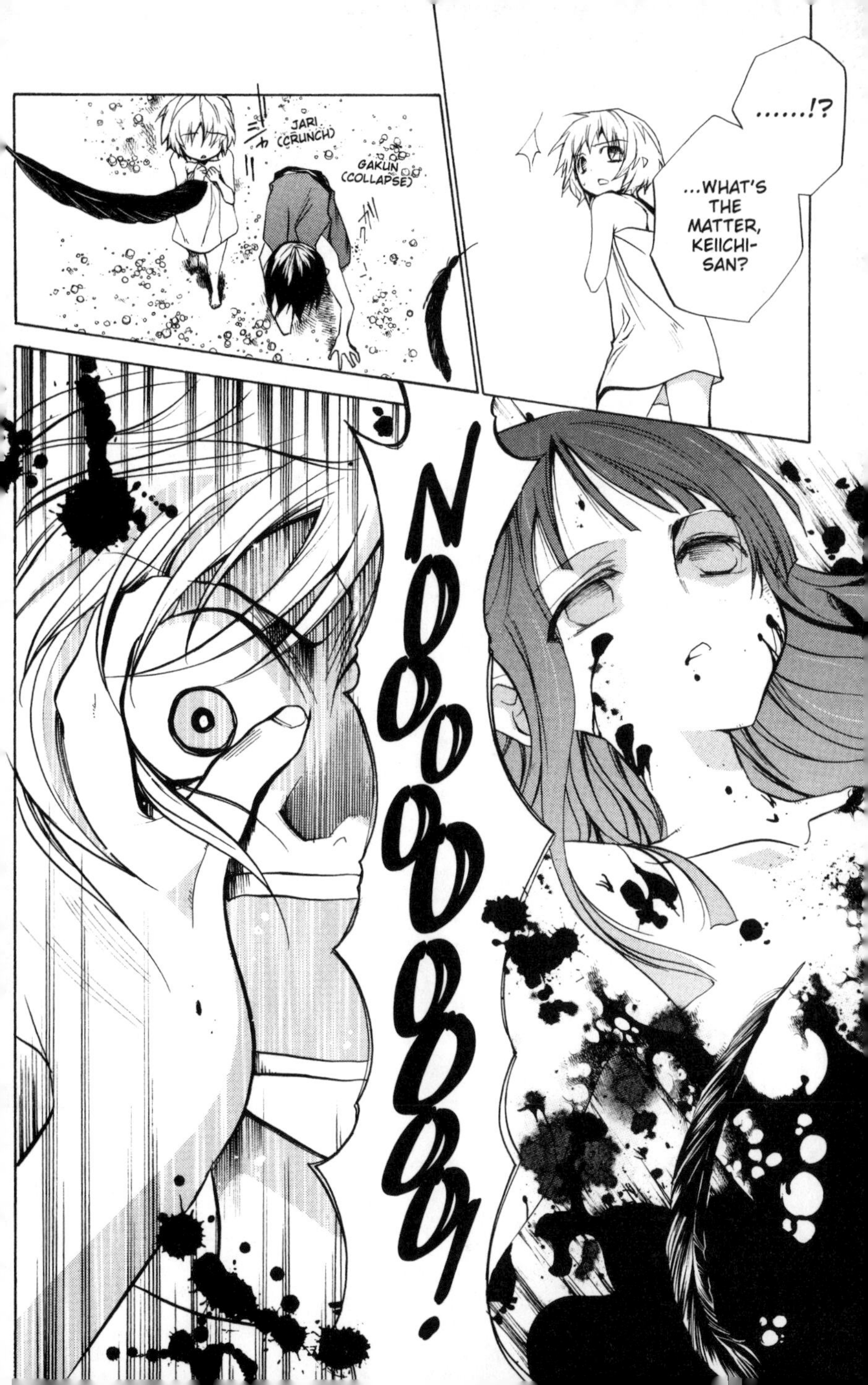
......!?
...WHAT'S THE MATTER, KEIICHI-SAN?
JARI (CRUNCH)
GAKUN (COLLAPSE)
NOOOOOOOOOOO!

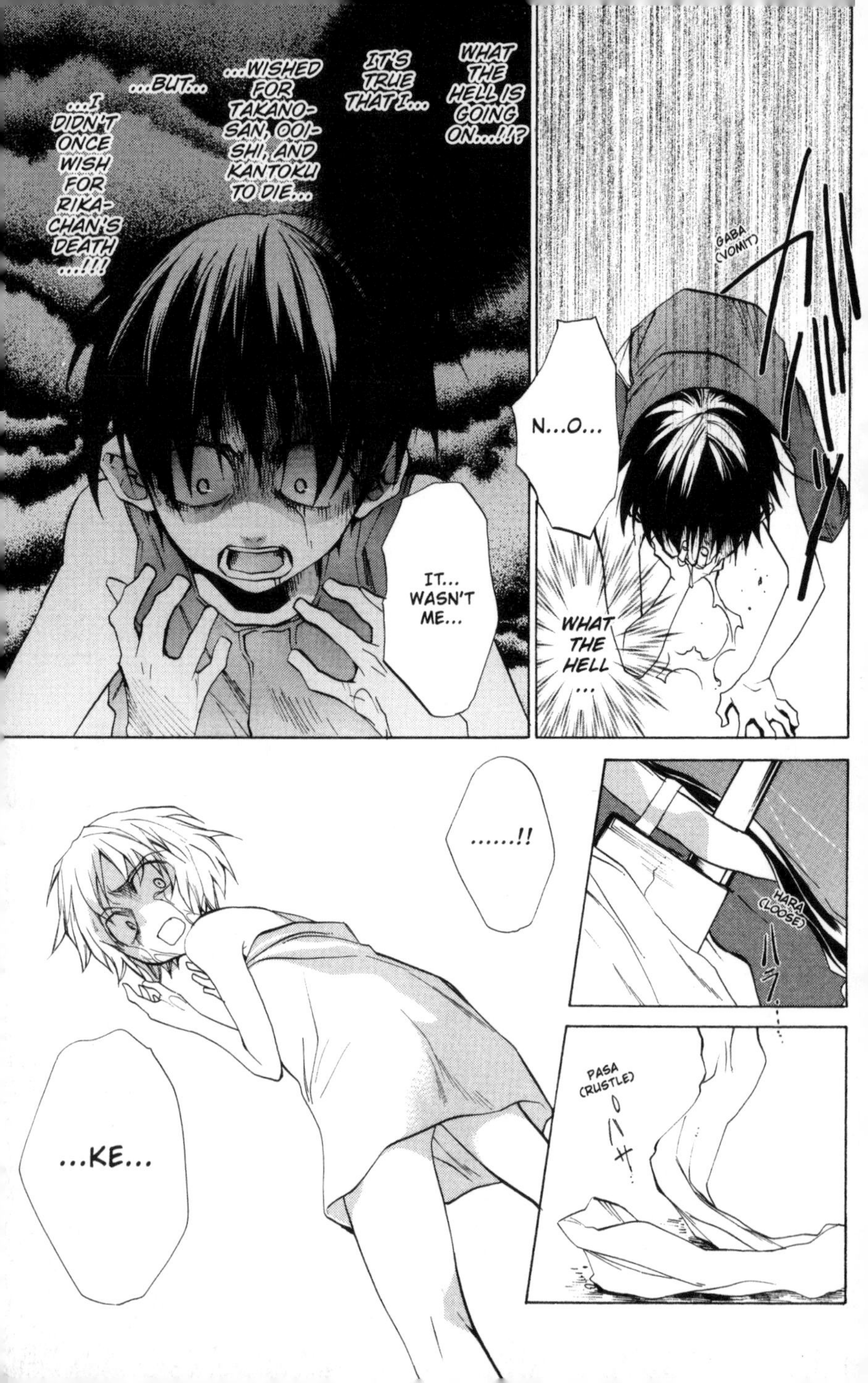
GABA (VOMIT)
N...O...
WHAT THE HELL ...
WHAT THE HELL IS GOING ON...!!?
IT'S TRUE THAT I...
...WISHED FOR TAKANO-SAN, OOI-SHI, AND KANTOKU TO DIE...
...BUT...
...I DIDN'T ONCE WISH FOR RIKA-CHAN'S DEATH ...!!!
IT... WASN'T ME...
HARA (LOOSE)
PASA (RUSTLE)
......!!
...KE...

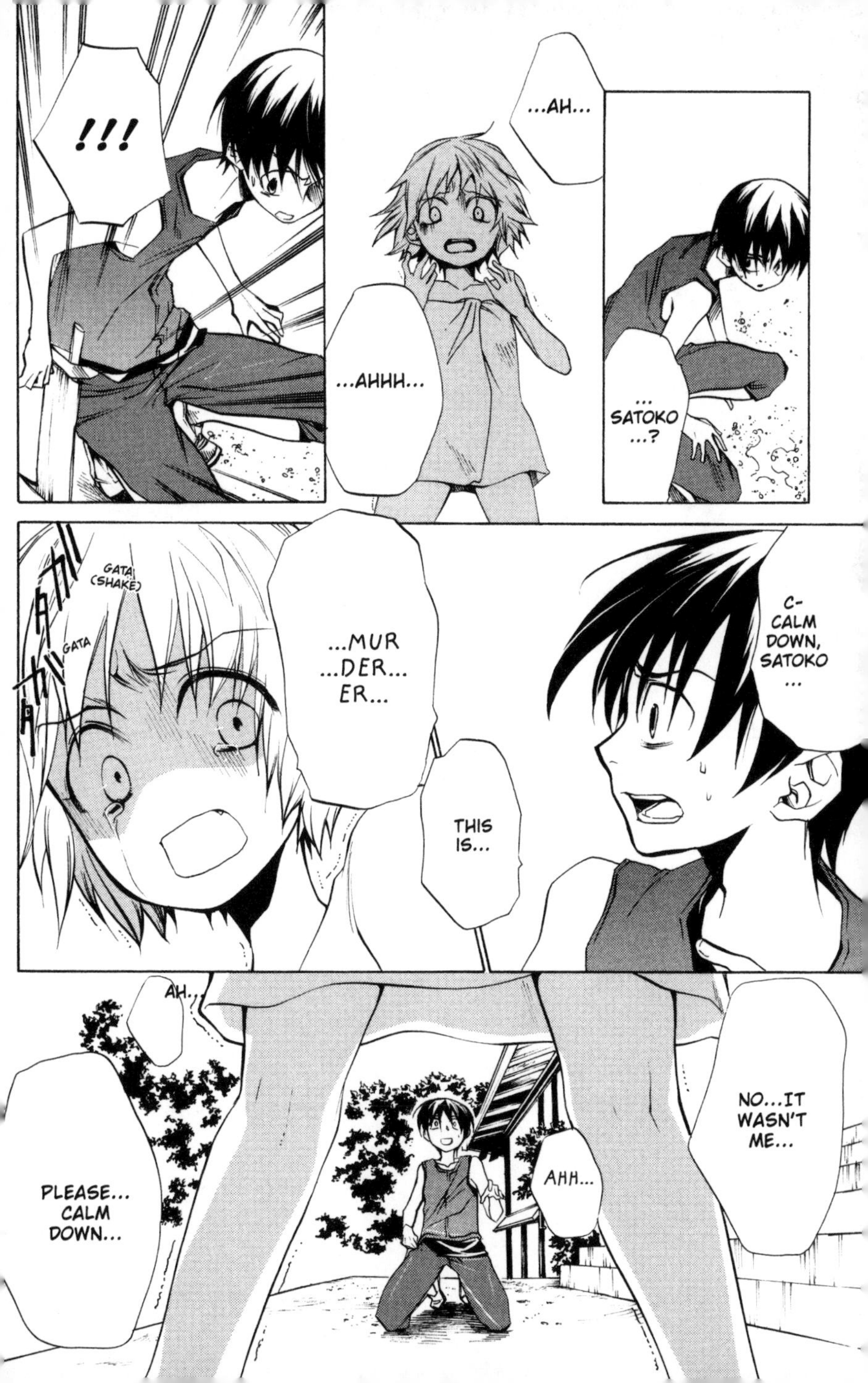

...SATOKO...?
...AH...
...AHHH...
!!!
C-CALM DOWN, SATOKO...
...MUR...DER...ER...
GATA (SHAKE)
GATA
THIS IS...
NO...IT WASN'T ME...
AHH...
AH...
PLEASE... CALM DOWN...

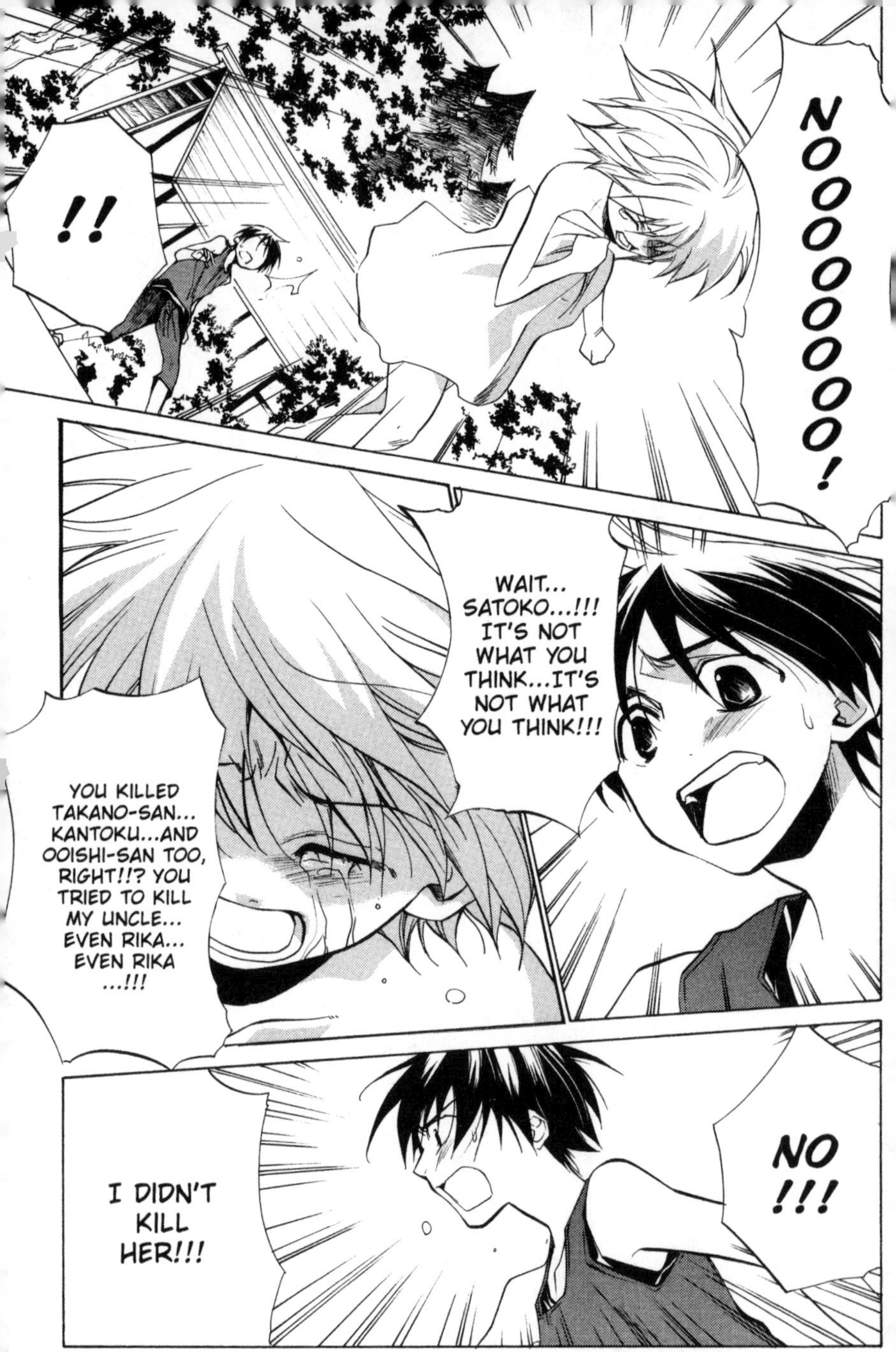
NOOOOOOOOOO!
!!
WAIT... SATOKO...!!! IT'S NOT WHAT YOU THINK...IT'S NOT WHAT YOU THINK!!!
YOU KILLED TAKANO-SAN... KANTOKU...AND OOISHI-SAN TOO, RIGHT!!? YOU TRIED TO KILL MY UNCLE... EVEN RIKA... EVEN RIKA ...!!!
NO !!!
I DIDN'T KILL HER!!!

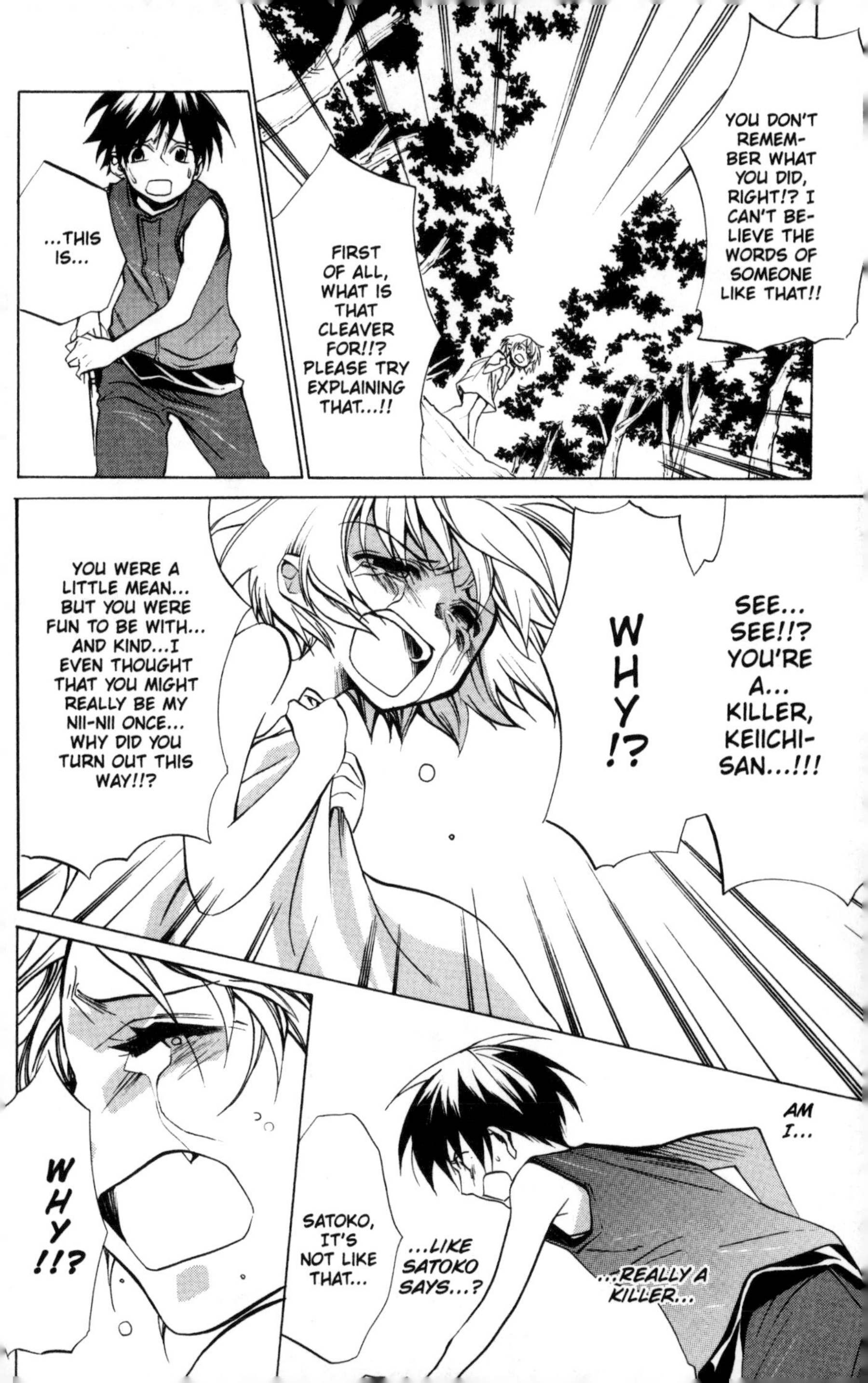
YOU DON'T REMEMBER WHAT YOU DID, RIGHT!? I CAN'T BELIEVE THE WORDS OF SOMEONE LIKE THAT!!
FIRST OF ALL, WHAT IS THAT CLEAVER FOR!!? PLEASE TRY EXPLAINING THAT...!!
...THIS IS...
SEE... SEE!!? YOU'RE A... KILLER, KEIICHI-SAN...!!!
WHY!?
YOU WERE A LITTLE MEAN... BUT YOU WERE FUN TO BE WITH... AND KIND...I EVEN THOUGHT THAT YOU MIGHT REALLY BE MY NII-NII ONCE... WHY DID YOU TURN OUT THIS WAY!!?
AM I...
...REALLY A KILLER...
...LIKE SATOKO SAYS...?
SATOKO, IT'S NOT LIKE THAT...
WHY!!?

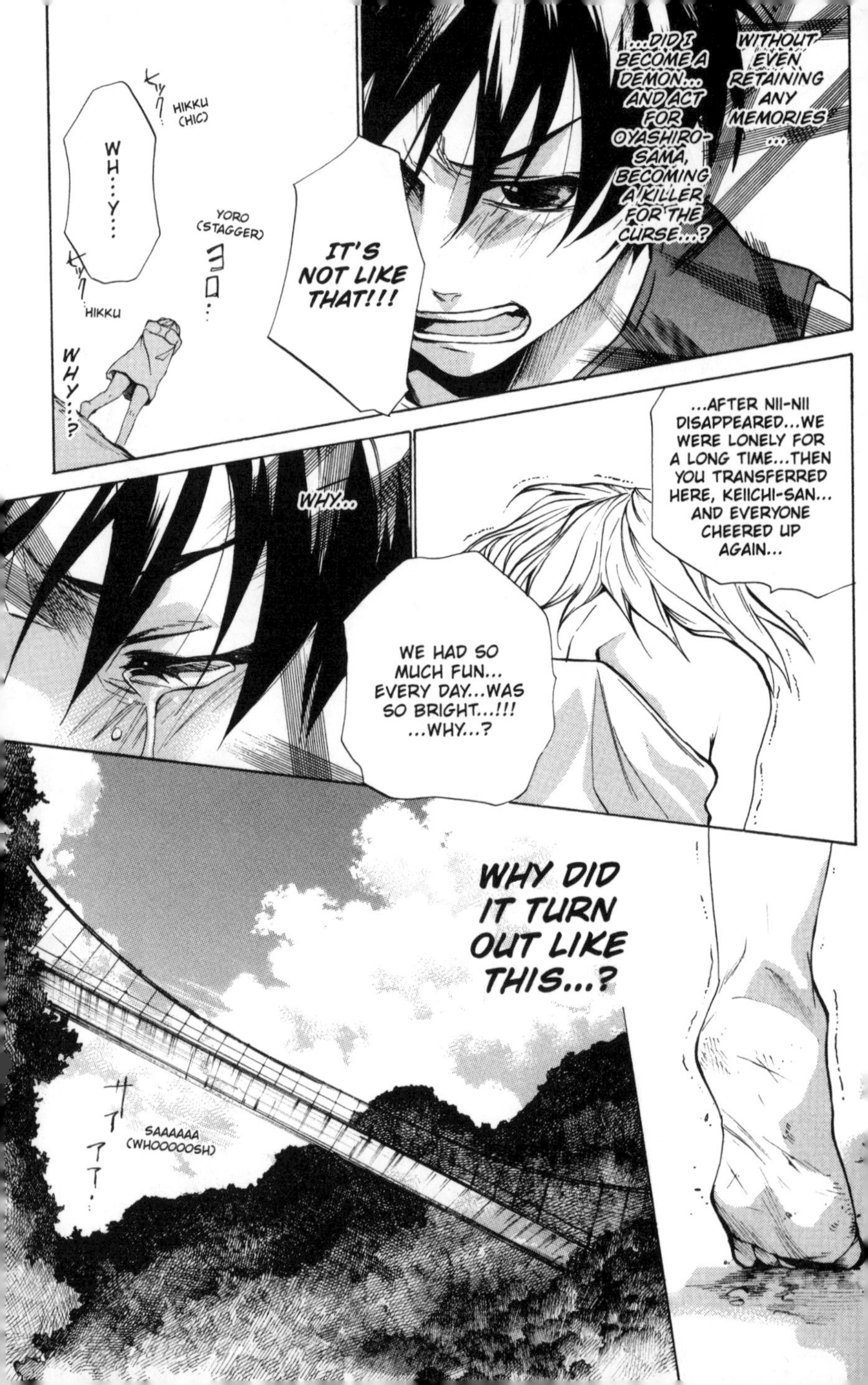
WITHOUT EVEN RETAINING ANY MEMORIES...
...DID I BECOME A DEMON... AND ACT FOR OYASHIRO-SAMA, BECOMING A KILLER FOR THE CURSE...?
IT'S NOT LIKE THAT!!!
HIKKU (HIC)
WH...Y...
YORO (STAGGER)
HIKKU
WHY...?
...AFTER NII-NII DISAPPEARED...WE WERE LONELY FOR A LONG TIME...THEN YOU TRANSFERRED HERE, KEIICHI-SAN... AND EVERYONE CHEERED UP AGAIN...
WE HAD SO MUCH FUN... EVERY DAY...WAS SO BRIGHT...!!! ...WHY...?
WHY...
WHY DID IT TURN OUT LIKE THIS...?
SAAAAAA (WHOOOOOSH)

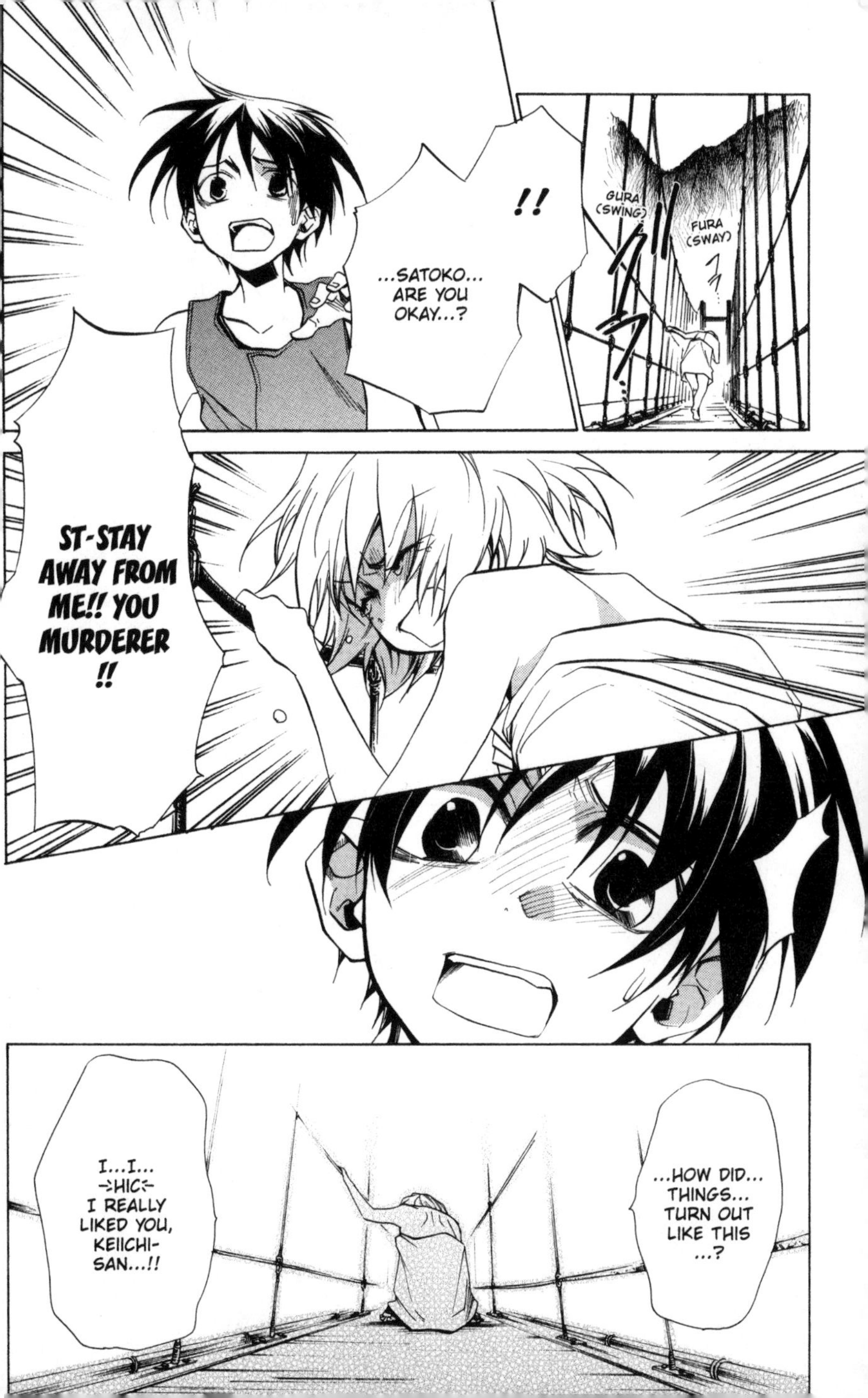
GURA (SWING)
FURA (SWAY)
!!
...SATOKO... ARE YOU OKAY...?
ST-STAY AWAY FROM ME!! YOU MURDERER!!
...HOW DID... THINGS... TURN OUT LIKE THIS...?
I...I... HIC I REALLY LIKED YOU, KEIICHI-SAN...!!

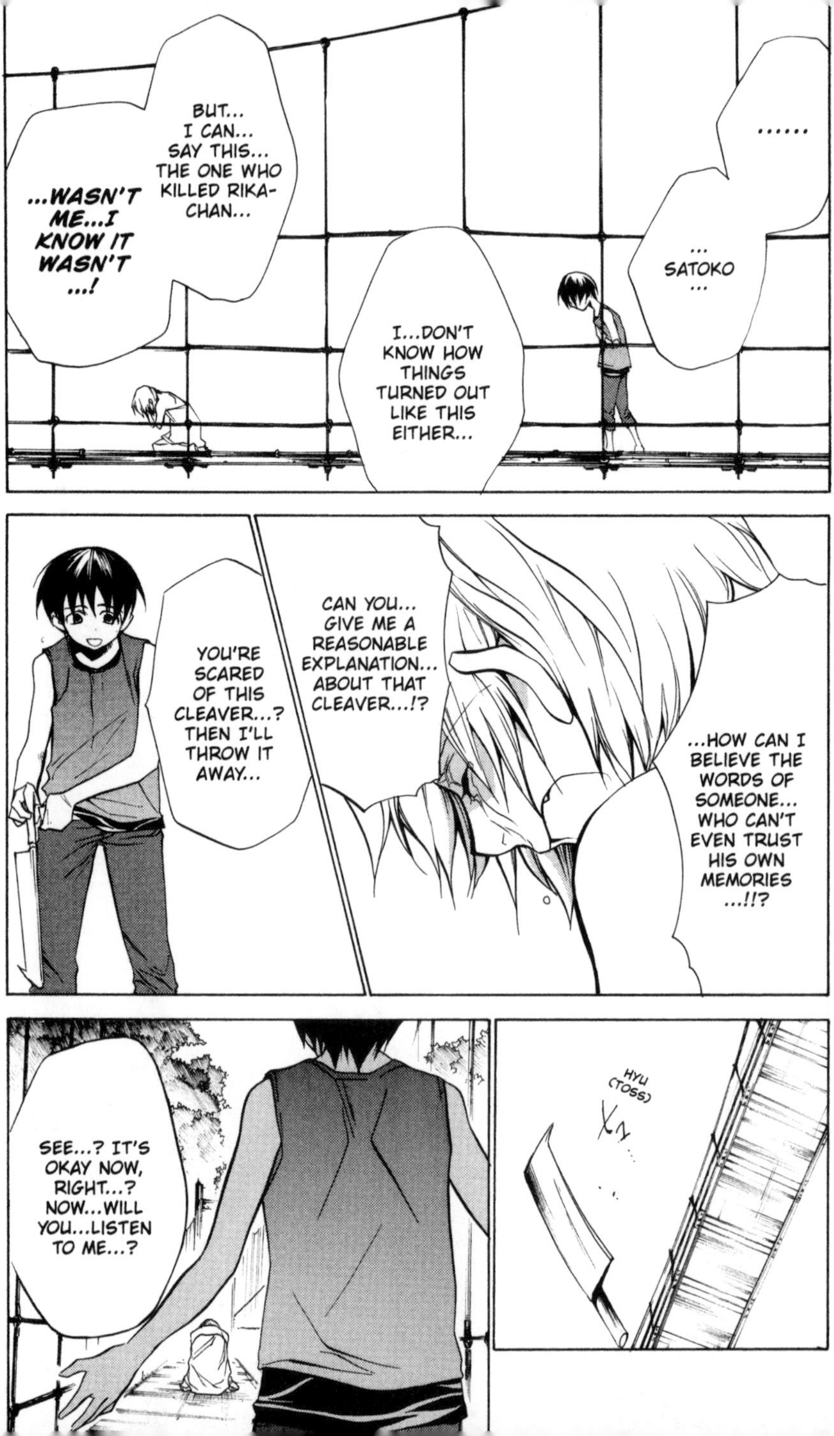
......
...SATOKO...
I...DON'T KNOW HOW THINGS TURNED OUT LIKE THIS EITHER...
BUT... I CAN... SAY THIS... THE ONE WHO KILLED RIKA-CHAN...
...WASN'T ME...I KNOW IT WASN'T ...!
CAN YOU... GIVE ME A REASONABLE EXPLANATION... ABOUT THAT CLEAVER...!?
...HOW CAN I BELIEVE THE WORDS OF SOMEONE... WHO CAN'T EVEN TRUST HIS OWN MEMORIES ...!!?
YOU'RE SCARED OF THIS CLEAVER...? THEN I'LL THROW IT AWAY...
HYU (TOSS)
SEE...? IT'S OKAY NOW, RIGHT...? NOW...WILL YOU...LISTEN TO ME...?

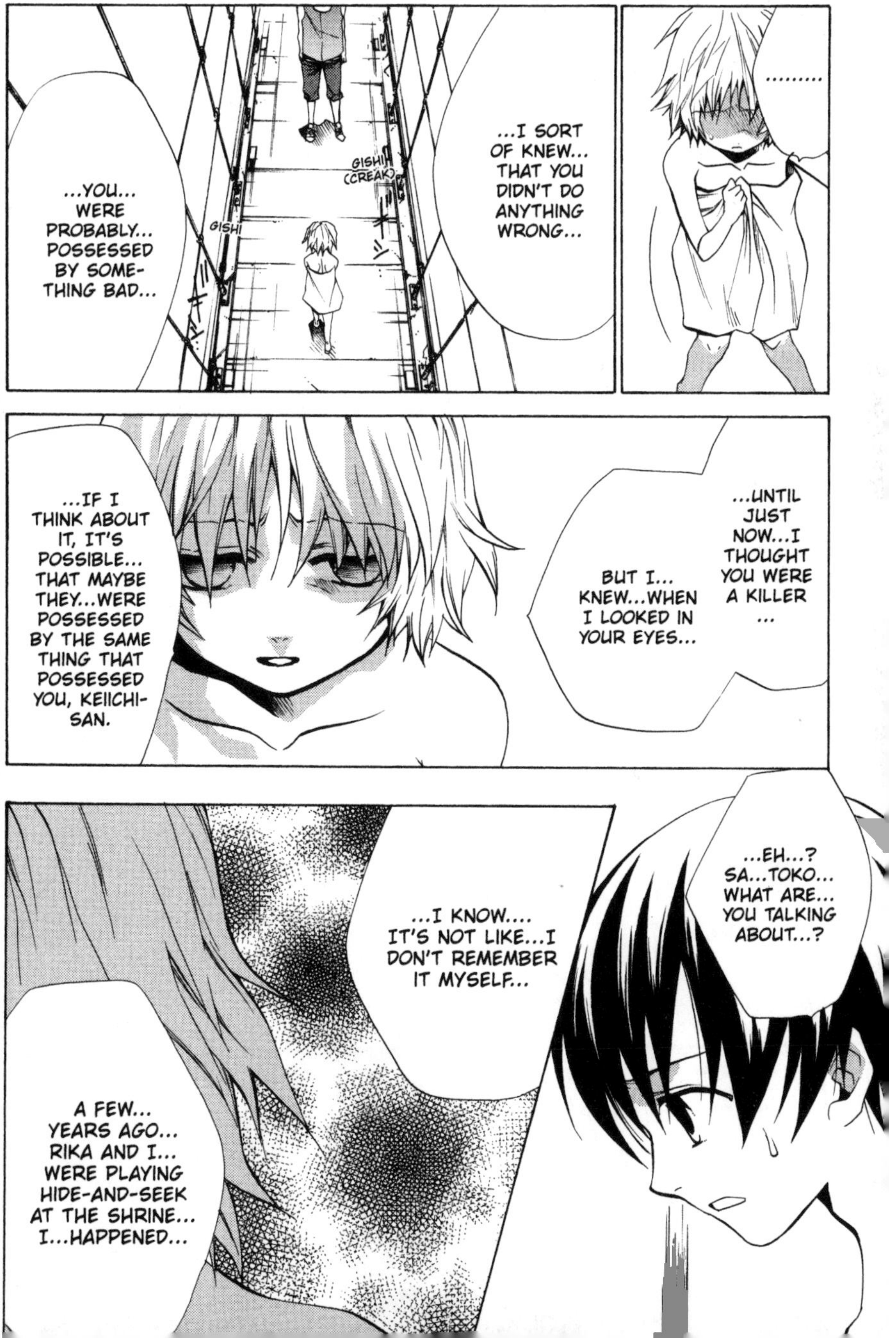
....
...I SORT OF KNEW... THAT YOU DIDN'T DO ANYTHING WRONG...
GISHI (CREAK)
GISHI
...YOU... WERE PROBABLY... POSSESSED BY SOME-THING BAD...
...UNTIL JUST NOW...I THOUGHT YOU WERE A KILLER ...
BUT I... KNEW...WHEN I LOOKED IN YOUR EYES...
...IF I THINK ABOUT IT, IT'S POSSIBLE... THAT MAYBE THEY...WERE POSSESSED BY THE SAME THING THAT POSSESSED YOU, KEIICHI-SAN.
...EH...? SA...TOKO... WHAT ARE... YOU TALKING ABOUT...?
...I KNOW.... IT'S NOT LIKE...I DON'T REMEMBER IT MYSELF...
A FEW... YEARS AGO... RIKA AND I... WERE PLAYING HIDE-AND-SEEK AT THE SHRINE... I...HAPPENED...

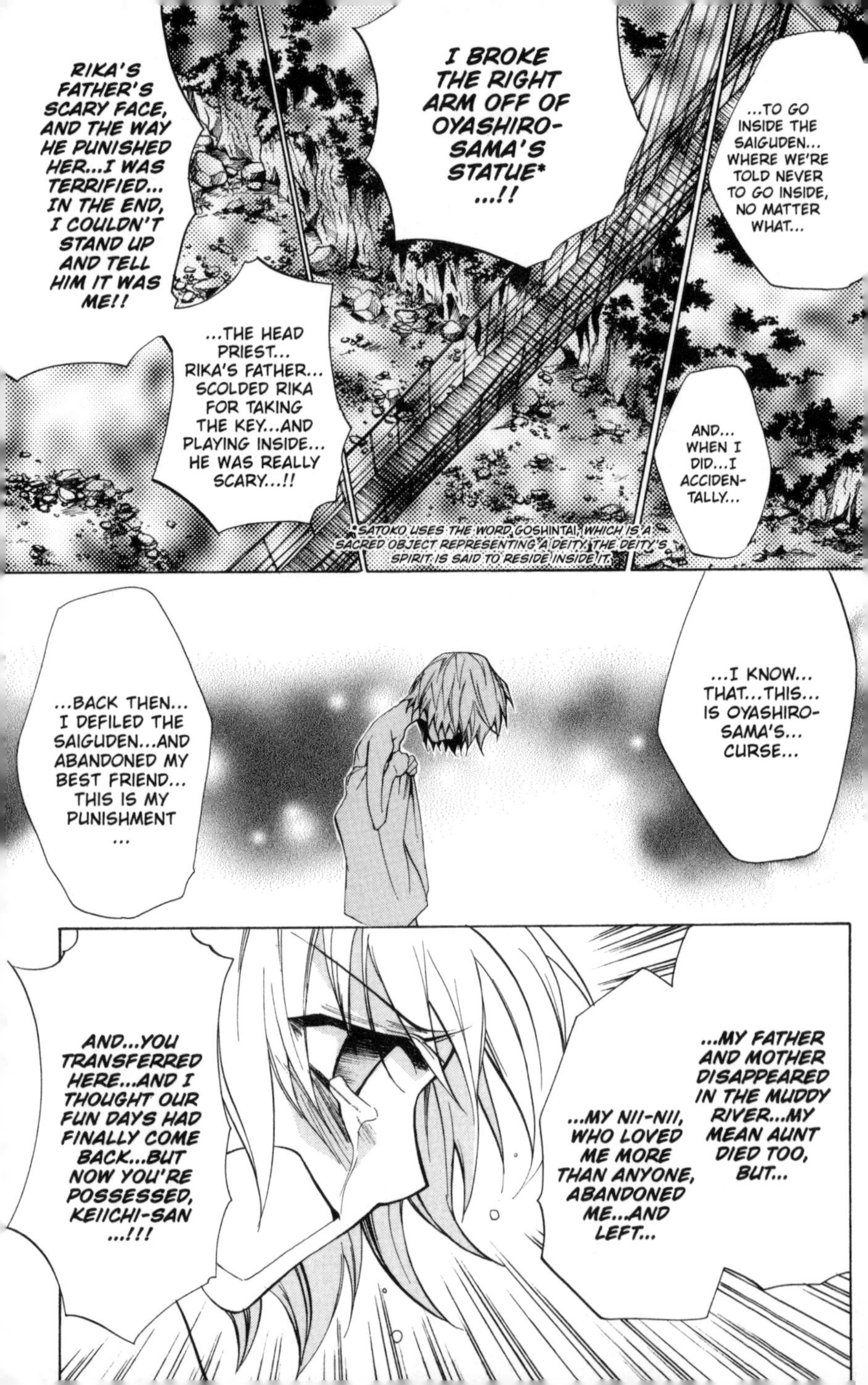
...TO GO INSIDE THE SAIGUDEN... WHERE WE'RE TOLD NEVER TO GO INSIDE, NO MATTER WHAT...
AND... WHEN I DID...I ACCIDEN-TALLY...
I BROKE THE RIGHT ARM OFF OF OYASHIRO-SAMA'S STATUE* ...!!
*SATOKO USES THE WORD GOSHINTAI, WHICH IS A SACRED OBJECT REPRESENTING A DEITY. THE DEITY'S SPIRIT IS SAID TO RESIDE INSIDE IT.
...THE HEAD PRIEST... RIKA'S FATHER... SCOLDED RIKA FOR TAKING THE KEY...AND PLAYING INSIDE... HE WAS REALLY SCARY...!!
RIKA'S FATHER'S SCARY FACE, AND THE WAY HE PUNISHED HER...I WAS TERRIFIED... IN THE END, I COULDN'T STAND UP AND TELL HIM IT WAS ME!!
...I KNOW... THAT...THIS... IS OYASHIRO-SAMA'S... CURSE...
...BACK THEN... I DEFILED THE SAIGUDEN...AND ABANDONED MY BEST FRIEND... THIS IS MY PUNISHMENT ...
...MY FATHER AND MOTHER DISAPPEARED IN THE MUDDY RIVER...MY MEAN AUNT DIED TOO, BUT...
...MY NII-NII, WHO LOVED ME MORE THAN ANYONE, ABANDONED ME...AND LEFT...
AND...YOU TRANSFERRED HERE...AND I THOUGHT OUR FUN DAYS HAD FINALLY COME BACK...BUT NOW YOU'RE POSSESSED, KEIICHI-SAN ...!!!

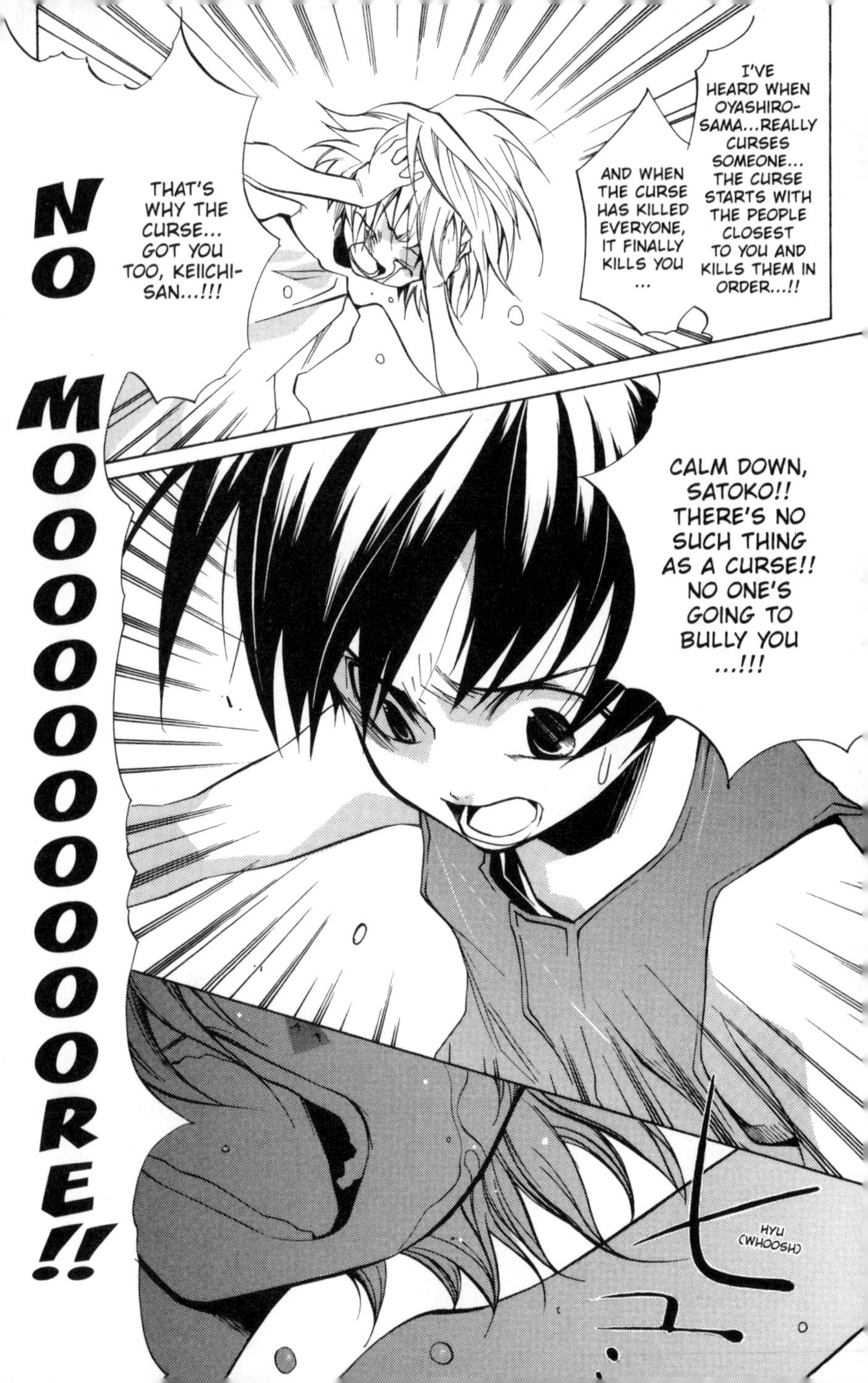
I'VE HEARD WHEN OYASHIRO-SAMA...REALLY CURSES SOMEONE... THE CURSE STARTS WITH THE PEOPLE CLOSEST TO YOU AND KILLS THEM IN ORDER...!!
AND WHEN THE CURSE HAS KILLED EVERYONE, IT FINALLY KILLS YOU ...
THAT'S WHY THE CURSE... GOT YOU TOO, KEIICHI-SAN...!!!
NO MOOOOOOOOOOOOORE!!
CALM DOWN, SATOKO!! THERE'S NO SUCH THING AS A CURSE!! NO ONE'S GOING TO BULLY YOU ...!!!
HYU (WHOOSH)

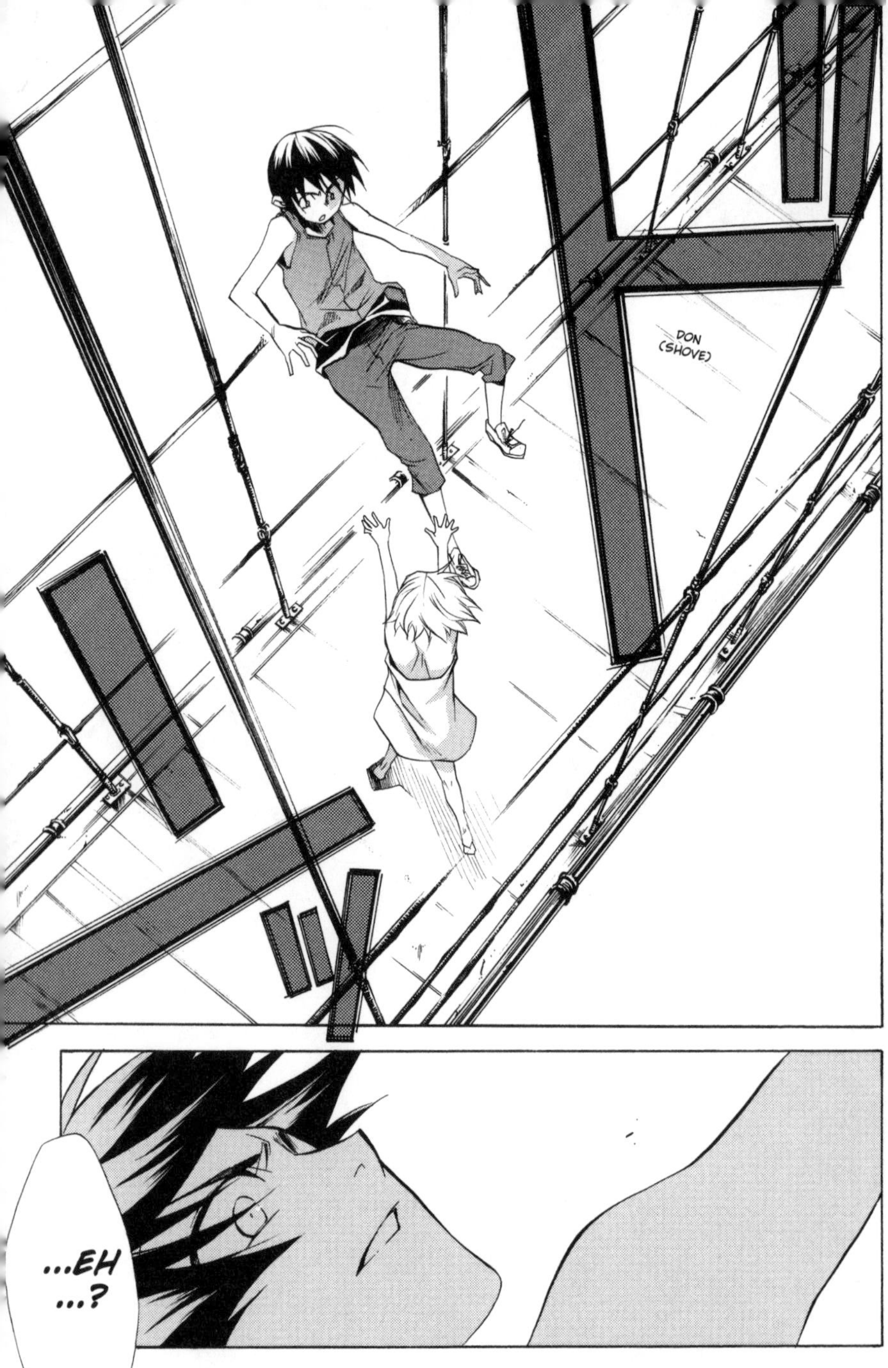
DON
(SHOVE)
...EH
...?

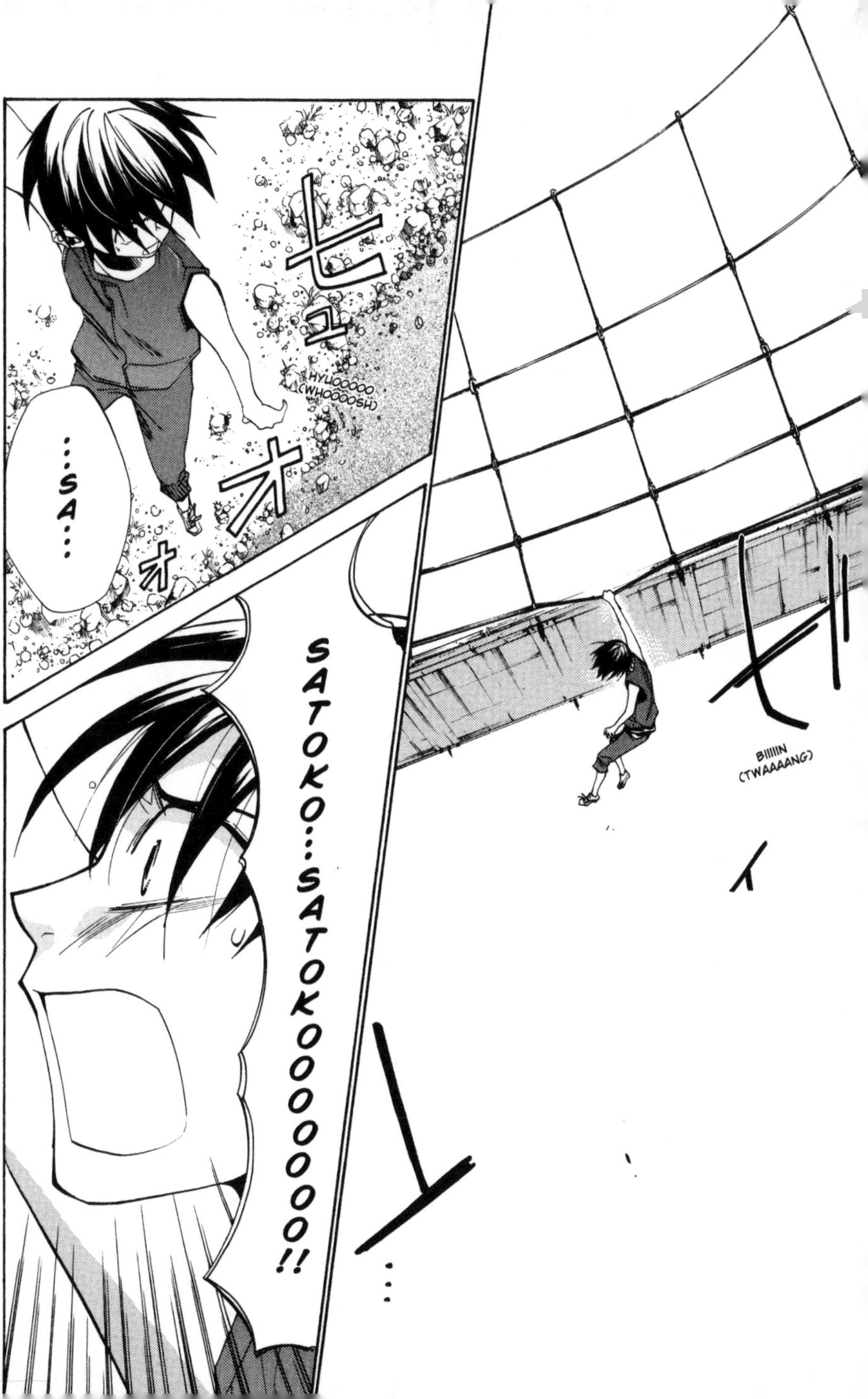

BIIIIIN (TWAAAANG)
ヒュオオ
HYUOOOOO (WHOOOOSH)
...SA...
SATOKO...SATOKOOOOOOOO!!
...

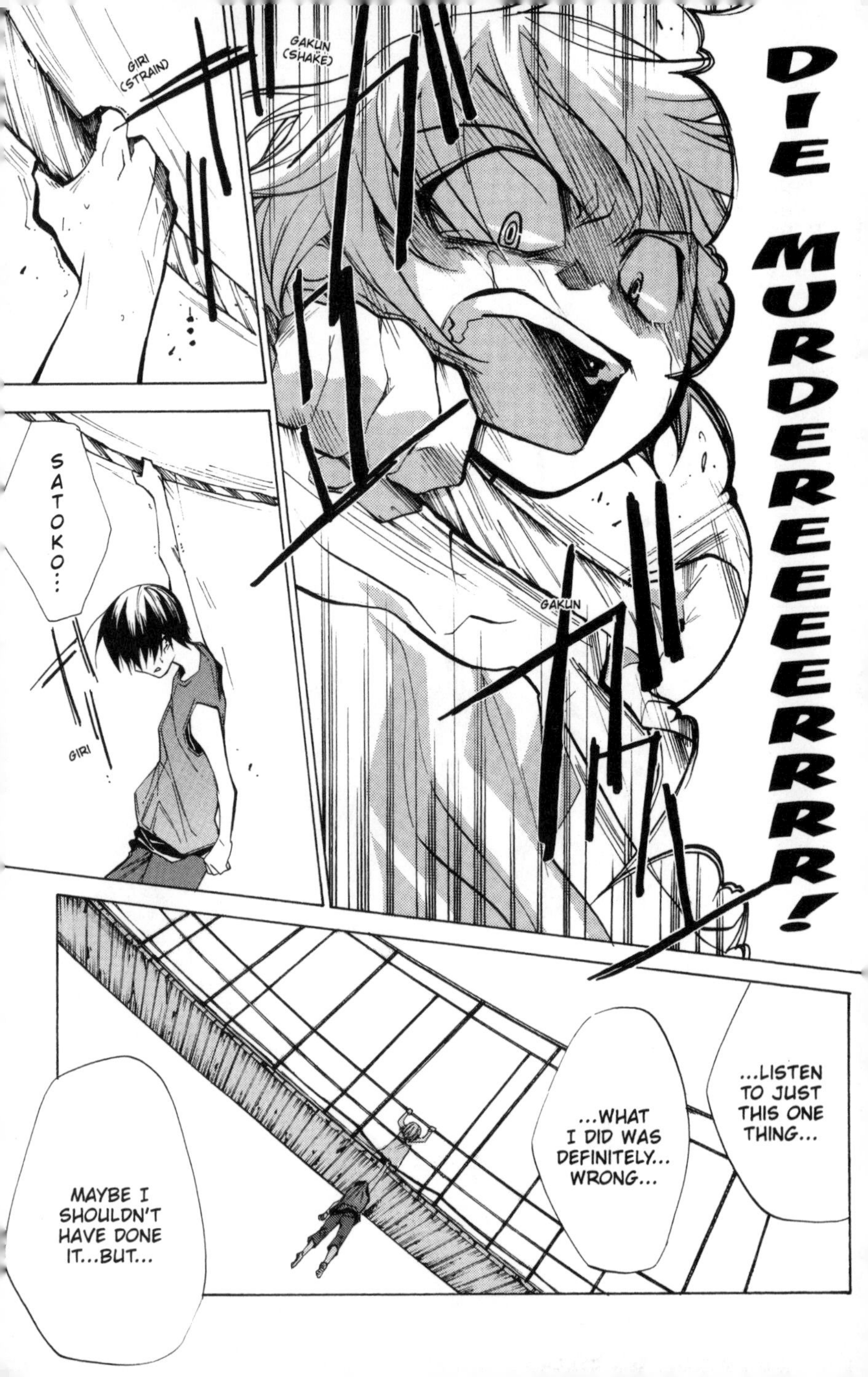
DIE MURDEREEEERRRR!
GAKUN (SHAKE)
GAKUN
GIRI (STRAIN)
SATOKO...
GIRI
...LISTEN TO JUST THIS ONE THING...
...WHAT I DID WAS DEFINITELY... WRONG...
MAYBE I SHOULDN'T HAVE DONE IT...BUT...

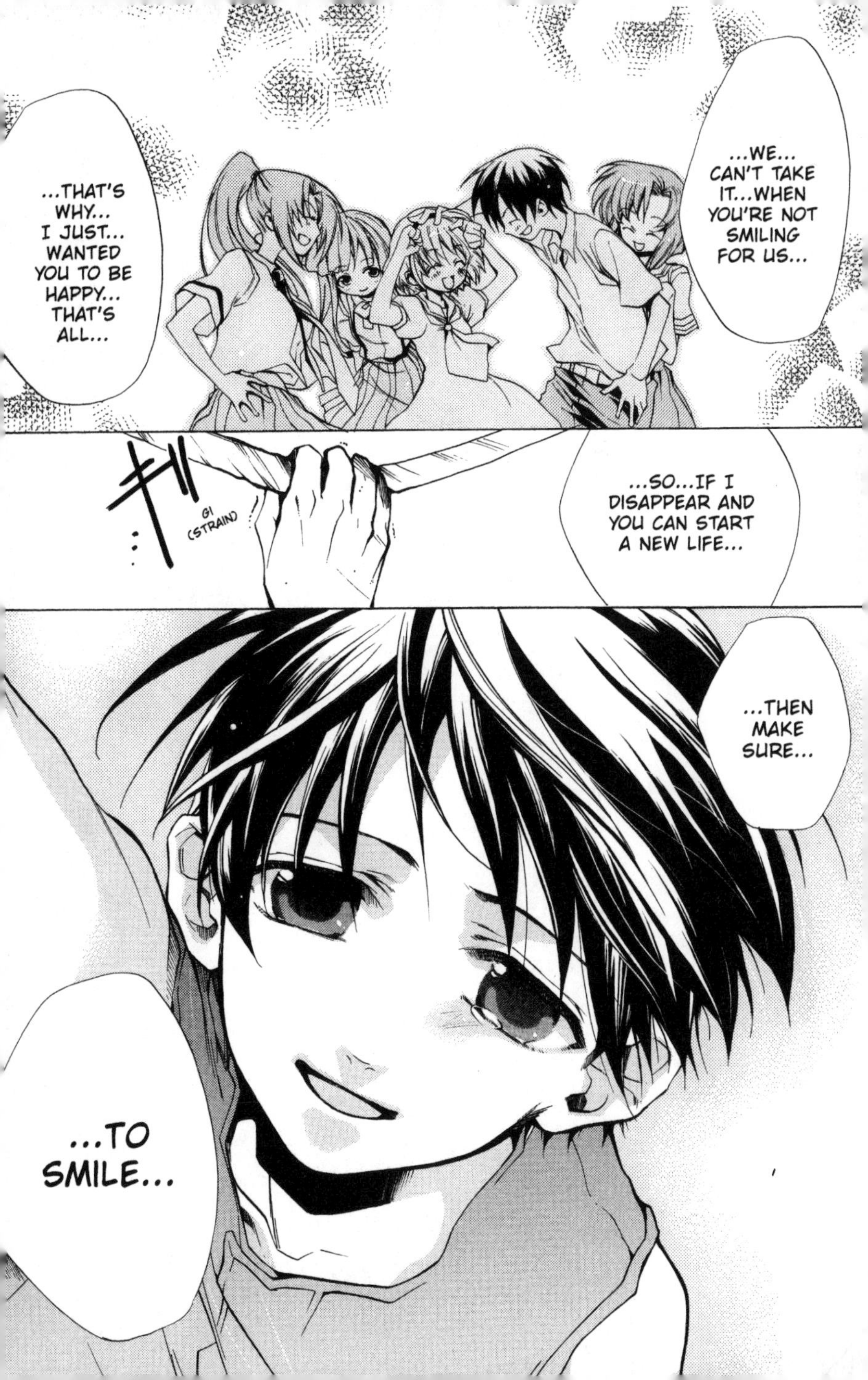
...WE... CAN'T TAKE IT...WHEN YOU'RE NOT SMILING FOR US...
...THAT'S WHY... I JUST... WANTED YOU TO BE HAPPY... THAT'S ALL...
...SO...IF I DISAPPEAR AND YOU CAN START A NEW LIFE...
GI (STRAIN)
...THEN MAKE SURE...
...TO SMILE...

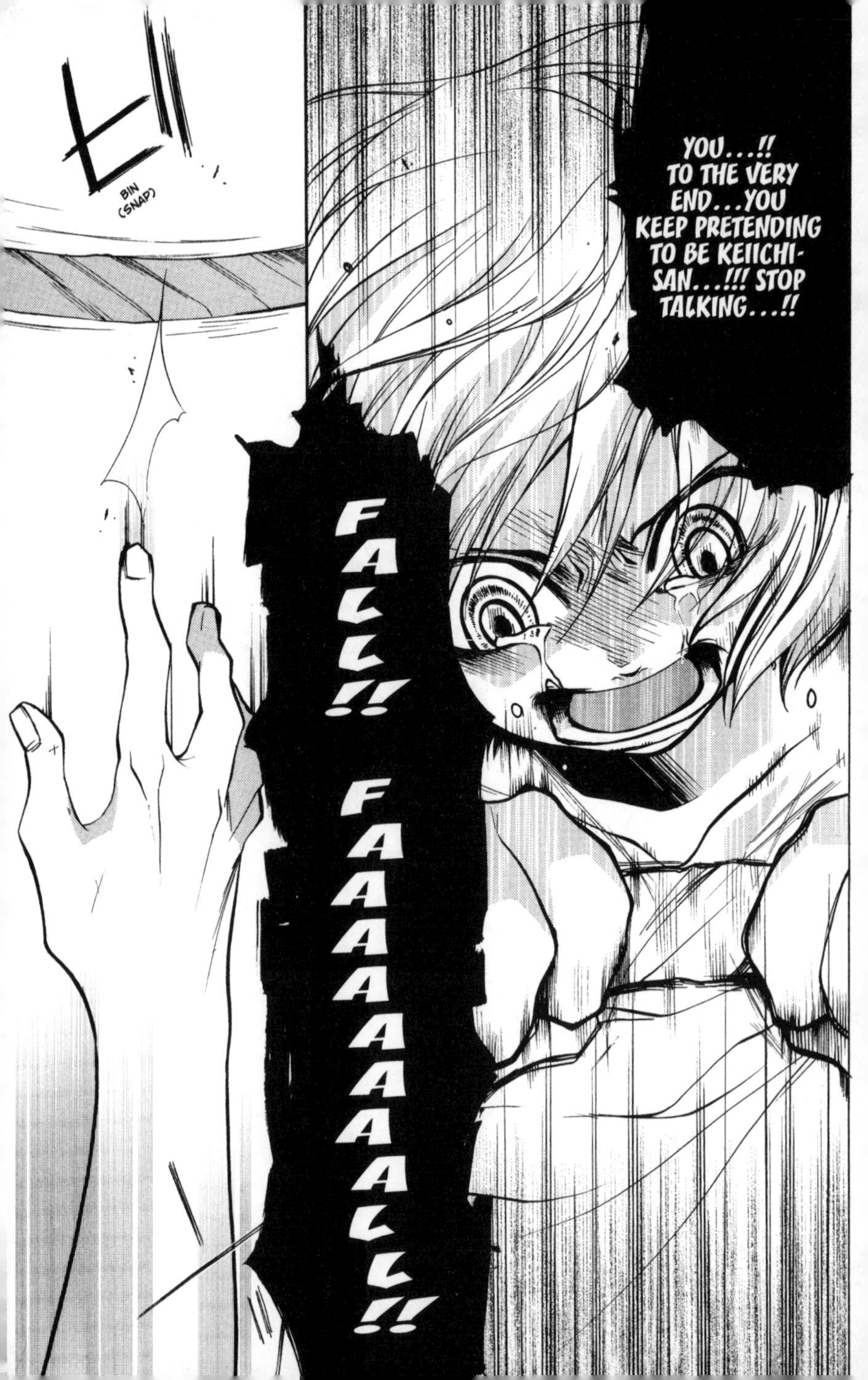
YOU...!! TO THE VERY END...YOU KEEP PRETENDING TO BE KEIICHI-SAN...!!! STOP TALKING...!!
FALL!! FAAAAAAAAAALL!!
BIN (SNAP)

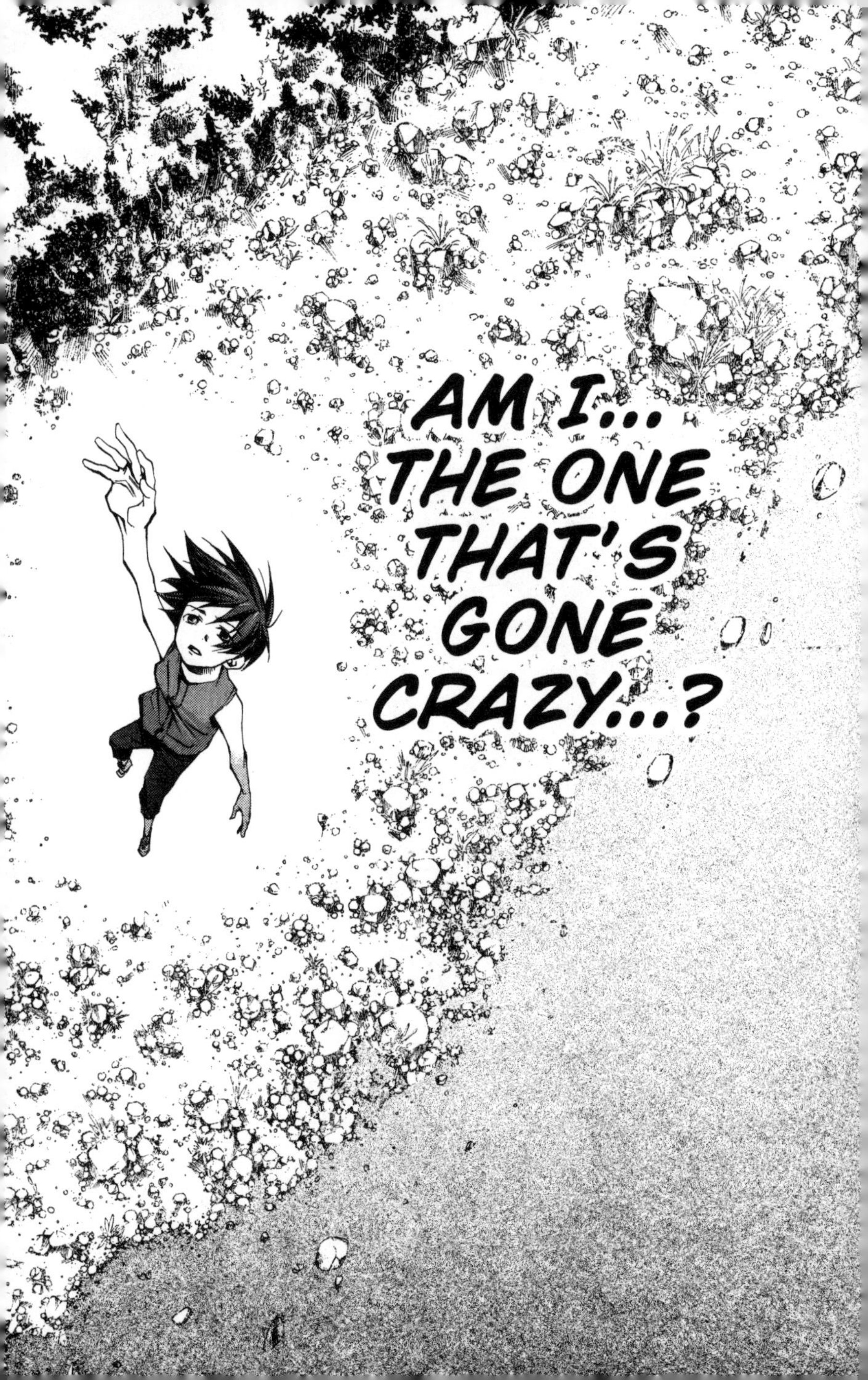
AM I...
THE ONE
THAT'S
GONE
CRAZY...?

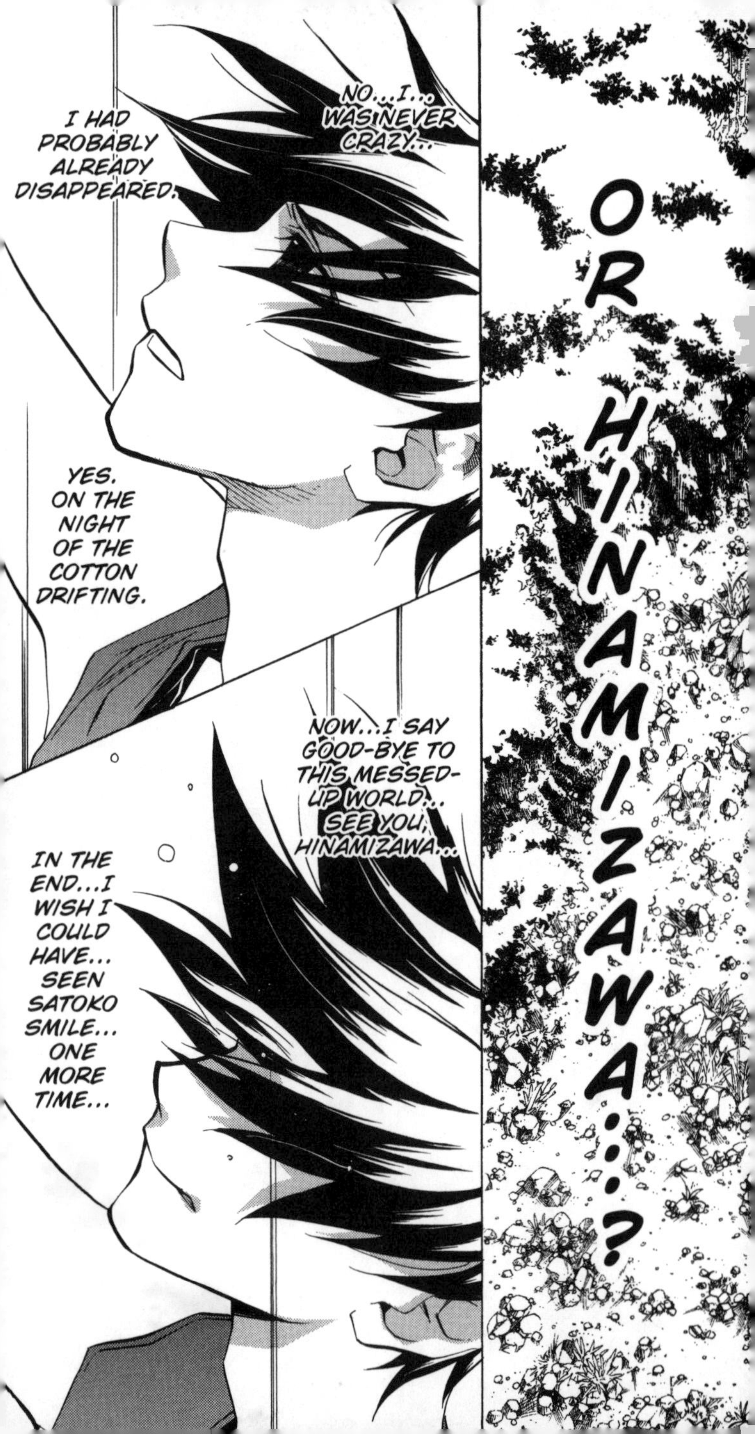
OR HINAMIZAWA...?
NO...I... WAS NEVER CRAZY...
I HAD PROBABLY ALREADY DISAPPEARED.
YES. ON THE NIGHT OF THE COTTON DRIFTING.
NOW...I SAY GOOD-BYE TO THIS MESSED-UP WORLD... SEE YOU, HINAMIZAWA...
IN THE END...I WISH I COULD HAVE... SEEN SATOKO SMILE... ONE MORE TIME...

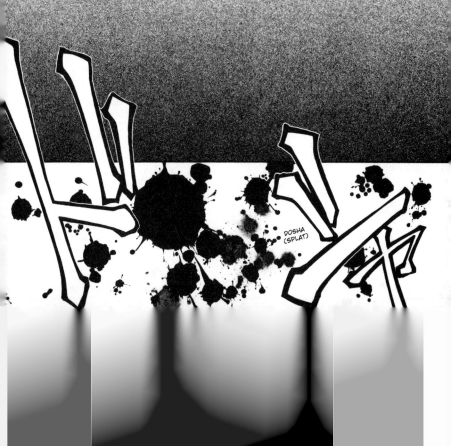

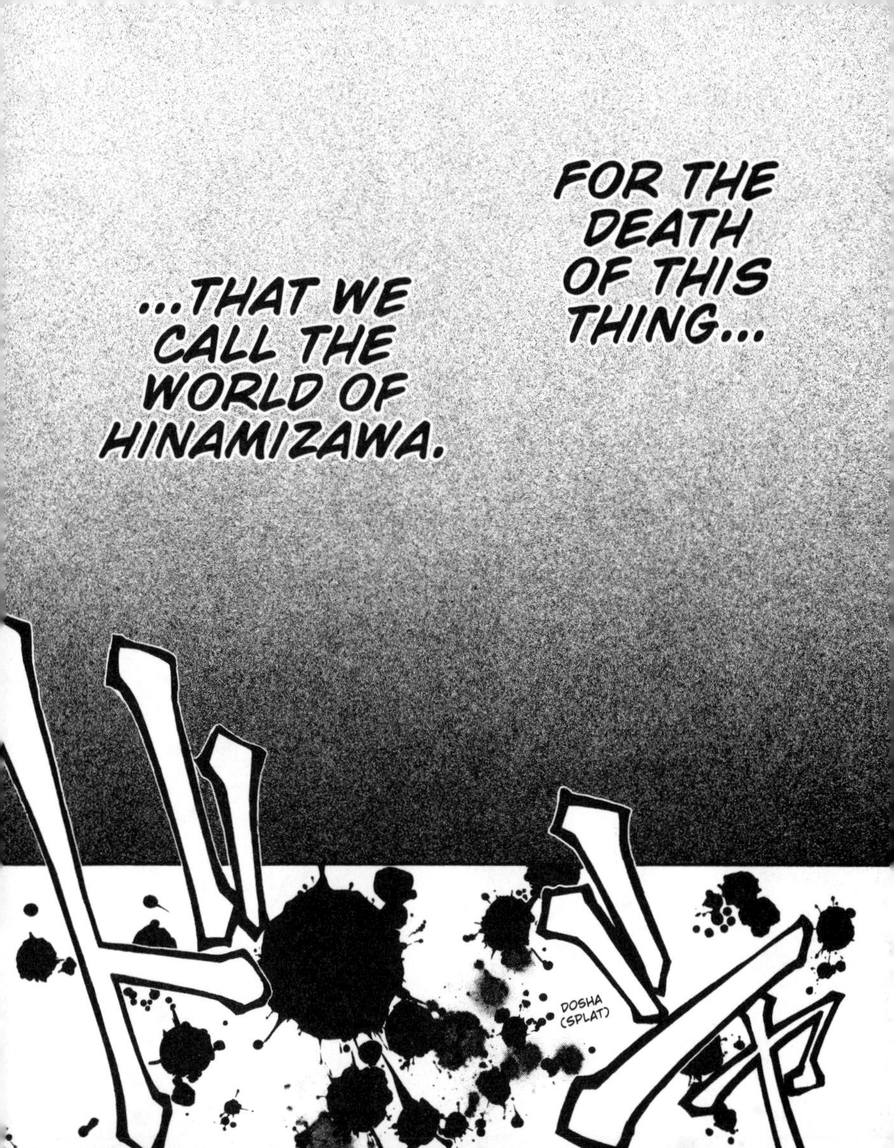
FOR THE DEATH OF THIS THING...
...THAT WE CALL THE WORLD OF HINAMIZAWA.
DOSHA (SPLAT)

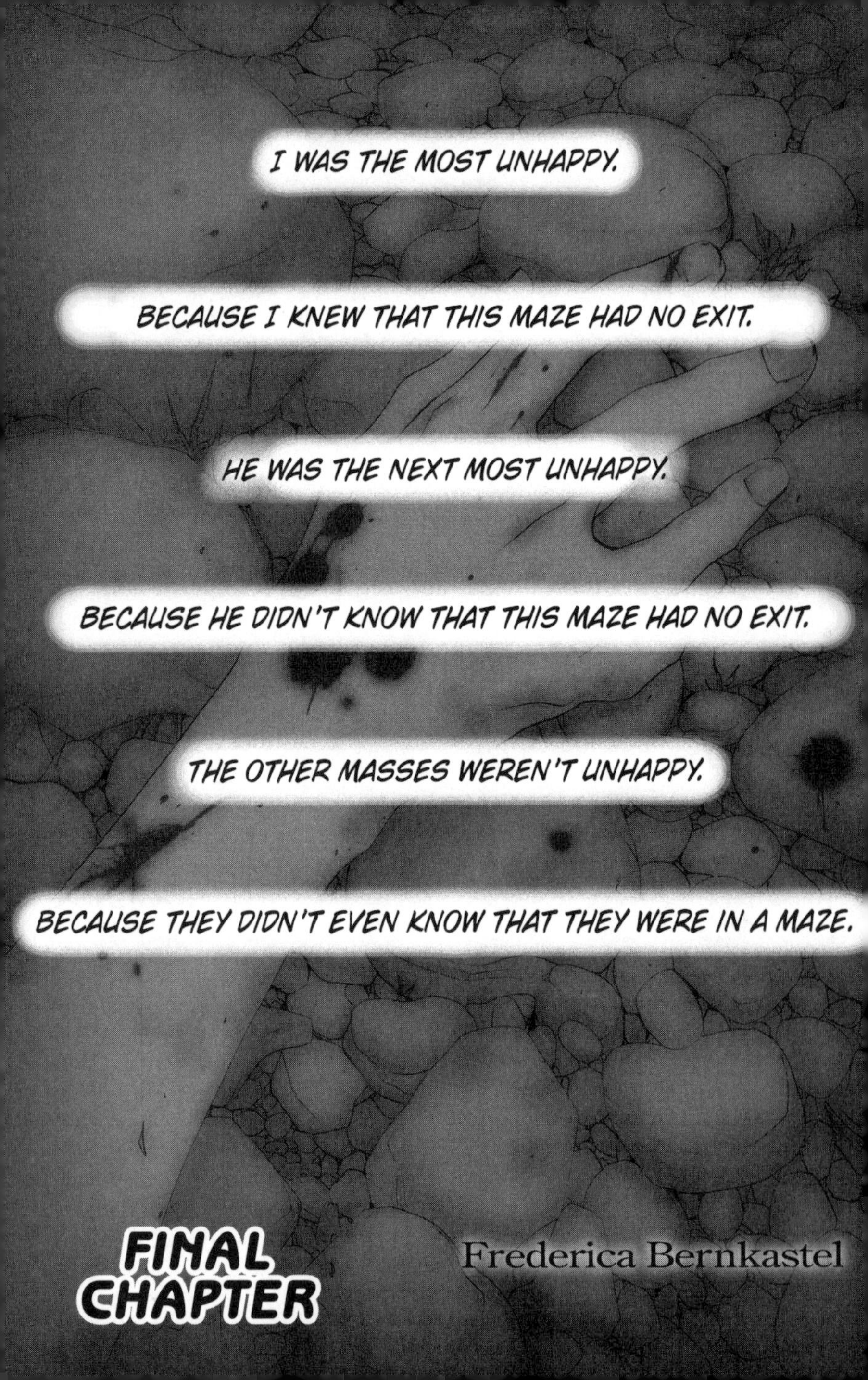
I WAS THE MOST UNHAPPY.
BECAUSE I KNEW THAT THIS MAZE HAD NO EXIT.
HE WAS THE NEXT MOST UNHAPPY.
BECAUSE HE DIDN'T KNOW THAT THIS MAZE HAD NO EXIT.
THE OTHER MASSES WEREN'T UNHAPPY.
BECAUSE THEY DIDN'T EVEN KNOW THAT THEY WERE IN A MAZE.
FINAL CHAPTER
Frederica Bernkastel

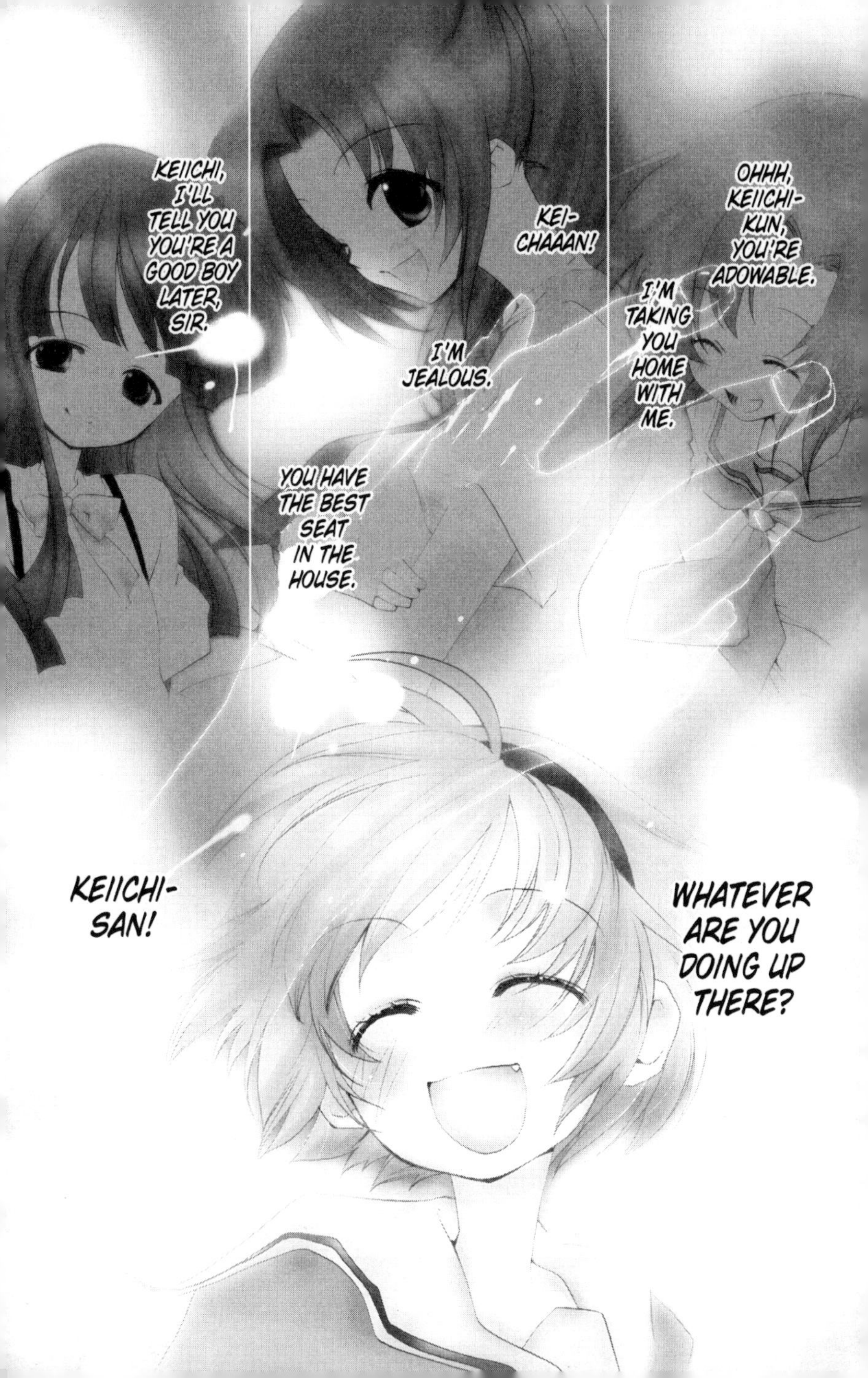
OHHH, KEIICHI-KUN, YOU'RE ADOWABLE.
I'M TAKING YOU HOME WITH ME.
KEI-CHAAAN!
I'M JEALOUS.
YOU HAVE THE BEST SEAT IN THE HOUSE.
KEIICHI, I'LL TELL YOU YOU'RE A GOOD BOY LATER, SIR.
WHATEVER ARE YOU DOING UP THERE?
KEIICHI-SAN!

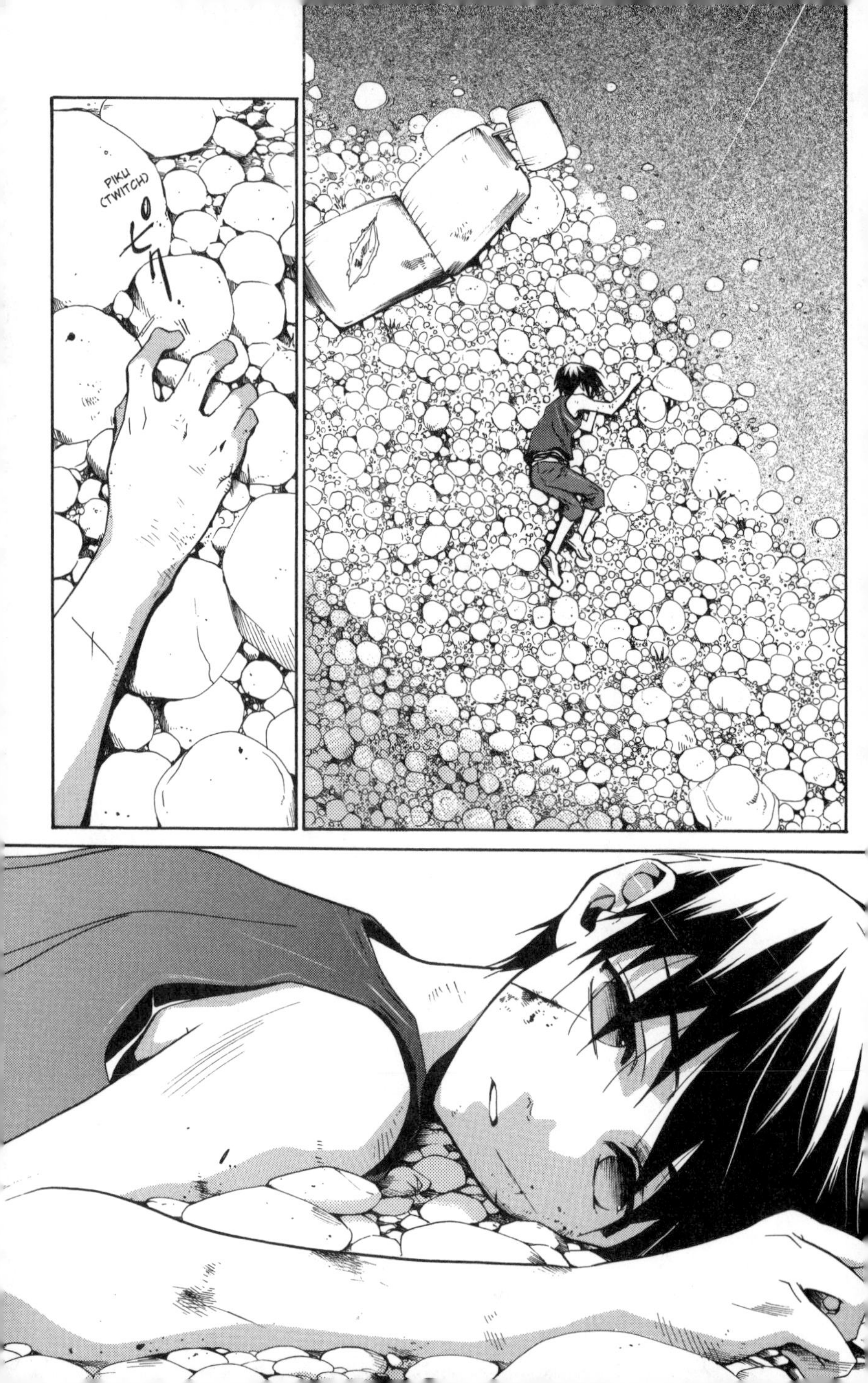
PIKU
(TWITCH)

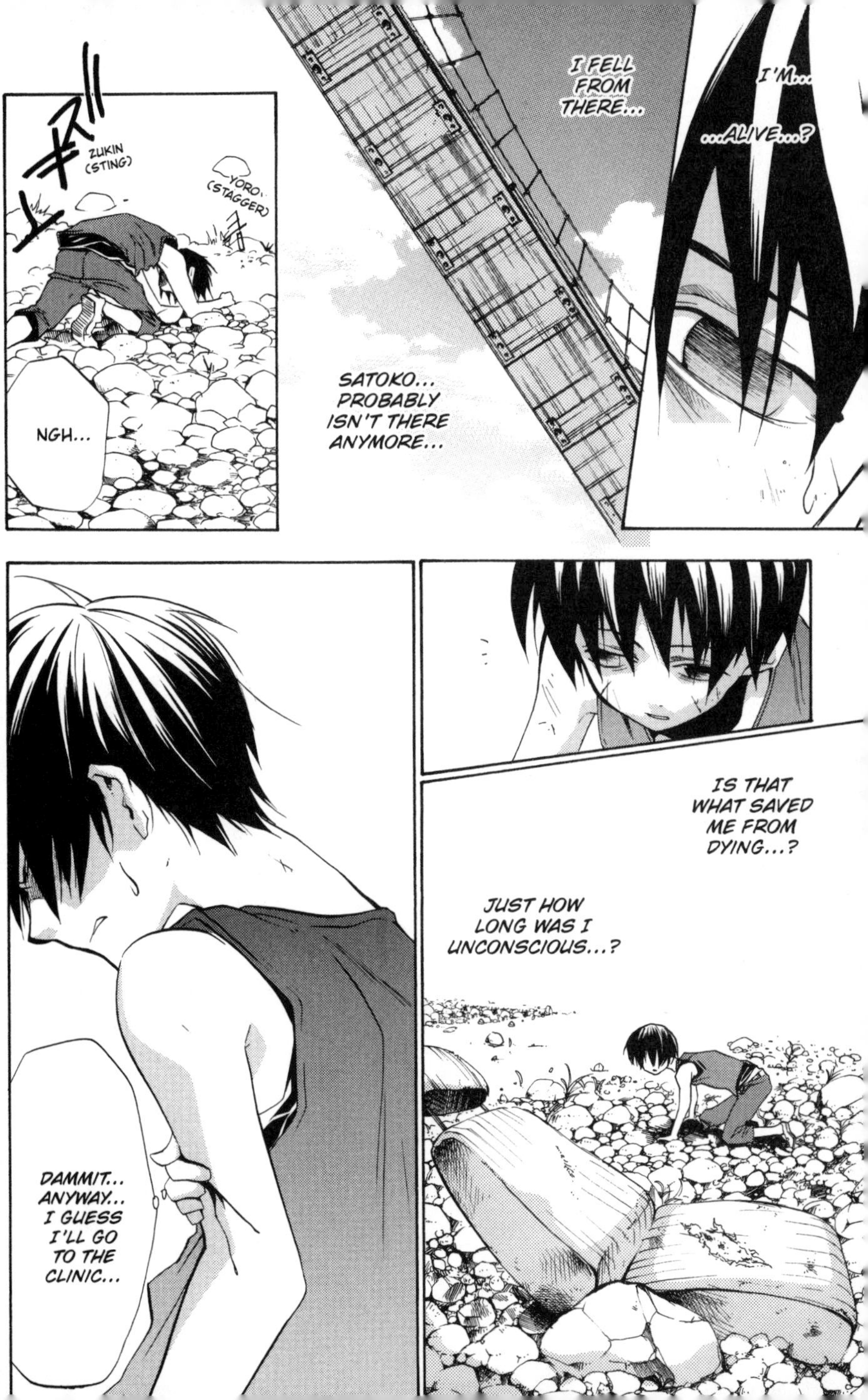
I'M...
...ALIVE...?
I FELL FROM THERE...
SATOKO... PROBABLY ISN'T THERE ANYMORE...
ZUKIN (STING)
YORO (STAGGER)
NGH...
IS THAT WHAT SAVED ME FROM DYING...?
JUST HOW LONG WAS I UNCONSCIOUS...?
DAMMIT... ANYWAY... I GUESS I'LL GO TO THE CLINIC...

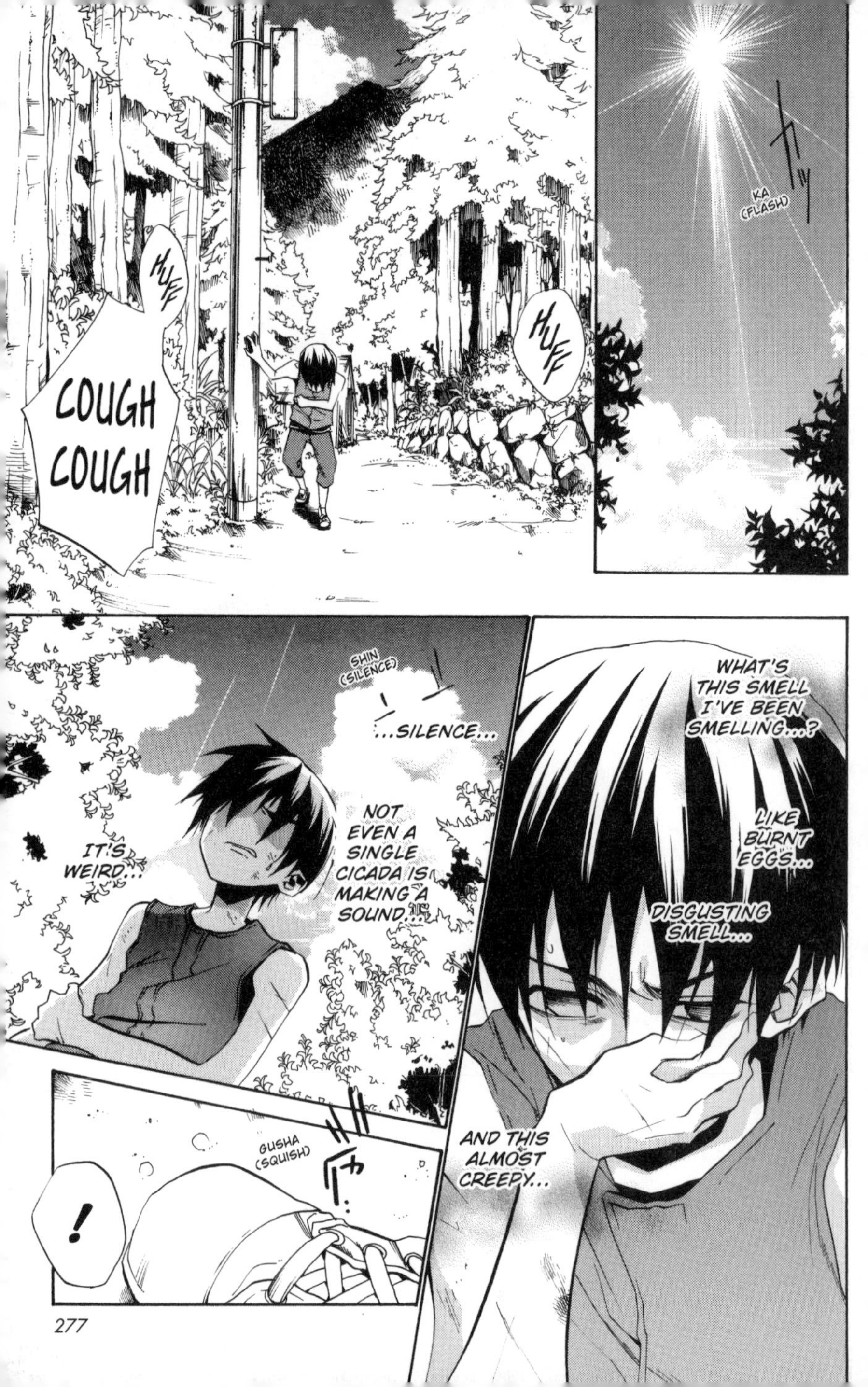

KA (FLASH)
HUFF
HUFF
COUGH COUGH
WHAT'S THIS SMELL I'VE BEEN SMELLING...?
LIKE BURNT EGGS...
DISGUSTING SMELL...
AND THIS ALMOST CREEPY...
SHIN (SILENCE)
...SILENCE...
NOT EVEN A SINGLE CICADA IS MAKING A SOUND...
IT'S WEIRD...
GUSHA (SQUISH)
!

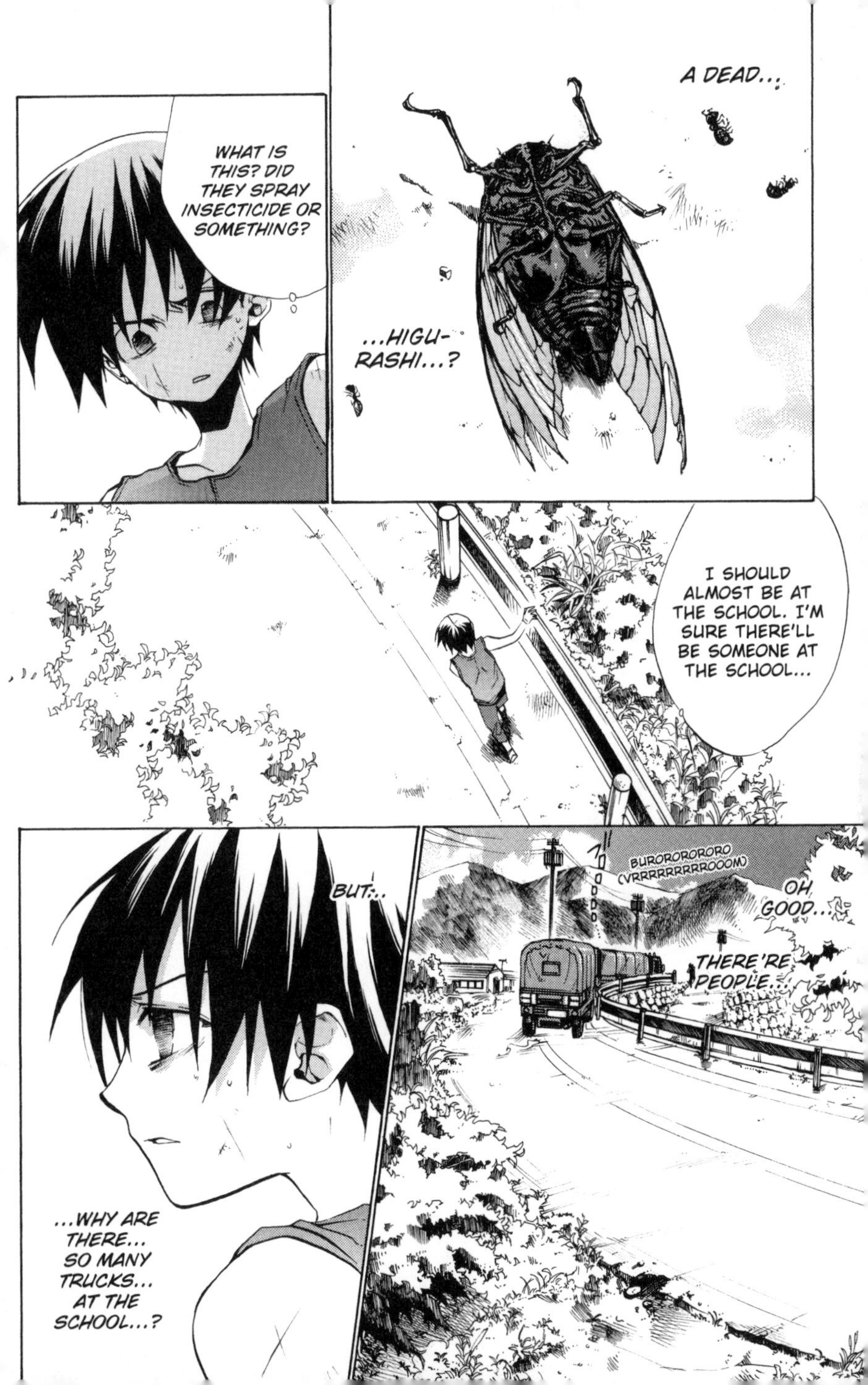
A DEAD...
...HIGU-RASHI...?
WHAT IS THIS? DID THEY SPRAY INSECTICIDE OR SOMETHING?
I SHOULD ALMOST BE AT THE SCHOOL. I'M SURE THERE'LL BE SOMEONE AT THE SCHOOL...
BURORORORORO (VRRRRRRRRROOOM)
OH, GOOD...
THERE'RE PEOPLE...
BUT...
...WHY ARE THERE... SO MANY TRUCKS... AT THE SCHOOL...?

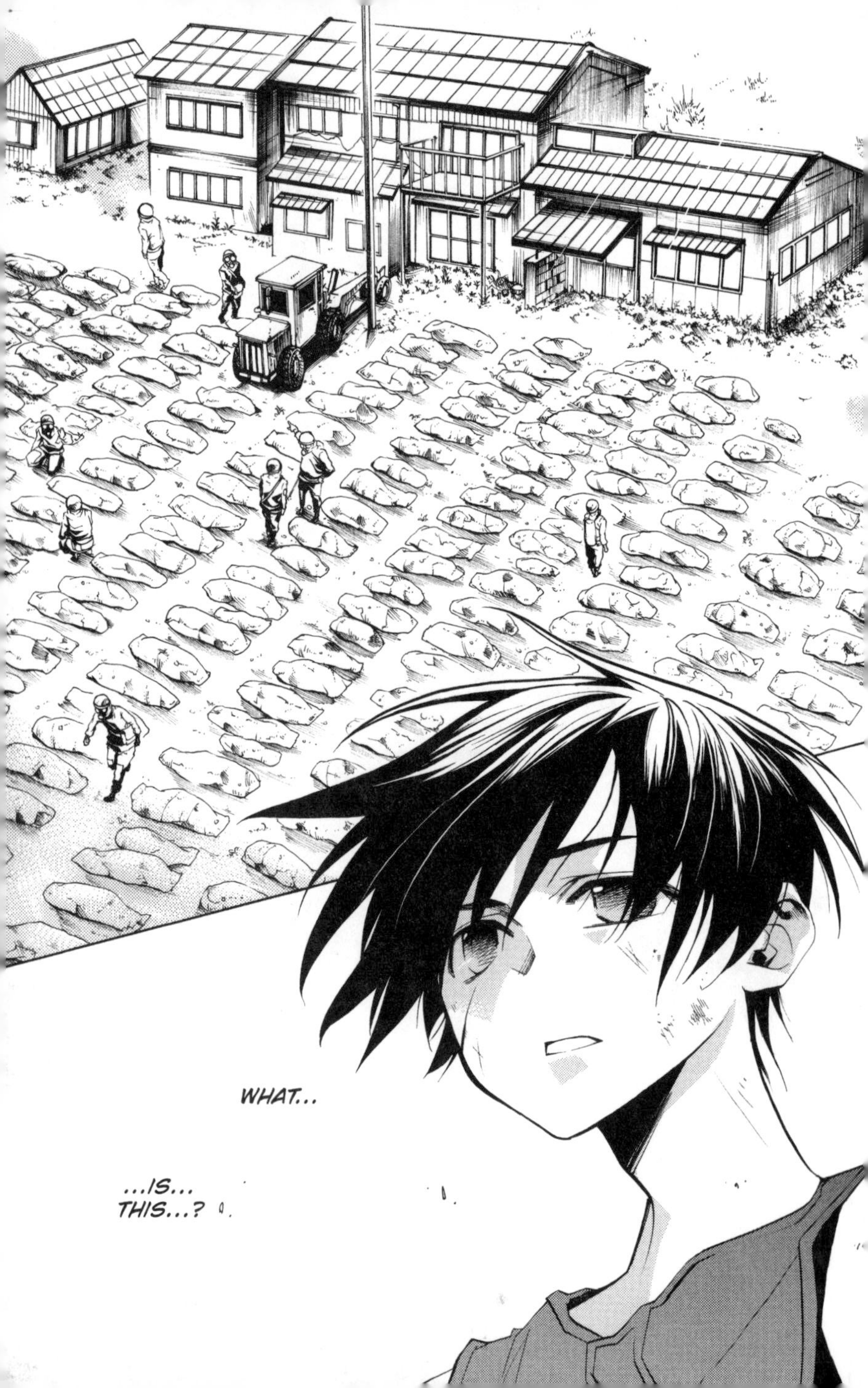
WHAT...
...IS... THIS...?

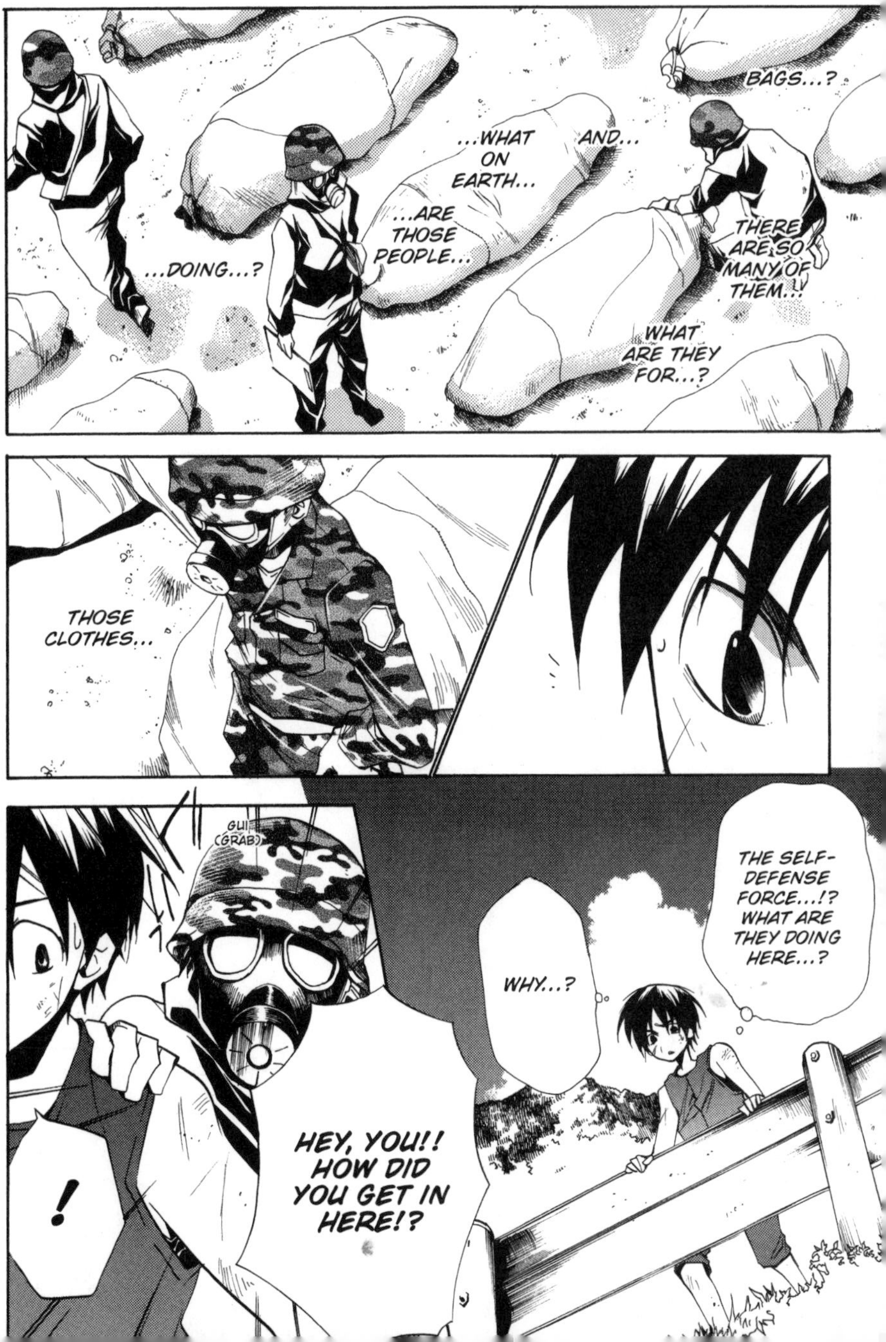
...WHAT ON EARTH...
...ARE THOSE PEOPLE...
...DOING...?
AND...
BAGS...?
THERE ARE SO MANY OF THEM...
WHAT ARE THEY FOR...?
THOSE CLOTHES...
THE SELF-DEFENSE FORCE...!? WHAT ARE THEY DOING HERE...?
WHY...?
GUI (GRAB)
HEY, YOU!! HOW DID YOU GET IN HERE!?
!

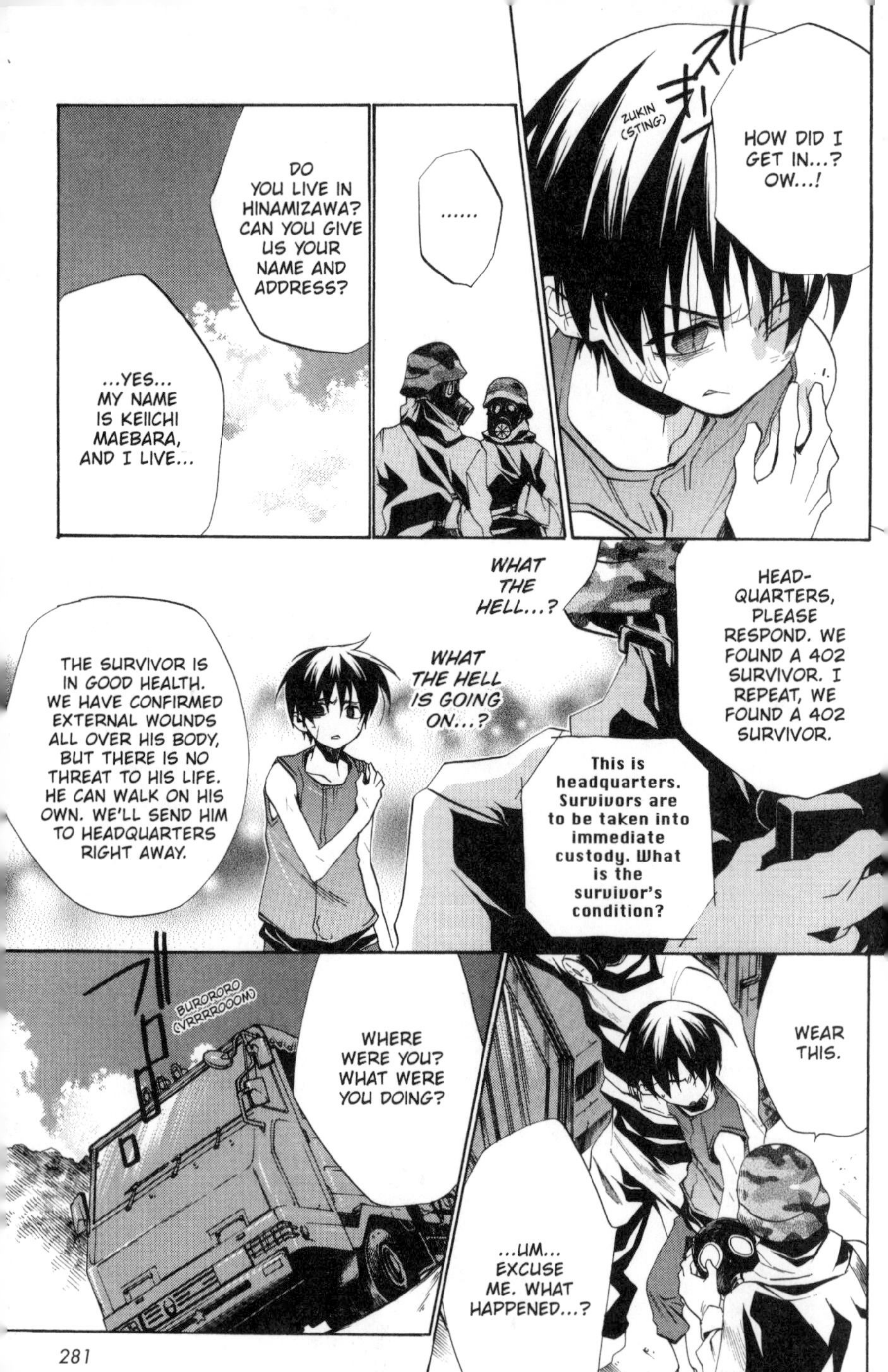

ZUKIN (STING)
HOW DID I GET IN...? OW...!
......
DO YOU LIVE IN HINAMIZAWA? CAN YOU GIVE US YOUR NAME AND ADDRESS?
...YES... MY NAME IS KEIICHI MAEBARA, AND I LIVE...
HEAD-QUARTERS, PLEASE RESPOND. WE FOUND A 402 SURVIVOR. I REPEAT, WE FOUND A 402 SURVIVOR.
WHAT THE HELL...?
WHAT THE HELL IS GOING ON...?
This is headquarters. Survivors are to be taken into immediate custody. What is the survivor's condition?
THE SURVIVOR IS IN GOOD HEALTH. WE HAVE CONFIRMED EXTERNAL WOUNDS ALL OVER HIS BODY, BUT THERE IS NO THREAT TO HIS LIFE. HE CAN WALK ON HIS OWN. WE'LL SEND HIM TO HEADQUARTERS RIGHT AWAY.
WEAR THIS.
...UM... EXCUSE ME. WHAT HAPPENED...?
BURORORO (VRRRROOOM)
WHERE WERE YOU? WHAT WERE YOU DOING?

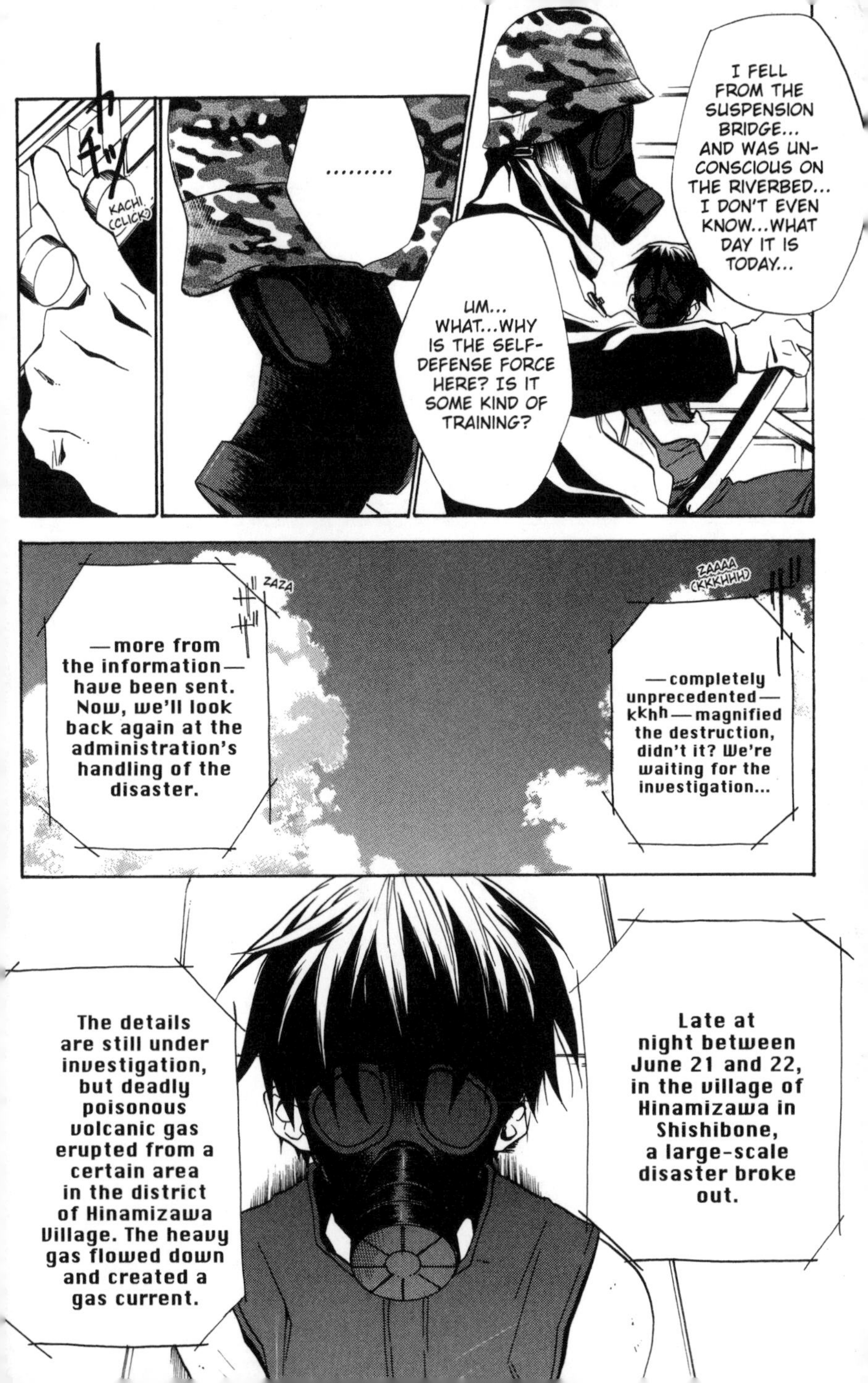
I FELL FROM THE SUSPENSION BRIDGE... AND WAS UN-CONSCIOUS ON THE RIVERBED... I DON'T EVEN KNOW...WHAT DAY IT IS TODAY...
UM... WHAT...WHY IS THE SELF-DEFENSE FORCE HERE? IS IT SOME KIND OF TRAINING?
....
KACHI (CLICK)
ZAAAA (KKKHHH)
—completely unprecedented—kkhh—magnified the destruction, didn't it? We're waiting for the investigation...
ZAZA
—more from the information—have been sent. Now, we'll look back again at the administration's handling of the disaster.
Late at night between June 21 and 22, in the village of Hinamizawa in Shishibone, a large-scale disaster broke out.
The details are still under investigation, but deadly poisonous volcanic gas erupted from a certain area in the district of Hinamizawa Village. The heavy gas flowed down and created a gas current.

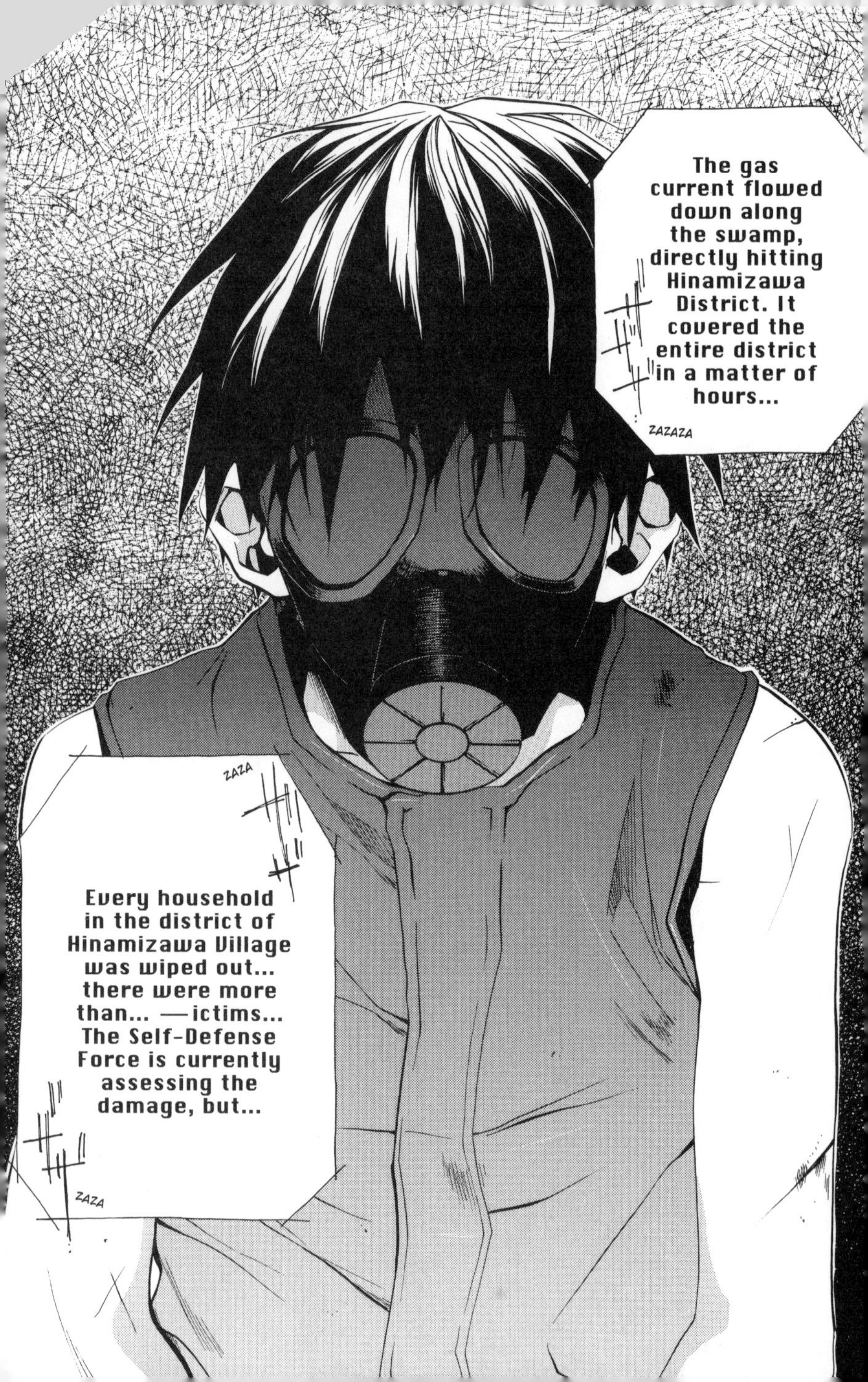
The gas current flowed down along the swamp, directly hitting Hinamizawa District. It covered the entire district in a matter of hours...
ZAZAZA
ZAZA
Every household in the district of Hinamizawa Village was wiped out... there were more than... —ictims... The Self-Defense Force is currently assessing the damage, but...
ZAZA

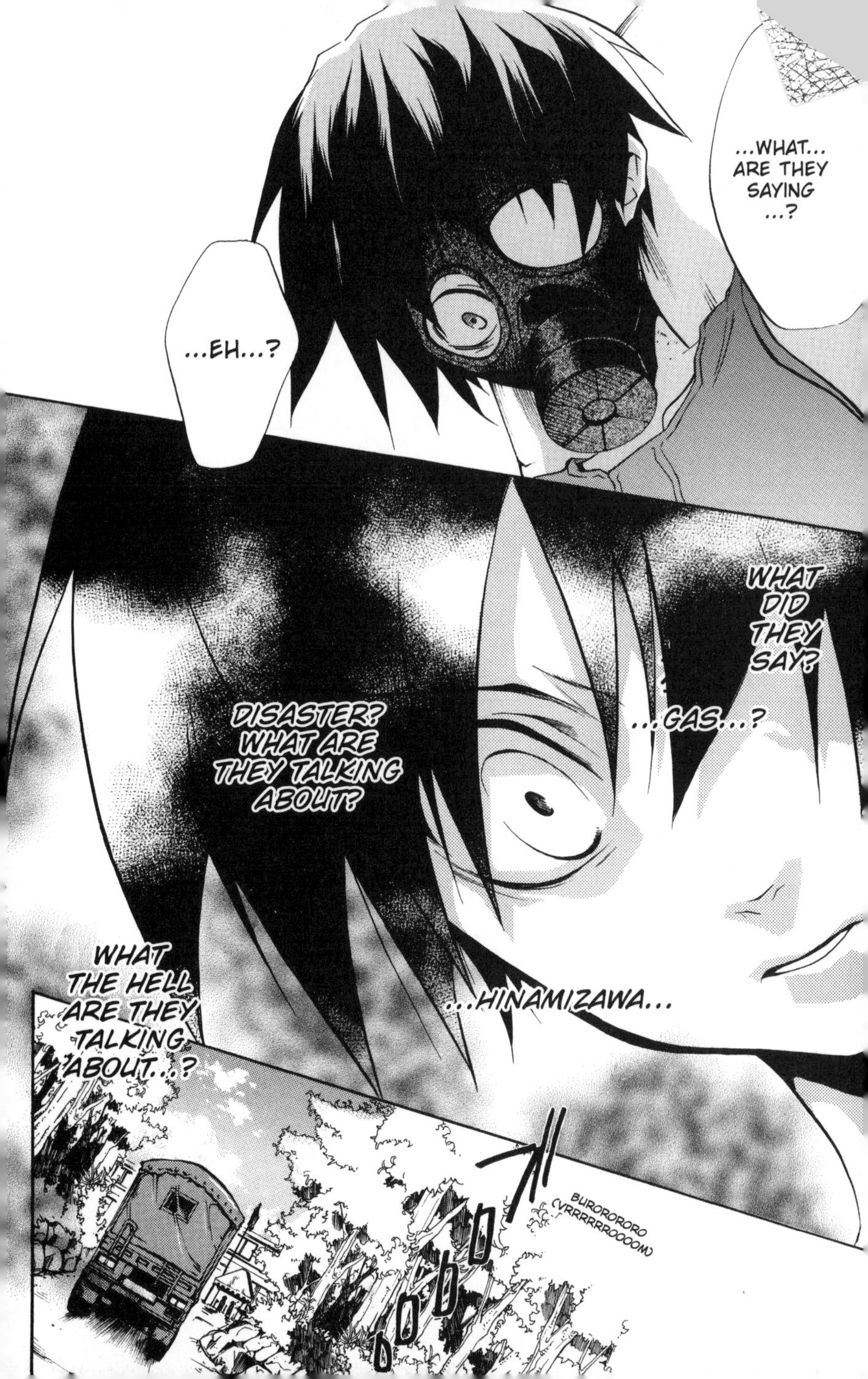
...WHAT... ARE THEY SAYING ...?
...EH...?
WHAT DID THEY SAY?
...GAS...?
DISASTER? WHAT ARE THEY TALKING ABOUT?
...HINAMIZAWA...
WHAT THE HELL ARE THEY TALKING ABOUT...?
BURORORORO (VRRRRRROOOOM)

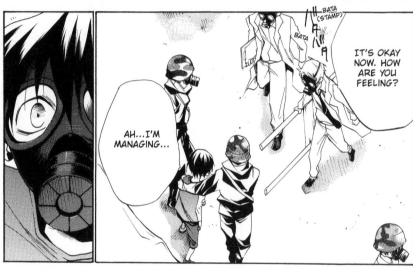

IT'S OKAY NOW. HOW ARE YOU FEELING?

BATA BATA (STAMP)

AH...I'M MANAGING...

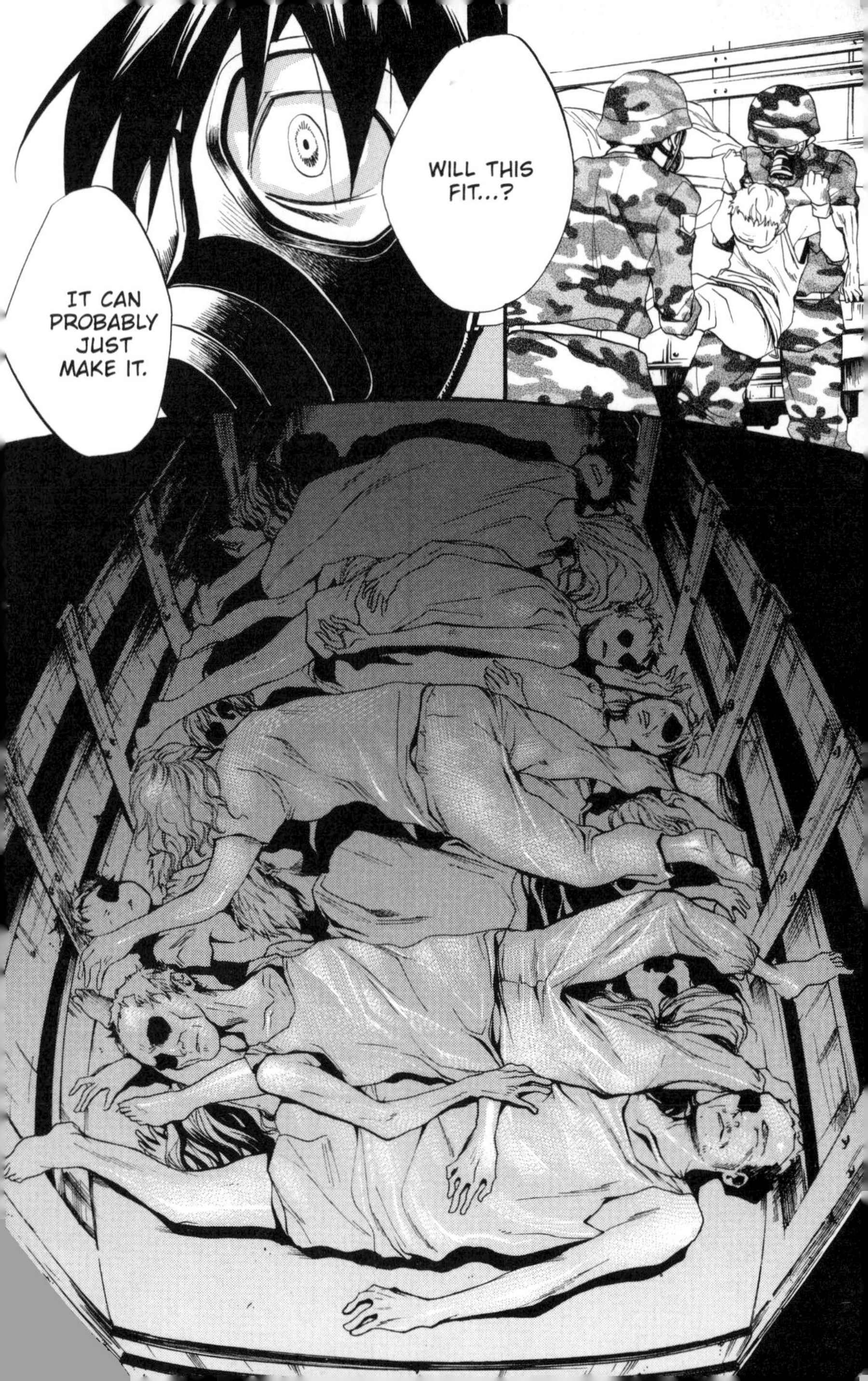
WILL THIS FIT...?
IT CAN PROBABLY JUST MAKE IT.

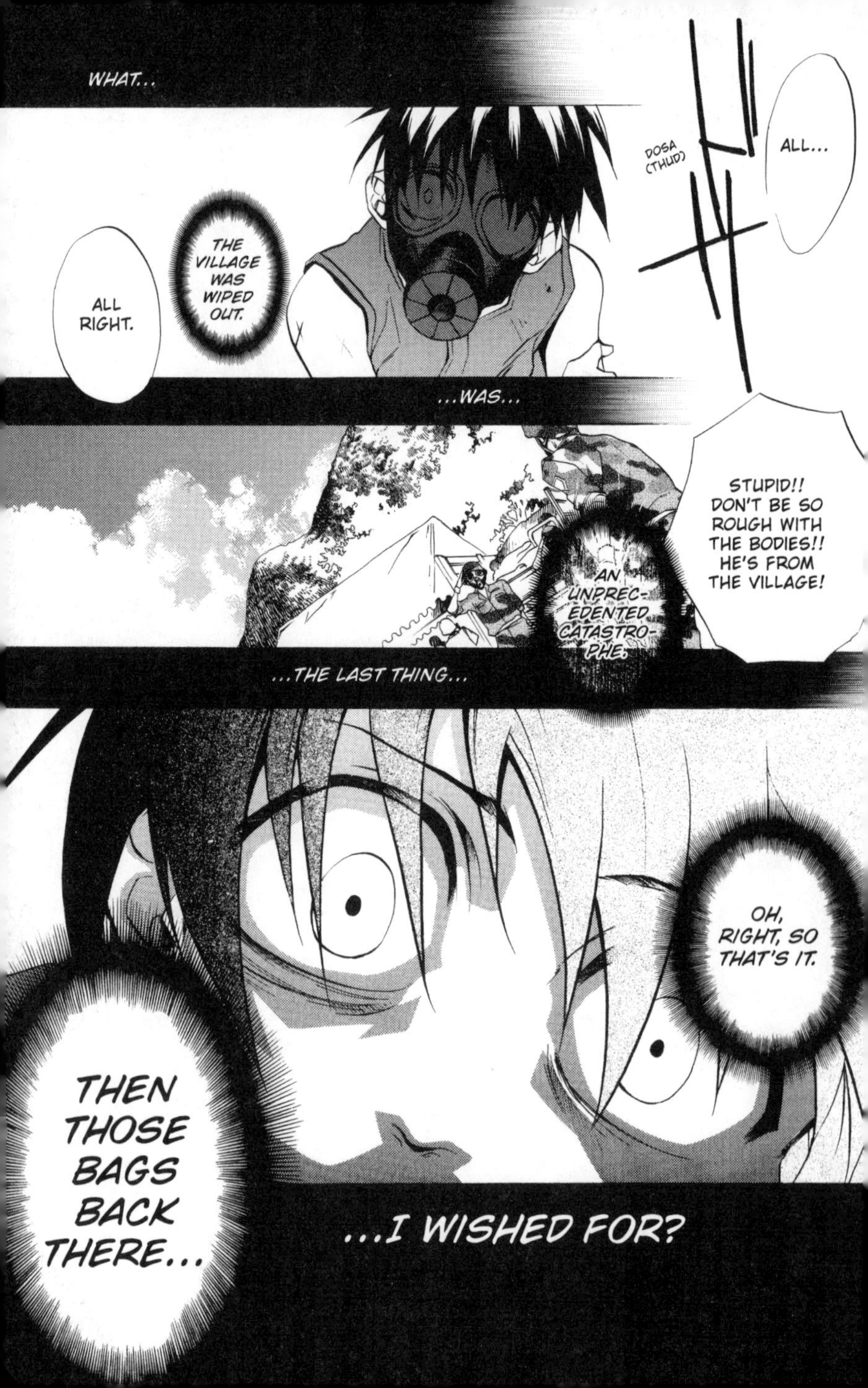
WHAT...
ALL...
DOSA (THUD)
THE VILLAGE WAS WIPED OUT.
ALL RIGHT.
...WAS...
STUPID!! DON'T BE SO ROUGH WITH THE BODIES!! HE'S FROM THE VILLAGE!
AN UNPRECEDENTED CATASTROPHE.
...THE LAST THING...
OH, RIGHT, SO THAT'S IT.
THEN THOSE BAGS BACK THERE...
...I WISHED FOR?

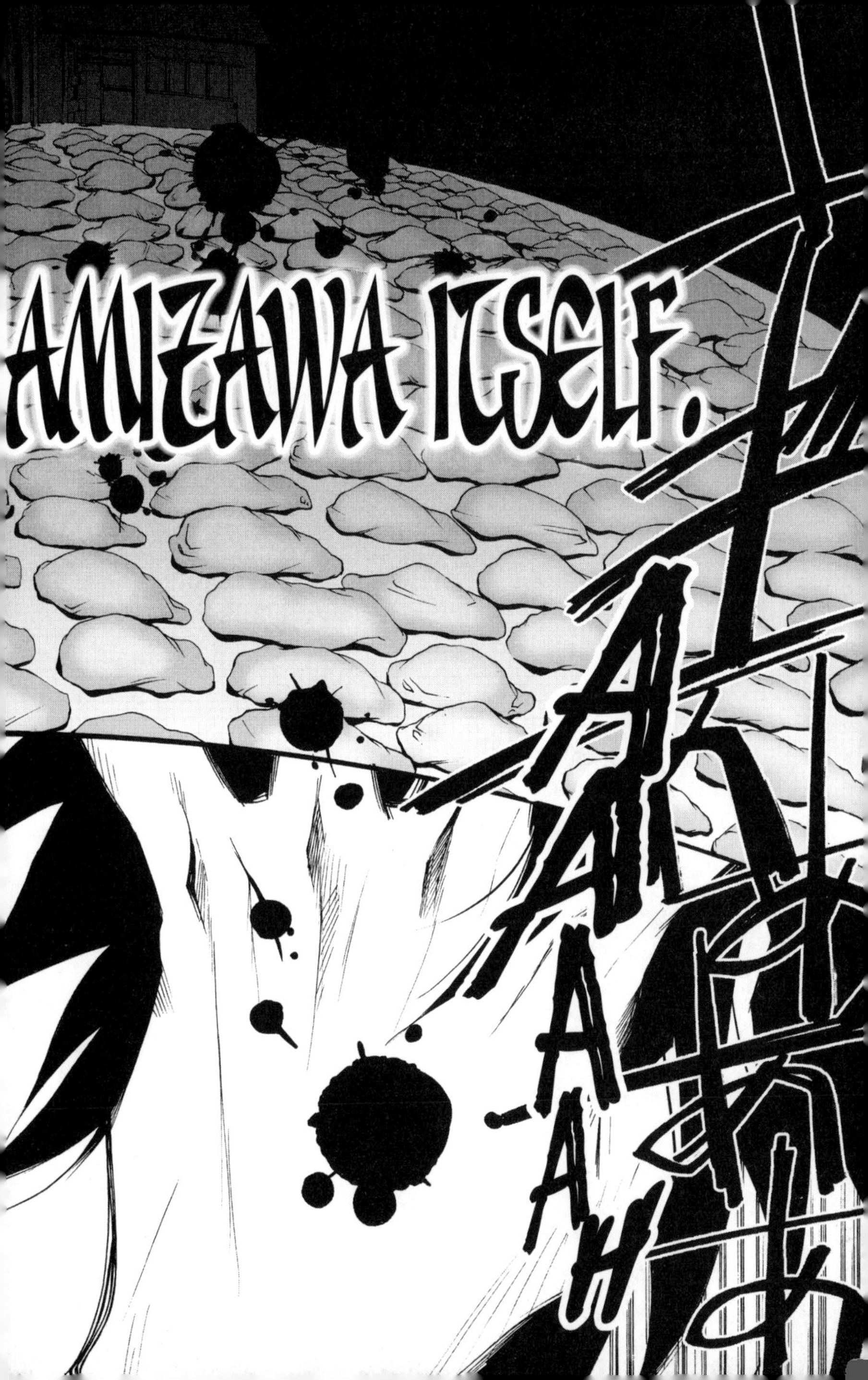
AMIZAWA ITSELF.
AAAAH

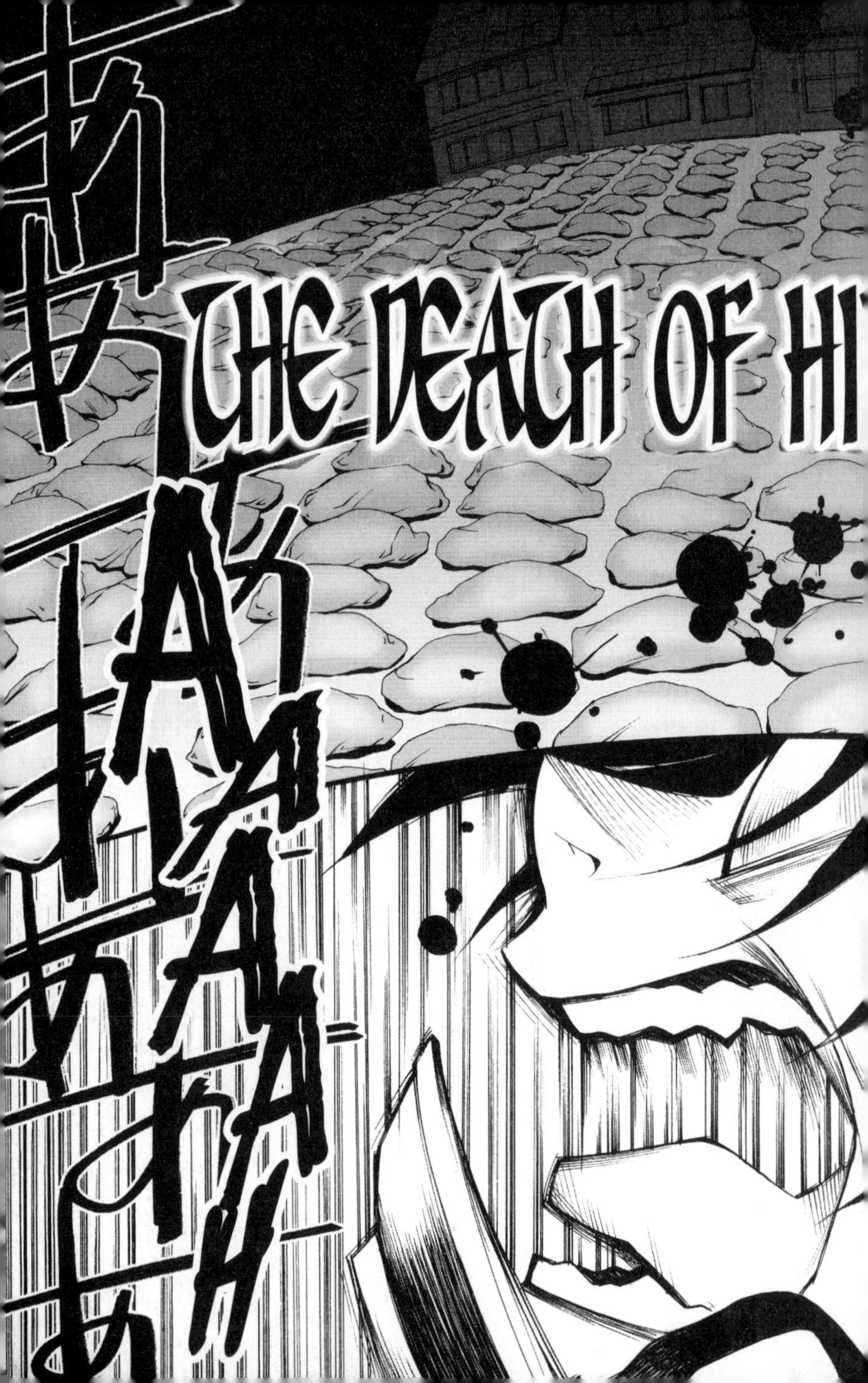
THE DEATH OF HI
AAAAAH
ああああ

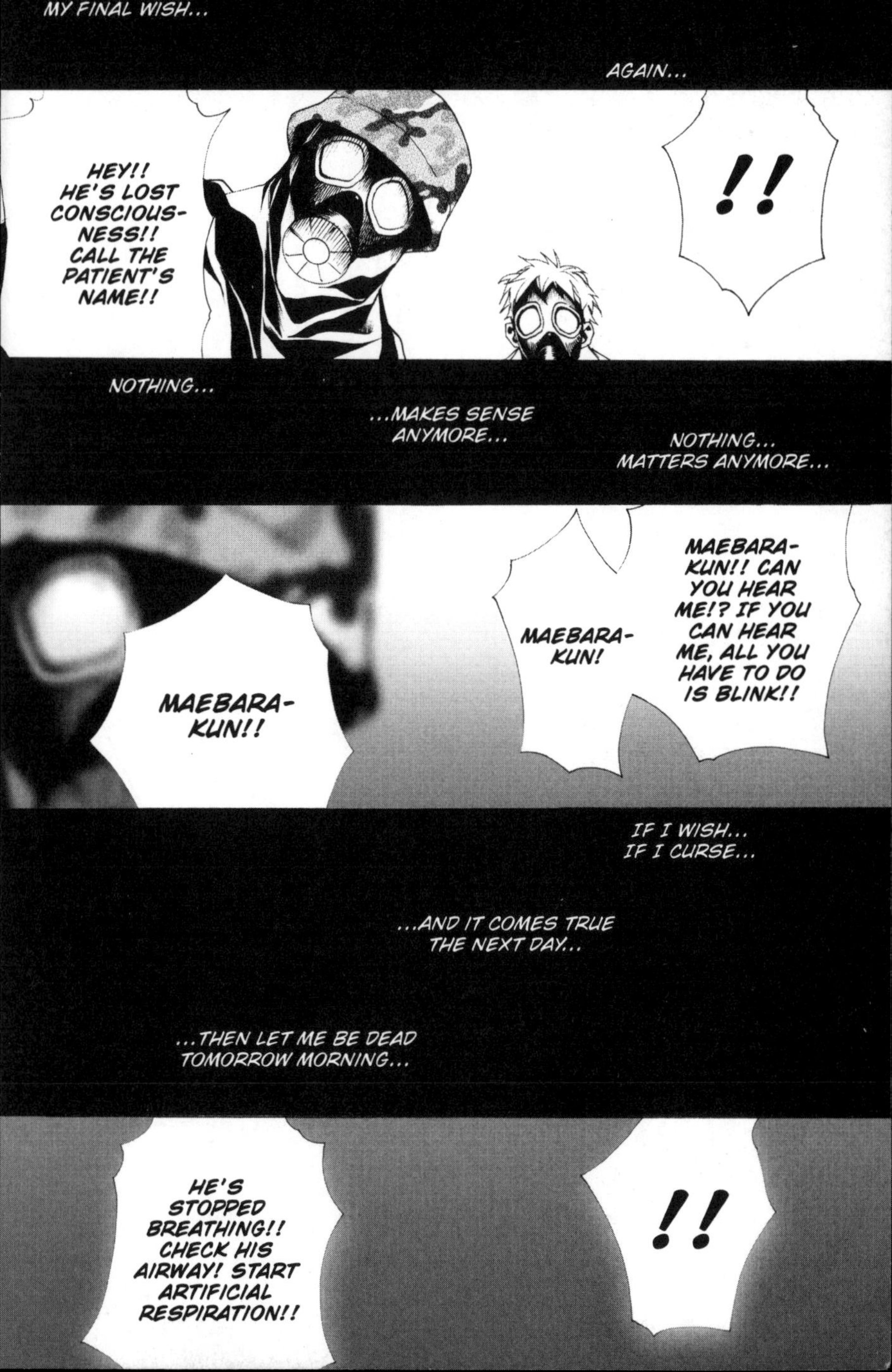
MY FINAL WISH...
AGAIN...
!!
HEY!! HE'S LOST CONSCIOUSNESS!! CALL THE PATIENT'S NAME!!
NOTHING...
...MAKES SENSE ANYMORE...
NOTHING... MATTERS ANYMORE...
MAEBARA-KUN!! CAN YOU HEAR ME!? IF YOU CAN HEAR ME, ALL YOU HAVE TO DO IS BLINK!!
MAEBARA-KUN!
MAEBARA-KUN!!
IF I WISH... IF I CURSE...
...AND IT COMES TRUE THE NEXT DAY...
...THEN LET ME BE DEAD TOMORROW MORNING...
!!
HE'S STOPPED BREATHING!! CHECK HIS AIRWAY! START ARTIFICIAL RESPIRATION!!

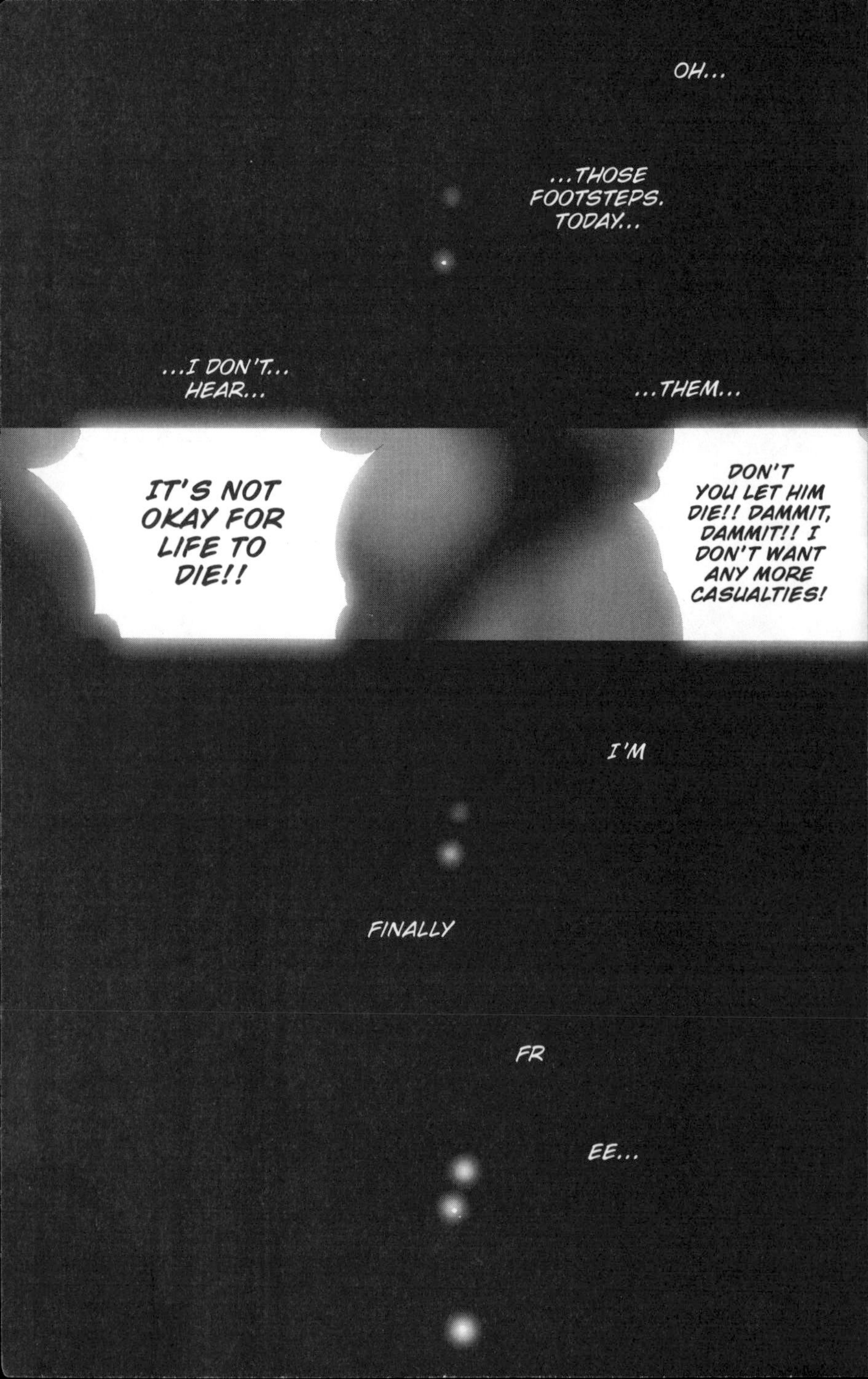
OH...
...THOSE FOOTSTEPS. TODAY...
...I DON'T... HEAR...
...THEM...
DON'T YOU LET HIM DIE!! DAMMIT, DAMMIT!! I DON'T WANT ANY MORE CASUALTIES!
IT'S NOT OKAY FOR LIFE TO DIE!!
I'M
FINALLY
FR
EE...

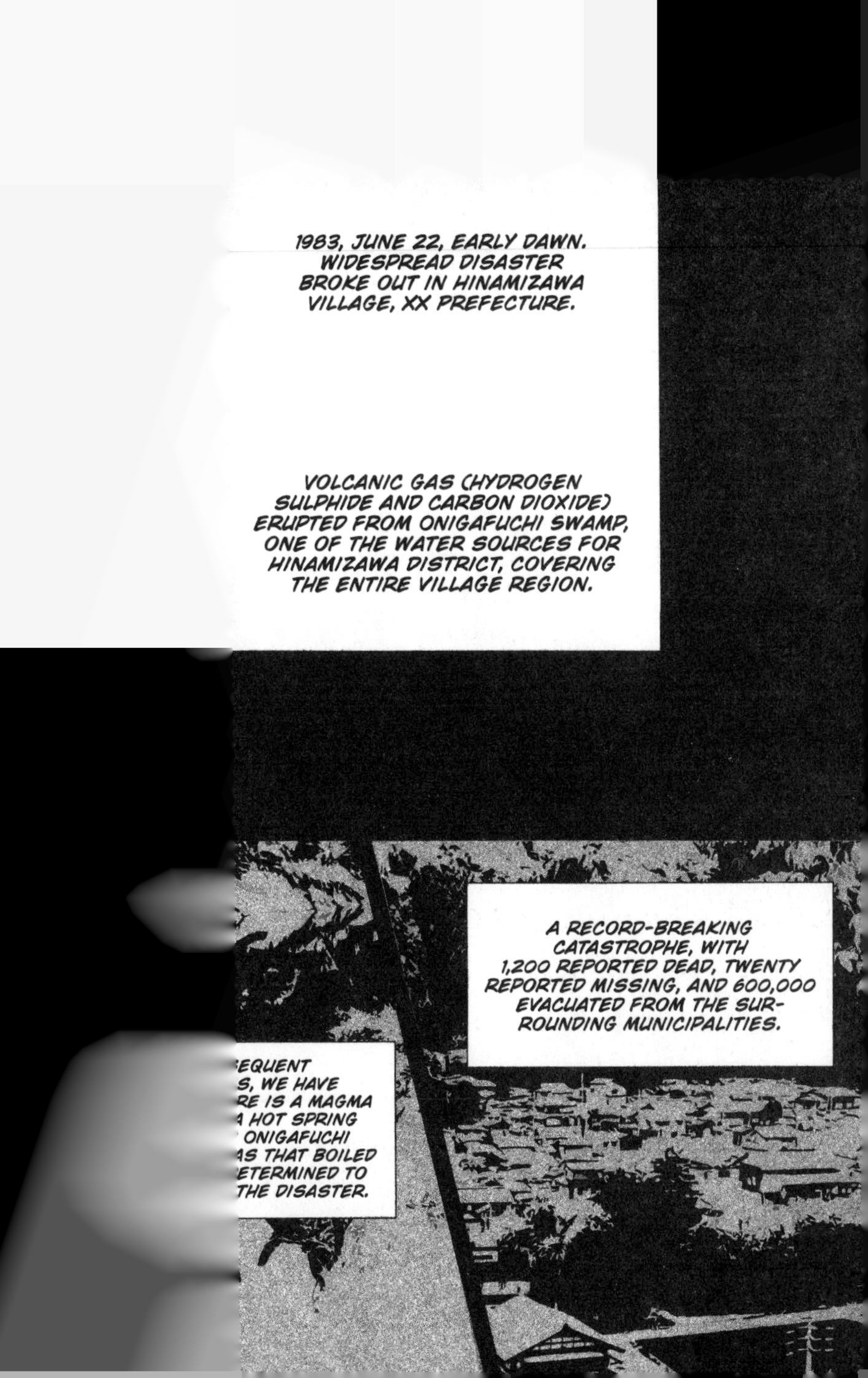
1983, JUNE 22, EARLY DAWN. WIDESPREAD DISASTER BROKE OUT IN HINAMIZAWA VILLAGE, XX PREFECTURE.
VOLCANIC GAS (HYDROGEN SULPHIDE AND CARBON DIOXIDE) ERUPTED FROM ONIGAFUCHI SWAMP, ONE OF THE WATER SOURCES FOR HINAMIZAWA DISTRICT, COVERING THE ENTIRE VILLAGE REGION.
A RECORD-BREAKING CATASTROPHE, WITH 1,200 REPORTED DEAD, TWENTY REPORTED MISSING, AND 600,000 EVACUATED FROM THE SURROUNDING MUNICIPALITIES.
EQUENT
S, WE HAVE
RE IS A MAGMA
A HOT SPRING
ONIGAFUCHI
AS THAT BOILED
ETERMINED TO
THE DISASTER.

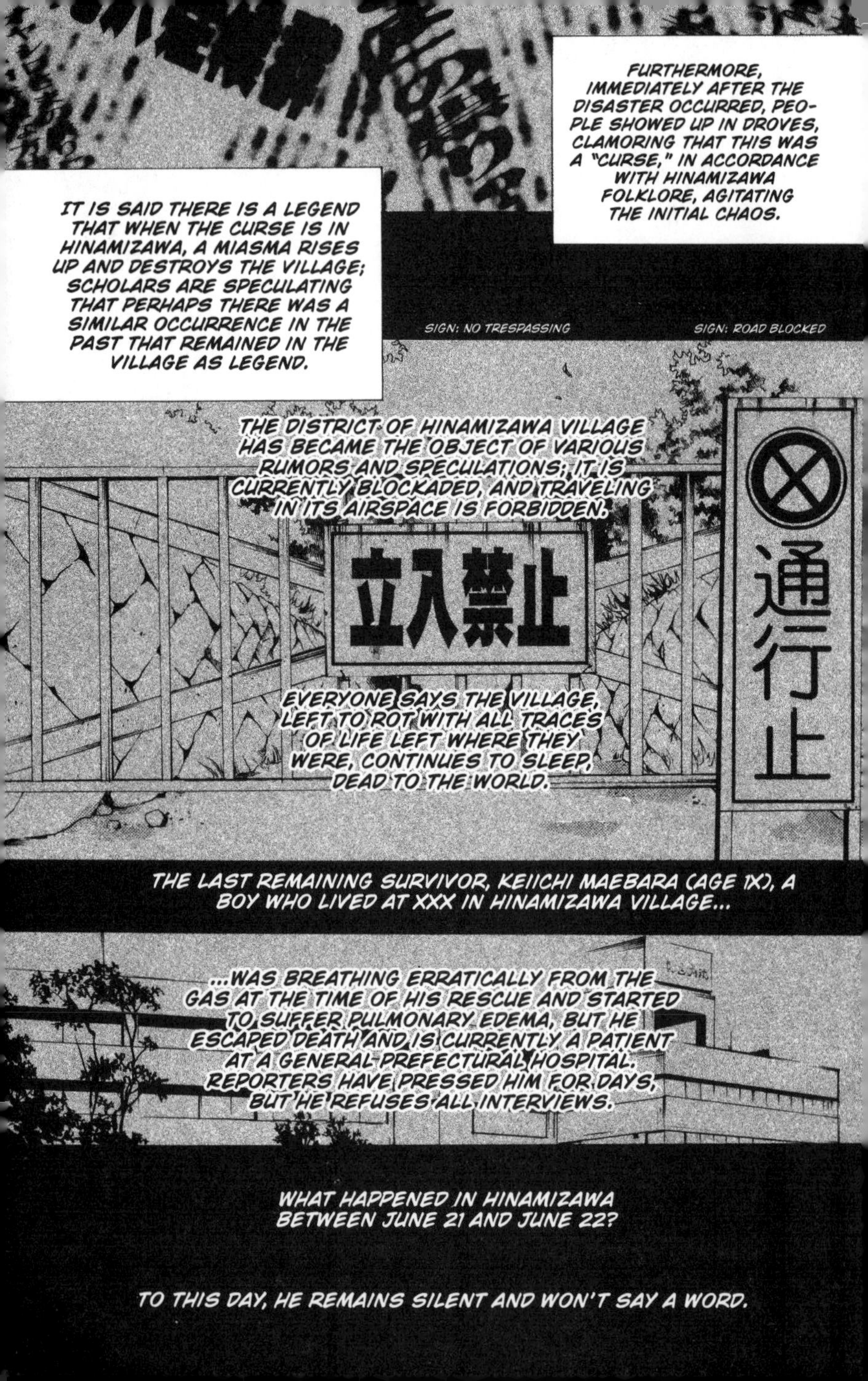
FURTHERMORE, IMMEDIATELY AFTER THE DISASTER OCCURRED, PEOPLE SHOWED UP IN DROVES, CLAMORING THAT THIS WAS A "CURSE," IN ACCORDANCE WITH HINAMIZAWA FOLKLORE, AGITATING THE INITIAL CHAOS.
IT IS SAID THERE IS A LEGEND THAT WHEN THE CURSE IS IN HINAMIZAWA, A MIASMA RISES UP AND DESTROYS THE VILLAGE; SCHOLARS ARE SPECULATING THAT PERHAPS THERE WAS A SIMILAR OCCURRENCE IN THE PAST THAT REMAINED IN THE VILLAGE AS LEGEND.
SIGN: ROAD BLOCKED
SIGN: NO TRESPASSING
通行止
立入禁止
THE DISTRICT OF HINAMIZAWA VILLAGE HAS BECAME THE OBJECT OF VARIOUS RUMORS AND SPECULATIONS; IT IS CURRENTLY BLOCKADED, AND TRAVELING IN ITS AIRSPACE IS FORBIDDEN.
EVERYONE SAYS THE VILLAGE, LEFT TO ROT WITH ALL TRACES OF LIFE LEFT WHERE THEY WERE, CONTINUES TO SLEEP, DEAD TO THE WORLD.
THE LAST REMAINING SURVIVOR, KEIICHI MAEBARA (AGE 1X), A BOY WHO LIVED AT XXX IN HINAMIZAWA VILLAGE...
...WAS BREATHING ERRATICALLY FROM THE GAS AT THE TIME OF HIS RESCUE AND STARTED TO SUFFER PULMONARY EDEMA, BUT HE ESCAPED DEATH AND IS CURRENTLY A PATIENT AT A GENERAL PREFECTURAL HOSPITAL. REPORTERS HAVE PRESSED HIM FOR DAYS, BUT HE REFUSES ALL INTERVIEWS.
WHAT HAPPENED IN HINAMIZAWA BETWEEN JUNE 21 AND JUNE 22?
TO THIS DAY, HE REMAINS SILENT AND WON'T SAY A WORD.

Hinamizawa Disaster Victims List

Jirou Tomitake (real name unknown)
June 19, 1983; suicide within the village?
Investigation suspended.

Miyo Takano
June 19, 1983; hanged in the mountains in Gifu Prefecture.
The corpse was burned. Investigation pending.

Kuraudo Ooishi
June 20, 1983; went missing during an investigation.
Investigation pending.

Katsuya Kumagai
June 20, 1983; went missing during an investigation.
Investigation pending.

Kyosuke Irie
June 21, 1983; suicide inside his clinic?
Investigation suspended.

Rika Furude
June 21, 1983; murdered at the shrine?
Investigation suspended.

Reina Ryugu
June 22, 1983; died in the Hinamizawa Disaster.

Mion Sonozaki
June 22, 1983; died in the Hinamizawa Disaster.

Oryou Sonozaki
June 22, 1983; died in the Hinamizawa Disaster.

Satoko Hojo
June 22, 1983; missing in the Hinamizawa Disaster.

Teppei Hojo
June 22, 1983; missing in the Hinamizawa Disaster.

Ichiro Maebara
June 22, 1983; died in the Hinamizawa Disaster.

Aiko Maebara
June 22, 1983; died in the Hinamizawa Disaster.

Daiki Tomita
June 22, 1983; died in the Hinamizawa Disaster.

Suguru Okamura
June 22, 1983; died in the Hinamizawa Disaster.

Rumiko Chie
June 22, 1983; died in an accident while evacuating
from the Hinamizawa Disaster.

Kiichiro Kimiyoshi
June 22, 1983; died in the Hinamizawa Disaster.

Yukikazu Kameda
June 22, 1983; died in an accident while evacuating
from the Hinamizawa Disaster.

Tatsuyoshi Kasai
August 11, 1983; died at the hospital where he was admitted.

Shion Sonozaki
August 27, 1983; killed herself at the hospital where
she was admitted. Investigation complete.

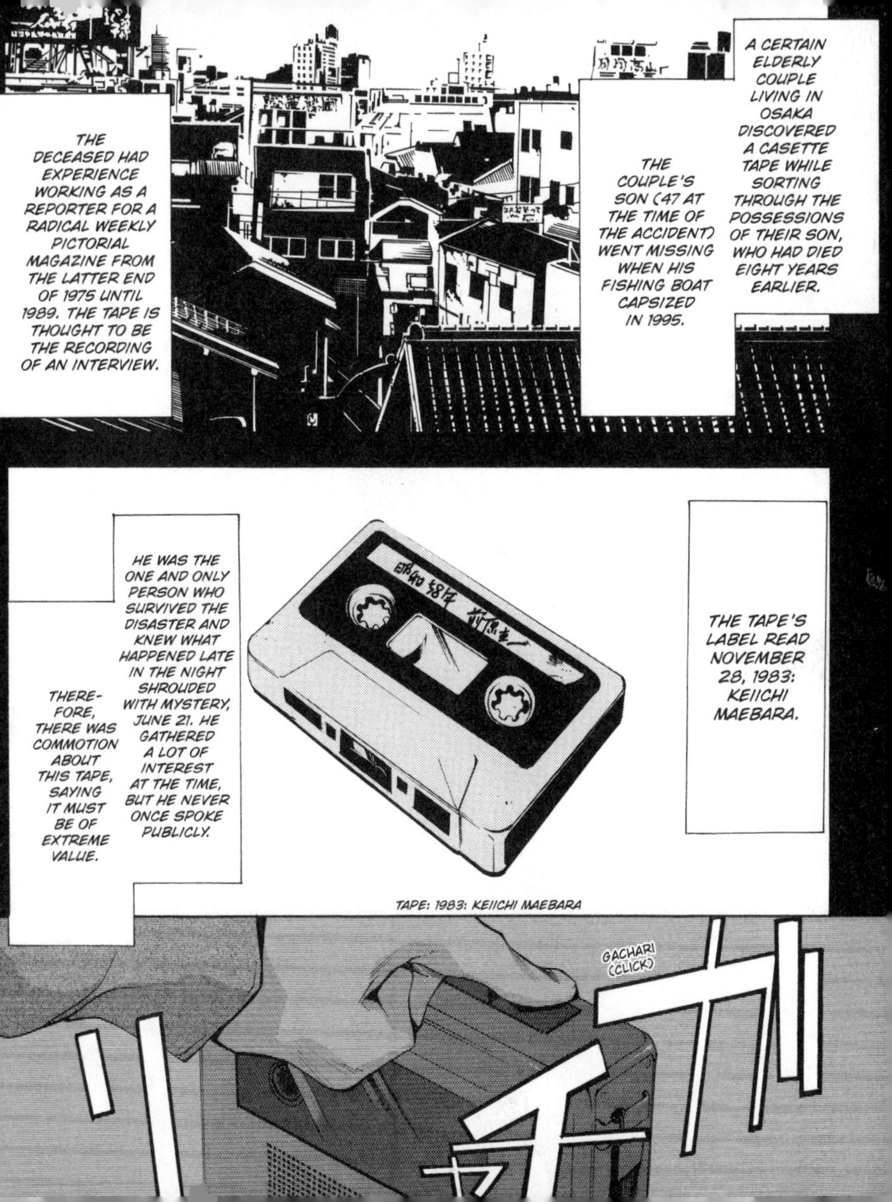
A CERTAIN ELDERLY COUPLE LIVING IN OSAKA DISCOVERED A CASETTE TAPE WHILE SORTING THROUGH THE POSSESSIONS OF THEIR SON, WHO HAD DIED EIGHT YEARS EARLIER.
THE COUPLE'S SON (47 AT THE TIME OF THE ACCIDENT) WENT MISSING WHEN HIS FISHING BOAT CAPSIZED IN 1995.
THE DECEASED HAD EXPERIENCE WORKING AS A REPORTER FOR A RADICAL WEEKLY PICTORIAL MAGAZINE FROM THE LATTER END OF 1975 UNTIL 1989. THE TAPE IS THOUGHT TO BE THE RECORDING OF AN INTERVIEW.
THE TAPE'S LABEL READ NOVEMBER 28, 1983: KEIICHI MAEBARA.
HE WAS THE ONE AND ONLY PERSON WHO SURVIVED THE DISASTER AND KNEW WHAT HAPPENED LATE IN THE NIGHT SHROUDED WITH MYSTERY, JUNE 21. HE GATHERED A LOT OF INTEREST AT THE TIME, BUT HE NEVER ONCE SPOKE PUBLICLY.
THERE-FORE, THERE WAS COMMOTION ABOUT THIS TAPE, SAYING IT MUST BE OF EXTREME VALUE.
TAPE: 1983: KEIICHI MAEBARA
GACHARI (CLICK)

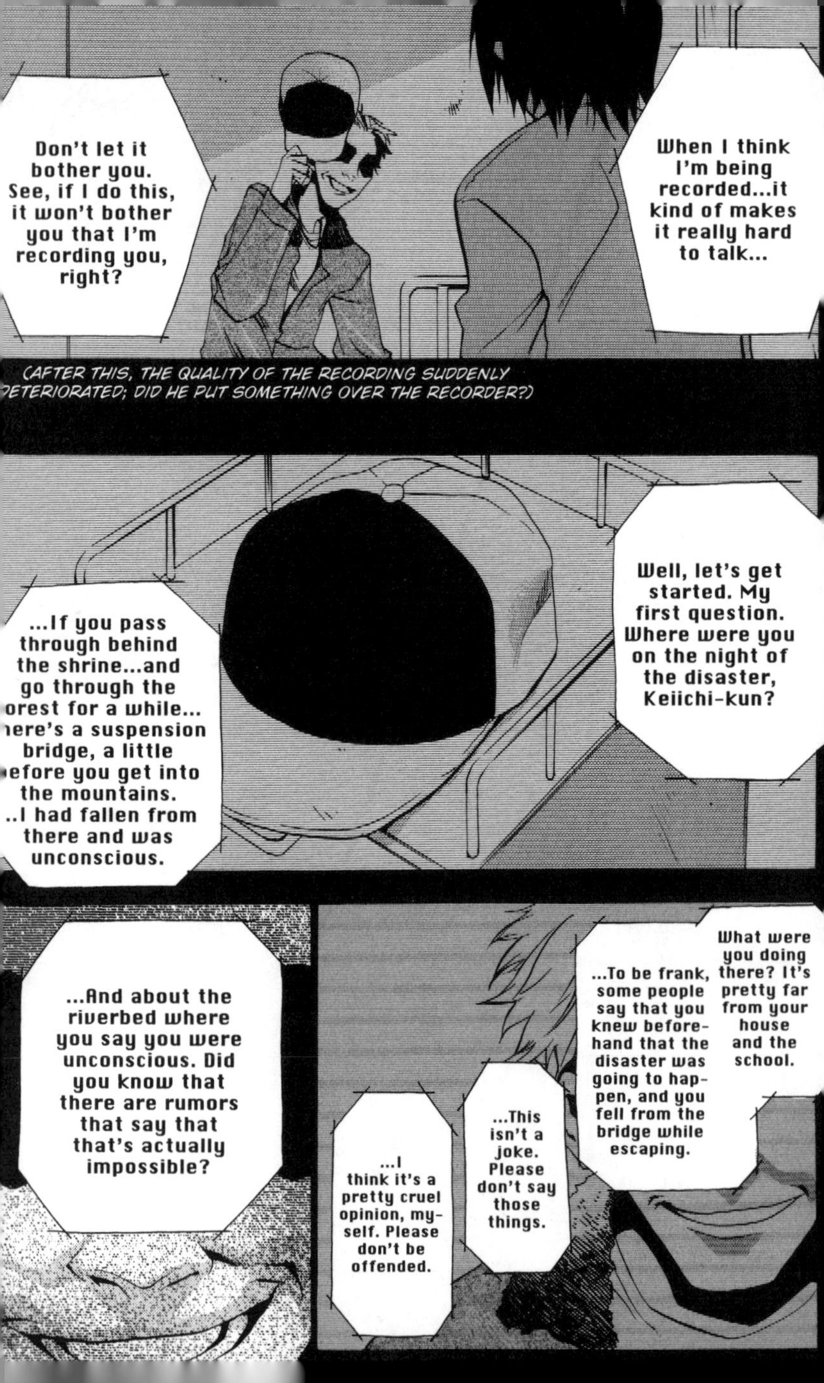
When I think I'm being recorded...it kind of makes it really hard to talk...
Don't let it bother you. See, if I do this, it won't bother you that I'm recording you, right?
(AFTER THIS, THE QUALITY OF THE RECORDING SUDDENLY ETERIORATED; DID HE PUT SOMETHING OVER THE RECORDER?)
Well, let's get started. My first question. Where were you on the night of the disaster, Keiichi-kun?
...If you pass through behind the shrine...and go through the orest for a while... ere's a suspension bridge, a little efore you get into the mountains. ..I had fallen from there and was unconscious.
What were you doing there? It's pretty far from your house and the school.
...To be frank, some people say that you knew before-hand that the disaster was going to hap-pen, and you fell from the bridge while escaping.
...This isn't a joke. Please don't say those things.
...I think it's a pretty cruel opinion, my-self. Please don't be offended.
...And about the riverbed where you say you were unconscious. Did you know that there are rumors that say that that's actually impossible?

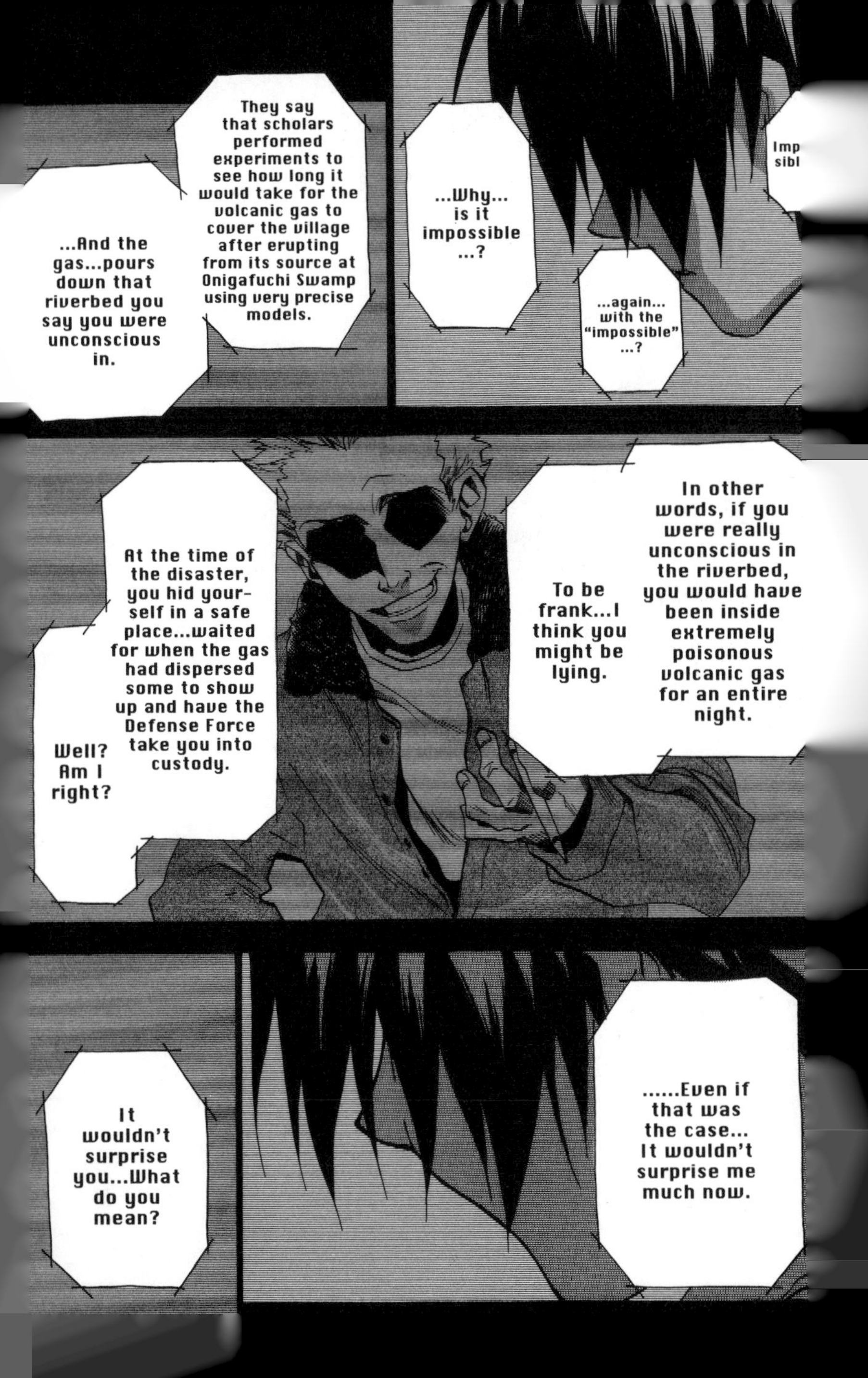
Imp sibl
...Why... is it impossible ...?
...again... with the "impossible" ...?
They say that scholars performed experiments to see how long it would take for the volcanic gas to cover the village after erupting from its source at Onigafuchi Swamp using very precise models.
...And the gas...pours down that riverbed you say you were unconscious in.
In other words, if you were really unconscious in the riverbed, you would have been inside extremely poisonous volcanic gas for an entire night.
To be frank...I think you might be lying.
At the time of the disaster, you hid your-self in a safe place...waited for when the gas had dispersed some to show up and have the Defense Force take you into custody.
Well? Am I right?
......Even if that was the case... It wouldn't surprise me much now.
It wouldn't surprise you...What do you mean?

THERE ARE OPINIONS THAT DOUBT WHETHER IT IS ACTUALLY KEIICHI MAEBARA RECORDED ON THIS TAPE.
...You just said it, didn't you? That it's "impossible." In that village of Hinamizawa, a lot of impossible things happen.
...Someone who should not be in one place is, and someone who should be dead is alive...It's not anything unusual.
I should be dead, and I'm alive...To try to prove that...ha-ha...
AH-HA-HA-HA-HA-HA-HA-HA-HA!
TO CONFIRM THE AUTHENTICITY OF THE TAPE, WE HAD THEM MATCH IT AGAINST THE VOICE ON TAPES FROM MAEBARA FAMILY RELATIVES, BUT THE RECORDING ISN'T VERY CLEAR, AND MANY YEARS HAD PASSED, SO WE WERE UNABLE TO GAIN ANY DEFINITIVE PROOF.
Ah-ha...ha-ha-ha...All right, Keiichi-kun, let's change the subject. What do you think about the talks that maybe the disaster was the fifth year of the curse, the series of mysterious deaths in Hinamizawa?
No, that's not true. Because the fifth year's curse was me.
Eh? Ah-ha-ha-ha-ha. What do you mean?
What do I mean...? I'm answering your question.
FURTHER, THERE ARE STILL DOUBTS AS TO THE DATE WRITTEN ON THE TAPE, NOVEMBER 28.
That disaster... Well, you probably won't believe me if I tell you. But I caused it.
...You see, I... wished that the entire village would die, so it happened.

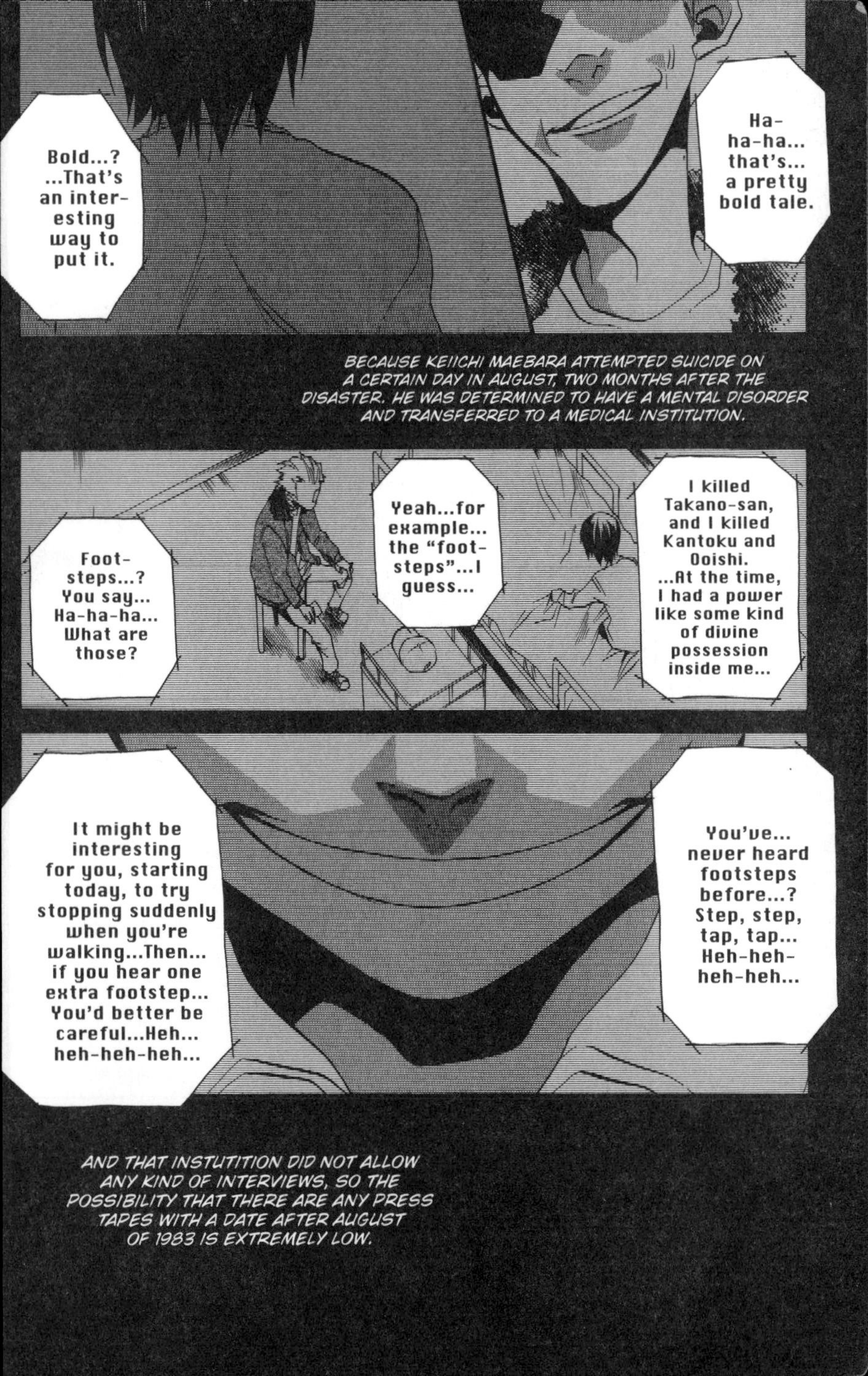
Ha-ha-ha... that's... a pretty bold tale.
Bold...? ...That's an interesting way to put it.
BECAUSE KEIICHI MAEBARA ATTEMPTED SUICIDE ON A CERTAIN DAY IN AUGUST, TWO MONTHS AFTER THE DISASTER. HE WAS DETERMINED TO HAVE A MENTAL DISORDER AND TRANSFERRED TO A MEDICAL INSTITUTION.
I killed Takano-san, and I killed Kantoku and Ooishi. ...At the time, I had a power like some kind of divine possession inside me...
Yeah...for example... the "footsteps"...I guess...
Footsteps...? You say... Ha-ha-ha... What are those?
You've... never heard footsteps before...? Step, step, tap, tap... Heh-heh-heh-heh...
It might be interesting for you, starting today, to try stopping suddenly when you're walking...Then... if you hear one extra footstep... You'd better be careful...Heh... heh-heh-heh...
AND THAT INSTUTITION DID NOT ALLOW ANY KIND OF INTERVIEWS, SO THE POSSIBILITY THAT THERE ARE ANY PRESS TAPES WITH A DATE AFTER AUGUST OF 1983 IS EXTREMELY LOW.

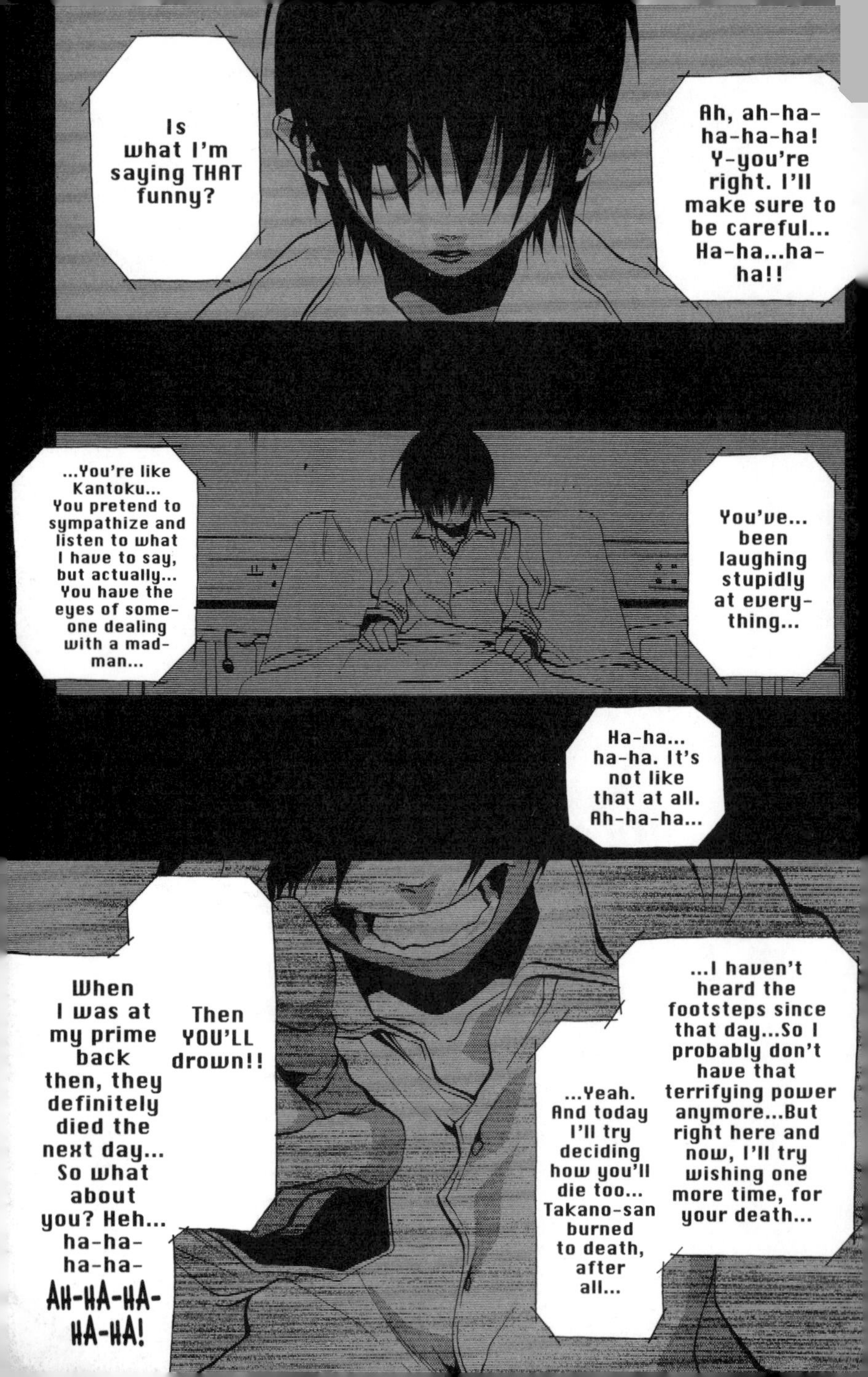
Ah, ah-ha-ha-ha-ha! Y-you're right. I'll make sure to be careful... Ha-ha...ha-ha!!
Is what I'm saying THAT funny?
You've... been laughing stupidly at every-thing...
...You're like Kantoku... You pretend to sympathize and listen to what I have to say, but actually... You have the eyes of some-one dealing with a mad-man...
Ha-ha... ha-ha. It's not like that at all. Ah-ha-ha...
...I haven't heard the footsteps since that day...So I probably don't have that terrifying power anymore...But right here and now, I'll try wishing one more time, for your death...
...Yeah. And today I'll try deciding how you'll die too... Takano-san burned to death, after all...
Then YOU'LL drown!!
When I was at my prime back then, they definitely died the next day... So what about you? Heh... ha-ha-ha-ha-AH-HA-HA-HA-HA!

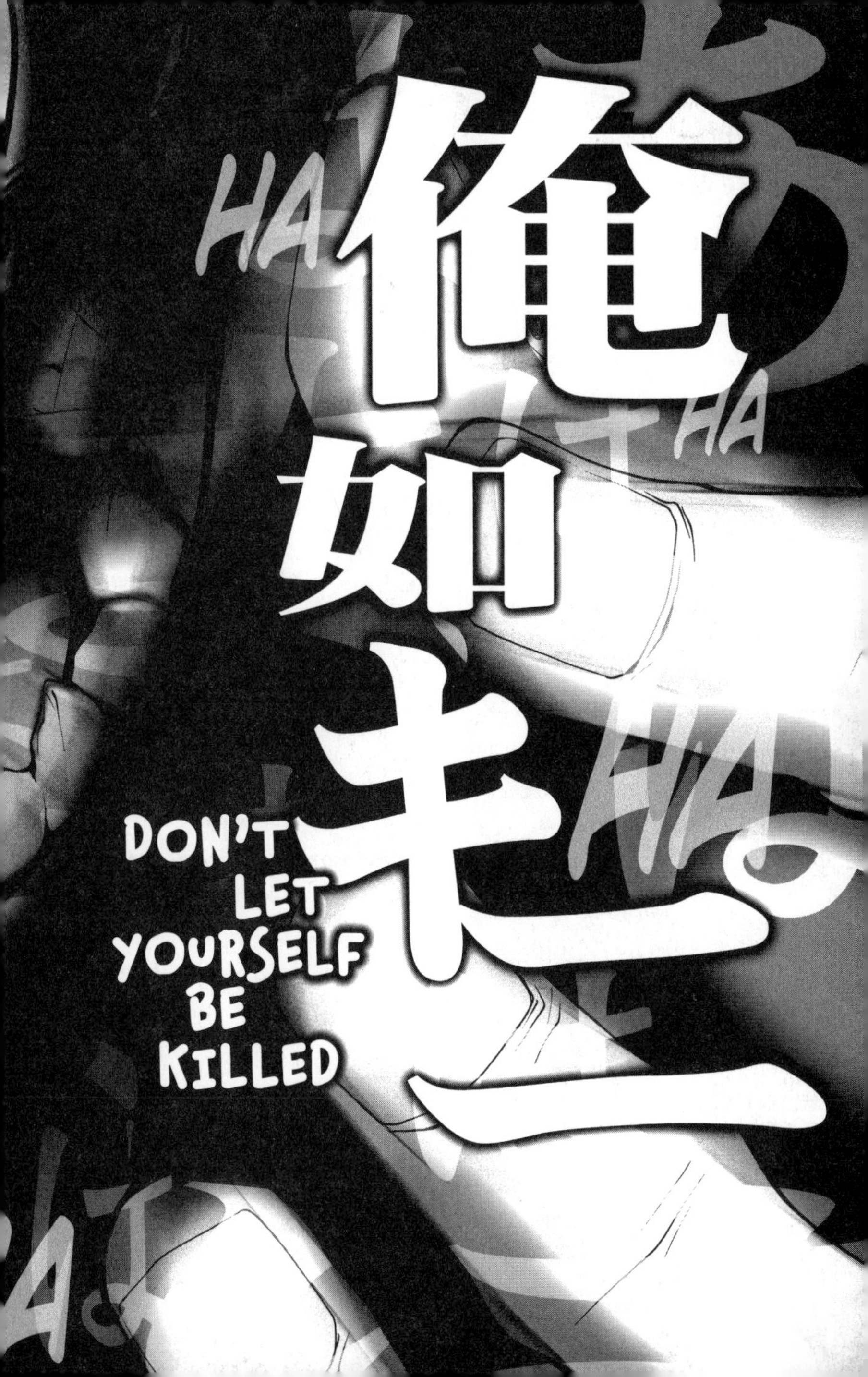
俺如き
DON'T LET YOURSELF BE KILLED
HA
HA
HA

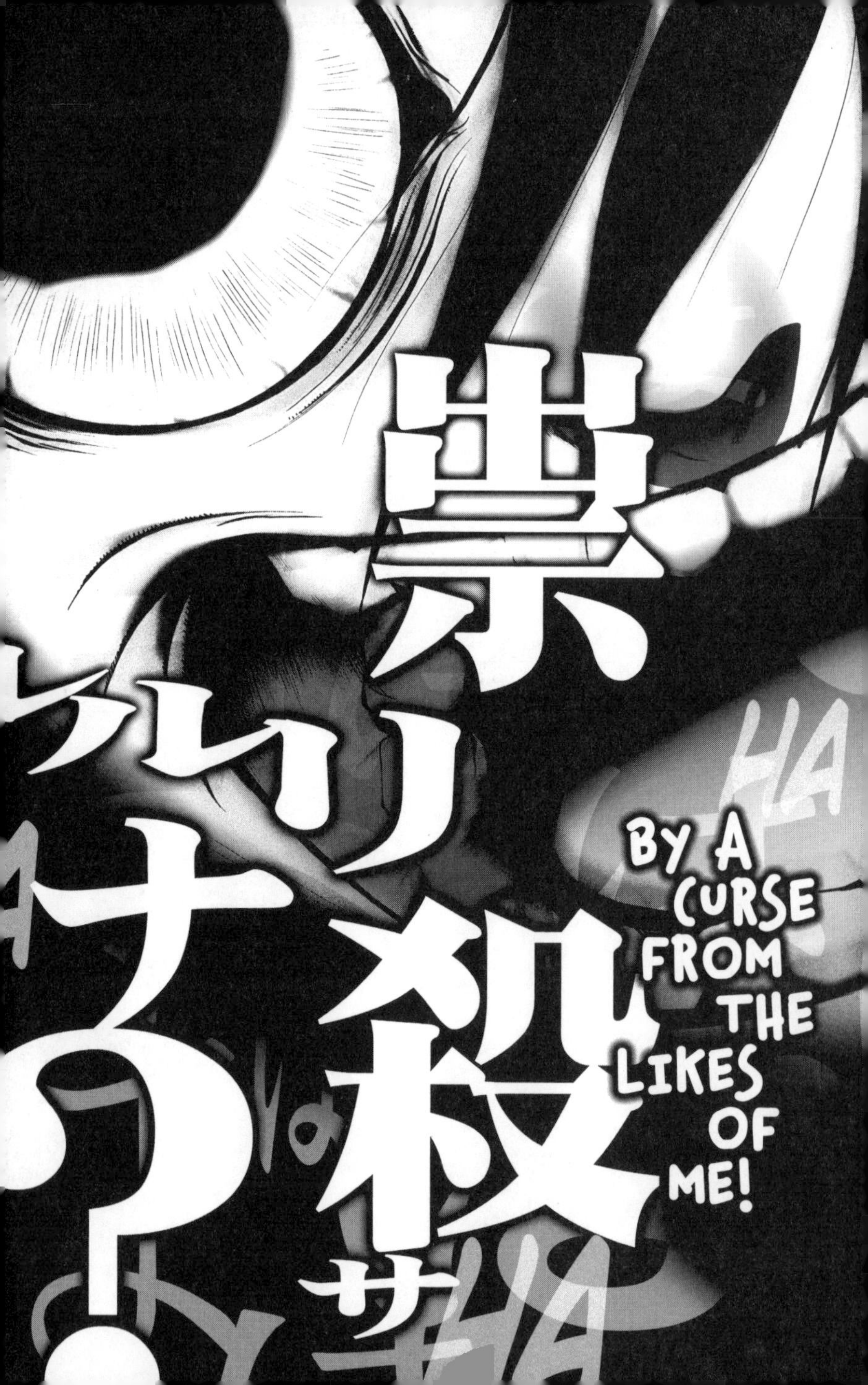
祟り殺サ
BY A CURSE FROM THE LIKES OF ME!
HA
HA

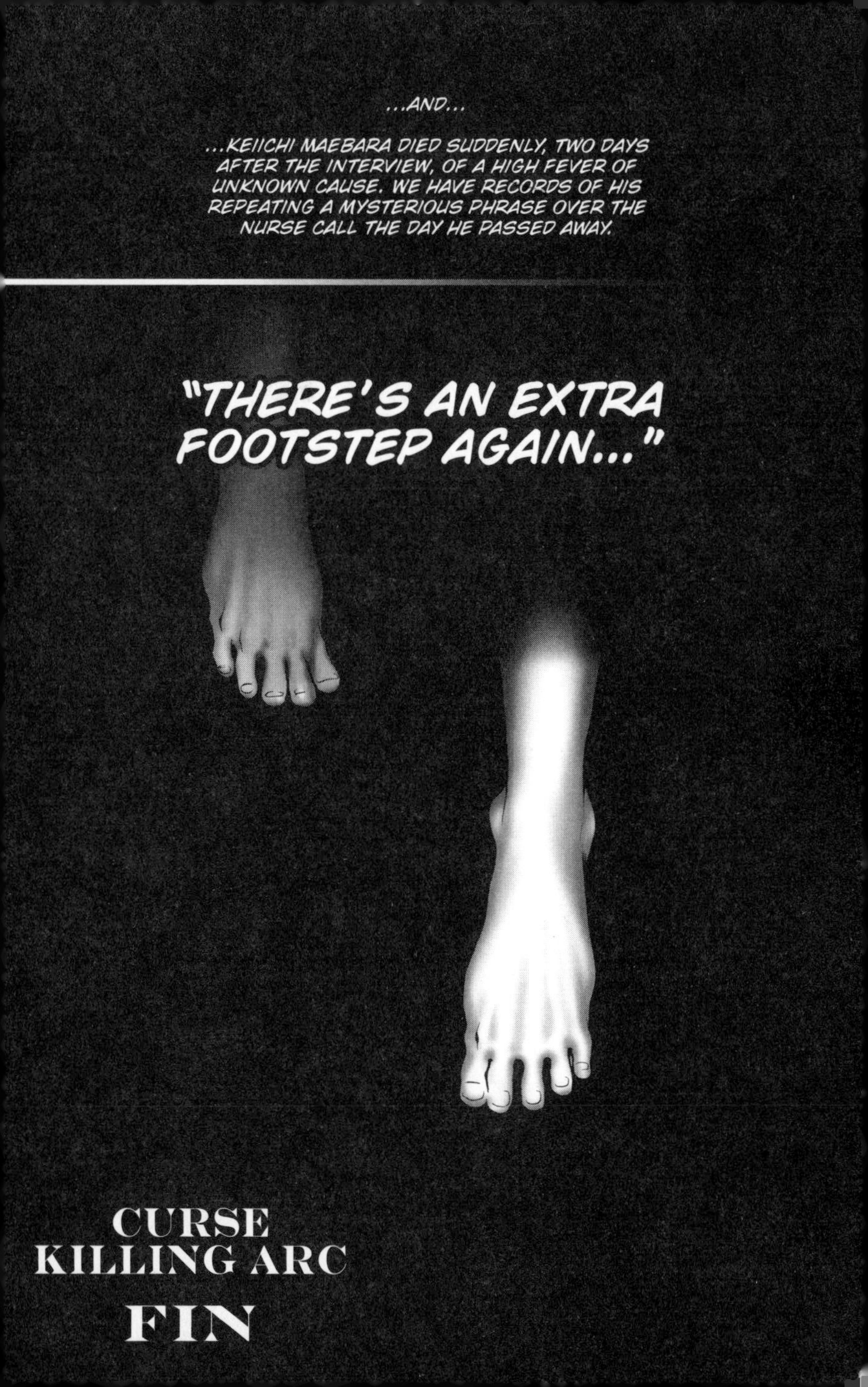
...AND...
...KEIICHI MAEBARA DIED SUDDENLY, TWO DAYS AFTER THE INTERVIEW, OF A HIGH FEVER OF UNKNOWN CAUSE. WE HAVE RECORDS OF HIS REPEATING A MYSTERIOUS PHRASE OVER THE NURSE CALL THE DAY HE PASSED AWAY.
"THERE'S AN EXTRA FOOTSTEP AGAIN..."
CURSE KILLING ARC
FIN

HIGURASHI WHEN THEY CRY

©07th Expansion presents. Welcome to Hinamizawa.. "WHEN THEY CRY.."

ABOUT THE "CURSE KILLING ARC"

IN ORDER TO BREAK THROUGH THE TRAGEDY

ORIGINAL STORY, SUPERVISOR: RYUKISHI07

THE "CURSE KILLING ARC" IS THE THIRD SCENARIO IN "HIGURASHI WHEN THEY CRY" AND IS AN IMPORTANT STORY THAT FINISHES OFF THE THREE "HIGURASHI" QUESTION ARCS. ALSO, IN THE SENSE OF SEEKING WHAT'S NECESSARY TO BREAK THROUGH THE TRAGEDIES OF THIS WORLD, IT IS THE MOST IMPORTANT SCENARIO.

SATOKO'S SUFFERING IS DEPICTED EXTREMELY HEART-BREAKINGLY IN THIS SCENARIO. AND MORE FRIGHTENING THAN ANYTHING, I THINK IT BRINGS WITH IT THE RAW SENSE OF REALITY THAT SOMETHING SIMILAR COULD SUDDENLY HAPPEN CLOSE TO ANYONE AT ANY TIME.

IN A WAY, THE "CURSE KILLING ARC" IS THE MOST LIGHTHEARTED OF THE "HIGURASHI" ARCS, AND IN A WAY, PERHAPS IT COULD BE SAID THAT IT'S THE MOST DIFFERENT FROM THE MAIN WORLD OF "HIGURASHI." BUT THE KEY HIDDEN IN THIS SCENARIO IS ANOTHER VERY IMPORTANT ONE. IT'S SO IMPORTANT THAT IT WOULDN'T BE AN EXAGGERATION TO SAY THAT IT'S FAR MORE IMPORTANT THAN THE KEYS OF ALL THE THREE QUESTION ARCS, AND IT'S THE MASTER KEY OF THE "HIGURASHI" WORLD.

UNFORTUNATELY, KEIICHI WASN'T ABLE TO OBTAIN THAT KEY IN THIS INSTANCE. HE'LL FINALLY GAIN THIS KEY IN A LATER SCENARIO. I WONDER IF ALL OF YOU WERE ABLE TO FIND IT...?

HIGURASHI
WHEN THEY CRY
CURSE KILLING ARC ②

RYUKISHI07
JIRO SUZUKI

Translation: Alethea Nibley and Athena Nibley

Lettering: AndWorld Design

Higurashi WHEN THEY CRY Curse Killing Arc, Vol. 2 © RYUKISHI07 / 07th
Expansion © 2006 Jiro Suzuki / SQUARE ENIX CO., LTD. All rights reserved.
First published in Japan in 2006 by SQUARE ENIX CO., LTD. English trans-
lation rights arranged with SQUARE ENIX CO., LTD. and Hachette Book
Group through Tuttle-Mori Agency, Inc. Translation © 2009 by SQUARE
ENIX CO., LTD.

Yen Press
Hachette Book Group
237 Park Avenue, New York, NY 10017

www.HachetteBookGroup.com
www.YenPress.com

Yen Press is an imprint of Hachette Book Group, Inc. The Yen Press name
and logo are trademarks of Hachette Book Group, Inc.

First Yen Press Edition: February 2010

ISBN: 978-0-7595-2988-5

10 9 8 7 6 5 4 3 2 1

BVG

Printed in the United States of America